MW00850352

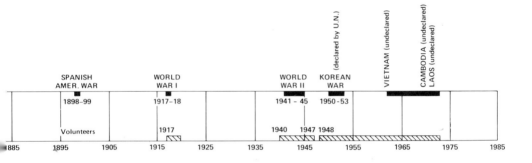

SPANISH
AMER. WAR

WORLD
WAR I

WORLD
WAR II

KOREAN
WAR

(declared by U.N.)

VIETNAM (undeclared)

CAMBODIA (undeclared)
LAOS (undeclared)

1898–99

1917–18

1941 – 45

1950 - 53

Volunteers

1917

1940   1947 1948

1885   1895   1905   1915   1925   1935   1945   1955   1965   1975   1985

■■■■■ WAR

▨▨▨ DRAFT

The Military Draft

★ ★ ★

OTHER BOOKS BY MARTIN ANDERSON

The Federal Bulldozer: *A Critical Analysis of Urban Renewal, 1949–1962*

Conscription: *A Select and Annotated Bibliography*

Welfare: *The Political Economy of Welfare Reform in the United States*

Registration and the Draft: *Proceedings of the Hoover-Rochester Conference on the All-Volunteer Force*

UB
340
.M55
1982

The Military Draft

★ ★ ★

Selected Readings on Conscription

Edited by

Martin Anderson

with Barbara Honegger

HOOVER INSTITUTION PRESS
Stanford University, Stanford, California

GOSHEN COLLEGE LIBRARY
GOSHEN, INDIANA

The Hoover Institution on War, Revolution and Peace, founded at Stanford University in 1919 by the late President Herbert Hoover, is an interdisciplinary research center for advanced study on domestic and international affairs in the twentieth century. The views expressed in its publications are entirely those of the authors and do not necessarily reflect the views of the staff, officers, or Board of Overseers of the Hoover Institution.

Hoover Press Publication 258

© 1982 by the Board of Trustees of the Leland Stanford Junior University
All rights reserved under International and Pan–American Copyright conventions.

Library of Congress Cataloging in Publication Data
Main entry under title:

The military draft.

Includes index.
1. Military service, Compulsory—Addresses, essays, lectures. 2. Military service, Compulsory—United States—Addresses, essays, lectures. I. Anderson, Martin. II. Honegger, Barbara.
UB34.M55   355.2'2363   81-84641
ISBN 0-8179-7581-0   AACR2

The text of this book was set by computer in a version of a type face called Baskerville. The face is an adaptation of types cast from molds first used by John Baskerville in England about 1760. Baskerville's original face was one of the forerunners of the modern faces of the nineteenth and twentieth centuries.
Composition by Computer Typesetting Services, Glendale, California.
Printed and bound in the United States of America by Braun-Brumfield, Inc., Ann Arbor, Michigan.

Grateful acknowledgment is made and credit given as follows for permission to reprint copyrighted selections included in this book:

"Posse Comitatus," by David Dawson, from *Persuasion*, Volume 3, Number 4 (April 1966), pages 43–52. Reprinted by permission of the author's estate. Copyright © 1966 Persuasion, Inc.

"Plain Truth, &c," by Benjamin Franklin, from *The Papers of Benjamin Franklin*, Volume 3, edited by Leonard W. Labaree (New Haven and London: Yale University Press, 1961), pages 188–204. Reprinted by permission of the publisher, Yale University Press. Copyright © 1961 by the American Philosophical Society Held at Philadelphia for Promoting Useful Knowledge and by Yale University.

"Conscription," by Mark Sullivan. Used by permission of Charles Scribner's Sons from *Our Times: The United States, 1900–1925*, Volume 5, *Over Here, 1914–1918*, by Mark Sullivan. Copyright 1933 Charles Scribner's Sons; renewal copyright © 1961 Mark Sullivan, Jr.

"Why Don't We Learn from History?" by B. H. Liddell Hart. Reprinted by permission of George Allen & Unwin and by permission of Hawthorn Properties (Elsevier-Dutton Publishing Company, Inc.), from the book *Why Don't We Learn from History?* by B. H. Liddell Hart. [Originally published in 1944 by George Allen & Unwin, London; reissued in 1969 by Meredith Press (Hawthorn Books), New York.] Copyright © 1969 by B. H. Liddell Hart.

"The Origins of American Military Policy," by Louis Morton. Reprinted from *Military Affairs*, Summer 1958, Volume XII, Number 2, pages 75-82, with permission. Copyright © 1958 by the American Military Institute. No additional copies may be made without the express permission of the author and of the editor of *Military Affairs*.

"Raising Armies Before the Civil War," by William G. Carleton, from *Current History*, Volume 54, Number 322 (June 1968), pages 327-332, 363. Copyright © 1968 Current History, Inc. Reprinted by permission of the publisher.

"The Peacetime Draft: Voluntarism to Coercion," by Richard Gillam, from *The Yale Review*, Volume 57, Number 4 (June 1968), pages 495-517. Copyright © 1968 by Yale University. Reprinted by permission of *The Yale Review*.

"The Volunteer Army," by Donald Smith, from *The Atlantic Monthly*, Volume 234, Number 1 (July 1974), pages 6-12. Copyright © 1974 by The Atlantic Monthly Company, Boston, Massachusetts. Reprinted with permission of the publisher and the author.

"Civil Rights and Conscription," by D. H. Monro, from *Conscription in Australia*, edited by Roy Forward and Bob Reece, published by University of Queensland, St. Lucia, Queensland, 1968. Copyright © 1968 University of Queensland Press. Reprinted with permission.

"Political Alienation and Military Service," by Michael Walzer. Reprinted by permission of the publishers from *Obligations: Essays on Disobedience*, by Michael Walzer, Cambridge, Massachusetts: Harvard University Press. Copyright © 1970 by the President and Fellows of Harvard College.

"The Wreckage of the Consensus" from *Capitalism: The Unknown Ideal* by Ayn Rand. Copyright © 1967 by The Objectivist, Inc. Reprinted by arrangement with the New American Library, Inc., New York, New York. Used by permission of the author.

"Military Service and Moral Obligation," by Hugo Adam Bedau. From *Philosophy and Political Action: Essays Edited for the New York Group of the Society for Philosophy and Political Affairs*, edited by Virginia Held, Kai Nielson, and Charles Parsons. Copyright © 1972 by Oxford University Press, Inc. Reprinted by permission of Oxford University Press, New York.

"Selected Draft Law Cases: A Supreme Court Decision," by Edward White, from *Current History*, Volume 54, Number 322 (June 1968), pages 359-363. Copyright © 1968 Current History, Inc. Reprinted by permission of the publisher.

"Conscription and the Constitution: The Original Understanding," by Leon Friedman, from *Michigan Law Review*, Volume 67, Number 7 (May 1969), pages 1493-

1552. Copyright © 1969 The Michigan Law Review Association. Reprinted with permission of the original publisher, The Michigan Law Review Association.

"The Economic Cost of the Draft," by Walter Y. Oi, from *American Economic Review*, Volume 57, Number 2 (May 1967), pages 39–62. Copyright © 1967 American Economic Association. Reprinted by permission of the publisher and the author.

Ryan C. Amacher, James C. Miller III, et al., *The Economics of the Military Draft* (Morristown, New Jersey: General Learning Corporation, 1973). Copyright © 1973 General Learning Corporation. Reprinted by permission of Silver Burdett Company.

"The Logic of National Service," by Morris Janowitz; "A National Service System as a Solution to a Variety of National Problems," by Margaret Mead; "The Draft in the Light of History," by William H. McNeill; and "Selection for Military Service in the Soviet Union," by Raymond L. Garthoff. Reprinted by permission of the publisher from *The Draft: A Handbook of Facts and Alternatives*, edited by Sol Tax (Chicago: University of Chicago Press, 1967), pages 73–90, 99–109, 117–121, 167–170. Copyright © 1967 The University of Chicago.

"The Basic Purpose and Objective of the U.S. Selective Service" (extract), by Lewis B. Hershey; "The Draft: Unjust and Unnecessary," by Thomas B. Curtis; and "The Courage to Compel," by Terrence Cullinan. Reprinted by permission of *The Forensic Quarterly* and (for the articles by Curtis and by Cullinan) the authors from *The Forensic Quarterly*, Volume 42, Number 1–3 (May 1968), pages 71–72, 165–179, 211–224. [Originally published in *Compulsory Service Systems: A Critical Discussion and Debate Source Book* (Columbia, Missouri: Artcraft Press, Publishers, 1968), the contents of which were also published, under the title *Compulsory Service Systems*, as the May 1968 issue of *The Forensic Quarterly*.] Copyright © 1968 The Forensic Quarterly.

"The Social and Political Aspects of Conscription: Europe's Experience," by Herman Beukema, from *War as a Social Institution: The Historian's Perspective* (New York: Columbia University Press, 1941), pages 113–129. Copyright © 1941 Columbia University Press. Reprinted by permission of the publisher.

"Inequities in the Draft," by Edward M. Kennedy, from *The New York Times*, February 24, 1971, page 41. Copyright © 1971 by The New York Times Company. Reprinted by permission.

"Doubts About an All-Volunteer Army," by Joseph A. Califano, Jr., from *The New Republic*, Volume 168, Number 9 (March 3, 1973), pages 9–11; with reply by Roger T. Kelley and rejoinder by Joseph A. Califano, Jr., from *The New Republic*, Volume 168, Number 16 (April 21, 1973), pages 30–32. Reprinted by permission of *The New Republic*, copyright © 1973, The New Republic, Inc.

"Conscription and Conscience," by A. J. Muste, from *Sourcebook on Conscience and Conscription and Disarmament*, compiled by American Friends Service Committee (Wallingford, Pennsylvania: Pendle Hill, 1943), pages 3–8. Copyright © 1943 American Friends Service Committee. Reprinted with permission of the American Friends Service Committee, Philadelphia, Pennsylvania.

"Why the Draft Should Go," by John M. Swomley, Jr., from *The Nation Magazine*, Volume CCIX, Number 4 (August 11, 1969), pages 108–110. Copyright © 1969 The Nation Associates. Reprinted by permission.

"Why Not a Volunteer Army?" by Milton Friedman, from *New Individualist Review*, Volume 4, Number 4 (Spring 1967), pages 3–9. Copyright © 1967 Liberty Fund, Inc. Reprinted by permission of the author and the Liberty Fund.

To Milton Friedman

Contents

Part VIII | Conscription: Con

Foreword

The issue of the proper relationship between citizen and state is one of the oldest questions in the history of the West. It grows out of the tension between the state's need to survive and the freedom that Western civilization believes makes life worth living, the freedom that is one of the fundamental reasons for the state's existence in the first place. Thus, it is not surprising that the United States, as the modern field on which the classical ideas of the state are practiced, should reflect this tension. Indeed the debate over conscription is at the heart of this matter and has been with us since the time our Constitution was written.

For our first hundred and fifty years we generally depended on a small standing volunteer professional armed force. The first major step away from this practice came just after World War II with the realization of America's world leadership role. It became clear then that conscription was needed for the standing forces that mission required. It is important, however, to remember that historically America's reliance on conscription has been the exception rather than the rule for manning our Army. So our return in the past decade to a volunteer force is no less than a return to tradition.

The task of maintaining a *large* peacetime standing force wholly through volunteers is very challenging. In fact it may be the most critical challenge facing the Department of Defense for the next decade. The transition to reinstating the volunteer concept and abolishing the draft has not been smooth. It has been the subject of continued debate and study. For example, after President Nixion announced the decision in favor of the All-Volunteer Force on 23 April 1970, it took almost three years to begin implementing it.

Once we moved to the All-Volunteer Force in July 1973, the question then shifted to whether we could successfully meet the challenge. Could the armed forces continue to attract and retain the numbers and kinds of people needed to maintain a strong defense? Most Americans and average citizens believe that in a democratic society, men and women will serve their country voluntarily when given the proper encouragement, incentives, and respect. In the past, these have not always been forthcoming.

With the All-Volunteer Force came an implicit commitment to maintain levels of military pay that were competitive with civilian sectors of the economy. However, this implicit contract was broken in 1975 by a pay cap and abrogated by successive pay caps in 1978 and 1979. In addition, the elimination of the GI Bill in 1976, combined with the expansion of federally sponsored scholarship programs and large-scale CETA programs available to nonmilitary people, made military service even less attractive. And, as though all this were not enough, Congress actually imposed substantial reductions in the FY 1976 recruiting budget. The results were predictable. Career retention rates declined to the lowest levels experienced since the All-Volunteer Force was established. Significant shortfalls in recruiting appeared in all the services, and the Army fell below its authorized strength.

The decline in retention and in the ability to recruit in the late 1970s was even greater than could be expected from the pay caps and competing programs. The reductions, coupled with an atmosphere of perceived indifference—even hostility—to our Vietnam veterans and the well-being of our military personnel, led many people in uniform as well as those considering enlistment to believe they should expect the worst in military service. The generally negative attitude on the part of the American public toward our military was in part a manifestation of the "Vietnam syndrome." The attitude was helped along by negative media comments about the quality of enlistees and the declining quality of life among service members. A self-fulfilling prophecy had taken effect. Fortunately, Congress began, none too soon, to reverse the trend of the later 1970s. A 25 percent pay increase over two years (FY 1981 and FY 1982), additional recruiting resources and educational initiatives, President Reagan's leadership in securing an increasing awareness of and appreciation for the role of our people in uniform, and his leadership in improving the effectiveness of the Volunteer Force have made it clear to military personnel that the neglect of the late 1970s is over.

As a result of these efforts, FY 1981 became an important milestone in the history of America's All-Volunteer armed forces. It demonstrated that the ideas guiding the Gates Commission were sound—young men and women will serve their country freely when given the proper encouragement, incentives, and respect.

All the services met their recruiting goals in FY 1981; test scores improved dramatically; and recruits included the highest proportion of high school graduates ever—even greater than during the draft years. In fact, the median test scores and high school graduate rates for enlistees were higher than those in the general youth population.

There were also dramatic increases in the reenlistment programs of the services. The first term reenlistment rates were among the highest ever experienced, and career reenlistment rates are on an upward trend after several years of decline.

These excellent recruiting and retention results have continued through the first half of FY 1982.

There are two other aspects of the All-Volunteer Force that are often discussed by both its proponents and critics. These are the issues of representation and patriotism.

Many analysts say that the military should contain a generally balanced cross section of society so that the burdens of service can be shared relatively equally. America's armed forces meet that criterion. Although evidence about recruits is difficult to develop, surveys show that those in the very highest and lowest economic brackets are somewhat underrepresented on a strict percentage basis. But the force is otherwise balanced. In addition, if we look at regional- or state-level distributions, our surveys show that we are obtaining a proportionate share of enlistees from each state. A recent study conducted by the Departments of Labor and Defense has also addressed the question of representation. It compared first-term enlistment military personnel to their fully employed counterparts in the civilian sector. Without minimizing some difficulties in the Army, which are being corrected, the study concluded that the All-Volunteer Force is attracting young men and women with backgrounds and abilities comparable to those youth who are employed full time in the labor market. In fact the IQ scores of those volunteering for the services are higher than the national average.

Questions about conscription invariably lead to the issue of whether a volunteer army is as patriotic as an army of conscripts. We have found that service to country is, in general, an important reason for enlistment. However, during an era of relative peace other attributes of service such as job training, opportunities to better one's life, and good benefits for self and family are also very important.

Our research and common sense alike suggest that patriotism, though not always uppermost in the minds of our young people, is related to their view of the threat the nation faces. But nothing even hints that service members who are attracted by motives other than patriotism are any less effective in the performance of their military duty.

The Department of Defense is optimistic about the underlying patriotism of our youth in the face of national crisis. We do not see any logic in the argument that holds that conscription or coercive national service during peacetime would encourage patriotism. Rather than increasing patriotism, a peacetime draft that is not perceived as necessary may result in a backlash by the youth against their government, just as happened in the late 1960s.

In summary, while the volunteer force has had problems, those problems were related not to voluntarism itself as much as to the nation's breaking those commitments necessary to sustain the volunteer force. The volunteer system is not an end in itself. It is a valid program to meet manpower requirements and thus deserves every opportunity to succeed. One of the more important points to recall is that the volunteer concept is consistent with our democratic heritage. It means, in short, that under normal, peacetime conditions each soldier, sailor, airman, and marine is in the armed forces of the United States out of a freely given commitment.

The All-Volunteer Force will continue to receive our highest priority. The real issues are whether in peacetime the nation can man its forces with the numbers and kinds of people needed to perform their missions and whether those forces can be increased quickly enough in an emergency. We believe that the All-Volunteer Force is the most appropriate way during peacetime to meet military manpower requirements.

The final and key element of success for the volunteer force is the American public's attitude towards it. Happily, the American people support our men and women in uniform and appreciate more than ever the part they have in keeping the United States at peace. That continued encouragement, that respect for our service members, will ultimately be the strongest factor in making the All-Volunteer Force work.

At the moment, the All-Volunteer concept is working extraordinarily well.

CASPAR W. WEINBERGER
Secretary of Defense

Preface

Over the years, a great deal has been written about conscription. Some of this work has been exceptional, offering powerful insights into the labyrinth of controversy that pervades this national policy issue.

Since the late 1960s, I have been involved in this controversy in a number of ways—developing issue positions in presidential campaigns, helping to formulate the policy and legislation that ended the draft in the early 1970s, compiling a comprehensive bibliography on conscription, and researching and writing about it. Of the hundreds of writings I have perused and studied, a few are notable for the way they help the reader understand various aspects of the policy debate on conscription—both pro and con.

These are the ones selected for inclusion in the following collection. They deal with the history, philosophy, constitutionality, and economics of conscription; with universal national service; with the practices of other nations; and, finally, with the powerful, emotional arguments that both foes and friends of conscription have mounted over the centuries.

I think you will like them.

MARTIN ANDERSON

Washington, D.C.
January 26, 1982

Acknowledgments

This select collection of works on conscription constitutes part of the results of a longtime research effort at the Hoover Institution, supported patiently by Dr. W. Glenn Campbell, the director, and many of my colleagues.

A special note of recognition should be given to my research assistants Judy Gans and Jeanne Crispen, who, over the years, worked on the volume from time to time.

Special thanks and acknowledgment go to Barbara Honegger, my research assistant from 1976–77 and 1980–82. Much of the work on the abstracts, the author biographies, and tracking down and obtaining all the necessary reprint permissions was done by her. Without her diligent work in these areas and her useful editing suggestions, this work would still undoubtedly be another "work in progress." I, of course, take responsibility for the organizational structure, selection of works included, and final editing.

I should also like to acknowledge the crucial role of Lise Hofmann, whose careful proofreading, as always, was invaluable, and to the Hoover Press, under the direction of Phyllis Cairns, which did its usual exemplary job of turning a rough manuscript into a polished, professional volume.

Part I

History

1

Posse Comitatus

by
David Dawson

Dawson traces the historical roots of modern conscription to the late Roman institutions of patrocinium *and* precarium *and the related Germanic barbarian tradition of* posse comitatus.

In patrocinium, *defenseless individuals provided military, agricultural, and other services to strong, local patrons in exchange for protection. Originally this was a contractual relationship between patron and client, but as conditions worsened,* patrocinium *evolved into* precarium, *in which small landowners relinquished their land as well as services for protection. Because of the widespread acceptance of these institutions, fearful, landless Europeans were easily absorbed into the Germanic barbarian system of* posse comitatus, *"power of the community," when Rome fell. Key to* posse comitatus *was the unquestioned obligation of each vassal to serve his liege lord's purposes in battle.*

Dawson details how the tradition of posse comitatus *became codified in postfeudal English law and was used to legitimate naval impressment in Britain in the sixteenth and seventeenth centuries and early compulsory conscription in the American colonies. Since that time, the ancient tradition has been called upon, implicitly or explicitly, to rationalize the usurpation of constitutionally protected individual rights of U.S. citizens.*

There was a time in Europe when most individuals were, in effect, classed with fruit trees and grapevines and vegetables—they were in law attached to the land. What amounted to ownership of them went with the land, should it be conquered, or sold, or given away, or inherited. The most important fact about the serf was the land in which he was rooted. In case of war with a neighboring baron a few miles away, or a princeling a hundred miles away, or a Mohammedan Sultan a thousand miles away, his person could be (and was) required to attend his liege lord, to carry a spear, to care for armor, to prepare supplies, or to do whatever was necessary to make war according to the fashion of the time. Always he suffered, often he died, and it was not recognized that he was anything more than a walking, talking, rather useful plant.

Were you to ask any liege lord, "Is this fair?" most would not even have understood the question. An especially thoughtful one of them might well have said that nothing is totally fair, but society must be served or it will not survive. Of course he would mean his society, that best of all possible worlds, feudal Europe.

One thing we must note—feudalism was consistent. Liege lords never made grand statements about the rights of man as they dragged off human battle fodder. If you're owned, then you are there to be used and disposed of.

Naturally all this has long passed. The rights of man are now recognized beyond argument—as part of this republic's basic legal assumptions. Man no longer exists for the land; rather, the land is there for man. Man is no longer considered a vegetable to be harvested for the purposes of his liege lord.

One thing has been established. Man is more than a plant. Or has it?

We live today with a contradiction whose seeds were laid down long ago, one might say, in prehistory. But the direct lineage of this contradiction, now presently codified in the Selective Service Act, goes back to the last days of the Roman Empire and the institutions called *patrocinium* and *precarium,* and to a related idea held by the Germanic barbarians, that of the *posse comitatus.*

Rome ruled by law, even though the concept of rights had not yet been developed. The establishment of universal peace (the *Pax Romana*), coupled with a great deal of freedom of action, resulted in an empire of prosperity, of protection of citizens, and of commercial activity.

Rome did not die in a day—it ceased to be an effective governing force, first in one district, then in another, sometimes to reassert itself and then collapse again. Local lawfulness and justice disintegrated; individual citizens were subjected to more and more robbery and extortion; districts were pillaged by bandits or ravaged by quasi-legal local governments that came and went like shifts in the direction of the wind. In the end, no one had anyone but himself to look to for the protection of his person and property.

And so an old Roman relationship, that of patron and client (*patrocinium*), expanded and gained new meaning. Lacking protection from his government, the powerless individual escaped the consequences of anarchy by putting himself under the protection of a local strong man, a patron. It was, at first, a contractual relationship. Protection was granted for military, agricultural, clerical, domestic, or other services rendered.

As conditions worsened, the institution of *precarium* came on the scene. Here the small landowner, unable to protect himself, would swear over, not services, but ownership of his land to a nearby patron. In return he received protection and the use of the land that once was his, but only for his lifetime. His children were landless, and if they wished to use the land and to gain protection, they had to swear to provide services and produce for the patron.

When the tribal barbarians finally and permanently occupied the lands of previous Roman dominion in Western Europe, the foundations of what was to become feudalism were there in the institutions of *patrocinium* and *precarium*. Through these already existing institutions (and through the conditions that gave them sway), the fear-ridden, landless, de-individualized population was prepared to be absorbed into the collectivist traditions of the barbarians. In fact, these institutions fitted neatly into a concept of the barbarians signified in Latin by the phrase *posse comitatus*, meaning literally "the power of the community." This tradition was grounded in ceremonies of fealty which through vows and ceremonies subordinated the individual to the tribe. The key tenet was the obligation of each member of the tribe to make himself a part of the tribe's power; specifically, each member was at all times to answer his chieftain's call to arms.

In a few generations, man the citizen and landowner and free artisan became man the tribalized vegetable, part of that structure of fealties, privileges, and powers that froze Europe into near-immobility for centuries.

Some apologists for feudalism praise the era by saying that it was one of order, where each man "knew his place." I agree. But it was an order like that of the prison, each man in his cell—a cell his son and his son's sons would have to occupy into eternity, bound to the land, bound also to the performance of certain inescapable duties. Feudal Europe at its most orderly was not totally changeless. There were many shifting traditions, many exceptions; and eventually the inherent necessity for change that is in the nature of a social system led to its end. But one duty ran as a binding chain through all the variations of feudalism—the obligation of each vassal to serve on the battlefield. You owed your patron (now a feudal noble) that, or else you were not protected, nor could you have a living from your patron's lands, nor could you leave the land. Should you refuse, most likely you would die, perhaps hoisted in a cage near the castle entrance to starve in the sight of your fellow serfs. *Patrocinium* and *precarium,* blended into the guiding spirit of *posse comitatus,* had made you but a plant growing for tribes within tribes: the immediate manor, the barony, the duchy, the princedom, and, over all, Christendom.

Eventually the tradition of *posse comitatus,* codified and verbalized, became part of post-feudal English law. In 1626 it was translated from the Latin as "the force of the county . . . the body of men above the age of fifteen in a county (exclusive of peers, clergymen, and infirm persons) whom the sheriff may summon or raise to repress a riot or for other purposes" (*The Oxford Universal Dictionary*, third edition, revised, 1955).

Thus do we have the long antecedents to that characteristic remark of the American Western, "Let's get a posse together and go after him."

It was from this same tradition that Great Britain derived impressment, a system of draft applied primarily in the 1700's and early 1800's to fill out the crews of naval vessels. (It was abandoned in the mid-nineteenth century in favor of long-term volunteer enlistments and the development of naval service as a career.)

When Britain's North American colonies rebelled against the crown, after a long and fruitless attempt by colonial leaders to gain redress of grievances through petition and other legal means, they issued a document in which they explained themselves. In it they said that "all men are . . . endowed . . . with certain unalienable Rights, that among these are Life, Liberty, and the Pursuit of Happiness."

There was no hue and cry of tyranny, of "abuses and usurpations," when in 1777 Massachusetts and Virginia instituted compulsory military service to pursue the values laid out in that document.

Posse comitatus was so assumed to entail the obligation of the citizen to the state (even to one which had come into being through rebellion) that George Washington in 1778 wrote to the President of the Continental Congress, "I believe our greatest and only aid will be derived from drafting, which I trust may be done by the United States."

I do not doubt Washington's sincere support of the political ideals in the Declaration of Independence. In the face of a tradition going back at least to the last days of the Roman Empire, he simply could not see an inconsistency between those ideals and a draft. Nor did his fellow revolutionaries. The idea of a political system based on rights which *all* men had from birth was a very new one. So Congress did recommend a draft to all the colonies. Supposedly only the fortuitous aid of the French made it unnecessary.

What the feudal tradition set was the precedent. In principle, this precedent went largely unchallenged by the thinkers of the Enlightenment. Worse, it was sanctioned by some of the most brilliant activists of that movement. A few men, off in what was then an obscure corner of the world, pledged "our Lives, our Fortunes, and our sacred Honor" to secure the rights of man—and saw no contradiction in forcing men to fight for the tribe, as long as the tribe fought tyranny.

But feudal levies, impressment, colonial drafts are little things beside the all-encompassing grasp of modern conscription.

It was in a cataclysm that modern conscription came into being. And it was born in the name of *liberté, fraternité,* and *égalité.*

In 1789 the *Ancien Régime* of France crumbled. An old-fashioned absolutism was succeeded by one in a newer fashion, one that used mass ideology, mass arrests, mass murders, and mass armies.

The first experiment in conscription ended in disastrous failure. In 1789 the concept of *égalité* was held to mean equality in one's obligation to serve in the military with "every able-bodied man liable." The enforcement of such universality was impossible. By 1792 "able-bodied" men by the tens of thousands had deserted their homes. The district of Vendée rose in revolt almost to a man.

Clearly, the design had not yet been perfected. The first refinement was one of utmost simplicity: in effect, a majority ganged up on a minority. The law was changed. Liability for service was restricted to young men only, men between the ages of eighteen and twenty-five. This group simply was not strong enough politically to prevent coercion. Only one other refinement was needed to produce a workable design. It was noted that the nation suffered when too many skilled artisans were taken. So the institutions of deferment and exemption were incorporated. (The English had excused London fishing masters and others from impressment many years earlier, on the grounds that they were of too great a service to the nation.)

The military instrument of modern dictatorship now ready, there arose the first modern dictator: the first to apply the modern principle derived from *posse comitatus*. He was, of course, Napoleon Bonaparte. It was he who said to Metternich that all he needed was 25,000 men a month. He got them. Eventually his total draftees numbered well over two million men. With them, he first conquered and then lost Europe, leaving the bodies of conscripts strewn across the continent from Madrid to Moscow.

Under Napoleon, France became a human breeding farm which turned out a crop of up to 116,000 young men a month: the youth which made the campaigns of Napoleon possible.

He ended at Waterloo, but mass conscription did not. Prussia used it, as she welded the hodgepodge of German-speaking principalities of mid-Europe into an empire.

Napoleonic conscription came to the United States in World War I (when some even wanted to broaden it to include the conscription of workers for industry and agriculture). Essentially, this system is the law of the United States today.

And its purpose is the same as it was for Napoleon and for Bismarck—the pursuit of state-chosen ends, ends which are held to be higher than those chosen by individuals for themselves.

Mass conscription did not embody a contradiction in states which had accepted the idea of a dictator-emperor, whether set up by plebiscite (France) or openly affirmed by a privileged nobility and military caste (Prussia).

But in the United States the contradiction is so open it is like a grand purloined letter on the table of history; open and apparent and obvious, and yet few have chosen to declare it so. This is the republic whose basic law and legal tradition emphasize the inviolability of rights: of life, liberty, and property. Nowhere in the Constitution is the explicit power given the government to conscript coercively. It takes an act of imagination to read this power as being implied by the power given Congress to raise armies. Further, it takes a mind-boggling act of reverse-think to see the right to bear arms as really the duty to be an arms bearer. No, quite clearly there is no objective, unequivocal foundation for the draft in the Constitution.

And yet in the American Revolution itself, in the Civil War (on both sides), and then massively and with Napoleonic scope in the wars of the twentieth century, this nation's government has violated rights in order to raise armies.

Suppose we put the principle behind American draft laws into words. In words, here it is in all its deceptive simplicity; here is our legacy from *patrocinium* and *precarium* and *posse comitatus:*

TO BE PERMANENTLY FREE, WE MUST TEMPORARILY ENSLAVE.

Is "enslave" too strong a word for a system that takes a man for a few years only, pays him at least something, and upon discharge gives him scholarships and guaranteed loans and special privileges? It is not, if we take the term literally. To enslave is to seize the person of some-one and put his person and services under the control of another as owner or master (*Webster's New International Dictionary*, second edi-tion, Springfield, 1937). It is in the nature of soldiering that, once in-ducted, the use and disposal of the soldier's person by his commanding officers is practically unlimited. The volunteer has agreed to this. The conscript has been ordered to agree. In the final analysis, when he goes to war he could not choose any other action. If he refuses to go, his liberty and property are indeed precarious.

It is strange to think that a tradition with its roots in the dissolution of an empire and in the tribal traditions of the hordes which sup-planted it still operates among us, whether acknowledged in so many words or not.

It is the spirit behind *posse comitatus* that rules the destinies of our young men, calling them to serve our tribe just as the chieftains did over a millennium ago in the black forests and foggy plains of the bar-barian lands outside the Roman Empire.

Here it is, almost in so many words, in a quote from the Secretary of War of the United States in 1917:

> The bill makes certain the raising and maintenance of the required forces with the utmost expedition. It establishes the principle that all arms-bearing citizens owe the nation the duty of defending it. It selects only those who by reason of their age and physical capacity are best fitted to receive the training and withstand the actual hard-ship of campaigns and who, happily, can be taken with least distur-bance of normal economic and industrial conditions.

So the principle of *posse comitatus,* which should have gone the way of serfdom and special privilege and levies, lives on, dressed in its more modern clothes. Conscription is but another form and application of tribal collectivism, but another application of the moral position that service to the values of the group is fundamentally prior to service to the values of oneself. In the present Selective Service Act, this principle is carried out to the last detail and with great consistency.

To see that this is so, take this test. First read the two following cases:

Case #1: A twenty-year-old man has made a down payment on a bulldozer. He has started a business—earth moving as a subcontractor. He sees no point in going to college; instead he is taking technical courses, both at night and from a correspondence school. He expects that in a few years his income will be over $10,000 a year, and then he will be able to marry. Beyond that, he sees the day when he'll own his own contracting firm, and he hopes (no, is certain) that one day he will build some of the biggest buildings in the country.

Case #2: A twenty-year-old man, in college, is uncertain of what he really wants to be. However, officially he's becoming an electrical engineer and will go for his doctorate in order to teach. Presently, he attends college on a state scholarship; his grades average in the high B's. Any higher, and, as he says, "There's no time for real living." He plans to marry in a few months, won't be a bit surprised if the first baby comes near the end of his senior year.

This test has only one question. Which young man will be drafted first? Do you need to refer to the Selective Service Act in order to answer?

The standard for exemption and deferment is the degree of actual or potential service to others. It is simply held to be obvious that doctoral candidates in engineering who want to teach are much much more valuable than entrepreneurial earth movers—and, anyway, there'll be that wife and baby when the time comes for the local board to reconsider Case #2. Not only does he serve the nation, but he has a family, too. The only way he could more certainly establish his draft-exempt status would be to become a student for the ministry, taking evening courses in medicine, with the eventual goal of becoming an overseas Peace Corps electronic medical missionary.

There is virtually no one reading this article who does not know [at least one] young man who has twisted his life into a counterfeit of his real purposes in order to conform to the official state morality and thus avoid the draft. Tens of thousands of young men take college courses they don't want, enter careers that are a torture to them, attend graduate schools that are a bore to them, marry women they love with a love most fortunate in its timing, and, with similar timing, have children. All of this, as supposedly free citizens in a free country where basic law says no man may have his freedom of speech abridged, his home invaded without warrant, his property taken without due process, his liberty taken away without formal charge and trial by jury. Young men, who are supposed inheritors of all this, by the thousands seek to avoid the forced seizure of their persons by using fraud, deceit, evasion, connivance, conspiracy, and self-deception.

And, in doing this, they often bring down upon themselves an incalculable burden of undeserved guilt.

It is time that our present institutions made a step or two beyond the semi-mystical, semi-tribal barbarities of prehistorical savagery. It is time; it has been for centuries. It is time simply to see that it is wrong to enslave, even if your goal is to preserve freedom.

But much of this has been said before. It may not have been said enough; it quite obviously has not convinced a sufficient number of people. The draft goes on, with virtually all of those screaming in the streets protesting, not the principle of conscription, but the fact of war. Or rather, only the latest war that conscription has made possible.

Once before this country tried to make a contradiction in principle work. It didn't. Ultimately two million men died. The republic itself nearly bled to death; today it still bleeds. That contradiction was the simultaneous recognition both of rights and of the institution of slavery. How we have paid and are paying for those few words in the Constitution!

Are the consequences potentially as grave if the nation persists with this other peculiar institution, conscription? At first glance, have results been so terrible?

The U.S. has been victorious in two major wars and in a lesser war, all in the last fifty years. Still using conscription, it bodes well to win this latest of its lesser wars. All it has cost has been several hundred thousand men, and many of these were volunteers.

Can't we just continue to evade the fact of injustice? After all, statistically, only a few are affected. They can't do much politically; the French administrators made that discovery some time ago. So the republic will go on.

Or will it?

"Posse Comitatus," by David Dawson, from *Persuasion*, Volume 3 (April 1966), pages 43–52. Reprinted by permission of the author's estate. Copyright © 1966 Persuasion, Inc.

DAVID J. DAWSON (1925–1979) was a Canadian-born editor, playwright, and sculptor who became a U.S. citizen after volunteering at age seventeen to serve in the U.S. Navy during World War II. He actively opposed military conscription on American college campuses and on radio and television from 1964 to 1968, during which time he was president of the Metropolitan Young Republican Club of New York City, chairman of its Committee for the Abolition of the Draft, and publisher of the early libertarian magazine *Persuasion*.

2

Plain Truth

by

Benjamin Franklin

In 1747, Pennsylvanians—most of them pacifist Quakers—found them-
selves vulnerable to imperialist attack by French and Dutch privateers.
In Plain Truth, *Benjamin Franklin attempts to persuade his compla-*
cent fellow colonists of the practical necessity for self-defense. His elo-
quent essay calls for a volunteer militia to protect the colony and reflects
American policy on war and defense at that time.

It is said the wise Italians make this proverbial Remark on our Nation,
viz. *The English* FEEL, *but they do not* SEE. That is, they are sensible
of Inconveniencies when they are present, but do not take sufficient
Care to prevent them: Their natural Courage makes them too little
apprehensive of Danger, so that they are often surpriz'd by it, un-
provided of the proper Means of Security. When 'tis too late they are
sensible of their Imprudence: After great Fires, they provide Buckets
and Engines: After a Pestilence they think of keeping clean their
Streets and common Shores: and when a Town has been sack'd by their
Enemies, they provide for its Defence, &c. This Kind of AFTER-

WISDOM is indeed so common with us, as to occasion the vulgar, tho' very significant Saying, *When the Steed is stolen, you shut the Stable Door.*

But the more insensible we generally are of publick Danger, and indifferent when warn'd of it, so much the more freely, openly, and earnestly, ought such as apprehend it, to speak their Sentiments; that if possible, those who seem to sleep, may be awaken'd, to think of some Means of Avoiding or Preventing the Mischief before it be too late.

Believing therefore that 'tis my DUTY, I shall honestly speak my Mind in the following Paper.

War, at this Time, rages over a great Part of the known World; our News-Papers are Weekly filled with fresh Accounts of the Destruction it every where occasions. Pennsylvania, indeed, situate in the Center of the Colonies, has hitherto enjoy'd profound Repose; and tho' our Nation is engag'd in a bloody War, with two great and powerful Kingdoms, yet, defended, in a great Degree, from the French on the one Hand by the Northern Provinces, and from the Spaniards on the other by the Southern, at no small Expence to each, our People have, till lately, slept securely in their Habitations.

There is no British Colony excepting this, but has made some Kind of Provision for its Defence; many of them have therefore never been attempted by an Enemy; and others that were attack'd, have generally defended themselves with Success. The Length and Difficulty of our Bay and River has been thought so effectual a Security to us, that hitherto no Means have been entered into that might discourage an Attempt upon us, or prevent its succeeding.

But whatever Security this might have been while both Country and City were poor, and the Advantage to be expected scarce worth the Hazard of an Attempt, it is now doubted whether we can any longer safely depend upon it. Our Wealth, of late Years much encreas'd, is one strong Temptation, our defenceless State another, to induce an Enemy to attack us; while the Acquaintance they have lately gained with our Bay and River, by Means of the Prisoners and Flags of Truce they have had among us; by Spies which they almost every where maintain, and perhaps from Traitors among ourselves; with the Facility of getting Pilots to conduct them; and the known Absence of Ships of War, during the greatest Part of the Year, from both Virginia and New-York, ever since the War began, render the Appearance of SUCCESS to the Enemy far more promising, and therefore highly encrease our DANGER.

That our Enemies may have Spies abroad, and some even in these Colonies, will not be made much doubt of, when 'tis considered, that such has been the Practice of all Nations in all Ages, whenever they

were engaged, or intended to engage in War. Of this we have an early
Example in the Book of Judges (too too [sic] pertinent to our Case, and
therefore I must beg leave a little to enlarge upon it) where we are told,
Chap. xviii, v. 2, That *the Children of Dan sent of their Family five
Men from their Coasts to spie out the Land, and search it, saying, Go,
search the* LAND. These Danites it seems were at this Time not very
orthodox in their Religion, and their Spies met with a certain idolatrous Priest of their own Persuasion, v. 3, and they said to him, *Who
brought thee hither? what makest thou in this Place? and what hast
thou here?* [Would to God no such Priests were to be found among
us.][1] And they said unto him, verse 5, *Ask Counsel of God, that we may
know whether our Way which we go shall be prosperous? And the
Priest said unto them, Go in Peace; before the Lord is your Way
wherein you go.* [Are there no Priests among us, think you, that might,
in the like Case, give an Enemy as good Encouragement? 'Tis well
known, that we have Numbers of the same Religion with those who of
late encouraged the French to invade our Mother-Country.] *And they
came,* Verse 7, *to Laish, and saw the People that were therein, how they
dwelt* CARELESS, *after the Manner of the Zidonians,* QUIET *and*
SECURE. They *thought* themselves secure, no doubt; and as they *never
had been* disturbed, vainly imagined they *never should.* 'Tis not unlikely that some might see the Danger they were exposed to by living in
that *careless* Manner; but that if these publickly expressed their Apprehensions, the rest reproached them as timorous Persons, wanting
Courage or Confidence in their Gods, who (they might say) had hitherto protected them. But the Spies, Verse 8, returned, and said to their
Countrymen, Verse 9, *Arise that we may go up against them; for we
have seen the Land, and behold it is very good! And are ye still? Be not
slothful to go.* Verse 10, *When ye go, ye shall come unto a People*
SECURE; [that is, a People that apprehend no Danger, and therefore
have made no Provision against it; great Encouragement this!] *and to a
large Land, and a Place where there is no Want of any Thing.* What
could they desire more? Accordingly we find, in the following Verses,
that *Six hundred Men* only, *appointed with Weapons of War,* undertook
the Conquest of this *large Land;* knowing that 600 Men, armed and
disciplined, would be an Over-match perhaps for 60,000, unarmed,
undisciplined, and off their Guard. And when they went against it, the
idolatrous Priest, Verse 17, *with his graven Image, and his Ephod, and
his Teraphim, and his molten Image,* [Plenty of superstitious Trinkets]
joined with them, and, no doubt, gave them all the Intelligence and
Assistance in his Power; his Heart, as the Text assures us, *being glad,*
perhaps for Reasons more than one. And now, what was the Fate of

poor Laish! The 600 Men being arrived, found, as the Spies had reported, a People QUIET and SECURE, Verse 20, 21.[2] *And they smote them with the Edge of the Sword, and burnt the City with* FIRE; *and there was no* DELIVERER, *because it was far from Zidon.* Not so far from Zidon, however, as Pennsylvania is from Britain; and yet we are, if possible, more *careless* than the People of Laish! As the Scriptures are given for our Reproof, Instruction and Warning, may we make a due Use of this Example, before it be too late!

And is our *Country,* any more than our City, altogether free from Danger? Perhaps not. We have, 'tis true, had a long Peace with the Indians: But it is a long Peace indeed, as well as a long Lane, that has no Ending. The French know the Power and Importance of the Six Nations, and spare no Artifice, Pains or Expence, to gain them to their Interest. By their Priests they have converted many to their Religion, and these* have openly espoused their Cause. The rest appear irresolute which Part to take; no Persuasions, tho' enforced with costly Presents, having yet been able to engage them generally on our Side, tho' we had numerous Forces on their Borders, ready to second and support them. What then may be expected, now those Forces are, by Orders from the Crown, to be disbanded; when our boasted Expedition is laid aside, thro' want (as it may appear to them) either of Strength or Courage; when they see that the French, and their Indians, boldly, and with Impunity, ravage the Frontiers of New York, and scalp the Inhabitants; when those few Indians that engaged with us against the French, are left exposed to their Resentment: When they consider these Things, is there no Danger that, thro' Disgust at our Usage, joined with Fear of the French Power, and greater Confidence in their Promises and Protection than in ours, they may be wholly gained over by our Enemies, and join in the War against us? If such should be the Case, which God forbid, how soon may the Mischief spread to our Frontier Counties? And what may we expect to be the Consequence, but deserting of Plantations, Ruin, Bloodshed and Confusion!

Perhaps some in the City, Towns and Plantations near the River, may say to themselves, *An Indian War on the Frontiers will not affect us; the Enemy will never come near our Habitations; let those concern'd take Care of themselves.* And others who live in the Country, when they are told of the Danger the City is in from Attempts by Sea, may say, *What is that to us? The Enemy will be satisfied with the Plunder of the Town, and never think it worth his while to visit our*

---

*The Praying Indians.

Plantations: Let the Town take care of itself. These are not mere Suppositions, for I have heard some talk in this strange Manner. But are these the Sentiments of true Pennsylvanians, of Fellow-Countrymen, or even of Men that have common Sense or Goodness? Is not the whole Province one Body, united by living under the same Laws, and enjoying the same Priviledges? Are not the People of City and Country connected as Relations both by Blood and Marriage, and in Friendships equally dear? Are they not likewise united in Interest, and mutually useful and necessary to each other? When the Feet are wounded, shall the Head say, *It is not me; I will not trouble myself to contrive Relief!* Or if the Head is in Danger, shall the Hands say, *We are not affected, and therefore will lend no Assistance!* No. For so would the Body be easily destroyed: But when all Parts join their Endeavours for its Security, it is often preserved. And such should be the Union between the Country and the Town; and such their mutual Endeavors for the Safety of the Whole. When New-England, a distant Colony, involv'd itself in a grievous Debt to reduce Cape-Breton, we freely gave *Four Thousand Pounds* for *their* Relief. And at another Time, remembering that Great Britain, still more distant, groan'd under heavy Taxes in Supporting the War, we threw in our Mite to their Assistance, by a free Gift of *Three Thousand Pounds.* And shall Country and Town join in helping Strangers (as those comparatively are) and yet refuse to assist each other?

But whatever different Opinions we have of our Security in other Respects, our TRADE, all seem to agree, is in Danger of being ruin'd in another Year. The great Success of our Enemies, in two different Cruizes this last Summer in our Bay, must give them the greatest Encouragement to repeat more frequently their Visits, the Profit being almost certain, and the Risque next to nothing. Will not the first Effect of this be, an Enhauncing of the Price of all foreign Goods to the Tradesman and Farmer, who use or consume them? For the Rate of Insurance will increase in Proportion to the Hazard of Importing them; and in the same Proportion will the Price of those Goods increase. If the Price of the Tradesman's Work and the Farmer's Produce would encrease equally with the Price of foreign Commodities, the Damage would not be so great: But the direct contrary must happen. For the same Hazard, or Rate of Insurance, that raises the Price of what is imported, must be deducted out of, and lower the Price of what is exported. Without this Addition and Deduction, as long as the Enemy cruize at our Capes, and take those Vessels that attempt to *go out,* as well as those that endeavour to *come in,* none can afford to trade, and Business must be soon at a Stand. And will not the Consequences be, A discouraging of many of the Vessels that us'd to come from other Places to purchase our Produce, and thereby a Turning of the Trade to Ports that can be entered with less Danger, and capable of furnishing them with the same Commodities, as New-York, &c? A Lessening of Business to every Shopkeeper, together with Multitudes of bad Debts; the high Rate of Goods discouraging the Buyers, and the low Rates of their Labour and Produce rendering them unable to pay for what they had bought: Loss of Employment to the Tradesman, and bad Pay for what little he does: And lastly, Loss of many Inhabitants, who will retire to other Provinces not subject to the like Inconveniencies; whence a Lowering of the Value of Lands, Lots, and Houses.

The Enemy, no doubt, have been told, That the People of Pennsylvania are Quakers, and against all Defence, from a Principle of Conscience; this, tho' true of a Part, and that a small Part only of the Inhabitants, is commonly said of the Whole; and what may make it look probable to Strangers, is, that in Fact, nothing is done by any Part of the People towards their Defence. But to refuse Defending one's self or one's Country, is so unusual a Thing among Mankind, that possibly they may not believe it, till by Experience they find, they can come higher and higher up our River, seize our Vessels, land and plunder our Plantations and Villages, and retire with their Booty unmolested. Will not this confirm the Report, and give them the greatest Encouragement to strike one bold Stroke for the City, and for the whole Plunder of the River?

It is said by some, that the Expence of a Vessel to guard our Trade, would be very heavy, greater than perhaps all the Enemy can be supposed to take from us at Sea would amount to; and that it would be cheaper for the Government to open an Insurance-Office, and pay all Losses. But is this right Reasoning? I think not: For what the Enemy takes is clear Loss to us, and Gain to him; encreasing his Riches and Strength as much as it diminishes ours, so making the Difference double; whereas the Money paid our own Tradesmen for Building and Fitting out a Vessel of Defence, remains in the Country, and circulates among us; what is paid to the Officers and Seamen that navigate her, is also spent ashore, and soon gets into other Hands; the Farmer receives the Money for her Provisions; and on the whole, nothing is clearly lost to the Country but her Wear and Tear, or so much as she sells for at the End of the War less than her first Cost. This Loss, and a trifling one it is, is all the Inconvenience; But how many and how great are the Conveniencies and Advantages! And should the Enemy, thro' our Supineness and Neglect to provide for the Defence both of our Trade and Country, be encouraged to attempt this City, and after plundering us of our Goods, either *burn it,* or put it to Ransom; how great would that Loss be! Besides the Confusion, Terror, and Distress, so many Hundreds of Families would be involv'd in!

The Thought of this latter Circumstance so much affects me, that I cannot forbear expatiating somewhat more upon it. You have, my dear Countrymen, and Fellow Citizens, Riches to tempt a considerable Force to unite and attack you, but are under no Ties or Engagements to unite for your Defence. Hence, on the first Alarm, *Terror* will spread over All; and as no Man can with Certainty depend that another will stand by him, beyond Doubt very many will seek Safety by a speedy Flight. Those that are reputed rich, will flee, thro' Fear of Torture, to make them produce more than they are able. The Man that has a Wife and Children, will find them hanging on his Neck, beseeching him with Tears to quit the City, and save his Life, to guide and protect them in that Time of general Desolation and Ruin. All will run into Confusion, amidst Cries and Lamentations, and the Hurry and Disorder of Departers, carrying away their Effects. The Few that remain will be unable to resist. *Sacking* the City will be the first, and *Burning* it, in all Probability, the last Act of the Enemy. This, I believe, will be the Case, if you have timely Notice. But what must be your Condition, if suddenly surprized, without previous Alarm, perhaps in the Night! Confined to your Houses, you will have nothing to trust to but the Enemy's Mercy. Your best Fortune will be, to fall under the Power of Commanders of King's Ships, able to controul the Mariners; and not into the Hands of *licentious Privateers.* Who can, without the utmost Horror, conceive the Miseries of the Latter! when your Persons, Fortunes, Wives and Daughters, shall be subject to the wanton and unbridled Rage, Rapine and Lust, of *Negroes, Molattoes,* and others, the vilest and most abandoned of Mankind.* A dreadful Scene! which some may represent as exaggerated. I think it my Duty to warn you: Judge for yourselves.

'Tis true, with very little Notice, the Rich may shift for themselves. The Means of speedy Flight are ready in their Hands; and with some previous Care to lodge Money and Effects in distant and secure Places,

---

*By Accounts, the ragged Crew of the Spanish Privateer that plundered Mr. Liston's, and another Plantation, a little below Newcastle, was composed of such as these. The *Honour* and *Humanity* of their Officers may be judg'd of, by the Treatment they gave poor Capt. Brown, whom they took with Martin's Ship in Returning from their Cruize. Because he bravely defended himself and Vessel longer than they expected, for which every generous Enemy would have esteem'd him, did they, after he had struck and submitted, barbarously *stab* and *murder* him, tho' on his Knees begging Quarter!

tho' they should lose much, yet enough may be left them, and to spare. But most unhappily circumstanced indeed are we, the middling People, the Tradesmen, Shopkeepers, and Farmers of this Province and City! We cannot all fly with our Families; and if we could, how shall we subsist? No; we and they, and what little we have gained by hard Labour and Industry, must bear the Brunt: The Weight of Contributions, extorted by the Enemy (as it is of Taxes among ourselves) must be surely borne by us. Nor can it be avoided as we stand at present; for tho' we are numerous, we are quite defenceless, having neither Forts, Arms, Union, nor Discipline. And tho' it were true, that our Trade might be protected at no great Expence, and our Country and our City easily defended, if proper Measures were but taken; yet who shall take these Measures? Who shall pay that Expence? On whom may we fix our Eyes with the least Expectation that they will do any one Thing for our Security? Should we address that wealthy and powerful Body of People, who have ever since the War governed our Elections, and filled almost every Seat in our Assembly; should we intreat them to consider, if not as Friends, at least as Legislators, that *Protection* is as truly due from the Government to the People, as *Obedience* from the People to the Government; and that if on account of their religious Scruples, they themselves could do no Act for our Defence, yet they might retire, relinquish their Power for a Season, quit the Helm to freer Hands during the present Tempest, to Hands chosen by their own Interest too, whose Prudence and Moderation, with regard to them, they might safely confide in; secure, from their own native Strength, of resuming again their present Stations, whenever it shall please them: Should we remind them, that the Publick Money, raised *from All,* belongs *to All;* that since they have, for their own Ease, and to secure themselves in the quiet Enjoyment of their Religious Principles (and may they long enjoy them) expended such large Sums to oppose Petitions, and engage favourable Representations of their Conduct, if they themselves could by no Means be free to appropriate any Part of the Publick Money for our Defence; yet it would be no more than Justice to spare as a reasonable Sum for that Purpose, which they might easily give to the King's Use as heretofore, leaving all the Appropriation to others, who would faithfully apply it as we desired: Should we tell them, that tho' the Treasury be at present empty, it may soon be filled by the outstanding Publick Debts collected; or at least Credit might be had for such a Sum, on a single Vote of the Assembly: That tho' *they* themselves may be resigned and easy under this naked, defenceless State of the Country, it is far otherwise with a very great Part of the People; with *us,* who can have no Confidence that God will protect those that neglect the Use of rational Means for their Security; nor have any Reason to hope, that our Losses, if we should suffer any, may be made up by Collections in our Favour at Home? Should we conjure them by all the Ties of Neighbourhood, Friendship, Justice and Humanity, to consider these Things; and what Distraction, Misery and Confusion, what Desolation and Distress, may possibly be the Effect of their *unseasonable* Predominancy and Perseverance; yet all would be in vain: For they have already been by great Numbers of the People petitioned in vain. Our late Governor did for Years sollicit, request, and even threaten them in vain. The Council have since twice remonstrated to them in vain. Their religious Prepossessions are unchangeable, their Obstinacy invincible. Is there then the least Hope remaining, that from that Quarter any Thing should arise for our Security?

And is our Prospect better, if we turn our Eyes to the Strength of the *opposite Party,* those Great and rich Men, Merchants and others, who are ever railing at Quakers for doing what their Principles seem to require, and what in Charity we ought to believe they think their Duty, but take no one Step themselves for the Publick Safety? They have so much Wealth and Influence, if they would use it, that they might easily, by their Endeavours and Example, raise a military Spirit among us, make us fond, studious of, and expert in Martial Discipline, and effect every Thing that is necessary, under God, for our Protection. But ENVY seems to have taken Possession of their Hearts, and to have eaten out and destroyed every generous, noble, Publick-spirited Sentiment. *Rage* at the Disappointment of their little Schemes for Power, gnaws their Souls, and fills them with such cordial Hatred to their Opponents, that every Proposal, by the Execution of which *those* may receive Benefit as well as themselves, is rejected with Indignation. *What,* say they, *shall we lay out our Money to protect the Trade of Quakers? Shall we fight to defend Quakers? No; Let the Trade perish, and the City burn; let what will happen, we shall never lift a Finger to prevent it.* Yet the Quakers have *Conscience* to plead for their Resolution not to fight, which these Gentlemen have not: *Conscience* with you, Gentlemen, is on the other Side of the Question: *Conscience* enjoins it as a DUTY on you (and indeed I think it such on every Man) to defend your Country, your Friends, your aged Parents, your Wives, and helpless Children: And yet you resolve not to perform this Duty, but act *contrary* to *your own* Consciences, because the Quakers act *according* to *theirs.* 'Till of late I could scarce believe the Story of him who refused to pump in a sinking Ship, because one on board, whom he hated, would be saved by it as well as himself. But such, it seems, is the Unhappiness of human Nature, that our Passions, when violent, often are too hard for the united Force of *Reason, Duty* and *Religion.*

Thus unfortunately are we circumstanc'd at this Time, my dear Countrymen and Fellow-Citizens; we, I mean, the middling People, the Farmers, Shopkeepers and Tradesmen of this City and Country. Thro' the Dissensions of our Leaders, thro' *mistaken Principles* of *Religion,* join'd with a Love of Worldly Power, on the one Hand; thro' *Pride, Envy* and *implacable Resentment* on the other; our Lives, our Families and little Fortunes, dear to us as any Great Man's can be to him, are to remain continually expos'd to Destruction, from an enter-prizing, cruel, now well-inform'd, and by Success encourag'd Enemy. It seems as if Heaven, justly displeas'd at our growing Wickedness, and determin'd to punish* this once favour'd Land, had suffered our Chiefs to engage in these foolish and mischievous Contentions, for *little Posts* and *paltry Distinctions,* that our Hands might be bound up, our Understandings darkned and misled, and every Means of our Security neglected. It seems as if our greatest Men, our *Cives nobilissimi*† of both Parties, had *sworn the Ruin of the Country, and invited the French, our most inveterate Enemy, to destroy it.* Where then shall we seek for Succour and Protection? The Government we are immediately under denies it to us; and if the Enemy comes, we are *far from* ZIDON, *and there is no Deliverer near.* Our Case indeed is dangerously bad; but perhaps there is yet a Remedy, if we have but the Prudence and the Spirit to apply it.

If this now flourishing City, and greatly improving Colony, is de-stroy'd and ruin'd, it will not be for want of Numbers of Inhabitants able to bear Arms in its Defence. 'Tis computed that we have at least (exclusive of the Quakers) 60,000 Fighting Men, acquainted with Fire-Arms, many of them Hunters and Marksmen, hardy and bold. All we want is Order, Discipline, and a few Cannon. At present we are like the separate Filaments of Flax before the Thread is form'd, without Strength because without Connection; but UNION would make

---

*When God determined to punish his chosen People, the Inhabitants of Jerusalem, who, tho' Breakers of his other Laws, were scrupulous Observers of that ONE which required keeping holy the Sabbath Day; he suffered even the strict Observation of that Command to be their Ruin: For Pompey observing that they *then* obstinately refused to fight, made a general Assault on that Day, took the Town, and butcher'd them with as little Mercy as he found Resistance.   JOSEPHUS.

---

†Conjuravere cives nobilissimi Patriam incendere; GALLORIUM GENTEM, infes-tissimam nomini Romano, ad Bellum·arcessunt.   CAT. in SALUST.

us strong and even formidable: Tho' the *Great* should neither help nor join us; tho' they should even oppose our Uniting, from some mean Views of their own, yet, if we resolve upon it, and it please GOD to inspire us with the necessary Prudence and Vigour, it *may* be effected. Great Numbers of our People are of BRITISH RACE, and tho' the fierce fighting Animals of those happy Islands, are said to abate their native Fire and Intrepidity, when removed to a Foreign Clime, yet with the People 'tis not so; Our Neighbours of New-England afford the World a convincing Proof, that BRITONS, tho' a Hundred Years transplanted, and to the remotest Part of the Earth, may yet retain, even to the third and fourth Descent, that *Zeal* for the *Publick Good,* that *military Prowess,* and that *undaunted Spirit,* which has in every Age distinguished their Nation. What Numbers have we likewise of *those brave People,* whose Fathers in the last Age made so glorious a Stand for our Religion and Liberties, when invaded by a powerful French Army, join'd by Irish Catholicks, under a bigotted Popish King! Let the memorable SIEGE OF LONDONDERRY, and the signal Actions of the INISKILLINGERS, by which the Heart of that Prince's Schemes was broken, be perpetual Testimonies of the *Courage* and *Conduct* of those *noble Warriors!* Nor are there wanting amongst us, Thousands of *that Warlike Nation,* whose Sons have ever since the Time of Caesar maintained the Character he gave their Fathers, of joining the most *obstinate Courage* to all the other military Virtues. I mean the *brave* and *steady* GERMANS. Numbers of whom have actually borne Arms in the Service of their respective Princes; and if they fought well for their Tyrants and Oppressors, would they refuse to unite with us in Defence of their *newly acquired* and most precious *Liberty* and *Property?* Were this Union form'd, were we once united, thoroughly arm'd and disciplin'd, was every Thing in our Power done for our Security, as far as human Means and Foresight could provide, we might then, *with more Propriety,* humbly ask the Assistance of Heaven, and a Blessing on our lawful Endeavours. The very Frame of our Strength and Readiness would be a Means of Discouraging our Enemies; for 'tis a wise and true Saying, that *One Sword often keeps another in the Scabbard.* The Way to secure Peace is to be prepared for War. They that are on their Guard, and appear ready to receive their Adversaries, are in much less Danger of being attack'd, than the supine, secure and negligent. We have yet a Winter before us, which may afford a good and almost sufficient Opportunity for this, if we seize and improve it with a becoming Vigour. And if the Hints contained in this Paper are so happy as to meet with a suitable Disposition of Mind in his Countrymen and Fellow Citizens, the Writer of it will, in a few Days, lay before them a

Form of an ASSOCIATION for the Purposes herein mentioned, together with a practicable Scheme for raising the Money necessary for the Defence of our Trade, City, and Country, without laying a Burthen on any Man.

May the GOD *of* WISDOM, STRENGTH *and* POWER, *the Lord of the Armies of Israel, inspire us with Prudence in this Time of* DANGER; *take away from us all the Seeds of Contention and Division, and unite the Hearts and Counsels of all of us, of whatever* SECT *or* NATION, *in one Bond of Peace, Brotherly Love, and generous Publick Spirit; May he give us Strength and Resolution to amend our Lives, and remove from among us every Thing that is displeasing to him; afford us his most gracious Protection, confound the Designs of our Enemies, and give* PEACE *in all our Borders, is the sincere Prayer of*

A TRADESMAN of Philadelphia.

"Plain Truth, &c.," by Benjamin Franklin, from *The Papers of Benjamin Franklin*, Volume 3, edited by Leonard W. Labaree (New Haven and London: Yale University Press, 1961), pages 188–204 (most editorial notes have been omitted). Reprinted by permission of the publisher, Yale University Press. Copyright © 1961 by the American Philosophical Society Held at Philadelphia for Promoting Useful Knowledge and by Yale University.

BENJAMIN FRANKLIN (1706–1790) is best remembered for his role in framing the Declaration of Independence and the United States Constitution. An accomplished author and publisher as well as scientist, inventor, and diplomat, Franklin designed the first official U.S. coin and devoted his life to promoting the public interest.

Notes

1. Brackets in this paragraph in the original.
2. Should be: verses 27, 28.

3

Conscription

by
Mark Sullivan

Reversing a long-standing tradition of volunteer military service in America proved one of the most formidable tasks of Woodrow Wilson's presidency. Though Wilson was personally predisposed against coercion, the realities of a declared war and pressure from his army chiefs quickly convinced him of its necessity. In this essay, Sullivan details the often extreme measures that Secretary of War Newton Baker and Judge Advocate General Enoch Crowder used to shape public opinion in an attempt to ensure passage and acceptance of the Conscription Act of 1917.

I

Vaguely, but only vaguely as yet, America realized that war on Germany involved something more grim than the thrill of hearing the declaration. Somebody must fight the war. A number of young men would be glad to—about the proportion that in any war would volunteer, the adventurous, the romantic, those who found their ordinary life dull, those having associations they would be glad to get away from, those without jobs, those who preferred the routine of military life above the self-responsibility of civil life—in any country in any time there is always a ratio who will volunteer in any war. In America at this time the proportion to volunteer would be smaller than normal, for nearly three years of watching the Western front had brought realization that war under modern conditions meant hardship, dirt and death, and very little glamour or romance. As for economic motive, there was none; every man in America who wanted a job could have one, and at high wages—America was furiously busy turning out munitions for the Allies. Moreover, of those who would normally volunteer, a considerable proportion had already gone forward. A few, the most dashing, had gone early in the war to Canada, and managed to get into the fighting. Many had enlisted in our own Regular Army or Navy or National Guard in the moderate expansion which Congress had authorized at Wilson's request a year before. Those volunteer enlistments had been slow. It was not likely that a call for volunteers to fight Germany would bring numbers adequate for this major war. There must be conscription, but art would be needed to lead the country to accept it, an art with which both President Wilson and Secretary Baker were exceptionally endowed.

II

Wilson personally did not like conscription, he preferred the spirit of volunteering. In his early discussions of preparedness he had emphasized the volunteer system, and his faith in it:

> I have been asked by questioning friends, whether I thought a sufficient number of men would volunteer for the training or not. Why, if they did not, it is not the America that you and I know; something has happened. If they did not do it, I should be ashamed of America. I am sorry for the skeptics who believe that the response would not be tremendous; not grudging, but overflowing in its abundant strength.[1]

Not only had Wilson been, by temperament and conviction, personally unsympathetic to conscription. He knew that America as a whole did not like it—indeed it never occurred to the masses of the country that conscription would be attempted. Conscription, in the

American mind, was associated with autocracy. Never in any war of ours had conscription been suggested at the outset; only once had it been tried at all, and when, after two years of the Civil War, an attempt had been made to draft, rioting mobs in New York had sacked the provost marshal's office, burned and smashed the wheels and lists and the other paraphernalia for taking Americans to war against their wills. In this war, not only would there be the usual American repugnance; further, 13 per cent of our people were of German birth or descent, and a considerable percentage more were of peoples embraced in the Austrian Empire. In the war in Europe so far, the precedent we most respected had been against conscription—Britain had relied on volunteers for the first eighteen months, her government unwilling or afraid to attempt conscription.

All this Wilson knew. But Germany had flouted him and America; he had a high purpose in which, since Germany had forced him to it, crushing of German arms was now the first and indispensable step. Wilson could be hard; "like most reformers," said Doctor Charles W. Eliot, "Wilson had a fierce and unlovely side."

III

Wilson's decision to conscript America was made before he called on Congress to declare war, and more than two months before Congress passed the Act that legalized the draft. By agreement,[2] kept secret, of Wilson, Secretary of War Baker, and Judge Advocate General (later Provost-Marshal) Enoch H. Crowder, the colossal machinery for enforcing the draft was set up and made ready long before the country knew[3] there would be a draft—while, indeed, the country continued to take it for granted that only the volunteer system would be used.

Anticipating the country would be shocked, that it might refuse to submit to conscription, a procedure was devised that would be least offensive to the people, that would indeed give the process to some extent the color of volunteering. The direct act of taking young men from their homes would not be done by army officers in uniform; the process would be carried out by civilians, so far as possible by neighbors of the conscripted man. "Instead of having soldiers . . . ride the country side going from door to door and listing men of draft age" the draft would be made to appear "like going to the polls to vote."[4] The order, so soon as, and if, Congress should pass the Act, would be that all men of draft age register at the place in the local precinct where it was their custom to vote. Out of those thus registered—it would be all of draft age—

local civilian officials would pick the ones to be turned over to the army for service, would say who was exempt, who must go. The process would be one, not of the army walking into the draftee's home, but of civilian officials, mainly neighbors, delivering the draftee to the army. It would be supervised by civilian sheriffs and governors, officials holding their offices by popular vote. But the draftee would reach the army just as surely as if the army had come and taken him.

This depriving the draft of the appearance of compulsion, but at the same time getting the advantage of compulsion, is attributed to Secretary of War Baker. Baker, like Wilson, knew the importance of appearances, had much of Wilson's skill with words. Both had exceptional understanding of the art of causing popular psychology to be what they wished it to be.

In the same spirit, it was decided to have the draft machinery ready to start in motion the day when Congress should pass the Act. Setting up of the immense mechanism would consume two months—and two months before public knowledge of the intention to draft and actual drafting might provide time for resistance to generate.

Baker, before Congress had passed the Draft Act, before it had appropriated the money for what he was about to do—indeed with care to prevent Congress from knowing—Baker, acting through General Crowder and he through Major Hugh S. Johnson, arranged with the head of the Government Printing Office to print secretly the more than ten million blanks that would be required to put the draft in effect when and if Congress should enact it. To the Public Printer, secrecy was easy; it was an ordinary incident of his duty in printing advance copies of Presidents' messages and Supreme Court decisions. He went ahead with printing the blanks, wrapping and sealing them. He "did not realize how much space the millions of forms would occupy; the corridors were so full he had to find storage elsewhere; the local Washington postmaster now became a conspirator; soon the cellar of the city post office was stacked to the ceiling. Still no word of the operation reached the public or Congress."[5]

Then Baker, April 23, wrote a confidential letter to every State governor: "The President desires [not directs] that I bring to your attention the following considerations which he is not at present ready to give to the press. . . ."

In the letter Baker explained to the governors the secret preparations being made for the draft, and asked them to be ready to co-operate, so soon as Congress should pass this Act. "Then all the sheriffs of the land were taken into confidence; to each was mailed his quota of blanks, accompanied by a slip saying that it was a matter of urgent government secrecy that there be no mention of their existence until the word of release came from Washington."[6] Every sheriff kept the secret. After the sheriffs, the men chosen to compose the local draft boards were secretly notified and "eagerly awaited the signal."[7]

IV

All this was before Congress had passed the Draft Act, before it was certain they would. The opposition was strong; Congress knew the country would not like the draft, and Congress reflected the country. Wilson, in his request for the Act, used words designed to rob it, in appearance, of some of its unpalatability: "The necessary men will be secured . . . by volunteering as at present, until . . . a resort to a selective draft is desirable." Congressmen who were friends of the measure sought further camouflage. Representative Richard Olney of Massachusetts observed that "the words 'draft' and 'conscription' are rather unpopular," and suggested the wording of the bill be altered to say, "personal obligation to service." Congressman John Q. Tilson of Connecticut asked Baker if there was not "something to be said in favor of accepting a system, volunteering, that is known to be bad, inefficacious and inadequate, rather than to create the effect which might be created by a very unpopular measure."

In the public debate on the floor of House and Senate, opponents of the draft used the harshest words: "Prussianize America" . . . "destroy democracy at home while fighting for it abroad" . . . "a sulky, unwilling, indifferent army" . . . "abject or involuntary servitude" . . . "un-American" . . . "conscription makes the term 'sovereign citizen' irony" . . . "conscription is another name for slavery" . . . "rioting all over the United States will add more joy to the German heart." Champ Clark, Democratic Speaker of the House, said: "I protest with all my heart and mind and soul against having the slur of being a conscript placed upon the men of Missouri; in the estimation of Missourians there is precious little difference between a conscript and a convict."[8]

Chairman Dent of the House Military Affairs Committee declined to introduce the draft bill; a majority of the committee were opposed to it. Wilson, sending for the House leaders, informed them that he would not "yield an inch of any essential part of the programme for raising an army by conscription." A Congressman friend of Provost-Marshal Crowder warned him, "Your name will become the most odious in America." Senator Reed of Missouri said to Baker, "You will have the streets of our American cities running red with blood on Registration day." But Baker knew his art and went on with his plan for robbing the draft of its unpalatability.

The bill passed and was signed by the President May 18. "The singularly brief act delegated to the President more power than any of his predecessors had been granted over the lives and destinies of their fellow-citizens."[9]

V

Meanwhile, May 1, sixteen days before Congress acted, Baker, carrying out his project of making the draft seem what he conceived it,[10] rather than what the public felt it to be, described to Wilson some of his plans:

> I am exceedingly anxious to have the registration and selection by draft . . . conducted under such circumstances as to create a strong patriotic feeling and relieve as far as possible the prejudice which remains to some extent in the popular mind against the draft. With this end in view, I am using a vast number of agencies throughout the country to make the day of registration a festival and patriotic occasion. Several Governors and some mayors of cities are entering already heartily into this plan, and the Chamber of Commerce of the United States is taking it up through its affiliated bodies.

"As a part of this programme," Baker added, to Wilson, "I am anxious to have you issue a proclamation when you sign the bill, and I submit herewith a draft for your revision."

The proclamation, written by Baker, modified slightly by Wilson and then signed, was shrewdly designed to create an intended atmosphere. As published in many papers it was captioned "Call to Arms" and surrounded with a border of American flags. Its paragraphs began with "𝔚𝔥𝔢𝔯𝔢𝔞𝔰," and "𝔑𝔬𝔴, 𝔗𝔥𝔢𝔯𝔢𝔣𝔬𝔯𝔢," and "𝔍𝔫 𝔚𝔦𝔱𝔫𝔢𝔰𝔰 𝔚𝔥𝔢𝔯𝔢𝔬𝔣," in the Gothic type associated with religion and legal documents. Wilson's phrases were carefully composed to bear out the lofty atmosphere:

> *Now, Therefore, I, Woodrow Wilson,* President of the United States, do proclaim and give notice to all persons . . . and I do charge . . . the day here named is the time upon which all shall present themselves. . . . It is essential that the day be approached in thoughtful apprehension of its significance and that we accord it the honor and the meaning that it deserves. . . . Carried in all our hearts as a great day of patriotic devotion and obligation, when the duty shall lie upon every man to see to it that the name of every male person of the designated ages is written on these lists of honor. . . .

In Witness Whereof, I have hereunto set my hand and caused the seal of the United States to be affixed. Done at the City of Washington this 18th day of May in the year of our Lord one thousand nine hundred and seventeen, and of the independence of the United States of America the one hundred and forty-first.

By the President:

WOODROW WILSON.

That proclamation brought the war home to America—literally "home," for it was to the homes that its meaning went.

Within the aura of lofty phrasing, the grim fact that every one sought and many disliked to find, was that on June 5, 1917, between 7 A.M. and 7 P.M. every American male between the ages of 21 and 30 (inclusive)[11] must register; and the registration was surrender of their persons to the government. So far as they and their families were dismayed or sullen, expression of individual feeling was kept down by the success of Wilson and Baker in "turning of registration day into a joyous pilgrimage. . . . The sweep of public opinion smothered critical questioning. The cozening glove concealed the reminder of the steel gauntlet to enforce the penalty for failure to register."[12] Beneath the lofty phrases designed to evoke a national spirit of patriotic exaltation, lay iron words informing the individual that the penalty of fleeing from the draft was imprisonment for one year.

But if the youth, taking his way to the registration place along the mountain roads of West Virginia or the city streets of New York, had any sullenness, it was dissipated in most cases by finding shortly that Baker's art had made him, unexpectedly, a hero. Presently, under the influence of the national spirit, he began to believe it. Speeches from the mayor, the clergyman, and the Chamber of Commerce head; congratulations by star-eyed committees of women, more intimate attentions from young girls, turned most of the draftees to feeling the war would be a grand adventure.

The method by which the draft was brought about, this use of immense organized propaganda by government to make the public mind receptive to what the government planned to do, coupled with elaborate, secret, advance preparation of a mechanism which should put the draft in effect, without delay that might permit opposition to generate—this was a new thing in America. Essentially it was a process of causing the mass of the public to move in a direction in which the government wished them to go, a direction which the public, if left alone, would not take. The technique included, as a principle or as a condition that arose in practice, exercise of pressure by the majority to compel the minority to conform. In the case of the draft, any who attempted dissent were called "slackers," and subjected to odium by the public as well as to formal punishment by the government.

The device, starting with the draft, was used, with variations, again and again during the war, in drives to sell "Liberty Bonds," in compulsion of business to conform to regulations laid down by the War Industries Board, in requirement of dealers in food to follow regulations laid down by the Food Administration.

The close of the war brought an end to the use of organized propaganda by the government to bring about mass movements. For some fifteen years it lapsed. In 1933, the technique was revived to cause the country to accept a new relation between government and business, called the National Recovery Act. (Abbreviated to N. R. A., and symbolized by a Blue Eagle.) On this occasion, as during the war, the process included compulsion exercised by the majority upon the minority. The majority who accepted N. R. A. agreed to exclude from their patronage the minority who did not. The technique of N. R. A. in 1933 was a duplicate of that of conscription in 1917. The General Johnson who administered N. R. A. in 1933 was the same man who as Major Johnson had managed preparation for the draft in 1917.*

"Conscription," by Mark Sullivan. Used by permission of Charles Scribner's Sons from *Our Times: The United States, 1900–1925*, Volume 5, *Over Here, 1914–1918*, by Mark Sullivan. Copyright 1933 Charles Scribner's Sons; renewal copyright © 1961 Mark Sullivan, Jr. (Some notes have been omitted.)

MARK SULLIVAN (1874–1952) received his law degree from Harvard University in 1903 but soon left practice to become a free-lance writer. He was editor of *Collier's* magazine and served as Washington correspondent for both the *New York Evening Post* and the *New York Tribune/Herald-Tribune*. Sullivan was a colonel in the U.S. Marine Corps Reserve and author of a number of books and articles on the American political scene.

Notes

1. From Wilson's preparedness speech at Chicago, January 31, 1916. Wilson was speaking of a volunteer system for building up the regular army through two months of training each year for three years.

---

*[Editor's note]: The final three paragraphs are a footnote in the original.

2. The genealogy of the Draft Act, according to Frederick Palmer's biography of Newton D. Baker, began with recommendations by Generals Leonard Wood and Hugh Scott, the latter Chief of Staff during the period preceding our entry into the Great War. These recommendations convinced Baker. Baker took the recommendations to Wilson and, with these and his own arguments, convinced Wilson. The bill was written by conferences in which the participants were Generals Scott, Tasker H. Bliss, Crowder, McCain, and other army officers—"Newton D. Baker, America at War," by Frederick Palmer.

3. "Six weeks before the enactment of the Selective Service bill, the plans for its execution had been formulated in minute detail." Provost-Marshal Enoch H. Crowder in "The Spirit of Selective Service."

4. "Newton D. Baker, America at War," Frederick Palmer.

5. Quoted from "Newton D. Baker, America at War," by Frederick Palmer.

6. Quoted from "Newton D. Baker, America at War," by Frederick Palmer.

7. Quoted from "Newton D. Baker, America at War," by Frederick Palmer.

8. *Congressional Record*, April 25, 1917.

9. Quoted from "Newton D. Baker, America at War," by Frederick Palmer.

10. Baker made a distinction between conscription practised by some other countries and conscription practised by the United States. "Militarism," he wrote, "is . . . the designation given to a selfish or ambitious political system which uses arms as a means of accomplishing its objects. The mobilization and arming of a democracy in defense of the principles on which it is founded, and in vindication of the common rights of man, is an entirely different thing."

11. By two subsequent acts the age limit was extended to take in all between 18 and 45.

12. Quoted from "Newton D. Baker, America at War," by Frederick Palmer.

4

Why Don't We Learn from History?

by
B. H. Liddell Hart

Hart's main argument is that coercion stifles the creative enthusiasm from which all great and lasting changes flow. He places conscription, as an example of a highly coercive system, in broad historical context and concludes that it is never justified. Hart argues that whereas compulsion may sometimes be practical to prevent actions, positive, permanent social transformation is never achieved through the application of force. The one way to achieve it is through the relatively slow, but sure dissemination of ideas.

The Fallacy of Compulsion

We learn from history that the compulsory principle always breaks down in practice. It is practicable to *prevent* men doing something; moreover that principle of restraint, or regulation, is essentially justifiable in so far as its application is needed to check interference with others' freedom. But it is not, in reality, possible to *make* men do something without risking more than is gained from the compelled effort. The method may appear practicable, because it often works when applied to those who are merely hesitant. When applied to those who are definitely unwilling it fails, however, because it generates friction and fosters subtle forms of evasion that spoil the effect which is sought. The test of whether a principle works is to be found in the product.

Efficiency springs from enthusiasm—because this alone can develop a dynamic impulse. Enthusiasm is incompatible with compulsion—because it is essentially spontaneous. Compulsion is thus bound to deaden enthusiasm—because it dries up the source. The more an individual, or a nation, has been accustomed to freedom, the more deadening will be the effect of a change to compulsion.

These logical deductions are confirmed by analysis of historical experience. The modern system of military conscription was born in France—it was, ironically, the misbegotten child of Revolutionary enthusiasm. Within a generation, its application had become so obnoxious that its abolition was the primary demand of the French people following Napoleon's downfall. Meanwhile, however, it had been transplanted to more suitable soil—in Prussia. And just over half a century later, the victories that Prussia gained led to the resurrection of conscription in France. Its re-imposition was all the easier because the renewed autocracy of Napoleon III had accustomed the French people to the interference and constraints of bureaucracy. In the generation that followed, the revival of the spirit of freedom in France was accompanied by a growth of the petty bureaucracy, parasites feeding on the body politic. From this, the French could never succeed in shaking free; and in their efforts they merely developed corruption—which is the natural consequence of an ineffective effort to loosen the grip of compulsion by evasion.

It is generally recognized today that this rampant growth of bureaucratically-induced corruption was the dry-rot of the Third Republic. But on deeper examination the cause can be traced further back—to the misunderstanding of their own principles which led a section of the creators of the French Revolution to adopt a method fundamentally opposed to their fulfilment.

It might be thought that conscription should be less detrimental to the Germans, since they are more responsive to regulation, and have no deeply rooted tradition of freedom. Nevertheless, it is of significance that the Nazi movement was essentially a voluntary movement—exclusive rather than comprehensive—and that the most important sections of the German forces—the air force and the tank force—have been recruited on a semi-voluntary basis. There is little evidence to suggest that the ordinary "mass" of the German army has anything like the same enthusiasm; and considerable evidence to suggest that this conscripted mass constitutes a basic weakness in Germany's apparent strength.

Twenty-five years spent in the study of war, a study which gradually went beyond its current technique to its well-springs, changed my earlier and conventional belief in the value of conscription. It brought me to see that the compulsory principle was fundamentally inefficient, and the conscriptive method out of date—a method that clung, like the ivy, to quantitative standards in an age when the trend of warfare was becoming increasingly qualitative. For it sustained the fetish of mere numbers at a time when skill and enthusiasm were becoming ever more necessary for the effective handling of the new weapons.

Conscription does not fit the conditions of modern warfare—its specialized technical equipment, mobile operations, and fluid situations. Success increasingly depends on individual initiative, which in turn springs from a sense of personal responsibility—these senses are atrophied by compulsion. Moreover, every unwilling man is a germ-carrier, spreading infection to an extent altogether disproportionate to the value of the service he is forced to contribute.

Looking still further into the question, and thinking deeper, I came to see, also, that the greatest contributory factor to the Great Wars which had racked the world in recent generations had been the conscriptive system—the system which sprang out of the muddled thought of the French Revolution, was then exploited by Napoleon in his selfish ambition, and subsequently turned to serve the interests of Prussian militarism. After undermining the eighteenth century "age of reason," it had paved the way for the reign of unreason in the modern age.

Conscription serves to precipitate war, but not to accelerate it—except in the negative sense of accelerating the growth of war-weariness and other underlying causes of defeat. Conscription precipitated war in 1914, owing to the way that the mobilization of conscript armies disrupted national life and produced an atmosphere in which negotiation became impossible—confirming the warning, "mobilization means war." During that war its effect can be traced in the symptoms which preceded the collapse of the Russian, Austrian, and German armies, as well as the decline of the French and Italian armies. It was the least free States which collapsed under the strain of war—and they collapsed in the order of their degree of unfreedom. By contrast, the best fighting force in the fourth year of war was, by general recognition, the Australian Corps—the force which had rejected conscription, and in which there was the least insistence on unthinking obedience.

The Spread of Compulsion

The prolonged security of our island home made us slow to perceive the external danger of the growth of this system abroad. And the fact that we had a better instinct for naval than for military matters made us equally slow to realize the internal danger of its more insidious effects. The very degree to which we are sea-minded has made us prone, as regards the army, to catch the infection of a foreign fashion. Before the last war we were fond of imitating Continental types of headdress—with somewhat ludicrous effects. We also imitated what was under the headdress—with much more dangerous effects. It led us to discard the historic tradition of English strategy, on which our prosperity and security had been built up through the centuries. And it led us into a morass—from which we emerged so exhausted as to lose the power of influencing the post-war settlement on lines that could establish an enduring state of peace.

When one comes to examine the way we adopted conscription in the last war, and to embrace it again precipitately on the verge of this war, one finds that it was really a case of rushing to borrow a fashionable remedy without pausing to enquire about its effects, or even whether it suited our condition and constitution. To put it in the opposite way, long immunity from the disease had made us the more susceptible to its effects, so that when we caught it late in the epidemic, we caught it all the worse.

The effects far transcend the military sphere. Bemused by the cry of total warfare, we have tried to make ourselves totalitarian—with the maximum of inefficiency for the minimum of productivity in proportion to the effort.

At the same time we risked the shortening of our maximum measure of endurance by imposing excessive restrictions and hardships in the name of "total war." In a long war, the issue turns above all on the question of which people first becomes tired of the struggle. Realizing this, wise statesmanship would try to maintain normal conditions of life as long and as far as possible, compatibly with the development of its military forces to a carefully gauged *optimum* level. The less a people feel the strain of war, the greater is likely to be their staying power in a test of endurance. This principle has received all too little attention.

The best way to fight Fascism effectively is to fight it with a conscious faith in Freedom. We have been foolish enough to forfeit that dynamic. While professing to fight for freedom we have put no faith in it—preferring to trust in compulsion, the enemy's principle. It is futile to talk of the need for fighting the war as a crusade under such conditions. The crusading spirit cannot be generated by compulsion. You cannot make crusaders out of conscripts.

If, in this imitation of the German way, we have not yet become such a slave-State in practice, it is only because our instinctive autocrats and bureaucrats have hitherto shown more restraint, or been made conscious of more resistance from the long-inherited instinct for freedom among the people. But we have allowed them to shackle us with the fetters of State-slavery in theory; with such a rigid set of regulations that we could be rendered helpless to protest or to recover our freedom if, with the continuance and intensification of the struggle, the present Government were replaced or displaced by one of a more dictatorial tendency.

Some of these regulations constitute a betrayal of our inheritance that would have shocked those who fought the long battle for freedom during the seventeenth, eighteenth, and nineteenth centuries. A grave responsibility is borne by the members of a Parliament which allowed, and even encouraged, officialdom to impose such unconstitutional measures while at the same time turning this country into a potential prison-house, from which in case of defeat or a *coup d' état* it might be impossible for anyone to escape and start a "Free British" movement. The most charitable explanation is that in giving the executive such sweeping powers they were doped by the talk of "total war"—in a war which they did not understand. For efficiency in modern war *can* be reconciled with proper respect for the basic rights of the individual and his freedom. Indeed, this produces the soil in which initiative, itself essential to true efficiency, grows best.

The present Parliament already bears the onus of bringing us into the war inadequately prepared. Its responsibility would be still graver if, in its belated attempt to redeem the consequences of this negligence, it should be forgetful that it is trustee for the liberties of the people— for this is the foundation-stone of its own existence. Any form of government can suffice for the purpose of carrying on a war; the justification for parliamentary government lies in the purpose of upholding freedom. If it fails to maintain the basic conditions of civil liberty in the course of maintaining war, it stultifies its distinctive purpose and value. And that is the quickest way for it to commit *felo de se.*

If we are to convince the peoples of the world that we are really fighting for freedom, we ought to lose no time in examining our own current condition, and conscience. To make our propaganda meet for consumption abroad, we need to ensure the production at home of freedom *from* want and fear; freedom *for* truth and progress.

The Perpetuation of Compulsion?

We have become so habituated to military and civil conscription in the wartime years that a large body of opinion is now favourable to its peacetime continuance. Significantly, the advocacy of it can be traced back to the years immediately before the war, and even prior to the adoption of military conscription—to a time when an influential section of people in this country were more impressed by the social developments of the Nazi system than alarmed by its dangers. A campaign for "universal national service" was launched in the winter before Munich. As defined by Lord Lothian, in a letter to *The Times* in March 1938, it embodied the "allocation of every individual" to a particular form of service "whether in peace or in emergency." It was visualized then, and is being freshly urged now, as an "educational" measure.

Such a system entails the suppression of individual judgment—the Englishman's most cherished right. It violates the cardinal principle of a free community: that there should be no restriction of individual freedom save where this is used for active interference with others' freedom. Our tradition of individual freedom is the slow-ripening fruit of centuries of effort. To surrender it within after fighting to defend it against dangers without would be a supremely ironical turn of our history.

In upholding the idea of compulsory service, its advocates have often emphasized that the principle was adopted in our Statute Law in certain times of alarm, and applied in a haphazard way to the poorer classes of the community, during the eighteenth and the early nineteenth century. Here they fail to take due account of the progressive development in our national principles, and of the way our concept of freedom has been enlarged during the last century.

It was an advance in British civilization which brought us, first to question, and then to discard, the press-gang as well as the slave-trade. The logical connection between the two institutions, as violations of our principles, was obvious. Is the tide of our civilization now on the ebb? In respect of personal service, freedom means the right to be true to your convictions, to choose your course, and decide whether the cause is worth service and sacrifice. That is the difference between the free man and the State-slave.

Unless the great majority of people are willing to give their services there is something radically at fault in the State itself. In that case the State is not likely or worthy to survive under test—and compulsion will make no serious difference. We may be far from having attained an adequate state of freedom as yet, of economic freedom in particular, but the best assurance of our future lies in advancing conditions in which freedom can live and grow, not in abandoning such essentials of freedom as we have already attained.

Another false argument is that since conscription has long been the rule in the continental countries, including those which remain democracies, we need not fear the effect of adopting it here. But the deeper I have gone into the study of war and the history of the past century, the further I have come towards the conclusion that the development of conscription has damaged the growth of the idea of freedom in the continental countries, and thereby damaged their efficiency, also—by undermining the sense of personal responsibility. There is only too much evidence that our temporary adoption of conscription in the last war had a permanent effect harmful to the development of freedom and democracy here. For my own part, I have come to my present conviction of the supreme importance of freedom through the pursuit of efficiency. I believe that freedom is the foundation of efficiency, both national and military. Thus it is a practical folly as well as a spiritual surrender to "go totalitarian" as a result of fighting for existence against the totalitarian States. Cut off the incentive to freely given service, and you dry up the life-source of a free community.

We ought to realize that it is easier to adopt the compulsory principle of national life than to shake it off. Once compulsion for personal service is adopted in peace-time, it will be hard to resist the extension of the principle to all other aspects of the nation's life, including freedom of thought, speech, and writing. We ought to think carefully, and to think ahead, before taking a decisive step towards totalitarianism. Or are we so accustomed to our chains that we are no longer conscious of them?

Progress by Compulsion?

It is only just to recognize that many of those who advocate such compulsory service are inspired by the desire that it should, and belief that it will, be a means to a good end. This view is one aspect of the larger idea that it is possible to *make* men good; that they must not only be shown the way to become better, but compelled to follow it. That idea has been held by many reformers, most revolutionaries, and all busybodies. It has persisted in generation after generation, although as repeatedly contradicted by the experience of history. It is closely related—cousin at least—to the dominant conception of the Nazi and Fascist movements.

While pointing out the analogy, and the fallacy, we should draw a distinction, however, between the positive and negative sides of the principle. The negative side comprises all laws which are framed to remove hindrances to progress and prevent interference by a selfish or naturally obstructive section of the community. It may be defined as a process of regulation, as contrasted with actual compulsion—which is, strictly, the positive process of forcing people to do some action against their will. Regulation, in the negative or protective sense of this definition, may be both necessary and helpful in promoting true progress. It does not infringe the principle of freedom, provided that it is wisely applied, for it is embraced in the corollary that freedom does not give license for interference with others' freedom. Moreover, it accords with the philosophical law of progress that the negative paves the way for the positive: that the best chance of ensuring a real step forward lies in taking care to avoid the mistakes that, in experience, have wrecked or distorted past attempts at progress.

At the same time history warns us that even in the negative regulatory sense, if much more in the positive compulsory sense, the effort to achieve progress by decree is apt to lead to reaction. The more hurried the effort, the greater the risk to its endurance. The surer way of achieving progress is by generating and diffusing the *thought* of improvement. Reforms that last are those that come naturally, and with less friction, when men's minds have become ripe for them. A life spent in sowing a few grains of fruitful thought is a life spent more effectively than in hasty action that produces a crop of weeds. That leads us to see the difference, truly a vital difference, between influence and power. . . .

Some Conclusions

The germs of war find a focus in the convenient belief that "the end justifies the means." Each new generation repeats this argument—while succeeding generations have had reason to say that the end their predecessors thus pursued was never justified by the fulfilment conceived. If there is one lesson that should be clear from history it is that bad means deform the end, or deflect its course thither. I would suggest the corollary that if we take care of the means the end will take care of itself.

Only second to the futility of pursuing ends reckless of the means is that of attempting progress by compulsion. History shows how often it leads to reaction. It also shows that the surer way is to generate and diffuse the idea of progress—providing a light to guide men, not a whip to drive them. Influence on thought has been the most influential factor in history, though, being less obvious than the effects of action, it has received less attention—even from writers of history. There is a general recognition that man's capacity for thought has been responsible for all human progress, but not yet an adequate appreciation of the historical effect of contributions to thought in comparison with that of spectacular action. Seen with a sense of proportion, the smallest permanent enlargement of men's thought is a greater achievement, and ambition, than the construction of something material that crumbles, the conquest of a kingdom that collapses, or the leadership of a movement that ends in a rebound.

In the conquest of mind-space it is the inches, consolidated, that count. Also for the spread and endurance of an idea the originator is dependent on the self-development of the receivers and transmitters—far more dependent than is the initiator of an action upon its executants. In the physical sphere subordination can serve as a substitute for co-operation, and, although inferior, can go a long way towards producing effective action. But the progress of ideas, if it is to be a true progress, depends on co-operation in a much higher degree, and on a higher kind of co-operation. In this sphere the leader may still be essential, but instead of fusing individuals into a mass through the suppression of their individuality and the contraction of their thought, the lead that he gives only has effect, lighting-effect, in proportion to the elevation of individuality and the expansion of thought. For collective action it suffices if the mass can be managed; collective growth is only possible through the freedom and enlargement of individual minds. It is not the man, still less the mass, that counts; but the many.

Once the collective importance of each individual in helping or hindering progress is appreciated, the experience contained in history is seen to have a personal, not merely a political, significance. What can the individual learn from history—as a guide to living? Not what to do, but what to strive for. And what to avoid in striving. The importance and intrinsic value of behaving decently. The importance of seeing clearly—not least of seeing himself clearly.

To face life with clear eyes—desirous to see the truth—and to come through it with clean hands, behaving with consideration for others, while achieving such conditions as enable a man to get the *best* out of life, is enough for ambition—and a high ambition. Only as a man progresses towards it, does he realize what effort it entails, and how large is the distance to go.

It is strange how people assume that no training is needed in the pursuit of truth. It is stranger still that this assumption is often manifest in the very man who talks of the difficulty of determining what is true. We should recognize that for this pursuit any one requires at least as much care and training as a boxer for a fight or a runner for a Marathon. He has to learn how to detach his *thinking* from every desire and interest, from every sympathy and antipathy—like ridding oneself of superfluous tissue, the "tissue" of untruth which all human beings tend to accumulate, for their own comfort and protection. And he must keep fit, to become fitter. In other words, he must be true to the light he has seen.

He may realize that the world is a jungle. But if he has seen that it could be better for everyone if the simple principles of decency and kindliness were generally applied, then he must in honesty try to practice these consistently and to live, personally, as if they were general. In other words, he must follow the light he has seen.

Since he will be following it through a jungle, however, he should bear in mind the supremely practical guidance provided nearly two thousand years ago—"Behold, I send you forth as sheep in the midst of wolves: be ye therefore wise as serpents, and harmless as doves."

Reprinted by permission of George Allen & Unwin and by permission of Hawthorn Properties (Elsevier-Dutton Publishing Company, Inc.), from the book *Why Don't We Learn from History?* by B. H. Liddell Hart. [Originally published in 1944 by George Allen & Unwin, London; reissued in 1969 by Meredith Press (Hawthorn Books), New York.] Copyright © 1969 by B. H. Liddell Hart.

Sir Basil Henry Liddell Hart (1895–1970) was a British military officer, strategist, and historian well known for his unpopular advocacy of mechanized warfare. A number of Liddell Hart's proposed reforms were eventually implemented, especially the addition of air power and mechanized tank warfare. He was, however, opposed to the concept of total, nuclear war. He was knighted in 1966 by Queen Elizabeth II.

GOSHEN COLLEGE LIBRARY
GOSHEN, INDIANA

5

The Origins of American Military Policy
by
Louis Morton

The roots of American military policy lie deep in English tradition, dating from Saxon times. Carried to the colonies by the earliest settlers, this tradition formed the basis of an unquestioned obligation of every able-bodied male to rise to the emergency defense of his community. Though initially most men volunteered for service, the ancient tradition became codified into civil law by the end of the seventeenth century, forming the basis of the early militia systems in each of the colonies. Surviving in various guises for nearly two centuries, the idea of universal service obligation is still strong today.

All too often those who write about the American military tradition start with the Revolution, or with the beginning of the Federal government. They would have us believe that the founders of our nation created and formulated out of thin air a military policy at once complete and perfect.

To represent the origins of American military policy in this way is of course a distortion. The roots of our military policy, like the beginnings of our representative government and political democracy, are to be found in the early settlements at Jamestown, Plymouth, and elsewhere—in the arrangements the settlers made for their defense. The seeds of our policy go back even further in time—to the experience of the English people.

In this three hundred and fiftieth anniversary year of the founding of Jamestown, it is perhaps not out of place to review some of the origins of our national defense establishment. Not only will we understand better why certain things are as they are today. We will also be struck by the fact that many of the problems and solutions of those earlier days are still with us in different form.

Before the new world settlers left their homes in the old world, they provided for their defense on the unknown continent of America. The businessmen who financed the colonizing ventures had invested too much money to risk the destruction of their property. The religious leaders were practical men, not visionaries, and their hope of attaining freedom from persecution was too strong to allow them to be negligent of their military strength. The British crown, which authorized the expeditions and granted lands, but which took no risks, empowered the colonists to take whatever measures were required (in the words of the Massachusetts Charter of 1628) "to incounter, expulse, repell, and resist by force of armes, as well by sea as by lands" any effort to destroy or invade the settlement.

Weapons and military stores were therefore included in the cargo of the ships that came to Virginia and Massachusetts. Among the settlers were experienced soldiers, men specifically engaged to train the colonists in the use of arms, organize them into military formations, and direct them in battle if necessary. Such a man was Captain John Smith, an adventurer and veteran of the religious wars on the Continent. Such a man was Captain Myles Standish, hired by the Pilgrims to accompany them to Plymouth.

Not even a John Smith or a Myles Standish could fight off an Indian attack by himself. The settlers had to do that together, and every able-bodied man became in times of military emergency a frontline soldier. There was never any question about this. The obligation of every male who could carry arms to perform military service in the defense of his community was an ancient English tradition dating back to Saxon times. Such documents as the Assize of Arms (1181), the Statute of Westminster (1285), and the Instructions for General Musters (1572) rooted the obligation of military service firmly in English law. As late as 1588, when the Grand Armada threatened invasion, "the rugged miners poured to war from Mendip's sunless caves . . . and the broad streams of pikes and flags rushed down each roaring street" of London to defend the nation against the approaching Spanish fleet.

According to this tradition, which became organized into the militia system, every able-bodied man was considered a potential soldier. He had to train and drill in military formation at stated intervals. By law, he was required to possess arms and equipment and to have them ready for immediate use.

The system was local in character and organized on a geographical basis. It was administered by county and town officials who had full authority to impose punishment and collect fines. Yet English law also restricted the use of the militia to inhibit the crown from using it as an instrument of despotism and from employing it outside the kingdom. The militia, thus, was a military system for emergencies of short duration in defensive situations.

Since this was the military tradition of the colonists, this was the basis of the military system they employed in the New World. It was admirably suited to their needs. But there was an important difference. In England there had been but a single militia organization; in America there were as many militias as there were colonies. No man would serve in any but his own. "Let the New Yorkers defend themselves," said a North Carolinian of a later day. "Why should I fight the Indians for them?"

Arrived in the New World, the colonists were as much concerned with preparations for defense as with food and shelter. Acting in accordance with instructions from home, the original settlers of Jamestown—100 men and 4 boys—split into three groups upon landing. One group provided fortifications for defense, another furnished a guard and planted a crop, the third explored the nearby area. Within a month after their arrival, they had built a primitive fort, a triangular stockade of "Planckes and strong Posts, foure foot deepe in the ground."

The Puritans, similarly instructed in England, were also militant in defense of their property. As one of their number remarked, "they knew right well" that their church "was surrounded with walls and bulworks and the people of God, in re-edifying the same did prepare to resist their enemies with weapons of war, even while they continued building."

Probably the first military legislation in the English colonies was the code of laws proclaimed in Jamestown by Sir Thomas Dale in 1612. On military leave from his post in the Netherlands, Dale assumed the governorship of Virginia at a time when the colony was in danger of extinction, its inhabitants on the verge of starvation. The strict regime he imposed, based on existing military regulations and on "the laws governing the Armye in the Low Countreys," was even more severe than the English laws of the period. But it accomplished its purpose. Order was restored, crops were planted, and peace was made with the Indians. "Our people," wrote John Rolfe, "yearly plant and reape quietly, and travell in the woods a-fowling and a-hunting as freely and securely from danger or treacherie as in England."

Martial law soon outlived its usefulness. As soon as the colony ceased to be a military outpost, the Virginians wrote into civil law the requirements for military service. The Massacre of 1622, which almost destroyed the colony, was still fresh in mind when the General Assembly in 1623 required all inhabitants "to go under arms." Three years later, Governor Yeardley specified that all males between 17 and 60 years of age were to serve when necessary and perform military duty when required. Changes were afterwards made in the law, but the obligation of universal service was never abandoned. Failure to comply subjected the offender to punishment and fine, as one John Bickley discovered when, for refusing to take up arms, he was sentenced to be "laid neck and heels" for 12 hours and pay a fine of 100 pounds of tobacco.

A local official known as the Commander controlled the militia in each district. He was charged with responsibility for seeing that his men were properly armed and supplied with powder and shot. Later, as the population grew and his duties increased, a lieutenant commander was appointed to assist him. The Commander's duties were so varied and extensive as to make him the most important person in the community, its chief civilian as well as military official. Not only did he supervise the construction of defenses, drill his units, and have custody of the public gunpowder, but he also saw to it that everyone attended church services and observed the laws relating to the tobacco trade. Though the commissioning of officers remained in the hands of the governor, the commander appointed his own subordinates. Once a man acquired a military title he retained it. So numerous were the officers produced by this system and so fond were the Virginians of their titles that a visitor in a later period, struck by the abundance of military rank, remarked that the colony seemed to be "a retreat of heroes."

The Pilgrims too lost no time in organizing their defenses. Captain Standish was designated military commander of the colony. Under him were formed four companies, each with its own commander and designated area of responsibility. A visitor at Plymouth in 1627 noted approvingly the defensive works and the careful preparations to meet an attack. "They assemble by beat of drum," he explained, "each with his musket or firelock in front of the captain's door; they have their cloakes on and place themselves in order, three abreast, and are led by a sergeant without beat of drum. Behind comes the governor in a long robe; beside him, on the right hand, comes the preacher with his cloak on, and on the left hand the captain with his side-arms and cloak, and with a small cane in his hand; and so they march in good order, and each sets his arms down near him. Thus they are constantly on their guard night and day."

By the middle of the seventeeth century Plymouth had established a military system based on universal service. Each colonist was required to own and maintain his own weapons, and the governor was authorized by law to prescribe military training. As new towns grew up along the frontier, they were brought into the defensive organization by the requirement to maintain their own companies under the central control of the government at Plymouth. The local companies elected their own officers, subject to approval of the government, and the officers appointed subordinates, selected training days, and drilled their units. Regulations were enforced by fines, collected by the clerk of the company or the local constable, and these fines often supported the military activities of the community. If the General Court (the legislature) required it, each town provided a quota of men for military expeditions.

The military system of the Puritans was much like that of Plymouth and Jamestown. According to a law of 1631, all males between 16 and 60, whether freemen or servants, were to provide themselves with weapons and to form into units for training. A council was established for the specific purpose of supervising military matters, for, declared the General Court, "the well ordering of the militia is a matter of great concernment to the safety and welfare of this commonwealth." Additional regulations were issued from time to time and in 1643, after the Pequot War, the entire militia system was overhauled. One of the results was the selection of 30 soldiers within each company "who shall be ready at halfe an hour's warning upon any service they shall be put upon." Here in essence are the Minutemen of the Revolution, more than a century later.

As in the other colonies, provision was made in the law to excuse from military service those with "natural or personal impediment" such as "defect of mind, failing of sences, or impotence of Limbes." Certain professions were also exempted—public officials, clergymen, school teachers, and doctors—as were those who practiced critical trades.

The companies established in Massachusetts numbered from 65 to

200 men, two-thirds of whom were musketeers and one-third pikemen. When the number exceeded 200, a new unit was formed; when it was less than 65, several towns combined to form a single unit. The officers elected by the men consisted of the captain, a lieutenant as his principal assistant, an ensign, sergeants, and corporals. The company clerk kept the roster of men liable for military service, checked attendance at drills, and collected the fines.

At an earlier date than any other colony, Massachusetts formed the militia into regiments. The Act of 1636 divided the military companies then in existence into three regiments and required regimental training at first once a year and then every three years. Commanded by a sergeant major, who was assisted by a muster master, the regiment came ultimately to comprise all the units in a county and its strength consequently varied. Plymouth adopted the regimental organization in 1658 when Josiah Winslow was given the rank of major and designated "chief officer over the military companies of this jurisdiction." "All Captains, inferior officers and soldiers," read his orders, "are hereby required to be in ready subjection to you during your continuance in the said office."

Training was the primary activity of the militia, and regular training periods were an integral part of the system. The first drills at Jamestown were held shortly after the colony was founded. Captain Smith, when he became President of the Council, held drills and target practice on a level stretch of ground within plain view of the Indians, who could see for themselves the effect of cannon shot on the trunk of a tree.

Training exercises in Virginia were initially held, by custom, on holy days. In 1639, when a muster master-general was appointed to enforce the militia regulations, even though the captain remained immediately responsible for training his men, no specific time was set by law for drills. In some districts they were held monthly, in others every three months. Failure to attend brought a fine, but absence was apparently so common that the General Assembly finally set a stiff penalty of 100 pounds of tobacco, declaring that the offenders were bringing about the "ruin of all military discipline." By the end of the seventeenth century the militia regulations in Virginia required an annual drill for the entire regiment and quarterly exercises for companies and troops.

Training in New England was put on a regular basis earlier than in Virginia. In Plymouth drills were held six times a year to assure, in the words of the General Court, "that all postures of pike and muskett, motions, ranks and files . . . skirmishes, sieges, batteries, watches, sen-

tinells; bee always performed according to true military discipline."
The first military law of the Puritans called for weekly training periods, held every Saturday. In 1637, when conditions had become more
settled, the number of training days per year was fixed at eight, and
this number remained in effect for the next forty years.

From the weekly training of the first settlers to the monthly sessions a few decades later can be measured the decreasing threat of Indian attack. Before the century was out, the number of drills per year
had dropped to four, with provisions for two extra days if the unit
commander thought them necessary. Regimental drills, when held,
were deductible from the total. But during times of emergency, interest
in military matters revived phenomenally; during King Philip's War
drills were held as often as twice a week.

The military code of the day enforced a strict discipline. A militiaman in Virginia guilty of three offenses of drunkenness had to ride the
"wooden horse," an ingeniously uncomfortable and ignominious seat;
if drunk on post he was liable to the death sentence. Drunk or sober, if
he lifted his hand against an officer, he lost the hand; if he raised a
weapon, the penalty was death. Should he express discontent with his
lot during a march, complain about the ration, or sell his gun, he was
treated as a mutineer.

Imposed freely, fines provided one of the sources of defraying militia expenses. All the colonies had laws fining those who failed to supply
themselves with arms or to maintain them properly. Failure to attend
drill as well as quarreling and drunkenness during the drill were also
punishable by fines.

The drill was usually held in a public place, such as the commons
in Boston, and began early in the day. After roll call and prayer, the
men practiced close order drill, the manual of arms, and other formations to the accompaniment of drums. Then followed a review and inspection by higher officers and public officials. After that, the units
might form into smaller groups for target practice and extended order
drill. Training closed with a sham battle and final prayers. By now it
was early in the afternoon and the militiamen retired for food and
other refreshment. The rest of the day was spent in visits, games, and
social events.

The manuals provided for a remarkably complicated series of motions for forming troops, marching, fixing the pike, and firing the musket. These were standard in European armies, where the perfection of
mechanical motions governed warfare, but they bore no relation to Indian fighting in the forests of North America. Nevertheless, the militiamen in the New World had to go solemnly through the prescribed

movements on each training day. Fifty-six separate motions were required to load and fire the matchlock musket; only eleven for the pike, a fact which may account in part for its retention as a weapon and its popularity among troops. It was also a case, not altogether unusual in a more recent day, of the failure of training to keep pace with changing conditions.

The militia was not limited to foot soldiers; horsemen too were included. From the start, cavalry was the favored arm, and cavalrymen acquired special privileges that gave them higher status. Few men could afford to supply the horse and equipment required, a fact that limited membership to the well-to-do. Massachusetts, for example, restricted service in the cavalry to those with property valued at 100 pounds sterling.

Many advantages accrued to members of a horse unit. The trooper was exempted from training with the foot companies and from guard duty. He enjoyed special tax privileges; he could not be impressed into another service; he did not have to pay the customary fees for pasturage on common grounds.

The number as well as the quality of militia units varied widely in different periods and among the various colonies. Governor Berkeley of Virginia estimated in 1671 that he could put 8,000 horse in the field if needed, and the following year the militia of the colony consisted of 20 foot regiments and 20 horse, a proportion marking clearly the southerner's preference for cavalry.

Second only to Virginia was Massachusetts, which in 1680 had about the same number of foot companies but fewer companies of horse. Since the number of men in the companies varied so widely, exact comparisons are impossible. For Connecticut exact figures appear in the report made by the governor in 1650. "For the present," he wrote, "we have but one troope settled, which consist of about sixty horse, yet we are upon raysing three troopes more. . . . The whole amount to 2,507."

Though the militia was organized into units, it rarely fought that way. It was not intended to. The system was designed to arm and train men, not to produce military units for combat. Thus, it provided a trained and equipped citizen-soldiery in time of crisis. In this sense it was a local training center and a replacement pool, a county selective service system and a law enforcing agency, an induction camp and a primitive supply depot.

The forces required for active operations against the Indians came usually from the militia. The legislature assigned quotas to the local districts. Volunteers usually filled them. But if they did not, local authorities had the power to impress or draft men, together with their arms and equipment (including horses), into service. The law on this point was specific. The Virginia Assembly in 1629 gave the commanders power to levy parties of men and employ them against the Indians. In Plymouth during the Pequot War, when each town was required to furnish a quota, some of the men volunteered only on the understanding that if they did not, they would be conscripted.

Service was usually limited to expeditions within the colony, but there were numerous occasions when militiamen were employed outside. This right was specifically recognized in the law. Thus, in 1645, the Massachusetts General Court empowered the governor and council "to raise and transport such part of the militia as they shall find needful" outside the Commonwealth "without their free and voluntary consent" for a period of six months. When the term of service was over, the forces thus raised were dissolved and the men returned to their homes where they resumed their place in the militia.

There was no central command for the militia of all the colonies; each had its own organization and its own commander. Supreme authority within each colony rested usually with the legislative body and was based on the charter. In practice, however, the legislature left the administration of the militia system to other groups, sometimes the Upper House and at other times to various committees or commissions on military affairs or martial discipline.

The utmost care was exercised to maintain civilian supremacy. The General Court of Massachusetts repeatedly asserted its authority over military officials and representatives of the crown. The establishment of the Artillery Company of Boston in 1638 caused some suspicious officials to liken it to the Praetorian Guard in Roman times and to the Knights Templar; care was taken to make certain that the Artillery Company would not become "a standing authority of military men, which might easily in time overthrow the civil power."

The actual management of war was delegated to the governor and a small group of advisers usually, but the legislature in almost every case retained control of the funds and watched expenditures with a suspicious eye. When an expedition was formed, it was the legislature that gave approval, furnished the money—and later appointed a committee to look carefully into the conduct of operations.

The principal officer of the militia and the only single individual who could be considered to exercise supreme command was, in Massachusetts, the sergeant major-general; in Virginia, the governor.

When New Hampshire, New York, and Massachusetts came under royal authority late in the century, command of the militia there passed to the governor also.

The office of sergeant major-general—later shortened to major general—was an elective post and carried with it extensive powers and excellent opportunities for personal profit. In addition to general supervision of the militia, the sergeant major-general mobilized the militia, moved units to threatened areas, and procured arms and supplies. He commanded one of the regiments and had the unique privilege of training his own family. In wartime he commanded the colonial forces in the field, which, on occasion, he himself had raised and equipped.

To overcome the absence of a single unifying military authority in the New World, the colonies of New England formed a confederation in 1643. Representatives of Massachusetts, Connecticut, New Haven, and Plymouth came together in Boston and agreed that "inasmuch as the Natives have formerly committed sundry insolencies and outrages upon several Plantations of the English, and have of late combined themselves against us ... we therefore doe conceive it our bounden duty to enter into a present Confederation among ourselves, for mutuall help and strength." Two commissioners from each colony met as a body, which had authority to declare war, call on the member colonies for funds and troops, select commanders, and unify in other ways the military efforts of the colonies in time of emergency.

Though it lasted 42 years, the Confederation ran into trouble immediately and foundered finally on the rocks of jealousy and conflicting interest. From the outset, Massachusetts contested the right of the Confederation to declare war or draft Massachusetts troops. The dispute came to a head in 1653 when Massachusetts refused to obey a Confederation ruling. There was considerable feeling also about the choice of commander, for no colony was agreeable to placing its troops under an outsider. Like sovereign powers of a later day, each colony was jealous of its prerogatives and quick to object to seeming encroachment on its authority.

In no colony was there a group that resembled a military staff. The need did not exist. In peacetime the various officials of the militia system sufficed; in war the Assembly and the Council of War exercised control over military operations and procured the equipment and supplies needed by the troops. The commander was always adjured to take counsel of his assistants, and he was expected to abide by their advice. In this sense the various councils were policy-making bodies rather than staffs.

Supplying the military forces of the colonies was a comparatively simple matter. The first procurement agencies were joint stock companies that had financed the original settlements, but by the middle of the century responsibility had devolved upon the colonists. The procurement of individual arms and equipment was, in general, the responsibility of each militiaman. Every colony required each householder to provide for himself and his family weapons and equipment, and specified the type and condition of both. The community itself provided for the poor who served out the cost of their arms in labor. In addition, most colonies required the local authorities to keep on hand a supply of weapons and powder for emergencies, to be paid for by the town or county.

Normally there was no need for commissary or quarter-master in Indian warfare. Operations were of brief duration and the militiaman provided his own weapons, ammunition, clothing, and provisions, for which he was usually recompensed.

Extended operations, though uncommon, could hardly be supported in so informal a manner and there were in each colony various regulations and officials to provide the materials of war. In Massachusetts there was from earliest time an officer—variously known as surveyor of ordnance, overseer of the arms, or surveyor general—who had charge of weapons and ammunition. The officer was responsible for making certain that the towns had a supply of powder and ammunition; he also kept records and made purchases for the colony. Commissaries were appointed when required and were given authority to collect provisions. Two such officers designated for a force numbering 200 men sent against the Indians in 1645 were directed to procure bread, salted beef, fish, flour, butter, oil, cereals, sugar, rum, and beer. Only occasionally were such officials required to purchase arms.

When the colony needed funds for an expedition, it could fix quotas for the counties, borrow from private individuals, or impose special taxes. All methods were followed. The General Assembly in Virginia customarily set levies on the counties and imposed taxes payable in tobacco. In 1645 the expense of an expedition of 80 men to Roanoke was met by a levy of 38,000 pounds of tobacco to pay for the hire of boats, the purchase of provisions, powder and shot, and the payment of surgeons' salaries. The pay of the men alone amounted to 8,000 pounds of tobacco. Those suffering injuries received special compensation. The levy was made against three counties, each tithable person paying about 30 pounds of tobacco.

Even in that era war was a costly business and a fearful drain on the economy. In the greatest Indian war of the century—against King Philip—Massachusetts spent 100,000 pounds sterling an enormous sum for that day. And though the legislature fixed prices and dealt harshly with profiteers, the war debt at the close of hostilities was larger than the aggregate value of all the personal property in the colony.

By the end of the seventeenth century, the militia system was firmly established in the American colonies. Though the training it afforded was less than adequate and the number of training days had steadily declined as the frontier moved westward, the system had become deeply imbedded in the traditions and laws of the colonists. Under this system they had defended their settlements, driven back the Indians, and pre-empted the most desirable lands along the Atlantic seaboard. A century of military experience had made little impression on the method of instruction, but it had demonstrated to the colonists that a military system based upon the obligation of every able-bodied citizen to bear arms provided a practical solution to their defense needs. Other problems would arise later that could not be solved by this method alone, but the militia system, in one form or another, remained an integral part of the nation's military policy for almost two more centuries. The obligation of universal service on which it was based, though often ignored, has never been abandoned. It constitutes yet today the basis of our military organization.

"The Origins of American Military Policy," by Louis Morton. Reprinted from *Military Affairs*, Summer 1958, Volume XII, Number 2, pages 75–82, with permission. Copyright © 1958 by the American Military Institute. No additional copies may be made without the express permission of the author and of the editor of *Military Affairs*.

LOUIS MORTON (1913–1976), an educator and prolific American historian, was deputy chief historian for the U.S. Army's Office of Military History; professor of history at Dartmouth College; a member of the U.S. Air Force History Advisory Group; historical adviser to the secretary of the Army and of the Air Force; and a member of the Council on Foreign Relations and of the Institute for Strategic Studies. He wrote a number of books, including *War in the Pacific: Strategy and Command* and *Writings on World War II*, and edited two series, *The United States Army in World War II* (eleven volumes) and *Military Institutions of the United States* (seventeen volumes).

6

The Draft in the Light of History

by
William H. McNeill

*McNeill concludes this broad historical survey of the relationship be-
tween military power and civilian power with the assertion that
effective political power is impossible to maintain without at least the
implicit consent of the military establishment. He argues that traditional Anglo-American insistence on political-military separatism becomes increasingly unrealistic and dangerous for a civilian population
the larger, more autonomous, and more professional its military establishment becomes. Universal military service can reduce these dangers,
McNeill maintains, if it incorporates individuals from the highest ranks
of civilian political leadership.*

As public discussion of the draft law assumes a new urgency it seems
worthwhile to ask how other peoples in other times and places have
regulated civil-military relations and defended themselves. Humanity's
long experience with armed men ought to add to our wisdom in confronting the current dilemmas of American military policy.

To begin with, it is important to understand that an army is not simply a tool of foreign policy or an instrument of defense. It also and inevitably plays an important role in domestic politics, since no regime unacceptable to the military establishment can long endure. Divorce between those with the power to affect public policy and those who bear arms is at best precarious, being dependent on the good will of those who do control weapons. Viable political regimes have therefore tended throughout history to confine effective political rights to those who had arms and knew how to use them. A survey of the historical record may help to revive for us this cliché of eighteenth-century political wisdom.

In early times the relationship between military and civil communities was harsh but simple. Organized armies came into existence by conquest. Really successful conquerors overwhelmed local resistance by gathering an army that was too large to find food and other supplies for very long in any one place. Such armies lived by plunder. Accordingly, from the time of Sargon of Akkad (about 2250 B.C.) to that of Tamerlane (died 1405) and Wallenstein (died 1634) ever-victorious, predatory armies repeatedly arose whose numbers both guaranteed success in the field and required incessant campaigning year after year after year.

Seldom, however, did the cohesion of such an army long survive the captain around whom it formed. In relatively poor societies a more stable arrangement was to scatter small groups of warriors across the countryside. Such a "feudal" system made the armed establishment into a privileged class, supported locally by goods and services extracted from the inhabitants. In the relatively stable, face-to-face situations that resulted, law and custom soon defined who owed what to whom. The destructive and irregular depredation characteristic of primitive centralized armies could thus give way to relatively predictable rents and taxes, sustaining a military system which maintained most of the advantages of centralization. Tax collectors were able to concentrate enough goods and services at a single center to allow a monarch to maintain an armed establishment far superior to any merely local opposition. The ancient Assyrian, Persian, Chinese, and Roman empires sustained themselves on this principle. Indeed, as the subject peoples got used to paying taxes to an unseen and distant monarch, it became possible to station troops in outlying parts of the empire, far from the royal person. This simplified supply and improved frontier guard. It also invited rebellion, as the history of the ancient empires repeatedly demonstrated.

Nevertheless, from the iron age to the present, the prevailing form of military establishment among civilized states has been a tax-supported professional army, organized and supplied along lines first worked out by the ancient Assyrians. This kind of army prevailed quite simply because it was usually stronger than alternatives or rivals.

Needless to say, a tax-supported standing army was not a perfect solution to the problems arising from divergences between civilian and military interests. On the one hand, the sovereign had to guard against military usurpation. Court rituals designed to surround the person of the monarch with awe and mystery helped; so did the hereditary principle of succession and religious sanctions against rebellion. But these devices—the best which long centuries of imperial government ever discovered—were never effective for very long in any large state.

A second and almost equally difficult problem was how to prevent soldiers from oppressing the subject populations so harshly as to arouse their antagonism and persuade them to welcome almost any invader as a liberator. Here the principle of divide and rule came richly into play. Military bureaucracy could be paralleled by a civil bureaucracy, and the civil bureaucracy could be split up between administrative, judicial, and tax-collecting branches—each checking the others and each liable to inspection from above and vulnerable to appeals from below. In this fashion the army could be made to depend on supplies doled out by civilian officials, and any gestures on the soldiers' part toward helping themselves directly by plundering the civilian population could be detected from the start. But despite every administrative ingenuity, collaboration between local civil and military officials to fleece the population always remained possible. The history of all the world's great empires—especially during their later phases—demonstrates how widespread this phenomenon has been.

The conclusion to be drawn from such a survey of the historic record is that a citizen army of the sort we have been accustomed to taking for granted is rare and entirely atypical of civilized states. To be sure, most barbarian tribes expected every able-bodied man to bear arms But such forces were militias rather than armies in the civilized sense. The Greek cities of antiquity did raise and train citizen armies during a period of about three hundred years; so did the Roman republic. In the corners and coulisses of history a considerable number of other tribal republics and city states can be discovered that depended for varying lengths of time upon a citizen army. This was the case, for example, in towns of medieval Italy and Germany, in parts of Japan before the Tokugawa period, in northern India before the time of Buddha, and in Palestine during the time of the Hebrew Judges.

However important some of these communities were for the world's cultural and religious history, in matters of war and politics they remained puny and of merely secondary significance. The reasons are not far to seek. An effective citizen army required (and requires) very special conditions to flourish. First, the technical level of warfare must be such that no elaborate or expensive equipment that is beyond the reach of ordinary citizens can have decisive effect in battle. Until the introduction of firearms, this meant that infantry tactics and training had to be superior to cavalry—a circumstance only sporadically and locally the case. In the second place, a citizen army can only be effective as long as most citizens trust one another enough to fight side by side and back to back—not face to face against one another.

Since socioeconomic differentiation has been and continues to be a mark of civilized society, political or economic success with concomitant territorial expansion puts enormous strain upon such consensus. In fact, it proved easier to collect taxes from a disfranchised population than to maintain political consensus among a citizen majority. Accordingly, the great imperial states of history all fell back upon a professionalized army, separated from the general body of the subject population by a distinct ethos and, often, by distinct ethnic origin as well.

Western Europeans worked a remarkable variation upon these themes in the late eighteenth century. Prior to that time the European experience remained within the general patterns I have attempted to describe. With the invention of missile weapons that were effective against armor—first the cross bow and then guns—medieval feudal lords gave way to mercenary bands that lived mainly by plunder, just as Sargon of Akkad had done millennia before. In the course of the seventeenth century, royal bureaucratic administration converted these bands into royal standing armies that were organized along the same lines as the Assyrian army had been more than two thousand years earlier. The French revolutionaries broke away from these ancient patterns, however, by summoning all Frenchmen to the defense of the *patrie* in 1793. During the next twenty years innumerable French victories demonstrated the new power that mass armies could command in an age of incipient industrialism.

The subsequent military history of Europe is the history of more and more thorough mobilization for total wars—and the increasing awkwardness of citizen armies for the conduct of anything except all-out warfare. From this point of view the hesitations of the French, Austrian, and Prussian governments in military matters between 1815 and 1870 are most instructive. To fight limited wars abroad and maintain a dubiously popular regime at home clearly called for long-service professional troops. But such a force put a heavy strain on finances. A short-service conscript army cost less, since draftees did not get paid, but required the government to be popular or risk overthrow. Prussia's victories over Austria in 1866 and over France in 1870–71 seemed to prove that a conscript army of citizen soldiers could make even a conservative regime popular. This assuaged the scruples of aristocratic officers against more and more radical mobilization of social resources for war. The unparalleled efforts of World Wars I and II resulted.

British and American military experience departed from this European pattern in significant and important fashion. First of all, the British did not build up a large royal standing army. The seventeenth-century experience of Cromwell's military dictatorship soured king and Parliament, not to mention the people at large, against soldiers garrisoned at home. As a result, after the Glorious Revolution of 1688, the British army was legally subordinated to Parliament, not to the king; and its officers were recruited from the county families who simultaneously dominated Parliament and English society at large. Rank and file came mainly from the subject nationalities of the British Isles, the Irish and Scots, and secondarily from the English lower classes. The army was garrisoned abroad; home stations were used for training recruits. The result was an imperial army that had remarkably little independent weight in politics. Coincidence between the social origins and consciousness of the officers and of the ruling classes of Great Britain was so close that no independent military interest ordinarily made itself felt; and nearly all of the rank and file were kept overseas where their behavior could bring no harm and their weapons could hold no threat to the social order of Great Britain.

As for the United States, until very recently we stayed close to the militia tradition characteristic of barbarian and simple agrarian peoples. Thirty years ago the professional army of the United States was minuscule—less than 100,000 in a population of 120 million. Local police forces, National Guard units commanded by state governors, together with widespread possession of firearms by ordinary citizens all meant that no centralized monopoly of armed force existed within the country. This, indeed, was the hope and intention of the Founding Fathers, among whom a close and indissoluble relation between the exercise of political rights and the possession of arms and practice in their use was taken for granted.

Nothing that has changed since the eighteenth century invalidates the wisdom of the men who fought the revolutionary war and drafted the Constitution. In the long run it still is true that the possession of arms and practice in their use must coincide with the effective exercise of political rights. This is so because the leaders of those who do have arms in their hands can always exercise a veto over any action proposed by public officials if they have the will to do so and command the support, or at least the obedience, of their troops.

Fortunately, the American officer corps has a strong tradition against involvement in politics, and as long as civilian government does nothing to offend the corporate interest or pride of the officer corps this tradition will undoubtedly continue to inhibit open intervention in political decision-making, as it has in the past. Yet the military veto is still there; hidden perhaps, but not so far from the surface as it used to be. This is the case not because army officers have changed or become greedy for power, but because, as the military establishment has become larger and more professionalized, it has become both more expensive and more distinct from the general body of the citizenry. This increases the risk of open divergence between civil and military interests in a way which the United States has not known in earlier times.

If such a confrontation should develop openly in future, citizens without arms obviously risk the loss of their political rights—in fact if not in form. In cases of stubborn disagreement between civil and military leaders it is simply not safe to cut off the pay and decree the dissolution of an aggrieved army. As Sulla and Caesar demonstrated to Roman republicans, such acts of civic virtue invite military usurpation. Nor does it require a great stretch of our imaginations to envisage a time when half a million disgruntled Americans might return from Vietnam, or from some future battleground, with the conviction that they had been betrayed by the fat cats at home. On high patriotic grounds some general might then refuse to defer to civilian authority— as General MacArthur was sorely tempted to do in Korea.

I conclude that military service is, always has been, and seems likely to remain, the ball and chain attached to political privilege. Political privilege, in this connection, means the exercise of an effective voice in the determination of public policy. It follows that either the armed services must remain very small or some sort of universal military service is required to provide a secure basis for democracy. And if it is true that technical conditions no longer permit a citizen army to attain high efficiency, then the democratic political order is at least potentially endangered by that fact.

If the United States decides nevertheless to accept the risks of relying upon long-term-service professional troops of the sort suited for conducting distant, low-grade wars and for garrison duty overseas, then devices must be found for linking military leadership more closely with the leadership of civil society. The existing policy of exempting the future leaders of civilian life from military service positively invites divergence of viewpoint and seems almost suicidal in a democracy. In case a selective draft continues to be necessary—assuming that we do not wish to invite a coup d'etat—then it is precisely those who go to college and are headed for the privileged places in our society who should be drafted. Unwillingness to qualify for social leadership at such a price amounts to abdication.

Preservation of democratic government will be difficult in future as it always was in the past. The success or failure of this enterprise in the United States will depend in very significant part upon the military policy we adopt. The debate now opening in congress should therefore command the very best wisdom and attention of citizens and legislators alike. No more important issue has confronted us since World War II.

"The Draft in the Light of History," by William H. McNeill, from *The Draft: A Handbook of Facts and Alternatives*, edited by Sol Tax (Chicago: University of Chicago Press, 1967), pages 117–121. Copyright © 1967 The University of Chicago. Reprinted by permission of the publisher.

WILLIAM H. MCNEILL (1917–) is a Canadian-born American historian. He is known for his diffusionist theory of history, which holds that civilizations form when people organize in response to outside threat, after which they tend to absorb originally alien ideas, technology, and institutions.

7

Raising Armies Before the Civil War

by

William G. Carleton

Before the Civil War the regular army of the United States was little more than a token force, as wartime armies were largely volunteer. Volunteerism not only expressed basic American values of freedom and equality; it worked. The Revolutionary War had been won without benefit of a large, professional standing army that the British themselves had taught the colonists to distrust; and, profoundly religious, the colonists wanted to believe in the superiority of a nonprofessional force. Not until the deep divisions that led to the Civil War did Americans begin to question the supremacy of right spirit over sheer strength, and, even then, volunteers were considered naturally superior to draftees.

Pre-twentieth-century Americans had strong feelings against military professionalism. Their regular army was little more than a token force. They despised conscription, and until the Civil War they rejected it. Even in the Civil War the draftees were secondary to the volunteers. In fighting their wars, Americans traditionally relied on voluntary and temporary military service.

Before the Revolution, each of the 13 colonies had its own militia, and all able-bodied males from 16 to 60 were subject to service. Universal service, however, was ill enforced. The militia did very well in quelling local disturbances and fighting local Indian wars; but in waging the large-scale wars of the late seventeenth century and of the eighteenth century with the Spanish, the French, and their Indian allies (King William's War, Queen Anne's War, King George's War, and the Great War of 1754–1763), every colony found it necessary to resort to special recruitments of volunteers.

Colonials recoiled from fighting outside their own colony, and recruitments lagged except when local frontiers were harassed—and often even then. The British complained that the colonies did not act enough in their own defense; they prodded them to do more; and yet they held colonial military efforts in contempt. That contempt was largely justified. Colonial expeditions against the French in Canada during all four of the French and Indian wars bogged down again and again; and the pacifism of Pennsylvania's Quaker leaders exposed the frontiers of the keystone colony to repeated disasters. Those remarkable British victories in North America in 1759 (climaxing in James Wolfe's taking of Quebec), which resulted in the expulsion of the French from the continent, were largely the work of the British regulars.

Yet the Americans, forgetting their poor records in the colonial wars, seized upon two events of those wars to fortify their developing belief in the superiority of non-professionalism over professionalism. One was the improvised New England expedition of a fleet of fishing smacks and 4,000 volunteers which, in 1745, captured Louisbourg, in Nova Scotia, the mightiest fort in North America. The other was the spectacular defeat, in 1755, at the forks of the Ohio, of Edward Braddock's crack British regulars by a handful of Frenchmen and their Indian allies.

At the time of the Revolution (1775–1783), the Americans had no regular army; they were compelled to rely on improvisation and volunteers; and since they won that war, Americans were confirmed in the tradition of military non-professionalism. George Washington's Continental Army was composed of companies of riflemen from several states (enlisted for the duration), companies of musketmen from various states (enlisted for short terms, often for one year), and attached state militia units. Militiamen also fought in various parts of the country, independent of the Continental Army. Clusters of irregulars and minutemen often operated as guerrillas, especially in the backcountry.

How the Volunteer System Operated

After they had won their independence, the Americans depended on a small peacetime regular army, employed mostly to defend their frontiers and to fight Indians. This army was recruited from volunteers who enlisted for longer terms than the wartime volunteers, many of whom reenlisted repeatedly. Hardened by Indian fighting and long experience, these old regulars and their officers trained the raw recruits who joined the army in time of war. Following the War of 1812, the peacetime regular army was limited to a maximum of 10,000 men, but it usually fell far short of that; and on the eve of the Mexican War its actual strength was little more than 7,000.

In time of war, the regular army was enlarged with volunteer recruits who enlisted for short terms—often for one year and sometimes for only six months. During the War of 1812 (1812–1814), the regular army rose to around 34,000 men; and during the Mexican War (1846–1848), it rose to around 31,000. When wartime volunteering slackened, cash bounties were sometimes paid to new volunteers to encourage enlistments. Veteran volunteers, who had been paid no bounty, resented this. A similar situation in 1781 had sparked the famous mutiny of the Pennsylvania Line in the Continental Army.

There was a marked distinction between the experienced "old regulars" and the wartime "new regulars." Even the officers of the new men were often a different breed from the officers of the old men. As the regular army expanded in time of war, so also did the officerships, and the new officerships often went to prominent laymen who had taken the lead in their local communities in enlisting the war volunteers. Hence it frequently fell to the lot of the officers of the old regulars to train and direct the new men and their officers as well.

In time of war, there was also much dependence on military units outside the regular army. During the War of 1812, state militia units, enlarged by wartime volunteers, were important and carried on a number of campaigns. (Their records, however, were generally poor.) Militia officers were commissioned by the state's governor, although these appointments often merely confirmed the elections already made by the men, and they almost always reflected popular sentiment. Following the War of 1812, the states increasingly neglected their militias for a variety of reasons, but militia units were kept alive in various localities by young men interested in military affairs and by prominent citizens.

During the Mexican War some militia units were used, but far more numerous and important were the volunteer units which were not connected with the militia. These volunteer units were composed of men who did not want to join the regular army. They wanted to serve with men of their own neighborhood, or class, or ethnic or religious group; or they wanted to be sure of serving under local leaders who had recruited them and whom they admired. These volunteer units elected their own officers, often even those at the very top.

When mustered into the federal service, militia units and volunteer units came under the direction of the federal government and were paid, equipped, and supplied by that government. Assigned to campaign along with the regular army, militia units and volunteer units were often the last to be used, and generally they were given less important and less vulnerable positions in battle formation. Sometimes such units were under orders to campaign on their own, independent of the regular army. During the Mexican War, the number of men in the volunteer groups outside the regular army was double the number of the "new" and the "old" regulars combined.

An example, taken from the Mexican War, of how this haphazard system operated—at its best—is furnished by Colonel Alexander W. Doniphan's First Regiment of Missouri Mounted Volunteers. This regiment of 860 riflemen was recruited from Missouri farm boys by Doniphan, a frontier lawyer with no formal knowledge of military science. All of its officers, including Doniphan, were elected by the men in the outfit. Along with some other volunteer units, Doniphan's regiment was attached to some regulars for service in Colonel S. W. Kearny's expedition, which conquered New Mexico. After the fall of Santa Fe, Doniphan's regiment was allowed to operate on its own. Cutting itself off from all supply bases, it traversed 3,000 miles of wasteland, mostly in enemy country, to take El Paso and then the city of Chihuahua deep in Mexico—one of the great sagas of military history.

In time of war, then, the United States military establishment was complicated; much of it was improvised and decentralized; frequently it was short of manpower, equipment, and supplies. Washington's Continental Army never exceeded 20,000 men. The War of 1812 was waged over many fronts, yet when the regular army's ceiling was raised to 62,000 men, the appeals for volunteers resulted in an increased army of little more than half the ceiling. President James Madison's proposal to raise 100,000 men by conscription was unacceptable to Congress and public alike. During the Mexican War, the various battlefronts ranged from California to Vera Cruz, but the total military manpower (old regulars, new regulars, volunteer groups) was never much more than 90,000 men. Winfield Scott's army, which fought its way from Vera Cruz to Mexico City, usually had only 10,000 men, and sometimes fell below that.

During the Revolution, the War of 1812, and the Mexican War, army pay was often in arrears and supplies were meager. Washington's awful winter at Valley Forge is well known, but there were a number of "little Valley Forges" in all these wars. On many occasions, American armies were forced to forage, not only in enemy territory but also in friendly territory. Americans made it a general rule to avoid battle, if possible, unless they had a preponderance of men and materials.

Why the niggardliness in the general day-to-day military operations? There were a number of reasons: the disinclination of Americans to dislocate civilian life; the perennial optimism that every war would be a short one; the traditional American resistance to taxation; the invariable unpreparedness of ordnance, quartermaster, and other administrative agencies at the beginning of every war; the enormous difficulties of communication and transportation over vast distances and long stretches of wilderness.

The Weaknesses of the Volunteer System

Not only did the volunteer system (as applied to the regular army and to units outside the regular army) fail to provide sufficient wartime manpower, but it also gave free rein to certain abuses of localism. When the fighting was near home, there was a marked increase in militiamen and volunteers; but when it was elsewhere, there was a sharp decline. Many localities remained remote from the scenes of fighting, and these did not do their part in contributing manpower to the national defense. Even when wars were fought outside the United States, those nearest the scene (in the Mexican War, for example, the men of the lower Mississippi Valley and Texas) did a disproportionate share of the fighting. In the War of 1812, there were a number of cases in which state militiamen refused to invade Canada or even to carry their operations into another state, on the plea that the terms of their service did not require them to fight beyond the borders of their own state.

The practice of recruiting wartime volunteers for short terms played havoc with military operations. Most volunteers insisted on being relieved at the end of their stipulated term, even though this might occur during a critical campaign and involve the release of a number of companies and regiments simultaneously. Appeals for reenlistments usually went unheeded. The attitude was: "I have served my time, now let the other fellow serve his." At the worst, this practice resulted in the depletion of manpower at a crucial juncture; at the best, it meant hastily training batches of raw replacements. General Washington always dreaded the approach of December 30, for that was the date most one-year enlistments in his Continental Army ran out. During the Mexican War, Scott had to halt his perilous march from Vera Cruz to Mexico City in order to arrange for the safe return to the states of several thousand volunteers whose enlistments had expired. He was left, for the time, deep in enemy country with only 7,000 men.

There was never enough time to train the men or even the officers for war. Most recruits were rural youths who had free-wheeling frontier or semi-frontier habits; they were not accustomed to cooperating with other people. They were handy with guns, but they thought that individual marksmanship was all that counted. They disdained organized discipline, parades, drills, and maneuvering as so much playacting. Baron Friedrich Wilhelm von Steuben, on Washington's staff, anticipated the headaches of future drillmasters in America when he blurted out: "Goddam de gaucheries of dese badauts. Je ne puis plus. I can curse dem no more." When militiamen and volunteer units elected their own officers, these elections often took on the aspects of political campaigns back home. Sometimes the officers seemed to be more afraid of their men than the men were of their officers. Foreigners often commented that Americans made good fighters but poor soldiers. Discipline and experience *did* count, for the battle casualties of the volunteers were usually higher than those of the old regulars.

Recruits hated building camps and draining ditches; when they bothered to dig latrines, they dug them too close to camp. They drank too much, brawled too much, and wasted food, drinking water, bedding, clothing, and ammunition. They drank water from stagnant ponds and buffalo wallows. Prior to the twentieth century, all armies suffered more casualties from disease and epidemics than from battles; but United States armies seem to have suffered more from disease than did European armies; and such casualties were usually higher among the volunteers than among the old regulars.

The volunteers boasted of their resistance to discipline; they said that they joined the army not to work but to fight. The slogan of a North Carolina company during the Mexican War was: "Soldier, will you work?" "Sell my shirt first." "Soldier, will you fight?" "Twell I die." When they were admonished for their slovenly and nondescript dress, volunteers bragged that they would fight for their country but not dress for it.

The lack of discipline also accounted for the large number of desertions from United States armies. Again, desertions were higher among volunteers than among old regulars. America's frontier culture produced a large number of rovers, so when one became dissatisfied with army life he often simply disappeared. Because of the lack of communications, few deserters were apprehended.

It was on foreign soil, particularly in Mexico, that the American volunteer showed himself at his worst. President James Polk was distressed by the rowdy, bullying way the volunteers treated Mexican civilians, for he had hoped to win the people of the northern Mexican provinces to United States annexation. The roistering, rip-roaring conduct of the volunteer troops in New Mexico helped spark revolts in Santa Fe and Taos that were more troublesome than the original conquest.

The United States army was neither a class army nor a professional army; instead it became a political army. Men with political ambitions recruited volunteers in order to be chosen to high officerships and thereby get wide publicity for their martial activities. Officers sought to be popular with the rank-and-file, for army popularity would later help win civilian elections back home. The President, the war department, and Congress "played politics" with the army. Even Washington was not immune to the animosities and ambitions of politicians, as the Conway Cabal in the Continental Congress revealed. During the undeclared war with France in 1798, President John Adams, against his better judgment, was forced by Federalist party politicians to make Alexander Hamilton head of the temporarily expanded army. At the beginning of the War of 1812, many of those given high commands were superannuated Revolutionary War veterans with political "names." The Mexican War was honeycombed with politics. The number of Democratic politicians who overnight became colonels and brigadiers was astonishing. President Polk was irritated that the war's two leading generals, Zachary Taylor and Winfield Scott, were both Whigs; yet he could not dispense with their services, so he surrounded them with restrictions and "court-favored" officers. While they were waging the war, both Taylor and Scott were in effect running for the Whig nomination for President, but Taylor allowed his presidential ambitions to affect his military conduct far more than did Scott.

Our Military System: An Expression of American Culture

Despite the weaknesses of a repeatedly improvised volunteer system, the Americans clung to it because it expressed basic American conditions and values—localism, pluralism, non-professionalism, devotion to liberty, and a folksy egalitarianism.

The Americans inherited the British distrust of a large professional standing army. They regarded such an army as a threat to their liberties. Americans could afford to indulge their distrust of militarism more than could the British, for the Americans faced fewer wars and world involvements. Americans associated a professional army with the armies in Europe, where the soldiers were drawn from the distressed classes and the officers from the aristocracy and the gentry. Americans regarded the "frills and folderol" of European armies as combinations of medieval chivalry and caste privilege. But they abhorred the military draft even more than they did a professional army. Despite the use of conscription by revolutionary France, Americans thought of it as a monstrous violation of individual freedom and a relic of the feudal lord's mass levy.

In the United States, men were jacks-of-all-trades, and the successful forged ahead without formal education or training. If this were true in civil life, why not also in military life? To the Americans, the prerequisites of a good officer were simple—courage, common sense, native ability, quickness of mind, some boning up on mathematics and surveying, and a reading of Caesar's *Commentaries*. Nathanael Greene had been a farmer and smith, Francis Marion a modest planter, Daniel Morgan a teamster, John Sullivan a lawyer, Anthony Wayne a farmer and land surveyor. Prior to the Civil War, the nation's two outstanding military heroes were George Washington and Andrew Jackson, and both had been largely self-taught amateurs with some prior experience in backwoods fighting.

If so little formal training was necessary to make an officer, it was thought that even less was necessary to make an ordinary soldier. Native Americans were not much attracted to service in America's regular peacetime army anyway, and in the years from the Revolution to the Civil War a substantial portion of that small force—often more than one-third of it—was composed of foreign-born immigrants.

It was not until 1802 that Americans finally founded at West Point a military academy for the training of professional officers, and for years that institution was starved for funds. On the eve of the Mexican

War, Congress was debating a measure to abolish West Point. West Pointers were characterized as "puppets and aristocrats." On the other hand, General Scott, who was not a West Pointer, expressed the professional view when he declared that without his junior officers who were graduates of the Academy, the United States army could never have set foot in Mexico City. Many of these junior officers would become famous commanders in the Civil War.

At the time of the Mexican War, it appeared that the American preference for the non-professional had become, under the impact of Jacksonian democracy, a veritable anti-professionalism. The American people rejected both Stephen Kearny and Scott, the most competent commanders of that war. Winfield Scott was derided by the populace as "Old Fuss and Feathers" although he had done more than any other individual to win the war, and was the idol of the junior professionals. On the other hand, the people made heroes of John C. Frémont, who was little better than a military impostor, and Zachary Taylor, a veteran of the regular army but never respected by those well versed in military science. The people said that "Old Zach" was "folksy" and "as plain as an old shoe"; they hailed him as "Old Rough and Ready" and made him President.

American military practices also expressed the American society's localism and pluralism. The volunteer system allowed those localities most affected by a war to support it wholeheartedly, but that system also allowed those localities less affected by a war and even hostile to it (as was New England to the War of 1812) to escape its military burdens. (In those days when the Americans were less nationalistic than they later became, there was some wisdom in this.) Again, the volunteer system permitted one to choose whether he would serve with his neighbors, or fellow members of his social class, or fellow members of his ethnic or religious group. During the Mexican War, there were German-American units, Irish-American units, even a Mormon battalion. (One of the Irish-American units deserted to the Mexicans and fought valiantly under Santa Anna.) This practice did not appear to the Americans of that time as segregation or hyphenated Americanism but as a pragmatic recognition of American diversity.

Americans erected their haphazard and improvised way of waging war into a national legend. They played down the achievements of the professionals and exalted the exploits of the non-professionals—the swarming of the minutemen at Lexington and Concord, the victories of backwoodsmen at Bennington and King's Mountain, the feats of the Revolutionary guerrillas of the Carolinas, the seizure of an empire by a handful of frontiersmen under George Rogers Clark, the sensational victory of Andrew Jackson's militiamen over Redcoat regulars at New Orleans, the "big win" of "General" Sam Houston at San Jacinto, the odyssey of Doniphan's gamecocks.

Why the Americans Escaped Disaster

The professionals had a less romantic view. To General Washington, the American victory in the American Revolution was almost inexplicable. In 1783, he observed that anyone who attempted to write a history of the Revolution would run the risk of having his work called fiction. He put his finger on the American weakness:

> To bring men to be well acquainted with the duties of a soldier requires time. . . . To expect the same service from raw and undisciplined recruits as from veteran soldiers is to expect what never did and perhaps never will happen.

What Washington said about the American military weakness during the Revolution would also help explain the poor showing of the Americans in the War of 1812, and why even in the War with Mexico a number of the American "victories" were so precariously won (Monterey, Churubusco) or were actually a draw (Buena Vista).

For a number of reasons Americans were able to continue many unorthodox military practices without bringing disaster to the nation. All United States wars, up to the Mexican War, were fought mostly on United States territory, where the Americans had the defensive advantages of great distances, wilderness spaces, and a thorough knowledge of the terrain. (In the Revolution, they also had powerful aid from France.) In the Mexican War, the Americans were pitted against a people who were scarcely a nation and whose government was a travesty. There was also considerable truth in the belief that Americans needed less formal training than the fighting men of other nations, for the large majority of Americans of the preindustrial age lived hardy, out-of-doors existences.

During the Revolution, the Americans made the first general use of the light, thin skirmish line, a deployment of infantry in open formation. This was a "natural" for American frontier riflemen, and it proved less burdensome in equipment, more flexible and mobile, and easier for inexperienced troops to learn than the traditional infantry practices of European armies—the Swiss phalanx, the Spanish square, and the British heavy infantry in mass formation. Even in the preindustrial age the Americans showed a remarkable capacity for technology and technological innovation. During the Revolution, the superiority of the American rifle over the British smoothbore musket, both in range and in accuracy, was demonstrated again and again. During the Mexican War, foreign military experts repeatedly praised the excellence of the American field artillery.

Professional Military Practice

Finally, although the Americans, in line with their concept of war as high-spirited amateurism, always expected quick victories and short wars (and Presidents Madison, Polk, and Abraham Lincoln shared this optimism), most military men who conducted United States wars—whether their own backgrounds were professional or non-professional—succeeded in imposing on the American military tradition a cautious and practical view of war and a highly professional military practice.

To most high-level officers in the actual field of operations, remote from the original sources of supplies and equipment, war was not a matter of brilliant risks and strokes of daring but the prosaic business of winning the last battle. The best guarantee of victory was to have a sure flow—if possible, a superiority—of manpower and materials to the main scene of action. This underscored the importance of industrial production, engineering, logistics, and open lines of communications and supply.

General George Washington was a master of Fabian tactics, and he was called "the old fox" because he eluded the British and would never fight unless there seemed more than a fair chance of success. All United States wars down through the Civil War and including the many Indian wars involved, above everything else, maintaining supply lines over vast distances where communication and transportation facilities were precarious and often primitive. Hence the American maxim became: It is not always important to get there "the firstest," but it is always important to get there, if possible, with "the mostest."

WILLIAM G. CARLETON (1901–) is emeritus professor of history and political science at the University of Florida in Gainesville. He is the author of *Revolution in American Foreign Policy* and has published numerous articles in periodicals in the United States and abroad.

"Raising Armies Before the Civil War," by William G. Carleton, from *Current History*, Volume 54, Number 322 (June 1968), pages 327–332, 363. Copyright © 1968 Current History, Inc. Reprinted by permission of the publisher.

8

Women and the Draft
by
M. C. Devilbiss

As a background to the present controversy over compulsory military service for women, Devilbiss traces the history of women in the U.S. military. Women have played a unique military role because they have served in and with the U.S. armed forces solely as volunteers and never as conscripts. And though a few women have, at various times, served as warriors, most have typically been relegated to "combat support" rather than combat-related roles. Thus they have seldom actually been in the military but rather have merely been attached to it.

Devilbiss suggests five explanations for women's historical exclusion from conscription and, in presenting public opinion data from 1940 to 1980, shows that there is no consistent historical consensus regarding compulsory military service for women. In tackling the reasons both the potential draft of women and their use in combat roles have now become focal issues, Devilbiss notes in particular the effects of changes in the definition of "citizen-soldier" and in the concepts of gender roles.

In the complex web of issues concerned with women in the U.S. military, one issue that has recently drawn much attention—and generated confusion and consternation—is that of compulsory military service for women. We must try to clearly identify and delineate the questions and assumptions involved in order to avoid confounding the issues. Specifically, the questions "Should there be a draft" and "If there is a draft, should women be included in it?" are two analytically separate, but related issues. This paper will address the latter issue only, using the historical role of American women in the military as a stepping-stone.

The Past Role of Women in and with the Armed Forces

Women have played a unique role in U.S. military history. Unlike men, whose service has been either voluntary or conscripted, women have served in and with the armed forces solely as volunteers.[1]

During the American Revolution there were three major categories of military participation for women: "first, those serving in a distinct branch of the Continental Army referred to as 'women of the army,' or 'army women'; second, those enlisted as regular troops fighting in uniform side by side with male Continentals; and third, women serving as irregular fighters affiliated with local militia companies."[2] Far from being "camp followers" or "battlefield domestics,"[3] the "women of the army" performed duties with artillery units on the battlefield and served as medics in the field and in military hospitals. In the former capacity, they carried water for the gun crews.[4] (The water was *not* for the men to drink, as is commonly believed, but for swabbing out the cannons before reloading them after firing.)[5] In the latter capacity, they served in what was then the most dangerous military occupation, for the risk of dying from the diseases they were exposed to was far greater than the risk of death on the battlefield.[6] In utilizing women, the Continental Army was not being innovative but merely following the precedent of the eighteenth-century European armies and navies, which accepted a quota of "regulated wives" who were paid a small sum and drew half-rations in return for their work.[7]

Of those women, perhaps a few hundred, who served in combat with the Continental Army as regularly enlisted soldiers, some disguised themselves as males—they wore male clothing and enlisted under male names—while others made no effort to conceal their sex, and received pay, rations, and pensions under their own names. Finally, local militia units (as opposed to "regulars") were often composed partly or entirely of women and were employed as local defense forces. Women also served routinely on board warships at this time.[8]

During the period of expansion of the American frontier, the military employed women, as well as men, as scouts and also attached them to frontier outposts. As for the civilian frontierswoman, she was just as important, aggressive, and skilled in fighting Indians in defense of home and land as was the frontier male.[9]

At least 400 women posed as soldiers during the Civil War, presumably carrying out regular duties that included engaging and being engaged by the enemy in combat. Women also served on the battlefield and aboard Navy ships as physicians, nurses, and medical corpsmen. Dr. Mary Walker, a combat surgeon, was awarded the Medal of Honor by Congress for her heroism, the only woman in U.S. history ever to be thus honored.[10]

During this period women were also involved in activities that today would be called "combat support" or "combat service support": supplying ammunition, cooking, laundering, and engaging in camp maintenance.[11] Women again served in units of irregulars and were prominent in such covert activities as espionage and sabotage.[12]

The Spanish-American War in 1898 was the last war in which women assumed male names and clothing while serving in the armed forces.[13] During this conflict, women also served as nurses under contract to the War and Navy Departments. But they, like their predecessors in the Civil War, were civilians who were not actually *in* the military but instead were said to be attached *to* it. They served with distinction alongside the "regular" troops, enduring many of the same conditions—in the United States, Cuba, Puerto Rico, Hawaii, Japan, China, the Philippines, and aboard troopships.[14] In part because of the quality of the service of these women, nurse corps were subsequently established in the Army and the Navy in 1901 and 1908, respectively. But nurses were not given full military status, privileges, or equal pay and benefits until World War II.

The first women in "line" (nonmedical) roles in the armed forces of the twentieth century were enlisted women in the Navy and the Marine Corps in World War I. Called Yeoman (F)'s and Marine (F)'s, and numbering 12,500 and 305, respectively, they were brought into the services through a policy loophole that specified that "persons" (subsequently interpreted as not necessarily "male persons") could be enlisted *into* the service. These women served primarily in communications specialties stateside as well as overseas. They were brought *into* the Navy and Marine Corps mainly because of pressing personnel needs, and required little training, for they brought their skills with them. This era saw the beginning of the philosophy that a woman's role in the military was to do a particular job so that the man who usually did that job could perform other duties. This "free a man to fight" notion lived on in slogans and recruiting literature in World War II and is still prevalent in the military forces.

The Army during World War I decided that it could not put women *into* the service (that is, women could not be enlisted in the Army as they were in the Navy and Marine Corps) but that it could use them in uniform—as civilians. And as such they served, both in the United States and overseas, as clerks in the Quartermaster Corps (supply) and as bilingual telephone operators in the Signals Corps. In 1980 a tri-service review board considered the service performed by these women and ruled that they were entitled to veterans' benefits.[15] During this period about 22,000 women also served in the Army Nurse Corps and 1,400 in the Navy Nurse Corps, both at home and abroad. After World War I, when the armed forces demobilized generally, all women except nurses were transferred to inactive status and eventually discharged; their participation in the military had been viewed as a temporary emergency measure and no continuing role for them was officially foreseen.[16]

During World War II there were again unusually pressing personnel needs and women were taken *into* the armed services, this time in all branches. Over the course of the war, about 350,000 women served in the military, both stateside and overseas. Some held medical and administrative jobs; others became pilots,[17] truck drivers, airplane mechanics, air traffic controllers, naval air navigators, metalsmiths, and electricians.[18] The aftermath of World War II brought the Women's Armed Services Integration Act of 1948 (Public Law 625), which provided for a reorganized, regular, continuing, and institutionalized role for women in the U.S. armed forces. This time the women were not all discharged following a war. But the law set a 2 percent ceiling on their total numbers in the military, restricted certain job assignments, made enlistment standards and some military benefits different for men than for women, and excluded women from flag rank. Beginning in 1967, most of these prohibitions were modified or eliminated, but the job assignment restrictions are still in effect today.[19]

During the post–World War II era, punctuated by the Korean War, the Berlin Crisis, and the Vietnam War, women continued to serve, most of them engaging in medical and administrative work, but some holding communications, training, and supply jobs, and their numbers remained steady at about 1–2 percent of the total force. In 1973, with the end of the draft, and consequent *man*power shortfalls, the number of women in the military rose dramatically. This increase spurred a broadening of job categories, although some jobs—mainly those defined as "combat-related" —remained closed to women. But women were admitted to "nontraditional" jobs, primarily crafts and skilled trade occupations.[20] In addition, women were admitted into the National Guard in 1967 and into the service academies in 1976.[21] On December 12, 1980, Congress passed Public Law 96–513, the Defense Officer Personnel Management Act, which equalized the treatment of female and male commissioned officers as part of a broader standardization of personnel policies in the Army, Navy, Air Force, and Marine Corps. Currently there are some 150,000 women in the military, about 8 percent of the total force.

In summary, women have always served in and with the U.S. armed forces. But they have not historically been subject to *compulsory* military service; they have served voluntarily. This has not been the case with other nations, notably Germany, the Soviet Union, Israel, and England, which did conscript women into their armed forces during World War II. During this time, some of these women served as combatants in mixed-gender or all-female units.[22] One nation, Israel, continues today to specify military service as compulsory for both women and men.

That women in the United States have not been subject to the draft is not to say, however, that the issue of women and conscription has not been historically considered. During the American Revolution, women who served in local militia units may have been subject to call-up for service in the Continental Army.[23] Moreover, a draft of women was formally proposed at least twice in the nation's history: in 1942 within the War Department and in 1944 when a debate on the issue reached the floor of Congress.[24] Tangential to this was the voluntary and involuntary recall of Women's Army Corps reservists (especially enlisted women and junior officers) to active duty during the Korean War. And in January 1980 President Carter proposed registration (not conscription) for military service for both men and women. Congress approved the measure for males, but a like proposal for females was referred to a committtee, which shelved it.

Women and the Draft: Why Is This Becoming an Issue Now?

We have seen that whereas women have been utilized by the U.S. military, they have not as a class been *conscripted*. Why? We can construct some answers to this question by first analyzing five major points.

Concepts of defense and of international relations are changing. For most of its preindustrial history, the United States relied on a strategy of defensive domestic retaliation. Wars were fought principally on domestic lands and waters, and armies and navies were typically small, localized forces. So it was relatively easy for women to take part in and with the uniformed forces, although the exact extent of their participation and the roles they assumed were dictated largely by the perceptions of those who were in charge (men) and the concept of military need, variously defined.

With the advent of industrialization, however, military strategy concepts and international relationships altered dramatically. Many Americans were forced to think in more macroscopic terms. Defense could no longer be restricted to the home front or conceptualized as a localized boundary. Through many technological advances, the world had gotten smaller. Now defense was a global issue. The small, localized armed forces of the past gave way to large, standing military forces and the perceived need for a global presence. If there were more personnel spaces available in the military and not enough qualified men to fill them, women could be looked to as an important alternative source of supply. But this could occur only if military roles could be legitimated for women. This indeed did happen because, coterminus with the change in concepts of defense/international relations, there was a change in the structure of the military organization.

The structure of the military is changing. The rise of industrialization in the twentieth century created drastic changes in the military as an organization. It became larger, more differentiated, and increasingly complex, as did many other social institutions at the time. The modern military required new, more, and different kinds of jobs. Whereas the military forces of the eighteenth and nineteenth centuries were made up primarily of persons with combat jobs, those of the twentieth century came to be composed largely of persons in support, service, and *non*combat specialties.[25] This is referred to as a change in the "tooth-to-tail ratio." And it relates to the idea of "allowing" women to fight: If women cannot or are not permitted to fight, there is little room for them in a military organization in which most jobs involve fighting; but if most jobs in a military organization are those which women can do or are permitted to do, there is naturally more room for them.

The U.S. military of the late twentieth century has not only become more dependent on greater numbers of women, but has also been compelled to rely upon the "outside" skills that an increasing number of women possess. One reason for this is that there are fewer combat roles. Another reason is that jobs in the military are becoming increasingly technological, and civilian skills are therefore more readily transferable to military needs, and vice versa. Because many women have acquired skills in the civilian sector that the military needs—or have indicated an interest in and/or aptitude to learn critical skills deemed "acceptable" for women—they have been increasingly utilized by the armed forces when *man*power skills have been in short supply. Thus, women have become a more visible resource for the military in "other-than-combat" roles.

In this context it is interesting to speculate about the combat infantryman role and its virtual nontransferability, in the legitimate sense, to civilian life. (Even the Army openly admits this nontransferability, listing no counterpart civilian job for military occupational specialty "11B," combat infantryman. The skills of a Navy seaman, on the other hand, are more transferable.) If women, for example, dominated a civilian occupation called "combat infantryman," the Army would be literally forced to use women in such a role. There is, however, little opportunity for women to develop combat skills in a comparable civilian job category, and the combat role is proscribed to military women. The result is a military Catch 22: Women do not have an opportunity to learn and therefore cannot be utilized in such a role; women cannot be thus utilized and therefore cannot learn the necessary skills. Some opening in the argument does exist, however, since weapons familiarization and marksmanship skills (two aspects of the combat infantryman role) can be acquired by women through legitimate avenues—for instance, in sporting clubs and in police training. Moreover, some weapons familiarization is provided by the armed forces to its basic trainees, both male and female. The snag in this argument is that men go on to utilize and perfect these skills in the military while women cannot (they are not permitted to do so). Related to this is a third point, concerning "fighting" itself.

The nature of combat is changing. During the American Revolution and the Civil War, battle lines were hard to draw and define. Women joined men in battle when fighting occurred in their midst. In the modern era, the World War I concept of trench warfare came into being: warfare with clear-cut battle lines and a definite forward edge of the battle area, flanks, and rear area. In such a situation, it was easier to designate areas of fighting and of nonfighting. The advent of long-range weaponry, however, has now made areas other than front lines vulnerable.

Combat has changed in another way. In earlier conflicts, hand-to-hand fighting was often the rule. Today, again through technological development, opposing forces are often discharged from many yards or even many miles away.[26] Indeed, if the opposing force is in an aircraft, a tank, or a ship, what is discharged is the vessel itself—face-to-face combat may never even occur. Combat has become increasingly technological and decreasingly personal. In considering the case for women, however, we must examine the issue of combat with the related concepts of gender roles, of spheres of defense, and of citizenship.

Gender roles and "spheres of defense" are changing. In the early history of the United States, and on the American frontier, gender roles were more diffuse than they are now. In preindustrial eighteenth-century America "in every occupation open to men there also were women working. . . . There was no occupation in which men were engaged that did not include women acting either as practitioners or [as] owners of the business."[27] (Recall that "businesses" were *family* businesses—in the truest sense of the word—at this time.) With industrialization came the separation of work from the home. Men and low-status women moved into the cities to take on new jobs. This was the time when "the cult of true womanhood" was born, a philosophy that assigned to a (high-status) woman a special place, that is, in the home and *outside* the economic order. It was deemed that, owing to characteristics attributed to her gender, economic pursuits were unsuitable for her and she must be protected (by men) from such activities. This was the beginning of the "separate-sphere" philosophy in which each sex had power in a certain area—women in the home, men in the labor force.[28]

Thus, going into the twentieth century, many women were unemployed or underemployed and constituted a potential *reserve* of labor power, to be drawn on when labor was in short supply. This happened, of course, during the two world wars, when many men left their jobs to enter the armed forces and these jobs were taken over by women.[29] At this time also, industrialization and standardization made it possible to mass-produce the food, clothing, weapons, and equipment necessary to support enormous armies in the field for prolonged periods. But this required a national effort. Thus it was a "man's job" to fight in the military and a "woman's job" to work in support and service positions so that men could be "freed" from such jobs to do the "main" job. Thus, it was supposed, women and men "fought" in different ways, dictated by their capacities and natures.

As women have come to participate more extensively in the educational and economic institutions of the United States, gender roles have begun to change and the cult of true womanhood has waned. Much concern has been expressed over the appropriate roles for modern women. Perhaps no issue in this area has been more debated than that of women as warriors and, by implication, the role of women in the military in general. Because it is so tied to the topic of women and conscription, we must examine this issue of women in combat roles before we can get a complete answer to the question of why women have historically been excluded from compulsory military service.

As we have noted, the Continental Army of the American Revolution needed every fighting person it could get. The war was waged on home soil and women fought alongside men. Moreover, the nation's economic base was an agricultural one in which gender roles were somewhat more diffuse than was later the case during industrialization. Thus, because it was a crisis (an emergency during which usual norms might be temporarily suspended), because it was a domestic conflict, and because gender roles were more overlapping, women could contribute to the war effort in both traditional and nontraditional (nontypical) ways. Women were "allowed" to fight. This "right to fight" was later taken away from them by the first-class citizens (men) who made the rules governing military service when the crisis was over. Congress did occasionally recognize the bravery of these female veterans and reward them with pensions, but it did not want them to continue their combat roles once the war was over. Of course, the easiest way to stop them was to prevent them from serving in the armed forces at all, since most of the jobs in the Army and Navy involved combat roles. Men wanted these jobs for themselves. Other supportive jobs, like logistical support and medical care, were just as necessary and probably no less difficult, but they were less glorified jobs and could be done by nonpersons, such as women volunteers, servants, blacks, and other minorities.

Why were these jobs desired by men? One argument is that the opposite of the cult of true womanhood, the cult of true *manhood,* exalted physical aggression and victory as a badge or mark of a man. Combat was seen as a test of virility. It was also a more generalized test of a person's ability to withstand a stress-filled environment for a prolonged period. This type of environment afforded an opportunity for a man to display traits of bravery and leadership (again considered to be marks of manhood), for which he could be recognized and glorified. Men knew that a combat environment might also prompt individual reactions and emotions of a sexually exciting nature, which, according to the cult of true womanhood, women should not experience. Thus, military service, but in particular, combat experience, was (and still is) conceptualized as a rite of passage to "manliness" and therefore to "manhood." It was unnecessary, then, to have women in combat because "manhood" by definition was something that women could never achieve, just as men, by definition, could never achieve "womanhood." The armed forces were thus deemed an exclusively (or predominately) male club to which women were denied admission, or, if admitted, a club in which they could not gain access to the highest ranks and "inner circle" because of this combat exclusion. As DePauw notes:

> This policy, which most people assume protects women, actually keeps them from entering a number of prestigious specialties that are considerably less dangerous and less demanding physically than some of the noncombat jobs women are presently eligible for. Although the overwhelming majority of today's generals are not in combat assignments, experience in such assignments is essential to get to the upper ranks at the Pentagon.[30]

Yet the matter is today, even more than in the past, definitional.[31] Women have "engaged or been engaged by an enemy in armed conflict," have been "in a geographical area designated as a combat/hostile fire zone by the Secretary of Defense," and have "received hostile fire pay and combat awards."[32] Therefore, even though women have been under the same conditions—and even fought—in battle as have men, their roles have not been considered to be "combat" *by definition,* thanks largely to the influence of the concept of separate spheres and the cults of true womanhood and true manhood. This leads us now to examine the final aspect of our question concerning women and conscription, the concept of the "citizen-soldier."

The concept of citizenship is changing. An individual's relationship to the State can find expression in several forms for "the term *citizen* serves to highlight and symbolize the dramatic transformation of the individual's relationship to the state that occurred with the breakdown of European feudalism and the rise of nationalistic democracies."[33] But citizenship, the privilege and status of only a minority of the population during the early days of the American Republic, has come to be a much more inclusive phenomenon. The "noncitizen" category historically encompassed such groups as slaves, servants, women, aliens, and other marginal and excluded populations.

Just as the concept of "citizen" underwent a period of considerable change during the fourteenth through eighteenth centuries, so did the concept of "soldier" —that is, an armed combatant of a nation or ruler. Historically, common soldiers serving in armies of a particular nation or ruler were not necessarily citizens of the State; rather, they were much more likely to be slaves, conquered peoples, mercenaries, or members of a warrior caste. Military *leaders,* on the other hand, were likely to be citizens and members of a ruling elite. In particular, armored knights were those who both held an hereditary title and could afford the proper regalia and entourage; likewise, the mounted cavalry who later held the place of honor on the battlefield, had to be members of the nobility.[34]

In the eighteenth century, the time of the American and French revolutions, the two previously distinct historical concepts of "citizen" and "soldier" merged into a new concept, the "citizen-soldier."[35] Citizens, however, were still a minority of the American population. That is, they were free white males—no woman could be a "citizen."[36] Because women were considered to be *outside* the citizen structure (nonpersons), they could not vote or take part in the political process or be in decision-making positions in the governmental and military spheres, lest they make laws and policies regarding their own roles and participation. Men in these positions made such decisions for them. Thus, women could not be "citizen-soldiers" because they could not be "citizens." The rights and obligations of citizens, including the citizen-soldier function, were extended neither to women nor to other non-citizen classes.

In the eighteenth and nineteenth centuries, the citizen-soldier role was finally extended to these groups. What is unique about the case of women, however, is that they were, and still are, offered only noncombat roles— "their 'right to fight' has been constrained."[37] It has been argued that women have not been subject to compulsory military service because they have the right *but not the obligation* to serve in the military.[38] This view merely supports the historical argument that women constitute a "special category" of citizens, those who do not have either the rights or the duties of full citizenship.[39]

The citizenship issue is, then, a clue to why women have not been included in draft legislation. But there is another angle to this. Service in the armed forces has actually been a pathway to citizenship for many groups who were thus "given the opportunity to prove their loyalty through defense of the state."[40] However, women have served in the armed forces both before and after becoming citizens, in the sense of their assumption of certain citizenship rights, such as property ownership, educational access, enfranchisement.[41] But if women have served in the armed forces, have they not then "proven their loyalty through defense of the state"? The argument here is that their loyalty has not been "proven" because they did not defend the State specifically by bearing arms.[42]

Besides the citizenship argument, other explanations can be advanced as to why women have historically been excluded from compulsory military service. One of these concerns spheres of defense. It was not necessary, for example, to draft women to engage in work that would help to support and maintain an army in the field (for example, wartime defense work and production) when women *as civilians* were doing the jobs that needed to be done. Another potential explanation takes changing international relationships into account. In an age when many conflicts are settled over the conference table rather than on the battlefield, the new "fighter" is becoming the ambassador and diplomat, and more and more women are appearing in such negotiating roles. This explanation, however, relates to the citizenship issue: Women are being increasingly—but not totally—recognized in these roles as legitimate representatives of the State.

There is still another important issue related to citizenship. It is argued that in the modern era only the State and, by extension, its legitimate agents have the power to take a life. The combat soldier, the police patrolman, and the judge, for example, are roles in which this power, under certain circumstances, can be exercised. Thus, the issue related to citizenship for women is this: Do women have the institutional right to take a life? If the answer is no, is this, then, one reason such roles are not seen as appropriate for women? Should women have the same rights and authority as men do? Should women, like men, be full citizens? Should women, like men, be legitimate agents of the State? Moreover, there remains the issue of "proving" loyalty: If women were armed ("allowed" to fight), would they use this new freedom in defense of the State or against it?

We have put forth some explanations for women's historical exclusion from compulsory military service. But why has the potential drafting of women become such an issue now? Perhaps the most compelling reason is the change in definitions of (and subsequent ambiguities surrounding) the "appropriate" roles for women in the latter twentieth century. In addition, for the *first* time the term "citizen-soldier" applies not only to men but potentially to women because (1) women are now "citizens" (though perhaps a special class thereof), whereas they were not in the past, and (2) changing definitions of appropriate jobs for women in the military, based on their historical duties, imply a *consideration* of their potential utilization in direct combat roles, whereas, in the early twentieth century at least, even when the proposal for women to be drafted was made, it was "understood" that they would be excluded from combat.[43]

The juxtaposition of changing social norms and definitions of the roles of the "citizen" and the "soldier" (and the "citizen-soldier") has vividly brought the issue of compulsory military service for women to public attention. Until the recent past, the issues involved were not problematic, either because women could fight but could not be citizens or because women could be citizens but could not fight. Indeed, today the very constitutionality of a draft law that includes men but excludes women is being brought under review. It is in the 1980s, marked by a press for equality with "no exceptions" for women and by changing gender roles, that the issue of gender and the draft, the question of compulsory military service, and the related issue of susceptibility to combat roles come at last to a watershed.

In summary, the issue of compulsory military service for women is obviously a complicated one. This issue and the related one of women in combat roles are symptomatic of our times. They speak to larger issues, not the least of which are the concepts of changing gender roles and a move toward a postindustrial, androgynous society. It is not overstating the case to say that how the issue of compulsory military service for women is ultimately decided will frame and dictate many of our attitudes about the nature of our society and of the roles and positions of the women and men in it for years to come.

This is the first publication of "Women and the Draft," by M. C. Devilbiss.

M. C. DEVILBISS (1948–) served on active duty in the U.S. Army from 1971 to 1973 and is currently a member of the Air National Guard. She received a doctorate in sociology from Purdue University in 1979 and has taught undergraduate sociology courses at Frederick Community College, Purdue University, and Ohio University. Now a postdoctoral fellow in the Department of Sociology at Yale University, she is at work on a book about the role of women in U.S. military service.

Notes

1. In the strictest sense, this statement is not true, owing to some unique historical conditions of women's service, as we shall see.

2. Linda Grant DePauw, "Women in Combat: The Revolutionary War Experience," *Armed Forces and Society*, Volume 7 (Winter 1981), pages 209–226.

3. DePauw notes: "Women did, of course, sew and cook—but they did this for themselves and occasionally for an officer who could afford to pay out of his own pocket for such special service. They did not do chores for enlisted men" (ibid., page 213). Cf. John Todd White, "The Truth About Molly Pitcher," in *The American Revolution: Whose Revolution?*, edited by James Kirby Martin and Karen R. Stubas (Huntington, New York: Robert E. Drieger Publishing Company, 1977).

4. The cannon of the American Revolution required a crew of three: gunner, assistant gunner, and water carrier. Compare this with the modern machine gun crew (all male): gunner, assistant gunner, and ammunition bearer.

5. DePauw, "Women in Combat: The Revolutionary War Experience," pages 210–217.

6. The risk of death from disease in war was dramatically reduced by sanitary measures, for which major credit has been given to Florence Nightingale, an English nurse, who introduced sanitation measures during the Crimean War. A decade later Clara Barton and the U.S. Women's Sanitary Commission carried on this work during the Civil War. See ibid., pages 209–210.

7. Ibid., page 212.

8. Ibid., pages 217–218; and Linda Grant DePauw, "Effects of the Increased Role of Women in the Armed Forces on American Women" (Paper presented at the Seminar on Women in the Armed Forces, Library of Congress, Washington, D.C., November 2, 1979).

9. DePauw, "Women in Combat: The Revolutionary War Experience," pages 222–225. In this context it should be pointed out that Native American women too exercised a good deal of power in waging war against *their* enemy. For example, one source notes: "Cherokee women exercised a decisive voice in the war plans of the tribe. If they opposed the war council's choice, they could negate a declaration of war by declining to provide food and clothing for the warriors. Some Cherokee women, such as Nancy Ward, attained a position on the war council by bravery in battle in the eighteenth century; another War-Woman had a street in Georgia named after her, commemorating the site of an engagement

which she helped win through her courage and skillful military strategy" (U.S. Army Center of Military History, Staff Support Branch, "Women in Combat and as Military Leaders: A Survey," Washington, D.C., March 1978), page 10.

10. DePauw, "Women in Combat: The Revolutionary War Experience," page 218; U.S. Department of Defense, Defense Advisory Committee for Women in the Service (DACOWITS), "Women in the Armed Forces" (Washington, D.C., 1976); and Leonard Berlow, "Mary Walker: Only Woman to Win the Medal of Honor," *The Times Magazine*, September 1, 1980, pages 60–61. See also note 4.

11. Martin Binkin and Shirley J. Bach, *Women and the Military* (Washington, D.C.: Brookings Institution, 1977), page 5; and Linda Grant DePauw, "Commentary," in *Military History of the American Revolution*, Proceedings of the Sixth Military History Symposium, U.S. Air Force Academy, Colorado Springs, Colorado (Colorado Springs: U.S. Air Force Academy, 1974), pages 176–178.

12. Linda Grant DePauw, "Women in Combat: Unwritten Chapters in American Military History" (Paper presented at the Conference on Sex Roles at the Crossroads, Dickinson College, Carlisle, Pennsylvania, February 16, 1981), page 10.

13. Elvira Virginia Mugarriette (known as "Babe Bean") reportedly served with the U.S. Navy as Lieutenant "Jack Garland." For a discussion of some historical "transvestite soldiers," their motives, and their methods, see DePauw, "Women in Combat: The Revolutionary War Experience," pages 217–219.

14. U.S. Department of Defense, DACOWITS, "Women in the Armed Forces," page 31.

15. The Department of Defense Civilian/Military Service Review Board awarded veterans' benefits to the female telephone operators in the Signal Corps who served primarily in France and to the female members of the Quartermaster Corps who served overseas *only*.

16. Two plans for establishing a "women's service corps" in the Army were suggested during the interwar years—the Phipps Plan in 1926 and the Hughes Plan in 1928-1930—but they were reviewed with less and less attention and finally filed away. See Binkin and Bach, *Women and the Military*, pages 5–6.

17. These were the WASP (Women's Airforce Service Pilots), civilian pilots in military uniform, whose major responsibilities were the ferrying of all types of military aircraft from the factories to their destinations for deployment, the testing of "red-lined" aircraft to detect problems, and two-target flying for artillery practice. In 1977, Congress granted these women their veterans' benefits. For an interesting history of this group, see Sally VanWagenen Keil, *Those Wonderful Women in Their Flying Machines* (New York: Rawson Wade Publishers, 1979).

18. See Binkin and Bach, *Women in the Military*, page 7; and Joy Bright Hancock, *Lady in the Navy* (Annapolis, Maryland: Naval Institute Press, 1972), pages 275–276.

19. In 1967, Public Law 90–130 removed the legal 2 percent ceiling on female participation in the armed forces. (However, this authority to prescribe the numbers and percentages of women in the military was merely *transferred* at this time from the letter of the law to the discretion of the individual Service Secretaries, so limits were still in fact imposed.) The 1967 law also removed the restrictions on the promotion of women to the ranks of general and admiral. But promotions have often depended on types of job skills and assignments (particularly combat and command) that were—and still are—restricted to women. Currently, women remain prohibited by Sections 6015 and 8649 of Title X of the U.S. Code from serving on permanent duty aboard combat ships and in combat aircraft. These sections apply to the Navy and the Air Force. The Army has no legal restrictions on the use of women in combat, but has adopted a service policy that excludes them from such duty. The Marine Corps is under the Navy restrictions. The Coast Guard, under the Department of Transportation, has no restrictions on the utilization of women. Benefits for men and women have moved in the direction of equalization. (Cf. Frontiero v. Richardson, 441 U.S. 677 [1973].) The two most pressing questions concerning women in the U.S. armed forces are (1) How many women can be utilized, and (2) in what kinds of jobs can/should they be employed?

20. These occupations were actually not "new" to women at all, as evidenced by the World War II period.

21. See Judith H. Stiehm, *Bring Me Men and Women: Mandated Changes at the U.S. Air Force Academy* (Berkeley: University of California Press, 1981), which, though focusing on the Air Force Academy, covers women's entry into all five service academies and also takes up the issue of women in combat roles.

22. Soviet women, for example, were in tank battalions and also served as pilots of fighter and bomber aircraft. See Binkin and Bach, *Women in the Military*, page 31; and U.S. Army Center of Military History, Staff Support Branch, "Women in Combat," p. 24.

23. Linda Grant DePauw, "Women in Combat," *George Washington University Times*, Volume 10 (January-February 1981), pages 1–2.

24. Mattie E. Treadwell, *The Women's Army Corps* (Washington, D.C.: Department of the Army, 1954).

25. See Barbara Allen Babcock et al., *Sex Discrimination and the Law: Causes and Remedies* (Boston: Little, Brown and Company, 1975).

26. Some exceptions to this occur in fighting insurgent or nonconventional forces.

27. DePauw, "Commentary," page 176.

28. Albie Sachs and Joan Hoff Wilson, *Sexism and the Law* (New York: Free Press, 1978), pages 52–66.

29. See DePauw, "Commentary," page 176.

30. DePauw, "Women in Combat," page 2.

31. The Combat Exclusion Policy of the Army, for example, is intended to preclude the utilization of women in combat units as combatants. However, a substantial percentage (currently about 20 percent) of women in the Army are *in* combat units. Were these units to become engaged in hostilities, women would be on the battlefield, exposed to the same risks of injury, capture, and death as men, and would be expected to defend themselves and their units. However, because the jobs in these units are performed by women, they are designated "noncombat" jobs. Men perform combat jobs and women do not, by definition. See U.S. Department of Defense, Office of the Assistant Secretary of Defense, (OASD), *Use of Women in the Military*, second edition (Washington, D.C., September 1978), pages F-3 and F-5; and Grace M. King, "Women in Combat—The New Reality" (Paper presented at the biennial meeting of the Inter-University Seminar on the Armed Forces and Society, Chicago, October 1980).

32. U.S. Department of Defense, OASD, *Use of Women in the Military*, page F-5.

33. James B. Jacobs and Leslie Anne Hayes, "Aliens in the U.S. Armed Forces: A Historico-Legal Analysis," *Armed Forces and Society*, Volume 7 (Winter 1981), page 198. Cf. Morris Janowitz, "Military Institutions and Citizenship in Western Societies," *Armed Forces and Society*, Volume 2 (Winter 1976), pages 185–204.

34. David R. Segal, Noral Scott Kinzer, and John C. Woelfel, "The Concept of Citizenship and Attitudes Toward Women in Combat," *Sex Roles*, Volume 3 (1977), page 470.

35. See ibid., page 469; and Morris Janowitz, *Military Conflict* (Beverly Hills, California: Sage Publications, 1975), pages 70–88.

36. In the mid-1800s in England, there were arguments over whether the term "persons" legally included women. It was ultimately decided that it did, but this decision was not reached until 1929 (Sachs and Wilson, *Sexism and the Law*, pages 38–40).

37. Segal, Kinzer, and Woelfel, "Concept of Citizenship," page 471.

38. Having the right to serve *in* the military, however, may be viewed as progress since, at times in U.S. history, women did not have the right to do so.

39. See Sachs and Wilson, *Sexism and the Law*, pages 87–94. The current debate over the Equal Rights Amendment (which provides for full

citizenship rights and duties for women) also lends support to this interpretation.

40. Segal, Kinzer, and Woelfel, "Concept of Citizenship," page 469. Included in the groups "given an opportunity to prove their loyalty" are black, Native American, and alien males. See Jacobs and Hayes, "Aliens in the U.S. Armed Forces," passim.

41. For example, all women who served in and with the armed forces before and during World War I did so before they could vote.

42. Segal, Kinzer, and Woelfel, "Concept of Citizenship," passim.

43. In fact, the whole concept of "citizen-soldier" is undergoing evolution. It is now being questioned whether the "soldier" role is an obligation and/or right of citizenship. In 1981 the U.S. Supreme Court is due to consider a case in which the constitutionality of a law that subjects men, but not women, to compulsory military service is being challenged.

9

The Peacetime Draft:
Voluntarism to Coercion

by
Richard Gillam

Following a subtle but profound shift in national values and nearly three decades of congressional debate, a century-and-a-half-long tradition of rejecting peacetime military conscription in America ended with the passage of the Selective Service Act of 1967. Though Americans had traditionally placed their highest peacetime priority on protecting freedom and individual rights against State coercion, radical changes after World War II and the Korean War moved Congress to emphasize national interests. Gillam documents the thoughts and events that transformed national peacetime military conscription from the unthinkable to the acceptable: it was eventually regarded as an indisputable cost of preserving national security. This change came within a totally new historical context—a state not of declared war, but of declared perpetual national emergency unmarked by the open hostilities traditionally necessary to justify the suspension of individual liberties.

The anomaly of peacetime military conscription, the puzzling contradiction posed by a highly coercive institution which exists in a presumably democratic and libertarian society, has recently made the draft a topic of intense and heated public debate. Yet the arena of this debate has been rather narrowly limited to administrative and political considerations. It is time, then, that intellectual historians should call attention to the critical ethical and intellectual dimensions of the issue in the hope of providing information and perspectives which may lift discourse to a more sophisticated level and perhaps free debate from the seeming impasse at which it now stands.

The passing of our particular national tradition of maintaining only a voluntary army in peacetime has, in fact, required a subtle, yet momentous, readjustment of national values to the perceived exigencies of new situations. The transition from voluntarism to coercion as a means of raising a military force has necessitated some essential modifications to that sometimes inarticulate, yet nevertheless discernible, philosophy underlying the American polity. With some oversimplification, we may see a change in emphasis from liberty and the protection of individual independence against state coercion to a view which stresses both the dark side of human nature and the need for increased state authority to preserve national order and collective security. Although this philosophical readjustment was accomplished in a relatively short period following the Second World War, it was not consummated without a great deal of uncertainty in the minds of concerned Americans, nor did our people easily succeed in exorcising the burden of guilt accompanying their disaffection from a long and venerable tradition.

In short, both a profound change in the national climate of opinion and a crisis of American thought resulted when Americans struggled to reconcile their traditional, democratic ideals concerning military recruitment with expedient, if not inevitable, action. As America broke sharply with her past, she sought desperately to resolve the manifest tensions born of her disaffection. The story of this inner struggle provides a fascinating chapter in American intellectual history.

Examination of previous national debates over coerced military service, for example, offers a needed corrective to certain misconceptions about the consensus or "seamlessness" underwriting our transition to peacetime military conscription and about the "inevitability" of this change. The idea of a "seamless" American culture cut from whole cloth, of a culture which flows gradually and inexorably from the mainstream of history with few dramatic bends or rapids to mar its splendid wholeness, is in fact a commonplace in the writing of American history. (Its major statement is in Daniel Boorstin's provocative work, *The Genius of American Politics.* The now classic attack on this school of history is John Higham's "The Cult of the 'American Consensus': Homogenizing Our History," in *Commentary*, February 1959.) Appealing as might be the gradualist vision of enlightened historical progress and endemic cultural harmony, however, it cannot bridge the chasm which separates the ethic of voluntarism from that of coercion; it cannot explain the current acceptance, indeed the fervent support, by a majority of Americans of an institution once viewed as profoundly anti-democratic in nature. In short, the national transvaluation of values which followed the dramatic change from voluntarism to coercion as a means of military manpower procurement may be viewed as a sharp and major new departure in American history There was, of course, an element of consensus in this process, but the abruptness and severity of our break with past tradition nevertheless goes far to obviate historical interpretations based on notions of gradualness or seamlessness.

Another conventional view, that because peacetime military conscription followed hard on the heels of the Second World War it was an "inevitable" product of that war, is certainly oversimple and inadequate. Previous American wars saw no necessary extension of peacetime conscription, while a nation such as England, one of the world's major belligerents, has recently found it possible to defy any idea of historical inevitability by ending her own system of compulsory military service. Indeed, during the postwar period the United States herself very nearly chose voluntarism and discarded coercion altogether. The very existence of this alternative and the respect given it for many years after the inception of the Second World War strikes another blow at the view of the peacetime draft as an institution which was brought into being by an inexorable determinism. America's acceptance of peacetime military conscription may, on the contrary, best be understood as the history of frustrated expectations, as an erosion of the will and a weakening of the spirit not completed until well after the war's end. Further, it was the product as much of cold as of hot war.

A major problem, of course, in any such examination of national attitudes is that of defining "popular opinion." I have relied for my information primarily upon a reading of the many and often acrimonious debates over peacetime military conscription to be found in the post-1940 volumes of the *Congressional Record*. By so doing, I have in part assumed that Congressional opinion largely coincided with that of the nation in general; but, in addition, my own reading of *The Nation*, *The New Republic*, and the *New York Times* after 1940, with particular emphasis on the period to 1951, has lent some factual credence to this assumption. Such evidence at least suggests that Congress mirrored a climate of opinion which also informed the content of popular attitudes. Another difficulty, however, is that my evidence relates primarily to the opinions of only the white middle class. The attitudes of the "Other America," especially those of the Negro community as expressed in such newspapers as the *Pittsburgh Courier*, frequently diverged. Negroes worried that they would once again be denied "first-class citizenship" by *not* being drafted and by thus not being allowed to serve in the American armed forces, which was yet another symbol of white privilege. To Negroes, conscription also sometimes seemed a likely solution to some problems of the ghetto, such as the massive unemployment of Negro youth. Despite such significant minority group concerns, however, white middle-class thought ran in different directions; and it is the direction of this thought which may be traced through the pages of the *Congressional Record*.

On August 12, 1940, near the beginning of the long and tortuous debate over the Burke-Wadsworth selective service bill, Senator Arthur Vandenberg of Michigan delivered the following illuminating plea to his fellow legislators:

> I am opposed to tearing up 150 years of American history and tradition, in which none but volunteers have [sic] entered the peacetime Armies and Navies of the United States, unless there is valid reason to believe that this reliance in 1940 has become a broken reed for the first time in a century and a half.
>
> There must have been sound reasons all down the years why our predecessors in the Congress always consistently and relentlessly shunned this thing which we are now asked to do. These reasons must have been related in some indispensable fashion to the fundamental theory that peacetime military conscription is repugnant to the spirit of democracy and the soul of Republican institutions, and that it leads in dark directions. That certainly is my view.

We of an age hardened by too frequent and often obstructionist appeals to the muse of history may lightly dismiss this as merely another rearguard attack by an unhappily atavistic politician. Yet it would be an error to interpret Vandenberg's argument as simple rhetorical extravagance, because the ensuing debates amply illustrate that many, including a large number of those eventually supporting the bill, well realized the historical verity of the Michigan senator's remarks. Among the legislators there was an uneasy and accurate sense that they were, indeed, tampering with a long and respectable tradition of American military voluntarism.

In fact, the voluntarist precedent issued from the earliest years of our Republic. While there existed some colonial examples of compulsory peacetime service on the militia level (of which the 1940 Congress was uniformly unaware), our national history was entirely free of such legislation. The Selective Service Series on the draft (No. I, Vol. II does exhaustively document colonial precedent for conscription. Because this collection was researched and published for the express purpose of justifying the peacetime draft, however, its usefulness as reliable history is strictly limited. It is further important that colonial laws, cited by the Selective Service Bureau, which required militia training for only a few days per year or which demanded service during periods of high emergency only are not strictly comparable to the kind of peacetime military conscription initiated after 1940 which required a long period of separation from home and family. But most significantly, even the selective service system does not claim that there was precedent in our *national* history for peacetime military conscription by the federal government. In this essay, I refer to this larger national tradition of military voluntarism.

To be sure, during our early national history George Washington had believed that a professional standing peacetime army was "indispensably necessary" and had advocated coercion of service if it were needed. The Congress, however, believed that such a proposal was outside the American pale and, despite the President's immense prestige, his wishes went unheeded. The Militia Act of 1792, which Washington's Congress finally did pass, contained no provisions for financing or enforcement and thus raised only a "paper army." Real emergencies, rather, were to be met by six-month volunteer "levies" raised directly by national authority. Yet in 1803, even this limited federal power of raising such levies was returned to the individual states, with the voluntarist principle remaining intact. After the burning of Washington, D.C., during the War of 1812, Daniel Webster also restated the deep national aversion to coerced military service. Peacetime military conscription, he argued, was "incompatible with any notion of personal liberty . . . a solecism, at once the most ridiculous and abominable that ever entered into the head of man."

The theory that the free citizen would voluntarily, by nature, spring to the defense of the nation during any hour of need remained current during at least the first half of the nineteenth century. Even during the less than necessary Mexican War, President Polk could confidently invoke voluntarism. "A volunteer force," he told Congress, "is beyond question more efficient than any other description of citizen soldiers; and it is not to be doubted that a number far beyond that required would readily rush to the field upon the call of their country."

Wartime conscription was a practice eventually adopted during the Civil War, yet even during this period of national peril, coercion was not popularly or passively accepted. The draft met widespread and violent resistance, especially in the North. The bloody anti-draft riots of 1863, for instance, raged for four days in New York City, causing millions of dollars of property damage and countless deaths. Walter Millis, the eminent military historian, has even concluded that the Civil War saw, not the mitigation, but the triumph of American voluntarism. "Both in the South and the North," he writes, "conscription acted more as a support for and encouragement to volunteering than as a substitute for it. On neither side did conscription work very well, whereas the volunteers carried the terrible burdens of the great battles." In his *Memoirs*, General William T. Sherman himself decried the efficacy of state coercion as the means of raising a military force. The "men who voluntarily enlisted at the outbreak of the war," he wrote, "were the best, better than the conscript and far better than the bought substitute." It is not surprising, then, that conscription terminated with the cessation of hostilities, leaving inviolate the traditional American enmity to peacetime military conscription. The Spanish-American War was fought entirely with volunteers, and thus it was not until the First World War that coerced military service once more made an appearance on the American scene. Yet, again, this was only a wartime measure which expired with the coming of peace.

Of course, the long-standing tradition of peacetime military voluntarism was not based merely upon intellectual whimsy or emotional caprice. From the Revolution to 1940, there were implicit and rather constant philosophical assumptions which underwrote the national animus toward federal coercion in the cause of peacetime military might. With some apologies for necessarily broad generalizations, we may isolate the main canons of voluntarist thought as it existed in 1940. The first might loosely be called anti-militarism, involving both a fear of a large standing army and the suspicion, derived initially from the course of British history, that such military establishments posed grave dangers to individual liberties and to democratic institutions. Related to this, and stemming in large part from traditional libertarian philosophy, were a number of assumptions regarding the individual and the state. Respect for individual liberties and fear of despotic authority led to the belief that only in the most necessary areas should individual volition be subordinated to state hegemony. Political authority was narrowly defined and when possible denied; excessive state power, it was believed, led to regimentation, and regimentation to the death of liberty. Indeed, to many, the great powers over the individual which peacetime conscription gave to the state seemed productive of totalitarianism. Voluntarism was further tightly bound up with the notion that society supported the state, or political order, rather than being based on the older notion that the political order sustained society. This implicit distinction between society and state was frequently extended; the former was seen as naturally expressing the will of a people, while the latter often assumed in the public mind the form of an alien and unnatural entity which operated largely by coercion rather than by consent. In a true emergency which endangered the existence of the polity, the argument went, society would naturally respond and military volunteers would abound. With this view went an understandable reluctance to lend the state a coercive power which, at best, seemed unnecessary. In time of war, conscription might be reluctantly and doubtfully subscribed to, but in time of peace it remained unthinkable.

By 1940, then, peacetime voluntarism and the philosophy underwriting it seemed often a sacrosanct and immutable part of the American heritage. In this light, the belief of Vandenberg and many of his colleagues that they were breaking with the national past was well founded. In another sense, however, the establishment of selective service in 1940 cannot be viewed as an intentional or a permanent repudiation of peacetime voluntarism. The basic change suggested by popular support for the peacetime draft in 1940 was that a measure previously accepted only in time of war could now be justified by an "emergency" not necessarily marked by open hostilities. In fact, the military draft was justified only by the existence of an emergency approximating a war crisis, and it was generally expected that the restoration of normal times would bring the end of conscription. Few legislators in 1940 harbored any thoughts of establishing the draft as a permanent policy, nor did many Congressmen expect or desire the creation of a large, perpetual military establishment.

Public opinion had moved from overwhelming opposition to military conscription in late 1939 to its support only after emergency war preparedness had seemingly been dictated by the Battle of Flanders and the ensuing fall of France. Yet even when faced with the threat of world conflagration, Congress suggested its uneasiness at abandoning traditional voluntarism by writing into the Burke-Wadsworth bill a one-year limit on inductions, a restriction on the number of draftees, and a prohibition against sending any conscripts out of the Western hemisphere. Again and again the troubled legislators emphasized the temporary nature of selective service. The cadence of disclaimers is a tribute to the recognized strength of the voluntarist ethic.

"This bill shows on its face," argued Senator Kenneth D. McKellar, "that the law is to be temporary and intended for the emergency only." The bill's co-sponsor, Congressman James Wadsworth, himself carefully explained "that this is an emergency measure. . . . It is not an attempt to establish a permanent policy in the United States."

That only the general sense of a war emergency had sanctioned the 1940 act was again indicated by a renewed debate over draft extension in 1941. In midyear, when the war in Europe to many seemed somewhat more remote than it had the previous year and no material threat to the United States had yet appeared, growing opposition to continuation of conscription was evident. Supporters of the draft spent their rhetorical energy proclaiming the existence of a real and imminent emergency which justified state coercion in the interest of national security. Again, however, none would argue for a peacetime military establishment founded on permanent conscription. It was not seriously doubted that the draft would end coterminously with the emergency. "We all know," contended Senator Alben Barkley, an advocate of conscription, "that when the emergency terminates there is not enough power in Christendom to keep the Congress from releasing these boys from the Army and sending them back home." Senator Josh Lee paid deference to the continuing strength of anti-conscription tradition when he promised that "the soldiers will not remain in service a single day longer than the necessity for their being in service exists. . . . The pressure of the people at home would demand it." Congressman Luther Patrick added just one of many other similar reservations about any explicit break with tradition: "When the time comes that we can restore these boys to civil life, as soon as conditions can justify it being done, you may be sure it will be done, of course. I do not believe anybody believes anything else." Yet despite such reassurances, despite such deference to historic American ideals, a troubled House of Representatives passed the draft extension by only a single vote, 203 to 202. It seems apparent, therefore, that during this one-year interlude of "peacetime" conscription, the American people had by no means accommodated themselves to any dramatic break with the past. The climate of opinion was still inexorably opposed to any system of permanent military conscription, and all expectations were for a return to voluntarism as soon as possible.

Yet we may perhaps wonder if America had not done more than she supposed. By justifying her departure from a previously pure tradition on the basis of a "national emergency," the nation had opened a closed issue to interpretation. What constituted an emergency, how great that emergency need be to legitimate coercion, who was to define that emergency, all became relevant questions. America had taken her first small but significant step down the long road toward a system of permanent peacetime conscription. Still, the real and lasting change in national attitudes toward coerced military service would wait until the postwar period.

The recent history of the peacetime draft has frequently been viewed as a continuous, evolutionary process stemming logically from the act of 1940 and from the war itself. A close examination of the period from 1945 to 1950, however, renders this a less than satisfactory explanation. Indeed, during the immediate postwar years there was a great deal more staggering and reeling than has commonly been supposed. By these years, some may have accepted the peacetime draft as inevitable; but another and perhaps more important group upon which I have chosen to focus remained reluctant to countenance such a sharp break with the American past. Even having just survived one of history's most sobering military events, such persons believed that military needs could be met by traditional, voluntary methods. This view changed only as America encountered what it perceived to be an irreconcilable conflict between venerated ideal and unhappy reality. As in virtually all such conflicts, it was not tradition which triumphed. Yet it may be fairly said that the eventual accommodation was not easily accomplished, nor was it consummated before producing what can perhaps be described as a psychological crisis of national thought.

In 1945, during the last months of a fading war, Congress had extended the selective service law into the following year. Finally, in 1946, however, America was able to review the concept of military conscription free from the exigencies of war and relieved in part of the necessary burden of maintaining a huge military establishment. It was generally assumed that the draft would terminate in 1947. "The people in the country at large wholeheartedly favor the volunteer system for the armed forces," observed the Senate Committee on Military Affairs in its report on the 1946 bill. "There is complete unanimity on this point." The committee recommended another one-year extension of selective service, but only in order to assure the continued efficacy of the volunteer method and to provide for an orderly transition to peace during a period of continued international tensions.

Congress itself yet more clearly intended to eliminate peacetime conscription from the American scene. It softened the existing law by exempting all fathers and by prohibiting the drafting of teen-agers.

Representative Carl Vinson, later to become one of the most hardened and lasting proponents of peacetime conscription, introduced an amendment to suspend the draft for five months before allowing it to operate into 1947. There "can be no justification in normal peacetimes," he declared, "for a draft in order to provide men to man the Army and Navy. The only justification for a draft is when there is a national emergency confronting the country." Senator Wayne Morse bluntly stated that "we should put the army on a voluntary basis as soon as possible."

Yet, by hindsight, we may perceive in even this terminal, one-year extension of selective service suggestions that a faithful national allegiance to voluntarism was being further eroded. While rejecting conscription at the time, Vinson had nevertheless said explicitly that an emergency short of war itself might justify continuation of the peacetime draft. Other Congressmen resorted frequently, sometimes almost compulsively, to a stylized pattern of rhetoric. Legislators voiced predictable sentiments: they proclaimed, first, allegiance to voluntarism, or, in alternate form, voiced simple regret that compulsion was necessary; next, they set forth the unusual conditions necessitating temporary abrogation of the American ideal; finally, they voiced confidence that the tradition would soon be restored. This type of formalized rhetoric issues from the tension between expectation and reality, and may well be characteristic of all periods involving a transition or reconstruction of values. Certainly such ritualized statements played an important part in the American debate over peacetime military conscription and in the transition from voluntarism to coercion. In later years, as American expectations of a voluntary army were continually thwarted, such rhetoric would become more strident; finally, it would become a simple lament as the nation broke with her past and could only sadly remember the ethic of a world she considered irrevocably lost.

In 1946, however, Congressional rhetorical form seemed sincerely hopeful, if uncertain. Thus, Senator H. Alexander Smith of New Jersey spoke to his colleagues:

I am in entire accord with those who argue that a volunteer Army and a volunteer Navy are far preferable to any form of conscription. . . . We are very definitely not a militaristic nation. We seek no conquest, and as a people we are wedded to the paths of peace and good will toward our neighbors. . . .

Why, then, should we even consider continuation of the Selective Service Act? . . . We have found rather definitely, after the experiences of World Wars I and II, that we as a people cannot live alone. Time and space have been annihilated; and the conquest of the air, coupled with the discovery and dreadful possibilities of the atomic bomb, make us realize that, whether we desire it or not, we have very definite responsibilities to cooperate in preserving the peace of the world. . . . I look upon this measure as an indication of our cooperation with the world to preserve the peace, not to strengthen ourselves for war with other countries. . . .

It is difficult for me to endorse a national policy which calls upon our young men, just at the moment when they are about to enter on their more advanced studies, to accept responsibility to be on call to help our country meet its international obligations. But I have come to the conclusion that our country and our international responsibilities are the primary consideration.

The next day, Smith added an important final addendum to his statement:

[B]y taking this action now to extend the Selective Service Act in this transition period from war to peace we are in no way establishing a policy of a draft army, an army by way of conscription.

In the House of Representatives, Congressman R. Ewing Thomason offered his own version of such ambiguous rhetoric:

I wish we did not have to extend selective service a single day. Heaven knows I wish we did not have to draft or bring into the military service by any means a single 18-year-old boy in this country. . . . There is not a man or woman among us who would not like to get these men by the volunteer method, if it is possible. In my opinion there is a very good chance to do that. . . .

I want this to be the last extension of selective service and I think it will be, but we can take no chances during the next few months.

Yet are there not here elements of doubt, of uncertainty? Is there not a suggestion that circumstances, while certainly not hopeless, might render voluntarism a more elusive ideal than had previously been assumed? In short, is there not a slight indication that expectations might have to be modified in the face of intractable necessity? Such thoughts were, in fact, to find abundant sustenance.

On March 3, 1947, President Harry Truman expressed "the earnest desire of placing our Army and Navy on an entirely volunteer basis at the earliest possible moment." As a result, and with no articulate opposition in either house of Congress, the peacetime draft was allowed to lapse at the end of that same month. Once again it was possible to reconcile theory with action, to bring the military back again to its historic principle of voluntary service. Truman's own basic commitment to voluntarism was questionable, however, since in December of the previous year he had appointed a nine-member Advisory Commission on Universal Military Training which, by virtue of its composition, was destined from the first to underwrite the principle of coercion, as it formally did in June 1947.

The commission report foreshadowed the further frustration of national expectations in 1948. With strikingly few attempts at public justification, the armed forces had raised the minimum acceptable intelligence-test scores of Army enlistees from 59 to 70, and in 1948 to 80, thus eliminating from service many previously acceptable volunteers and contributing to a temporary manpower shortage. This, and an increase in international tensions, combined to make the reestablishment of peacetime conscription seem to many necessary, to some inevitable.

In his address to a joint session of Congress on March 17, 1948, President Truman gave voice to a growing national suspicion of Soviet Russia. After cataloguing Communist bellicosity in Czechoslovakia, Finland, and Greece, he asked both for a renewal of the peacetime draft and for "universal training" (the President's very unwillingness to call the latter "military" training is testimony to his realization that it affronted certain national traditions). Universal training was rejected out of hand by both houses of Congress, but selective service itself was renewed for a two-year period. Even in acquiescing to the President's request, however, it was still generally anticipated that peacetime conscription was a temporary expedient which would end with the abatement of world tensions. Once again, examination of Congressional debate demonstrates that voluntarism was abandoned only after a great deal of timorous uncertainty.

The favorable House majority report on the new 1948 conscription bill stressed the "serious deterioration in the international situation" and the presumed inadequacy of voluntary recruitment. The minority report, on the other hand, found it more significant that peacetime conscription would be a "radical departure in American history," would "invade the family and disrupt its character," and eventually would become a permanent institution. On the last charge, however, there was significant dissent from those supporting the new draft bill. Senator J. Chandler Gurney assured his colleagues that he did "not wish permanently to saddle a selective service system on the youth of our nation." Senator Irving M. Ives contended that peacetime conscription was "fundamentally something of a very temporary nature."

While some of those who argued the temporary nature of selective service may actually have expected a type of universal military training to follow logically as a substitute, at least one of their number, Senator

Leverett Saltonstall, predicted a return to voluntarism. "If this bill is enacted," he argued, ". . . more and more volunteers will enter the armed services, and this bill will be used less and less." If this seems a perverse sort of voluntarism made efficacious only by a kind of psychological coercion, it nevertheless represents one of many distraught attempts to avoid a complete break with the American past and to preserve some alternatives to overt state conscription. In the hope that a sudden ground swell of youthful patriotism might at the last minute obviate the necessity of compulsory military service, the House wrote in a stipulation that delayed the implementation of the legislation until ninety days after its enactment. Under the leadership of Wayne Morse, the Senate further insisted on limiting selective service to a two-year trial rather than the requested five. It is perhaps indicative of deep-rooted Congressional reservations about the peacetime draft that many prominent Senators came to the support of Morse's two-year amendment. Suspicion of the military was also reflected in Senator James Kem's proposals to reform the military justice system, and in Congressman Edward Rees's amendments insisting that training under the act be carried out "on the highest possible moral, religious, and spiritual plane." Had Congress felt secure in the compatibility of military life with traditional civilian ideals, such a stipulation would scarcely have been necessary. In yet another attempt to vitiate some effects of peacetime conscription, the Congress lowered the required period of service from 24 to 21 months (the House had wanted only 12).

At the same time, Congressional rhetoric assumed a sadder quality, one mirroring the apparent, if seemingly necessary, disparity between theory and action, between ideal and fact. Hence, Congressman Leroy Johnson of California mused:

> What we propose to do today is, under ordinary conditions, contrary to our traditions—it is contrary to our democratic way of life—yet I believe that the wise step for us to take is to pass this bill. . . . We are not living in an ordinary time. We have not peace in the sense which we used and interpreted that word ten or more years ago. We are living in a world of fear, of chaos, of uncertainty, and to a certain extent of hopelessness. . . . It goes contrary to our ideals in peacetime to do a thing like this, but there is no greater mission that we have to perform than to try to make the peace. . . . You cannot have liberty unless you have security. This bill will help bring about world security, in my opinion.

Yet this was a curious turn, and one which obviously troubled thoughtful Americans. How long, they might have wondered, can ideal give way to necessity before falling into disuse, and to what extent might fear of the future dictate abandonment of the past? How long might it be until the nation had defined a state of permanent national emergency with conscription as a way of life and with liberty having largely given way to the quest for national security? Such questions were not truly answered until the middle of the next decade, although the nature of their answers had clearly been suggested earlier.

By 1950, the immediate postwar expectation of reestablishing a voluntary army had not yet been entirely abandoned. That a total of only 30,126 men had been drafted under the 1948 act, virtually none of them since January 1949, convinced many that they had been deliberately misled as to the necessity in 1948 for any conscription law at all. These circumstances convinced many more that voluntarism might still be a viable principle, even though Congress remained entirely unwilling to raise military salaries to the very lowest level of attractiveness. (Congressional unwillingness to spend the amounts necessary to raise armed-forces salaries to competitive levels was a constantly voiced reason for retaining the compulsory system after the Second World War; voluntarism, it was feared, would simply be too expensive.)

Despite such financial reservations, however, the 1950 Congress seemed ready to amend the conscription system. Both House and Senate were willing to sanction the continuation of the office of selective service as an administrative establishment. But the lower chamber hoped to suspend the compulsory features of the conscription law, which in effect would have terminated the draft; it could have been reactivated only upon Congressional approval of a concurrent resolution declaring a state of national emergency. The upper chamber would merely have stayed compulsory inductions until Congress had "by concurrent resolution declared that it [was] necessary to supplement voluntary enlistments in the armed forces of the United States in order to maintain the strength thereof to the extent appropriated for by Congress." Senator Harry P. Cain voiced a common expectation that "the armed forces can continue, exactly as they have for the past 18 months, to get the necessary men by voluntary enlistments."

Thus the differing House and Senate bills were sent to conference in the latter part of June 1950, with the general belief that compulsory peacetime inductions would be halted and only a skeleton selective service system held in reserve in case some future emergency should arise. As late as June 26, the principal consideration in conference was to preserve the administrative structure of the system without giving the President much power to use it. Yet again events interceded to frustrate this design. On June 27, when the conferees assembled, each had been informed of President Truman's decision to intervene militarily on behalf of South Korea, which over the previous weekend had been attacked from the North. Because of this development and what they called the "critical and momentous times," the conferees reported back to their respective houses a recommendation to extend the draft for a year and to give the Chief Executive broad discretionary power in its use.

If this single decision, made during a time of crisis, did not at one blow inevitably doom traditional peacetime voluntarism, it may nevertheless be seen as a watershed after which the old tradition never regained its former strength. The unsettled climate of American opinion was not in a moment clarified, but it was soon clear that new stability would be found in the support of coercion and not of voluntarism. After Korea the necessity of a large standing army, even in peacetime, was seldom questioned. From this assumption it followed logically that peacetime military conscription would at least periodically be necessary, and more important, it also meant that a majority of Americans would support such a draft policy.

The nature of this change may be well seen in the behavior of Dewey Short, the obstreperous Congressman from Missouri who had persistently and valiantly battled peacetime conscription throughout the 'forties and who a few days before Korea stood as the staunchest defender of conscription during periods of emergency only. On June 27, he performed his act of public contrition in the House of Representatives. "Events change one's outlook and position," he remarked. "We had to face brutal facts and meet a reality, unpleasant as that reality is. No longer can we continue to bury our heads like an ostrich in a sand dune with wishful thinking and expect peace to come to a shattered and war-torn world." As Short concluded his address supporting draft extension, his colleagues rose and gave him a standing ovation. In part, this was a gesture of respect for the speaker; in part, it was an expression of patriotic enthusiasm to be found in any nation embarking on a military venture. With the benefit of hindsight and some imagination, however, we may prefer to see an audience rising to applaud the final act of a play involving American voluntarism, a play pleasant and enjoyable in performance if somewhat old-fashioned and idealistically sentimental in content. Men hardened by angry and dangerous times could no longer respond to values which, for over one and a half centuries, had quickened the pulse of their ancestors.

During the next decade and a half, the efficacy of peacetime military conscription would not be seriously challenged on the floor of either house of Congress. Henceforth, discussion would center largely about the administrative rationalization of the draft. Men might speak of making conscription more "equitable" (although this would remain merely rhetoric), but very few would speak seriously of its elimination.

The 1951 debate over the extension of the conscription act lends support to my contention that the period of meaningful and substantive debate had passed, that Americans had adjusted their expectations to what they perceived as uncompromising reality. Men who previously had been adamant opponents of the draft now hoped merely to stave off the new threat of universal military training while accepting selective service itself as given. True, this debate took place in the midst of a legitimate national emergency, yet the change in attitude cannot be attributed solely to the storm and stress of the moment; during previous emergencies selective service had been extended only with reluctance and some trepidation, and always with the expectation of eventual termination, an expectation noticeably weaker in the 1951 debates. "True peace," suggested Congressman Charles Price in words typical of many, "is something living generations may dream about and remember, but may never know again. Armed truce is something we may yet bargain for, as being preferable to war." Senator Edward Martin of Pennsylvania articulated a new mood of bellicose preparedness in somewhat blunter terms. "America," he proclaimed to his fellow legislators, "must move forward with an atomic bomb in one hand, and the cross in the other." Senator Edwin Johnson's comment summarizes the general sentiment on conscription: "There is nothing controversial about selective service." It was an "equitable, and democratic, manner of mobilizing our manpower."

Congressional rhetorical form, while continuing to express a certain ritualistic antipathy to the principle of military conscription, subtly metamorphosed into a fatalistic statement of intent to do what was seen as necessary. Representative Edmund Radwan said:

> Of course the idea of compulsion is distasteful. There is no moral satisfaction that by law we shall compel the youth of our land to learn how to kill as well as to keep from being killed. There is no moral satisfaction that for the first time in our history we must resort to compulsory conscription, but we do not live in a world of our own choice, of our own comfort. We are faced today with an implacable adversary who does not and will not understand our honorable intentions unless these intentions are backed by unquestionable might.

The form, in essence, had become a lament, a hollow protestation accompanied by weary resignation. In addition, America judged herself free of guilt for the transition in value from voluntarism to coercion.

The sin was not hers but that of Russia and Communism in general, an "implacable adversary" which forced democracies into distasteful expedients. There existed a state of quiet consensus that America had entered a period of perpetual national emergency which demanded and justified creation of a garrison state based on peacetime military conscription.

By 1955, the conscription act passed four years previously could be extended after only a few hours of debate in each house. There was no objection to the principle of coercion, nor were there any appeals to the virtually dormant ethic of voluntarism. Most legislators remained entirely unwilling to spend the sums necessary to make a military career attractive, while assuming that volunteers would never fill the ranks of an organization offering such unsatisfactory salary inducements. John Kenneth Galbraith has commented that "the draft survives principally as a device by which we use compulsion to get young men to serve at less than the market rate of pay." In such terms, voluntarism could indeed seem little but a relic of the past. Thus, Carl Vinson asked with evident sincerity: "If we do not extend the draft law, what is our alternative?" The now-converted Dewey Short issued the perfunctory declaration to the effect that "no one is here voting for a draft because he likes it. It is really contrary to the spirit of freedom and to the lovers of liberty everywhere." Yet, as he observed, the policy was not determined by us, but by our enemy. Senator Richard Russell's comment in 1955 that "the regular draft is the keystone of the arch of our national defense," suggests the distance the nation had traveled from the voluntarism championed before the Second World War. During the 1956 presidential campaign, Adlai Stevenson did raise the possibility of abolishing the draft; Eisenhower, however, fell back upon the virtues of conscription and eventually the eruption of the Suez crisis brought an end to Stevenson's proposal.

How long theory and practice could remain bifurcated, how long America could view conscription as necessary without also persuading herself that it was good, was partly answered in 1959 by the House Armed Services Committee. In its report on the extension of selective service for another four years, it observed that the system was "vital to the preservation of the American way of life." Gone was any sense that conscription itself violated ideals which were once themselves seen as vital to that "way of life." If Congress's traditional rhetorical lament continued to appear sporadically during the debates of 1959, and later during those of 1963, it more and more often merely suggested that coercion was distasteful rather than undemocratic, more and more frequently it chose to emphasize the assets rather than the debits of compulsory military service. While the search for national security and world order were used initially to justify coerced military service, the nation for a time turned to other palliative ideals involving "equality" and "obligation" to institutionalize the new departure in American practice and values. A glance at such arguments may suggest the outlines of this new ethic.

Alexis de Tocqueville once perspicaciously observed that the great conflict in the American mind was between liberty and equality, one frequently existing at the expense of the other. The suggestion is indeed prophetic regarding national attitudes toward selective service. The rejection of that individual liberty of choice implicit in voluntarism was justified in the name of equality of obligation. Gradually the idea grew among the American people that every physically and mentally acceptable young man owed to his country and would have to fulfill many years of active and reserve military duty. This "universal military obligation" for many needed no justification in terms of national crises or war emergencies (in part because these existed continually), but was seen as the simple price of citizenship to be paid in time of peace as well as of war. This notion, new in American history, persuaded many that peacetime military conscription was democratic because it was equally imposed and presumably equally borne.

This justification of coercion by way of equality and universality, for example, had been accepted by a majority of both houses of Congress in 1951 when they voted in favor of the *principle* of universal military training and directed that a commission should later recommend a concrete proposal for such training to the Congress. In 1952, when the actual training proposal was voted upon, a majority of the House seems actually to have favored it; only a complicated series of parliamentary maneuvers by opponents of the plan prevented its passage. Despite the narrowness of this defeat, however, it is significant that even the theoretical, if coercive, equality of universal military training was not realized in fact.

To this specific failure may be added other qualifications to any justification of conscription by way of equality or universality. There is, initially, the clear inequity by which men who cannot vote are made to fight. In the interval since 1951, it has also become perfectly clear that military *service* (if not the "obligation") is in fact selective rather than universal, that the burden of its performance is more likely to be felt by certain socioeconomic, educational, and racial groups than by others. Also disconcerting has been the sight of a supposedly civilian selective service agency largely controlled by the military or by men closely associated with its interests. Thus, the all too visible face of reality has rendered the already vulnerable argument from equality yet more dubious. Still, many have remained reluctant to abandon this convenient justification of the peacetime draft. In 1955, for instance, Carl Vinson could still insist that "every man upon reaching the age of 18½ years has an obligation to serve; in other words the obligation to serve is universal; it applies to every boy in America alike." Yet it was also necessary for him to add the qualification that "the system upon which he is brought into service is selective."

Unsatisfactory as this argument might be, it maintained a tenuous existence with the aid of some administrative peculiarities of the selective service system. In fact, draft deferments, although perhaps not designed for the purpose, have proven philosophically important to the preservation of the egalitarian argument. By reducing the manpower pool, such deferments for a time allowed proponents of peacetime conscription to maintain the fiction of equality by arguing that virtually all "qualified nonfathers" eventually serve. As the Senate Armed Services Committee put it in 1959: "[V]irtually no 1-A nonfather who is qualified physically and mentally and not eligible for deferments can avoid military service." Relieved of its tortured array of qualifications, this statement meant that approximately one-half the eligible American youths would not have to meet their military "obligation."

Recently, however, the pressure of events again brought selective service into the public eye. In 1967 a number of reports were issued which recommended various changes in the existing draft system. Yet it is significant that all of the suggested modifications were merely ones of rationalization or administration; none seriously considered a return to traditional American voluntarism. The reversal of induction priorities so that the military might procure more malleable and less obstreperous manpower and so that uncertainty might be lifted from the lives of young men at an early age, as recommended by both the Burke Marshall and Mark Clark Commissions, hardly seemed a radical break with the existing system. The lottery suggested by the Presidential Advisory Commission on Selective Service (the Marshall Commission) seemed scarcely more than the product of an ephemeral hope that chance could somehow dispense a kind of random justice. Even the most daring of the recent proposals, supported by such disparate persons as then Defense Secretary Robert McNamara and anthropologist Margaret Mead, would simply have rendered coercion "democratic" by universalizing it in the form of "national service." In the face of such suggestions, Congress succumbed in general to the proposals of archconservative L. Mendel Rivers and adopted a conscription bill distinguished primarily by unfortunate and largely irrational strictures directed at America's small group of conscientious objectors. Burke Marshall, head of the Presidential Advisory Commission, noted bitterly that "the new bill makes the system worse than it was before."

Thus in 1967 coercion was perfunctorily accepted and the argument from equality laid quietly to rest with the ghost of American voluntarism. The nation no longer needed philosophical excuses to justify a practice which it felt was indisputably necessary and which, over a period of years, had become a familiar part of national life. At least for the moment, another ideal once central to American thought seemed of profound irrelevance.

"The Peacetime Draft: Voluntarism to Coercion," by Richard Gillam, from *The Yale Review*, Volume 57, Number 4 (June 1968), pages 495–517. Copyright © 1968 by Yale University. Reprinted by permission of *The Yale Review*.

RICHARD GILLAM (1943–) is a historian who has taught at Stanford University, San Francisco State University, and the University of California at Santa Cruz. He is the author of *Power in Post-War America* and numerous scholarly articles, and is working on a forthcoming biography of C. Wright Mills.

10

The Volunteer Army
by
Donald Smith

Smith outlines the events that led to President Nixon's program ending the military draft and establishing an all-volunteer armed force. He focuses on the transition period, graphically demonstrating the kinds of problems the army had to face as it groped its way from reliance on the draft to dealing with the more complex and demanding requirements of raising an armed force by persuasion rather than by force.

Fort Benning, Georgia, is a 285-square-mile ecological filigree of long-needle pine forests, ridges, swamps, clay banks, and foot-high anthills bordering lonesome pre-Civil War cemeteries, and networks of dirt trails and two-lane macadam highways named for long-forgotten heroes. It is one of America's last official sanctuaries of machismo, a place where middle-aged warriors direct textbook wars of their own design against imaginary enemies, using pistols loaded with blanks, with troopers who were adolescents when the officers were cursing real artillery falls in Vietnam. Fort Benning is the home of the 197th Infantry Brigade, one of the first and still best examples of the Nixon Administration's plan for an all-volunteer army, an end to the draft. As the plan goes into its second year of trial, all is not well at Fort Benning or with the Army.

Long Good-bye

Some of the more gung-ho generals up north at the Pentagon see the volunteer army as the hottest device since Moshe Dayan invented the Israeli Defense Forces. It has been a handy excuse for instituting reforms delayed by the war, such as overhauling training methods and trimming deadwood. But their opinion was not always thus. Until recently the signals coming out of the Pentagon said, clearly, don't commit yourself on the volunteer army. Stay loose and wait for the antiwar hysteria in Congress to pass and the retributions to play themselves out, and the draftees will be back. But the signals have changed. A warning has gone out from the Pentagon, and it is that the draft will not be back for a while. The volunteer army is the only army the generals are likely to have for some time, and they have received intimations that failure to make it work could bring personal retribution.

"We get some bad soldiers through the volunteer program, but we did in the draft system too," a battalion commander in the 197th remarked as our jeep bounced down a narrow dirt road in the middle of a Fort Benning forest after dusk. He was on his way to join the battalion for a night exercise. "I would say we're making the volunteer army work because we've got a lot of professional people who are taking the right attitude to make it work. Now, some of the noncommissioned officers and the lower-ranking commissioned guys are skeptical, and without the draft I don't get people with college degrees and skilled people like draftsmen to make pretty charts for me. I have to develop people to do that myself, and it makes me do a little more work." The officer, a stocky, graying lieutenant colonel from San Antonio named Charles Arneke, shrugged, as if it was of no consequence. As we lurched into the assembly area, I asked Arneke what he thought would happen if the volunteer army didn't work out. He wrinkled his nose, as if he smelled a trap.

"I think we can make a fighting unit out of the men we're getting now," he said.

"But what if you yourself come to a point where you can see it's just not working?"

Arneke thought for a long moment.

"We'll have to draft 'em," he allowed.

That is not likely to happen in the near future. If it even begins to appear that the draft will have to be restored because the volunteer army has flopped, there is every indication that supporters of the volunteer experiment in Congress would launch a hunt for scapegoats. Advocates of the plan in Congress and in the upper strata of President Nixon's Defense Department are chewing over a body of evidence suggesting that until about October, 1973, somebody in the Army was subtly undermining the system with the aim of provoking a quick restoration of the draft.

Sabotage?

"Nothing has been as traumatic for the Army since the removal of the Air Force in 1947," notes one civilian Defense official who asked not to be identified because he sees himself as being on the trail of saboteurs. "This is an institution that's in a state of virtual revolution. This thing is rocking the Army from top to bottom. Everybody's affected. It's hard to pinpoint where the resistance was coming from without saying who it was, which we can't do, simply because we're still trying to deal with the problem and solve it permanently. We would have had some firings long before this if Watergate hadn't gotten in the way. The case has to be proven to people who are not inclined to believe it, like [White House chief of staff Alexander M.] Haig, who was never a friend of the volunteer army. I don't know if the President knows how much harm Haig can do us over there or not, just by not letting the word get through."

The Army's failures since the last draft call went out in January, 1973, were mostly in the area of recruiting. For the first nine months of the year, the Army consistently missed its enlistment goals, falling as low as 49 percent in April. During the same period the Navy hit above 90 percent five times and 100 percent twice. The Marines made their monthly goals all but twice, and the Air Force hit every month.

As the Army's lag became noticeable, Defense Department officials began wondering about a number of curious circumstances.

Item: In June, 1973, the Army chose to move its recruiting command from Washington, D.C., to Chicago. June is the very month when the Army normally expects to recruit its greatest number of high school graduates, and it also happens to have been the month when the volunteer force officially came into being. Naturally, the shift in location threw the recruiting command's communications and coordination out of step.

Item: Until Assistant Secretary of Defense for Manpower William Brehm ended the practice, the Army routinely tacked onto the next month's goal the number of men by which it missed its recruiting goal during the month just ending, thereby systematically inflating the monthly recruiting failure—on paper, anyway.

Item: The Army had 6500 recruiters in the field in July, 1972, when the draft was still in effect. By September, 1973—nine months after the draft had ended—the Army had *reduced* its on-station recruiting force by almost 18 percent at the recommendation of the Army's audit agency. The Army later claimed that this reduction was an innocent error in managerial judgment.

Item: Out of eighteen colonels and eight lieutenant colonels in the recruiting command eligible for promotion last year, not one was promoted. Out of eighty-eight officers eligible for assignment to senior service schools, which are prerequisites for entry into the super ranks, not one was sent. This could be read as evidence either that the Army had picked unpromising officers to man its recruiting stations in the first place, or that it was deliberately discouraging promising officers from volunteering for recruiting duty.

"Adversaries"

One who holds the sabotage theory is Roger T. Kelley, a civilian whom a trial lawyer might call an expert witness. Kelley directed the Pentagon's switch to all-volunteer policies from 1969 to 1973 as Brehm's predecessor, and left the government last June. On his way out he set off a few explosions.

"As I leave I am very sensitive that the adversaries [of the volunteer system] are bolder and more frequent in their acts of sabotage against the system," Kelley told a wire service reporter as he was cleaning out his desk. And: "I found more cooperation than resistance, but certainly enough resistance that it's a danger signal to my successor." And: "[Enemies of the system] can demonstrate a need for the draft by letting failures occur and then observe once again the services have missed their goal."

Since then Kelley has calmed a bit. "On balance I would give the armed forces decidedly high marks for making as much progress as was made in a relatively brief period of time in which the whole system was being turned around," he says. But, "I very deliberately used the term sabotage because any lack of willingness or positive commitment to make it work under the circumstances would be sabotage of the system, and I saw plenty of evidence of that. The draft system was more comfortable and secure, since all you had to do was reach into the well and call up more people whenever you had shortages. Military careerists could count on always having a sufficient number of people. The volunteer system puts you in competition with other employers and therefore it demands considerably more leadership than does the draft system. I think—I know—some of the senior military leaders felt a good deal more secure with the draft."

Kelley refuses to name culprits, but he says he puts the responsibility for the Army's failures "squarely on those who are running the service," by which he clearly means to include General Creighton W. Abrams, the Army's chief of staff.

"Abrams has been very equivocal," says a Defense Department official. "There was no clear pattern, and his commanders and everybody else in the Army interested in getting ahead are very alert to picking up that kind of equivocation from their chief. If the chief of staff is talking volunteer force, they're going to talk volunteer force. If he's not, they're not. It's a follow-the-leader game. That's what it's all about."

Last October, Abrams called a conference of major commanders and ordered them—unequivocally—to get behind recruiting and push the volunteer system. Abrams' critics hold that this turnaround was a response to a visit to Army bases last August by Senator John C. Stennis, Democrat of Mississippi, chairman of the Armed Services Committee, after which Stennis publicly, and somewhat testily, warned that the volunteer system had better work because the draft was not going to be restored any time soon. Some sources believe that soon after the Stennis statement, former Secretary of Defense Melvin R. Laird, then Nixon's chief domestic counselor, either told Abrams directly or sent a warning to him that further deterioration would not be tolerated. In any case, the Army's performance suddenly took a radical turn. In November, the month after Abrams' conference, the Army hit its recruiting goal for the first time since the volunteer system had gone into effect. It surpassed its goal by 4 percent.

A spokesman for Abrams, Deputy Chief of Army Information Major General DeWitt C. Smith, Jr., discounts the talk of sabotage. "We began without knowing much," he says. "We've been feeling our way, and we began with very bad luck in July, August, and September [of 1973]. But we took a major number of initiatives in policies and programs and revitalizing people in the recruiting effort across the board. I don't expect the volunteer army not to work. That would represent a total failure by all of us. We're not trained to failure and not accustomed to failure."

Nixon's Ploy

The more fundamental question—whether the volunteer army should be made to work—remains.

The system traces its parenthood back to 1967, and the warm-up of Richard M. Nixon's presidential campaign. One new member of his entourage was Martin Anderson—then thirty—a Republican economist associated with Milton Friedman and Arthur Burns. Anderson was interested in the issue of the volunteer army from a theoretical and ideological viewpoint. He is a conservative libertarian who believes in minimum interference by government in the lives of individuals, and so opposed conscription as unwarranted interference. The military had argued over the years that a volunteer army would be a poorly motivated, untrainable, undisciplined army. With the help of some young Ripon Society Republicans, Anderson marshaled the arguments rebutting this view and drafted a paper claiming exactly the opposite.

Anderson circulated the paper among his colleagues in the Nixon policy group. Although some thought that an all-volunteer force would lead to problems associated with a mercenary army, the consensus was favorable. If the system were militarily feasible it would be a legitimate piece of conservative thought. The more pragmatic wing of the Nixon team was pleased by the prospect of Nixon embracing a plan that would attract war-weary voters, and confuse and divide the antiwar movement. Coupled with Nixon's vague pledge to "end the war and win the peace," the proposal seemed sure to confound further an already splintered and dispirited Democratic Party. Liberals in Congress were split on the issue, some fearing that a volunteer force would encourage a President to use the Army recklessly, since he would be less likely to come under the kind of public and congressional scrutiny that commitment of an Army of draftees would invite. For varying reasons, liberals and conservatives worried about the prospect of a volunteer army heavily manned by poor, ill-educated blacks. Some liberals sided with conservatives who oppose the draft as an invasion of civil liberties. On the other side of the divide, some congressmen simply saw the volunteer force proposal as a painless way to cast an antiwar vote. Important opposition to the plan came from traditional conservatives such as those on the House Armed Services Committee, including F. Edward

Hebert, Democrat of Louisiana, who is now the chairman; they felt that any such change would weaken the nation's military preparedness. Anderson's paper was a persuasive argument against that view—which Hebert, nevertheless, still holds.

Nixon endorsed the concept in late November, 1967, during an interview with a reporter on a campaign flight. He liked the response he got and continued to advocate the volunteer system all the way through the last weeks of the campaign, finally issuing a major policy declaration, written by Anderson, during a radio campaign speech in October, 1968.

Soon after his inauguration, Nixon appointed a commission headed by Eisenhower's Secretary of Defense Thomas S. Gates to make an official study of the military feasibility of the proposal. In due time the commission unanimously ratified the idea, and in April, 1970—at the height of student protests over U.S. involvement in the clandestine war in Laos and shortly before Nixon announced his decision to send U.S. forces into Cambodia—Nixon ordered the Defense Department to start planning for an all-volunteer force to go into effect by June, 1973. Though protests continued, an order that foreshadowed the end of the draft had obvious dampening effects.

"It's pretty simple," says General William C. Westmoreland, then the Army's chief of staff, when discussing the volunteer army's origins. "It was a campaign problem of the President."

Westmoreland, who retired in July, 1972, had always opposed the concept, partly on philosophical grounds and partly because he was convinced the absence of the draft would deplete the Army reserve system, which he still believes cannot survive without the motivation of the draft to produce enlistees.

"I opposed ending the draft—not just the volunteer army," Westmoreland said in an interview in Charleston, South Carolina, shortly before he announced his candidacy for the Republican gubernatorial nomination. "The two are related, but it's an entirely different approach. The approach I had hoped for was to take extraordinary steps to increase the number of volunteers through increasing the pay and improving service attractiveness, putting more effort into our recruiting program, and improving professionalism. It was my opinion that with the inducement of the draft we could attract the volunteers we needed and we would not have had to exercise the draft very often, to a point where it would become politically odorous. From a social standpoint it seemed to me that our armed forces should represent a cross-section of America from the standpoint of economic status and ethnic and racial status of our society."

Black and White

Defense Department officials praise Westmoreland for suppressing his doubts about the system once Nixon ordered the planning to proceed. He appointed one of his most innovative generals, Lieutenant General George I. Forsythe, who had commanded the First Air Cavalry Division in Vietnam, and gave him wide powers to develop a program and budget and to oversee testing of the system at three sites: Fort Carson, Colorado; Fort Ord, California; and Fort Benning. But bureaucratic resistance began to develop almost immediately.

"I don't think the Army is completely with it yet," says Forsythe, who has also since retired. "The performance is still spotty. But there are a lot of young generals coming along now who understand what needs to be done, and they are doing it. At first there was a sense of insecurity on the part of a lot of officers and noncommissioned officers. This is a frightening experience for many people."

"Everything we do here is geared toward professionalism," says Fort Benning's 197th Brigade Commander, Colonel William R. Steele, a tall, bushy-eyebrowed, forty-four-year-old veteran of twenty-three years in the Army. He has a polished manner that fits an officer who once served as Westmoreland's senior aide. Steele regards command of the 197th as "the best job in the Army."

The brigade intelligence and civil affairs officer, Lieutenant Colonel Douglas Snell, was standing at rigid parade rest between two easels, flipping charts as Steele flowed through his narration. Off to the side on a sofa were Steele's deputy commander, Lieutenant Colonel Watha J. Eddins, Jr., and the brigade information officer, a forty-one-year-old black major, Willie R. Cage, Jr.

Like most combat units, the 197th has a high proportion of black soldiers. Steele estimates that blacks account for 31 to 33 percent of the brigade's approximately 4300 men, compared to an Army-wide figure of 20 percent. Blacks form about 13 percent of the total U.S. population. Steele said he couldn't furnish statistics for the black-white ratio in the front-line rifle and mortar platoons, but from what I saw at Fort Benning I estimated some of these units were from 50 to 75 percent black.

Less than 11 percent of the unit's 275 officers are black, and Major Cage is the only black officer above the rank of captain. Race relations in the 197th appear to be good, however, with no racial incidents showing on Steele's charts so far in 1974, though there were two in 1973 and six in 1972. Steele credits the brigade's active race relations program of classes and seminars with this improvement. Good or bad, the upward trend of black enlistments in the Army has been more or less steady since February, 1973, peaking at 34.1 percent in August and averaging 27 percent in fiscal 1974. In 1970, 13.2 percent of the Army was black, compared to 17 percent in 1972 and the current figure of 20 percent.

Cage and I had lunch at the battalion's headquarters mess hall, a large, hollow room with linoleum floors, water pipes exposed along the ceiling, and furnished with wooden tables, covered with red plastic sheets, and molded turquoise plastic chairs. Cage broke into a group of black troopers who had just come in and were making their way through the cafeteria-style serving line. "Tony, are y'all waiting for hamburgers?" a distinctly white Southern voice called from behind us. "Yeah," replied one of the black privates.

The Southern voice belonged to Captain Harold E. McClelland, the headquarters company commander, a bony, twenty-seven-year-old native of Montgomery, Alabama. As we moved around the hamburger line he apologized for the confusion. "When the mess hall is redesigned, the short-order area will be moved so we don't have the mess we have here," he said.

After lunch McClelland took me upstairs for a look at the barracks. All the enlisted quarters are undergoing remodeling to conform more closely with the Army's recruiting poster promises. The rooms I saw still had a long way to go.

The first one we came to was painted a sort of traffic-signal yellow and had seven months' worth of *Playboy* centerfolds hanging on the walls. "We allow anything on the wall as long as they're not too ridiculous, like hard-core pornography," McClelland said. "They're allowed to decorate and paint their rooms any way they want."

As we entered, five black soldiers were gathered at the rear of the room near a portable radio that was playing soul music, very loud. One looked around at us, lowered his gaze, and turned back. After several moments McClelland said in a low, intense drawl that pierced the music, "Can you come to attention?" They turned and stiffened, faces blank. The one nearest the radio switched it off.

"Where do you belong? Where are you supposed to be right now?" McClelland asked in the same tone of voice.

One of the men made a muffled reply. After an awkward silence, they filed out one by one. When they were gone McClelland dropped his stern pose and grinned sheepishly. "They're some of our problem children," he said. He looked up at Cage and then amended, "Not really."

The room looked depressingly bare, despite two handsome Army-issued mahogany dressers and a desk, all of which Cage told me later were made by Duncan Phyfe. Other items included three plain wooden chairs and a pair of battered, dull gray metal lockers. The floor had no rug. Two metal frame bunks covered by sagging Army blankets projected from the wall. The other rooms looked much the same. Many had pinups, mostly of nude black women in provocative poses, and hand-painted posters carrying antidrug and religious slogans. There were also photographs of younger brothers and sisters, girlfriends, parents, and on a wall in one room a letter from something called the National Photographers Album Company. It began, "Dear ————: Your credit record is one of your most valuable possessions. . . . Your payment is past due. . . ."

What Can Money Buy?

Money is one of the keys to the volunteer force. In 1968 recruits received $102.30 a month. Now they get $326, a raise of more than 200 percent, and salaries go up to $363 after two months' service, plus, of course, free room, board, and medical care. Privates with dependents receive an additional $105 a month. There is a $2500 bonus for service in a combat unit, and everyone gets a bonus of up to $10,000 for reenlisting.

Supporters of the volunteer system say a soldier getting this kind of pay should be sufficiently motivated and well-disciplined, considering the fact that he volunteered. But it was the almost unanimous opinion of the noncommissioned officers and commissioned officers at the company level whom I talked to (when out of range of senior officers) that money has bought neither motivation nor discipline. One dissenter was a thirty-four-year-old staff sergeant from Kentucky whose platoon was practicing setting up mortars in a remote part of Fort Benning. The unit was the first he had been in charge of training since the end of the draft. "I haven't had any discipline problems," said Sergeant Billy M. Whitaker, a fifteen-year-veteran. "It surprised me. Usually you have a few bad eggs at least."

However, a black lieutenant in the field with a support battalion said, "We're getting immature soldiers and guys out of jail, where the judge orders him to join the Army or else. You can't do anything with them a lot of the time. Guys below the rank of Spec. 4 can't see the need for some of the things we do, and you can't get the backing of higher-ups when you call them for discipline problems.

"A couple of months ago I surprised some troopers who were trying to lift the hubcaps off my car, which was parked on one of the brigade streets," the lieutenant said. "One of them took a shot at me as they got away in another car. The Army refused to prosecute, even though I later identified the men, because there were no corroborating witnesses."

"I *think* there's a lot of politics involved in this," grumbled a thirty-seven-year-old sergeant first class who was in charge of a mortar platoon. "If you have a big scuttle and a whole bunch of guys are kicked out of the Army on account of discipline problems, it's going to be in the news real fast and people are going to be embarrassed. So the higher-ups are afraid. They take a private's word for something before they do a platoon leader's or even a company commander's."

One of the sergeant's squad leaders, a black Spec. 5, nodded in agreement. "Once I had to tell my squad in the unit I just came from in Korea [where the Army is about 90 percent volunteer] that we had orders to move a hundred meters to the rear and let the other two squads stay up on the line and make a lazy W. And what they said was, 'Why the hell does it have to be our squad? Why can't it be the one over there? How come we have to move this heavy thing? Let them come over and help us.' "

"If that happened, the man ought to be a private instead of a Spec. 5," snapped General Smith, the information deputy, when I told him that story. "There really is no connection at all between the volunteer army and permissiveness. I don't think the shout, kick, and shove school of discipline is necessary and I don't think it's effective. But when they say they can't get people to obey them with alacrity and sharpness and so on, I just think the people who say that are not effective leaders."

If so, the 197th has a serious leadership problem. The volunteers themselves, mostly eighteen- to twenty-year-olds from towns, cities, and farms in the Southeast, seem for the most part bewildered and unsure of themselves. Many acknowledged that they had spent their entire bonuses during short leaves and were left wondering what they had gotten themselves into.

Drug use appears to be rising at the 197th, though it involves mostly marihuana, Colonel Steele says, and the upward statistical trend may be due to better methods of detection such as the use of dogs trained to discern the odor of marihuana. In fiscal 1972, the battalion arrested 114 men for drug use, compared to 155 in fiscal 1973 and 114 in the first half of 1974. "Very seldom do we find a hard-drug user," Steele says, "and most of those get identified pretty quickly." The Department of the Army reported at the beginning of 1974 that the trend in identified drug use was "generally level" and that the Army's policy was to rehabilitate drug (and alcohol) abusers or to discharge them when they cannot be rehabilitated "within a reasonable period."

One person who is convinced the volunteer army is bound for failure is former Lieutenant Joe Hooper, thirty-six, the most decorated soldier to come out of Vietnam, according to the information officer at his last duty station, Fort Polk, Louisiana. Hooper's chestful of ribbons includes a Medal of Honor, delivered personally to him by President Nixon. Hooper quit the Army in January after seventeen and a half years of service, two and a half years short of eligibility for full retirement, partly because his battlefield commission was about to expire and partly because he couldn't stand the volunteer army.

"I would just as soon be a private as a general as long as I'm happy with what I'm doing," Hooper says. "But you see what's happening and you become discouraged. There's no discipline now, or it's just way, way, way down. The Army would fall apart if it had to go into combat now. We're a third-rate military power, and the officers are afraid to say anything because they're running scared."

Though much of what Hooper and others have to say about the volunteer army may be owing to natural resistance to change, one is still left with a dour picture.

The last time the United States had a volunteer army was shortly after World War II, when Harry S. Truman allowed the draft to die, to the general applause of a war-worn and politically hostile Congress. After a disastrous recruiting effort, Truman went back to Capitol Hill in 1947 and pleaded for restoration of the draft.

The problems haunting today's volunteer army experiment can be summed up this way. First, it seems clear that no army is likely to perform well in combat if officers and noncommissioned officers who are directing the fighting have to argue with troops about tactics. Second, assuming the volunteer army could be turned into a military success, one can't discount the danger of an essentially mercenary force at the disposal of a President given to arbitrary decisions. As Adam Yarmolinsky, who served in Robert McNamara's Defense Department, put it recently, "If this great hulking creature is allowed to go bumping about in American society and the rest of the world, the range of consequences runs from broken china to shattered civilizations." And yet, third, a return to the draft system, with its gross class inequities, would be almost impossible to legislate now. (If the volunteer army fails disastrously, there could be a move to a universal service system, under which a person could choose between spending two years in uniform or two years in a government-sponsored civilian occupation serving the public in some way, for example helping alleviate the shortage of health service manpower. This idea was dismissed by Congress without debate as it considered the volunteer army scheme.)

For now officers such as Lieutenant Colonel Arneke are likely to continue running volunteer troops through night operations and the like even though the operations look more and more like empty charades. Before I left Arneke's exercise around midnight, one of his soldiers collapsed and swallowed his tongue and had to be taken out of the field by helicopter. The medic who first looked at the soldier reported that it looked like a drug overdose.

I caught up with Arneke about 2 P.M. the next day. He seemed as energetic as before, even though he said he had slept only three and a half hours. He was poring over a map propped up on the hood of his jeep, which was parked near his command post tent on a bed of pine needles. His fatigues were starched to a marble finish and his boots were gleaming.

"We had a pretty good time last night," he said. "Alpha Company crossed the starting point, here, about 12:45, and Bravo went along Red Arrow Road to the north. Once they got moving we turned the scout platoon into aggressor troops and set up ambush sites. Bravo moved up so fast that they passed through before the aggressors got set up. Charlie came along seven hundred meters behind and was caught with an M-60 machine gun. Charlie dispersed along the road and sent out an element to find out what had fired on them, and as soon as they got squared away they were hit with tear gas."

Arneke stared at the map, and absentmindedly fingered his scarf.

"I had planned to start a voluntary night withdrawal tonight, leave a third of the people in position and deceptively withdraw the main force to another position, but I dunno. . . . I'm thinking now about trying a night attack. It's a much more complicated maneuver."

He looked around for his deputy commander and then remembered he was asleep in the tent.

"Go wake up Major Windham," Arneke said to a droopy-eyed soldier standing nearby.

The soldier wandered off.

"What the hell, I think I'll do a night attack."

"The Volunteer Army," by Donald Smith, from *The Atlantic Monthly*, Volume 234, Number 1 (July 1974), pages 6–12. Copyright © 1974 by The Atlantic Monthly Company, Boston, Massachusetts. Reprinted with permission of the publisher and the author.

DONALD SMITH (1941–) has been a reporter and editor for the *Washington Star* and managing editor of the *Washington Post Magazine*. He was White House correspondent for the *Congressional Quarterly* during the Nixon and Ford administrations, and is currently with Congressional Quarterly Inc. as editor of the newsletter *Congressional Insight* and executive editor of the weekly *Defense Policy Report*.

Part II

Philosophy

11

Civil Rights and Conscription
by
D. H. Monro

In this philosophical survey of potential grounds for conscription, Monro finds that conscription perpetuates the conditions of fear and distrust it is held to ameliorate. Further, it violates all four principles that might justify state interference with individual liberties: (1) The power exercised serves a policing function; (2) the extent of interference is more than offset by benefits gained; (3) sacrifices by some individuals and/or groups are not disproportionately great; and (4) individuals and/or groups are prevented from imposing their moralities on others. The two rational alternatives to conscription, Monro concludes, are no conscription at all or conscription for home service only.

Is conscription for military service an interference with the liberty of the subject? At first sight there may seem to be no doubt at all about the answer. A conscript is, after all, compelled to abandon his ordinary occupation, his wife and his family, his whole everyday life, and to spend years learning a completely new way of life which he may find uncongenial and which is not only physically arduous, but extremely dangerous. If all this may be done without encroaching upon the liberty of the subject, then, we may well ask, what would constitute such an encroachment? If the state may do this without overstepping the bounds of its authority, then, one may well suppose, there are in fact no such bounds and all talk of liberty in the sense of the right of the individual against the state is a mere mockery.

This is the short answer to our question and it is by no means without force; but it will hardly do as it stands. For, it will be said, desperate ills need desperate remedies, and on occasion even conscription may be the lesser of two evils. It is worth noticing at the outset, however (since familiarity may lead us to take even the most outrageous of abuses for granted), how very great an evil conscription is. Any man who expects another to kill and perhaps die at his bidding really has enormous cheek. The cheek is no less if the man is acting as a functionary of the state.

What could possibly justify the state in demanding so much of the individual? We may best answer this question by considering what justification there can be for any demand by the state. After all, any compulsion, any forcing of the individual to do something against his will, is an interference with his liberty. It may, however, sometimes be desirable to interfere with liberty. The burglar's liberty to burgle, for example, is not compatible with the property owner's liberty to own property. Here it is obviously necessary to decide which of these two liberties is more desirable. The way to decide it is to ask which of the two will cause less suffering to all concerned. Most of us prefer to live in a society in which men are free to own property and no-one is free to take it away from them. Generalizing from this example, it would seem that interference with liberty is justified when such interference is necessary in order to prevent greater harm being done to others.

In particular, the state is justified in interfering with the liberty of its citizens in the interests of law and order: that is to say, in order to protect those liberties which, by common agreement, do not cause harm to others. Since the whole police function of the state, with its apparatus of law courts, prisons, and the like, derives from this principle, it is obvious that the interference with liberty which it justifies is by no means inconsiderable. It would usually be said, however, that this power should be exercised only with certain specific safeguards. It must be clearly stated in advance what actions are, like burgling, prohibited, and police action should be taken only against those who have been proved, by certain recognized procedures, to be guilty of them.

Police action is not the only activity of the state which may be regarded as a justifiable interference with liberty. The tax collector, acting with the authority of the state, interferes with the liberty of individual citizens in much the same way as the burglar does. Why do we approve of the tax collector but not of the burglar? The answer is that we believe that the citizen may justly be compelled to contribute to those common amenities in which all members of society share. Even if he does not stand to benefit directly from some such amenity (if he is a bachelor, for example, and a tax is being levied for education) we may still think that he ought to be compelled to contribute, perhaps on the ground that he will benefit indirectly, or perhaps on the ground that there is such interdependence between all members of society that the welfare of one cannot be separated from the welfare of all. Clearly this last ground is a somewhat dubious one. In general, I believe that it would be appealed to only when the amenity being provided is of very great benefit to some sections of the community and when the contribution to be levied from the rest of the community will not be such as to cause serious hardship.

It may seem odd to say that the state is justified in interfering with the liberty of the individual only when it is exercising either the police power or the taxing power. Isn't this, it may be asked, a reversion to nineteenth-century views which we have now discarded? Even in these days of the welfare state, however, I believe that all the compulsions exercised by the state could be justified as necessary either to protect citizens from the harmful activities of others, or to provide amenities which will be (in a wide sense) generally beneficial.

Can conscription be justified on either of these grounds? At first sight, no. The citizen who is directed into the army has not been found guilty of any crime. Perhaps the army is a social amenity, though it does not usually present itself in that light; but even if it is, there is a big difference between being asked to contribute to its support and being compelled to sacrifice all one's other interests in order to maintain it.

But, it may be said, in the exercise of its police power the state may legitimately demand more of the citizen than simply that he shall obey the law, under penalty of fine or imprisonment. Laws require policemen to enforce them; and if in any given case the police find this task beyond their powers, they are entitled to call upon ordinary citizens to assist them. The army may be regarded as an extension of the police force. Its duty is to preserve law and order, not against internal law-breakers, but against the occasional incursions of foreign powers. In an emergency there is no reason, then, why the army should not have the same right as the police force to call upon the assistance of ordinary citizens. As the guardian of law and order the army is indeed an amenity. It is one of such great importance to society, indeed, that, while the citizen's contribution to it will normally be limited to helping to pay for it, he may reasonably be required to do more than that if more than that is necessary for its efficient functioning.

It is clear, however, that the rights so far accorded to the state are not without limitation. The state, we have said, may legitimately use force to prevent one citizen from harming another and may legitimately require all citizens to help in providing common amenities. Nobody thinks, however, that the state would be justified in punishing very severely a very minor injury to another. We now think it unjust to hang a man for a petty theft or for parking in the wrong place. We would also think it unjust of the tax collector to deprive a taxpayer of his whole income even for the sake of financing a very worthy government project. The general principle, in short, is that even when the state has an admitted right to interfere with the liberties of the subject, the extent of its interference must be proportionate to the benefit to be gained from such interference. This is admittedly vague and attempts to state it more precisely have run into some notorious difficulties. It is tempting to say, with the Utilitarians, that the suffering caused by the state's interference must be less than the suffering that would be caused (to all concerned) if the state did not interfere. Suppose, however, that the state, grappling with the twentieth-century problem of recruiting labour to repair the damage inflicted daily on the public highways by the quantities of trucks and cars which use them, were to revive the eighteenth-century remedy of the press-gang. Able-bodied men might be seized as they went about their daily business, on the wharves or on the stock exchange, and condemned to a life of virtual slavery in the road gangs. Suppose further that these men were used to build a grand new highway made of some durable material which, once built, would last practically for ever. This practice would cause great suffering to some individual men and no doubt to their wives and relatives. It would also cause a rather different type of suffering to a vast number of other men who would live in constant insecurity because they would be afraid that next time they ventured forth into the streets they too might be shanghaied. All this suffering, however, would be over once the highway had been built. Since we are supposing it to last practically for ever, the highway might be expected to cause satisfaction to millions of motorists, both in our time and in the quite distant future. Although the pleasure felt by any individual motorist might be small, the accumulated pleasure of all the millions through all the years would in time come to outweigh the quite considerable pain of the much smaller number of road makers. Yet we would not think the press-gangs justified. Clearly, then, the Utilitarian formula needs some modification. Even when there will be a gain in human happiness in the long run, there is a limit to the extent of the sacrifice that may justly be required.

Without going further into the very difficult theoretical questions that have been touched on, we can now have a fairly good idea of the grounds on which it might be possible to justify conscription. Conscription may be justified, it would appear: (*a*) if the army is engaged in what amounts to police action; (*b*) if the malefactors against whom it is acting cannot be restrained without the assistance of civilians; (*c*) if the necessity of restraining them is so great as to warrant very considerable sacrifices on the part of individuals; (*d*) if the sacrifice required of any particular individual or group of individuals is not disproportionately great.

Does conscription for modern war satisfy these conditions? To begin with, is the soldier a kind of policeman maintaining law and order against the deliberate lawbreaker? Most official accounts of any given war would no doubt represent him as one. In any given war the citizen (on both sides) is likely to be told that he is being called to arms in order to resist the wicked actions of a band of men who are going about killing men and raping women, and all with the avowed object of subjecting him and his fellow citizens to the rule of a tyrannical foreign government. The details will, of course, vary with the circumstances of each individual war, but something like this will be the general impression conveyed. If a band of men did behave in this way, it would of course be the duty of the police to stop them, and if their efforts were unavailing they might very well call upon the rest of the citizens for assistance. Moreover, it is undoubtedly the case that when war does break out there will be bands of men (on both sides) behaving more or less in this way. It is also true that if any country loses a war it will find itself subjected to the will of a foreign government. There is, however, a difference between saying that this is what will happen once war has actually broken out, and saying that war breaks out in the first place in order to prevent happenings of this kind.

Apart altogether from the causes of war, there are several respects in which the comparison between war and police action breaks down. The policeman proceeds only against individuals who, there is good reason to believe, have been guilty of some specified illegal act. Having proceeded against them, he is bound to use only sufficient force to apprehend them and bring them to trial. None of this applies very well to the war situation. The airman who drops a bomb on enemy territory, for example, is not proceeding against a specific guilty individual, though he may cause death or injury to thousands of individuals, nor is he using just sufficient force to apprehend certain individuals and bring them to trial. Even if we ignore the bombing of civilians and consider only the old-fashioned type of war which consisted of pitched battles between combatants, there is still no very close resemblance to police action. In the first place, the soldier on each side is likely to regard himself as the policeman and his opponent as the malefactor. In the second place, few individuals on either side will have committed any specific act that could be regarded as illegal, except the act of taking part in war. But it seems odd to justify war as a means of preventing the illegal action of taking part in war. It is even odder to justify conscription in this way, since conscription consists in making it illegal *not* to take part in war.

Perhaps, however, this is a spurious objection. After all, the actions of policemen would often be illegal if done by private citizens. In every war, it will perhaps be said, those on one side have committed an aggressive act which, if not formally illegal by the laws of their own country, may nevertheless be justly resisted by those against whom it is directed. Those on the other side, then, are in the position of policemen. This argument brings us back again to the causes of war. All that need be said here is that comparatively few wars fit the simple pattern of there being a clear aggressor and a clear victim. Each nation takes part in war because it regards the other as doing something which it is not prepared to tolerate.

It might be thought that a simple and obvious test of aggression is the territory on which the war is fought: the owner of this territory must be the victim and his opponent the aggressor. Few Australians, however, would accept it as beyond question, that, for example, the Anzacs were the aggressors at Gallipoli. Even if one goes back to the beginning of a war, it can hardly be said that those who fire the first shot are necessarily in the wrong. Certainly it cannot be said that every individual soldier on that side is justly to be treated as a criminal. Particularly, it may be added, if he has been conscripted; for, ironically enough, this justification of conscription largely loses its force when there has been conscription on both sides. The truth is, of course, that any realistic account of what happens in war makes it very different from what happens when the policeman arrests a known criminal. Instead of the policeman on the one hand and the criminal on the other, we have confronting each other two bewildered young men, each of whom has been led to believe that he is fighting in defence of his country and his loved ones. The point might seem too obvious to be worth making. In fact, however, it is continually overlooked. One of the stock questions put to conscientious objectors, for example, is about what they would do if they saw a criminal attacking somebody with a gun or a knife, or, perhaps, raping a defenceless woman. The proper answer is, of course, that whether or not the objector thinks violence justified in such circumstances, the situation has no relevance to what he is called upon to do in time of war. In most wars there are rights and wrongs on both sides which make it plausible for the individual on either side to believe that he is acting to resist aggression; particularly since he will usually have heard only his own side of the case with any thoroughness. Once the war has actually begun, indeed, it will often be a criminal offence to try to find out what can be said on the other side.

Whatever may be the mental processes of those who interrogate conscientious objectors, most people will agree that the individual soldier on the other side cannot justly be regarded as a criminal. They will, however, possibly say that the comparison with police action has been misinterpreted. It is not that the individual soldier on one side is to be considered a policeman and the individual soldier on the other as a criminal: it is rather that one nation is to be regarded as a criminal nation and the other as a peaceful nation acting in defence of law and order.

This switch from individuals to nations is a highly significant one and demands careful attention. It may sometimes be useful to refer to nations, or to commercial firms, trade unions, or cricket clubs, as if they were separate persons with individualities of their own. The statement that a given firm has gone bankrupt, for example, is far from being equivalent to the quite different statement that the directors of the firm have gone bankrupt; nor is it even equivalent to saying that the shareholders have, or that the employees of the company have lost their jobs. Perhaps the statement that the firm is bankrupt can, ultimately, be reduced to a series of statements about the activities of individuals in which the firm, as a separate entity, is not mentioned. Such a reduction, however, would often be complex and difficult. In much the same way many statements about nations cannot easily be reduced to statements about individuals. Although it is convenient, consequently, to speak of nations as if they were single entities, or even persons, it would be a mistake to suppose that a nation actually is a kind of superman and not merely a convenient way of referring to a number of individuals and a quite complex network of relations which exist between them. Quite absurd consequences can follow from taking the personality of nations too literally. There is a book called *Psycholex*,[1] for example, in which the author, in all seriousness, discusses the behaviour of nations from the point of view of psychoanalysis. He distinguishes between "masculine" (aggressive, power-loving, dominating) nations and "feminine" (submissive, peaceful) ones. There are also young nations which have just emerged from the childish condition of being colonies. Having divided nations into these categories, the author goes on to describe cases of such aberrations as transvestism (when a "feminine" nation behaves on a particular occasion in an uncharacteristically aggressive way), paedophilia (when an older nation shows undue concern for the welfare of a newly emergent state) and so on. It may be doubted whether this is any more absurd than much current talk or writing about international affairs in which China or Russia (as it is now) or Germany or Japan (as it used to be) are regarded as big bullies, to be dealt with, in the best tradition of boys' adventure stories, by a manly sock in the jaw. It might, indeed, be a refreshing change if nations were to interfere in each other's affairs with psychoanalysts' couches instead of guns or bombs. It makes just a little more sense to talk of a guilty nation than to talk of a homosexual one, since moral terms can be meaningfully applied to the official acts of statesmen (ordering the dropping of an atomic bomb, for example) whereas the action of one "masculine" nation in forming an alliance with another normally aggressive nation cannot properly be described in sexual terms at all. Nevertheless, to talk of punishing a guilty nation (as distinct from punishing individual statesmen) makes no more sense than to talk of stretching a nation out on a couch. The author of *Psycholex* begins with a quite plausible analogy between the behaviour of nations and the characteristics of men and women: he ends with a wild, if somewhat engaging, fantasy in which we are invited to look upon international affairs as the cavorting of a mixed assembly of lesbians and transvestites. Similarly, the chairman of the conscientious objectors' tribunal begins with the simple concept of a gallant young man protecting his sister from a wicked violator: he ends with a situation, fantastic enough, though unfortunately real, in which conscientious young men, each convinced that he is doing no more than his duty, kill and maim one another.

The argument that conscription is justified as an extension of police action, then, breaks down. What one individual soldier is called upon to do to another is not at all like what the policeman does to a known criminal. One can sustain the analogy only by shifting from talk of individuals to talk of nations. Unfortunately, however, it is not nations that are shot or blown to pieces with bombs, but individuals. Consequently the first of the conditions which we said would be necessary to justify this argument has not been fulfilled. This being so, it might be thought unnecessary to consider the other conditions. It may be worth pointing out, however, that the second and third of them (that the alleged malefactors cannot be restrained without the assistance of civilians and that the need to restrain them is so great as to warrant very great sacrifices on the part of individuals), though they may be satisfied in some war situations, are by no means satisfied in all. What these conditions require is that all attempts to recruit the armed forces from volunteers shall have failed and that the consequences of fighting a war with only such volunteers as are available will be plainly catastrophic. While it is the purpose of this paper to discuss general principles rather than their application to particular cases, it is worth mentioning that it is far from clear that the present situation in Vietnam, for example, is one to which these conditions apply.

The fourth condition, it will be remembered, was that no individual should be required to make a disproportionately great sacrifice. It may be doubted whether this condition is ever satisfied in any war. It is difficult to discuss this question calmly and clearly because it is usually clouded by appeals to emotion. Through the centuries successive generations of priests, poets, and politicians have assured young men that they should be willing, and perhaps even glad, to die for the sake of their country and that the consequences of being defeated in war are always such that any man would gladly lay down his life to prevent it. The truth is, of course, that in most wars one side or the other is defeated. Consequently large numbers of people do in fact endure the fate that is said to be worse than death. They seem to manage somehow. This is not to say that the consequences of being a member of a defeated nation may not be very unpleasant indeed, or that it might not be rational, in some circumstances, for a man to say that he would rather die than endure those consequences. All that need be insisted on is that this is such a grave decision that a man may very well be left to make it for himself. It is at least doubtful whether anybody else has the right to force such a decision on him.

This last argument may be thought a selfish and cynical one. The world might, however, be a very much more pleasant place to live in if more people were selfish and cynical in this matter. Any politician will tell you that his power is limited by the fact that there are some things, however desirable in themselves, which he knows his electors will not stand for. In Australia, for example, it would probably be politically impossible to devote even as much as 2 per cent of the national income to aid for undeveloped countries, or to make a gesture of goodwill towards Asia by admitting any large number of coloured migrants, or to increase taxes very considerably in order to spend more on education, or even to tax beer and tobacco to the extent that is endured by the people of Britain. Nor is it only the politicians of democratic countries who have to keep a careful eye on what their people will stand for; this is necessary even in totalitarian countries, as is shown by the enormous propaganda machines which it is found necessary to maintain in such countries. It seems surprising, then, that one of the things that is not politically impossible is to force men to risk their lives in war. It is of course utopian to hope that the day may ever dawn when the young men of all nations, confronted by the usual exhortations to die in the defence of the fatherland, will meet them with the simple reply: "Who, me? Come off it, mate." If cynicism and selfishness should ever increase to that extent, however, we might well feel that the new Jerusalem had arrived. Until that happy day we would seem to be stuck with a world which is fit only for heroes to live in.

In this idealistic and miserable world, those who refuse to take part in war do not usually do so because they object to dying for their country, but because they object to killing for it. This too is a perfectly reasonable objection. It is in one way a more realistic one, since killing rather than dying is in fact what the conscript is being asked to do. The good soldier is not one who dies for his country, but one who remains alive and sees that the enemy does the dying. The objection to killing in war, as has already been pointed out, does not necessarily depend on an objection to killing in all circumstances. The objection to war is simply an objection to being embroiled in the intolerable situation in which men of perfect good will are compelled to kill one another.

But, it will be asked, even if all this is true, even if there are no just wars, since war is itself unjust, even if war is an undoubted evil, may it not sometimes be the lesser of two evils? So far the argument has been that in conscripting for military service the state interferes quite drastically in the private lives of its citizens and that such interference cannot be justified as an extension of either the police power or the taxing power. Very well, it may be answered, let us admit that. Let us grant that the right of the state to conscript goes beyond the other rights claimed for it, and cannot be justified on precisely the same grounds. The state may still have this further right. It has it simply because there is no other way of averting a disaster which will not only cause widespread suffering to all its citizens but may threaten the very existence of the state itself. It is not now suggested that the enemy are wicked men who may justly be killed. They are to be regarded much as a natural force, say a bush fire or an earthquake, might be regarded; to be resisted, to be overcome, but not to be blamed. No doubt, it will be said, it is distasteful to have to dispose of human lives in this way; but the harsh truth is that unless we are prepared to take up this attitude there are some things that the state will simply be unable to do. The British government, for example, might have sent troops to Rhodesia in 1965. If they had been sent, no doubt some young Englishmen and some young Rhodesians, each convinced of the rightness of their respective causes, would have died. The failure to send them, however, means that the British government no longer has any effective control over the ruling minority in Rhodesia. The rule of that minority may yet result in riots and bloodshed, with possibly greater loss of life than the prompt sending of troops would have caused. Whether Mr. Wilson made the right decision or not, his problem was the typical one which confronts governments. If another government insists on doing something which his own government dislikes, a statesman has only two alternatives. He may give way, or he may use (or threaten to use) force. If force is always to be ruled out, then there is simply no way of preventing other governments from doing whatever they choose. And what they choose may very well include taking over one's own country and subjecting its inhabitants to alien domination.

This argument at least has the merit of stripping the subject of much of the mythology with which it is usually beclouded. Instead of the cartoonist's symbols of knights and dragons, gallant young heroes with faces like film-stars pitted against sub-human gorillas, international cops and robbers, pure young maidens and side-whiskered villains determined to rape them, we have the much more familiar and much less edifying spectacle of nations jockeying for advantage. War (including the threat of war) is an instrument of national policy: one of the means by which nations endeavour to secure what they conceive to be their interests against the conflicting interests of other nations. To say this is, of course, not to deny that in any given dispute one nation may be in the right, and the other in the wrong (though it is much more likely that each of them will be partly right and partly wrong) or even that one or the other of them may be relatively disinterested. I believe, for example, that Britain is in the right in the Rhodesian dispute and that Egypt was in the right in the Suez affair. In neither case does it in the least follow that their opponents were inhuman monsters or even particularly wicked men. The point is that war is seen in perspective when it is realized that it is simply a means (and a peculiarly wasteful, brutal, and clumsy means) of resolving disputes between men.

As such, it will be said, it may still be the lesser of two evils. No doubt this is the case much less often than patriots would have us believe; no doubt, too, the advent of nuclear weapons makes it increasingly unlikely that war should ever be the lesser evil; but the possibility cannot be completely ruled out. In this essay, however, we are not asking whether war as such can ever be justified, but whether conscription can. And about this several things need to be said.

The stock case in which it is usually taken for granted that a nation is not only right to wage war, but is clearly justified in conscripting its citizens to serve in that war, is that in which it is invaded by a foreign power intent upon establishing sovereignty over it. Actually this occurs less often than is usually alleged: it is much more likely to be a consequence rather than a cause of the outbreak of war. Let us suppose however that it has occurred. Is it absolutely certain that in all such cases resisting the invasion by force of arms will always be a lesser evil than submitting to it? It may perhaps be said that it will be the lesser evil only if the resistance is successful; and that is why it is necessary that all available men shall be pressed into service. Even a successful resistance, however, is not necessarily the lesser evil. When people talk of "the very existence of the nation being at stake" it is very often forgotten that the existence of the nation is not the same thing as the existence of its individual citizens. After all, the nation is a corporate body like any other. Cricket clubs, churches, or universities, although they would no doubt very much resent their extinction, do not take it for granted that they are justified in calling upon their members to fight and die in order to keep them in existence. Nor is the extinction of the nation the same thing as the extinction of all ordered society. I am not denying, of course, that the members of nations which are absorbed by other nations often do have a very hard time indeed; no-one in Australia, with the fate of the aboriginals before him, need doubt that. The fact remains, however, that not even national extinction is necessarily the greatest of all evils, or necessarily a fate worse than death. Even in this situation the question of which evil is the lesser one needs to be determined on its merits, with careful attention to the particular circumstances.

Moreover, if the nation's territory is actually being involved, if the attackers are bent on domination, and if the state is one that commends itself to its citizens, so that they do not in fact prefer alien rule, then conscription is hardly likely to be necessary. The very fact that conscription is resorted to may very well be taken as evidence that quite a considerable number of citizens do have doubts, which may well be legitimate ones, about whether taking part in war is actually the lesser evil.

But, it will be objected, the nation cannot afford to wait until the invaders have actually landed; their wicked schemes must be nipped in the bud well in advance. This means that the ordinary citizen may very well not be aware of the full extent of the danger. Consequently his more far-sighted political leaders, knowing what his decision about the greater evil would be if he were in possession of all the facts, benevolently saves him the trouble of making that decision and makes it for him. At this point mythology begins to raise its head again. Just as the zealous recruit, eager to save his sister from rape, finds himself assigned to dropping bombs on somebody else's sister, so the patriot, burning to fight the invader on the beaches and the barricades, finds himself instead landing on somebody else's beaches as part of an expedition that looks, to the local inhabitant, suspiciously like a jackbooted invasion.

We have become accustomed to thinking of the world as divided into two armed camps, each watching the other nervously and wondering whether this or that move should not be interpreted as the first act of aggression, as the bud that needs to be nipped. Moreover, each side is (understandably) anxious that the governments of the relatively "uncommitted" nations should be friendly, or at least not hostile, to themselves. Both China and the United States, for example, feel like this about Vietnam. And friendliness to one side is likely to be interpreted as hostility to the other. In this situation it may not be easy to tell whether a government which veers to the right or the left has or has not been influenced by pressure from outside. Consequently, there will be plenty of moves on either side that can plausibly be interpreted as aggressive interference in the affairs of other nations and so the prelude to wider aggression. The concept of "aggression," accordingly, gets stretched. We begin with the contention that taking part in war is a lesser evil than being invaded. This becomes transformed into the quite different contention that any military action intended to prevent a step which might conceivably be a prelude to aggression at some time in the future is also the lesser of two evils. Clearly this cannot be taken for granted.

Whether in any given situation taking part in war is or is not a lesser evil than any available alternative is, then, a question which must be settled according to the merits of each individual case. In settling it, attention should of course be paid to all the likely consequences of war, including the well-attested fact that wars usually leave a legacy of bitterness and hatred which leads to still more wars. The present point, however, is simply that the decision is not likely to be an easy one. Honest and conscientious men may very well decide it differently. That being so, can it be said that any man, whether or not he is acting as a government official, has the right to decide it for another? It is, after all, a moral question and a peculiarly tricky one. Should moral questions, especially difficult ones, not be left to individuals to decide for themselves?

But, it may be retorted, don't governments settle moral questions for their citizens every day? The morality of theft, of murder, of duelling, of driving when drunk, is not left to the individual to decide for himself. Yet all these clearly are moral matters. Nor will it do to say that these are all questions about which there can be no serious disagreement. The ordinary thief, no doubt, does not seriously disapprove of the institution of property. But there might be a thief who would be prepared, quite sincerely, to justify his theft on Robin Hood's principles and be perfectly ready to share his wealth with men poorer than himself. Similarly, a murderer might believe, quite sincerely, that his victim had behaved in a way that merited death and might be quite willing to lose his own life if he himself should ever behave similarly. It was once thought self-evident that any man of honour should be prepared to fight a duel if challenged, much as many people now believe it self-evident that any man of honour should be prepared to fight in defence of his country. In these examples the thief, the murderer, and the duellist all hold moral beliefs which differ from the official morality of the community, the morality that is enforced by the laws. However sincerely they hold them, they are not permitted to act on their respective moralities. The state forces them to accept the official morality, or at least to behave as if they did. And most people would say that in doing this the state is acting rightly.

It is important to realize that even if we believe that the law punishes such men rightly, we do regard them differently from the ordinary criminal. The reason for compelling them to conform is that their moralities not only differ from the accepted morality but are incompatible with it. The two moralities are incompatible not merely in the sense that one man cannot consistently believe in both, but in the sense that it is not practicable for some members of the community to act in accordance with the one morality while the others act in accordance with the other. To practise Robin-Hoodery, for example, is to enforce a system of property in which goods will be shared roughly in equal amounts. Whatever the merits of this system of property, it is different from the prevailing one; and it is hardly possible for a society to have two conflicting sets of rules about property in operation at the same time. Rules about property, in short, must be settled collectively. Those who want a different system may urge a change, but they may not, without causing confusion, attempt to force their own system of property upon others. In the same way the conscientious murderer is attempting to enforce a system of capital punishment different from the one prevailing in the community. This too is a matter on which there is no room for diversity of practice as distinct from diversity of opinion.

The principle that would seem to emerge, then, is that the state has a right to enforce a morality on those who do not share it only when it would be impossible in practice for different members of the community to act upon different moralities. Otherwise each individual citizen should be allowed to practise his own morality. The state should not enforce an alien morality on him; but he in his turn must not force his morality upon others. The Christian fundamentalist, for example, who, for queer reasons of his own, thinks blood transfusions immoral may be permitted to refuse this operation on his own behalf, but not to sacrifice his child's life to his scruples. The disciple of Robin Hood is not prevented from giving his own goods to the poor if he wants to; he is merely prevented from forcing others to do the same.

What will follow about conscription from the application of this principle? We have already seen that the question of participation in war is indeed a moral question which arises afresh with each particular war (unless of course it is decided, as it may well be, that the evils of modern war are such that it will always be a greater evil than any alternative). Is the decision one that can only be taken collectively, like the decision about the property rules to be applied in any given community? In one way perhaps it is: war, especially modern war, is inflicted upon a whole community, so that if a nation is at war every member of it is likely to feel the effects. Those who decide in favour of taking part in war, then, are forcing their decision upon all their fellow citizens. It does not follow, however, that those who take the opposite decision, at least in the sense of refusing as individuals to have a hand in the actual killing, are forcing their decision upon everyone else. All that would result from their refusal would be that the war would be fought only by those who were in favour of it: only, that is to say, by volunteers. And this is certainly possible; wars have been fought by volunteers in the past.

But, it may be objected, the foregoing argument does not establish a case against conscription: at best, it is merely a plea for the exemption of conscientious objectors, an exemption which is, in this country at least, already allowed by the law. For many of those who refuse to fight may resemble, not the man who genuinely disagrees with (say) the laws about property but the thief who accepts them when they work in his favour and breaks them when they work against him. In other words, the man who would like to avoid military service for himself but has no genuine objection to war as such may, on this view, be justly conscripted.

Before this objection is answered, it may be pointed out that exemption for conscientious objectors is not, in fact, adequately provided for by the existing law. The law exempts only those who object to war under any conceivable circumstance, and not those who object only to the particular war they are being asked to fight,[2] or even to all wars except a very unlikely, but remotely possible, one. This is plainly absurd. If it is held that some wars are just and others unjust, it is clearly a duty not to take part in unjust wars. There is no ground whatsoever for saying that simply because a man believes that he has a duty to take part in a just war he does not have a perfectly genuine conscientious objection to taking part in a war which he believes to be unjust. Yet most of those who enforce the existing law do in fact believe that some wars are just and others unjust.

There are, moreover, very strong practical objections to the present procedure. Ordinary legal processes are well adapted to establishing matters of fact, but not to the probing of beliefs. How can a man prove the sincerity of his professed opinions? Cross-examination by counsel may show that he is unready in argument, or inarticulate, or even muddled, but it does not follow from any of these that he is insincere. Some tribunals, indeed, have been known to adopt the principle that an appellant who stands up well to cross-examination must be insincere, since (they argue) only a muddled man could really be a pacifist. The same tribunals may very well, when faced with a different appellant, take muddlement to be a sign of insincerity. In the light of this, it is natural enough that the only evidence that most tribunals are prepared to take very seriously goes to such matters of fact as that the objector has been, for a lengthy period, a member of some religious sect which specifically forbids its members to take part in war. The result is that in practice exemption tends to be given, not to any individual who genuinely disbelieves in war, but to a few religious organizations.

There is, then, a strong practical reason for opposing conscription as such, and not merely the conscription of those who can prove that they have a moral objection to fighting. The practical reason is that the law which demands such proof has been found to be unworkable. There is also, however, another and stronger reason. The actions the soldier is asked to do are those which, if done in any other circumstances, would be accounted the worst of crimes. It is not unreasonable, therefore, to presume that any normal man would have a conscientious objection to doing them. The onus of proof might well be placed on those who are prepared to kill, not on those who are not. In civilian life, after all, this principle is taken for granted. Even in war, it may be regarded as established by the Nuremberg trials.

If the punishment of "war criminals" is to be justified at all, it can only be on the assumption that, when an action is normally a crime, the individual cannot escape responsibility for it on the ground that he is merely obeying the orders of his civil or military superiors. There seems no reason why this principle should not be applied, not merely to the worst excesses of warfare, but to the act of taking part in war itself. Whether or not this follows from the principles adopted at Nuremberg does not matter: it would seem to be the merest common sense that no man has a right to kill, maim, and dismember other men unless he is very sure indeed that the circumstances justify these acts. To put the onus of proof on the man who says he is not sure seems quite unwarranted.

Many people will, I suspect, feel that this argument ignores the realities of the international situation. The question, they will protest, is not whether war is an evil, but whether it is the lesser of two evils. It may, however, be doubted whether the evil that conscription is intended to meet is not, at least in part, brought about by the existence of conscription.

What I mean is this. In western countries we are accustomed to thinking of ourselves as menaced by totalitarian communist regimes which require their citizens to sacrifice everything else to the good of the state. In communist countries they regard themselves as menaced by the ruthlessness of capitalist countries determined to destroy any non-capitalist regime. Asian and African countries regard themselves as menaced by the arrogance and callousness of the white man, who looks on men of any other colour as his natural inferiors. None of these beliefs is simply silly. Each is no doubt exaggerated, but each does receive a good deal of support from history, including recent history. The net result is that statesmen in every country feel that military preparedness, generally including conscription, is forced upon them in self-defence. Each believes that his country cannot abandon it so long as the others do not, and that it would be hopelessly naïve to expect the others (ruthless bigots that they are) to do so.

There is no easy way out of this situation. But it is at least aggravated by the fact that, in all countries, men accept the right of the state to force them to fight at its bidding. Men do, after all, behave much worse in war than most of them behave in peace. One reason for this is that the actions they perform in war are, in a sense, no longer their actions; they do not feel individually responsible for them. Conscription, indeed, exacerbates the situation in two ways: by encouraging the individual to sink his judgment in that of the state, and by making it easier to think of the enemy as a faceless mass forced into the service of an inhuman ideology rather than as men and women with the ordinary human aspirations.

At the very least it would be a step forward if it were generally accepted that conscription should be regarded as very much a last resort, to be adopted only when a country is faced by an actual invasion. This is, of course, the policy of no conscription for overseas service. It is said that this policy would make it possible for an unscrupulous power to pick off its victims one by one, instead of having to meet their combined forces; but this is hardly true, since the sending of volunteers overseas is not ruled out. What is true is that no government holding to such a policy could embark successfully on overseas adventures without convincing its soldiers that these adventures were necessary: a quite salutary state of affairs. When it is argued that conscription is the lesser of two evils, it is nearly always assumed that the other evil is invasion; so that the restriction of conscription to home service would seem to follow logically enough. On the other hand, conscription for home service may be unnecessary, since, if there were an actual invasion, probably almost every eligible person would agree to serve, except those convinced pacifists whose exemption is in any case provided for. There is, then, a strong case for opposing conscription altogether; but, as has been said, a policy of no conscription for overseas service would at least be a step forward, and might help to reduce the danger of action being taken which seems, to those who take it, to be merely defensive and, to their opponents, clearly offensive. In the present atmosphere of mutual fear and suspicion, a clear demarcation between these two is perhpas the first essential.

This essay may seem to have wandered some way from the question with which it started, whether conscription for military service is an interference with the liberty of the subject. It may be as well, then, to recapitulate its main contentions.

1. Conscription goes beyond the other legitimate powers of the state to interfere with the individual. In particular, it cannot be justified on the ground that war is merely an extension of police action, and that any citizen may rightly be called upon to help the police.

2. Conscription can be justified, therefore, only as being *sui generis:* a very special case of an admitted evil which is, nevertheless, the lesser of two evils. The greater evil is usually taken to be foreign invasion: an argument that would seem to justify conscription for home service only.

3. But the question of whether one evil is greater than another is a moral question, which should be left to the individual to decide. It is not legitimate for the state to impose an alien morality on its citizens, though it may prevent them from imposing their morality on others.

4. All that may seem to follow from 3 is that conscientious objectors should be exempted from conscription, not that conscription should be abandoned. But the attempt to exempt conscientious objectors does not work well in practice, and is, moreover, exposed to the grave objection that it puts the onus of proof in the wrong place. It is not the refusal to kill that needs justification, but killing.

5. Conscription for any military purpose is, then, a breach of individual liberty. But the restriction of conscription to home service would at least be a step forward, in helping to lessen the mutual fear and suspicion that is one of the chief causes of war.

6. The central tragedy of war is that men of good will on both sides, each convinced that he is doing no more than his duty, are compelled to kill one another. Conscription helps to bring about this situation by removing from the individual the responsibility for his own actions.

"Civil Rights and Conscription," by D. H. Monro, from *Conscription in Australia*, edited by Roy Forward and Bob Reece, published by University of Queensland, St. Lucia, Queensland, 1968. Copyright © 1968 University of Queensland Press. Reprinted with permission.

D. H. MONRO (1911–) received his graduate education in New Zealand at the University of Auckland and is emeritus professor of philosophy at Monash University in Australia. He has published a number of articles and books on moral philosophy, including *Empiricism and Ethics* and *Ethics and the Environment*.

Notes

1. Paul Shepard, *Psycholex* (New York: Megwa, 1960).
2. The law has not been interpreted in this way in every case.

12

Political Alienation and Military Service

by
Michael Walzer

Examining the relationship between obligations and rights in political society, Walzer considers how governments become legitimized, the distinction between state and society, and the distinction between express and tacit consent. He shows that, whereas conscription originally became legitimized through the express consent of adult male, native-born property holders, today democratic governments justify it by considering the absence of express dissent as express consent. Walzer argues that this practice is devious and unjustified.

Despite the conventional claims of the authorities, it is not at all easy to determine the precise extent of the obligations owed by an individual citizen to the modern state. The authorities claim what they have, as far as I can tell, always claimed: that citizens must, if necessary, fight and die for the state. But this view of every citizen as a potential soldier, rushing to arms at his government's call, has its origins in states and societies very different from our own; above all, very much smaller than our own. It was in the polis of ancient Greece and in the medieval commune that the notion of the citizen-soldier was born, and the idea was elaborated by theorists like Rousseau who still thought in terms of small participant communities. The extraordinary transformation in social scale which has occurred in the past century and a half has created a radically different kind of political community—one in which relations between individual and state are so attenuated (at least their moral quality is so attenuated) as to call into question all the classical and early democratic theories of obligation and war. The individual has become a private man, seizing pleasure when he can, alone, or in the narrow confines of his family. The state has become a distant power, captured by officials, sometimes benevolent, sometimes not, never again firmly within the grasp of its citizens. If this is so, what do these citizens owe to this state?

In an important sense, only liberal (I mean, chiefly, Lockeian) theory is capable of answering this question, for only the liberals have been entirely accepting of the transformation in scale and of the new individualism it has generated. I want to argue that the liberal concept of tacit consent provides a key to understanding the new relations between citizens, or rather, some citizens, and the state. Because the man most often described as having yielded tacit consent and no more is the resident alien, I want to examine the (limited) obligations such a man incurs. It is a commonplace of contemporary social thought that the modern state breeds aliens, whereas older political societies could only import them. We can learn something about this modern alienation, I think, if we begin with the older notion of alienage.

All the philosophers of consent have realized what their critics have in any case told them quickly enough, that the possibility of express consent to a political system—even a democratic system—is rarely available to all men and sometimes is available only to a few. If consent theory is to be taken seriously, it must suggest some way of submitting oneself to a government other than by pledging allegiance to it, taking out naturalization papers, or becoming an active participant in its politics. Liberal writers have generally argued that there is such a way; there is a kind of silence that may be construed as consent. This is the silence of the unsworn, inactive resident, who enjoys the benefits conferred by the state and lives amidst its citizens without ever publicly acknowledging its authority. The acceptance of benefits, even if their rejection would require such extreme courses of action as emigration or hermitic retreat, involves, we are told, an unspoken agreement to maintain the conditions that make the benefits possible, for oneself and others. That means, most importantly, to obey the laws and keep the public peace. This seems to me a reasonable doctrine; I would only add that the obligations incurred by silence are not owed exclusively to the state but to society as well, that is, to the population in whose midst the resident resides. They have their origin not only in the acceptance of benefits but also in the daily round of social activities and the expectations of peaceful conduct which that round inevitably produces in the minds of all the other residents.

The immediate difficulty with this merely tacit consent is, as Locke wrote in his *Second Treatise*, to know "how far it binds." It was Locke's view that any "enjoyment"—of property, lodging, or the bare freedom of the highways—bound a man to an obedience no different in character from that of a full-fledged citizen. A visitor to England or a resident alien was as committed as any "denizen," as any natural-born or legally sworn subject of the king. Tacit consent produced a temporary bond, while express consent made a man "perpetually . . . and unalterably a subject," but the nature of the obligation for the respective durations is, according to Locke, precisely the same.[1] This is a curious view, and, as Locke's expression of it is casual and cursory, it need not be taken as an important feature of his political theory. Surely the moral situations of a mere visitor and a long-term resident are different in significant ways, and one might say the same thing about a resident alien and a citizen—especially in a liberal society. The citizen, after all, participates in his government and shares to some degree in the making of decisions about such crucial matters as taxation, conscription, and war. A resident alien does not participate: how far can he be bound to pay taxes, to serve in the army, to risk death in battle?

Before attempting to answer this question, it will be useful to consider an older distinction between temporary and perpetual obligation, made by the English common lawyers and summarized in Blackstone's *Commentaries*. Blackstone distinguishes the allegiance owed by a natural-born subject, which "cannot be forfeited, cancelled, or altered by any change of time, place, or circumstance," and the allegiance of an alien and stranger which "ceases the instant such a stranger transfers himself from this kingdom to another." A natural-born subject can, of course, "transfer himself" as easily as can an alien, but not with the same results. "An Englishman who removes to France, or China, owes the same allegiance to the king of England there as at home and twenty years hence as well as now."[2] This is a view that makes a good deal more sense than Locke's, since it is founded on a whole set of ideas about birth that lend themselves to talk of perpetual obligations. A man does not choose and cannot change his native land as he can choose a political system and later change his mind about its merits. A natural-born subject is like a son or daughter—a comparison implicit in Black-stone's discussion—whose parents are his willy-nilly and who has per-manent commitments. If this comparison is rejected, as it explicitly is by Locke, it would seem that the notion of perpetual obligation must also be rejected. Perpetuity is an awkward notion when intruded into a consensual universe. The possibility of reconsideration is surely inher-ent if not in the idea of consent itself, then in the idea of government by consent. In the latter phrase both terms refer to series of acts over time (possibly, in the case of a radical democracy, to the same series), and the two together do not suggest an agreement made at some single mo-ment or for all time. A theorist may reasonably want to make recon-sideration a similar series of acts, prescribing some lengthy process for terminating consent and so making the bonds established by consent as firm as he can. However, he cannot bar entirely the possibility of a political divorce.

If this is so, then Locke's effort to distinguish tacit and express consent must be called a failure. It is not in the duration of the bond established but in its character for whatever duration that the dif-ference must be sought. In fact, a difference of precisely this kind has been worked out, once again by the lawyers, and it is of enormous relevance to political theory, though it has not, so far as I know, been discussed by political theorists. In the course of the eighteenth and nineteenth centuries, it became a principle of international law that resident aliens were obligated differently than citizens: they were bound to a more narrow range of actions.

> Until a foreigner has made himself by his own act a subject of the state into which he has come, he has politically neither the priv-ileges nor the responsibilities of a subject . . . He is merely a person who is required to conform himself to the social order of the com-munity in which he finds himself, but who is politically a stranger to it, obliged only to the negative duty of abstaining from acts inju-rious to its political interests or contrary to its laws.[3]

This is a far-reaching assertion. It suggests that tacit consent pro-duces only "negative" duties, and it might require a political society to include within its territorial confines men whom it could neither tax nor conscript for any public service whatsoever. When stated more concretely, however, the argument is also more limited, and it tends to focus on the issue of military service. The same writer I have quoted above argues that "aliens may be compelled to help maintain social order, provided that the action required of them does not overstep the limits of police, as distinguished from political, action."[4] This is the common distinction: because they enjoy the benefits of social order, aliens may be required to maintain that order, to pay taxes, to serve as police deputies, to join a fire brigade, and so on. But they cannot be bound to fight in either a civil or an international war (unless the country where they live is "threatened by an invasion of savages . . ."). The distinction is nicely illustrated by the behavior of the British government during the American Civil War:

> The British government in 1862 [insisted] that as a general principle of international law neutral aliens might not be compelled to perform any military service . . . [but] in 1864 the British government saw no reason to interfere in the case of neutral foreigners . . . enrolled as a local police for New Orleans.[5]

This argument by the international lawyers has a double rationale, only the first part of which is of interest to us, though the second may well be of greater interest to them. The resident alien is conceived both as an individual who has made a limited commitment and so incurred only limited obligations, and as the subject of another state which retains, so to speak, rights in his person. Hence the precise limits of his obligation to the state within whose jurisdiction he resides is often a matter of negotiation between that state and his own (and so not merely of his "own acts").[6] He is protected in his residence *here* by his citizenship *there,* and this protection is often confirmed by explicit bilateral treaties. It is important to stress, however, as an American Secretary of State did in 1918, that the existence of treaties exempting subjects of the contracting parties from military service abroad does not constitute "evidence of a practise among nations to draft aliens into their forces."[7] The treaties do not, in this regard at least, create a right, but merely protect a right already established. Aliens cannot be compelled to serve (though they can be subjected to considerable pressure to do so, as we shall see). Nor is the condition of a stateless person any different from that of a foreign citizen, though such a person, unprotected by treaty, is all too often treated differently.[8]

The condition of a resident alien in international law suggests two distinctions of major importance to political theory. The first is a distinction between ultimate obligation—the obligation to fight and risk death—and all other, lesser duties. The second is between obligations owed to society and those owed to *political* society or to the state. International law seems to suggest that a man can incur ultimate obligations to society, he can bind himself to defend its population against devastation and destruction even at the risk of his own life, simply by residence and daily intercourse. But he cannot commit himself to the polity, he cannot bind himself to risk his life for "ordinary national or political objects," except through those expressions of consent and participation (which may, of course, be variously defined) that make him a citizen. So tacit and express consent have different moral consequences, and the difference suggested by the lawyers, it seems to me, illuminates the precise character of political membership far better than Locke's *Second Treatise*. To be a citizen is to be committed to a political system, not merely to the survival of the society that system organizes, but to the survival of the particular organization and also to all those purposes beyond survival that the organization sets for itself. Residence alone cannot and does not generate such a commitment.

I do not doubt that this is a difficult distinction to apply in practice, for the "ordinary" purposes of the state are not necessarily political in the narrow sense of that term, concerned, that is, with power manipulation and aggrandizement or with the fostering of some secular ideology. One of the purposes of any state is the defense of "its" society, and it is probably true that certain sorts of societies can only be defended by certain sorts of states. There are likely to be moments, then, when all residents, aliens and citizens alike, are morally obligated to defend the state that defends their everyday social life—against barbarian invasion, as the lawyers have suggested, and conceivably against any invasion likely to entail serious disruption and devastation. If this is so, it is not difficult to imagine a variety of borderline cases—which I cannot even attempt to resolve here—when the invasion is only threatened and the state takes one or another kind of preventive action. But it is important to stress that the existence of borderline cases does not call the original distinction into question, since it is only by making such distinctions that we know which are the borderline cases. The cases on either side of the line are clear enough.

Because the rights of hospitality and asylum are also established in international law, though not necessarily in the practice of nations, it would appear that the lawyers intend that any given state at any given time include men who have only limited obligations toward its own survival and its "ordinary political objects." And it is not difficult to imagine a state that includes a large number of resident aliens—as Athens did, for example, after the days of Solon. In 434, when the Peloponnesian war broke out, Athens had a population of one resident alien for every two citizens; one-third of the free men of the city were foreigners. The Athenian case is especially instructive, because citizens and aliens were treated differently with regard to military service: the aliens were organized into separate military units and used only for the defense of the city and its immediate environs.[9] But the condition of Athenian aliens was different from that of aliens in a modern nation-state in that it was virtually impossible for them to become citizens; they constituted something very near a hereditary political caste, with carefully limited rights and duties. The opening up of the possibility of naturalization, and the steady pressure of modern governments to establish a uniformity of obligation among their subjects, raise moral issues which, so far as I know, never arose in the classical polis. These issues can be seen clearly in the history of conscription in the United States.

Consent theorists have one fundamental problem with the obligation to perform military service: the young men conscripted for that service are often below the age of consent. They are asked not so much to fulfill their obligations as to anticipate them. There are some good reasons for this strange request, beyond its obvious practical reason. Ideally, wars ought to be fought by old men—they might then be less bloody as well as less frequent—but young men perform with markedly greater efficiency and have always been required to serve. It can be said that these young men have already enjoyed years of peace, as well as all the other benefits their state confers, and moreover that their parents, who are presumed to love and protect them, have had a say in determining the policies of their country. This last cannot be said of the young resident alien, even if he has been resident for all or most of his life. Still, he can only serve when he is young, and if he is exempted now on the grounds of his alienage and later becomes a citizen, as he may well do or try to do, he will have escaped military service altogether.

This is the calculation that led U.S. officials, beginning in 1863, to require military service of any alien who had formally declared his intention of becoming a citizen, that is, who had taken out first naturalization papers.[10] This requirement was sharply protested by the treaty nations, on the reasonable grounds that intentions, even declared intentions, do not make a man a citizen and that many of the draftees were in fact citizens elsewhere and so not liable for conscription in the U.S. As a result of these protests, new procedures were adopted which permitted "declarant" aliens (whether citizens of treaty nations or not) to withdraw their declarations, provided they had not exercised political rights under state law and provided also that they left the country within sixty-five days. Both these conditions are of interest. Many states at that time permitted residents of one year to vote in state elections even if they were not yet U.S. citizens. The federal government claimed the right to draft all persons who had exercised this suffrage and so illustrated nicely the close connection between express consent and military obligation. Clearly, the voting aliens of 1863 were thought to have committed themselves to the U.S. in some more significant way than any other declarant aliens had done. Hence the others could leave rather than serve; the voting aliens were given no option. The requirement that the others leave if they wished to escape service (this did not apply to nondeclarant aliens, who were exempt in the first place) was unusually harsh and so far as I know without precedent. It was not repeated in the World War I regulations, which went through an evolution similar to that just described. Once again, an effort was made to draft all declarant aliens; once again, there were protests from the treaty nations; once again, the U.S. yielded and established procedures for the discharge or exemption of aliens who withdrew their declarations, with the provision that such men would be "forever . . . debarred from becoming citizens of the U.S."[11] They were not, however, required to leave the country. Efforts to bar from future citizenship all nondeclarant aliens who refused military service failed in Congress in 1917. In 1941, however, the distinction between the two kinds of alienage was dropped. After that, no resident aliens were automatically exempt; they could claim exemption only by forswearing U.S. citizenship.

Like the native-born young, then, aliens were required to anticipate their obligations, even though they might not have enjoyed two decades of benefits and even though neither they nor their parents had any political rights. If this seems unfair, however, aliens had one striking advantage over the native-born: they were required to serve only if they hoped one day to become citizens. They could refuse to serve if they were willing to accept a perpetual alienage. This last has never been an option open to the native-born, at least not in their "own" country. If they wish to be aliens, they must go somewhere else.

In 1952, during the Korean War, a law was adopted requiring military service of every male alien admitted to permanent residence (that is, holding an immigrant's visa) and actually resident in the U.S. for more than one year.[12] The same rule has held during the war in Vietnam. This effectively turns conscription into a kind of enforced naturalization, since it requires an alien to assume the same burdens as a citizen whatever his own hopes and intentions with regard to citizenship. Clearly it lies within the power of Congress to do this, but it may be argued that it does not lie within its right. The present legislation represents a sharp break with the established rules of international law and also with the legal traditions of our own country.[13] It is particularly strange and disturbing, though also perhaps revealing of the motives of the legislators, that this dramatic shift should have come during the Korean and Vietnamese wars. For these are precisely the kinds of war—distant struggles in which the safety of the country and the lives of its inhabitants are not at stake—that the rule against alien service was most clearly intended to bar. Indeed, the bar was first expressed in terms of a simple, no doubt an overly simple, distinction between external and internal service—the first (as Americans once were more ready to admit than they are today) being likely to have some political motive beyond mere survival. Thus Secretary of State Madison in 1804 said: "Citizens or subjects of one country residing in another, though bound . . . to many common duties, can never be rightfully forced into military service, *particularly external service.*"[14]

I want to fasten for a moment on this anomaly: according to international law and American legal tradition, foreign-born residents of the U.S. can refuse that express consent which provides the only moral basis for conscription, while native-born residents cannot. It would appear that the distinction between tacit and express consent is meaningful only in the life of an alien. But this was surely not the intention of those theorists, like Locke, who originally worked out the idea of tacit consent. For them the alien was only a convenient example of a group of men in fact much larger than the population of aliens, who had yielded nothing more than a silent acquiescence to the polity, and this larger group included native-born men and women. I should think that for Locke it included all those men (the poor and the landless, for example) who were not required to take oaths of allegiance, and if he thought of them at all, it included most women since they also were generally not sworn. It would also include all young men, whatever the economic condition of their families, for a young man below the "age of discretion" clearly cannot be thought to have expressed consent in any binding way and " 'tis evident there is no tie upon him by his father being a subject of this kingdom, nor is he bound up by any compact of his ancestors."[15] For Locke the population that has expressed its consent is thus likely to coincide with the population of adult, male property owners. Of course, he would almost certainly have conscripted young men without regard to the quality of their consent, since he distinguished the two kinds of consent, as we have seen, in a different way. But this leads him into a very curious position: he requires express consent for taxation, in fact, he requires a double consent, since property owners are individually sworn to the king and then collectively represented in Parliament, but he would require men to fight who are neither sworn nor represented. Perhaps he would have been willing to call this draft what it so obviously is, a simple impressment.[16] In any case, Locke's view of tacit consent suggests the existence of a kind of moral proletariat whose members have nothing to give to the state—neither advice nor consent—except their lives. Such a proletariat did in fact exist in Locke's time. Does it exist in our own?

This is not an easy question to answer, because it requires that one suggest first what consent and citizenship mean or what they ought to be taken to mean in a modern democratic state—a state in which oaths have neither the social currency nor the moral weight that they had in the seventeenth century. It seems to me that the best expression of consent available to the resident of a democratic state is political participation after coming of age. Perhaps I should add, meaningful participation, for a man clearly does not incur the obligations of citizenship through actions about whose effectiveness and significance he is deceived. Meaningful is a vague word and one much abused, but for the moment it will have to serve. Just as the oath of allegiance in a monarchy was a pledge to acknowledge and abide by the commands of a sovereign lord, so meaningful participation in a democracy is a kind of pledge to acknowledge and abide by the decisions of the sovereign people. I doubt that this is a pledge often given without some awareness of what is being done. Actual participants in a democratic political process are generally not surprised to be told that they have committed themselves to abide by its results (or to refuse to do so, if they think they must, in a civil fashion, accepting whatever punishment their fellow citizens impose). War is simply one of the possible results and the obligation to fight one of the possible commitments.[17] Surely no one need feel hesitant about telling citizens this if they ever act as if they do not know it.

What of nonparticipants? I think we must say that resident nonparticipants have refused this express consent (and those whose participation is not meaningful have simply failed or been unable to give it) and have yielded only tacit consent to the political system. Though such persons have no legal status, their moral situation is not in any significant way different from that of resident aliens who could, but do not, apply for naturalization papers. The same applies to young men, especially if we assume with Locke that they are not commited by the commitments of their parents (and leave aside the question whether their own political activity can be called meaningful while they are below voting age). Native-born young men are not obviously different from young aliens. Before they are conscripted, then, they ought to be asked, as aliens traditionally were, whether they "intend" to become citizens, that is, whether they intend to exercise their political rights. If they say no, then we must at least consider the possibility that they be allowed, like aliens again, to avoid the draft and continue their residence, that is, to become *resident aliens at home,* acknowledging their obligation to defend society against destruction, but refusing to defend or aggrandize the state.

Now this may be taken as a monstrous suggestion. Even to talk of resident aliens at home, it may be said, is to misunderstand the meaning of "home." A man has enormous debts to his native land and to his polity. He receives from them both not merely physical security but moral identity. *Extra patria, nullum nomen.*[18] It is surprising how quickly we are back to Blackstone, for arguments of this sort necessarily suggest obligations akin to those we have to our parents. I do not want to deny the value of living permanently in one's native land and enjoying a secure political membership there, but I do want to deny the relevance of either of these to the question of ultimate obligation to the state. There is more than one reason for arguing irrelevance here, but I think it will be useful to stress a distinction that I have already made: the society into which we are born is not the same entity as the state that governs us, and neither of these is adequately described by the Latin word *"patria."* That word blurs the distinction between state and society and is thereby faithful, perhaps, to the world of the polis, but radically divorced from the experiences of modern men. Liberalism from its beginning has emphasized the distinction, not merely in order to subject the state to certain sorts of social control, but also in order to free society and its individual members from the restraints of active citizenship and patriotic fervor. Liberal society is conceived as a voluntary association of private men, egotists and families of egotists, a world not of friends and comrades but of strangers. And the liberal state, though it permits a limited kind of membership and solidarity, really has another purpose. With its impersonal administration, its equality before the law, its due process, it represents the triumphant solution to the problem of governing a society of strangers. There is a sense, then, in which no one is at home in the modern state; we are all nameless aliens, *extra patria.*

That is an exaggeration, of course, even a gross exaggeration, though just how gross I really do not have to say. The modern liberal state is most often a democratic state, and through the mechanisms of mass self-government it seeks, with some success, to integrate and obligate its citizens. Nevertheless, that vivid sense of cooperating with one's fellows and governing oneself, which is so crucial to democratic legitimacy, has in fact been lost to many of those citizens. Whatever the reasons for that loss, its effects are fairly clear: an indeterminate number of men and women "drop out" of political life; a larger, but equally indeterminate number never join.[19] It is not the case that they simply do not vote, nor do I believe that nonvoting can be taken as anything but a very rough indication of political withdrawal or nonparticipation. Something more is involved: these people never have "Roman thoughts." They do not join in any of the actions available to democratic citizens; they do not participate in parties, sects, or movements; they do not take part in political debate; they do not inform themselves on public issues. In all these ways they refuse or neglect or proclaim their inability to consent to the political system and to the various purposive actions it generates. These are the alienated residents of the modern democratic state, and they are probably far more numerous than are the resident aliens. I should stress that what these people suffer from (or endure or enjoy) is political and not, or not necessarily, moral alienation. They are strangers only to the state, and it does not follow from this either logically or psychologically that they refuse or neglect the obligations produced by their silence.

Liberal theory knows nothing of an alienation more profound than political alienation, but that is a condition it seems almost designed to specify. The politically alienated man has incurred social obligations by his residence, by the everyday contacts he maintains with other men and women, and by the benefits he accepts. But these obligations do not involve what the ancients called political "friendship" and do not bind him to share the political purposes or the political destiny of his fellow residents, or of those of his fellows who are active in state affairs. He has incurred limited, essentially negative duties to the state that regulates and protects his social life. He is bound to respect the regulations and to join at critical moments in the protection. But that is all he is bound to do. His only politics is the everyday politics of his personal life.

There is no established right to yield only tacit consent to the state. A resident alien need yield no more, but no state is bound to permit aliens to live permanently or even temporarily under its protection. Even the right of asylum might be qualified by the requirement that all refugees become citizens as soon as the law permits. A declaration of intention to become a citizen might well be made a requirement for admission. But if the legal status of resident alien could thus be eliminated, the moral condition of the alienated resident probably cannot be, at least not in the modern state. Nor can alienated residents simply be asked to leave; their condition is, after all, not their own "fault." It is some reflection on the quality of the state in which they find themselves. Yet, so far as I can discover, there are no states willing to admit the reality of alienation among their inhabitants or to recognize the alienated resident as a moral person. Just what this refusal means, what its reasons are, is not entirely clear to me. There are a number of possibilities. First, the rulers of the state may be claiming, with Blackstone, that obligation in fact derives from birth and upbringing and that the voluntary actions or inactions of adults have no significance in the formation or destruction of moral bonds. Or, second, they may be assuming express consent on the part of all native-born men and women in the absence of express dissent—perhaps on the grounds that such consent would probably be given were it somehow required, though the requirement itself would be administratively and politically difficult to enforce. Or, third, they may be denying that there is any moral difference between tacit and express consent and no special value to be assigned to the exercise of political rights. The first of these reasons is simply a denial of consent theory, and while I appreciate its consistency and force I am not going to discuss it here. The second and third quietly replace the notion that government is legitimized by consent with another notion: that government is legitimized by the absence of active and express dissent. People who hold this second view would, in effect, force all residents to choose between full-scale commitment on the one hand and emigration or revolution on the other. And when large numbers of men and women refuse to choose, as in fact they do, and rest, so to speak, in a position of tacit consent, they would allow the authorities to assume the commitment and to act accordingly. But surely this is to deny to those men and women their moral weight in the community and to treat them as children, that is as persons whose choices are not morally or politcally effective.[20]

How might the force of tacit consent to be recognized? It would of course be possible, as I have suggested, to allow native-born young men the same choice that young aliens have, or have had in the past. They could be invited at age nineteen or twenty either to declare their intention of becoming citizens, thereby accepting conscription, or to become resident aliens at home, losing forever their political rights and avoiding military service except in specified conditions of social emergency. There is, however, an obvious objection to this: it imposes a very difficult choice on very young men. Though it is true that we do this already, and by denying the possibility of voluntary alienage at home make the choice even more difficult, that does not make it a good thing to do. There may be nothing wrong with forcing young men to make hard choices, but forcing them to make permanent choices, with no possibility of reconsideration, places a burden on them that is clearly unjustified. On the other hand, the possibility that, if reconsideration were permitted, few men would choose citizenship until they were past the age for military service may be sufficiently strong to warrant the harshness of perpetual alienage. If this is so, another objection follows: perpetual alienage means the division of the members of state and society into two classes, with different rights and obligations. The whole tendency of modern legislation and of contemporary social struggle, however, is to establish a single class of citizens with precisely equal rights and obligations. A two-class system is not necessarily incompatible with democratic government, as the Athenian case demonstrates, but there is something repugnant in the spectacle of a group of men denied political rights because of a decision made in their late adolescence or very early manhood. The spectacle becomes especially repugnant when it is realized that not all men will face the same choice when it comes their turn to decide. Women will presumably not have to decide at all, nor will men who reach the age of military service during years when conscription is not thought necessary, and the choices of men in peacetime and wartime will be radically different. So the division of the classes will be as arbitrary and unjust as such divisions have always been in the past.

It seems clear to me that tacit and express consent must be regarded as producing different degrees of obligation, and yet it seems equally clear that legal recognition of these differences, or rather any recognition that makes them permanent, is undesirable. There is one way out of this dilemma, and that is to suggest that the state, while not legally establishing or perpetuating the differences, must do nothing to override them. That means, above all, that it cannot simply assume the express consent of its citizens and press them into its service, as it does today. For some of its citizens at least, and perhaps many of its citizens, have never yielded or will never yield such consent. For them conscription, except in cases of social emergency, is nothing more than impressment; it has no moral basis at all. But the group of alienated residents or silent citizens neither has nor ought to have any determinate membership. There are degrees of alienation, and even if the state were determined to recognize and measure these degrees, it is hard to see how it could do so. Nor does the group of alienated residents have a stable membership. In a democracy, at least, there is always the possibility of rejoining the polity. Individuals move, and should certainly be allowed to move, in and out of the political system.[21] Hence the principle "respect the differences between tacit and express consent" must establish a presumption against any conscription at all, except when the country as a whole or some part of it is threatened with devastation.

I am inclined to think that the presumption is very strong indeed and that military conscription at any other time or for any other purpose—for political crusades, foreign interventions, colonial repressions, or international police actions—is virtually certain to be unjust to many individuals, even if the war itself is entirely justified. Conscription, then, is morally appropriate only when it is used on behalf of, and is necessary to the safety of, society as a whole, for then the nature of the obligation and the identity of the obligated persons are both reasonably clear. But the state must rely on volunteers and can only hope (a genuine and vital democracy might expect) that commited citizens, whether they can readily be identified or not, will choose to come forward.[22] Clearly, they are obligated to come forward, though they may have other obligations as well.

The myths of common citizenship and common obligation are very important to the modern state, and perhaps even generally useful to its inhabitants, but they are myths nonetheless and cannot be allowed to determine the actual commitments of actual men and women. These commitments depend upon their own actions, and their actions, presumably, upon their previous moral experience: both actions and commitments are bound to be diverse in character. If the whole gamut of possible commitments cannot be specified in law, it can be understood in theory, and law can be adjusted on the basis of that understanding. I have argued that the notion of alienage provides a useful theoretical parallel to the moral experience of alienation and to the commitment or lack of commitment that follows from that experience. It suggests a way of recognizing the political strangers among us and of doing them justice as moral persons. I do not mean, once again, that justice will or can be done by assigning a legal status or creating a determinate class of individuals exempt from certain obligations and deprived of certain rights. So far is this from being the case, that whenever conscription is enforced in the absence of social emergency, alienated residents (or those of them sufficiently self-aware to make claims on account of their alienation) should probably be treated as conscientious objectors are at present—exempted but not deprived, so as not to create a second-class citizenship. Perpetual alienage would be almost as bad as permanent exile, the only alternative to conscription available today to these same people. It can be argued, of course, that estrangement from the day-to-day self-government of society ought not to be tolerated in a democracy, for in the long run it undermines the sense of political obligation altogether and endangers the everyday mutuality and peacefulness of social life. Alienation is not a desirable human condition. That is no

168 | MICHAEL WALZER

reason, however, for refusing recognition to those men and women whose condition it is.

"Political Alienation and Military Service," by Michael Walzer. Reprinted by permission of the publishers from *Obligations: Essays on Disobedience*, by Michael Walzer, Cambridge, Massachusetts: Harvard University Press. Copyright © 1970 by the President and Fellows of Harvard College.

MICHAEL WALZER (1935–) is professor of government at Harvard University and the author of a number of books, including *The Revolution of the Saints*, *Political Action*, and *Just and Unjust War*.

Notes

1. John Locke, *The Second Treatise of Government*, pars. 119–122.

2. William Blackstone, *Commentaries on the Laws of England*, bk. I, chap. 10.

3. William Edward Hall, *International Law* (Oxford, 1880), p. 43.

4. Ibid., pp. 171–173; he is following J. C. Bluntschli, *Le Droit international codifié* (Paris, 1874), section 391, but the argument is common to virtually every writer on international law since Emerich de Vattel's *Droit des gens* (1758).

5. Francis Wharton, *A Digest of the International Law of the United States* (Washington, 1886), section 202.

6. Thus the phrase "neutral aliens" in the statement of the British government cited above; *allied* aliens have often been conscripted with the consent of their governments. See Ministry of Labor and National Service, *The Obligations of Allied and Other Foreign Nationals in Great Britain* (London, 1943).

7. G. H. Hackworth, *Digest of International Law* (Washington, 1942), vol. III, section 282.

8. International meetings held before and after World War II attempted to guarantee to stateless persons the status and privileges of neutral aliens. See the *Convention on the Status of Refugees* (1938) and Geneva Convention IV (1949). These are discussed in F. Lafitte, *The Internment of Aliens* (Hammondsworth, England, 1940), p. 221; and Morris Greenspan, *The Modern Law of Land Warfare* (Berkeley, 1959), p. 51.

9. There is some disagreement about this among historians. I am fol-

lowing Michel Clerc, *Les Métèques athéniens* (Paris, 1893), p. 48; for another view, see H. H. M. Jones, *Athenian Democracy* (New York, 1958), p. 164.

10. For the following paragraph I am relying chiefly on Wharton, *A Digest*, section 202, and John Houck, "Comment," *Michigan Law Review* 52:265–276 (December 1953).

11. Hackworth, *Digest*, section 282, amendment of July 9, 1918, to Selective Service Act of May 18, 1917.

12. Houck, "Comment," p. 275.

13. I have been unable to discover any court cases under the new law. This is probably because it affects so many fewer people than did previous legislation with regard to alien service, the number of resident aliens having fallen sharply during the past thirty years. I should add that many recent immigrants are from Puerto Rico, and they are not regarded as aliens at all. They are, strangely enough, equally subject to conscription at home and in the U.S., before and after they have become citizens.

14. Quoted in Ernst W. Puttkammer, "Alien Friends and Alien Enemies in the U.S.," *Public Policy Pamphlet* No. 39 (Chicago, 1943).

15. Locke, *Second Treatise*, par. 118.

16. Locke writes explicitly only of the obligation of soldiers, and says nothing of the obligation of citizens or subjects to become soldiers. I am here assuming what seems most likely, that he accepted contemporary recruitment practices. See *Second Treatise*, par. 139.

17. The argument holds only if the decision to go to war is in fact made democratically; this is obviously not always the case, even in formally democratic systems.

18. The psychological importance of "having" a native land is stressed by Sebastian de Grazia, *The Political Community: A Study of Anomie* (Chicago, 1948), but his argument helps to explain only the *sense* of obligation, not its reality. Exactly what arguments of this sort imply about being as distinct from feeling obligated is unclear to me.

19. Some people never join because they are prevented from doing so, or from doing so in any meaningful way; they are excluded from citizenship by one or another form of oppression. Oppressed minorities in a democratic state may perhaps be regarded as alienated residents, but more needs to be said about them than I can say here.

20. Joseph Tussman has argued that there is no significant difference between express and tacit consent so far as their moral consequences go. He does believe, however, that there are many citizens who have not consented at all: "They are political child-brides who have a status they do not understand and which they have not acquired by their own consent" (*Obligation and the Body Politic* [New York, 1960], p. 37). I am made uneasy by the presumption here that large numbers of adults can be

passed off as children, and I doubt very much that these people have no understanding at all of their status, though they may have a different understanding of it than Professor Tussman does. I should add that Tussman is by no means content with his child-brides; he would prefer adult marriages. But what if the adults fight shy?

21. But note Rousseau's qualification in Jean Jacques Rousseau, *The Social Contract*, bk. III, chap. 18. It is generally easier to incur obligations than to renounce them.

22. There is one way of making this distinction in law that I want to notice, but not necessarily to endorse. In Australia during World War II, young men were conscripted for home service, while only volunteers were sent overseas. It is not the case, of course, that the defense of Australian (or any other) society could never require overseas service. Still, this is a rough and often acceptable way of guaranteeing that conscripts never be forced to wage a political war.

13

The Wreckage of the Consensus
by
Ayn Rand

Rand challenges the idea that a man's life belongs to the state, which she claims is the fundamental principle of statism and the root of innumerable evils. Instead, she maintains that the only proper function of government is to protect individual rights, the most fundamental of which is the right to life. The military draft, as an abrogation of this most fundamental right, thereby abrogates every other right. It is the one means a government has of initiating and perpetuating wars for reasons other than self-defense and for purposes its citizens neither approve nor understand. Volunteers, Rand emphasizes, have never been lacking to fight wars of legitimate self-defense. A volunteer army, therefore, is the only proper, moral, and practical way to defend a free society.

The institution that enables our leaders to indulge in such recklessly irresponsible ventures is the military draft.

The question of the draft is, perhaps, the most important single issue debated today. But the terms in which it is being debated are a sorry manifestation of our anti-ideological "mainstream."

Of all the statist violations of individual rights in a mixed economy, the military draft is the worst. It is an abrogation of rights. It negates man's fundamental right—the right to life—and establishes the fundamental principle of statism: that a man's life belongs to the state, and the state may claim it by compelling him to sacrifice it in battle. Once that principle is accepted, the rest is only a matter of time.

If the state may force a man to risk death or hideous maiming and crippling, in a war declared at the state's discretion, for a cause he may neither approve of nor even understand, if his consent is not required to send him into unspeakable martyrdom—then, in principle, *all* rights are negated in that state, and its government is not man's protector any longer. What else is there left to protect?

The most immoral contradiction—in the chaos of today's anti-ideological groups—is that of the so-called "conservatives," who posture as defenders of individual rights, particularly *property* rights, but uphold and advocate the draft. By what infernal evasion can they hope to justify the proposition that creatures who have no right to life, have the right to a bank account? A slightly higher—though not much higher—rung of hell should be reserved for those "liberals" who claim that man has the "right" to economic security, public housing, medical care, education, recreation, but no right to life, or: that man has the right to *livelihood,* but not to *life.*

One of the notions used by all sides to justify the draft is that "rights impose obligations." Obligations, to whom?—and imposed, by whom? Ideologically, that notion is worse than the evil it attempts to justify: it implies that rights are a gift from the state, and that a man has to buy them by offering something (his life) in return. Logically, that notion is a contradiction: since the only proper function of a government is to protect man's rights, it cannot claim title to his life in exchange for that protection.

The only "obligation" involved in individual rights is an obligation imposed, not by the state, but by the nature of reality (i.e., by the law of identity): *consistency,* which, in this case, means the obligation to respect the rights of others, if one wishes one's own rights to be recognized and protected.

Politically, the draft is clearly unconstitutional. No amount of rationalization, neither by the Supreme Court nor by private individuals, can alter the fact that it represents "involuntary servitude."

A *volunteer* army is the only proper, moral—and practical—way to defend a free country. Should a man volunteer to fight, if his country is attacked? Yes—if he values his own rights and freedom. A free (or even semi-free) country has never lacked volunteers in the face of foreign aggression. Many military authorities have testified that a volunteer army—an army of men who know what they are fighting for and why—is the best, most effective army, and that a drafted one is the least effective.

It is often asked: But what if a country cannot find a sufficient number of volunteers? Even so, this would not give the rest of the population a right to the lives of the country's young men. But, in fact, the lack of volunteers occurs for one of two reasons: (1) If a country is demoralized by a corrupt, authoritarian government, its citizens will not volunteer to defend it. But neither will they fight for long, if drafted. For example, observe the literal disintegration of the Czarist Russian army in World War I. (2) If a country's government undertakes to fight a war for some reason other than self-defense, for a purpose which the citizens neither share nor understand, it will not find many volunteers. Thus a volunteer army is one of the best protectors of peace, not only against foreign aggression, but also against any warlike ideologies or projects on the part of a country's own government.

Not many men would volunteer for such wars as Korea or Vietnam. Without the power to draft, the makers of our foreign policy would not be able to embark on adventures of that kind. This is one of the best practical reasons for the abolition of the draft.

Consider another practical reason. The age of large, mass armies is past. A modern war is a war of *technology;* it requires a highly trained, scientific personnel, not hordes of passive, unthinking, bewildered men; it requires brains, not brawn—intelligence, not blind obedience. One can force men to die; one cannot force them to think. Observe that the more technological branches of our armed services—such as the Navy and the Air Force—do not accept draftees and are made up of volunteers. The draft, therefore, applies only to the least efficacious and—in today's conditions—the least essential part of our armed forces: the infantry. If so, then is national defense the main consideration of those who advocate and uphold the draft?

The practical question of the country's military protection is *not* the issue at stake; it is not the chief concern of the draft's supporters. Some of them may be motivated by routine, traditional notions and fears; but, on a national scale, there is a deeper motive involved.

When a vicious principle is accepted implicitly, it does not take long to become explicit: pressure groups are quick to find practical advantages in its logical implications. For instance, in World War II, the military draft was used as a justification for proposals to establish labor conscription—i.e., compulsory labor service for the entire population, with the government empowered to assign anyone to any job of its choice. "If men can be drafted to die for their country," it was argued, "why can't they be drafted to work for their country?" Two bills embodying such proposals were introduced in Congress, but, fortunately, were defeated. The second of those bills had an interesting quirk: drafted labor, it proposed, would be paid a union scale of wages—in order not to undercut union scales—but, in "fairness" to the military draftees, the labor draftees would be given only the equivalent of army pay, and the rest of their wages would go to the government.(!)

What political group, do you suppose, came up with a notion of this kind? Both bills were introduced by Republicans—and were defeated by organized labor, which was the only large economic group standing between us and a totalitarian state.

Now observe the terms in which the draft is being debated today. The main reason advanced for the continuation of the draft is not military, but financial. (!) It is generally conceded that the draft is unnecessary, but, it is argued, a volunteer army would cost too much.

As matters stand, the army is one of the lowest paid groups in the country; a drafted soldier's pay, in cash or equivalent (i.e., including room and board), amounts to about *one dollar* an hour. To attract volunteers, it would be necessary to offer higher pay and better conditions, thus making an army career comparable to the standards of the civilian labor market.

No exact estimates of the cost of a volunteer army have been offered, but the approximate estimates place it at about four billion dollars a year.

Hold this figure in mind. Hold it while you read about our national budget in the daily papers—and while you hold also, clearly and specifically, the image of what this figure would buy.

The years from about fifteen to twenty-five are the crucial formative years of a man's life. This is the time when he confirms his impressions of the world, of other men, of the society in which he is to live, when he acquires conscious convictions, defines his moral values, chooses his goals, and plans his future, developing or renouncing ambition. These are the years that mark him for life. And it is *these* years that an allegedly humanitarian society forces him to spend in terror—the terror of knowing that he can plan nothing and count on nothing, that any road he takes can be blocked at any moment by an unpredictable power, that, barring his vision of the future, there stands the gray shape of the barracks, and, perhaps, beyond it, death for some unknown reason in some alien jungle.

A pressure of that kind is devastating to a young man's psychology, if he grasps the issue consciously—and still worse, if he doesn't.

The first thing he is likely to give up, in either case, is his intellect: an intellect does not function on the premise of its own impotence. If he acquires the conviction that existence is hopeless, that his life is in the hands of some enormous, incomprehensible evil, if he develops a helpless, searing contempt for the hypocrisy of his elders, and a profound hatred for all mankind—if he seeks to escape from that inhuman psychological pressure by turning to the beatnik cult of the immediate moment, by screaming: "Now, now, now!" (he has nothing else but that *"now"*), or by dulling his terror and killing the last of his mind with LSD—don't blame him. Brothers, you asked for it!

This is what four billion dollars would buy—*this* is what it would spare him and every other young man in the country and every person who loves them. Remember down what drains our money is being poured today: according to the Federal budget for fiscal year 1968, we will spend 4.5 billion on foreign aid and allied projects, 5.3 billion on space programs, 11.3 billion on just one of the many, many departments dealing with public welfare—yet we claim that we cannot afford four billion dollars to save our youth from the agony of a mangling, brutalizing psychological torture.

But, of course, the real motive behind that social crime is not financial; the issue of costs is merely a rationalization. The real motive may be detected in the following statement made by Lt. Gen. Lewis B. Hershey, Director of the Selective Service System, on June 24, 1966: "I am not concerned with the uncertainty involved in keeping our citizenry believing that they owe something to their country. There are too many, too many people that think individualism has to be completely recognized, even if the group rights go to the devil."

The same motive was made fully clear in a proposal which was advanced by Secretary of Defense Robert S. McNamara and is now being plugged with growing insistence by the press.

On May 18, 1966, Mr. McNamara said the following: "As matters stand, our present Selective [Service] system draws on only a minority of eligible young men. That is an inequity. It seems to me that we could move toward remedying that inequity by asking every young person in the United States to give two years of service to his country—whether in one of the military services, in the Peace Corps or in some other volunteer developmental work at home or abroad."

"Developmental" work—devoted to *whose* development?

Apparently, planting rice or digging ditches in Asia, Africa, and South America constitutes service to the United States—but preparing oneself for a productive career does not. Teaching our own illiterates in hill-billy regions or city slums constitutes service to the United States—

but going to college does not. Teaching retarded children to weave baskets constitutes service to the United States—but acquiring a Ph.D. does not.

Isn't the unnamed principle clear? Developing yourself into a productive, ambitious, *independent* person is not regarded as a value to the United States; turning yourself into an abject sacrificial animal is.

This, I submit, is a moral obscenity.

Whatever country such a principle could apply to, it is *not* the United States. It is not even Soviet Russia—where they do destroy the minds of their youth, but not in so mawkishly, wantonly senseless a manner.

That proposal represents the naked essence of *altruism* in its pure and fully consistent form. It does not seek to sacrifice men for the alleged benefit of the state—it seeks to sacrifice them *for the sake of sacrifice*. It seeks to break man's spirit—to destroy his mind, his ambition, his self-esteem, his self-confidence, his *self*, during the very years when he is in the process of acquiring them.

Mr. McNamara's trial balloon did not go over too well, at first. There were outcries of protest and indignation, which compelled the government to issue a hasty disclaimer. "The Johnson Administration," said *The New York Times* of May 20, 1966, "quickly made it plain today that it had no plans to draft young Americans for civilian duty or to let such duty become an alternative to military service." The same news story said that "officials called upon to interpret his [McNamara's] words stressed that he had suggested 'asking' rather than 'compelling' young people to serve." Well, *I* want to stress that if a government intends to "ask" rather than "compel," it does not choose the Secretary of Defense to do the "asking," and he does not "ask" it in the context of a passage dealing with the military draft.

The suggestion of "voluntary service" under a threat to one's life is *blackmail*—blackmail directed at the entire American youth—blackmail demanding their surrender into explicit serfdom.

After that initial suggestion—obviously, as an intermediary step, to "condition" the sacrificial animals—the statist-altruist gangs began to plug the notion of "voluntary" social service. On September 14, 1966, James Reston, of *The New York Times*, quoted President Johnson as saying: "I hope to see a day when some form of voluntary service to the community and the nation and the world is as common in America as going to school; when no man has truly lived who only served himself."

The motivation of all this is obvious. The draft is not needed for military purposes, it is not needed for the protection of this country, but the statists are struggling not to relinquish the power it gave them and the unnamed principle (and precedent) it established—above all, not to relinquish the principle: that man's life belongs to the state.

This is the real issue—and the only issue—and there is no way to fight it or to achieve the abolition of the draft except by upholding the principle of man's right to his own life. There is no way to uphold that right without a full, consistent, moral-political ideology. But that is not the way the issue is now debated by the frantic anti-ideologists of all sides.

It is the "conservatives," the alleged defenders of freedom and capitalism, who should be opposing the draft. They are not; they are supporting it. Early in the presidential election campaign of 1964, Barry Goldwater made a vague suggestion favoring the abolition of the draft, which aroused the public's hopeful attention; he promptly dropped it, and devoted his campaign to denouncing the morals of Bobby Baker. Who brought the issue of the draft into public focus and debate, demanding its repeal? The extreme *left*—the Vietniks and Peaceniks.

In line with the anti-ideological methods of all other groups, the Vietniks—whose sympathies are on the side of Russia, China and North Vietnam—are screaming against the draft in the name of their "individual rights"—*individual rights,* believe it or not. They are proclaiming their right to choose which war they'll fight in—while sympathizing with countries where the individual does not even have the right to choose and utter a thought of his own. What is still worse is the fact that they are the only group that even mentions individual rights (if newspaper reports are to be trusted).

But of all this anti-ideological mess, I would pick one small incident as, morally, the worst. I quote from *The New York Times* of February 6, 1967:

Leaders of 15 student organizations representing both political extremes as well as the center called today for the abolition of the draft and the encouragement of voluntary service in humanitarian pursuits. In a resolution ending a two-day conference on the draft and national service at the Shoreham Hotel [Washington, D.C.], the student leaders declared: "The present draft system with its inherent injustices is incompatible with traditional American principles of individual freedom within a democratic society, and for this reason the draft should be eliminated. An urgent need exists within our society for young people to become involved in the elimination of such social ills as ignorance, poverty, racial discrimination and war." Among those who signed the resolution were leading members of the leftwing Students for a Democratic Society, the rightwing Young Americans for Freedom, and the moderate Youth and

College Division of the National Association for the Advancement of Colored People. . . . Although no unanimity on concrete recommendations was arrived at, Mr. Chickering [the sponsor of the conference] said he believed that most of the student leaders favored his proposal for the creation of a system of voluntary national service. Under this proposal . . . students at campuses throughout the country will be asked to fill out cards expressing their willingness to serve in humanitarian work.

(Observe the formulation "traditional American principles of individual freedom within a democratic society"—instead of "individual *right* to life." What is "individual freedom within a democratic society"? What is a "democratic society"? "Individual freedom" is not a primary political principle and cannot be defined, defended or practiced without the primary principle of individual rights. And a "democratic society," *traditionally,* means: unlimited majority rule. This is an example of the method by which today's anti-ideologists are obliterating the concept of rights. Observe also that the leaders of the "conservative" Young Americans for Freedom signed a document of that kind.)

These are not men who are being whipped: these are men who take the lash obediently and whip themselves.

Politically, that proposal is much worse than the draft. The draft, at least, offers the excuse that one is serving one's own country in time of danger—and its political implications are diluted by a long historical tradition associated with patriotism. But if young men accept the belief that it is their duty to spend their irreplaceable formative years on growing rice and carrying bedpans—they're done for psychologically, and so is this country.

The same news story carried some shocking statistics on the attitude of college students at large. It quoted a poll conducted by the National Students Association at twenty-three campuses throughout the country. If that poll is to be trusted, "Approximately 75 per cent said they preferred the establishment of some means to allow work in the Peace Corps, the Teacher Corps or Volunteers in Service to America as an alternative to military service. About 90 per cent, however, said they believed that the Government has a right to conscript its citizens, and 68 per cent thought such conscription was necessary in periods other than those of a declared national emergency."

This is an example, on a grand scale, of what I call "the sanction of the victim." It is also an example of the fact that men cannot be enslaved politically until they have been disarmed *ideologically.* When they are so disarmed, it is the victims who take the lead in the process of their own destruction.

Such is the swamp of contradictions swallowing the two most immediately prominent issues of today—Vietnam and the draft. The same is true of all the other issues and pseudo-issues now clogging all the avenues of public communication. And, adding insult to injury, the anti-ideologists, who are responsible for it, are complaining about the public's lethargy.

Lethargy is only a precarious psychological cover for confusion, disgust and despair.

The country at large is bitterly dissatisfied with the status quo, disillusioned with the stale slogans of welfare statism, and desperately seeking an alternative, i.e., an intelligible program and course. The intensity of that need may be gauged by the fact that a single good speech raised a man, who had never held public office, to the governorship of California. The statists of both parties, who are now busy smearing Governor Reagan, are anxious not to see and not to let others discover the real lesson and meaning of his election: that the country is starved for a voice of consistency, clarity and moral self-confidence—which were the outstanding qualities of his famous speech, and which cannot be achieved or projected by consensus-seeking anti-ideologists.

As of this date, Governor Reagan seems to be a promising public figure—I do not know him and cannot speak for the future. It is difficult to avoid a certain degree of skepticism: we have been disappointed too often. But whether he lives up to the promise or not, the people's need, quest for and response to clear-cut ideas remain a fact—and will become a tragic fact if the intellectual leaders of this country continue to ignore it.

Since the elections of 1966, some commentators have been talking about the country's "swing to the right." There was no swing to the right (except, perhaps, in California)—there was only a swing against the left (if by "right," we mean capitalism—and by "left," statism). Without a firm, consistent *ideological* program and leadership, the people's desperate protest will be dissipated in the blind alleys of the same statism that they are opposing. It is futile to fight *against,* if one does not know what one is fighting *for.* A merely negative trend or movement cannot win and, historically, has never won: it leads nowhere.

The consensus-doctrine has achieved the exact opposite of its alleged goal: instead of creating unity or agreement, it has disintegrated and atomized the country to such an extent that no communication, let alone agreement, is possible. It is not unity, but intellectual coherence that a country needs. That coherence can be achieved only by fundamental principles, not by compromises among groups of men—by the primacy of ideas, not of gangs.

The task of defining ideas and goals is not the province of politicians and is not accomplished at election time: elections are merely consequences. The task belongs to the intellectuals. The need is more urgent than ever.

(*Postscript to our readers.* Once in a while, I receive letters from young men asking me for personal advice on problems connected with the draft. Morally, no one can give advice in any issue where choices and decisions are not voluntary: "Morality ends where a gun begins." As to the practical alternatives available, the best thing to do is to consult a good lawyer

There is, however, one moral aspect of the issue that needs clarification. Some young men seem to labor under the misapprehension that since the draft is a violation of their rights, compliance with the draft law would constitute a moral sanction of that violation. This is a serious error. A forced compliance is not a sanction. All of us are forced to comply with many laws that violate our rights, but so long as we advocate the repeal of such laws, our compliance does not constitute a sanction. Unjust laws have to be fought ideologically; they cannot be fought or corrected by means of mere disobedience and futile martyrdom. To quote from an editorial on this subject in the April 1967 issue of *Persuasion*: "One does not stop the juggernaut by throwing oneself in front of it . . .")

"The Wreckage of the Consensus" from *Capitalism: The Unknown Ideal* by Ayn Rand. Copyright © 1967 by The Objectivist, Inc. Reprinted by arrangement with The New American Library, Inc., New York, New York. Used by permission of the author.

AYN RAND (1905–1982), novelist and philosopher, is the author of a number of books, including *The Fountainhead, Atlas Shrugged, We the Living, Capitalism: The Unknown Ideal,* and *The Virtue of Selfishness.*

14

Military Service and Moral Obligation
by
Hugo Adam Bedau

Bedau takes as given that men are legally *obligated to render military service under a valid law of a government whose constitution is itself morally sound. He questions, however, whether they also have a* moral *obligation, in the absence of volunteering, to do so. Analyzing and rejecting a number of assumptions on which past claims of the morality and obligatory nature of conscription have been based, he concludes there is no plausible theory that guarantees that a legitimate military obligation is or is not also a moral obligation. Bedau maintains that decisions as to moral obligation are personal decisions, especially in large, modern nation-states where original foundations of communal obligation in familial or tribal ties no longer exist. Each man must be prepared to decide individually and directly the moral validity of each of his legitimate military obligations.*

I

Since 1948, thanks to Congressional legislation and presidential policy, compulsory military service has been the law in this country.

Every male resident, upon reaching the age of eighteen, has been subject to the provisions of the draft law. Unless a registrant could produce evidence to warrant some other classification, deferment, or exemption, the law required him to be classified 1-A. Depending upon the manpower needs of the Defense Department, he was liable to be inducted into the armed services (usually, the Army) for two years. In the past generation millions of men have been drafted under the authority of the Selective Service Act. Hundreds of thousands of draftees have seen combat service in Korea and Indochina.

An integral feature of the draft throughout its history has been the idea that every American male has an *obligation* to render military service to the nation. The idea is found already in the first court case on selective service, which upheld President Lincoln's authority to draft men into the Union armies in 1863.[1] It reappeared during the First World War; in 1916, one Massachusetts congressman unsuccessfully urged deletion of the term 'draft' from the title of the proposed legislation then under debate, in favor of the phrase 'personal obligation to service.'[2] Two years later, the Supreme Court vindicated the draft law by declaring, in part, that "the very concept of a just government and its duty to the citizen includes the reciprocal obligation of the citizen to render military service in case of need."[3] Within the past decade, the Supreme Court has again spoken of the "imperative obligations of citizenship," including military service "in time of war and national emergency."[4] The president of Yale University has referred to our "national obligation" and "national duty" to serve.[5] Several of the invited speakers at the University of Chicago's Conference on the Draft in 1966 alluded to our "obligations of military service."[6] In his message to Congress in 1967 recommending renewal of the Selective Service Act, President Johnson invoked on behalf of that legislation what he called "the obligations and benefits of military service."[7] Congress, too, in prefacing the Military Selective Service Act of 1967 (the law in force at the time of this writing), spoke of "the obligations and privileges of serving in the armed forces" and declared that these "should be generally shared." The unpopularity of the war in Vietnam has not wholly effaced this century-old style of talk. Earlier this year, President Nixon's Commission on an All-Volunteer Armed Force referred to "the traditional belief that each citizen has a moral responsibility to serve his country."[8] And of course General Hershey, for thirty years the director of Selective Services, has assured us that "military service," in our "American heritage," is both "an obligation and privilege."[9] The idea that we have a military obligation, therefore, is not merely invented and propagated by recruiting sergeants, draft boards, and the

American Legion. It is an essential feature of how we understand our Selective Service System—of how we talk about it, appraise its claims upon us, gauge our response to it.

That the lawyers, soldiers, politicians, behaviorial scientists, and scholars who have written so much on the draft in the last few years have ignored this language is all the more surprising. One would have thought that this putative obligation raised questions at least as fundamental as other moral questions about the draft (such as whether its statutory provisions and administration are fair and efficient) and like all such assumptions it would receive its proper review.[10] Instead, all these writers have looked right past this much-touted military obligation. The interested reader may well wonder whether these authorities are cautious cynics (not caring whether there is any such obligation, but having no intention of challenging the conventional wisdom either way) or hypocrites (taking for granted in their public discussions that there is such obligation, but in private not believing it), or whether they are simply blind to this matter.

I propose to look at this issue squarely: do we in fact have an obligation to render military service (a military obligation, as I shall usually call it, for brevity's sake)? If so, what is the source of this obligation? What makes this obligation universal among American men (and only men!) today? What fault accrues to us if by evasion or repudiation we fail to discharge this obligation? The matter is a grave one for anyone concerned with moral conduct, because to have a moral obligation to do something is always to have a special kind of good reason for doing it. Today, few things can have greater moral urgency for young men in this country than to be assured whether they have that kind of good reason for accepting the military draft. To anticipate my conclusion, I shall argue that there is not any plausible theory in terms of which we can understand our military obligation as a moral obligation, and I am prepared to draw the inference that in all likelihood there is no such moral obligation at all.

II

At the threshold of my argument, it is necessary to supply some elementary clarifications so that the issue and my position on it are not grossly misunderstood. In the first place, when I say that the topic of this inquiry is whether men have a military obligation, I mean to challenge their obligation to obey the Selective Service Act. Since I concede that the Selective Service Act is valid law, I do not intend to dispute or cast into doubt whether that body of law imposes *legal* obligations on all who are subject to it. (The possible unconstitutionality of that law, however, I do not foreclose; see below, section III.) My question, therefore, is not whether men have a military obligation in the sense of a legal obligation to render military service if ordered to do so. Rather, I am concerned with whether that legal obligation is in any sense a *moral* obligation, and how it is to be shown that it is a moral obligation. I am aware that many Americans subject to the draft think that a man's military obligation is a moral obligation, and that many others not subject to the draft also think so. Far from denying these beliefs, I insist upon them because they point up the genuineness and relevance of the questions we are to discuss. What I do not concede is (a) that this legal obligation is *ipso facto* a moral obligation, (b) that this legal obligation is decisive evidence that there is a concurrent, antecedent, or subsequent moral obligation, and (c) that the source of this legal obligation also causes the obligation to be moral. All three points, (a)–(c), should be clear, for they do not arise only in the present context. Few legal obligations are *ipso facto* moral obligations; e.g. the legal obligation to pay a monthly interest charge of one and one-half percent of the unpaid balance on one's charge account is not anything a person is morally obligated to do just because it is enforceable against him as a legal obligation. Nor does the existence of a legal obligation, e.g. for a tenant to give thirty days notice prior to terminating a lease, show that there is some antecedent moral obligation to which this legal duty gives shape or substance. In general, then, persons can have a legal obligation without having any correlative moral obligation of the same sort or to the same end. In the present context, it is even possible that a man's legal obligation to render military service to his country is contradicted by a moral obligation not to fight his nation's declared enemies, a possibility of considerable interest in light of the Vietnam war, but not something there is space to pursue here.

Secondly, the question I am raising is related to but is not identical with the question whether men *ought* to render military service. Whether someone is *obligated* to do something, and whether he *ought* to do it, are in general two very different kinds of questions—as many philosophers have been trying to show for some years.[11] In general, sentences of the form 'You are obligated to do *x*' and 'You ought to do *x*' do not have the same meaning. Nor do the kinds of reasons which show that one of these utterances is true always show that the other is true. In general, we establish obligations for ourselves and others in virtue of making promises, voluntarily accepting benefits from others, incurring debts to them, placing ourselves in roles with defined duties, and so forth. But what persons ought to do will be determined by a much wider range of considerations, including selfish and prudential considerations. Thus, perhaps a person ought to take his umbrella with him (because it looks like rain), but only if something very different is true (he promised his wife) will he have an obligation to take his umbrella. We are often blinded to this distinction because, normally, if a man has an obligation to do *x,* then (barring certain contravening considerations of a moral sort) he ought to do *x.* Whether a man's moral obligations are always and only what we "morally ought" to do[12] is also dubious. Morally, a person ought to help someone in need if he can do so without grave risk or cost to himself; only under unusual circumstances (the person is his companion in a joint venture, e.g. spelunking) will it be thought that he has a moral obligation to help him here and now. The reason for insisting here on a distinction between obligatoriness and oughtness is to allow for the possibility that even though there may be no moral obligation whatever to serve one's nation militarily, still it might be true that a man ought to (and, conversely, even if there were a moral obligation to serve it might still be true that a man ought not to). I shall not attempt to argue to this conclusion (or its converse). Though much of what I say against the morality of military obligation will count as well against military service being what a man ought (or morally ought) to render to his country, the two issues are separate, and to distinguish them is not to indulge in an evasive quibble.

Finally, when I challenge the nature and basis of a man's military *obligation,* I do not mean to put in doubt whether some American men today are *obliged* to render such service. There is no doubt that they are, viz., most of those who are ordered to report for induction. It is true that anyone who is so ordered has alternatives. He can "go underground" into the "dropout culture," or emigrate, or suffer imprisonment. But none of these alternatives (save the last) is legally permitted, much less officially encouraged, and for most inductees all are practically out of the question. It is these facts, deriving from the imposition of sanctions for draft law violators, which oblige them to serve. This is what makes their service compulsory; it does not make it morally obligatory, however. Nor can we explain or justify what is called a man's military obligation by invoking the fact that he is obliged to such service. Although obligations may have an aroma of something onerous, of requirements contrary to the desires of the person bearing the obligation, and not of benefit to him nor desired for their own sake in the normal course of events, we are in trouble if we try to identify *being obliged* with *being obligated.*[13] Were we to do so, in this case, we could not understand the words of all those quoted earlier (the courts, the

Congress, the president, the director of Selective Service) who speak for the larger society. We could not understand why, for example, the public high schools so readily cooperate with the military recruiting officers but reject would-be draft counselors, why volunteering for military service is so widely esteemed whereas seeking an exemption as a conscientious objector has been stigmatized as evasive and little short of disloyal. The putative morality of one's military obligation would be hidden, perhaps completely destroyed, if it were collapsed into being obliged.

In sum, then, I concede that there is at present a *legal obligation* on American men to serve in the armed forces, and that many of them are *obliged* to render military service; I leave open whether anyone *ought* to serve in the armed forces—and I question whether anyone is *morally obligated* to such service.

III

The most convenient way to proceed would be as follows. First, we should identify what in general are the defining conditions of a moral obligation; then we should determine whether our alleged military obligation meets all of these conditions; finally, we should draw the inference that it does, or that it does not, with the consequences in either case. Regretfully, moral philosophers, as recent discussions show,[14] are far from agreement on what a moral obligation is. The explanation of this disagreement is complex; it lies partly in the heterogeneous uses to which 'obligate' and its cognates are subject, in the vagaries in the idea of the moral itself,[15] and in the evident heterogeneity of the things which morally obligate a person. These together allow different interpretation and emphasis, so that a clear and coherent theory of moral obligation has yet to emerge. Some features about moral obligation do seem to be generally accepted: the personality of obligations (only persons or their organizations are obligated), their universalizability (whatever serves to obligate one person would serve equally well to obligate anyone else, were he in the same situation), the inequivalence of feeling obligated and being obligated, of being obligated and being obliged, of a thing's being what one is obligated to do and its being what one ought to do, the notion that to have a moral obligation to do something is to have a special reason for doing it. Beyond this, however, it is difficult to go, and these agreements are not of much help here. Short either of inventing an entire theory of moral obligation for use in the present context, or of accepting one of the existing theories, warts and all, we will have to abandon the plausible way to proceed which I outlined above in favor of a less straightforward strategy.

Let us begin, then, in a different way. It seems quite clear that a man can come under a moral obligation to serve by volunteering for military service. In the absence of defeating conditions (e.g. his failure to understand the consequences of being sworn in) such a man would have a moral obligation to serve his country; how could this be disputed? For centuries men have understood that for a man to give his consent (to agree, to promise) to do something is to undertake a moral obligation to do it, to be morally bound to render a certain performance as a consequence of his promise. A man's word is his moral bond, and in his giving his word we have the paradigm of how a moral obligation is created.

The trouble with this line of thought in the present context is twofold. The most obvious difficulty is its inapplicability in the overwhelming number of cases, since we know that most men do not volunteer for military service. No doubt the boldest attempt which history records to disguise this fact was contributed by President Wilson in 1917, when he said on behalf of the pending draft bill in Congress that it provided "in no sense a conscription of the unwilling; it is, rather, selection from a nation which has volunteered in mass."[16] The simple truth, of course, is that if it were a necessary and sufficient condition of a man's having a military obligation that he be a volunteer, then not all servicemen and only a small proportion of draft registrants would have any such obligation at all. This unwelcome conclusion cannot be surprising, since no one really believes that the morality of the military obligation young men are supposed to have is something which their volunteering for service creates. At most, the act of volunteering is thought to ratify a man's recognition of his being morally obligated to serve, and to bring the volunteer under the legal obligation to serve. Or, it might be argued, the act of volunteering adds a further and special moral obligation (derived from an explicit promise) to serve, over and above the standing moral obligation of service which all men have. Whereas the ordinary citizen has only the standing obligation to serve if needed, and the draftee has his obligation to serve because he has been ordered to do so, the volunteer has both the standing obligation and a special obligation because he offered to serve. These possibilities, however, do show that insofar as volunteers, draftees, and ordinary citizens all have a common moral obligation to serve, then that obligation cannot arise from any volunteering. It must arise in a totally different way. The problem is, what is that way; what is the way in which a person without doing anything special (such as volunteering) incurs a moral obligation to serve his country? I am not, it should be noted, implying that the model of consent is irrelevant to understanding the morality of this obligation. I am only showing that acts of volunteering (and the same could be said for the act of oathtaking performed by all servicemen, volunteers and draftees alike) for military service will not be the relevant, or obligation-making, feature.

If we proceed on the assumption (a) that the moral obligation we want to account for is shared equally by draftee and volunteer, it will be plausible to assume also (b) that this obligation is simply a special case of the citizen's general legal or societal obligations, all of which are moral obligations for the same reasons. Philosophers have provided many theories to account for the morality of legal and political obligations, including these:[17] (i) the government is the earthly representative of a divine power, and whatever the earthly power commands (not expressly contrary to the divine will) imposes a moral duty on those subject to it (Thomism); (ii) the government has the rightful authority to command military service, because whatever the government commands imposes a moral duty upon those subject to it (positivism); (iii) the government is the creation of the members of the body politic, who have voluntarily covenanted to create it in authority over themselves, and whatever issues from such a government the members are morally obligated to obey (contractualism); (iv) the government is the device through which the society secures the greatest good of the greatest number, and this makes strict obedience to the law a moral obligation (utilitarianism); (v) the nation has a life and purpose logically independent of, and morally superior to, the lives and purposes of its individual citizens, and this moral superiority legitimizes the authority of the state over the individual and imposes an obligation of obedience by the latter to the former (organicism); (vi) through social organizations, including the nation-state, unique benefits are secured to all citizens, but only by the willing acceptance of various burdens by all, chief among which is dutiful obedience to the law; so that it is unfair to accept these benefits without accepting one's share of the burdens—including military service—which alone make the benefits possible.[18]

I shall not attempt to assess the merit of these theories, one by one, as they relate to the problem at hand; what that might gain in thoroughness it would surely lose in tedium. Besides, all of these theories share in common one vulnerable feature which can be isolated for direct scrutiny. I shall call it *the transitivity of morality*. The point of all these theories is to show the citizen in general and in advance why he has a moral obligation to obey particular laws independent of any further moral test for those particular laws. Each theory proceeds on the assumption that if the purpose, end, system, or structure—the *constitution*, in short—of the society meets certain tests of moral worthiness, then every valid or legitimate act of the government in that society must be no less morally worthy.[19] The transitivity of morality guarantees that it would be inconsistent both to grant the morality (by whatever test is deemed appropriate) of the political structure and still doubt or deny the morality, including the moral obligatoriness, of a particular policy, statute, or court decision which some appropriate agency in that structure issues.

We may illustrate the difficulty of accepting any theory which relies on this assumption by considering two questions: Is the constitutional structure under which our society operates, including the avowed and tacit ends to be secured by that constitution, morally acceptable? Are the particular laws and policies which create our legal obligation for military service valid? On the theory we are considering, only if the answer to both questions is in the affirmative will the legal obligation in question also be a moral obligation. What we are considering, in other words, is simply an application of the thesis that a person has a moral obligation to obey whatever law is validly enacted by whatever political authority is constitutionally authorized to do so, provided only that constitutional structure itself has moral authority.

In the present case, it is impossible to give a fully convincing answer to either question; all I can do is sketch the outline of an answer. As to the first question, the moral acceptability of our constitutional system is chiefly to be determined by whether it is founded on principles of justice and equality, and whether it gives operating effectivenss to those principles.[20] If only for the sake of argument here, let us concede that our constitutional structure is not an unjust one, and that it does operate effectively. As for the second question, an affirmative answer depends to some extent on accepting a distinction between what is legitimate (or valid) law and what is constitutionally permissible. The former is to be determined chiefly by reference to whether the legislation in question arises in the constitutionally authorized way. The latter, however, is to be settled by reference to whether the legislation is in violation of any constitutional prohibition as determined by the courts. More than one statute has clearly passed the former of these tests, and yet failed the latter, as the history of state and federal legislation before the bar of appellate courts will testify. I am unwilling, as I have already made clear, to challenge the validity or legitimacy of the draft legislation as such. I have, however, doubts about its constitutional permissibility, as do many others. I do not concede, for example, that a perpetual peacetime military draft is consistent with the constitution, nor that the constitution permits the use of draftees in overseas combat with foreign nationals in the absence of a declaration of war.[21] Even if the Supreme Court were to continue to evade these "political questions" (as I expect it will), that evasion need not be construed as a favorable judgment on these constitutional questions. Nevertheless, we may be required to give an affirmative answer to the second question before us.

But surely the more interesting question in the argument we are assessing is not the truth of the two premises we have been discussing but the validity of the inference, which depends on the transitivity of morality. Such transitivity is dubious at best. I believe that we do not and should not accept the argument that a given law creates not only a legal but a moral obligation because it is a valid law and it issues from a government authorized by a constitution that is morally sound. The chief objection to accepting such a form of argument is the best reason for rejecting any form of argument as invalid: it would allow one to infer false conclusions from true premises. Consider some examples of the moral obligations we would find it necessary to recognize if we were to accept the transitivity of morality: the manufacture of intoxicating liquors during the reign of the Volstead Act would have violated not only a legal but also a moral obligation; today, it would be not only legally but morally impermissible to travel to North Vietnam and China, given current State Department directives; all persons having taxable income would be under a moral as well as a legal obligation to pay that portion of their taxes which finances the Vietnam war, CBW research, endless stockpiling of nuclear weapons, etc. There is no end to these examples, but is not any one of them too much to accept? In order to avoid such counter-intuitive consequences, we must abandon the assumption I have called the transitivity of morality and be prepared to face directly and piecemeal, in each case where we have a legal obligation, whether we also have a moral obligation.

Some may object that any society which would permit such preposterous things as cited in my examples cannot be founded on a morally sound constitution. One recalls Thoreau's explicit condemnation of the constitution of his day for its tolerance of slavery. This line of objection claims that my examples quite fail to establish their point. For I am purporting to prove by examples that morality is not transitive, and to do that I must rely on the morality of the constitution, which my own examples impeach! There is some truth in this objection, and it prompts two comments. Perhaps the transitivity of morality is theoretically a tenable assumption; even so, it remains practically useless because at no stage in history has any constitution been sufficiently just to entitle inferences of the sort we are discussing. If, however, transitivity of morality is accepted, despite the existence of morally obnoxious laws, we are entitled to reverse the argument, with the result that we destroy the moral authority of the constitution itself. For example, anyone in 1859 who judged that he had no moral obligation to assist in the return of fugitive slaves, but who accepted the transitivity of morality, would have had to judge the constitution grossly immoral (as Thoreau said he did). The lesson is that one must be cautious in insisting upon the transitivity of morality lest the immoralities sanctioned by law turn out to destroy the truth of the major premiss (that the constitution is just).

IV

Another line of interpretation ancillary to the foregoing line of argument is the possibility that a military obligation is made moral by being a *status* obligation, an obligation on those who hold the status of citizen in a republic. This idea emerged from the development of conscript armies in the Napoleonic era. The military historian, B. H. Liddell Hart, no admirer of conscription, once described it as "the misbegotten child of [French] revolutionary enthusiasm."[22] An armed citizenry (so this view would hold) is the natural result of an egalitarian and democratic basis of political authority and at the same time the best protection against counterrevolutionary efforts by reactionary elements in society or in neighboring nations. So, along with our right to vote and other rights of citizenship there are certain responsibilities, duties, or obligations, including the defense of the society in which we are full and equal members, Citizens. That this line of thought is still pertinent can be seen from the recent remark of an American military officer: "To divorce military service from the duties of citizenship would be the height of folly, inviting ultimate disaster."[23] The Supreme Court has already been quoted in its endorsement of this idea of citizen soldiers, in language hardly less categorical.

The idea that status provides (indeed, is to be defined in terms of the exercise of) certain responsibilities, privileges, rights, duties, is generally accepted. Elective and appointive offices in all organizations, roles earned by dint of qualifications and merit, jobs assigned or otherwise obtained, titles inherited and awarded—all these amply illustrate the notion that with certain status go certain duties. Do we then have in the role or status of citizen a special case of this general idea, and if so, can it be used to show why a citizen's military obligation is also a moral obligation? So long as we extend general moral approval to the ends and constitutional structure of political society, the morality of the ensuing rights and duties of citizen membership in that society is guaranteed—at least, if we accept the transitivity of morality. But the only way to guarantee that there is a universal moral obligation upon (male) citizens to render military service is by stipulating that this is one of the duties of their citizenship. Historically, something like this may be seen in the claim that citizens have a moral duty to volunteer when their country needs them (the theory on which England raised its first armies in World War I). Logically, however, the status of citizenship can bear the weight being put on it by this argument only if the question is begged, or else if there is tacit reliance on other notions such as those criticized elsewhere in this essay.

V

The argument of the two preceding sections has relied on the assumption that a man's military obligation is simply a special case of a more general legal or political obligation. Natural though it may be, this assumption is neither historically sound nor logically necessary. Traditionally, moral obligations have often been divided into three categories: obligations to God, to others, and to oneself. A man's military obligation to serve his country presumably would be a special case of the second sort of obligation, and all other legal or political obligations would also fall into this category. The distinctive thing about military service is that it creates a cadre of persons subject to military orders and (in that sense) ready to fight so that the community in which they live can preserve its integrity, including its own legal, political, and social institutions. Now, suppose one thinks of the protection and defense of other persons, in particular of one's family and neighbors, as something which one is morally obligated to provide. Thus, a recent critic of pacifism has asserted that "the draft is morally justifiable if the defense of persons is considered a basic obligation of the citizen."[24] As such, it would be natural to think of this defense as being derived from his other obligations to other persons. In this way one might come to see the morality of a man's military obligation as a consequence of all his other legal or political obligations.

This, or something like it, seems to me to be a line of thought behind much talk of a military obligation as a moral obligation. In order to establish this obligation upon particular persons by means of this kind of argument, one must be relying on certain empirical assumptions. Chief among these is the belief that the presence of men in military service can and will in fact protect the rest of the community from aggression, in ways or with effectiveness superior to any alternative, e.g. by deterring aggressors, defeating attempted invasion, forcing a stronger aggressor to negotiate a less than unconditional surrender. Should this factual situation not obtain, then there seems no reason on this argument why anyone should see himself as morally obligated to provide what amounts to ineffective or futile military service.

In the present social and political climate, what can we say about this argument as establishing a moral obligation upon young American men to serve in the armed services today? Frankly, it strikes me as the moral detritus from a half-imagined and hardly to be reestablished period in human history when familial, tribal, communal, and civic loyalties dictated the chief features of civilized life, and from which recognizable political relationships eventually grew. This antique mode of thought about the fundamental nature of a person's military obligation has little if any relevance to the morality of a young American's rendering military service to the United States in the current decade of the present century. No one can seriously think of treating this nation as a community to which communal-like obligations are borne by each of us (or at least by each male during a certain period of his young manhood). Nor is it reasonable to see our economic, social, political, legal institutions—insofar as they are worthy of preservation and pride—both as seriously threatened by any nation or people outside (or inside) our borders and as defendable only by conscripted citizen service in the armed forces.

It must be kept in mind that the obligation whose morality we are attempting to establish is an obligation to others (insofar as it is to anyone) as defined by the limits of the nation-state. Obligations to one's neighbors as human beings, obligations to defend the weak and helpless, obligations to run risks for those in danger, obligations to come to the aid of the innocent, obligations to preserve the community—all these obligations are wholly indifferent to the nation-state system. But national territory, national citizenship, and the national state are of the essence in characterizing the military obligation we are discussing. It is not, after all, the town of Concord, the county of Middlesex, the Commonwealth of Massachusetts—nor the Anglo-American community,

the English-speaking people of the world, nor even the United Nations—that propose to draft my sons if their volunteered service cannot
be secured. No doubt it would be easier to establish the morality of our
military obligation if the morality of the nation-state system could be
established. In any case, it is military obligation within the framework
of that system which is in question.

If I may hazard the idea, I suggest that if there were a universal
moral obligation upon persons to defend their community, their duties
would be confined to the protection of neighborhoods and towns, to
keep them liveable and healthy, safe and available for the use of all,
both today and in the future. The community's defenses, in other
words, would be raised against polluters and despoilers, not only
against criminals, and least of all against foreign enemies. Moral considerations adequate to justify a domestic police force cannot suffice to
justify as well a conscript standing army in present international conditions. A nation's army is not a police force, after all, and least of all is it
an international police force. It is not, therefore, a moral obligation to
render community service which I dispute. I object only to the attempt
to see in such a moral obligation the source or rationale of the morality
of a military obligation to serve the present nation-state.

It must be clear by now that my attack on the morality of military
obligation as derivative from the moral obligation to defend persons
depends essentially on the insufficiency of this consideration in the economic, political, and social conditions which exist in this country and in
the world today. Under altered domestic or international circumstances, approaches which I reject here might in fact prove sufficient to
establish the morality of a military obligation. Thus, I would not argue
from the absence of a military obligation which is also a moral obligation among young Americans today to the conclusion that their Israeli
counterparts, faced possibly with a genuine struggle for ethnic survival,
also have no moral obligation to serve in their nation's armed forces; or
that Cubans have no moral obligation to provide the armed forces
needed to defend their socialist society against a counterrevolutionary
invasion by imperialistic neighbors to the north. The moral obligation
of military service in such cases as these is not settled by my criticism of
possible ways whereby that obligation might be established in American society. What I have been relying upon throughout this discussion
is that having a moral obligation depends not only upon certain general
principles and practices and conceptual truths, but also upon circumstances and situations which alter through history as economic, social,
and other contingent relationships vary.

VI

Could it be argued that although the obligation to serve in the armed forces is imposed on young men, it is none the less moral? Is it possible to impose a moral obligation upon someone, to thrust upon him without his consent or desire the moral duty to perform or forbear certain undertakings? Are these circumstances under which I could *make* you morally obligated to do something, without your doing anything to undertake or acknowledge the obligation? Can you become liable to the imposition of an obligation without any offering (as the lawyers say) on your part? Surely, it seems, children have their status as children of their parents through no act of their own. Yet this status traditionally carries with it certain obligations beginning with the duty to "honor one's father and mother." Surely, this is an obligation which is a moral obligation, and it is imposed on all children without their consent.

There is, no doubt, something slightly archaic and quaint in the above reasoning. In earlier generations, to be sure, it would have been generally granted that children have obligations to their parents which are imposed on them and are yet moral. Locke, for example, certainly believed this (as his *Second Treatise* shows) and he did not speak for himself alone. But it is doubtful that many would grant this conclusion in the same way today. Normally, it would be agreed, children are much obliged to their parents for the benefits and blessings of tender loving care. Also, children are obliged by their infancy to obey their parent's wishes. Perhaps for some philosophers this would be sufficient to establish that children have imposed on them moral obligations toward their own parents.[25] Yet most philosophers today, I venture, would grant both the premise and the conclusion but deny the inference.

Even if the inference were granted, and it provided us with a clear case of the imposition of a moral obligation, it is not clear that it would provide us with a plausible model of the imposition of a moral obligation which could be used to explain how it is that the government (or Congress, by passing the Selective Service Act) imposes a moral obligation of military service on all eligible men. For it is not parents who impose moral obligations upon their children, but the circumstances in which children normally find themselves with respect to their parents: parents do not *make* children morally obligated to them merely by the act of procreation, but by the (usually, subsequent) things they do and forego for their children. If so, then we have not been brought to understand how it is that the government makes those subject to the draft morally obligated to obey it. Instead, we are again forced back upon one or another of the theories we have already examined, because it is those arguments which incorporate the circumstances in which the community finds itself and the previous acts of its members through which moral obligations arise.

VII

I have reviewed and found wanting three different arguments *for* the view that our military obligation is a moral obligation. Now I want to consider much more briefly three different arguments *against* that conclusion, arguments which I also reject.

The first of these arguments would destroy any possibility of a military obligation ever being a moral obligation. Again, we must assume that a military obligation is simply a special case of a legal or political obligation—an obligation unlike ordinary family or contractual obligations, in not being owed to another person or specific organization, but owed to some abstract entity, such as the State or Society, and so akin to the obligation to pay one's taxes, obey traffic regulations, and assist the police when ordered to do so. Now, some philosophers have urged that there simply are *no* such obligations at all; they have advanced arguments to show that it is absurd to suppose anyone ever has *any* legal or political obligation.[26] Other philosophers have gone even further; they have urged us to abandon the concept of obligation, whether legal, political, or otherwise, insofar as these obligations are to be thought of as *moral* obligations.[27] These are large-scale and bold challenges, but there is not space here to give them the scrutiny they deserve. These extreme objections may be true, though I believe and have assumed that they are not. If I am wrong, and these objections are well-founded, of course, any such investigation along the lines I have taken would be obviated at the onset, and the falsity of a military obligation being a moral obligation would be guaranteed.

A second line of argument urges that the very fact of compelling performance of military service, as is done by arraying the forces of the law against known evaders and draft resisters, shows conclusively that there is nothing moral in obeying the body of law thus sanctioned. That is, from the fact that the obligation to serve is made into a legal obligation backed by coercive force, it is inferred that whatever may have been moral in the obligation in the first place is now destroyed. To this objection I have two replies. (a) The idea of community or patriotic obligations being exacted from us, because the ordinary citizen cannot ordinarily be expected to render what he properly owes unless he is compelled to do so (or is subject to legal sanctions for failing to do so), is old and very familiar. For Americans, paying taxes, jury duty, and school attendance are all illustrations. All of these obligations are provided for by law, and a citizen may find himself coerced into performing any one of them against his will. But all three obligations have usually been thought to be moral obligations of good citizenship, and this conception of them has not been thought weakened or destroyed by their legal enforceability. The law, it would ordinarily be said, merely gives form, efficiency, and force to the moral obligation. So the fact that a man's military obligation is exacted from him by the coercive instrumentalities of the Selective Service System, the Federal Bureau of Investigation, the federal criminal courts, and the Bureau of Prisons will not of itself suffice to show that a military obligation is not a moral obligation. At the very least, it will have this consequence only if many other obligations enforceable as law which are thought to be moral cease to be so regarded. (b) While it is clear that no one general relation holds between law and morals, it is reasonably clear that the use of force to exact performance or compliance does not of itself—except on the most saintly ethic—destroy the putative morality of the conduct. Many philosophers would join John Stuart Mill in insisting that one of the distinctive characteristics of a moral obligation is that "we should be gratified to see . . . [it] enforced by anybody who had the power."[28] Now it is true that the fact that someone complies with a certain order or directive because it is backed by a threat to use coercive force to secure compliance tends to show that there is little or nothing moral in the compliance. But it does not tend to show that there is no moral obligation to comply with the directive or that it is morally wrong to use force to back it up. Perhaps it is a failure to distinguish the way coercion supplies a (nonmoral) motive from the way reasons may (morally) justify the use of force that leads us to disagree with the position Mill defends.

A third and very different line of criticism might be extracted from the apparent theory on which conscientious objection exemptions are established.[29] The exemption for conscientious objection is founded upon the language and intent of Congress as embodied in the Selective Service Act beginning with the legislation passed in 1940.[30] Although the basis of the exemption is not constitutional but statutory, and what Congress can grant Congress can deny, the statutory exemption seems to acknowledge the existence of a moral claim upon persons superior to any man-made law. The underlying theory of the statutory exemption seems to be that there is a different source of moral regulation, indeed, an obligation more ultimate than any provided by statute (or constitutional) law, i.e. God-given commandments forbidding men to raise their arms in anger against their brothers, and by implication forbidding a man to do so at the behest of a secular government on behalf of policies the man may not understand (or may understand only to repudiate) and against persons he has never seen and who have done him no harm. The "ultimacy" of military obligation,[31] therefore, is tacitly denied by the very instrument which gives legal authority to that obligation. On the strength of this analysis, one might argue that the statutory exemption for conscientious objectors shows that there is nothing moral in the legal obligation to serve in the armed forces, because these statutes acknowledge a superior moral claim as the basis of a moral exemption to such service.

On at least two different grounds this is an inconclusive argument. (a) This objection simply assumes that moral obligations cannot conflict with each other, as though what a moral obligation overrides cannot be another moral obligation. Much moral philosophy in this century, however, has relied upon the notion that there are "prima facie" moral obligations, that they can and do conflict, and that a man's ultimate moral obligation in each situation (or, to put it another way, what he morally ought to do) is determined by a rational resolution of this conflict.[32] It would be argued by these philosophers that a man has prima facie moral obligations to obey the laws of his country, to obey the orders of those in authority over him, to avoid harming other men, and to do whatever he conscientiously believes he ought to do. But these prima facie obligations can conflict; a given act which satisfies some of these obligations can violate others, and there might be no act open to the agent (at least in certain situations) which will satisfy them all. If this is the way in which one understands the intersection of the legal obligation to serve and conscientious objection to such service, then it is quite consistent to maintain that there is at least a prima facie moral obligation to serve in the armed forces. (b) The exemption for conscientious objectors has always carried with it the statutory requirement of alternative civilian service "in the national interest."[33] So it could be argued that a man's military obligation is really a special case of a more general moral obligation to render service to the nation, and that *this* obligation is one to which there is *no* legal or moral exemption in principle. As the law stands, this, too, is a perfectly consistent interpretation of the conscientious objector exemption, which does not undercut the putative morality of a man's military obligation. I should add that I do not advocate the interpretations relied upon in (a) and (b); I am only pointing out that they are plausible and that they show the original argument to be far from conclusive.

VIII

I hope I have shown why I believe that there is no route whereby persons incur or create or undertake moral obligations which, if used as a pattern or model for the morality of the obligation to serve in the armed forces, will show that young men in our country are morally obligated to serve in the armed forces at this time. The consequence is that we must either develop some new theory which will produce this result, or reassess the many factual judgments I have (admittedly) all too briefly identified and rendered, or confess that we have no adequate reason for supposing that a man's military obligation is at present also a moral obligation.

As we contemplate the last alternative, we should note that some recent commentators on the Selective Service System now describe it as a system of "impressment,"[34] deliberately using the term of opprobrium from previous centuries to reveal the true status of the system we have embraced during the past generation. Our draft boards have become little more than genteel press gangs, and our draftee army simply battalions of men dragooned into rendering a service which they are told on all sides they owe their country.

Impressment is strictly the forced contribution of private service in the public interest; it has its occasions and justifications. Imminent threat of community or public disaster (flooding waters, forest fire, volcanic eruption, famine, epidemic) can leave the authorities with no feasible alternative, in the face of the collapse of community life and essential social services, but to press all able-bodied persons in the vicinity into public service immediately. Whether one should invoke the doctrine of necessity to justify or only to excuse the use of force to secure compliance with orders in such situations will depend on one's theory of how a justification differs from an excuse. In either case, necessity makes it not wrong for the authorities to act as they do. Yet even the extreme circumstances and the extreme measures made morally appropriate in this way are appropriate only because of certain background assumptions which, conceivably, may be missing. For example, it cannot be right to impress persons into labor on behalf of preserving institutions which in normal times have exploited or otherwise unjustly treated them.

The problem with the draft for the past generation is whether one can reasonably invoke any such necessities on its behalf. American life and institutions do not seem, since 1948, to have been in jeopardy and saved from destruction thanks only to millions of draftees, in the way some village might have been lost if its mayor and council had not used the police to force all able-bodied persons to fill and haul sandbags to bolster sagging dikes against a rampaging river. Our much-touted "foreign policy commitments" have not created (nor been undertaken in response to) social needs tantamount to the necessities which alone could justify the conclusion that American men have a moral obligation to meet those needs with their personal military service.[35]

If I am right, then, a man's military obligation today looks, from a moral point of view, not significantly different from his obligation to get his dog a license. His obligation is a creature of the law, so that once a certain law is passed he has this (legal) obligation, but in the absence of the law he has no such obligation at all. One result of this is that the obligation men have today to serve in the armed forces may not be at all like the obligation their fathers or grandfathers had to render comparable service. *There simply is no standing and universal moral obligation upon persons to render military service which can be invoked to give a moral reason why a young man ought to obey a draft board.*

While I am unable to offer any fruit of research into American history to bolster the point, it is irresistible to speculate that the popularity of the idea of a military obligation in this country is chiefly a function of the actual imposition of a draft law over the past century: first, at the height of the Civil War (1863); next, immediately after American entry into the war in Europe (1917); again, a few days before the fall of France to the Nazi invaders (1940); finally, in our time, with the onset of the Cold War (1948), its subsequent quadrennial Congressional renewal always accompanied by predictable alarums and excursions. Is it not more likely that the presence of the draft in our midst explains the talk about our obligation to serve, rather than being explained by that alleged obligation? Is it not that the permanent military establishment in this nation encourages moralistic belief in our obligation to military service, rather than that our sense of obligation causes us to create our permanent military establishment?

What we are left with, then, is this. The Selective Service Act places on those subject to it a legal obligation to render military service if called upon to do so. Even if this law were to be abolished, there would remain the political capacity in Congress and the president to reestablish such a legal obligation at almost any time irrespective of the factual warrant for doing so (though this would not have been true in any other epoch of American history). The circumstances in community life, or in national survival, which alone could justify impressment are simply missing from the scene today and probably have not existed at any time in this century.

My arguments, as I have already implied, should not be construed as an attempt to show that we have a moral obligation to resist or repeal the draft. These possibilities go beyond my interests here, even if my arguments help pave the way for facing them. What I have tried to show is that repudiation, violation, or evasion of the legal obligation to serve in the armed forces today, if it incurs any moral taint at all, does not incur that taint brought upon a person who repudiates, violates, or evades his moral obligations.[36]

"Military Service and Moral Obligation," by Hugo Adam Bedau. From *Philosophy and Political Action: Essays edited for the New York Group of the Society for Philosophy and Political Affairs*, edited by Virginia Held, Kai Nielsen, and Charles Parsons. Copyright ©1972 by Oxford University Press, Inc. Reprinted by permission of Oxford University Press, New York.

HUGO ADAM BEDAU (1926–) received his graduate education from Boston and Harvard universities and is professor of philosophy at Tufts University. He is the author of *The Courts, The Constitution and Capital Punishment*, coauthor of *Victimless Crimes*, and author/editor of a number of articles and anthologies on social, political, and legal philosophy.

Notes

1. Kneedler v. Lane, 45 Pa. St. 238 (1863).

2. Quoted in Warren S. Tyron, "The Draft in World War I," *Current History* XIV (1968), p. 342.

3. *Selective Draft Law Cases*, 245 U.S. 366 (1918).

4. United States v. Mendoza-Martinez, 372 U.S. 144, 159–60 (1963).

5. Quoted in Harry A. Marmion, "A Critique of Selective Service with Emphasis on Student Deferment," in Sol Tax, ed., *The Draft* (Chicago: University of Chicago Press, 1967), p. 55.

6. Samuel H. Hays, "A Military View of Selective Service," in Tax, ed., op. cit., p. 14; S. L. A. Marshall, "The Search for an Ideal Solution in a Natural Game of Chance," in Tax, ed., op. cit., p. 62; and Donald J. Eberly, "Guidelines for National Service," in Tax, ed., op. cit., p. 110.

7. "The President's Message on Selective Service to the Congress," in Tax, ed., op. cit., p. 466.

8. *Report of the Commission on an All-Volunteer Armed Force* (Washington, D.C.: Government Printing Office, 1970), p. 14.

9. Lewis B. Hershey, "The Operation of the Selective Service System," *Current History* LIV (1968), p. 3.

10. The only exception I have noticed is Michael Walzer, "Political Alienation and Military Service," in J. Roland Pennock and John W. Chapman, eds., *Political and Legal Obligation: Nomos XII* (New York: Atherton Press, 1970), pp. 401–20, also published in his *Obligations* (Cambridge: Harvard University Press, 1970). The draft, of course, has been much criticized from a moral point of view as in, for example, American Friends Service Committee, Peace Education Division, *The Draft?* (New York: Hill and Wang, 1968).

11. See, for example, P. H. Nowell-Smith, *Ethics* (London: Penguin Books, 1954), pp. 190–212.

12. Cf. Kurt Baier, "Obligation: Political and Moral," in Pennock and Chapman, eds., op. cit., pp. 132 ff.

13. See, for example, H. L. A. Hart, *The Concept of Law* (Oxford: The Clarendon Press, 1961), pp. 80–81.

14. See, for example, H. L. A. Hart, "Legal and Moral Obligation," in A. I. Melden, ed., *Essays in Moral Philosophy* (Seattle: University of Washington Press, 1958), pp. 82–107; Richard Brandt, "The Concepts of Obligation and Duty," *Mind* LXXIII (1964), pp. 374–93; Kurt Baier, "Moral Obligation," *American Philosophical Quarterly* III (1966), pp. 210–26; John Ladd, "Legal and Moral Obligation," in Pennock and Chapman, eds., op. cit., pp. 3–35.

15. See G. Wallace and A. D. M. Walker, eds., *The Definition of Morality* (New York: Barnes and Noble, 1970).

16. Quoted in Tyron, op. cit., p. 342.

17. A. J. Ayer, *Philosophy and Politics* (Liverpool: Liverpool University Press, 1969), identifies no less than a dozen attempts by philosophers to answer the question, 'What is the ground of political obligation?' (pp. 9–10). All of these theories, he implies, are intended to show that political obligation is in general a moral obligation, but none of them, as he rightly remarks, is "very impressive."

18. Theory (vi) is the Hume-Kant-Rawls theory summarily stated by John Rawls, "Legal Obligation and the Duty of Fair Play," in Sidney

Hook, ed., *Law and Philosophy* (New York: New York University Press, 1964), p. 17. For a criticism different from but consistent with mine, see Richard A. Wasserstrom, "The Obligation to Obey the Law," *U.C.L.A. Law Review* X (1963), pp. 790–807, reprinted in Robert Summers, ed., *Essays in Legal Philosophy* (Oxford: Blackwells, 1968), pp. 293–302.

19. An instructive instance of the pervasiveness of this assumption can be seen in the theory of why political obligations are moral obligations advanced by J. R. Pennock, "The Obligation to Obey the Law and the Ends of the State," in Hook, ed., op. cit., pp. 77–85, and the critique therein of Rawls' rival theory. Pennock and Rawls share this assumption, and by comparison with this tacit agreement their differences shrink into relative insignificance.

20. By far the best attempt to show what is involved in this question (though not an attempt to answer it, even implicitly, for the United States) is to be found in the essays by John Rawls: "Justice as Fairness," *Philosophical Review* LXVII (1958), pp. 164–94; "Constitutional Liberty and the Concept of Justice," in C. J. Friedrich and J. W. Chapman, eds., *Justice: Nomos VI* (New York: Atherton Press, 1963), pp. 98–125; and "The Justification of Civil Disobedience," in H. A. Bedau, ed., *Civil Disobedience* (New York: Pegasus, 1969), pp. 240–55.

21. That Congress has the power to conscript men into military service during wartime was settled by the Supreme Court in *The Selective Draft Law Cases* (1918). Subsequently, however, only lower court holdings and Supreme Court dicta have endorsed the power of Congress to draft in peacetime and of the president to send draftees overseas into combat in an undeclared war. An unusually explicit avowal from the bench of these powers as constitutional may be found in the opinion of Judge Charles Wyzanski, Jr., in United States v. Sisson, *Selective Service Law Reporter* I (1969), pp. 3354 ff. For further discussion, see Carl Brent Swisher, "The Supreme Court and Conscription," *Current History* LIV (1968), pp. 351–55, 365–66; *Selective Service Law Reporter* (1968), p. 1005; and American Civil Liberties Union, "Memorandum of Points and Authorities in Support of Motion to Dismiss the Indictment," United States v. Zimmerman (S.D.N.Y., 1969) (mimeographed).

22. Quoted from B. H. Liddell Hart, *Why Don't We Learn From History?* (London: Allen and Unwin, 1944), by Senator Mark O. Hatfield, in *The Congressional Record* (July 7, 1970), p. S10634.

23. Hays, op. cit., p. 20.

24. Jan Narveson, "Pacifism: A Philosophical Analysis," *Ethics* LXXV (1965), pp. 259–71, reprinted in Richard Wasserstrom, ed., *War and Morality* (Belmont, Calif.: Wadsworth Publishing Co., 1970), p. 77. Narveson's statement would be more plausible if for 'if' he had written 'only if,' and if for 'persons' he had written 'fellow-citizens.'

25. Cf. Alan R. White, "On Being Obliged to Act," in G. N. A. Vessey, ed., *The Human Agent* (London: Macmillan, 1968), pp. 66 ff.

26. See T. N. Macpherson, *Political Obligation* (New York: Humanities Press, 1969), p. 84, and Ladd, op. cit., p. 4.

27. G. E. M. Anscombe, "Modern Moral Philosophy," *Philosophy* XXXIII (1958), pp. 5–26, reprinted in W. D. Hudson, ed., *The Is-Ought Question* (London: Macmillan, 1969), pp. 179 ff.

28. J. S. Mill, *Utilitarianism* (1861), chap. 5. Cf. Hart, "Legal and Moral Obligation," in Melden, ed., op. cit., pp. 102 ff.; Ladd, op. cit., pp. 14–15; and Brandt, op. cit., p. 391.

29. Quite apart from defects in the underlying theory of political obligation, the actual structure of exemptions is open to moral criticism, too. See John de J. Pemberton, Jr., "Equality in the Exemption of Conscientious Objectors," in Tax, ed., op. cit., pp. 66–69; Carl Cohen, "Conscientious Objection," *Ethics* LXXVIII (1968), pp. 269–79; and James Finn, ed., *Conflict of Loyalties* (New York: Pegasus, 1969).

30. 54 Stat. 885, Sec. 5(g) (1940).

31. The term is from Michael Walzer, *Obligations*, pp. 89, 97, 105.

32. The doctrine originated with W. D. Ross, *The Right and the Good* (Oxford: The Clarendon Press, 1930), pp. 19–47.

33. See, for example, Military Selective Service Act (1967), Sec. 6(j).

34. Bruce Chapman, "Politics and Conscription: A Proposal to Replace the Draft," in Tax, ed., op. cit., p. 208; and Walzer, op. cit., pp. 177 f.

35. See, for example, Gabriel Kolko, *The Roots of American Foreign Policy* (Boston: Beacon Press, 1969), and William Appleman Williams, *Roots of the Modern American Empire* (New York: Random House, 1969).

36. A revised version of a paper originally presented at the Ripon College Conference on Rights and Political Action, October 10, 1970. I am grateful to Constance Putnam for comments on an early draft, and to Virginia Held for comments on a later version published in *Inquiry* (1971).

Part III

Constitutionality

15

Thoughts on the Conscription Law of the United States

by

Roger B. Taney

Drawing from the U.S. Constitution, Chief Justice Roger B. Taney demonstrates the unconstitutionality of the Federal Conscription Act of 1863. This act gave the federal government authority to conscript and subject to military law any congressionally nonexempt, able-bodied male citizen of the United States. Insisting on two points—that the Constitution should be consistently interpreted (that all inferences should be consistent with express provisions) and that the United States possesses no original or inherent sovereignty over the states—Taney cites provisions that support his opinion. He argues that, as only the states have constitutional power to determine the composition of their militias, the president therefore has authority only to call state militias as composed by the states to supplement the national force. He concludes that the Conscription Act should be declared void because it abrogates constitutional government, substituting a provisional government with arbitrary power to dissolve the state governments that created it.

Taney accurately foresaw the deeper issue at stake in conscription challenges—the survival of states' rights. His timely and powerful opinion was never delivered.

By the Act of Congress entitled an Act for enrolling and calling out the national forces and for other purposes (generally called the conscription law) all able bodied male citizens of the United States between the ages of twenty and forty-five years except as thereinafter excepted are declared to constitute the national forces and liable to perform military duty in the service of the United States when called out by the President for that purpose.

The 2nd Section excepts and exempts from operation of the Law the Vice President of the United States, the Judges of the various Courts of the United States, the head of the various executive departments of the government, and the governors of the several States, sundry other descriptions of persons are also exempted from family considerations, or want of health, whose exemption is not material to the matter now before the Court.

The 18th Section provides that the persons called out shall be liable to serve for a period not exceeding three years.

The question to be decided is,—Does Congress under the Constitution of the United States possess the power it has in this instance exercised?

In determining this question it is necessary that we should fix clearly in our minds the relative powers of the general and State governments, and the attitude in which they stand to each other when exercising their respective powers.

The confederation which existed prior to the adoption of the present constitution was a mere league of independent States. Each State retained the entire sovereignty within its own territorial limits, and the confederate power could not exercise forcibly any authority civil or military by its own officers within the territories of a State without its consent nor did it possess any power within these limits in any case paramount and superior to that of a State.

It was under these circumstances and in this state of things that the present Constitution was formed.

By adopting this Constitution, the people of the several States created the government of the United States and delegated to it certain specified powers of sovereignty within their respective territories; but in express terms retained all the powers not thereby conferred on the U. States, in their own hands. Two separate governments are thus to exercise powers of sovereignty over the same territory and the same people at the same time. The line of division between them is marked out. Each of them is altogether independent of the other in the sphere of action assigned to it. The power of the Federal government is paramount to that of the State within the limits of its delegated powers. The authority of the several States is equally paramount within the limits retained by the States—neither owes allegiance to, or is inferior to the other, being both sovereignties they stand on equal ground—and the Citizen owes allegiance to the General government to the extent of the powers conferred on it and no further—and he owes equal allegiance to the State to the extent of the sovereign powers they reserved.—The rule as to allegiance and the reason of the rule are clearly stated in I Blackstone's Commentaries, 366, in the following words: "Allegiance is the tie or ligament which binds the subject to the King in return for that protection which the King affords to the subject." — And as neither the Federal government, nor that of a State, could lawfully afford protection to the Citizen beyond the limits of their respective powers, no allegiance can be claimed or is due from the Citizen to either government beyond those limits. It is a divided allegiance but not inconsistent—the boundaries of each sovereignty being defined and established, and not interfering with one another, and each independent of the other in its own sphere of action.

These principles were decided by this Court unanimously and upon much consideration in the case of Ablemore vs. Booth, 21 How. 366. But the great importance of the case now before the Court makes it proper that I should again refer to the clauses in the Constitution which bear upon the subject. Clause 16, S. 8, Article I. authorizes Congress "to make all laws which shall be necessary and proper for carrying into execution the foregoing powers and all other powers vested by this Constitution in the government of the United States, or in any Department or officer thereof.["] And again the second clause of the 6 article declares that ["]this constitution and the laws of the United States which shall be made in pursuance thereof, and all treaties made or which shall be made under the authority of the United States shall be the supreme law of the land, and the Judges in every State shall be bound thereby, anything in the Constitution or laws of any State to the contrary notwithstanding.["]

And Article [10] of the amendments to the Constitution declares "that the powers not delegated to the United States by the Constitution nor prohibited by it to the States are reserved to the States respectively or to the people.["]

These clauses show that the sovereignty of the general government is not a general & pervading one—but is confined to the powers delegated by the Constitution. And all the rights and powers of sovereignty not delegated are reserved to the States. The sovereignty of the State therefore to the extent of this reservation is wholly independent of the general government.

The last mentioned clause it will be observed was an amendment to the original Constitution after it had been fully discussed before the people and in the conventions of the different States, and was manifestly adopted to show more clearly than the original instrument was supposed to do, that no general supremacy over the States was intended to be conferred on the Federal government, and to show by the plainest and most positive words that the States were still sovereignties in their character.

Indeed the sovereignty of the States is expressly recognized in the 2d clause of the 2d Sect. of the 4th Article which provides that "a person charged in any State with treason, felony or other crime who shall flee from justice and be found in another State shall on demand of the Executive authority of the State from which he fled, be delivered up to be removed to the State having jurisdiction of the crime." The State must be sovereign, and the party accused must owe it allegiance in return for the protection it affords him, or the crime of high treason could not be committed against it, nor its Courts have jurisdiction of the offence.

It follows from what is above stated, that the Federal government has no inherent, and original powers of sovereignty. It has only what the States delegated—and any exercise of sovereign power beyond these limits would be a usurpation of State sovereignty—and consequently illegal.

This brings me to inquire whether the power exercised in passing the Conscription Act above mentioned has been delegated to the Federal government.

In pursuing this inquiry we must not confine our attention to a single clause and construe it as if it stood by itself apart from all other provisions. The whole instrument must be taken together—general words in one clause may be restrained in the meaning by other provisions in the instrument and no construction can by any just rule of construction, be given to any one clause, that would make it repugnant to the plain words of another and make the Constitution so carefully and deliberately prepared inconsistent with itself.

Guided by this well established and familiar rule of construction—I proceed to examine the clauses in the Constitution which bear directly on the question.

The Constitution establishes and recognizes two kinds of military force entirely different from each other in their character, obligations and duties.—The 12th clause of the 8th Section of the 1st Article gives to Congress the power to raise and support armies. The power is general,—the number is not limited and it embraces times of peace as well as times of war, when raised it is exclusively subject to the control of the United States authorities.—It is a body of men separated from the general mass of citizen—subject to a different code of laws liable to be tried by Military Courts instead of the Civil Tribunals—and may be employed at all times in or out of the United States, at the pleasure of Congress—and willing or not willing forced to obey the orders of their superior officers. And in the 3rd clause of the 10th Section of the 1st Article it is provided that "no State shall without the consent of Congress [. . .] keep troops or ships of war in time of peace."—The powers given to the general government to raise and support armies, necessarily carries with it the power to appoint their officers, and the power to make rules and regulations for its government is given by the 14th clause of the Section and Article last above referred to.* These rules and regulations so far as they concern the individuals who compose the army are altogether independent of State authority,—and the control of the whole body is exclusively and absolutely in the general government.—They compose the national forces,—or what is called in the Constitution the land forces of the United States.

The other description of military force is the militia over which by the express provisions of the Constitution the general government can exercise no power in time of peace, and but a limited and specified power in time of war.—It will be observed that as relates to the Army the power is given to raise and support it, a power which Congress in its discretion may or may not exercise. But the militia is spoken of, as a known military force, always existing and needing no law to bring it into existence and merely requiring organization, discipline and training to make it efficient.

Thus the clause 16—in the Section and Article aforesaid declares that Congress shall have power "to provide for organizing, arming and disciplining the militia and [for] governing such part of them as may be employed in the service of the United States, reserving to the States respectively the appointment of the officers and the authority of training the militia according to the discipline prescribed by Congress."

The clause immediately preceding (15) gives Congress the power to provide for calling forth the militia to execute the laws of the Union, suppress insurrection, and repel invasion. But what description of persons composes the militia who are thus to be officered and trained by the State,—and may be called to aid the general government in the

---

*[Editor's note]: That is, Article 1, Section 8.

emergencies above mentioned? The answer will be found in the 2d amendment to the Constitution which declares that "A well regulated militia being necessary to the security of a free State, [the] right of the people to keep and bear arms shall not be infringed." The militia is therefore to be composed of Citizens of the States, who retain all their rights and privileges as citizens who when called into service by the United States are not to be fused into one body—nor confounded with the Army of the United States, but are to be called out as the militia of the several States to which they belong and consequently commanded by the officers appointed by the State. It is only in that form or organization that they are recognized in the Constitution as a military force.

The United States can exercise no authority over them except only in the contingencies specified in the Constitution.

This . . . is plainly and distinctly expressed in the 1st clause of the 2nd Section of the Second Article which declares that—

"The President shall be commander in chief of the Army and Navy of the United States and of *the militia of the several States* when called into the actual service of the United States."

The distinction between the Army of the United States and the Militia of the several States and the power which the President may exercise over them respectively is here clearly stated. He has no power over the Militia unless when called into the actual service of the United States. They are then called out in the language of the Constitution, as the militia of the several States. The General government has no militia, it has only the Army and Navy—The militia force duly organized and ready to be called out belongs to the several States and may be called on in the emergencies mentioned to aid the land and naval forces of the United States.

But if the act of Congress of which I am speaking can be maintained all of the clauses in the Constitution above referred to are abrogated. There is no longer any militia—it is absorbed in the Army.— Every able bodied Citizen, not exempted by that law, belongs to the national forces—that is to the Army of the United States. They are not to be called out as the Militia of a State—but as a part of its land forces—and subject as soon as called on to all the obligations of a private soldier, in the ranks of the regular army.

The Generals, Colonels and other Officers appointed by the State according to the provisions of the Constitution are reduced to the ranks, and compelled to march as private soldiers and obey the orders of such persons as the President may select to command them, and they and every other able bodied citizen except those whom it has been the pleasure of Congress to exempt, are compelled against their will to subject

THOUGHTS ON THE CONSCRIPTION LAW | 213

themselves to military law, to be tried by military Courts instead of the civil tribunals—and to be treated as deserters if they refuse to surrender their civil rights.

It appears to me impossible to believe that a Constitution and form of government framed by such men can contain provisions so repugnant to each other. For if the conscription law be authorized by the Constitution, then all of the clauses so elaborately prepared in relation to the militia, coupled as they are with the declaration "that a well regulated militia is necessary for the security of a free State," are of no practical value and may be set aside and annulled whenever Congress may deem it expedient.

The power to do this is, I understand, claimed under the clause which gives Congress the power to raise and support armies.

It is true that the power is delegated without specifying the manner in which the armies are to be raised. But no inference can be drawn from these general words that would render null and inoperative the plain and specific provisions in regard to the militia, to which I have above referred. No just rule of construction can give any weight to inferences drawn from general words, when these inferences are opposed to special and express provisions, in the same instrument.

But apart from this consideration the words themselves, even if they stood alone, will not, according to their known and established use and meaning in the English language, justify this construction.

During the period when the United States were English Colonies, the Army of England,—the standing army,—was always raised by voluntary enlistments,—and the right to coerce all the able bodied subjects of the Crown into the ranks of the Army and subject them to military law, was not claimed or exercised by the English government—and when the power to raise and support armies was delegated to Congress, the words of the grant necessarily implied that they were to be raised in the usual manner.—And the general government has always heretofore so understood them and has uniformly by its own officers recruited the ranks of its "land forces" by voluntary enlistments for a specified period.

The general words "to provide and maintain a navy" could with much more apparant plausibility be construed to authorize coercion when a sufficient number of volunteer seamen could not be obtained. For at the time the Constitution was adopted and long before it had been the practice of the British government to compel by force seamen to serve on board its ships of war whenever there was a deficiency of volunteers—and it might be said with some appearance of reason, that the power to provide and maintain a navy, implied that it was to be provided and maintained in the same manner that it had been provided and maintained by the government under which we had before lived.— I do not think the Whalers and Fishermen, and Seamen of the Northern States would assent to such a construction or admit it to be correct.—It certainly would not be correct—for such a power over landsmen or seamen would have been repugnant to the principles of the government which was then framed and adopted.

It is true also that the act recites in the preamble that an insurrection and rebellion exists against the authority of the United States, and that it is its duty to suppress it.—But this is the very crisis which the framers of the Constitution foresaw might happen and has given to the general government the powers they deemed adequate to meet it, or safe to grant.

It is the state of things in which Congress is authorized to provide for calling out the militia of the several States and if that course was pursued, the forces called out would be commanded by officers appointed by the State,—and it can hardly be maintained that where a specific power is given to Congress in a certain contingency, Congress may when the contingency happens repudiate the means prescribed in the Constitution and adopt others which it may deem more effectual,— such a construction would make the Constitution of no higher authority than an act of Congress,—and every provision in it liable to be repealed and altered or disregarded whenever in the judgment of a majority of the Legislature the public interest would be promoted by the exercise of powers not conferred.

Much has been said in Courts of Justice as well as elsewhere of the war powers of the general government, and it seems to be assumed that the Constitution was made for a time of peace only and that there is no provision for a time of war. I can see no ground whatever for this argument. The war power of the Federal government is as clearly defined in the Constitution as its powers in time of peace.—Congress may raise and support armies,—it may provide and establish a Navy,—it may lay an embargo,—it may provide for calling out the militia of the several States—it may grant letters of marque and reprisal,—it may suspend the habeas corpus,—it may quarter soldiers in a house without the consent of the owner, in a manner to be regulated by law, which it cannot do in time of peace. These are all war powers—powers to be exercised in time of war—or in preparation for war.—And when we find these powers and none others enumerated and conferred for war purposes, it is conclusive proof that they are all that were deemed necessary, and that it was not deemed safe or prudent to trust more in the hands of the new government. This conclusion seems inevitable when we find that all powers not delegated to the general government or forbidden to the States were reserved to the States and the people. The same considerations apply with equal force to the case of an insurrection or rebellion against the authority of the United States. The Habeas Corpus may be suspended and the militia called out to suppress it.—The Constitution has armed the general government with these powers to meet the emergency mentioned in the preamble to this law. But it seems to be supposed that these measures are not adequate to meet the crisis,—and that the Federal government may for the time disregard the limitations of power contained in the Constitution and adopt any measures it may deem necessary to put down the rebellion. This view of the subject, in its effect, puts aside the government created by the Constitution and establishes a temporary or provisional government in its place.—But the Judiciary who derive all the power they possess from the Constitutional government—and have all sworn to support it, would hardly be justified in violating any of its provisions—or in sanctioning their violation by any other Department of the government.—They can never be called on to execute or enforce unconstitutional laws or recognize as justifiable assumptions of power which the Constitution has not conferred.

But there is a more serious objection to this act of Congress—than those above stated.—It enables the general government to disorganize at its pleasure the government of the States,—by taking forcibly from them the public officers necessary to the execution of its laws.

I have already spoken of the sovereignty reserved to the States, as altogether independent of the sovereignty of the United States and in no respect subordinate to it. It had high duties to perform in the protection of the persons and property of the citizen in preserving the peace and promoting the prosperity of the Citizens of the State. And as the militia when called into the service of the United States were to be taken from the people of the State it is essential to the existence of State Sovereignty that its governors, judges and civil officers necessary for the purpose of carrying on the government should not be taken away, and the government thereby disorganized and rendered incapable of fulfilling the duties for which it was created, what officers are required for that purpose, the State sovereignty alone can judge, accordingly we find in the clause of the Constitution herein before referred to, that no power is granted to the Federal government to determine what description of persons shall compose the military force called the militia; the power to provide for organizing, arming and disciplining the militia, was necessarily delegated to Congress to make that arm of the military force efficient by conforming that organization and discipline to that of the army, so that when called into the service of the United States they might conveniently act together.

But the power prescribed who shall be liable to be called on and who exempted, is not given, not any power from which it can be inferred, on the contrary the right to appoint the officers and train the men is reserved to the State.—The State must therefore determine who are to be trained, and they are to be selected from the people or the State.—It would necessarily happen that many from age or infirmity were unfit for military duty—and many would hold official stations essential to the existence and exercise of the State government; of this the people of the State have the sole right to judge. And such persons would not be enrolled and trained by the State because their duties required them to be elsewhere. And if the services of the militia were called for by the United States those only who were enrolled and trained under the State officers would be required by the State to respond to the call, and the State government would go on fulfilling its functions without interruption or inconvenience.

But the Act of Congress assumes the right of the General government to enroll in the national forces of the United States, and in the army or "land forces" as they are called in the Constitution, every able bodied male citizen of the State without regarding the position he may hold in the State government—neither the judges nor executive officers, except the governor, are exempted and are made liable to trial by military court, and to punishment as deserters, if they refuse to march when ordered by the President.—What is to become of the people of a State if their executive officers and judges are taken away, and their Courts of Justice shut up? It will hardly be said in defence of the law that the Governor may appoint others to fill their places; for I believe it will be found that the people of no one of the States anticipated the possibility of such a state of things and have not therefore made provisions in their respective Constitutions to meet it. And indeed if every able bodied citizen is liable to the Conscription unless exempted by Congress, the Governors of the States, if they had not been specially exempted, might be forced into the army, and find themselves standing by the side of their generals and Judges as privates in the ranks and commanded and disciplined by officers appointed by a different sovereignty.

Neither does the privilege of hiring substitutes or paying $300. lessen the constitutional objections to the law. For the State Officers could not be required to furnish substitutes or pay $300. unless the power exists to compel them to serve in person.

There can be no actual government without proper officers to exercise its powers and execute its laws. The act in question shows that Congress was fully sensible of this,—and has exempted all of the executives and judicial officers of the United States, whose services are required to carry on the government.—That government is preserved in the full, free and uninterrupted exercise of all its powers. But it exempts none of the Officers of the State governments, but the Governor—and it leaves him without any other officer, executive or judicial. How is the peace of the State to be preserved, and the laws efficiently executed, if the whole or even a part of the officers of the State to whom these duties have been assigned are taken away and forced into the Army of the United States? No one I think can believe that the men who framed the Constitution could have intended to give to the new sovereignty they then created the power to paralyze or cripple the old ones, so as to disable them from executing the power expressly reserved to them,—powers essential to the safety of the people of the State and which the State government alone could exercise under the provisions of the Constitution.

I speak of the Constitutional and lawful power, not of the physical power which the Constitution has placed in the hands of the Federal government.

For in a contest of mere force, a State would meet the United States upon very unequal terms—prepared as the latter always is with a disciplined army and navy at its command.—But so far from intending to give the general government the power to disorganize the government of a State they have carefully and jealously excluded it from any right to interfere in the domestic controversies and difficulties of a State, even where its aid might be supposed to be useful. For in the case of rebellion or insurrection against the State government, the United States is not allowed to interfere in it, to support the State authority, unless its assistance is applied for by the Legislature of the State or by the Executive where the Legislature cannot be convened (Art.—4, S. 4.) scarcely any provision could more strongly show how anxiously and jealously the sovereignty of the States was guarded from any interposition by the United States.—It is not permitted even to defend it, unless their assistance is asked for by the State authorities.

The circumstance that the Federal government pervades the whole union, and that its power within the sphere of action assigned to it, is supreme over that of the States, is perhaps calculated to create an impression upon the minds of those whose pursuits have not led them to examine particularly the provisions of the Constitution,—that its supremacy over the State extends to all cases where the general government may choose to exercise it.—The character of the powers assigned to it, and in which its power is supreme, is also calculated to attract the public attention far more than the quiet exercise of State powers, in any single State.—But it must be remembered that State Sovereignty also pervades every part of the Union and in that respect is coextensive with that of the United States.—In every part of the Union (except the territories) there is a State government, exercising independently of the general government, all the powers not delegated to the United States. These powers although not so striking as those exercised by the general Government are not less important to the happiness of the people.— For while the powers conferred on the general government contain mainly our foreign relations and the intercourse between the different States, it is the State Sovereignty which preserves tranquillity in the State, and guards the life, liberty and property of the individual Citizen, and protects him in his home and in his ordinary business pursuits.

It cannot be that the men who framed the Constitution, or the people who adopted it could have regarded these interests as of less value than those committed to the care of the Federal government,—and could have intended on that account to give the latter the power, whenever it deemed it expedient to paralyze the action of the State governments,—and leave the people to choose between anarchy on the one side, or a purely unlimited military despotism on the other, to be coerced by the U. States.

For the reasons above stated, I am of opinion that this Act of Congress is unconstitutional and void,—and confers no lawful authority on the persons appointed to execute it.

"Thoughts on the Conscription Law of the U. States—Rough Draft Requiring Revision," by Roger B. Taney, Copied from the Unpublished Manuscript (in His Own Handwriting) by M. L. York for Geo. Bancroft, 7 May 1886 [document caption]. For permission to use this material, grateful acknowledgment is extended to the New York Public Library, Astor, Lenox and Tilden Foundations, Manuscripts and Archives Division, Bancroft Collection.

ROGER BROOKE TANEY (1777–1864) was attorney general of the United States under President Jackson and fifth chief justice of the Supreme Court (1836–1864). A member of the Southern landed gentry, he is principally associated with the *Dred Scott* decision, in which Scott, a slave, was declared a noncitizen and therefore without the right to sue, and for related decisions barring Negroes from U.S. citizenship and forbidding Congress the power to exclude slavery from U.S. territories.

16

Selective Draft Law Cases:
A Supreme Court Decision

by
Edward White

The Supreme Court delivered its unanimous landmark decision of 1918 in response to the political pressures of World War I and legal cases challenging the constitutionality of presidential authority to draft citizens directly and call up state "National" Guard and Reserve units into the regular national force. The decision was of an advocacy nature. Citing historical arguments where it should have cited constitutional ones, assuming points it should have scrutinized, and arguing that the Fourteenth Amendment provides for the dominance of federal over state citizenship that it expressly does not, the High Court summarily ratified an alleged power of the federal executive and legislative branches to directly call U.S. citizens to raise a national army. This decision circumvented the constitutionally explicit right of states to act as intermediaries in the decision whether to provide their individual militias.

Though the Constitution allows for direct manpower procurement under a clause granting Congress general power to declare war and raise and support armies, under the consistency principle it provides this power only for citizens not actively participating in a state militia (now our National Guard and Reserves) at the time of the call. These points were avoided by the justices, whose decision struck a powerful blow to states' rights.

This is the full text of the decision—minus citations—as delivered by Chief Justice White.

We are here concerned with some of the provisions of the Act of May 18, 1917, entitled, "An Act to authorize the President to increase temporarily the Military Establishment of the United States." The law, as its opening sentence declares, was intended to supply temporarily the increased military force which was required by the existing emergency, the war then and now flagrant. The clauses we must pass upon and those which will throw light on their significance are briefly summarized:

The act proposed to raise a national army, first, by increasing the regular force to its maximum strength and there maintaining it; second, by incorporating into such army the members of the National Guard and National Guard Reserve already in the service of the United States (Act of Congress of June 3, 1916), and maintaining their organizations to their full strength; third, by giving the President power in his discretion to organize by volunteer enlistment four divisions of infantry; fourth, by subjecting all male citizens between the ages of twenty-one and thirty to duty in the national army for the period of the existing emergency after the proclamation of the President announcing the necessity for their service; and fifth, by providing for selecting from the body so called, on the further proclamation of the President, 500,000 enlisted men, and a second body of the same number should the President in his discretion deem it necessary. To carry out its purposes the act made it the duty of those liable to the call to present themselves for registration on the proclamation of the President so as to subject themselves to the terms of the act and provided full federal means for carrying out the selective draft. It gave the President in his discretion power to create local boards to consider claims for exemption for physical disability or otherwise made by those called. The act exempted from subjection to the draft designated United States and state officials as well as those already in the military or naval service of the United States, regular or duly ordained ministers of religion and theological students under the conditions provided for, and, while relieving from military service in the strict sense the members of religious sects as enumerated whose tenets excluded the moral right to engage in war, nevertheless subjected such persons to the performance of service of a non-combatant character to be defined by the President.

The proclamation of the President calling the persons designated within the ages described in the statute was made, and the plaintiffs in error, who were in the class and under the statute were obliged to present themselves for registration and subject themselves to the law, failed to do so and were prosecuted under the statute for the penalties for which it provided. They all defended by denying that there had been conferred by the Constitution upon Congress the power to compel military service by a selective draft, and asserted that even if such power had been given by the Constitution to Congress, the terms of the particular act for various reasons caused it to be beyond the power and repugnant to the Constitution. The cases are here for review because of the constitutional questions thus raised, convictions having resulted from instructions of the courts that the legal defenses were without merit and that the statute was constitutional.

The possession of authority to enact the statute must be found in the clauses of the Constitution giving Congress power "to declare war; . . . to raise and support armies, but no appropriation of money to that use shall be for longer term than two years; . . . to make rules for the government and regulation of the land and naval forces." Article I, §8. And of course the powers conferred by these provisions like all other powers given carry with them as provided by the Constitution the authority "to make all laws which shall be necessary and proper for carrying into execution the foregoing powers." Article I, § 8.

As the mind cannot conceive an army without the men to compose it, on the face of the Constitution the objection that it does not give power to provide for such men would seem to be too frivolous for further notice. It is said, however, that since under the Constitution as originally framed state citizenship was primary and United States citizenship but derivative and dependent thereon, therefore the power conferred upon Congress to raise armies was only coterminous with United States citizenship and could not be exerted so as to cause that citizenship to lose its dependent character and dominate state citizenship. But the proposition simply denies to Congress the power to raise armies which the Constitution gives. That power by the very terms of the Constitution, being delegated, is supreme. Article VI. In truth the contention simply assails the wisdom of the framers of the Constitution in conferring authority on Congress and in not retaining it as it was under the Confederation in the several States. Further it is said, the right to provide is not denied by calling for volunteer enlistments, but it does not and cannot include the power to exact enforced military duty by the citizen. This however but challenges the existence of all power, for a governmental power which has no sanction to it and which therefore can only be exercised provided the citizen consents to its exertion is in no substantial sense a power. It is argued, however, that although this is abstractly true, it is not concretely so because as compelled military service is repugnant to a free government and in conflict with all the great guarantees of the Constitution as to individual liberty, it must be assumed that the authority to raise armies was intended to be limited to the right to call an army into existence counting alone upon the willingness of the citizen to do his duty in time of public need, that is, in time of war. But the premise of this proposition is so devoid of foundation that it leaves not even a shadow of ground upon which to base the conclusion. Let us see if this is not at once demonstrable. It may not be doubted that the very conception of a just government and its duty to the citizen includes the reciprocal obligation of the citizen to render military service in case of need and the right to compel it. To do more than state the proposition is absolutely unnecessary in view of the practical illustration afforded by the almost universal legislation to that effect now in force. In England it is certain that before the Norman Conquest the duty of the great militant body of the citizens was recognized and enforcible. It is unnecessary to follow the long controversy between Crown and Parliament as to the branch of the government in which the power resided, since there never was any doubt that it somewhere resided. So also it is wholly unnecessary to explore the situation for the purpose of fixing the sources whence in England it came to be understood that the citizen or the force organized from the militia as such could not without their consent be compelled to render service in a foreign country, since there is no room to contend that such principle ever rested upon any challenge of the right of Parliament to impose compulsory duty upon the citizen to perform military duty wherever the public exigency exacted, whether at home or abroad. This is exemplified by the present English Service Act.

In the Colonies before the separation from England there cannot be the slightest doubt that the right to enforce military service was unquestioned and that practical effect was given to the power in many cases. Indeed the brief of the Government contains a list of Colonial acts manifesting the power and its enforcement in more than two hundred cases. And this exact situation existed also after the separation. Under the Articles of Confederation it is true Congress had no such power, as its authority was absolutely limited to making calls upon the States for the military forces needed to create and maintain the army, each State being bound for its quota as called. But it is indisputable that the States in response to the calls made upon them met the situation when they deemed it necessary by directing enforced military service on the part of the citizens. In fact the duty of the citizen to render military service and the power to compel him against his consent to do so was expressly sanctioned by the constitutions of at least nine of the States, an illustration being afforded by the following provision of the Pennsylvania constitution of 1776. "That every member of society hath a right to be protected in the enjoyment of life, liberty and property, and therefore is bound to contribute his proportion towards the expense of that protection, and yield his personal service when necessary, or an equivalent thereto." While it is true that the States were sometimes slow in exerting the power in order to fill their quotas—a condition shown by resolutions of Congress calling upon them to comply by exerting their compulsory power to draft and by earnest requests by Washington to Congress that a demand be made upon the States to resort to drafts to fill their quotas—that fact serves to demonstrate instead of to challenge the existence of the authority. A default in exercising a duty may not be resorted to as a reason for denying its existence.

When the Constitution came to be formed it may not be disputed that one of the recognized necessities for its adoption was the want of power in Congress to raise an army and the dependence upon the States for their quotas. In supplying the power it was manifestly intended to give it all and leave none to the States, since besides the delegation to Congress of authority to raise armies the Constitution prohibited the States, without the consent of Congress, from keeping troops in time of peace or engaging in war. Article I, §10.

To argue that as the state authority over the militia prior to the Constitution embraced every citizen, the right of Congress to raise an army should not be considered as granting authority to compel the citizen's service in the army, is but to express in a different form the denial of the right to call any citizen to the army. Nor is this met by saying that it does not exclude the right of Congress to organize an army by voluntary enlistments, that is, by the consent of the citizens, for if the proposition be true, the right of the citizen to give consent would be controlled by the same prohibition which would deprive Congress of the right to compel unless it can be said that although Congress had not the right to call because of state authority, the citizen had a right to obey the call and set aside state authority if he pleased to do so. And a like conclusion demonstrates the want of foundation for the contention that, although it be within the power to call the citizen into the army without his consent, the army into which he enters after the call is to be limited in some respects to services for which the militia it is assumed may only be used, since this admits the appropriateness of the call to military service in the army and the power to make it and yet destroys the purpose for which the call is authorized—the raising of armies to be under the control of the United States.

The fallacy of the argument results from confounding the constitutional provisions concerning the militia with that conferring upon Congress the power to raise armies. It treats them as one while they are different. This is the militia clause:

> The Congress shall have power . . . To provide for calling forth the militia to execute the laws of the Union, suppress insurrections and repel invasions; To provide for organizing, arming, and disciplining the militia, and for governing such part of them as may be employed in the service of the United States, reserving to the States, respectively, the appointment of the officers, and the authority of training the militia according to the discipline prescribed by Congress. Article I, § 8.

The line which separates it from the army power is not only inherently plainly marked by the text of the two clauses, but will stand out in bolder relief by considering the condition before the Constitution was adopted and the remedy which it provided for the military situation with which it dealt. The right on the one hand of Congress under the Confederation to call on the States for forces and the duty on the other of the States to furnish when called, embraced the complete power of government over the subject. When the two were combined and were delegated to Congress all governmental power on that subject was conferred, a result manifested not only by the grant made but by the limitation expressly put upon the States on the subject. The army sphere therefore embraces such complete authority. But the duty of exerting the power thus conferred in all its plenitude was not made at once obligatory but was wisely left to depend upon the discretion of Congress as to the arising of the exigencies which would call it in part or in whole into play. There was left therefore under the sway of the States undelegated the control of the militia to the extent that such control was not taken away by the exercise by Congress of its power to raise armies. This did not diminish the military power or curb the full potentiality of the right to exert it but left an area of authority requiring to be provided for (the militia area) unless and until by the exertion of the military power of Congress that area had been circumscribed or totally disappeared. This, therefore, is what was dealt with by the militia provision. It diminished the occasion for the exertion by Congress of its military power beyond the strict necessities for its exercise by giving the power to Congress to direct the organization and training of the militia (evidently to prepare such militia in the event of the exercise of the army power) although leaving the carrying out of such command to the States. It further conduced to the same result by delegating to Congress the right to call on occasions which were specified for the militia force, thus again obviating the necessity for exercising the army power to the extent of being ready for every conceivable contingency. This purpose is made manifest by the provision preserving the organization of the militia so far as formed when called for such special purposes although subjecting the militia when so called to the paramount authority of the United States. But because under the express regulations the power was given to call for specified purposes without exerting the army power, it cannot follow that the latter power when exerted was not complete to the extent of its exertion and dominant. Because the power of Congress to raise armies was not required to be exerted to its full limit but only as in the discretion of Congress it was deemed the public interest required, furnishes no ground for supposing that the complete power was lost by its partial exertion. Because, moreover, the power granted to Congress to raise armies in its potentiality was susceptible of narrowing the area over which the militia clause operated, affords no ground for confounding the two areas which were distinct and separate to the end of confusing both the powers and thus weakening or destroying both.

And upon this understanding of the two powers the legislative and executive authority has been exerted from the beginning. From the act of the first session of Congress carrying over the army of the Government under the Confederation to the United States under the Constitution down to 1812 the authority to raise armies was regularly exerted as a distinct and substantive power, the force being raised and recruited by enlistment. Except for one act formulating a plan by which the entire body of citizens (the militia) subject to military duty was to be organized in every State which was never carried into effect, Congress confined itself to providing for the organization of a specified number distributed among the States according to their quota to be trained as directed by Congress and to be called by the President as need might require. When the War of 1812 came the result of these two forces composed the army to be relied upon by Congress to carry on the war. Either because it proved to be weak in numbers or because of insubordination developed among the forces called and manifested by their refusal to cross the border, the Government determined that the exercise of the power to organize an army by compulsory draft was necessary and Mr. Monroe, the Secretary of War (Mr. Madison being President), in a letter to Congress recommended several plans of legislation on that subject. It suffices to say that by each of them it was proposed that the United States deal directly with the body of citizens subject to military duty and call a designated number out of the population between the ages of 18 and 45 for service in the army. The power which it was recommended be exerted was clearly an unmixed federal power dealing with the subject from the sphere of the authority given to Congress to raise armies and not from the sphere of the right to deal with the militia as such, whether organized or unorganized. A bill was introduced giving effect to the plan. Opposition developed, but we need not stop to consider it because it substantially rested upon the incompatibility of compulsory military service with free government, a subject which from what we have said has been disposed of. Peace came before the bill was enacted.

Down to the Mexican War the legislation exactly portrayed the same condition of mind which we have previously stated. In that war, however, no draft was suggested, because the army created by the United States immediately resulting from the exercise by Congress of its power to raise armies, that organized under its direction from the militia and the volunteer commands which were furnished, proved adequate to carry the war to a successful conclusion.

So the course of legislation from that date to 1861 affords no ground for any other than the same conception of legislative power which we have already stated. In that year when the mutterings of the dread conflict which was to come began to be heard and the Proclamation of the President calling a force into existence was issued it was addressed to the body organized out of the militia and trained by the States in accordance with the previous acts of Congress. That force being inadequate to meet the situation, an act was passed authorizing the acceptance of 500,000 volunteers by the President to be by him organized into a national army. This was soon followed by another act increasing the force of the militia to be organized by the States for the purpose of being drawn upon when trained under the direction of Congress, the two acts when considered together presenting in the clearest possible form the distinction between the power of Congress to raise armies and its authority under the militia clause. But it soon became manifest that more men were required. As a result the Act of March 3, 1863, was adopted entitled "An Act for enrolling and calling out the National Forces and for other purposes." By that act which was clearly intended to directly exert upon all the citizens of the United States the national power which it had been proposed to exert in 1814 on the recommendation of the then Secretary of War, Mr. Monroe, every male citizen of the United States between the ages of twenty and forty-five was made subject by the direct action of Congress to be called by compulsory draft to service in a national army at such time and in such numbers as the President in his discretion might find necessary. In that act, as in the one of 1814, and in this one, the means by which the act was to be enforced were directly federal and the force to be raised as a result of the draft was therefore typically national as distinct from the call into active service of the militia as such. And under the power thus exerted four separate calls for draft were made by the President and enforced, that of July, 1863, of February and March, 1864, of July and December, 1864, producing a force of about a quarter of a million men. It is undoubted that the men thus raised by draft were treated as subject to direct national authority and were used either in filling the gaps occasioned by the vicissitudes of war in the ranks of the existing national forces or for the purpose of organizing such new units as were deemed to be required. It would be childish to deny the value of the added strength which was thus afforded. Indeed in the official report of the Provost Marshal General reviewing the subject it was stated that it was the efficient aid resulting from the forces created by the draft at a very critical moment of the civil strife which obviated a disaster which seemed impending and carried that struggle to a complete and successful conclusion.

Brevity prevents doing more than to call attention to the fact that the organized body of militia within the States as trained by the States under the direction of Congress became known as the National Guard. And to make further preparation from among the great body of the citizens, an additional number to be determined by the President was directed to be organized and trained by the States as the National Guard Reserve.

Thus sanctioned as is the act before us by the text of the Constitution, and by its significance as read in the light of the fundamental principles with which the subject is concerned, by the power recognized and carried into effect in many civilized countries, by the authority and practice of the colonies before the Revolution, of the States under the Confederation and of the Government since the formation of the Constitution, the want of merit in the contentions that the act in the particulars which we have been previously called upon to consider was beyond the constitutional power of Congress, is manifest. Cogency, however, if possible, is added to the demonstration by pointing out that in the only case to which we have been referred where the constitutionality of the Act of 1863 was contemporaneously challenged on grounds akin to if not absolutely identical with, those here urged, the validity of the act was maintained for reasons not different from those which control our judgment. And as further evidence that the conclusion we reach is but the inevitable consequence of the provisions of the Constitution as effect follows cause, we briefly recur to events in another environment. The seceding States wrote into the constitution which was adopted to regulate the government which they sought to establish, in identical words the provisions of the Constitution of the United States which we here have under consideration. And when the right to enforce under that instrument a selective draft law which was enacted, not differing in principle from the one here in question, was challenged, its validity was upheld, evidently after great consideration, by the courts of Virginia, of Georgia, of Texas, of Alabama, of Mississippi and of North Carolina, the opinions in some of the cases copiously and critically reviewing the whole grounds which we have stated.

In reviewing the subject, we have hitherto considered it as it has been argued, from the point of view of the Constitution as it stood prior to the adoption of the Fourteenth Amendement. But to avoid all misapprehension we briefly direct attention to that Amendment for the purpose of pointing out, as has been frequently done in the past, how completely it broadened the national scope of the Government under the Constitution by causing citizenship of the United States to be paramount and dominant instead of being subordinate and derivative, and therefore, operating as it does upon all the powers conferred by the Constitution, leaves no possible support for the contentions made, if their want of merit was otherwise not so clearly made manifest.

It remains only to consider contentions which, while not disputing power, challenge the act because of the repugnancy to the Constitution supposed to result from some of its provisions. First, we are of opinion that the contention that the act is void as a delegation of federal power to state officials because of some of its administrative features, is too wanting in merit to require further notice. Second, we think that the contention that the statute is void because vesting administrative officers with legislative discretion has been so completely adversely settled as to require reference only to some of the decided cases. A like conclusion also adversely disposes of a similar claim concerning the conferring of judicial power. And we pass without anything but statement the proposition that an establishment of a religion or an interference with the free exercise thereof repugnant to the First Amendment resulted from the exemption clauses of the act to which we at the outset referred, because we think its unsoundness is too apparent to require us to do more.

Finally, as we are unable to conceive upon what theory the exaction by government from the citizen of the performance of his supreme and noble duty of contributing to the defense of the rights and honor of the nation, as the result of a war declared by the great representative body of the people, can be said to be the imposition of involuntary servitude in violation of the prohibitions of the Thirteenth Amendment, we are constrained to the conclusion that the contention to that effect is refuted by its mere statement.

Affirmed.

"Selected Draft Law Cases: A Supreme Court Decision," by Edward White, from *Current History*, Volume 54, Number 322 (June 1968), pages 359–363. Copyright © 1968 Current History, Inc. Reprinted by permission of the publisher.

EDWARD DOUGLASS WHITE (1845–1921) was U.S. senator and ninth chief justice of the Supreme Court (1911–1921). He is principally remembered for his 1911 decision that restraint of trade by a monopoly must be judged "unreasonable" to be illegal. He wrote important decisions favoring federal emergency powers during World War I and upheld military conscription in the 1917 Selective Draft Law case of *Arver* v. *U.S.*

17

Conscription and the Constitution: The Original Understanding

by

Leon Friedman

Friedman attempts to assess exactly what the framers of the Constitution had in mind when they gave Congress express power to "raise and support armies." He concludes that, within the historical context in which the Constitution was written, Congress was never intended to have the power to conscript. Friedman then examines the 1918 Supreme Court decision, which first upheld the constitutionality of congressional conscription, and argues that the decision was unsound. He

This Article is based upon a study which was prepared for the New York Civil Liberties Union as a basic memorandum on the military clauses of the Constitution. Its purpose was to show that the Military Selective Service Act of 1967 is unconstitutional since it exceeds the powers granted to the federal government. This Article does not purport to examine the desirability or undesirability of any system of federal conscription; it attempts only to marshal the available historical evidence to demonstrate that the framers of the Constitution did not intend to grant Congress the power to conscript.

The author wishes to acknowledge the editorial suggestions of Alan H. Levine of the New York Civil Liberties Union, and the invaluable assistance in researching and preparing this Article provided by Edwin G. Burrows, David Osher, and Dennis Van Essendelft, of the Columbia University Graduate Department of History.

claims it was based on superficial arguments, disregarded substantial historical evidence, and gave undue deference to the exigencies of World War I.

I. Introduction

The general words of the Constitution—famous phrases such as "due process," "freedom of speech," "interstate commerce," and "raise and support armies"—are not self-evident concepts. As Justice Frankfurter said, "The language of the [Constitution] is to be read not as barren words found in a dictionary but as symbols of historic experience illumined by the presuppositions of those who employed them. Not what words did Madison and Hamilton use, but what was it in their minds which they conveyed?"[1] While the framers obviously could not have foreseen the discovery of electromagnetic radio waves or atomic energy, and had no "intent" concerning the regulation of television stations or uranium piles, they knew only too well the dangers of a professional army and the need for training and mobilizing the citizens for defense. They considered these problems in more detail than those of virtually any other governmental function, and thus the plans they made for our nation's military forces deserve detailed inquiry. Such a study reveals that the military structure presently existing in the United States, which depends primarily upon direct conscription of citizens into the federal army, fails to meet the standards established by the framers of the Constitution in 1787.

Arguments about conscription produce rather strange alliances. The left has traditionally opposed the draft on the grounds that it violates the conscientious beliefs of those opposed to war, compels participation in military adventures against reform movements throughout the world, and generally lays the heavy hand of government too forcefully on the shoulders of every citizen. The continuing viability of this tradition is exemplified by Senator Mark Hatfield's recent assertion that a volunteer army would "preserve individual liberty and freedom as much as possible from unjustified intrusion by the government" and still provide "maximum national security with the greatest efficiency and economy."[2] The far right also has frequently called for a volunteer army, but for markedly different reasons. Many conservatives and military men prefer a professional army since regulars are more easily trained and controlled, and a permanent corps is more efficient in the long run because of the lower turn-over in personnel. Such a professional force also fits traditional elitist ideas held by the right about the organization of society.

Others have argued that a federal draft is necessary not only to mobilize the nation's manpower most efficiently in an emergency, but also to serve as a check upon military adventures that offend the political conscience of the country. While a volunteer army would necessarily be "composed of the poor and the black,"[3] a conscripted army is made up of all classes. And, to the extent that the sons of the middle class are unwilling hostages of the military, their parents will want to know exactly where they will be sent and why. Opposition to the Vietnam war seems to be growing even among the traditionally conservative areas of the Midwest for precisely this reason. President Nixon, who reads the political pulse very clearly, has pressed for an end to the war and an end to the draft[4] because he is aware of these sentiments.

Thus, the basic organization of our military forces involves problems that are crucial to the democratic process. The worries and concerns that troubled the framers of the Constitution are still with us, and, as the debate on the draft continues, another look backward may be worthwhile.

II. The Selective Draft Law Cases

A. Background of the Cases

In the 1918 decision of the *Selective Draft Law Cases* (*Arver v. United States*),[5] the United States Supreme Court first upheld the constitutionality of congressional conscription. These decisions have never been seriously challenged, and have been cited repeatedly as determining that question once and for all time. This Article will attempt to show that the *Selective Draft Law Cases* were based upon superficial arguments, disregard of substantial historical evidence, and undue deference to the exigencies of the First World War—in short, that they were incorrectly decided.

The cases arose in the midst of World War I and were decided only eight months after passage of the 1917 draft law.[6] The Selective Draft Act had been signed into law on May 18, 1917, and June 5 was set as registration day for all young men of draft age. Two who refused to register were Joseph F. Arver and Otto H. Wangerin; they were indicted on June 8, 1917, tried the following month before a United States district court in Minnesota, found guilty, and sentenced to one year in prison. The Supreme Court granted a writ of error directly to the trial court,[7] and argument was presented on December 13 and 14, 1917, along with the cases of other draft resisters from New York. At the same time the Court heard the appeals of Alexander Berkman and Emma Goldman,[8] two noted anarchist leaders who had been found guilty of conspiring to counsel resistance to the draft law in New York, and the appeals of Charles E. Ruthenberg, Alfred Wagenknecht, and Charles Baker, prominent Ohio Socialists who were convicted of encouraging a young man not to register.[9]

In asserting the invalidity of the draft, the defendants pressed two primary arguments: that the thirteenth amendment's prohibition of involuntary servitude deprived Congress of any power to conscript; and that the draft conflicted with the militia clauses of the Constitution since the federal government had effectively destroyed the state forces by drawing all the members of the state militia into federal service and shipping them overseas. In the course of their argument, the defendants traced the history of English military organization, emphasizing that no general conscription law had been passed in England prior to the twentieth century. They also claimed that the acts and regulations of the draft unlawfully delegated legislative authority to the President.

The Government's case was argued by John W. Davis, then Solicitor General, later Democratic presidential candidate, and one of the greatest advocates ever to practice before the Supreme Court. Davis submitted a joint brief for all of the cases, and Chief Justice Edward White carefully followed it in his opinion upholding the law. Davis characterized the power to conscript as an essential attribute of sovereignty. He cited the large number of nations enforcing compulsory military service in 1917, concluding: "It would be a contradiction in terms to declare the Government of the United States a sovereign, endowed with all the powers necessary for its existence, yet lacking in the most essential of all—the power of self-defense."[10] The Government also cited the many colonial and state laws in force before 1787—almost 200 were listed—calling for compulsory militia service by all male citizens. Davis argued that the fact that a federal draft was proposed (although not passed) in 1814 and the fact that a conscription law was enacted during the Civil War showed the practical exercise of the power and was therefore a recognition of it.

Nor were the militia clauses of the Constitution[11] relevant, he claimed, since men were taken directly into a federal army by the 1917 law rather than as members of a federalized state militia. Finally, the Government dismissed the thirteenth amendment argument by pointing out that the sole purpose of the amendment was to abolish chattel slavery, not to eliminate compulsory governmental service.

Surprisingly, none of the parties in the *Selective Draft Law Cases* relied to any extent on precedent or history. There had been a few remarks about conscription in earlier federal cases,[12] and a Pennsylvania Supreme Court case, *Kneedler v. Lane*,[13] had upheld the Civil War draft. But no Supreme Court decision that was on point had ever been handed down. Even though the Government's brief was 137 pages long, only three pages were devoted to the Constitutional Convention of 1787 and to the various state ratifying conventions while an additional three pages contained citations from *The Federalist Papers*. Yet these sources are traditionally the most important aid to constitutional interpretation. Moreover, the petitioners' briefs in *Arver* discussed the same subject matter in only one paragraph. Thus, the Court was deprived of the most crucial materials on which to base its decision.

The Supreme Court's unanimous opinion upholding the conscription law followed the government's presentation closely. In essence, Chief Justice White found that the constitutional provisions granting Congress power "to declare war"[14] and "to raise and support armies,"[15] combined with the necessary and proper clause, permitted the Government to draft citizens directly into a federal army.[16]

The Chief Justice's opinion placed principal reliance on five points. (1) The constitutional language allowing Congress to raise armies permitted a compulsory draft, since Congress must have the power to procure men by any means for those armies. (2) All nations as attributes of sovereignty have the right to conscript. (3) The English had compelled military service throughout their history. (4) The colonies had also used conscription into the militia. (5) The Continental Congress' lack of power to raise and control its own army was one of the reasons for the formation of the new Constitution. The Court then went beyond the Federalist period and noted that in 1814 Secretary of War James Monroe had proposed a plan for conscription, and that a conscription law had been passed during the Civil War. An analysis of each constituent part of the Court's opinion shows how the political pressures of World War I produced a chain of errors in this most crucial case concerning the federal government's relationship to its citizens.

B. Constitutional Language

Chief Justice White began his opinion by quoting the various military clauses in the Constitution. He then wrote:

As the mind cannot conceive an army without the men to compose
it, on the face of the Constitution the objection that it does not give
power to provide for such men would seem to be too frivolous for
further notice. . . . [I]t is said, the right to provide is not denied by
calling for volunteer enlistments, but it does not and cannot include
the power to exact enforced military duty by the citizen. This however but challenges the existence of all power, for a governmental
power which has no sanction to it and which therefore can only be
exercised provided the citizen consents to its exertions is in no substantial sense a power.[17]

However, as shown below,[18] the proposed grant of power to raise a
federal army by any means was questioned or opposed by a substantial
political group when the Constitution was submitted for ratification.
The Antifederalists did not wish a standing army of any kind to be
established by the central government; thus the bare power to *enlist* a
military force was significant in terms of the Confederation experience
and in terms of the restrictions suggested by the critics of the Constitution. Furthermore, none of the federal government's enumerated
powers can be exercised "without the men to compose" the offices involved. Did the grant of authority "to establish Post Offices" carry with
it the power to conscript postmen? Does the power to "coin money"
include the power to conscript employees for the mint? Without the
specific grants in article I, Congress might not be able to expend public
monies to build post offices or mints or to buy arms, and might not
even be able to pay its employees in these branches of government. But
no one ever suggested before the *Arver* case that any other enumerated
power included authority to compel service in the governmental organization involved.

C. Universality of Conscription

To show that compulsory service was required by the Constitution,
the Court noted that in 1918 most of the nations of the world had
compulsory military service.[19] However, the fact that every other nation in the world may have enforced conscription during World War I
is irrelevant if the framers of the Constitution did not grant Congress
that power. The United States may be the only nation with an electoral
college system of choosing its chief executive or with a federal system
with prohibitions on local interference with interstate commerce. The
fact that virtually every other jurisdiction in the world permits the use
of illegally seized evidence in criminal trials is of no relevance when an
interpretation of our Constitution is at issue.

Compulsory military service was not enacted in any modern nation until more than ten years after the ratification of the Constitution. A leading authority on conscription has described it as "something characteristically modern [which] occurred for the first time in France [in] 1798."[20] Moreover, to argue that the Constitution does not permit a draft does not deny the "obligation of the citizen to render military service in case of need and the right to compel it." The framers knew that the nation's manpower might have to be marshalled in an emergency; but, as shown below, the system they selected was one requiring mobilization through the state militia system, not direct conscription into a federal army. Finally, at present, a much smaller group of nations enforces direct conscription than did in 1918; for example, Great Britain, Canada, India, and Pakistan do not have a direct draft today.[21] But clearly the Constitution does not change as a larger or smaller number of foreign states pass laws on military service, and thus the *Arver* Court's reliance on the universality of conscription is at best marginally relevant.

D. The English Experience

The next argument advanced in the *Selective Draft Law Cases* was drawn from the military history of Great Britain. In one rather terse paragraph, the Court concluded:

> In England it is certain that before the Norman Conquest the duty of the great militant body of the citizens was recognized and enforcible. . . . It is unnecessary to follow the long controversy between Crown and Parliament as to the branch of the government in which the power resided, since there never was any doubt that it somewhere resided. So also it is wholly unnecessary to explore the situation for the purpose of fixing the sources whence in England it came to be understood that the citizen or the force organized from the militia as such could not without their consent be compelled to render service in a foreign country, since there is no room to contend that such principle ever rested upon any challenge of the right of Parliament to impose compulsory duty upon the citizen to perform military duty wherever the public exigency exacted, whether at home or abroad. This is exemplified by the present English Service Act.[22]

To cite the English experience before the Norman Conquest as a precedent for the American Constitution is far fetched at the very least. Similarly, the fact that the English Service Act of 1916 may have compelled service abroad has little relevance to the intention of the framers in 1787. But, ignoring these difficulties, the Court leaped over a thousand years of English history in a few brief sentences and disregarded the crucial period preceding the Revolutionary War. The latter omission is particularly unfortunate, for an examination of the relevant historical period clearly demonstrates that during colonial times the regular army forces in England were always composed of volunteers.

In Cromwell's time, the Levellers and other republican supporters had demanded specific protection against conscription as part of the basic freedoms of all Englishmen. The original "Agreement of the People" presented to the Council of the Army in 1647 contained a section which proclaimed that "constraining any of us to serve in the wars is against our freedom; and therefore we do not allow it in our Representatives."[23]

The Agreement of the People which was finally passed by the House of Commons in 1648 specifically provided:

> We do not empower [Parliament] to impress or constrain any person to serve in foreign war, either by sea or land, nor for any military service within the kingdom; save that they may take order for the forming, training and exercising of the people in a military way, to be in readiness for resisting of foreign invasions, suppressing of sudden insurrections, or for assisting in execution of the laws; and may take order for the employing and conducting of them for those ends; provided, that even in such cases, none be compellable to go out of the county he lives in, if he procure another to serve in his room.[24]

The behavior of Cromwell's troops in suppressing Parliament and taking command of the government proved to later commentators that a standing military force, independent of legislative control, was the most dangerous enemy of liberty. John Trenchard, one of the great liberal pamphleteers and an important influence on American colonial thought, wrote in 1698 that Cromwell's reign was

> a true and lively Example of a Government with an Army; an Army that was raised in the Cause, and for the sake of Liberty; composed for the most part of Men of Religion and Sobriety. If this Army could commit such violences upon a Parliament always successful, that had acquired so much Reputation both at home and abroad, at a time when the whole People were trained in Arms, and the Pulse of the Nation beat high for Liberty; what are we to expect . . . in a future Age.[25]

Trenchard described the subsequent excesses of Charles II's time—the bribery of Parliament, the dissolution of the municipal corporations, the defiance of the Constitution—as a direct outgrowth of the king's control of a professional army.[26] Seizing upon the pretext of a war with Holland, Charles raised a force of 12,000 men but kept half of them near London so that they would be available for use against the legislative leaders. When the House of Commons ordered the Army disbanded, Charles dissolved Parliament; a new House again voted to disperse the army, and passed a resolution stating that *"the continuance of any Standing Forces in this Nation other than the Militia, was illegal, and a great Grievance and Vexation to the People."*[27]

Charles' successor, James II, continued the effort to maintain his own armed forces. When the Duke of Monmouth attempted to overthrow him in 1685, James increased the army to 15,000 men and later 30,000. To strengthen his position against Parliament, he sought allies among the Protestant dissenters and filled the army with Irish Catholics until they constituted about one third of his total forces. According to Trenchard, James "violated the Rights of the People, fell out with the Church of *England,* made uncertain Friends of the Dissenters and disobliged his own Army; by which means they all united against him."[28] William of Orange and Mary ascended to the English throne in 1689, and shortly thereafter Parliament passed a Declaration of Rights, the basic Bill of Rights in the English Constitution. The sixth article of the Declaration stated: "That the raising or keeping a standing army within the kingdom in time of peace, unless it be with consent of parliament, is against law."[29] In Trenchard's view, however, even William went too far in organizing his army. War in Ireland led Parliament to grant the king 50,000 men and Trenchard wrote: "I will venture to say, that if this Army does not make us Slaves, we are the only People upon Earth in such Circumstances that ever escaped it, with the 4th part of their number."[30]

John Trenchard and his later collaborator Thomas Gordon were significant transmitters of English liberal thought to the colonies. Historian Bernard Bailyn wrote of the English "coffeehouse radicals":

> More than any other single group of writers they shaped the mind of the American Revolutionary generation. To the colonists the most important of these publicists and intellectual middlemen were those spokesmen for extreme libertarianism, John Trenchard . . . and Thomas Gordon.[31]

The overreachings of Cromwell, Charles II, and James II through their control of standing armies were prominent in the minds of the colonists as examples of the destruction of freedom; as Trenchard had written, "in no Country, Liberty and an Army stand together; so that to know whether a People are Free or Slaves, it is necessary only to ask, whether there is an Army kept amongst them."[32] The answer to this threat lay in a militia system in which the "Nobility and chief Gentry of England are the Commanders, and the Body of it made up of the Freeholders, their Sons and Servants."[33] To Englishmen who shared this belief that a professional army was an instrument of tyranny, the idea of direct conscription into that force was unthinkable.

Proposals to conscript for the regular Army were advanced in Parliament in 1704 and 1707, but were rejected.[34] Moreoever, under the military laws passed in 1756,[35] 1757,[36] 1778,[37] and 1779,[38] only idle and disorderly persons were pressed into service, and then only as punishment. This too was strongly condemned. It is true that compulsory service for the British militia system was theoretically established during this period; the act of 1757 provided an elaborate structure for choosing the militia on a territorial basis.[39] However, an extensive system of exemptions or substitutes made it extremely unlikely that a nonvolunteer would be taken. Professor J. R. Western, the leading expert on the English militia system, has noted:

> The development of the law on the raising of militiamen can be summed up by saying that the principle of obligatory personal service receded farther and farther into the background. Every facility and encouragement was given for the discharge of the obligation by some means of voluntary enlistment, and few balloted men seemed to have had to serve in person save by their own free will.[40]

Professor Western also points out that a great many Englishmen found compulsory military service so "profoundly distasteful" that there were numerous riots against service in the militia after passage of the act of 1757, but that popular unrest abated when it became understood that the law could be avoided and "real conscription was not to be introduced."[41] This strong popular opposition to conscription occurred despite the fact that the English militia acts specifically provided that no militiamen would be forced to serve abroad and that only a limited amount of service was required at home.[42] Nonetheless popular hostility to military service was widespread and the people's aversion to forced military service, even in the militia, continued for many years.

The American colonial leaders were steeped in this anti-military tradition; the available evidence indicates that they were extremely sensitive to the dangers of a professional army and that they saw clearly the distinction between regular forces and the armed citizenry composing the militia. They were also conscious of the fact that no general compulsory conscription law for the regular army was in force in England during the eighteenth century.

E. The Colonial Militia

After discussing the English experience, the Supreme Court in the *Selective Draft Law Cases* cited the colonial militia system as a precedent for conscription:

> In the Colonies before the separation from England, there cannot be the slightest doubt that the right to enforce military service was unquestioned and that practical effect was given to the power in many cases. Indeed the brief of the Government contains a list of Colonial acts manifesting the power and its enforcement in more than two hundred cases. . . . [I]t is indisputable that the States in response to the calls made upon them [by the Continental Congress] met the situation when they deemed it necessary by directing enforced military service on the part of the citizens. In fact the duty of the citizen to render military service and the power to compel him against his consent to do so was expressly sanctioned by the constitutions of at least nine of the States.[43]

However, the colonial militia system has only the most tenuous connection to any modern conscription program. In the first place, the militia was thought of as the armed citizenry as a whole; that is, every able-bodied man was expected to own a weapon and to use it for the protection of his colony. Second, the primary duty expected of each militiaman was merely that he enroll, arm, muster, and attend periodic general training sessions.[44] This system hardly qualifies as a precedent for forced conscription of a citizen for an uninterrupted period in a regular army.

As Professor Russell F. Weigley points out, a distinction soon developed between the "Common Militia"—the entire population of able-bodied men—and the "Volunteer Militia," which in fact performed the functions required of an armed force:

> When troops were needed for a campaign, the legislatures assigned quotas to the local militia districts. The local officials then called for volunteers and could impress or draft men when sufficient numbers did not come forward. Usually, compulsory service was limited to expeditions within the colony. . . . Out of these methods there naturally grew more or less permanent formations of those persons willing to volunteer for active duty. . . .[45]

The Selective Service System in its 1947 monograph *The Backgrounds of Selective Service* attempted to expand the *Arver* opinion's collection of compulsory colonial laws, citing hundreds of statutes which it claimed were precedents for federal conscription. But the laws show that the only element of compulsion in the colonial militia related to mustering and training. The training itself was often extremely lax, except in times of emergency.[46] Furthermore, most of the colonial statutes requiring periods of actual military service rather than mere training stipulated that the power existed only for defensive purposes. The Virginia statutes, for example, provided that men could be raised only in case of attack or upon certain knowledge of Indian presence.[47]

Initially, most of the colonial laws restricted militia service to duty within the colony except in emergency situations, when the governor could permit service outside the borders for limited purposes.[48] In later years the laws restricted to nonfreeholders compulsory service which would lead to expeditions outside the colony. A Virginia law passed in 1752[49] gave the colony power to levy vagrants or nonvoters, but no person who had a right to vote could be forced to serve outside of Virginia. A later Virginia statute[50] also provided that only vagrants and the unemployed could be impressed for service beyond the borders of the colony. This restriction was congruent with the English practice, which made the militia strictly a county force except in time of invasion and excluded all peacetime service outside the immediate borders of the organizing province.

The Massachusetts laws were comparable. Special legislation was necessary to permit service outside the colony,[51] and service was required only against an "attempt or enterprise [at] the destruction or invasion, detriment or annoyance of our province."[52] Similarly, South Carolina passed a law in 1778 permitting "all idle, lewd, disorderly men," "sturdy beggars," and "vagrants" to go out of the state into the Continental Army ranks to fill the state's quotas.[53]

In many states personal service from each citizen was not required. Liberal laws existed which provided for either substitution or payment of a small fine in lieu of service. For example, in Massachusetts there were five laws passed between 1740 and 1781 allowing a man to arrange for a substitute to take his place in the militia.[54] Other states, including Connecticut, Virginia, and New York, passed legislation providing for a small fine which freed citizens from virtually all forms of militia service. This practice became increasingly frequent in later years of the colonial period.[55]

By the 1750's and the 1760's the need for even minimal universal training of all the males of the colonies had receded, and the trend was away from any kind of compulsion. No fewer than nine states abandoned compulsory military establishments in this period.[56] The fact that vagrants and the unemployed were swelling the ranks of the militia, as they had filled the ranks of the British standing army following the statute of 1756, made military service less and less desirable. A recent commentator has noted:

> It is difficult to believe that the colonial volunteers of the eighteenth century had more in common with the pityable [*sic*] recruits of the contemporary European armies than with the militia levies of an earlier period; nevertheless, changes in the social composition of American forces between about 1650 and 1750 were in that direction. . . .
>
> Perhaps the vital change was in the tone of active service: with more social pariahs filling the ranks and military objectives less clearly connected to parochial interests, respectable men felt not so impelled by a sense of duty or guilt to take up arms. Only when a war approached totality (as in the Puritan crusade to Louisbourg in 1745, when an impressive percentage of Massachusetts manpower served in the land and sea forces) might the older attitude appear.[57]

Only during the emergency of the Revolution was this trend reversed and compulsory service reintroduced. But every effort was made to fill the Continental Army quotas with nonvoters and nonfreeholders.

Thus, the colonial experience showed only that (1) the primary compulsory aspect of the militia was the requirement to train; (2) the militia was fundamentally a defensive force; (3) continuous service was required solely during periods of emergency; (4) service outside the colony was for outcasts only; and (5) the trend was away from compulsion in the years preceding the Revolution. It is therefore not surprising that the Selective Service System was obliged to admit that the "evidence reveals no preconstitutional systems valuable as models" for a universal draft.[58]

F. Formation of the Constitution

Another proposition which the Supreme Court relied upon to uphold the constitutionality of the draft related to the creation of a new government in 1787. The Court noted:

> When the Constitution came to be formed it may not be disputed that one of the recognized necessities for its adoption was the want of power in Congress to raise an army and the dependence upon the States for their quotas. In supplying the power it was manifestly intended to give it all and leave none to the States, since besides the delegation to Congress of authority to raise armies the Constitution prohibited the States, without the consent of Congress, from keeping troops in time of peace or engaging in war.[59]

This statement, however, completely jumbles a very complicated political process which began before the Revolution. The experience of the nation during the war and the dangers which the Constitution-makers were concerned about cannot be telescoped in the offhand way that the Court attempted in the *Selective Draft Law Cases*. A more detailed analysis of that period is necessary.

III. Formulation of the Military Clauses of the Constitution

A. Political Background

As noted above, widespread revulsion existed in the American colonies against a standing professional army. Almost all of the colonial statesmen were familiar with John Trenchard's essays, in which he repeatedly sought to demonstrate that "unhappy Nations have lost that precious Jewel *Liberty* . . . [when] their Necessities or Indiscretion have permitted a Standing Army to be kept amongst them."[60] The behavior of British troops in America during the ten years before the Revolution confirmed their worst fears of this danger. When British troops landed in Boston in 1768 Andrew Eliot, a leading statesman, wrote: "To have a standing army! Good God! What can be worse to a people who have tasted the sweets of liberty!"[61] The Boston Massacre of 1770 and passage of the Quartering Act in 1774, which permitted the seizure of all buildings for the use of British troops, showed the colonists how accurate Trenchard had been. Indeed, one of the principal complaints expressed in the Declaration of Independence was that George III "has kept among us, in times of peace, standing armies without the consent of our legislatures," and "has affected to render the military independent of and superior to the civil power."

As a result of the popular apprehensions about the military, the Continental Congress imposed strict control over the army that it organized to fight the Revolutionary War. Marcus Cunliffe, the distinguished English historian, has recently concluded that: "[T]he Continental Congress and the majority of Americans were sometimes more concerned with the danger of military overlordship than the danger of military inefficiency. From a combination of doctrine and habit they were reluctant to create their own version of a standing army."[62] Examples of the distrust are plentiful; for instance, the Continental Congress insisted on regular reports from its commanding officer, George Washington, appointed his staff officers, and obliged him to consult with his generals in council before any major military decision was made.[63] Even in the midst of the war, Connecticut proposed that no peacetime army should be allowed.[64]

Furthermore, throughout the Revolution, Congress was never given any power to conscript soldiers directly into the Continental ranks. It had to rely primarily on the militia forces of the various states for the bulk of its fighting men. These forces were occasionally supplemented by enlistments; in June 1775, Congress permitted the enlistment of ten companies into the Continental Army to help New England militia forces around Boston. Although Congress later authorized increased musters, the enlistments, which ran generally for one year, always fell far below expectations. Short-term enlistments seemed an unnecessary leniency in the face of the national emergency, but as Professor Weigley has observed, "the basic cause of that policy was not Congressional folly but the caution necessary in creating a professional army among a people who had fled Europe partly to escape such armies."[65]

When the states were called upon for levies or quotas of troops to meet specific campaign needs, the Continental Congress could not even compel them to deliver the number of troops requisitioned; as might be expected, some were notoriously slow in providing manpower. George Washington suggested a direct draft system in 1777, 1778, and 1780, but "Congress did not dare invoke the instrument in any year of the war."[66] The most that the Continental Congress was prepared to do was to urge the states to deliver their quotas "by draughts, or in any other manner they shall think proper."[67]

However, the states were reluctant to rely upon conscription as a means of satisfying their congressional quotas. In part, this hesitancy may have resulted from the feeling that the state militia systems contained safeguards for the individual which would be vitiated when state forces were put under the control of the central government. While the militia laws had a compulsory element in that all the male citizens had to enroll, train, and muster, the militiamen were usually enrolled with their friends under officers whom they had known most of their lives. As noted above, generous provisions existed for paid substitutes to take the place of those unwilling to serve, and the laws generally provided that the troops could not be sent outside their immediate borders without the consent of the legislature or the governor. The government leaders who controlled the militia were also subject to close electoral check. But none of these safeguards was present when a distant central authority in which the state had only one of thirteen voices decided whom or where the men had to fight. Thomas Jefferson expressed the prevailing sentiment in the states in a letter to John Adams, dated May 16, 1777:

> Our battalions for the Continental service was sometime ago so far filled as rendered the recommendation of a draught from the militia hardly requisite. And the more so as in this country it ever was the most unpopular and impracticable thing that could be attempted. Our people under the monarchical government have learnt to consider it as the last of all oppressions.[68]

The Continental Congress not only had to rely on the states for quotas of troops for each campaign; it also had to come hat-in-hand to them for money to pay for the troops it enlisted and the supplies it required, since Congress had no power to tax.[69] Each state was obliged to pay a proportion of the general expenses, based on its population. The states moved as slowly to supply money as they did to furnish men for the Continental cause; by 1780, fifty million dollars in quotas remained unpaid, and Congress was powerless to demand compliance.[70]

There was another reason why the states were not prepared to surrender control of their individual militias to the central authorities: they wished to insure that they would have sufficient manpower to protect their own borders. The generous bounties offered by the states often meant that their ranks were adequate at the same time that the Continental army was experiencing the greatest difficulties recruiting troops. The state bounties "almost put a stop to enlistments in the Continental Army, for few engaged to serve three years . . . when by volunteering to serve in the militia for a few months they received a bigger bounty and higher pay."[71] When the states did supply troops to the central government, they wanted to retain direct control over their own forces even in the field. Early in the war, for example, Samuel Adams of Massachusetts wrote to Elbridge Gerry that "the Militia of each Colony should be and remain under the sole Direction of its own Legislative which is and ought to be the sovereign and uncontroulable power within its own limits or Territory."[72] Gerry agreed with Adams, and responded: "We already see the growing thirst for Power in some of the inferior departments of the army, which ought to be regulated so far as to keep the military entirely subservient to the civil in every part of the United Colonies."[73] This combination of Congress' dependence on the states for men and money and the states' constant attempts to interfere with the military authorities nearly drove George Washington to distraction. In 1780 he wrote, "I most firmly believe that the Independence of the United States never will be established until there is an Army on foot for the War; that [if we are to rely on occasional or annual levies] we must sink under the expence; and ruin must follow."[74]

Thus, the American leaders emerged from the Revolution with four separate and conflicting ideas about organizing the military power of the United States:

1. Washington and other military leaders claimed that a federal, professional army, financed by the central government, had to be maintained.[75]

2. The political leaders continued to reflect the long-established popular fear of a standing army. Samuel Adams indicated the prevalence of this view even after the war when he wrote that a "standing army, however necessary it may be at some times, is always dangerous to the liberties of the people. Soldiers are apt to consider themselves as a body distinct from the rest of the citizens."[76]

3. The states continued to see the importance of maintaining as much control over their own militia as they possibly could.

4. The idea of a direct draft by a central government acting upon every citizen without the intervening authority of the state governments was firmly and totally rejected even at the darkest moments of the Revolution.

The experience of the new nation immediately after the Revolutionary War confirmed each of these notions. The deplorable state of the nation's finances made the members of the army uneasy about the bounties and pay allowances which had been promised them. In 1783, a group of officers in New Jersey drew up a list of complaints and hinted at mutiny if they were not fulfilled; later the same year eighty Pennsylvania soldiers marched from Lancaster to Philadelphia and barricaded the Continental Congress in the State House while demanding redress of their grievances.[77] The apprehension that these actions caused led Congress to reduce the federal army to fewer than one hundred men. However, because of the need to defend the large Northwest section of the country and to garrison the various forts in Indian territory, the army was increased to approximately seven hundred men in 1785. When Shays' Rebellion broke out in 1786 in western Massachusetts—near the Springfield arsenal where the bulk of the Continental military stores were located—the army was increased to two thousand men. But the Massachusetts militia, and not the federal army, finally dispersed the rebels. To George Washington, Secretary of War Henry Knox, and others, the uprising demonstrated that the Confederation had become so feeble that it was unable to defend even its forts and arsenals.[78]

The danger of popular uprisings such as Shays' Rebellion was one of the contributing factors leading to the call for the Constitutional Convention in the spring of 1787. But, while the weakness of the federal authorities during the Revolution and Shays' Rebellion disturbed many of the political leaders, they did not lose their well-established distrust of centralized government in general and of standing armies in particular.[79] The attempt by king and parliament to rule from across the seas through a professional army was not to be duplicated in the United States. Again and again during this period the people expressed their fear of too strong a central authority;[80] the constant refrain that "the purse and the sword" were not to be put in the same hands meant that the power to tax and spend the public monies and an unlimited power to control the military should not be combined. In general, it was felt that a new balance should be created, giving the federal authorities some power to raise money, to establish a uniform currency, and to exercise direct command over a small military force required for essential tasks. But under no circumstances did the people wish to invest a new centralized government, over which they had little control, with the power to build up a standing army like the one that had been the instrument of oppression before 1775.

B. The Philadelphia Constitutional Convention

The Philadelphia Convention commenced its proceedings on May 28, 1787. The presentation of credentials, election of a chairman and adoption of rules took place on the first and part of the second day; the main business of the Convention began on May 29 with a speech by Edmund Randolph, Governor of Virginia and leader of the largest and most prestigious delegation. In his lengthy discourse, he enumerated the defects of the Articles of Confederation and commented upon the troubles then facing the separate states, including Shays' Rebellion in Massachusetts, the "havoc of paper money," violated treaties, and commercial discord. He then introduced a fifteen-point plan for a new federal government which could correct these shortcomings.[81] The Randolph or Virginia Plan became the basis for discussing changes in the Confederation and served as the skeleton of the new Constitution. Randolph must therefore be considered one of the chief architects of the Constitution.

The very first defect of the government under the Articles of Confederation, according to Randolph, stemmed from its inability to defend itself against foreign invasion. As Madison reported his remarks, Randolph said the following:

> He then proceeded to enumerate the defects: 1. that the confederation produced no security agai[nst] foreign invasion; congress not being permitted to prevent a war nor to support it by th[eir] own authority—Of this he cited many examples; most of wh[ich] tended to shew ... that particular states might by their conduct provoke war without controul; and that *neither militia nor draughts being fit for defence on such occasions, enlistments only could be successful,* and these could not be executed without money.[82]

James McHenry of Maryland took down a more complete description of Randolph's speech. Elaborating on the enumerated defects, Randolph noted that the Confederation had no means of preventing the states from provoking foreign invasion.[83] The Confederation, he said, could not even support a war; the states were constantly in arrears to the federal treasury, and the journals of the Continental Congress showed that a series of feeble expedients had been employed in the attempt to raise money for the nation's defense. He continued:

> What reason to expect that the treasury will be better filled in the future, or that money can be obtained under the present powers of Congress to support a war. Volunteers not to be depended on for such a purpose. Militia difficult to be collected and almost impossible to be kept in the field. *Draughts stretch the strings of government too violently to be adopted.* Nothing short of a regular military force will answer the end of war, and this only to be created and supported by money.[84]

Thus, at the very outset Randolph phrased the problem of providing an army in terms of *money.* Volunteer companies who would enlist without bounties—a system urged by many leaders and included in some of the early military laws—were "not to be depended on." Since Congress had been totally dependent on the states for its revenues—including the money required for defense—a change was necessary in order to give the central government sufficient funds to support its army. The humiliating spectacle of Congress pleading with the states for money to defend the country could not continue; the "military force" to be raised under the new Constitution was one that had to be financed directly by the government. But Randolph, expressing the views of the strongest Federalist delegates—those who wished to give the national government the widest powers—excluded the power to conscript as too dangerous: it "stretch[ed] the strings of government too violently to be adopted." The debates in the Convention, and those that took place afterwards in the states, centered on the desirability of his fourth alternative, on "enlistments" which alone "could be successful."[85] The question to which the political leaders addressed themselves was whether federal officials should have the funds and authority to pay for a professional volunteer army and the right to control such a force.

Since the states had made every effort to retain command over their militia even when the troops were fighting under the Continental aegis, it was important to Randolph and other Federalists that direct control of a central army be in the hands of the new government. And, because the states had proved so reluctant to meet their quotas during the Revolution, it was important that the central authorities be free to enlist their forces directly from the people rather than being required to act through the states. But the delegates realized that they tread on dangerous ground by suggesting the formation of such a force in peacetime. What could be "worse to a people who have tasted the sweets of liberty" than a standing army? However, the idea of a direct draft of citizens into the national military was rejected on the very first day of the Convention as a matter too impossible to consider. No one—not the stanchest Federalist in the hall—was prepared to go that far.

Following discussion of the various elements of the Randolph Plan, which contained no specific military clause, attention focused on the alternative scheme introduced by William Paterson of New Jersey. It proposed that the executive "direct all military operations; provided that none of the persons composing the federal Executive shall on any occasion take command of any troops, so as personally to conduct any enterprise as General or in any other capacity."[86] The Committee of Detail, assigned to prepare the actual words of the new Constitution, in its fourth working draft of late July, suggested that the new government be empowered to "make war," "raise armies," and "equip Fleets."[87] For unknown reasons, the seventh draft recommended that "the Legislature of U.S. shall have the exclusive power—of raising a military Land Force—of equipping a Navy";[88] but the ninth draft returned to the original phraseology, "to make war; to raise armies, to build and equip Fleets." Shortly thereafter the Convention accepted a motion to change "raise armies" to "raise and support armies" and "build and equip" a navy to "provide and maintain."[89]

At this point the Convention encountered its first real difficulties with the Government's power to raise and support armies; the key issue was again the historic fear of standing armies. Madison had already warned:

A standing military force, with an overgrown Executive will not long be safe companions to liberty. The means of defense agst. foreign danger, have been always the instruments of tyranny at home. . . . Throughout all Europe, the armies kept up under the pretext of defending, have enslaved the people. It is perhaps questionable, whether the best concerted system of absolute power in Europe cd. maintain itself, in a situation, where no alarms of external danger cd. tame the people to the domestic yoke.[90]

Elbridge Gerry of Massachusetts also was greatly concerned about the military clause. He acknowledged that the chief defect under the Articles of Confederation was the fact that the "existing Congs. is so constructed that it cannot of itself maintain an army."[91] But, while many Antifederalists later advocated an absolute prohibition on a standing army in time of peace, Gerry was prepared to grant a limited power to Congress in this area.[92] His solution was to allow Congress to use funds for maintaining a specific number of troops: "He proposed that there should not be kept up in time of peace more than ——— thousand troups. His idea was that the blank should be filled with two or three thousand."[93] Discussion continued with several members offering solutions to this problem, but ultimately no limit was imposed.

The Convention hedged even the limited power that it granted to buy an army through enlistments by insisting that "no appropriation of money to that use shall be for a longer term than two years."[94] By making the army return to the people—the legislative branch—for funds every two years, the delegates sought to minimize the dangers of tyranny. They considered this method of control more appropriate than a restriction on the number of troops or a ban on any peacetime establishment.[95] Later, George Mason introduced a resolution to preface the militia sections of the Constitution with a clause stating "that the liberties of the people may be better secured against the danger of standing armies in time of peace."[96] The motion was seconded by Randolph, and James Madison spoke in favor of it: "It did not restrain Congress from establishing a military force in time of peace if found necessary; and as armies in time of peace are allowed on all hands to be an evil, it is well to discountenance them by the Constitution, as far as will consist with the essential power of the Govt. on that head."[97] The motion, however, did not pass.

In summary, article I, clause 12 gave Congress a power it lacked under the Confederation—the unlimited authority to use federal funds to enlist an army. The power was granted because, as Randolph had observed, the militias were "difficult to be collected and . . . kept in the field" and because no other alternative seemed feasible. But the historic fears of a standing army led the delegates to limit the power at what they considered its source—by restricting the funds available to maintain an army. Clause 12 answered the concern of those who wished the new government to have *some* authority to keep up *some kind* of independent military force which would be used for specific national purposes. But it was hardly a blank check for the government to use *all* authority to raise *any* forces it desired in *any* manner it chose. Certainly it did not grant the power to draft; even the Federalists believed that such authority would "stretch the strings of government too violently to be adopted."

The manner in which the militias were organized confirms the idea that the body of state militias consisting of the citizens at large, and not a national professional standing army, was intended to be the main military force of the United States. When Randolph introduced the original Virginia Plan, he suggested that "the national legislature" should have authority "to call forth the force of the Union agst. any member of the Union failing to fulfill its duty under the articles thereof."[98] The issue was proposed three times with one change: "the federal Executive," said the advocates of this modification, "shall be authorized to call forth ye power of the Confederated States, or so much thereof as may be necessary to enforce and compel an obedience to such Acts, or an Observance of such Treaties" that were passed by Congress.[99]

The Convention was caught between two conflicting imperatives. On the one hand, they did not want the national authorities to coerce citizens with a standing army; on the other hand, if the only alternative power, the militia, were used as the primary arm of the United States, would it not then become a mere tool of the federal government? Hamilton, indeed, had thought it desirable for "the Militia of all the States to be under the sole and exclusive direction of the United States."[100] But this idea, never formally submitted, was hardly acceptable. The states would not give up complete control over their own forces. The solution came in one of the many compromises made during the Convention. The Committee of Detail in reporting the third draft of the Constitution provided that no state shall keep a naval or land force, "Militia excepted to be disciplined, etc. according to the Regulations of the U.S."[101] This language was elaborated by James Wilson, who proposed a clause stating that the legislature of the United States "shall possess the exclusive Right of establishing the Government and Discipline of the Militia—and of ordering the Militia of any State to any Place within U.S."[102] By the time that the ninth draft was completed, the clause provided that Congress would have the power "to <make laws for> call<ing> forth the Aid of the Militia, in order to execute the Laws of the Union, <to> enforce Treaties, <to> suppress Insurrections, and repel invasions."[103] With the deletion of the reference to treaties,[104] this became clause 15 of article I, section 8 of the Constitution.

In the debate on the militia power, the delegates were quite concerned that there should be national uniformity in the regulation of the militia.[105] The matter was debated on August 18, 1787, with Oliver Ellsworth insisting that the whole authority of the militia should not be taken away from the states. Roger Sherman, John Dickinson, and George Mason attempted to work out a compromise allowing the government to exercise control over a certain portion of the Militia, one fourth to one tenth. Madison advocated national control, arguing: "If the States would trust the Genl. Govt. with a power over the public treasure, they would from the same consideration of necessity grant it the direction of the public force."[106] Moreover, Madison asserted, only the federal government had a full view of the general situation and could mobilize and marshal the necessary forces to meet any contingency. General C. C. Pinckney, on the basis of his military experience, had very "scanty faith in Militia. There must be also a real military force. . . . The United States had been making an experiment without it, and we see the consequence in their rapid approaches toward anarchy," a reference to Shays' Rebellion in Massachusetts the prior year.[107] Roger Sherman, however, insisted that the states would need their own militia for defense against invasion and insurrection and for enforcing obedience to their own laws. The matter was referred to a select committee at that point.

The debate on the matter was resumed on August 23, 1787. The select committee had proposed that Congress be given the power "to make laws for organizing, arming, disciplining the Militia, and for governing such parts of them as may be employed in the service of the U.S. reserving to the States respectively, the appointment of the officers, and authority of training the militia according to the discipline prescribed."[108] Once again Elbridge Gerry attacked the whole notion of giving the central government power over the militia[109] while Madison insisted that uniformity was necessary because the states neglected their militia. "The Discipline of the Militia is evidently a *National* concern," Madison said, "and ought to be provided for in the *National* Constitution."[110] The Convention passed the proposal by a vote of nine to two, agreeing to a provision which allowed Congress "[t]o make laws for organizing arming & disciplining the Militia, and for governing such part of them as may be employed in the service of the U.S."[111] During the debate on the question whether the states should be free to appoint officers of the militia, Madison observed:

> As the greatest danger is that of disunion of the States, it is necessary to guard agst. it by sufficient powers to the Common Govt. and as the greatest danger to liberty is from large standing armies, it is best to prevent them by an effectual provision for a good Militia.[112]

A clause allowing the states to appoint all of their officers was passed, and, with minor changes made by the Committee on Style, it remains in the Constitution substantially as recommended by the Committee of Detail.[113]

The debate over the organization of the militia again points out how unthinkable it was to the framers that the central government could have any direct power to draft individual citizens into the general army. Only with the greatest reluctance did the delegates allow the central government to call the militia into service for specific purposes. The reason was obvious—a tyrannical central government with a large army would be able to destroy the hard-won liberties of the people. On the other hand, some central control was necessary to mobilize the militia for defense purposes and to compel obedience to the laws. But all the restrictions which the Convention imposed on this power, the fact that the states would be able to appoint the officers and train the militia, and the fact that the general government could control the militia only for the purpose of executing the laws of the Union, suppressing insurrections, and repelling invasions indicate that the framers were quite concerned about the danger of the central government using its military forces to suppress the freedoms of the people.

After circumscribing the central government's power to draw the militia into federal service with such careful restrictions, the delegates could not possibly have allowed the federal government to exercise direct control over the citizens by permitting a draft into the regular army. The matter was so impossible to imagine, given the circumstances and ideological climate of the times, that no voice was raised against it. The only mention of the draft at the Convention was by Edmund Randolph, a leading Federalist figure and proponent of the Constitution, who denied that the new government should have that power. It is inconceivable that stanch Antifederalists like Elbridge Gerry, who strongly opposed the creation of any standing army, would not have raised the loudest protest about any general power to draft by the federal government if they had thought that it was contained within the general grant of authority "to raise and support armies." All that was given by the grant, therefore, was the power to organize and enlist a federal, professional army which—the delegates thought—would consist of a limited number of garrison troops. That power was given grudgingly, only in the light of the severe hardship Congress had experienced during the Revolution in depending solely on the states for manpower and military supplies. But the door was opened for that limited purpose only.

Differences in the language of the Constitution support this interpretation. When the word "armies" is used in article I, section 8, it does not encompass any organized body of the military; rather, it refers to an "army" in eighteenth century usage, a force far different from the "militia." The former existed as a highly specialized instrument of the central government, a body of trained and disciplined troops whose purpose was to protect the central government and execute its policies. The militia, on the other hand, was a quite different sort of military establishment, comprehending the whole mass of citizen-soldiers. Its principal function was to safeguard free men against foreign and domestic enemies—not the least of which was government itself. The idea that citizens have an obligation to bear arms for a national authority, and work against their own most profound interests, never occurred to the framers; it would have been a contradiction to their entire political heritage, manifestly inconsistent with their sense of the delicate balance between liberty and power, between the appetite for oppression and the instinct for resistance. If the citizen had any military obligation, it was to his local militia, where he and his compatriots might have to meet the advance of standing armies in the employ of even their own government.

C. The Federalist Papers

James Madison and Alexander Hamilton devoted a substantial portion of *The Federalist Papers* to the military clauses.[114] The picture they drew of the military establishment confirms the foregoing interpretation of the structure that was delineated in the Philadelphia Convention. In the first place, the main military force was to be the militia; the professional army that was to be raised and controlled by the central government had limited functions. Hamilton's description of the English structure, which he used as a model for the American system, is illustrative:

> A sufficient force to make head against a sudden descent, till the militia could have time to rally and embody, is all that has been deemed requisite [in England]. . . .

If we are wise enough to preserve the union, we may for ages enjoy an advantage similar to that of an insulated situation. . . . Extensive military establishments cannot, in this position, be necessary to our security.[115]

Besides bearing the initial shock of any sudden invasion until the militia could be mobilized, the regular army troops would guard the frontiers, "against the ravages and depredations of the Indians":

These garrisons must either be furnished by occasional detachments from the militia, or by permanent corps in the pay of the government. The first is impracticable; and if practicable, would be pernicious. The militia would not long, if at all, submit to be dragged from their occupations and families to perform that most disagreeable duty in times of profound peace. And if they could be prevailed upon, or compelled to do it, the increased expense of a frequent rotation of service and the loss of labor, and disconcertion of the industrious pursuits of individuals, would form conclusive objections to the scheme. It would be as burthensome and injurious to the public, as ruinous to private citizens. The latter resource of permanent corps in the pay of government amounts to a standing army in time of peace; a small one, indeed, but not the less real for being small.[116]

Thus Hamilton believed that the citizens at large would be enrolled in the militia while the regular army would consist of professionals enlisted for long periods. His statement is incompatible with any notion that the citizens could be taken directly into the regular army by a draft, "dragged from their occupations and families" in a "frequent rotation of service" to perform "disagreeable duty" in Indian territory.

As the preceding quotation indicates, Hamilton distinguished often between the citizens at large and the regular army. He noted that the art of war had progressed to the point at which specialization was necessary,[117] and that the people no longer wished to devote themselves to the military arts:

The industrious habits of the people of the present day, absorbed in the pursuits of gain, and devoted to the improvements of agriculture and commerce are incompatible with the condition of a nation of soldiers, which was the true condition of the people of those [Greek] republics. The means of revenue, which have been so greatly multiplied by the encrease of gold and silver, and of the arts of industry, and the science of finance, which is the offspring of modern times, . . . have produced an intire revolution in the system of war, and have rendered disciplined armies, distinct from the body of the citizens, the inseparable companion of frequent hostility.[118]

In a nation such as the United States, which was not subject to invasions or internal strife, armies would be small and the citizens would not be "habituated to look up to the military power for protection, or to submit to its oppressions"; instead, they would recognize professional armies as a necessary evil and would "stand ready to resist a power which they suppose may be exerted to the prejudice of their rights."[119]

Hamilton returned to this point in *The Federalist No. 29*, in which he again argued that a strong militia was the best protection against the dangers of a standing army.[120] Madision concurred in *The Federalist No. 46*:

> Let a regular army, fully equal to the resources of the country be formed; and let it be entirely at the devotion of the Federal Government; still it would not be going too far to say, that the State Governments with the people on their side would be able to repel the danger. The highest number to which, according to the best computation, a standing army can be carried in any country, does not exceed one hundredth part of the whole number of souls; or one twenty-fifth part of the number able to bear arms. This proportion would not yield in the United States an army of more than twenty-five or thirty thousand men. To these would be opposed a militia amounting to near half a million of citizens with arms in their hands, officered by men chosen from among themselves, fighting for their common liberties, and united and conducted by governments possessing their affections and confidence. It may well be doubted whether a militia thus circumstanced could ever be conquered by such a proportion of regular troops.[121]

These statements show that Hamilton and Madison envisioned the regular army that Congress could raise as a small professional force, distinct from the citizens at large, and possessing limited functions and responsibilities. The yeomen of the country, organized in their militia, would be called out for the specific purposes mentioned in the Constitution and would act as a constant check on the government and its regular army. But the idea that citizens could be impressed into that army against their wills is totally inconsistent with the military structure outlined by the two Federalist leaders. No direct comment on this question appears in *The Federalist Papers* because it was entirely alien to the thinking of the time.

To both Hamilton and Madison, the problem of raising an army was simply a matter of raising the revenue to support the army, just as Randolph stated on the first day of the Philadelphia Convention.[122] Since the Confederation lacked such a power, both men wanted to be sure that the new government would have independent means of securing funds for defense and would be given the authority to gather and support its own forces; but clearly nothing more was supposed to be granted by the Constitution. It is true that Hamilton was anxious to insure that the various limitations on the military power which existed under the Confederation or were suggested at the Convention would not be imposed, and at one point he used rather sweeping language to argue that position:

> The authorities essential to the care of the common defence are these—to raise armies—to build and equip fleets—to prescribe rules for the government of both—to direct their operations—to provide for their support. These powers ought to exist without limitation: *Because it is impossible to foresee or to define the extent and variety of national exigencies, or the correspondent extent & variety of the means which may be necessary to satisfy them.* The circumstances that endanger the safety of nations are infinite; and for this reason no constitutional shackles can wisely be imposed on the power to which the care of it is committed. This power ought to be coextensive with all the possible combinations of such circumstances; and ought to be under the direction of the same councils, which are appointed to preside over the common defence.[123]

These remarks are often cited to show the broad reach of the war power, and to support the assertion that this power necessarily includes the ability to conscript. However, those who rely on this language seldom note that Hamilton explains his meaning in the same paper. Two paragraphs after the quoted passage he states that "unless it can be shewn, that the circumstances which may affect the public safety are reducible within certain determinate limits" there should be "no limitation of that authority, which is to provide for the defence and protection of the community, in any matter essential to its efficacy; that is in any matter essential to the *formation, direction* or *support* of the NATIONAL FORCES."[124] In other words, Hamilton is simply declaring that any traditional or accepted way of forming a professional army (in terms of the number or manner of enlisting men) or directing it (through any command structure decided by the authorities) or supporting it (by any system of pay scales deemed desirable) must be allowed. His statements can be understood only as a response to the various restrictions on a federal army suggested by the Antifederalists: a ban on any peacetime establishment, an absolute numerical limit on the peacetime army, or a short-term period of enlistment for professional soldiers. These were the limitations that he wished to avoid and his expansive language was offered to counter these attacks on the military power. Since even the most violent Antifederalist never claimed that the new government would have the power to conscript,[125] his statements were not directed to that problem in any way.

The interpretation is confirmed still later in *The Federalist No. 23.* In denigrating the old revolutionary military system, Hamilton argues:

> We must discard the fallacious scheme of quotas and requisitions as ... impracticable and unjust. The result from all this is, that the Union ought to be invested with full power to levy troops; to build and equip fleets, and to raise the revenues, which will be required for the formation and support of an army and navy, in the customary and ordinary modes practiced in other governments.[126]

By "levy[ing] troops" Hamilton meant federalizing the state militia and bringing them into federal service by executive decree instead of requesting the states to furnish them under the quota system. Moreover, as stated earlier,[127] no government in the world had exercised a general power to conscript its citizens into its regular army—other than as punishment or as a means of removing paupers from the streets—at the time that the Constitution was drafted. Thus, it is clearly illogical to interpret Hamilton's statements as advocacy for a power beyond that which any other contemporary government had ever asserted; at most he must have been arguing only that the federal government should be given the same general powers which other states possessed, the ability to use unlimited funds to buy an army through enlistments. The juxtaposition of his remarks about the system of quotas and requisitions with a discussion of the power to raise troops shows the intent of his statement: the federal government should be able to compel the states to supply their militias and to enlist men directly without the interposition of the states.

In summary, *The Federalist Papers* must be interpreted in terms of the Confederation's inability to control the military and the Antifederalist arguments which Hamilton and Madison sought to counter. The broad language in *The Federalist Papers* met both of these problems. They are answers to specific questions raised at the time about the proper organization of the armed forces. But both men make clear in their remarks about the function and composition of the professional army that it would not be composed of the citizens at large.

D. State Ratifying Conventions

The arguments in the various state ratifying conventions also reflect strong popular sentiment against a standing army of any kind. Not only those attacking the Constitution but also some of its most forceful defenders repeated the maxim that a standing army was a potential instrument of tyranny although it was necessary to defend the nation against hostile invaders.[128] The grudging support which the military clauses received from those who must be regarded as its principal defenders is a good indication that everyone expected the standing army to be a small professional volunteer army and as Hamilton indicated, a mere holding force until the militia could be mobilized. Further evidence that none of the founders thought power had been granted to conscript into a federal army is the fact that even the most vociferous Antifederalists never raised this spectre in attacking the new Constitution.[129] They objected to the federal government's power to enforce its laws directly on the citizens of the states, to levy taxes upon them, or to have federal courts exercise jurisdiction over them, and they undoubtedly would have made reference to the power to conscript if they had had any idea that such a grant of authority was written into the new instrument. The absence of any claims in this area is strong evidence that the power was not present, since the Antifederalists drew on every conceivable source, particularly when the military clauses were in issue, to undermine ratification.

Indeed, many of the arguments which the Antifederalists asserted against the new Constitution, and many of the amendments which were recommended to correct alleged defects, were premised on the implicit assumption that the power to draft did not exist. For example, the delegates in a number of state conventions, proposed that the Constitution be amended to limit the term of *enlistments* for all members of the federal army.[130] If they thought that the federal government could conscript directly, they would surely have included a limit on the conscription term as well. In another state some delegates wished to include a conscientious objector clause in the Constitution. But they mentioned this problem not in connection with the power to raise a federal army but only in discussing the militia clauses[131]—a clear indication of the belief that compulsory service was possible only in the state militia. An examination of this pattern in the various state conventions confirms the universality of these sentiments.

1. Opposition to Standing Armies

Perhaps the most articulate attack upon the new Constitution was made by Luther Martin, one of Maryland's delegates to the Constitutional Convention. He delivered an address entitled "The Genuine Information" to the Maryland legislature on November 29, 1787, describing the proceedings in Philadelphia. His report, which ran for approximately forty printed pages in Elliot's *Debates,* was the most detailed Antifederalist challenge to the new Constitution. When he addressed himself to the section of the Constitution dealing with Congress' power to raise an army, Martin had the following comments:

> [T]he Congress have also a power given them to raise and support *armies,* without any limitation as to numbers and without any restriction in time of peace. Thus, sir, this plan of government, instead of guarding against a standing army,—that engine of arbitrary power, which has so often and so successfully been used for the subversion of freedom,—has, in its formation, given it an express and constitutional sanction, and hath provided for its introduction. Nor could this be prevented. I took the sense of the Convention on a proposition, by which the Congress should not have power, in time of peace, to keep imbodied more than a certain number of regular troops, that number to be ascertained by what should be considered a respectable peace establishment. This proposition was rejected by a majority, it being their determination that the power of Congress to keep up a standing army, even in peace, should only be restrained by their will and pleasure.[132]

The Antifederalists in Massachusetts took a similar view, placing particular emphasis on the danger inherent in the fact that the new Constitution granted Congress "the power of the purse and the sword."[133] General Thompson, a strong Antifederalist figure, cited the English experience, saying: "Congress will have power to keep standing armies. The great Mr. Pitt says, standing armies are dangerous—keep your militia in order. . . ."[134] And, in Pennsylvania, minority delegates who voted against ratification issued an address declaring their "Reasons of Dissent"; one of the principal grounds which they specified was the fear of the central government's military power:

> A standing army in the hands of a government placed so independent of the people, may be made a fatal instrument to overturn the public liberties; it may be employed to enforce the collection of the most oppressive taxes, and to carry into execution the most arbitrary measures. An ambitious man who may have the army at his devotion, may step up into the throne, and seize upon absolute power.[135]

On the other hand, the delegates in many states recognized the need for a small peacetime standing army, primarily as a frontier garrison force; but they frequently emphasized the limited nature of this exception. James Iredell, a leading advocate of ratification in North Carolina and later an Associate Justice of the Supreme Court, expressed the hope that "in time of peace, there will not be occasion, at anytime, but for a very small number of forces."[136] Similarly, James

Wilson of Pennsylvania supported the immediate creation of a small federal army to guard the frontier as a means of avoiding the possibility that a large force would be needed later; in his view, "[o]ur enemies, finding us invulnerable, will not attack us; and we shall thus prevent the occasion for larger standing armies."[137] In James Madison's opinion, however, "the most effectual way" to avoid standing armies was to strengthen the state forces and "to give the general government full power to call forth the militia, and exert the whole natural strength of the Union."[138]

In the New York ratifying convention several amendments were proposed which indicate the kind of army that contemporary statesmen thought would be organized by the federal government. John Lansing recommended the adoption of a clause which provided "That no standing army, or regular troops, shall be raised, or kept up, in time of peace, without the consent of two thirds of the members of both houses present."[139] Alexander Hamilton also proposed an amendment that was substantially similar.[140] An amended version of Lansing's proposal was eventually adopted by the New York convention,[141] and, in a preamble to the ratifying document, the delegates proclaimed:

> [T]hat a well-regulated militia, including the body of the people *capable of bearing arms,* is the proper, natural and safe defence of a free state.
>
> . . . .
>
> That standing armies, in time of peace, are dangerous to liberty, and ought not to be kept up, except in cases of necessity. . . .[142]

Proposals to amend the Constitution by adding a prohibition on standing armies continued even after ratification and were frequently supported by Thomas Jefferson in his correspondence.[143]

As these comments demonstrate, the leaders who ratified the Constitution believed that the militia—the armed body of all the citizens— was the prime source of the nation's defense, and that only a small professional army with limited functions could be created by the federal government. This contrast between a standing army and "the people" was often quite explicit in the debates of the Virginia convention,[144] which were recorded more extensively than those of any other state. James Madison made a particularly forceful assertion of this distinction in defending the federal government's power to call out the militia:

> If resistance should be made to the execution of the laws . . . it ought to be overcome. This could be done only in two ways—either by regular forces or by the people. . . . If insurrections should arise, or

invasion should take place, the people ought unquestionably to be employed, to suppress and repel them, rather than a standing army.[145]

Randolph concurred in the judgment that primary military duties should fall upon "the people" rather than a standing army; in his interpretation of the Constitution, defense was "left to the militia, who will suffer if they become the instruments of tyranny."[146]

2. Comparison with the Military Powers of the Confederation and Other Countries

Another indication that the Constitution did not purport to give the federal government the power of conscription can be found in the frequent comparisons made in state ratifying conventions between the new military system and the one established under the Articles of Confederation. In response to the Antifederalists' expressions of apprehension about standing armies, supporters of the Constitution argued that the military clauses were merely a recognition of the practices of the former government; thus, Chancellor Robert R. Livingston[147] of New York, James Wilson[148] and Thomas McKean[149] of Pennsylvania, and Alexander Hamilton[150] all asserted that the power to control the purse and the sword which was granted by the new instrument was essentially the same as that existing in the Confederation. That is, many defenders of the Constitution felt that the answer to the problem of national defense lay in the explicit grant of power to raise money for enlisting an army, and not in any system so radical as direct conscription into the federal forces. This distinction is particularly clear in James Wilson's discussion of Shays' Rebellion:

> It may be frequently necessary to keep up standing armies in time of peace. The present Congress have experienced the necessity, and seven hundred troops are just as much a standing army as seventy thousand. . . . They may go further, and raise an army, without communicating to the public the purpose for which it is raised. On a particular occasion they did this. When the commotion existed in Massachusetts, they gave orders for enlisting an additional body of two thousand men.[151]

In addition to comparing the new government's authority to that of the old Confederation, some delegates also claimed that the military power of the United States was to be the same as that practiced by other nations—and, as noted above,[152] no nation practiced conscription at the time that the Constitution was adopted. Thus, when Thomas Dawes of Massachusetts cited the English experience with standing armies under Charles II, James II, and William III as support for the proposition that national legislatures have the inherent authority "to raise armies,"[153] he must have been referring to the kind of professional volunteer army which Great Britain maintained throughout the eighteenth century. James Wilson's analogy to foreign governments also underscores what the delegates meant when they passed upon the power to "raise and support armies": "I have taken some pains to inform myself how the other governments of the world stand with regard to this power, and the result of my inquiry is, that there is not one which has not the power of raising and keeping up standing armies."[154]

3. Amendments on Military Jurisdiction

The possibility that citizens could be tried by courts-martial was of central concern to many statesmen of the time who thought that trial by jury was the individual's greatest safeguard against tyranny. Luther Martin, the Maryland Antifederalist, expressed considerable concern over this problem, but he mentioned it only with respect to the militia clause, and not in connection with the provision for federal armies:

> It was thought that not more than a certain part of the militia of any one state ought to be obliged to march out of the same . . . at any one time, without the consent of the legislature of such state. This amendment I endeavored to obtain; but . . . it was not adopted. As it now stands, the Congress will have the power, if they please, to march the whole militia of Maryland to the remotest part of the Union, and to keep them in service as long as they think proper, without being in any respect dependent upon the government of Maryland for this unlimited exercise of power over its citizens—all of whom, from the lowest to the greatest, may, during such service, be subjected to military law, and tied up and whipped . . . like the meanest of slaves.[155]

According to Martin, who was a delegate to the Philadelphia Convention, it was the federal government's power to call out the militia that created the danger of military control over Maryland citizens; he did not even mention this problem when he discussed the congressional power to raise and support armies. It seems probable that his failure to mention the issue in the latter context was due to the unarticulated assumption that the regular army would be composed of volunteers who would waive their right to jury trial by enlisting.

It is apparent that the members of the Maryland convention shared Martin's assumption, for they proposed an amendment providing "That the militia shall not be subjected to martial law, except in time of war, invasion or rebellion."[156] According to the Amending Committee:

> This provision to restrain the powers of Congress over the militia, although by no means so ample as that provided by the Magna Carta and the other great fundamental and Constitutional laws of Great Britain . . . yet it may prove an inestimable check; for all other provisions in favor of the rights of men would be vain and nugatory, if the power of subjecting all men, able to bear arms, to martial law at any moment should remain vested in Congress.[157]

A similar amendment was proposed in Virginia.[158] It hardly seems possible that the delegates in these two states would be concerned about the danger that state citizens forced into the militia could be subject to martial law, but would completely ignore the fate of state citizens conscripted directly into a national army. Rather, the conclusion seems inescapable that the Maryland and Virginia delegates believed that the militia clauses constituted the sole mechanism by which unwilling citizens could be brought under the jurisdiction of the federal military apparatus.

4. Amendments on Term of Enlistment

In addition to the amendment concerning military jurisdiction, the Maryland convention proposed several other limitations on the military power. Two of these amendments provided that soldiers could not be quartered in private houses and that no mutiny bill could continue in force longer than two years; a third stipulated that "no soldier be enlisted for a longer time than four years, except in time of war, and then only during the war."[159] Amendments which were virtually identical to the latter provision were also introduced in North Carolina[160] and Virginia.[161]

According to the proponents of the Maryland amendments, the three limitations on the federal government were necessary because "[t]hese were the only checks that could be obtained against the unlimited power of raising and regulating standing armies, the natural enemies of freedom."[162] But surely the amendment limiting terms of enlistment would be a failure in achieving this objective if the federal government had the power to conscript citizens for unlimited periods of time. Again, the conclusion seems inescapable that the delegates who proposed these limitations on the central government's military powers never imagined that the new Constitution granted Congress the greater power of direct conscription.

5. Proposals Concerning Conscientious Objectors

Since many Pennsylvania citizens were Quakers who opposed military service in any form, that state's convention was forced to deal with the problem of conscientious objection. Thomas McKean discussed this problem; but, significantly, he referred to conscientious objection only in the context of the federal government's control over the militia, and not in relation to Congress' power to raise and support armies.[163] The minority report issued by the Pennsylvania Antifederalists was also quite explicit in condemning the incursions on individual liberty that were possible under the militia clause:

> The absolute unqualified command that Congress have over the militia may be made instrumental to the destruction of all liberty. . . .
> First, the personal liberty of every man, probably from sixteen to sixty years of age, may be destroyed by the power Congress have in organizing and governing of the militia.[164]

The Pennsylvania dissenters did not mention the threat to "the personal liberty of every man" in connection with the federal government's power to raise armies; in their view, apparently, the only compulsory military service contemplated by the Constitution was through the state militias. The minority delegates advanced another objection:

> Secondly, the rights of conscience may be violated, as there is no exemption of those persons who are conscientiously scrupulous of bearing arms. These compose a respectable proportion of the community in the state. . . .
> [During the Revolution] the framers of our State Constitution made the most express and decided declaration and stipulations in favor of the rights of conscience; but now, when no necessity exists, those dearest rights of men are left insecure.[165]

The Pennsylvania dissenters' failure to relate the problem of conscientious objection to the provision for a standing army is easily explained by hypothesizing their belief that the regular army would be composed solely of volunteers who obviously would have no scruples about bearing arms.

6. Financial Aspects of the Military Power

The contemporary identification of "the power of the purse and the power of the sword" served to focus the attention of many state delegates upon the government's financial ability to support an army, and those who believed in the need for a strong system of national defense often asserted that Congress should be able to raise substantial sums of money quickly in the event of invasion or other emergency.[166] As a corollary to this proposition, however, proponents of a strong central government believed that the Congress would need financial power in order to buy an army through enlistments. Thus, James Wilson of Pennsylvania asked rhetorically:

> Have not the freest of governments those powers [of the sword and the purse]? And are they not in the fullest exercise of them? . . . Can we create a government without the power to act? How can it act without the assistance of men? And how are men to be procured without being paid for their services?[167]

On the other hand, Antifederalist Richard Henry Lee opposed granting the national government unrestricted power to "*engage* officers and men for any number of years"; it was his fear that "[w]e shall have a large standing army as soon as the monies to support them can possibly be found."[168] "An army is not a very agreeable place of *employment*," he added, "for the young gentlemen of many families";[169] apparently he was concerned that those who would be attracted to a professional army would be insensitive to the values of liberty.

Some delegates also were apprehensive about the impact that compulsory militia service would have upon the civilian economy. Since the vast majority of citizens were farmers by occupation, a call of the militia during the planting or harvesting season could cause great hardship. Thus, Edmund Randolph,[170] Henry Lee,[171] and Francis Corbin supported a professional army that would promote a more appropriate division of labor. Corbin argued to the Virginia convention:

> If some of the community are exclusively inured to its defence, and the rest attend to agriculture, the consequence will be, that the arts of war and defence, and of cultivating the soil, will be understood. . . . If, on the contrary, our defence be solely intrusted to militia, ignorance of arms and negligence of farming will ensue. . . . If we are called in the time of sowing seed, or of harvest, the means of subsistence might be lost; and the loss of one year's crop might have been prevented by a trivial expense, if appropriated to the purpose of supporting a part of the community, exclusively occupied in the defence of the whole.[172]

Thus in the eyes of Corbin, Lee, and Randolph, regular troops— "a part of the community, exclusively occupied in the defense of the whole"—would take the military burden off the militia—the yeomen of the country who would devote themselves to agriculture and the mechanic arts. In their view, the farmers—the citizens at large—could not be forced into the regular army. In that case men would be called out at sowing time or at the harvest, which all three men saw as dangerous to agricultural industry. Wilson Nicholas discerned another economic reason for relying upon a professional volunteer army. Even if the militia were adequate for national defense, he contended, reliance on state forces imposed an unequal burden upon the poor. "If war be supported by militia," he argued, "it is by personal service. The poor man does just as much as the rich. Is this just?" Moreover, the rich man could easily exempt himself by finding a substitute. But if the military duties were entrusted to a regular army, Nicholas said, the soldiers would be "paid by taxes raised from the people, according to their property; and then the rich man pays an adequate share."[173] Thus, according to Nicholas, when regular troops were used to carry on a war, personal service by the poor would not be required; professional soldiers would be used, paid for by taxes. This argument strikes an ironic note in light of current debates upon the desirability of a volunteer army;[174] but the clear import of the delegates' discussion of economic factors is that the regular army was viewed by all parties as a professional force procured by enlistments, not by forced service of the people.

E. Early Congresses and the Military Power

The actions of the first Congresses elected under the Constitution, which included many of the delegates to the Philadelphia Convention, support the view that conscription was not authorized by the Constitution. One of the most important items of business confronting the first Congress was, of course, the promulgation of a Bill of Rights, and, in June of 1789, James Madison introduced a series of proposed amendments to the Constitution. One of these, which eventually became the second amendment, stated:

> The right of the people to keep and bear arms shall not be infringed; a well-armed and well-regulated militia being the best security of a free country: but no person religiously scrupulous of bearing arms shall be compelled to render military service in person.[175]

The fact that Madison sought to insert a conscientious-objector clause into the Constitution indicates the significance he ascribed to freedom of conscience; yet, his proposed objector clause dealt only with the militia power. It seems difficult to believe that he would seek to limit the militia's power to compel service in this manner and ignore a comparable power in the federal government, if there was any serious possibility that the federal government could conscript citizens. Like the other statesmen of the time, he apparently thought that compulsory military service could take place only in the militia, and that was the only area about which he concerned himself.

Opponents of Madison's conscientious-objector clause argued that the problem was too difficult and uncertain to be dealt with by an inflexible constitutional provision,[176] and the clause was finally eliminated in September 1789 by the Senate.[177] However, the second amendment that was finally adopted emphasizes once again the sharp distinction that was made between the militia and the regular army at the time the Constitution was adopted. The amendment's assertions that the militia was "necessary to the security of a free state" and that "the right of the people to keep and bear arms shall not be infringed" can be traced to the Virginia ratifying convention. There, George Mason had argued that the federal government might "neglect" or "harass and abuse" the militia "in order to have the pretense of establishing a standing army."[178] Patrick Henry had agreed; in his opinion, the "militia . . . is our ultimate safety. We can have no security without it."[179] Thus, the people organized in the state militias were regarded as a counterforce against the threat that the regular army could be used as an instrument of oppression,[180] and service in the militia was a right of the citizen that could not be transgressed by the federal government.[181] Clearly, this balance of power could be upset, and the citizen's right to bear arms in the militia undermined, if the federal government had the power to compel large numbers of citizens to serve in the regular army.

Congress moved quickly to implement the military sections of the Constitution. At the instigation of Secretary of War Knox, a statute was passed in September of 1789 legalizing the existence of the 840-man army inherited from the Confederation;[182] about six months later the authorized force was increased to over a thousand men.[183] The statutes clearly dealt only with enlisted forces, but in spite of this fact, there was substantial opposition in Congress to the creation of a standing army.[184]

The size of the regular army was increased twice more during the next two years,[185] and in May of 1792 Congress passed a uniform militia law.[186] The latter provision had developed from a plan proposed by Secretary of War Knox in 1790 which would have obliged every male citizen to enroll and train for specific periods in a federally organized militia system. A select part of the militia—the "advanced corps" of younger men—would be extensively trained and ready for service on short notice. Congressional opposition to this proposal proved insurmountable,[187] and, after two years of consideration, Congress passed a law which required enrollment but did not specify any particular duration or type of training for the militia; these matters were left entirely to the states. Perhaps the most significant aspect of the episode is the fact that Knox, the foremost advocate of a strong military system, sought to establish compulsory universal military training not under the constitutional grant of power to raise and support armies, but under the militia clause.

The early debates on the military also reflect a perception by many congressmen that their control over the militia was secondary to the states' regulatory power. Thus, one representative asserted that "the States alone are to say of what description of persons the militia shall consist, and who shall be exempt from militia duty; Congress have only power to organize them, when thus designated."[188]

Questions about the proper size and composition of the military establishment were before Congress frequently during the early years of the Republic, particularly with regard to the kind of force that should be used to fight the Indians. Those who advocated the use of regular troops emphasized the adverse impact on agriculture that would result from use of the militia,[189] or the unreliability of poorly trained militiamen;[190] others contended that the regular troops were "trash" who "enlist for three dollars a month; which, in a country like the United States, is a sufficient description of their bodies as well as their minds."[191] When the Whiskey Rebellion erupted in 1794, it was the militia that was summoned to suppress it; Washington called out 12,000 militiamen from four states, and maintained a peacekeeping force of 2,500 in the area after order was restored.[192] Early Congresses also depended heavily on militia groups entering the federal service of their own choice. These volunteer units had a long tradition dating from the colonial period; frequently they furnished their own arms and elaborate uniforms, and were composed of social elites.[193] In 1794[194] and 1798,[195] Congress authorized the President to accept volunteer militia units, but the statutes maintained a distinction between these groups and the troops obtained by regular enlistments.

Thus, in the first ten years of the nation Congress evidenced its understanding of the military powers granted in the Constitution by: (1) debating a constitutional amendment on conscientious objection which focused on the militia as the only compulsory military force; (2) passing the second amendment, which was totally incompatible with any notion of federal conscription; (3) grudgingly increasing the size of its regular, enlisted army; (4) passing a tepid militia law because it did not wish to compel the citizens to train in the militia; and (5) distinguishing between the "trash" of the regular army and the industrious yeoman of the militia. At no time during this period—not even during the quasi-war with France in 1797–1800—was there the slightest hint that Congress might have the power to enforce direct conscription.

F. The Relationship Between the Militia and the Regular Army

In the *Selective Draft Law Cases*, the Supreme Court placed considerable reliance on the relationship between the militia and the regular forces. The Court opened this phase of its argument by citing the portion of article I, section 10 which prohibits the states from keeping "Troops, or Ships of War in time of Peace" without the consent of Congress. This provision, together with the difficulties experienced by the Continental Congress in trying to get the states to meet their troop quotas and the grant of power to raise armies, led the Court to infer that the framers had intended to vest all the military powers in Congress.[196] Therefore, Chief Justice White concluded, "[t]here was left . . . under the sway of the States undelegated the control of the militia to the extent that such control was not taken away by the exercise by Congress of its power to raise armies."[197]

It is undoubtedly true that the military clauses of the Constitution were designed in part to remedy the central government's lack of power under the Articles of Confederation; Alexander Hamilton's belief that a permanent military corps was needed to perform duties for which the militia was inappropriate[198] and his argument that sole reliance on the states for national defense could lead to unequal burdens or disastrous rivalries[199] clearly weighed heavily with those who assisted in drafting the Constitution. But these acknowledged facts hardly support the conclusion that Congress' power to raise and support armies extended to all attributes of state militia power, including the authority to conscript. Rather, the available historical evidence indicates that the Supreme Court in *Arver* did not pursue the distinction between the militia power and the army power far enough, and that the framers did not view the state militias and the federal army as simply complementary manifestations of the same power.

It is clear that the framers imposed no specific limitations on how the federal government could use its regular forces; in the opinion of some early statesmen, they could even be sent abroad to fight in foreign wars.[200] At the same time, the militia could be used only for the limited purposes enumerated in the Constitution, and the states could not maintain regular forces on duty. This differential treatment of the uses to which the army and the militia could be put provides a marked contrast to the prevailing understanding of how the manpower could be raised for each force. The fact that the states could compel militia service did not mean that Congress would have equivalent power with respect to the army. As the preceding discussion of the Philadelphia Convention, *The Federalist Papers*, and the state ratifying conventions indicates, the contemporary understanding was that the regular army would be composed of volunteers who could not legitimately object if they were exposed to the dangers of questionable domestic conflicts or foreign entanglements. Indeed, the fact that various restrictions were imposed upon the use of the militia reflects the framers' belief that the citizens should not be taken into the army against their wills and employed in any military venture that the federal government might undertake. Thus, if the Court in the *Selective Draft Law Cases* had been more sensitive to the historical context in drawing inferences from the constitutional distinction between the militia and the regular army, it would not have concluded that every attribute of one force necessarily attached to the other. Instead, history points to the conclusion that the framers gave the federal government wide powers to *use* its army but not to *gather* it, while the militia's *functions* were specified but its manpower source was unlimited.

IV. The Nation's Military History Under the Constitution

A. The War of 1812

A major portion of the Court's opinion in the *Selective Draft Law Cases* dealt with the federal government's attempts to implement universal conscription after the adoption of the Constitution. The first significant attempt to enact a draft law occurred during the War of 1812, according to the Court, "[e]ither because [the existing regular army and militia force] proved to be weak in numbers or because of insubordination developed among the forces called and manifested by their refusal to cross the border."[201] In response to these pressures, Secretary of War Monroe introduced a plan to "call a designated number out of the population between the ages of 18 and 45 for service in the army."[202] The Court conceded that congressional opposition against the bill developed, but states that "we need not stop to consider it because it substantially rested upon the incompatibility of compulsory military service with free government, a subject which from what we have said has been disposed of."[203]

In this manner, the Court blithely dismissed the most significant aspect of the Monroe Plan: not the fact that it was introduced, but the fact that Congress never passed the proposal because a substantial number of congressmen did not believe that the federal government had power to conscript. Senator Christopher Gore's assertion that the plan "never will and never ought to be submitted to by this country, while it retains one idea of civil freedom"[204] was representative of the tenor of remarks made by those who opposed conscription,[205] and came with particular force from a man who had been a strong proponent of the Constitution in the Massachusetts ratifying convention. Several congressmen made more detailed attacks upon the proposal. Senator Jeremiah Mason of New Hampshire addressed himself to the specific problem of "whether the Constitution gives to this Government the power contended for," and found several grounds for concluding that it did not. In the first place, he observed, nothing in the Constitution imposed limits upon the sweeping power that the Government sought:

> The power claimed is, doubtless, vastly greater and more dangerous than any other possessed by the Government. It subjects the personal freedom of every citizen, in comparison with which the rights of property are insignificant, to arbitrary discretion. Had there been the intention of granting such power, would there not have been some attempt to guard against the unjust and oppressive exercise of it, as was done in the granting of power of less importance?[206]

Furthermore, Mason argued, the constitutional grant of power "to provide and maintain a navy" could equally support the implication of a power to conscript, and the manpower need was, if anything, greater in the naval service; yet the government was not seeking the power to conscript for the navy. Indeed, Mason pointed out:

> The British Government, before the Revolution did attempt to exercise in this country the supposed right of impressment for the Navy, which it never did for the Army. . . . Yet the Government, in their instructions to our Envoys for treating of peace with Great Britain, say "impressment is not an American practice but it is utterly repugnant to our Constitution and laws." The honorable Secretary [Monroe] when he drafted those instructions, knew not how soon he should be directed to contend for the contrary doctrine.[207]

The most eloquent attack on the Monroe Plan was made by Daniel Webster, who addressed the House of Representatives on December 9, 1814. First, he noted, the proposal went beyond the acknowledged power to call out the militia according to its existing organization; it was, in effect, a plan to raise "a standing army out of the militia by draft."[208] Therefore, Webster stated, "The question is nothing less than whether the most essential rights of personal liberty shall be surrendered, and despotism embraced in its worst form."[209] He then proceeded to ask:

> Is this, sir, consistent with the character of a free government? Is this civil liberty? Is this the real character of our Constitution? No, sir, indeed it is not. The Constitution is libelled, foully libelled. The people of this country have not established for themselves such a fabric of despotism. They have not purchased at a vast expense of their own treasure and their own blood a Magna Charta to be slaves. Where is it written in the Constitution . . . that you may take children from their parents, and parents from their children, and compel them to fight the battles of any war in which the folly or the wickedness of government may engage it?[210]

Webster then turned his attention to the source of the power to conscript "which now for the first time comes forth . . . to trample down and destroy the dearest rights of personal liberty. . . ."[211] The Government's claim of constitutional power was summarily dismissed: "I almost disdain to go to quotations and references to prove that such an abominable doctrine has no foundation in the Constitution of the country. It is enough to know that the instrument was intended as the basis of a free government, and that the power contended for is incompatible with any notion of personal liberty."[212] Nor, argued Webster, could the Secretary of War justify his plan by saying that Congress could raise armies by any means not prohibited by the Constitution, and that "the power to raise would be granted in vain" if there were insufficient enlistments. "If this reasoning could prove anything," Webster retorted, "it would equally show, that whenever the legitimate power of the Constitution should be so badly administered as to cease to answer the great ends intended by them, such new powers may be assumed or usurped, as any existing administration may deem expedient."[213]

This strong opposition made passage of the Monroe Plan a practical impossibility. John C. Calhoun, then a young representative from South Carolina, summarized the alternatives that were available to the federal government: "[T]he military force by which we can operate consists of . . . the regular force, whose general character is mercenary, the soldiers enlisting for the sake of bounty and subsistence; draughted militia called into the field by patriotic motives only."[214] Congress eventually settled upon a plan under which volunteer militia units could enlist for specific short periods; if they engaged to serve for more than nine months, the volunteers could receive acreage from the public lands instead of monthly pay.[215] The threat of a system of federal conscription, however, had repercussions even outside the Congress. In January of 1815, representatives of various New England states that were opposed to the war met at the Hartford Convention. One of the resolutions which they passed recommended that the states "adopt all such measures as may be necessary effectually to protect the citizens of said states" against acts of Congress "which shall contain provision, subjecting the militia or other citizens to forcible drafts, conscriptions, or impressments, not authorized by the 'constitution of the United States.' "[216] Thus, a substantial group of influential political leaders, within three decades after the Constitution was ratified, vigorously asserted that the federal government did not have the power of direct conscription; yet the *Arver* Court, in a single sentence, dismissed their arguments as irrelevant.

B. The Civil War

A final major point relied upon by the Supreme Court in the *Selective Draft Law Cases* was the use of direct conscription during the Civil War. Chief Justice White noted that early in the war the Union government relied upon militia and volunteers; when more men were required, however, a draft law was proposed and passed.[217] There is some doubt as to whether the true purpose of the Civil War Enrollment Act was to procure men through conscription; it seems equally possible that, as one historian has asserted, the measure was designed merely to stimulate enlistments in the regular army.[218] In any event, it is clear that even during the exigencies of the Civil War, a large segment of the populace actively opposed the draft.

The act was quite lenient by today's standards; for example, a drafted man could hire a substitute to perform his service for him, or could purchase outright commutation from the draft.[219] Nevertheless, popular sentiment against conscription was so strong that protest riots occurred in many cities throughout the country. The largest disturbance, which took place in New York City, resulted in an estimated 1,200 deaths and millions of dollars in property damage. Fifteen regiments of regular troops were eventually required before the pillaging mobs could be subdued. A recent commentator has suggested several reasons for this violent reaction to the draft:

> There was something deeply disturbing about a national military draft at best. It was not unheard of for states to raise their army quotas by various forms of compulsion, true. But a state government in the 1860's exerted a neighborly, close-to-home sort of authority. Or at least it seemed so to most people. Washington was different—

distant and unfeeling, somehow alien. And for the average citizen, this new Act was the first effort the Federal government had ever made to reach out its long arm and lay its heavy hand directly on his—his!—shoulder.[220]

Some state and local governments joined the popular opposition to conscription. The state of Delaware and the city of Troy, New York, for example, passed laws authorizing the local government to pay the commutation fee for residents, and the Governor of Massachusetts asked the Secretary of War to suspend operation of the draft in that state for six or seven weeks because a sufficient number of substitutes could not be found. The people were also astute to find means of circumventing the draft law. Enrolling officers, who were required to canvass neighborhoods in order to find eligible males, were frequently lied to, avoided, and even physically attacked. Outright evasion was so widespread that a new word—"skedaddling"—was coined to describe it; new towns sprang up just across the northern borders in Canada, and many men took refuge in California or the mining towns of the western territories. In many parts of New England, so many farm laborers had deserted their employers and fled from the draft that crops were harvested only with great difficulty. The total number of "skedaddlers" may have been as high as 200,000.[221]

Fraudulent exemptions were another popular means of evasion, and approximately 316,000 exemptions were made under the conscription law. When firemen became exempt, some towns enrolled all of their able-bodied men into the fire brigade; in 1864 Congress had to pass special legislation to meet such wholesale attempts to avoid service.[222] Malingering of practically every variety occurred, even to the point that some men maimed themselves in order to fail the physical requirements for the army. The combination of evasion, exemptions, commutations, and armed resistance showed that a substantial portion of the nation was not prepared to accept conscription as a part of the citizen's obligation to the state. As the end of the war approached, Congress began to respond to this general opposition; in March of 1865, a law providing for more liberal substitution was passed,[223] and the following month the draft law was allowed to expire.

This history of inefficiency and evasion seems to cast doubt on the *Arver* Court's assertion that "[i]t would be childish to deny the value of the added strength which was . . . afforded"[224] by the Civil War draft. The court based this conclusion on "the official report of the Provost Marshall General," which claimed that "it was the efficient aid resulting from the forces created by the draft . . . which obviated a disaster . . . and carried that struggle to a complete and successful conclusion."[225] The available statistics, however, cast considerable doubt on this assertion:

> Altogether, only six per cent of the 2,666,999 men who served in the Union Army during the Civil War were secured directly through conscription. Of 249,259 persons "held to service" under the Enrollment Act of 1863, 86,724 escaped by payment of commutation, leaving 168,649 "men raised." But of the latter, 116,188 were substitutes, and only 46,347 were "held to personal service."[226]

No case questioning the Civil War draft was heard by the Supreme Court, but it is known that Chief Justice Roger Taney prepared a rough outline of an opinion declaring the act unconstitutional. Taney's draft opinion began by noting that congressional power to call out the militia for specified purposes, and asking "what description of persons composes the militia who . . . may be called to aid the general government in the emergencies . . . mentioned?"[227] The answer, he said, could be found in the second amendment's declaration that "a well regulated Militia; being necessary to the security of a free State, the right of the people to keep and bear Arms, shall not be infringed":

> The militia is therefore to be composed of Citizens of the States, who retain all their rights and privileges as citizens, who when called into service by the United States are not to be "fused into one body"—nor confounded with the Army of the United States, but are to be called out as the militia of the several states . . . and consequently commanded by the officers appointed by the State. It is only in that form or organization that they are recognized in the Constitution as a military force.[228]

Given this clear distinction between the army and the militia, Taney continued, the limitations on the President's power to control the militia are equally clear: "He has no power over the Militia unless [they are] called into the actual service of the United States. They are then called out in the language of the Constitution, as the militia of the several States."[229] This constitutional plan would be thwarted, Taney believed, if the government exercised the power of direct conscription:

> There is no longer any militia—it is absorbed in the Army. Every able bodied Citizen . . . belongs to the national forces—that is to the Army of the United States. . . .
> The Generals, Colonels and other Officers appointed by the State according to the provisions of the Constitution are reduced to the ranks, and compelled to march as private soldiers . . . and they and every other able bodied citizen except those whom it has been the pleasure of Congress to exempt, are compelled against their will to

subject themselves to military law . . . and to be treated as deserters if they refuse to surrender their civil rights.[230]

Thus, said Taney, implying the power of direct conscription would create an inconsistency among the military clauses of the constitution; the power of direct conscription into the federal army and the militia provisions would be "repugnant to each other" because "if the conscription law be authorized by the Constitution, then all of the clauses so elaborately prepared in relation to the militia . . . are of no practical value and may be set aside and annulled whenever Congress may deem it expedient."[231] Nor could this difficulty be overcome, Taney asserted, by claiming that no restrictions had been placed on the power to raise armies. "No just rule of construction," he wrote, "can give any weight to inferences drawn from general words, when these inferences are opposed to special and express provisions [governing the militia], in the same instrument."[232]

Chief Justice Taney also relied upon history to support his construction of the military clauses. "During the period when the United States were English Colonies," he observed, "the Army of England— the standing army—was always raised by voluntary enlistments—and the right to coerce all the able bodied subjects of the Crown into the ranks of the Army . . . was not claimed or exercised by the English government."[233] Against this historical background, Taney concluded, the words granting Congress the power to raise armies "necessarily implied that they were to be raised in the usual manner." Indeed, he added, "the general government has always heretofore so understood [the words] and has uniformly . . . recruited the ranks of its 'land forces' by volunteer enlistments for a specific period."[234]

Chief Justice Taney never had the opportunity to perfect or deliver his opinion because the Government never brought a draft case to the Supreme Court. However, the constitutionality of the Civil War draft was questioned in the courts of Pennsylvania and ultimately was upheld in *Kneedler v. Lane*.[235] The *Kneedler* case, upon which the *Arver* Court relied,[236] was decided under rather unusual circumstances. It arose when three young men sued the local enrolling board to enjoin the board members from enforcing the law; the United States did not defend these actions, and on November 9, 1863, the Pennsylvania Supreme Court announced in a three-to-two decision that the law was unconstitutional.

The first opinion for the majority was written by Chief Justice Walter Lowrie. He found that the Constitution recognized two distinct kinds of land forces, the militia and the army. The militia could be drawn into federal service only in the manner provided by the Constitution; if these forces were subject to paramount federal call, they could be effectively wiped out. Moreover, Lowrie said, the Constitution provides that taxes and duties must be raised according to a rule of "uniformity, equality, or proportion," but no such requirement is imposed by the army clause. If the army "may be recruited by force," he asserted, "we find no regulation or limitation of the exercise of the power, so as to prevent it from being arbitrary and partial, and hence we infer that such a mode of raising armies was not thought of, and was not granted." Lowrie dwelt at length on the dangers of implying such a broad power:

> If Congress may institute the plan now under consideration, as a necessary and proper mode of exercising its power "to raise and support armies," then it seems to me to follow with more force that it may take a similar mode in the exercise of other powers, and may compel people to lend it their money; take their houses for offices and courts; ... their mechanics and workshops for the different branches of business that are needed for army supplies; their physicians, ministers, and women for army surgeons, chaplains, nurses, and cooks. ... I am quite unable now to suppose that so great a power could have been intended to be granted, and yet to be left so loosely guarded.[237]

Judge George W. Woodward issued a concurring opinion which relied heavily on the English experience. The framers, he said, had borrowed freely from the English system, and were familiar with the struggles which had prevented universal conscription in Great Britain. The framers intended, he argued, to create "a more free constitution than that of Great Britain—taking that as a model in some things—but enlarging the basis of popular rights in all respects that would be consistent with order and stability." Thus Woodward concluded that "[a]ssuredly the framers of our constitution did not intend to subject the people of the states to a system of conscription which was applied in the mother country only to paupers and vagabonds."[238] Judge James Thompson's concurrence also emphasized that the customary mode of raising armies in England had been voluntary enlistments. He then pointed out that at the time the Constitution was ratified a substantial segment of public opinion opposed any form of standing army; "but what would have been thought," Thompson asked, "if it had been discovered or avowed that in its creation [the federal army] might be directly and openly destructive of the individual liberties of those who were to compose it, and that it might be extended to embrace all the able-bodied citizens in the states!"[239]

The injunctions prayed for were issued on November 9, 1863. However, Chief Justice Lowrie's term expired on December 12, and he was replaced by Daniel Agnew, who was known to favor the draft. The Government then moved to vacate the injunctions. On January 16, 1864, the court vacated the initial orders over a bitter dissent by Judge Woodward, who had just been elevated to the position of Chief Justice. The Government, he pointed out, had failed to appear in the first hearing even though every opportunity had been given them to present their views; nor had they made any effort to seek reargument while Chief Justice Lowrie was still on the bench. Moreover, he said, the decision granting the injunction was a final judgment which could have been appealed to the United States Supreme Court; in any event, the dissenting judges should have been bound by the initial decision since no new facts had been presented.[240] On this divisive note, the Government obtained a victory in the first case to pass upon the constitutionality of conscription; but the narrow margin of this victory is emphasized by the fact that three of the six Pennsylvania judges who considered the matter held that Congress lacked the power to enforce direct conscription.

C. World War I and After

After the expiration of the Civil War draft, the Government did not attempt to use conscription again until the outbreak of World War I. On April 5, 1917—the day before Congress declared war on Germany—the Wilson administration introduced its Army Bill, which provided for compulsory military service. Opposition arose immediately, with Speaker of the House Champ Clark insisting on a volunteer system. "I protest with all my heart and mind and soul," he proclaimed, "against having the slur of being a conscript placed upon the men of Missouri. In the estimation of Missourians there is precious little difference between a conscript and a convict."[241] The Senate opposition was led by Robert M. LaFollette. "[The] power once granted," he said, "will attach to the office [of the President], and will be exercised so long as the Nation shall last, by every successive incumbent, no matter how ambitious or bloody-minded he may be."[242] Nevertheless, on May 18, 1917, the Selective Service Act was passed by large majorities in both Houses. June 5, 1917, was set as registration day, and most Americans responded to the call.

The hysteria of World War I created what was probably the most serious erosion of political and civil liberty in our history. Zechariah Chafee, in his famed analysis of *Free Speech in the United States*, recounts numerous instances of official disregard for first amendment rights.[243] Under the Espionage Act,[244] any statement which tended to obstruct the draft became criminal,[245] and the courts enforced this provision vigorously. J. P. Doe, son of the great Chief Justice of New Hampshire, was convicted for writing a chain letter arguing that Germany had not broken its promise to the United States on submarine warfare. The producer of a film entitled "The Spirit of '76," which contained footage on Patrick Henry's speech, the Declaration of Independence, and scenes of British outrages committed during the Revolution, was also found guilty under the Espionage Act, since Britain was then our ally. Abraham Sugarman, Minnesota state secretary of the Socialist Party, told an open meeting: "This is supposed to be a free country. Like Hell it is." He then stated that the Selective Draft Act was unconstitutional and that no one had to obey it. He, too, was convicted, and a federal judge sentenced him to three years at Leavenworth.[246] Ministers who preached that it was against Christian principles to fight were prosecuted, as were vigorous political opponents of congressmen who had voted for conscription.[247] Twenty-seven farmers from South Dakota claimed that their county's draft quota was too high and argued against the war generally; they received one-year sentences. Socialists, I.W.W. members, and labor leaders opposed to the war were systematically rounded up, tried in the most perfunctory manner before judges who openly called them traitors, and given maximum sentences. Newspapers and magazines that editorialized against the war were denied mailing privileges; insufficiently patriotic teachers were removed from their posts.[248]

In this atmosphere the Supreme Court's decision in the *Selective Draft Law Cases* was almost inevitable. Suggestions by critics of the war that the draft was unconstitutional had led to indictments under the Espionage Act, and the overwhelming sentiment in the country was in favor of maximum mobilization to fight the hated Germans. The briefs in the *Arver* case never even touched on the early history of the military clauses; instead, they focused primarily on the thirteenth amendment's prohibition of involuntary servitude. It is most unfortunate that such an important question was resolved in such an unsatisfactory decision; yet, despite its manifest deficiencies and questionable arguments, the *Arver* opinion has survived unchallenged as part of our constitutional doctrine.

One reason for the survival of the *Selective Draft Law Cases* may be in the fact that conscription is a relatively rare phenomenon in this country. From 1789 until 1940—the first 151 years of the nation's history—draft laws were in force for a total of only four years, once during the Civil War and once during World War I. Proposals for compulsory military service were firmly rejected by Congress in the 1920's and 1930's.[249] Finally, when the German army overran France in 1940, Congress again assented to a conscription program—the first peacetime draft in our history—over vociferous opposition in both houses.[250] This was the last time that any substantial political opinion opposed conscription until January 1969, when nine senators introduced a bill to return to a volunteer system[251] and President Nixon recommended abolition of the draft.[252] Perhaps the growing public opposition to the most unpopular war in the nation's history will persuade Congress to revert to the kind of military establishment contemplated by the Constitution, or provide the Supreme Court with the opportunity to give the military clauses of the Constitution the full and impartial judicial consideration that they demand but have never received.

"Conscription and the Constitution: The Original Understanding," by Leon Friedman, from *Michigan Law Review*, Volume 67, Number 7 (May 1969), pages 1493–1552. Copyright © 1969 The Michigan Law Review Association. Reprinted with permission of the original publisher, The Michigan Law Review Association.

LEON FRIEDMAN (1933–) received his law degree from Harvard University in 1960 and is now professor of constitutional law at Hofstra Law School. He is the author of *Southern Justice, The Wise Minority,* and *Disorder in the Courts.*

Notes

1. Dennis v. United States, 341 U.S. 494, 523 (1950) (concurring opinion).

2. *A Volunteer Army Is the Answer,* N.Y. Times, March 30, 1969, § 6 (Magazine), at 34, 35.

3. G. REEDY, WHO WILL DO OUR FIGHTING FOR US? 56 (1969).

4. N.Y. Times, Jan. 31, 1969, at I, col. 8.

5. 245 U.S. 366. *Arver* was the principal decision among the three contemporaneous cases dealing with the question; *see* notes 8–9 *infra* and accompanying text. Hereafter *"Arver"* will be used interchangeably with *"Selective Draft Law Cases."*

6. Act of May 18, 1917, 40 Stat. 76.

7. At this time, a writ of error could be taken from the district court directly to the Supreme Court in any case involving "the construction or application of the Constitution of the United States." Act of March 3, 1911, ch. 231, § 238, 36 Stat. 1157.

8. Goldman v. United States, 245 U.S. 474 (1918).

9. Ruthenberg v. United States, 245 U.S. 480 (1918).

10. Brief for the United States at 10, Ruthenberg v. United States, 245 U.S. 480 (1918).

11. U.S. CONST., art. I, § 8, cl. 16; id., art. I, § 10.

12. See, e.g., In re Grimley, 137 U.S. 147, 153 (1890); Tarble's Case, 80 U.S. (13 Wall.) 397, 408 (1871).

13. 45 Pa. 238 (1863).

14. Art. I, § 8, cl. 11.

15. Art. I, § 8, cl. 12.

16. The Government cited an earlier federal case, United States v. Sugar, 243 F. 423, 436 (E.D. Mich. 1917), for the proposition that "power to declare war necessarily involves the power to carry it on, and this implies the means, saying nothing . . . of the express power 'to raise and support armies' as the provided means." Since war had been declared, it was not necessary to distinguish between the two sources of congressional power. Brief for the United States at 12, Ruthenberg v. United States, 245 U.S. 480 (1918).

17. 245 U.S. at 377–78.

18. See text accompanying notes 128–74 infra.

19. 245 U.S. at 378: "It may not be doubted that the very conception of a just government and its duty to the citizens includes the reciprocal obligation of the citizen to render military service in case of need and the right to compel it. . . . To do more than state the proposition is absolutely unnecessary in view of the practical illustration afforded by the almost universal legislation to that effect now in force."

20. Colby, Conscription in Modern Form, THE INFANTRY JOURNAL, June 1929, quoted in Freeman, The Constitutionality of Peacetime Conscription, 31 VA. L. REV. 40, 68 (1944).

21. Conscription, in 6 ENCYCLOPAEDIA BRITANNICA 366, 368 (1967 ed.).

22. 245 U.S. at 378–79.

23. S. GARDINER, THE CONSTITUTIONAL DOCUMENTS OF THE PURITAN REVOLUTION, 1625–60, at 334 (2d ed. 1899).

24. Id. at 368–69.

25. A Short History of Standing Armies, in 1 A COLLECTION OF TRACTS OF JOHN TRENCHARD AND THOMAS GORDON 71–72 (1751).

26. *Id.* at 74–75: "But he durst not have dreamt of all these Violations if he had not had an Army to justify them . . . . [H]e rais'd Guards in *England* (a Thing unheard of before in our *English* Constitution) and by degrees increas'd them, till they became a formidable Army. . . ."

27. *Id.* at 76–77.

28. *Id.* at 80.

29. 1 W. & M., 2d sess., c. 2 (1688 O.S.).

30. Trenchard, *supra* note 25, at 78.

31. THE IDEOLOGICAL ORIGINS OF THE AMERICAN REVOLUTION 35 (1967).

32. Trenchard, *An Argument Shewing That a Standing Army Is Inconsistent with a Free Government*, in 1 A COLLECTION OF TRACTS, *supra* note 25, at 14.

33. *Id.* at 23.

34. Freeman, *supra* note 20, at 68–69.

35. 29 Geo. 2, c. 4.

36. 30 Geo. 2, c. 8.

37. 18 Geo. 3, c. 53.

38. 19 Geo. 3, c. 10.

39. 30 Geo. 2, c. 25, §§ 19–21.

40. THE ENGLISH MILITIA IN THE EIGHTEENTH CENTURY 254 (1965).

41. *Id.* at 290–91.

42. *E.g.,* 30 Geo. 2, c. 25, §§ 19, 24, 51 (1757).

43. 245 U.S. at 379–80.

44. *See, e.g.,* R. WEIGLEY, HISTORY OF THE UNITED STATES ARMY 6 (1967): "The Massachusetts [militia] Law of 1631, passed when the colony was so new that it was extremely insecure, called for weekly drills, to be held every Saturday. Later it seemed safe enough to drill less often, and in 1637, training days were set at eight a year. When danger reappeared, training again intensified proportionately; there were twice-weekly drills during King Philip's War in 1675–76. On the training days, a town's militia company generally assembled on public grounds, held roll call and prayer, practiced the manual of arms and close order drill, and passed under review and inspection by the militia officers and other public officials. There might also be target practice and sham battles followed in the afternoon—when times were not too perilous—by refreshments, games, and socializing."

45. *Id.* at 8.

46. *Cf.* note 44 *supra.*

47. *See* SELECTIVE SERVICE SYSTEM, 2 BACKGROUNDS OF SELECTIVE SERVICE, pt. 14, at 4, 62, 76, 145, 166, 178–79 (Special Monograph No. 1, 1947) [hereinafter BACKGROUNDS].

48. R. WEIGLEY, *supra* note 44, at 8.

49. 2 BACKGROUNDS, pt. 14, at 123–24.

50. *Id.* at 186–87.

51. *Id.,* pt. 6, at 205, 214–15.

52. *Id.* at 137.

53. *Id.,* pt. 13, at 57.

54. *Id.,* pt. 1, at 45–46.

55. *See id.* at 34–69.

56. *Id.* at 5.

57. Shy, *A New Look at the Colonial Militia*, 20 WM. & MARY Q. 175, 182–83 (3d ser. 1963).

58. 2 BACKGROUNDS, pt. 1, at 2.

59. 245 U.S. at 381.

60. Trenchard, *supra* note 32, at 7.

61. B. BAILYN, *supra* note 31, at 114.

62. SOLDIERS AND CIVILIANS 40–41 (1968).

63. R. WEIGLEY, *supra* note 44, at 30.

64. M. CUNLIFFE, *supra* note 62, at 41.

65. R. WEIGLEY, *supra* note 44, at 38.

66. *Id.* at 38. Professor Weigley states that "Washington . . . had to recognize that compulsory service . . . imposed on an unlucky portion of the national manpower was a policy the country was not likely to accept." *Id.* at 41.

67. E. BURNETT, THE CONTINENTAL CONGRESS 390 (1941).

68. 2 PAPERS OF THOMAS JEFFERSON 18 (J. Boyd ed. 1950).

69. *See, e.g.,* J. ALLEN, THE AMERICAN REVOLUTION 216 (1954): "Taxes had come to be associated in patriot thinking with British tyranny, and in any event Congress lacked authority to collect them."

70. J. MILLER, TRIUMPH OF FREEDOM: 1775–1783, at 456–59 (1948).

71. *Id.* at 238.

72. E. BURNETT, *supra* note 67, at 107.

73. *Id.*

74. 20 THE WRITINGS OF GEORGE WASHINGTON 113–14 (J. Fitzpatrick ed. 1937).

75. *See id.* at 49–50: "Regular Troops alone are equal to the exigencies of modern war. . . . *No militia* will ever acquire the habits necessary to resist a regular force."

76. R. WEIGLEY, *supra* note 44, at 75.

77. *Id.* at 76–79.

78. *See, e.g.,* Letter to Henry Knox, in THE WASHINGTON PAPERS 229–31 (S. Padover ed. 1958). *See also* R. WEIGLEY, *supra* note 44, at 84; W. WILSON, GEORGE WASHINGTON 256 (1897).

79. *See, e.g.,* J. MAIN, THE ANTIFEDERALISTS 15 (1961): "The suspicion of a standing army and the Antifederal determination to keep in local hands the control over the military had important consequences during and after the Revolution. Equally important in its effects was the conviction that the power to tax must be retained by the people. The long struggle with the governors and the decade of controversy with king and parliament re-emphasized and intensified a doctrine shared by all Englishmen."

80. For example, the town of West Springfield, Massachusetts, reminded its representatives to guard against a Congress "which will form a design upon the liberties of the People & [it will not be] difficult to execute such a design when they have the absolute command of the navy, the army & the purse." *Id.* at 15–16.

81. RECORDS OF THE FEDERAL CONVENTION 7–14, 18–19 (M. Farrand ed. 1937) [hereinafter Farrand].

82. *Id.* at 19 (emphasis added).

83. *Id.* at 24–25: "If a state acts against a foreign power contrary to the laws of nations or violates a treaty, [the Confederation] cannot punish that State, or compel its obedience to the treaty. . . . It therefore cannot prevent a war."

84. *Id.* at 25 (emphasis added).

85. *Id.* at 25–26.

86. *Id.* at 244.

87. 2 *id.* at 143.

88. *Id.* at 158.

89. *Id.* at 323.

90. 1 *id.* at 465. George Mason of Virginia also expressed "hope there would be no standing army in time of peace, unless it might be for a few garrisons. The Militia ought therefore to be the more effectually prepared for the public defense." 2 *id.* at 326.

91. *Id.* at 329.

92. *Cf. id.:* "The people were jealous on this head, and great opposition to the plan would spring from such an omission. . . . He thought an

army dangerous in time of peace & could never consent to a power to keep up an indefinite number."

93. *Id.*

94. *Id.* at 508.

95. Elbridge Gerry objected even to that clause since it "implied there was to be a standing army which he inveighed against as dangerous to liberty, as unnecessary even for so great an extent of Country as this. And if necessary, some restriction on the number & duration ought to be provided." *Id.* at 509.

96. *Id.* at 617.

97. *Id.*

98. 1 *id.* at 21.

99. *Id.* at 244–45.

100. *Id.* at 293.

101. 2 *id.* at 135.

102. *Id.* at 159.

103. *Id.* at 168.

104. It is interesting to note that after the deletion of the phrase referring to treaties, the three instances in which the militia could be called out corresponded almost exactly to the provisions of the English Agreement of the People passed by the House of Commons in 1648. *See* text accompanying notes 23–24 *supra*.

105. For example, General C. C. Pinckney mentioned a case that had occurred during the war in which dissimilarity in the militia of different states "had produced the most serious mischiefs. Uniformity was essential. The States would never keep up a proper discipline of their militia." 2 Farrand 330.

106. *Id.* at 332.

107. *Id.*

108. *Id.* at 384–85.

109. "This power in the U.S. as explained is making the States drill-sergeants. He had as lief let the Citizens of Massachusetts be disarmed, as to take the command from the States, and subject them to the Genl. Legislature. It would be regarded as a system of Despotism." *Id.* at 385.

110. *Id.* at 387.

111. *Id.*

112. *Id.* at 388.

113. U.S. CONST. art. I, § 8, cl. 16.

114. *See generally* THE FEDERALIST Nos. 8, 23–29, 41.

115. THE FEDERALIST No. 8, at 48–49 (J. Cooke ed. 1961).

116. THE FEDERALIST No. 24, at 156–57 (J. Cooke ed. 1961).

117. *See, e.g.,* THE FEDERALIST No. 25, at 162 (J. Cooke ed. 1961): "The steady operations of war against a regular and disciplined army, can only be successfully conducted by a force of the same kind. . . . War, like most other things, is a science to be acquired and perfected by diligence, by perseverance, by time, and by practice." Madison makes the same point in THE FEDERALIST No. 41, at 270 (J. Cooke ed. 1961): "If one nation maintains constantly a disciplined army, ready for the service of ambition or revenge, it obliges the most pacific nations who may be within the reach of its enterprizes to take corresponding precautions."

118. THE FEDERALIST No. 8, at 47 (J. Cooke ed. 1961).

119. *Id.* at 47–48.

120. According to Hamilton, a well-trained militia " 'will not only lessen the call for military establishments; but if circumstances should at any time oblige the government to form an army of any magnitude, that army can never be formidable to the liberties of the people, while there is a large body of citizens little if at all inferior to them in discipline and the use of arms, who stand ready to defend their own rights and those of their fellow citizens.' " At 184 (J. Cooke ed. 1961).

121. At 321 (J. Cooke ed. 1961).

122. In THE FEDERALIST No. 41, at 276 (J. Cooke ed. 1961), Madison wrote: "The Power of levying and borrowing money, being the sinew of that which is to be exerted in the national defence, is properly thrown into the same class with it." At the beginning of THE FEDERALIST No. 30, at 187–88 (J. Cooke ed. 1961), the first paper after his discussion of the military clause, Hamilton stated: "It has been already observed that the Federal Government ought to possess the power of providing for the support of the national forces; in which proposition was intended to be included the expence of raising troops, of building and equipping fleets, and all other expences in any wise connected with military arrangements and operations."

123. THE FEDERALIST No. 23, at 147 (J. Cooke ed. 1961).

124. *Id.* at 147–48.

125. *See generally* text accompanying notes 128–74 *infra.*

126. At 148–49 (J. Cooke ed. 1961).

127. *See* text accompanying notes 19–21 *supra.*

128. *E.g.,* THE FEDERALIST No. 41, at 271 (J. Cooke ed. 1961) (Hamilton).

129. *See generally* text accompanying notes 128–74 *infra.*

130. *See* pt. 4 *infra.*

131. *See* text accompanying notes 163–64 *infra*.

132. 1 J. ELLIOT, DEBATES 370–71 (2d ed. 1836) [hereinafter DEBATES].

133. 2 DEBATES 57: "Congress, with the purse-strings in their hands, will use the sword with a witness."

134. *Id.* at 80.

135. J. MCMASTER & F. STONE, PENNSYLVANIA AND THE FEDERAL CONSTITUTION, 1787–1788, at 480 (1888).

136. 4 DEBATES 96.

137. 2 *id.* at 521.

138. 3 *id.* at 381.

139. 2 *id.* at 406.

140. 5 PAPERS OF ALEXANDER HAMILTON 185 (H. Syrett & J. Cooke ed. 1962): "That no Appropriation of money in time of Peace for the Support of an Army shall be by Less than two thirds of the Representatives and Senators present."

141. 1 DEBATES 330.

142. *Id.* at 328.

143. *See, e.g.,* 13 PAPERS OF THOMAS JEFFERSON 442–43 (J. Boyd ed. 1956): "I sincerely rejoice at the acceptance of our new constitution by nine states. It is a good canvas, on which some strokes only want retouching. What these are, I think are sufficiently manifested by the general voice from North to South, which calls for a bill of rights. It seems pretty generally understood that this should go to Juries, Habeas corpus, Standing armies. . . . If no check can be found to keep the number of standing troops within safe bounds . . . abandon them altogether, discipline well the militia, and guard the magazines with them. More than magazineguards will be useless if few, and dangerous if many. . . ." *See also* 12 *id.* 440; 14 *id.* 678.

144. *See, e.g.,* 3 DEBATES 425: "Mr. GEORGE MASON. . . . I ask, Who are the militia? They consist now of the whole people, except a few public officers." *See also id.* at 379, 385.

145. *Id.* at 378.

146. *Id.* at 401.

147. 2 DEBATES 278–79: "But, say the gentlemen, our present Congress have not the same powers. I answer, they have the very same. Congress have the powers of making war and peace, of levying money and raising men. . . . We are told that this Constitution gives Congress the power over the purse and the sword. Sir, have not all good governments this power? Nay, does anyone doubt that, under the old Confederation, Congress holds the purse and the sword? How many loans did they pro-

cure which we are bound to pay! How many men did they raise whom we are bound to maintain!"

148. *Id.* at 468: "Another objection is, 'that Congress may borrow money, keep up standing armies and command the militia.' The present Congress possesses the power of borrowing money and of keeping up standing armies."

149. *Id.* at 537: "The power of raising and supporting armies is not only necessary, but is enjoyed by the present Congress, who also judge of the expediency or necessity of keeping them up."

150. *Id.* at 352: "A government, to act with energy, should have the possession of all its revenues to answer present purposes. The principle for which I contend is recognized in all its extent by our old Constitution. Congress is authorized to raise troops, to call for supplies without limitation and to borrow money to any amount."

151. *Id.* at 520–21.

152. *See* text accompanying notes 19–21 *supra.*

153. 2 DEBATES 97–98.

154. *Id.* at 520.

155. 1 *id.* at 371.

156. 2 *id.* at 552.

157. *Id.*

158. 3 *id.* at 660: "That each state respectively shall have the power to provide for organizing, arming, and disciplining its own militia, whensoever Congress shall omit or neglect to provide for the same. That the militia shall not be subject to martial law, except when in actual service, in time of war, invasion or rebellion. . . ."

159. 2 DEBATES 552.

160. 4 *id.* at 245.

161. 3 *id.* at 660.

162. 2 *id.* at 552.

163. *Id.* at 537: "It is objected that the powers of Congress are too large, because 'they have the power of calling for the militia on necessary occasions, and may call them from one end of the continent to the other, and wantonly harass them; besides, they may coerce men to act in the militia whose consciences are against bearing arms in any case.' "

164. J. MCMASTER & F. STONE, *supra* note 135, at 480.

165. *Id.* at 480–81.

166. *See, e.g.,* 2 DEBATES 66–67 (remarks of Christopher Gore of Boston): "Is America to wait until she is attacked, before she attempts a preparation at defense? This certainly would be unwise; it would be

courting our enemies to make war upon us. The operations of war are sudden, and call for large sums of money." *See also id.* at 68, 189, 191.

167. 2 *id.* at 522.

168. *Letters from the Federal Farmer to the Republican* (Letter No. III), in ESSENTIAL WORKS OF THE FOUNDING FATHERS 282 (L. Kriegel ed. 1964).

169. *Id.* at 282–83.

170. 3 DEBATES 77: "The militia of our country will be wanted for agriculture. . . . It must be neglected if those hands which ought to attend to it are occasionally called forth on military expeditions."

171. *See id.* at 177. Henry "Light-Horse Harry" Lee should not be confused with his cousin Richard Henry Lee (*see* text accompanying note 168 *supra*). For biographies of the two men, *see* 11 DICTIONARY OF AMERICAN BIOGRAPHY 107, 117 (D. Malone ed. 1933).

172. 3 DEBATES 112–13.

173. *Id.* at 389.

174. *See, e.g.,* G. REEDY, WHO WILL DO OUR FIGHTING FOR US? 56 (1969): "When we say 'volunteer army' we are really saying an army composed of the poor and the black."

175. 1 ANNALS OF CONGRESS, 1st Cong., 434 (1834).

176. *See, e.g., id.* at 751 (remarks of Representative Benson of New York): "If this stands part of the Constitution, it will be a question before the Judiciary on every regulation you make with respect to the organization of this militia. . . . It is extremely injudicious to intermix matters of doubt with fundamentals. I have no reason to believe but the Legislature will always possess humanity enough to indulge this class of citizens in a matter they are so desirous of; but they ought to be left to their discretion."

177. *See* E. DUMBAULD, THE BILL OF RIGHTS AND WHAT IT MEANS TODAY 46 n.9 (1957). There was strong sentiment in the House for the provision. Elias Boudinot, once President of the Continental Congress and in 1789 a Representative from New Jersey, defended the conscientious-objector clause. "In forming a militia," he said "an effectual defence ought to be calculated, and no characters of this religious description ought to be compelled to take up arms." He added that "by striking out the clause, people may be led to believe that there is an intention in the General Government to compel all its citizens to bear arms." 1 ANNALS OF CONGRESS, 1st Cong., 767. Of course, since the clause in question related only to the militia, Boudinot's statements would make no sense if Congress had the power to conscript. For in that case the general government would be able "to compel all its citizens to bear arms," a power which Boudinot was denying.

178. 3 DEBATES 379.

179. *Id.* at 385.

180. *Cf.* R. WEIGLEY, HISTORY OF THE UNITED STATES ARMY 87 (1967): "It was possible to regard the state militias as a check against a federal standing army, since they had just accomplished a very similar purpose: they had given birth to the Continental Army to check the threat of military despotism from the British army."

181. Thus, Antifederalist Elbridge Gerry had argued against the inclusion of Madison's conscientious-objector clause in the Bill of Rights on the ground that Congress could declare large numbers of citizens religiously scrupulous "and thus prevent them from bearing arms" in the militia. 1 ANNALS OF CONGRESS, 1st Cong., 749–50 (1834).

182. Act of Sept. 29, 1789, ch. 25, 1 Stat. 95.

183. Act of April 30, 1790, ch. 10, 1 Stat. 119.

184. On March 30, 1790, Senator William Maclay confided to his diary: "This bill seems laying the foundation of a standing army. The justifiable reasons for using force seem to be the enforcing of law, quelling insurrections, and repelling invasions. The Constitution directs all these to be done by militia. Should the United States, unfortunately, be involved in war, an army for the annoyance of our enemy in their own country, (as the most effective mode of keeping the calamity at a distance . . .) will be necessary." THE JOURNALS OF WILLIAM MACLAY 221 (E. Maclay ed. 1965). It is interesting to note that Maclay's conception of a foreign expeditionary force is an extension of Hamilton's idea that the regular army would serve only as a frontier garrison and as a holding force to permit time for mobilization of the militia in the event of invasion; *see* text accompanying notes 115–16 *supra.*

185. Act of March 3, 1791, ch. 28, 1 Stat. 222; Act of March 5, 1792, ch. 9, 1 Stat. 241.

186. Act of May 8, 1792, ch. 33, 1 Stat. 271.

187. Thomas Fitzsimons of Pennsylvania, a member of the Philadelphia Convention, asked "whether it would be the most eligible mode to subject all the citizens . . . to turn out as soldiers. A much smaller number would, in his opinion, answer all the purposes of a militia." 2 ANNALS OF CONGRESS 1805 (1790). Elias Boudinot agreed that there was "a manifest propriety in the measure." *Id.* In his diary, Maclay wrote: "General Knox offers a most exceptional bill for a general militia law which excites (as it is most probable he expected) a general opposition." THE JOURNALS OF WILLIAM MACLAY 235 (E. Maclay ed. 1965).

188. ANNALS OF CONGRESS, 2d Cong., 419 (1849) (remarks of Representative Sturges). Congressman Samuel Livermore of New Hampshire concurred. "It is a militia of the several States that Congress have power to organize, and provide a mode of discipline for. It is not a militia to be

formed, or created—it already exists. He therefore thought it best to leave it to the respective States to make their own militia laws." *Id.*

189. *Id.* at 775–76.

190. *Id.* at 779.

191. *Id.* at 796.

192. Congress authorized these actions. Act of Nov. 29, 1794, ch. 1, 1 Stat. 403.

193. *See, e.g.,* R. WEIGLEY, *supra* note 180, at 8.

194. Act of May 9, 1794, ch. 27, 1 Stat. 367.

195. Act of May 28, 1798, ch. 47, 1 Stat. 558.

196. 245 U.S. at 382: "The right on the one hand of Congress under the Confederation to call on the States for forces and the duty on the other of the States to furnish when called, embraced the complete power of government over the subject. When the two were combined and were delegated to Congress all governmental power on that subject was conferred, a result manifested not only by the grant made but by the limitation expressly put upon the States on the subject. The army sphere therefore embraces such complete authority."

197. 245 U.S. at 383.

198. THE FEDERALIST No. 24, at 156–57 (J. Cooke ed. 1961).

199. THE FEDERALIST No. 25, at 158–59 (J. Cooke ed. 1961).

200. *See* note 184 *supra.*

201. 245 U.S. at 384.

202. 245 U.S. at 385.

203. 245 U.S. at 385.

204. ANNALS OF CONGRESS, 13th Cong., 3d Sess., 100 (1854).

205. Senator David Daggett of Connecticut opposed the bill because "it is utterly inconsistent with principles [of civil liberty] to compel any man to become a soldier for life, during a war, or for any fixed time. In Great Britain, a war-like nation . . . no such practice is, or can be, resorted to; the people would revolt at it. . . . It is alike odious here, and I hope it will remain so." *Id.* at 72. Similarly, Robert Goldsborough of Maryland challenged his fellow senators, saying "you dare not . . . attempt a conscription to fill the ranks of your regular army." *Id.* at 107.

206. *Id.* at 80.

207. *Id.* at 81.

208. 14 THE WRITINGS AND SPEECHES OF DANIEL WEBSTER 57 (1903).

209. *Id.*

210. *Id.* at 61.

211. *Id.*

212. *Id.* at 62.

213. *Id.* at 63–64.

214. ANNALS OF CONGRESS, 13th Cong., 3d Sess., 531 (1854).

215. *See* SELECTIVE SERVICE SYSTEM, 3 THE SELECTIVE SERVICE ACT 155 (Special Monograph No. 2, 1954).

216. A. FRIED, THE JEFFERSONIAN AND HAMILTONIAN TRADITION IN AMERICAN POLITICS 93 (1968).

217. 245 U.S. at 386: "By [the Act of March 3, 1863, ch. 75, 12 Stat. 731.], which was clearly intended to directly exert upon all the citizens of the United States the national power which it had been proposed to exert in 1814 . . . every male citizen of the United States between the ages of twenty and forty-five was made subject by the direct action of Congress to be called by compulsory draft to service in a national army at such time and in such numbers as the President in his discretion might find necessary."

218. 1 F. SHANNON, THE ORGANIZATION AND ADMINISTRATION OF THE UNION ARMY, 1861–1865, at 308 (1928): "Very clearly the law was never intended as a direct procurer of men but merely as a whip in the hands of the federal government to stimulate state activities. Even the name of conscription was avoided by its friends who always spoke of it as the 'enrollment bill.' Only its enemies called it a 'conscription bill,' which term was considered by the administration men as an unfair epithet. But they knew whereof they spoke for, as they shaped it, the bill was not a conscription bill in any general sense; it was merely a piece of class legislation designed . . . merely to stimulate mercenary establishments and to match the rich man's dollars with the poor man's life. None would have been more horrified than Henry Wilson [the act's author] at the suggestion that every able-bodied man drafted should be compelled to serve. . . ."

219. Civil War Enrollment Act, ch. 75, § 13, 12 Stat. 733 (1863). Subsequently the commutation fee was eliminated except for conscientious objectors (Act of July 4, 1864, ch. 237, §§ 2, 10, 13 Stat. 379–80), but enrollees were still permitted to furnish substitutes (Act of July 4, 1864, ch. 237, § 11, 13 Stat. 380).

220. J. McCAGUE, THE SECOND REBELLION 17 (1968).

221. 2 F. SHANNON, THE ORGANIZATION AND ADMINISTRATION OF THE UNION ARMY, 1861–1865, at 184–85 (1928).

222. Act of Feb. 24, 1864, ch. 13, 13 Stat. 6.

223. Act of March 3, 1865, ch. 79, 13 Stat. 487.

224. 245 U.S. at 387.

225. *Id.*

226. R. WEIGLEY, HISTORY OF THE UNITED STATES ARMY 210 (1967).

227. 18 TYLER'S QUARTERLY HISTORICAL AND GENEALOGICAL MAGAZINE 79 (1939).

228. *Id.*

229. *Id.* at 80.

230. *Id.*

231. *Id.*

232. *Id.* at 81.

233. *Id.*

234. *Id.*

235. 45 Pa. 238 (1863).

236. 245 U.S. at 388.

237. 45 Pa. at 248.

238. 45 Pa. at 254–55.

239. 45 Pa. at 267. The two judges who voted in favor of the act on first hearing were William Strong and John M. Read. Strong relied primarily upon the lack of constitutional restrictions on the power to raise armies, and upon the drafts imposed by the states during the Revolutionary War. Read depended upon the obligation of every member of society to defend the state; he cited the Knox plan of 1790, Monroe's 1814 draft proposal, and the English laws providing for a levy on idle and disorderly persons to show prior recognitions of the power.

240. 45 Pa. at 323–29.

241. H. PETERSON & G. FITE, OPPONENTS OF WAR, 1917–1918, at 22 (1957).

242. *Id.*

243. At 42, 51, 80 (1941). *See also* Kalven, *"Uninhibited, Robust, and Wide-Open"—A Note on Free Speech and the Warren Court,* 67 MICH. L. REV. 289, 290–91 (1968).

244. Ch. 30, 40 Stat. 217 (1917), *as amended,* ch. 75, 40 Stat. 553 (1918).

245. Ch. 30, tit. 1, § 3, 40 Stat. 219 (1917), *as amended,* ch. 75, § 1, 40 Stat. 553 (1918). *See also* CHAFEE, *supra* note 243, at 39.

246. H. PETERSON & G. FITE, *supra* note 241, at 37. *See also* Kalven, *supra* note 243, at 290–91.

247. *Id.* at 115–16, 155.

248. *Id.* at 43–60, 92–112, 203–04.

249. *See* SELECTIVE SERVICE SYSTEM, 3 THE SELECTIVE SERVICE ACT, 224, 232, 237 (Special Monograph No. 2, 1954).

250. For example, Senator Arthur Vandenberg of Michigan told the Senate: "I am opposed to tearing up 150 years of American history and tradition, in which none but volunteers have [sic] entered the peacetime Armies and Navies of the United States. . . . There must have been sound reasons all down the years why our predecessors in the Congress always consistently and relentlessly shunned this thing which we are now asked to do. These reasons must have been related in some indispensable fashion to the fundamental theory that peacetime military conscription is repugnant to the spirit of democracy and the soul of Republican institutions, and that it leads in dark directions." Gillam, *The Peacetime Draft,* 57 YALE REV. 495, 498 (1968). Even the Act's supporters insisted it was a temporary expedient. Representative James W. Wadsworth, who introduced the legislation, said: "This is an emergency measure. . . . It is not an attempt to establish a permanent policy in the United States." *Id.* at 502.

251. Voluntary Military Manpower Procurement Act of 1969, S. 503, 91st Cong., 1st sess. For reports of the introduction of this bill, *see* 115 CONG. REC. S691–99 (daily ed. Jan. 22, 1969); N.Y. Times, Jan. 23, 1969, at 1, col 8.

252. N.Y. Times, Jan. 31, 1969, at 1, col. 8.

Part IV

Economics

18

Of the Expence of Defence
by
Adam Smith

Adam Smith's The Wealth of Nations, *the cornerstone of the science of political economy, contains this discussion of the economics of military preparedness and defense. Smith analyzes the relative manpower, organizational needs, and arms requirements of societies from loosely knit, ill-equipped bands of hunter-gatherers to the highly regimented, technologically equipped professional standing armies of modern nation-states. He argues that settled commerce, increasing specialization, and technological advances result in increasing defense costs, a distinct advantage for rich over poor nations, and the superiority of professional standing armies over volunteer militia for long-term defense. Smith concludes that the development of weapons is favorable to both the survival and the expansion of civilized nation-states.*

The first duty of the sovereign, that of protecting the society from the violence and invasion of other independent societies, can be performed only by means of a military force. But the expence both of preparing this military force in time of peace, and of employing it in time of war, is very different in the different states of society, in the different periods of improvement.

Among nations of hunters, the lowest and rudest state of society, such as we find it among the native tribes of North America, every man is a warrior as well as a hunter. When he goes to war, either to defend his society, or to revenge the injuries which have been done to it by other societies, he maintains himself by his own labour, in the same manner as when he lives at home. His society, for in this state of things there is properly neither sovereign nor commonwealth, is at no sort of expence, either to prepare him for the field, or to maintain him while he is in it.

Among nations of shepherds, a more advanced state of society, such as we find it among the Tartars and Arabs, every man is, in the same manner, a warrior. Such nations have commonly no fixed habitation, but live, either in tents, or in a sort of covered waggons which are easily transported from place to place. The whole tribe or nation changes its situation according to the different seasons of the year, as well as according to other accidents. When its herds and flocks have consumed the forage of one part of the country, it removes to another, and from that to a third. In the dry season, it comes down to the banks of the rivers; in the wet season it retires to the upper country. When such a nation goes to war, the warriors will not trust their herds and flocks to the feeble defence of their old men, their women and children, and the old men, their women and children, will not be left behind without defence and without subsistence. The whole nation, besides, being accustomed to a wandering life, even in time of peace, easily takes the field in time of war. Whether it marches as an army, or moves about as a company of herdsmen, the way of life is nearly the same, though the object proposed by it is very different. They all go to war together, therefore, and every one does as well as he can. Among the Tartars, even the women have been frequently known to engage in battle. If they conquer, whatever belongs to the hostile tribe is the recompence of the victory. But if they are vanquished, all is lost, and not only their herds and flocks, but their women and children, become the booty of the conqueror. Even the greater part of those who survive the action are obliged to submit to him for the sake of immediate subsistence. The rest are commonly dissipated and dispersed in the desart.

The ordinary life, the ordinary exercises of a Tartar or Arab, prepare him sufficiently for war. Running, wrestling, cudgel-playing, throwing the javelin, drawing the bow, &c. are the common pastimes of those who live in the open air, and are all of them the images of war. When a Tartar or Arab actually goes to war, he is maintained, by his own herds and flocks which he carries with him, in the same manner as in peace. His chief or sovereign, for those nations have all chiefs or sovereigns, is at no sort of expence in preparing him for the field; and when he is in it, the chance of plunder is the only pay which he either expects or requires.

An army of hunters can seldom exceed two or three hundred men. The precarious subsistence which the chace affords could seldom allow a greater number to keep together for any considerable time. An army of shepherds, on the contrary, may sometimes amount to two or three hundred thousand. As long as nothing stops their progress, as long as they can go on from one district, of which they have consumed the forage, to another which is yet entire; there seems to be scarce any limit to the number who can march on together. A nation of hunters can never be formidable to the civilized nations in their neighbourhood. A nation of shepherds may. Nothing can be more contemptible than an Indian war in North America. Nothing, on the contrary, can be more dreadful than a Tartar invasion has frequently been in Asia. The judgment of Thucidides [sic], that both Europe and Asia could not resist the Scythians united, has been verified by the experience of all ages. The inhabitants of the extensive, but defenceless plains of Scythia of Tartary, have been frequently united under the dominion of the chief of some conquering horde or clan; and the havoc and devastation of Asia have always signalized their union. The inhabitants of the inhospitable desarts of Arabia, the other great nation of shepherds, have never been united but once; under Mahomet and his immediate successors. Their union, which was more the effect of religious enthusiasm than of conquest, was signalized in the same manner. If the hunting nations of America should ever become shepherds, their neighbourhood would be much more dangerous to the European colonies than it is at present.

In a yet more advanced state of society, among those nations of husbandmen who have little foreign commerce, and no other manufactures but those coarse and houshold ones which almost every private family prepares for its own use; every man, in the same manner, either is a warrior, or easily becomes such. They who live by agriculture generally pass the whole day in the open air, exposed to all the inclemencies of the seasons. The hardiness of their ordinary life prepares them for the fatigues of war, to some of which their necessary occupations bear a good deal of analogy. The necessary occupation of a ditcher prepares him to work in the trenches, and to fortify a camp as well as to enclose a field. The ordinary pastimes of such husbandmen are the same as those of shepherds, and are in the same manner the images of war. But as husbandmen have less leisure than shepherds, they are not so frequently employed in those pastimes. They are soldiers, but soldiers not quite so much masters of their exercise. Such as they are, however, it seldom costs the sovereign or commonwealth any expence to prepare them for the field.

Agriculture, even in its rudest and lowest state, supposes a settlement; some sort of fixed habitation which cannot be abandoned without great loss. When a nation of mere husbandmen, therefore, goes to war, the whole people cannot take the field together. The old men, the women and children, at least, must remain at home to take care of the habitation. All the men of the military age, however, may take the field, and, in small nations of this kind, have frequently done so. In every nation the men of the military age are supposed to amount to about a fourth or fifth part of the whole body of the people. If the campaign too should begin after seed-time, and end before harvest, both the husbandman and his principal labourers can be spared from the farm without much loss. He trusts that the work which must be done in the mean time can be well enough executed by the old men, the women and the children. He is not unwilling, therefore, to serve without pay during so short a campaign, and it frequently costs the sovereign or commonwealth as little to maintain him in the field as to prepare him for it. The citizens of all the different states of ancient Greece seem to have served in this manner till after the second Persian war; and the people of Peloponesus till after the Peloponesian war. The Peloponesians, Thucidides [sic] observes, generally left the field in the summer, and returned home to reap the harvest. The Roman people under their kings, and during the first ages of the republic, served in the same manner. It was not till the siege of Veii, that they, who staid at home, began to contribute something towards maintaining those who went to war. In the European monarchies, which were founded upon the ruins of the Roman empire, both before and for some time after the establishment of what is properly called the feudal law, the great lords, with all their immediate dependents, used to serve the crown at their own expence. In the field, in the same manner as at home, they maintained themselves by their own revenue, and not by any stipend or pay which they received from the king upon that particular occasion.

In a more advanced state of society, two different causes contribute to render it altogether impossible that they, who take the field, should maintain themselves at their own expence. Those two causes are, the progress of manufactures, and the improvement in the art of war.

Though a husbandman should be employed in an expedition, provided it begins after seed-time and ends before harvest, the interruption of his business will not always occasion any considerable diminution of his revenue. Without the intervention of his labour, nature does herself the greater part of the work which remains to be done. But the moment that an artificer, a smith, a carpenter, or a weaver, for example, quits his workhouse, the sole source of his revenue is completely dried up. Nature does nothing for him, he does all for himself. When he takes the field, therefore, in defence of the public, as he has no revenue to maintain himself, he must necessarily be maintained by the public. But in a country of which a greater part of the inhabitants are artificers and manufacturers, a great part of the people who go to war must be drawn from those classes, and must therefore be maintained by the public as long as they are employed in its service.

When the art of war too has gradually grown up to be a very intricate and complicated science, when the event of war ceases to be determined, as in the first ages of society, by a single irregular skirmish or battle, but when the contest is generally spun out through several different campaigns, each of which lasts during the greater part of the year; it becomes universally necessary that the public should maintain those who serve the public in war, at least while they are employed in that service. Whatever in time of peace might be the ordinary occupation of those who go to war, so very tedious and expensive a service would otherwise be by far too heavy a burden upon them. After the second Persian war, accordingly, the armies of Athens seem to have been generally composed of mercenary troops; consisting, indeed, partly of citizens, but partly too of foreigners; and all of them equally hired and paid at the expence of the state. From the time of the siege of Veii, the armies of Rome received pay for their service during the time which they remained in the field. Under the feudal governments the military service both of the great lords and of their immediate dependents was, after a certain period, universally exchanged for a payment in money, which was employed to maintain those who served in their stead.

The number of those who can go to war, in proportion to the whole number of the people, is necessarily much smaller in a civilized, than in a rude state of society. In a civilized society, as the soldiers are maintained altogether by the labour of those who are not soldiers, the number of the former never can exceed what the latter can maintain, over and above maintaining, in a manner suitable to their respective stations, both themselves and the other officers of government, and law, whom they are obliged to maintain. In the little agrarian states of ancient Greece, a fourth or a fifth part of the whole body of the people considered themselves as soldiers, and would sometimes, it is said, take the field. Among the civilized nations of modern Europe, it is commonly computed, that not more than one hundredth part of the inhabitants of any country can be employed as soldiers, without ruin to the country at whose expence they are employed.

The expence of preparing the army for the field seems not to have become considerable in any nation, till long after that of maintaining it in the field had devolved entirely upon the sovereign or commonwealth. In all the different republics of ancient Greece, to learn his military exercises, was a necessary part of education imposed by the state upon every free citizen. In every city there seems to have been a public field, in which, under the protection of the public magistrate, the young people were taught their different exercises by different masters. In this very simple institution, consisted the whole expence which any Grecian state seems ever to have been at, in preparing its citizens for war. In ancient Rome the exercises of the Campus Martius answered the same purpose with those of the Gymnasium in ancient Greece. Under the feudal governments, the many public ordinances that the citizens of every district should practise archery as well as several other military exercises, were intended for promoting the same purpose, but do not seem to have promoted it so well. Either from want of interest in the officers entrusted with the execution of those ordinances, or from some other cause, they appear to have been universally neglected; and in the progress of all those governments, military exercises seem to have gone gradually into disuse among the great body of the people.

In the republics of ancient Greece and Rome, during the whole period of their existence, and under the feudal governments for a considerable time after their first establishment, the trade of a soldier was not a separate, distinct trade, which constituted the sole or principal occupation of a particular class of citizens. Every subject of the state, whatever might be the ordinary trade or occupation by which he gained his livelihood, considered himself, upon all ordinary occasions, as fit likewise to exercise the trade of a soldier, and upon many extraordinary occasions as bound to exercise it.

The art of war, however, as it is certainly the noblest of all arts, so in the progress of improvement it necessarily becomes one of the most complicated among them. The state of the mechanical, as well as of some other arts, with which it is necessarily connected, determines the degree of perfection to which it is capable of being carried at any particular time. But in order to carry it to this degree of perfection, it is necessary that it should become the sole or principal occupation of a particular class of citizens, and the division of labour is as necessary for the improvement of this, as of every other art. Into other arts the division of labour is naturally introduced by the prudence of individuals, who find that they promote their private interest better by confining themselves to a particular trade, than by exercising a great number. But it is the wisdom of the state only which can render the trade of a soldier a particular trade separate and distinct from all others. A private citizen who, in time of profound peace, and without any particular encouragement from the public, should spend the greater part of his time in military exercises, might, no doubt, both improve himself very much in them, and amuse himself very well; but he certainly would not promote his own interest. It is the wisdom of the state only which can render it for his interest to give up the greater part of his time to this peculiar occupation: and states have not always had this wisdom, even when their circumstances had become such, that the preservation of their existence required that they should have it.

A shepherd has a great deal of leisure; a husbandman, in the rude state of husbandry, has some; an artificer or manufacturer has none at all. The first may, without any loss, employ a great deal of his time in martial exercises; the second may employ some part of it; but the last cannot employ a single hour in them without some loss, and his attention to his own interest naturally leads him to neglect them altogether. Those improvements in husbandry too, which the progress of arts and manufactures necessarily introduces, leave the husbandman as little leisure as the artificer. Military exercises come to be as much neglected by the inhabitants of the country as by those of the town, and the great body of the people becomes altogether unwarlike. That wealth, at the same time, which always follows the improvements of agriculture and manufactures, and which in reality is no more than the accumulated produce of those improvements, provokes the invasion of all their neighbours. An industrious, and upon that account a wealthy nation, is of all nations the most likely to be attacked; and unless the state takes some new measures for the public defence, the natural habits of the people render them altogether incapable of defending themselves.

In these circumstances, there seem to be but two methods, by which the state can make any tolerable provision for the public defence.

It may either, first, by means of a very rigorous police, and in spite of the whole bent of the interest, genius and inclinations of the people, enforce the practice of military exercises, and oblige either all the citizens of the military age, or a certain number of them, to join in some measure the trade of a soldier to whatever other trade or profession they may happen to carry on.

Or secondly, by maintaining and employing a certain number of citizens in the constant practice of military exercises, it may render the trade of a soldier a particular trade, separate and distinct from all others.

If the state has recourse to the first of those two expedients, its military force is said to consist in a militia; if to the second, it is said to consist in a standing army. The practice of military exercises is the sole or principal occupation of the soldiers of a standing army, and the maintenance or pay which the state affords them is the principal and ordinary fund of their subsistence. The practice of military exercises is only the occasional occupation of the soldiers of a militia, and they derive the principal and ordinary fund of their subsistence from some other occupation. In a militia, the character of the labourer, artificer, or tradesman, predominates over that of the soldier: in a standing army, that of the soldier predominates over every other character; and in this distinction seems to consist the essential difference between those two different species of military force.

Militias have been of several different kinds. In some countries the citizens destined for defending the state, seem to have been exercised only, without being, if I may say so, regimented; that is, without being divided into separate and distinct bodies of troops, each of which per-formed its exercises under its own proper and permanent officers. In the republics of ancient Greece and Rome, each citizen, as long as he remained at home, seems to have practised his exercises either sepa-rately and independently, or with such of his equals as he liked best; and not to have been attached to any particular body of troops till he was actually called upon to take the field. In other countries, the militia has not only been exercised, but regimented. In England, in Switzer-land, and, I believe, in every other country of modern Europe, where any imperfect military force of this kind has been established, every militia-man is, even in time of peace, attached to a particular body of troops, which performs its exercises under its own proper and perma-nent officers.

Before the invention of fire-arms, that army was superior in which the soldiers had, each individually, the greatest skill and dexterity in the use of their arms. Strength and agility of body were of the highest consequence, and commonly determined the fate of battles. But this skill and dexterity in the use of their arms, could be acquired only, in the same manner as fencing is acquired at present, by practising, not in great bodies, but each man separately, in a particular school, under a particular master, or with his own particular equals and companions. Since the invention of fire-arms, strength and agility of body, or even extraordinary dexterity and skill in the use of arms, though they are far from being of no consequence, are, however, of less consequence.

The nature of the weapon, though it by no means puts the awkward upon a level with the skilful, puts him more nearly so than he ever was before. All the dexterity and skill, it is supposed, which are necessary for using it, can be well enough acquired by practising in great bodies.

Regularity, order, and prompt obedience to command, are qualities which, in modern armies, are of more importance towards determining the fate of battles, than the dexterity and skill of the soldiers in the use of their arms. But the noise of fire-arms, the smoke, and the invisible death to which every man feels himself every moment exposed, as soon as he comes within cannon-shot, and frequently a long time before the battle can be well said to be engaged, must render it very difficult to maintain any considerable degree of this regularity, order, and prompt obedience, even in the beginning of a modern battle. In an ancient battle there was no noise but what arose from the human voice; there was no smoke, there was no invisible cause of wounds or death. Every man, till some mortal weapon actually did approach him, saw clearly that no such weapon was near him. In these circumstances, and among troops who had some confidence in their own skill and dexterity in the use of their arms, it must have been a good deal less difficult to preserve some degree of regularity and order, not only in the beginning, but through the whole progress of an ancient battle, and till one of the two armies was fairly defeated. But the habits of regularity, order, and prompt obedience to command, can be acquired only by troops which are exercised in great bodies.

A militia, however, in whatever manner it may be either disciplined or exercised, must always be much inferior to a well-disciplined and well-exercised standing army.

The soldiers, who are exercised only once a week, or once a month, can never be so expert in the use of their arms, as those who are exercised every day, or every other day; and though this circumstance may not be of so much consequence in modern, as it was in ancient times, yet the acknowledged superiority of the Prussian troops, owing, it is said, very much to their superior expertness in their exercise, may satisfy us that it is, even at this day, of very considerable consequence.

The soldiers, who are bound to obey their officer only once a week or once a month, and who are at all other times at liberty to manage their own affairs their own way, without being in any respect accountable to him, can never be under the same awe in his presence, can never have the same disposition to ready obedience, with those whose whole life and conduct are every day directed by him, and who every day even rise and go to bed, or at least retire to their quarters, according to his orders. In what is called discipline, or in the habit of ready obedience, a militia must always be still more inferior to a standing army, than it may sometimes be in what is called the manual exercise, or in the management and use of its arms. But in modern war the habit of ready and instant obedience is of much greater consequence than a considerable superiority in the management of arms.

Those militias which, like the Tartar or Arab militia, go to war under the same chieftains whom they are accustomed to obey in peace, are by far the best. In respect for their officers, in the habit of ready obedience, they approach nearest to standing armies. The highland militia, when it served under its own chieftains, had some advantage of the same kind. As the highlanders, however, were not wandering, but stationary shepherds, as they had all a fixed habitation, and were not, in peaceable times, accustomed to follow their chieftain from place to place; so in time of war they were less willing to follow him to any considerable distance, or to continue for any long time in the field. When they had acquired any booty they were eager to return home, and his authority was seldom sufficient to detain them. In point of obedience they were always much inferior to what is reported of the Tartars and Arabs. As the highlanders too, from their stationary life, spend less of their time in the open air, they were always less accustomed to military exercises, and were less expert in the use of their arms than the Tartars and Arabs are said to be.

A militia of any kind, it must be observed, however, which has served for several successive campaigns in the field, becomes in every respect a standing army. The soldiers are every day exercised in the use of their arms, and, being constantly under the command of their officers, are habituated to the same prompt obedience which takes place in standing armies. What they were before they took the field, is of little importance. They necessarily become in every respect a standing army, after they have passed a few campaigns in it. Should the war in America drag out through another campaign, the American militia may become in every respect a match for that standing army, of which in the last war* the valour appeared, at least not inferior to that of the hardiest veterans of France and Spain.

This distinction being well understood, the history of all ages, it will be found, bears testimony to the irresistible superiority which a well-regulated standing army has over a militia.

One of the first standing armies of which we have any distinct account, in any well authenticated history, is that of Philip of Macedon.

---

*[Editor's note]: The Seven Years' War (1756–1763).

His frequent wars with the Thracians, Illyrians, Thessalians, and some of the Greek cities in the neighbourhood of Macedon, gradually formed his troops, which in the beginning were probably militia, to the exact discipline of a standing army. When he was at peace, which he was very seldom, and never for any long time together, he was careful not to disband that army. It vanquished and subdued, after a long and violent struggle, indeed, the gallant and well-exercised militias of the principal republics of ancient Greece; and afterwards, with very little struggle, the effeminate and ill-exercised militia of the great Persian empire. The fall of the Greek republics and of the Persian empire, was the effect of the irresistible superiority which a standing army has over every sort of militia. It is the first great revolution in the affairs of mankind, of which history has preserved any distinct or circumstantial account.

The fall of Carthage, and the consequent elevation of Rome, is the second. All the varieties of the fortune of those two famous republics may very well be accounted for from the same cause.

From the end of the first to the beginning of the second Carthaginian war, the armies of Carthage were continually in the field, and employed under three great generals, who succeeded one another in the command; Amilcar, his son-in-law Asdrubal, and his son Annibal; first in chastising their own rebellious slaves, afterwards in subduing the revolted nations of Africa, and, lastly, in conquering the great kingdom of Spain. The army which Annibal led from Spain into Italy must necessarily, in those different wars, have been gradually formed to the exact discipline of a standing army. The Romans, in the mean time, though they had not been altogether at peace, yet they had not, during this period, been engaged in any war of very great consequence; and their military discipline, it is generally said, was a good deal relaxed. The Roman armies which Annibal encountered at Trebia, Thrasymenus, and Cannæ, were militia opposed to a standing army. This circumstance, it is probable, contributed more than any other to determine the fate of those battles.

The standing army which Annibal left behind him in Spain, had the like superiority over the militia which the Romans sent to oppose it, and in a few years, under the command of his brother, the younger Asdrubal, expelled them almost entirely from that country.

Annibal was ill supplied from home. The Roman militia, being continually in the field, became in the progress of the war a well disciplined and well exercised standing army; and the superiority of Annibal grew every day less and less. Asdrubal judged it necessary to lead the whole, or almost the whole of the standing army which he commanded in Spain, to the assistance of his brother in Italy. In his march he is said to have been misled by his guides; and in a country which he did not know, was surprized and attacked by another standing army, in every respect equal or superior to his own, and was entirely defeated.

When Asdrubal had left Spain, the great Scipio found nothing to oppose him but a militia inferior to his own. He conquered and subdued that militia, and, in the course of the war, his own militia necessarily became a well-disciplined and well-exercised standing army. That standing army was afterwards carried to Africa, where it found nothing but a militia to oppose it. In order to defend Carthage it became necessary to recall the standing army of Annibal. The disheartened and frequently defeated African militia joined it, and, at the battle of Zama, composed the greater part of the troops of Annibal. The event of that day determined the fate of the two rival republics.

From the end of the second Carthaginian war till the fall of the Roman republic, the armies of Rome were in every respect standing armies. The standing army of Macedon made some resistance to their arms. In the height of their grandeur, it cost them two great wars, and three great battles, to subdue that little kingdom; of which the conquest would probably have been still more difficult, had it not been for the cowardice of its last king. The militias of all the civilized nations of the ancient world, of Greece, of Syria, and of Egypt, made but a feeble resistance to the standing armies of Rome. The militias of some barbarous nations defended themselves much better. The Scythian or Tartar militia, which Mithridates drew from the countries north of the Euxine and Caspian seas, were the most formidable enemies which the Romans had to encounter after the second Carthaginian war. The Parthian and German militias too were always respectable, and upon several occasions, gained very considerable advantages over the Roman armies. In general, however, and when the Roman armies were well commanded, they appear to have been very much superior; and if the Romans did not pursue the final conquest either of Parthia or Germany, it was probably because they judged, that it was not worth while to add those two barbarous countries to an empire which was already too large. The ancient Parthians appear to have been a nation of Scythian or Tartar extraction, and to have always retained a good deal of the manners of their ancestors. The ancient Germans were, like the Scythians or Tartars, a nation of wandering shepherds, who went to war under the same chiefs whom they were accustomed to follow in peace. Their militia was exactly of the same kind with that of the Scythians or Tartars, from whom too they were probably descended.

Many different causes contributed to relax the discipline of the Roman armies. Its extreme severity was, perhaps, one of those causes. In the days of their grandeur, when no enemy appeared capable of opposing them, their heavy armour was laid aside as unnecessarily burdensome, their laborious exercises were neglected as unnecessarily toilsome. Under the Roman emperors besides, the standing armies of Rome, those particularly which guarded the German and Pannonian frontiers, became dangerous to their masters, against whom they used frequently to set up their own generals. In order to render them less formidable, according to some authors, Dioclesian, according to others, Constantine, first withdrew them from the frontier, where they had always before been encamped in great bodies, generally of two or three legions each, and dispersed them in small bodies through the different provincial towns, from whence they were scarce ever removed, but when it became necessary to repel an invasion. Small bodies of soldiers quartered in trading and manufacturing towns, and seldom removed from those quarters, became themselves tradesmen, artificers, and manufacturers. The civil came to predominate over the military character; and the standing armies of Rome gradually degenerated into a corrupt, neglected, and undisciplined militia, incapable of resisting the attack of the German and Scythian militias, which soon afterwards invaded the western empire. It was only by hiring the militia of some of those nations to oppose to that of others, that the emperors were for some time able to defend themselves. The fall of the western empire is the third great revolution in the affairs of mankind, of which ancient history has preserved any distinct or circumstantial account. It was brought about by the irresistible superiority which the militia of a barbarous, has over that of a civilized nation; which the militia of a nation of shepherds, has over that of a nation of husbandmen, artificers, and manufacturers. The victories which have been gained by militias have generally been, not over standing armies, but over other militias in exercise and discipline inferior to themselves. Such were the victories which the Greek militia gained over that of the Persian empire; and such too were those which in later times the Swiss militia gained over that of the Austrians and Burgundians.

The military force of the German and Scythian nations who established themselves upon the ruins of the western empire, continued for some time to be of the same kind in their new settlements, as it had been in their original country. It was a militia of shepherds and husbandmen, which, in time of war, took the field under the command of the same chieftains whom it was accustomed to obey in peace. It was, therefore, tolerably well exercised, and tolerably well disciplined. As arts and industry advanced, however, the authority of the chieftains gradually decayed, and the great body of the people had less time to spare for military exercises. Both the discipline and the exercise of the feudal militia, therefore, went gradually to ruin, and standing armies were gradually introduced to supply the place of it. When the expedient of a standing army, besides, had once been adopted by one civilized nation, it became necessary that all its neighbours should follow the example. They soon found that their safety depended upon their doing so, and that their own militia was altogether incapable of resisting the attack of such an army.

The soldiers of a standing army, though they may never have seen an enemy, yet have frequently appeared to possess all the courage of veteran troops, and the very moment that they took the field to have been fit to face the hardiest and most experienced veterans. In 1756, when the Russian army marched into Poland, the valour of the Russian soldiers did not appear inferior to that of the Prussians, at that time supposed to be the hardiest and most experienced veterans in Europe. The Russian empire, however, had enjoyed a profound peace for near twenty years before, and could at that time have very few soldiers who had ever seen an enemy. When the Spanish war broke out in 1739, England had enjoyed a profound peace for about eight and twenty years. The valour of her soldiers, however, far from being corrupted by that long peace, was never more distinguished than in the attempt upon Carthagena, the first unfortunate exploit of that unfortunate war. In a long peace the generals, perhaps, may sometimes forget their skill; but, where a well-regulated standing army has been kept up, the soldiers seem never to forget their valour.

When a civilized nation depends for its defence upon a militia, it is at all times exposed to be conquered by any barbarous nation which happens to be in its neighbourhood. The frequent conquests of all the civilized countries in Asia by the Tartars, sufficiently demonstrate the natural superiority, which the militia of a barbarous, has over that of a civilized nation. A well-regulated standing army is superior to every militia. Such an army, as it can best be maintained by an opulent and civilized nation, so it can alone defend such a nation against the invasion of a poor and barbarous neighbour. It is only by means of a standing army, therefore, that the civilization of any country can be perpetuated, or even preserved for any considerable time.

As it is only by means of a well-regulated standing army that a civilized country can be defended; so it is only by means of it, that a barbarous country can be suddenly and tolerably civilized. A standing army establishes, with an irresistible force, the law of the sovereign through the remotest provinces of the empire, and maintains some degree of regular government in countries which could not otherwise admit of any. Whoever examines, with attention, the improvements which Peter the Great introduced into the Russian empire, will find that they almost all resolve themselves into the establishment of a well-regulated standing army. It is the instrument which executes and maintains all his other regulations. That degree of order and internal peace, which that empire has ever since enjoyed, is altogether owing to the influence of that army.

Men of republican principles have been jealous of a standing army as dangerous to liberty. It certainly is so, wherever the interest of the general and that of the principal officers are not necessarily connected with the support of the constitution of the state. The standing army of Cæsar destroyed the Roman republic. The standing army of Cromwell turned the long parliament out of doors. But where the sovereign is himself the general, and the principal nobility and gentry of the country the chief officers of the army; where the military force is placed under the command of those who have the greatest interest in the support of the civil authority, because they have themselves the greatest share of that authority, a standing army can never be dangerous to liberty. On the contrary, it may in some cases be favourable to liberty. The security which it gives to the sovereign renders unnecessary that troublesome jealousy, which, in some modern republics, seems to watch over the minutest actions, and to be at all times ready to disturb the peace of every citizen. Where the security of the magistrate, though supported by the principal people of the country, is endangered by every popular discontent; where a small tumult is capable of bringing about in a few hours a great revolution, the whole authority of government must be employed to suppress and punish every murmur and complaint against it. To a sovereign, on the contrary, who feels himself supported, not only by the natural aristocracy of the country, but by a well-regulated standing army, the rudest, the most groundless, and the most licentious remonstrances can give little disturbance. He can safely pardon or neglect them, and his consciousness of his own superiority naturally disposes him to do so. That degree of liberty which approaches to licentiousness can be tolerated only in countries where the sovereign is secured by a well-regulated standing army. It is in such countries only, that the public safety does not require, that the sovereign should be trusted with any discretionary power, for suppressing even the impertinent wantonness of this licentious liberty.

The first duty of the sovereign, therefore, that of defending the society from the violence and injustice of other independent societies, grows gradually more and more expensive, as the society advances in civilization. The military force of the society, which originally cost the sovereign no expence either in time of peace or in time of war, must, in the progress of improvement, first be maintained by him in time of war, and afterwards even in time of peace.

The great change introduced into the art of war by the invention of fire-arms, has enhanced still further both the expence of exercising and disciplining any particular number of soldiers in time of peace, and that of employing them in time of war. Both their arms and their ammunition are become more expensive. A musquet is a more expensive machine than a javelin or a bow and arrows; a cannon or a mortar than a balista or a catapulta. The powder, which is spent in a modern review, is lost irrecoverably, and occasions a very considerable expence. The javelins and arrows which were thrown or shot in an ancient one, could easily be picked up again, and were besides of very little value. The cannon and the mortar are, not only much dearer, but much heavier machines than the balista or catapulta, and require a greater expence, not only to prepare them for the field, but to carry them to it. As the superiority of the modern artillery too, over that of the ancients is very great; it has become much more difficult, and consequently much more expensive, to fortify a town so as to resist even for a few weeks the attack of that superior artillery. In modern times many different causes contribute to render the defence of the society more expensive. The unavoidable effects of the natural progress of improvement have, in this respect, been a good deal enhanced by a great revolution in the art of war, to which a mere accident, the invention of gunpowder, seems to have given occasion.

In modern war the great expence of fire-arms gives an evident advantage to the nation which can best afford that expence; and consequently, to an opulent and civilized, over a poor and barbarous nation. In ancient times the opulent and civilized found it difficult to defend themselves against the poor and barbarous nations. In modern times the poor and barbarous find it difficult to defend themselves against the opulent and civilized. The invention of fire-arms, an invention which at first sight appears to be so pernicious, is certainly favourable both to the permanency and to the extension of civilization.

"Of the Expence of Defence," from *An Inquiry into the Nature and Causes of the Wealth of Nations*, by Adam Smith, 1st edition (London: Printed for W. Strahan and T. Cadell, 1776), Volume 2, pages 291–313.

ADAM SMITH (1723–1790) was a Scottish political economist and social philosopher who first won reputation with his *Theory of Moral Sentiments* (1759). He is best known for his monumental and highly influential work *An Inquiry into the Nature and Causes of the Wealth of Nations* (1776), in which he argues for the "invisible hand" of free competition to guide economic systems based on individual initiative and self-interest.

19

The Economic Cost
of the Draft*

by
Walter Y. Oi

Oi compares the direct economic cost to the general economy—the civilian value of goods and services relinquished to maintain a standing army—of two hypothetical military forces of 2.65 million men each: a purely voluntary force, and a mixed force of conscripts and reluctant as well as true volunteers. These costs—$13 billion for the mixed force and $14.2 billion for the all-volunteer force—are slightly higher than the actual payroll cost, $12.7 billion, of the mixed force in existence in 1967. To initiate an all-volunteer armed force of 2.65 million men, the author estimates the need for an annual $4 billion increase in the military budget and a recruitment requirement of 27.5 percent of males qualified for service in 1967—approximately half the percentage needed to maintain the mixed force.

Oi estimates the full economic cost of the draft for enlisted ranks,

*A considerable part of the research for this paper was done when I served as a consultant for the Office of the Assistant Secretary of Defense from June, 1964, to July, 1965. I am deeply indebted to the assistance and information which was provided by various members of the OASD staff. I would like to express my special thanks to Mr. William A. Gorham, Dr. Harold Wool, and Prof. Stuart H. Altman,

including opportunity costs of $1.3 billion (the increase in compensation required to attract otherwise reluctant enlistees into an all-volunteer service), at $5.3 billion. Regardless of cost, however, conscription inequitably distributes the tax burden of maintaining an army, substituting a hidden tax on reluctant volunteers in the case of the mixed force and higher explicit taxes on all citizens in the case of the all-volunteer service.

The draft represents one means of supplying the armed forces with qualified personnel. Under the current draft, accessions to military service are of three types: (1) true volunteers who freely choose military service over alternative civilian job opportunities, (2) reluctant volunteers who enlist in preference to being drafted, and (3) draftees who are involuntarily inducted. The last two groups are coerced to serve by the military service obligation that is imposed by the current draft law.

In times of war when nearly everyone must serve to assure the defense of the nation, alternatives to a draft are judged to be too costly or infeasible. Peacetime demands for military personnel are, however, considerably smaller, with the consequence that a draft becomes selective. Debates over the equity of the selection process (which under the current draft translates into deferment policies) are symptomatic of a search for an alternative to current military manpower procurement policies. To say that a particular alternative such as an all-volunteer force[1] is preferable to the current system implies that the cost of the alternative is, in some sense, lower than the cost of the current draft. If the draft were abolished, military pay and other recruitment incentives must be improved to attract sufficient recruits to meet prescribed military manpower objectives. In his statement before the House Armed Services subcommittee, the Hon. T. D. Morris (Assistant Secretary of Defense) indicated that an all-volunteer force of 2.65 million men

who provided counsel, encouragement, and assistance in my year of service on the manpower study. The statistical and clerical assistance supplied by Mr. W. M. Mahoney and Mrs. R. Catton is gratefully acknowledged. They are absolved of responsibility for any errors of fact or interpretation which may still remain in this paper. A fuller discussion of the material in section I, as well as the supporting data, are contained in a paper which I am presenting at the University of Chicago. See "The Costs and Implications of an All-Volunteer Force."

would increase the annual military payroll budget by $4 to $17 billions.[2] The military payroll of the Department of Defense (hereafter abbreviated DOD) is not the economic cost of labor resources allocated to the uniformed services. The draft has surely affected both the level and structure of military pay. Moreover, many of the men who serve are conscripted or are recruited under the threat of a draft liability. In addition to the costs borne by those who do serve, it is argued that the uncertainty of being drafted creates other real and psychic costs for those who avoid military service by obtaining deferments.

The cost of acquiring and retaining military personnel can be measured in several ways, of which the budgetary cost is one. The financial cost to the economy is defined in this paper as the value of civilian outputs that could have been produced by the labor resources which were allocated to the armed forces. This concept which completely ignores occupational preferences provides a measure of technical efficiency in terms of civilian outputs that were foregone to achieve given levels of military preparedness. The full economic cost of the draft must, however, acknowledge occupational preferences for military versus civilian employments. If an individual has an aversion to service life, he could, in principle, be compensated by enough to induce him to volunteer. Presently, individuals who would require such compensation are forced to serve by the draft law. In this paper, I propose to compare these costs for two hypothetical forces with the same active duty strength of 2.65 million men: one a purely voluntary force and the other a mixed force composed of conscripts, true and reluctant volunteers.

I. Force Strengths and Military Manpower Requirements

The labor resources demanded by the armed forces can be measured by force strengths. The force strength is simply a stock demand for military personnel unadjusted for the quality of servicemen or the proportion in an effective status.[3] The total defense establishment can conveniently be divided into three forces: (1) officers on active duty, (2) enlisted men on active duty, and (3) paid drill reserves. The last component engages in active duty for training only and is rarely used to bolster active duty strengths.[4]

In the six years prior to the Vietnam build-up, the average strength in all active and reserve components was just under 3.7 million men, of which 2.6 million were on active duty (see Table 19.1).

TABLE 19.1
FORCE STRENGTHS AND ACCESSIONS FROM CIVIL LIFE
(Actual FY 1960–65 and Projected FY 1970–75, in Thousands)

	1960	1961	1962	1963	1964	1965	Annual Averages 1960–65	Annual Averages 1970–75*
Force strengths†								
DOD (active duty) total	2,476.4	2,483.8	2,807.8	2,697.7	2,685.2	2,653.1	2,634.0	2,650.0
Officers	316.7	314.8	343.1	333.4	336.4	337.6	330.3	340.0
Enlisted	2,159.7	2,168.9	2,464.7	2,364.3	2,348.8	2,315.5	2,303.7	2,310.0
Army (active duty) total	873.1	858.6	1,066.4	975.2	972.4	968.3	952.3	969.5
Officers	101.2	99.9	116.1	107.8	110.3	111.5	107.8	112.5
Enlisted	771.8	758.7	950.4	867.4	862.2	856.8	844.6	857.0
Reserves and National Guard (paid drill)	1,079	1,086	958	964	1,048	1,006	1,023.5	–
All components total	3,555.4	3,569.8	3,765.8	3,661.7	3,733.2	3,659.1	3,657.5	–
Accessions from civil life								
DOD total	469.8	475.3	622.4	488.0	569.3	495.0	520.0	507.7
First enlistments‡	349	386	423	373	377	352	376.7	416.7
Inductions‡	90	60	158	74	151	103	106.0	55.3
Officers§	30.8	29.3	41.4	41.0	41.3	40.0	37.3	35.7

Army	206.3	188.6	303.2	203.0	285.8	221.0	234.5	228.5
First enlistment‡	106	118	127	113	117	103	114.0	159.0
Inductions‡	90	60	158	74	151	102	105.8	55.3
Officers§	10.3	10.6	18.2	16.0	17.8	16.0	14.8	14.2
Reserves and National Guard #	130.0	130.0	90.0	110.0	170.0	120.0	125.0	–
Total entries all components	599.8	605.3	712.4	598.0	739.3	615.0	645.0	–

*SOURCE: House Hearings, p. 9954.

†Active duty force strengths include both sexes as reported in *Statistical Abstract of the United States 1966*, Table 365, p. 261 (Government Printing Office: Washington, D.C., 1966). The paid drill reserve and National Guard strengths were obtained from unpublished data, DOD Statistical Office.

‡First enlistments include two-year reserve enlistments but exclude reserves recalled to active duty. Confer *Statistical Abstract*, ibid., Table 366, p. 262.

§Data for officer accessions taken from a special tabulation prepared by the DOD Statistical Office.

#*House Hearings*, p. 10C01.

The fluctuations in active duty strengths are largely due to international tensions. Since a discussion of the factors which determine force strength objectives is beyond the scope of this paper, the peacetime strength objectives are taken to be exogenous.

A more meaningful demand concept is provided by the gross flow demand for accessions from civilian life. It is the number of required accessions A_t that must be recruited or conscripted to replace losses during the year L_t and to achieve changes in stock demands $(S_t - S_{t-1})$.

$$A_t - L_t + (S_t - S_{t-1})$$

If force strength S_t is held constant, required accessions must equal losses which arise because of voluntary separations upon completion of obligated tours of duty, retirements, deaths, and discharges for medical and unsuitability reasons.

The military manpower procurement channels which have evolved under a draft have strongly influenced the characteristics of servicemen. Of the 645 thousand annual accessions to military service in FY 1960–65, 539 thousand (83.6 percent) entered through a variety of voluntary programs. An individual can discharge his service obligation by entering active duty forces as an enlisted man or officer. He can accomplish the former as a voluntary enlistment or as an involuntary draftee, usually to the Army.[5] Except for the doctors and dentists draft, all officer procurement programs are voluntary. Finally, the draft liability can be satisfied by entering a reserve or National Guard unit which requires active duty only for training. The historical trends in accessions and projected accessions in FY 1970–75 under a continued draft are shown in the lower panel of Table 19.1. In order to extrapolate the characteristics of men who are likely to enter military service in the future, it is convenient to study the service experience of age classes (cohorts) born in specific years.

The disposition of military service obligations by men born in 1938 was estimated from a sample of Selective Service registrants.[6] By July, 1965, 51.6 percent of this age class had some active or reserve military service, with the highest participation rate of 59.5 percent for men with some college education. Given current physical, moral, and mental qualification standards for military service, roughly 30.4 percent of these men would have been rejected.[7] From independent data, I estimated that 59.2 percent of qualified males entered active duty forces while another 14.4 percent served in reserve and Guard units. The incidence of active military service also varied across education groups from a high of 76.8 percent of qualified high school graduates to 32.3 percent of qualified college graduates.

The projected flows of accessions in FY 1970–75 under a continued draft were developed in the DOD study and appear in the last column of Table 19.1.[8] These projected flows were juxtaposed to a typical age class born in 1946–48, which is estimated to contain 1,880 thousand males. The estimated participation rate in active military service falls from 41.5 percent of men born in 1938 to 27.0 percent for the age class of 1947. Only 38.5 percent of qualified males will be needed to staff active duty forces in FY 1970–75.

Before turning to the characteristics of accessions to a voluntary force, it is desirable to assemble data on the structure of the entire mixed force. Higher qualification standards and secular gains in the educational attainment of the entire population have contributed to an upward trend in the average education of members of the armed forces. The percentage of enlisted men with high school degrees climbed from 55.2 to 72.8 percent between 1956 and 1963. Over the same period, the percentage of officers with college degrees rose from 55.5 to 69.4 percent. From the 1960 Population Census, it was possible to obtain the age and educational distribution of members of the armed forces stationed in the United States. If these data are expanded to the assumed force strength of 2.65 million men, I obtain the distribution shown in Table 19.2.[9] In relation to the male civilian labor force, the armed services have smaller fractions in the lowest educational level due to the mental qualification standards. The proportion of college graduates is also somewhat lower than in the civilian sector for the age groups above 30. Finally, since military pay is primarily a function of years of service, the age structure (in terms of years of service) of the force as of June 30, 1965, is presented in Table 19.3. Under a continued draft, it is probable that the retention profiles of enlisted and officer personnel will not alter, so that the mixed force of FY 1970–75 can be expected to exhibit a similar age structure.

The task of estimating the cost and composition of an all-volunteer force was approached in two steps. It was first assumed that the draft would be abolished with no accompanying changes in pay or other recruitment incentives. An implication of this exercise is that supplies of volunteers fall short of requirements for the strength objective of 2.65 million men. In the second step, military pay was advanced to attract enough volunteers to meet the strength objective.

If the draft is eliminated, the services would obviously lose the draftees who had accounted for 21 percent of accessions to enlisted ranks in FY 1960–65. In addition, the reluctant volunteers who had enlisted because of the draft liability are likely to remain in civilian life. To determine the probable number of reluctant volunteers, the Department of Defense made a survey in the fall of 1964 of servicemen and

TABLE 19.2

DISTRIBUTION OF ARMED FORCES BY AGE AND EDUCATION
(For Force Strength of 2,650; Figures in Thousands)

Age	Years of School Completed					
	0–8	9–11	12	13–15	16+	Total
Total DOD						
17 or less	11.3	55.2	6.7	.4	—	73.7
18–19	21.7	141.3	218.6	14.3	.2	396.2
20–21	18.4	111.3	235.1	48.3	2.7	415.8
22–24	30.8	97.9	238.3	81.1	79.6	527.7
25–29	34.7	89.3	181.0	47.4	63.1	415.5
30–34	38.2	67.8	124.3	34.7	28.5	293.5
35–44	44.2	67.2	178.2	81.2	59.9	430.8
45–54	12.3	12.0	21.2	14.9	21.3	81.8
55 and over	2.8	3.2	4.3	1.6	3.2	15.1
Total	214.5	645.2	1,207.8	323.9	258.5	2,650.0

SOURCE: Derived from *U.S. Census of Population, 1960*; Subject Report: "Educational Attainment," Code No. DC(2) 5B, Table 4, p. 54.

TABLE 19.3

ACTIVE DUTY FORCE STRENGTH BY YEARS OF SERVICE
(As of June 30, 1965, in Thousands)

Years of Service	Total	Officers	Enlisted
0	427.7	28.4	399.3
1	488.4	34.1	454.3
2	301.6	25.0	276.5
3	226.3	20.1	206.2
4	99.8	12.9	86.8
5–9	321.6	54.0	267.7
10–14	338.6	51.1	287.4
15–19	291.0	58.4	232.6
20–24	131.4	45.4	86.0
25 and over	17.7	9.4	8.1
Total	2,643.8	338.8	2,304.9

civilians in the military ages of 16–34. First-term regular enlisted men (who had all voluntarily entered service between 1960 and 1964) were divided into true and reluctant volunteers on the basis of their responses to the question: "If there had been no draft, and if you had no military obligation, do you think you would have volunteered for active military service?" Those who replied "no definitely" or "no probably" were classified as reluctant. The percentage of true volunteers in subgroups identified by age and education at time of enlistment are shown in the first column of Table 19.4. The proportion of true volunteers is highest in the youngest and least educated group and declines with age and educational attainment. The fourth column gives the estimated annual flows of voluntary enlistments in FY 1970–75 if the draft is continued, the mixed force case. Multiplying by the proportions of true volunteers, I obtain the estimated flows of enlistments if the draft were abolished with no pay changes.[10] The same question on draft-motivation was asked of officers on their first obligated tours and revealed that 41.3 percent of officer accessions were reluctant volunteers. In the absence of a draft, it is probable that officer procurement programs will be revised placing more reliance on noncollege graduate sources. Space precludes a fuller discussion of the supplies of officer personnel.

Depletions in supplies of initial accessions due to the loss of draftees and reluctant volunteers are offset to some degree by improvements in retention. Air Force studies show that first-term reenlistment rates are substantially higher for airmen whose primary reason for entry was unrelated to the draft.[11] If the reenlistment rate of reluctant volunteers is assumed to be the same as that of draftees, one can deduce probable reenlistment rates in an all-volunteer force.[12] Higher reenlistment rates imply lower personnel turnover which, in turn, leads to smaller required accessions to sustain a given force strength. If the transitional problems of moving to a voluntary force are ignored, I obtain the following estimates [Table 19.5] of gross flow demands (required accessions) to maintain a force of 2.65 million men. Voluntary supplies in the absence of a draft fall short of requirements for the strength objective, with the deficit being largest in the Army.

The manpower deficits can be eliminated by raising military pay to attract more volunteers. The responsiveness of enlistments to pay changes was estimated from cross-sectional data.[13] Of several functional forms which were fitted to the data, the most consistent fit was provided by a complement supply equation.[14].

(1) $$1 - E = \alpha Y^{-\beta}$$

where E is the enlistment rate and Y denotes relative pay, the ratio of

TABLE 19.4

Effect of the Draft on Voluntary Enlistments—Survey Responses
(Classified by Age and Education)

Age at Entry and Education	Percentage of True Volunteers*	Number of DOD Sample†		Voluntary Enlistments in FY 1970–75			
		Number	Percent	With Draft‡	No Draft		
					Number§	Percent	
17–19 years of age							
Less than high school	79.3	167.8	27.7	122.2	96.2	36.6	
High school graduate	63.7	247.1	40.8	188.0	119.7	45.5	
Some college	55.9	44.0	7.3	18.3	10.2	3.9	
Total	68.7	458.9	75.8	328.5	226.1	86.0	
20 and over							
Less than high school	60.2	20.2	3.3	14.3	8.6	3.3	
High school graduate	42.3	61.7	10.2	42.8	18.1	6.9	
Some college	32.7	64.4	10.6	31.1	10.2	3.9	
Total	40.5	146.4	24.2	88.2	36.9	14.0	
All ages							
Less than high school	77.4	31.1	31.1	136.5	104.8	39.8	
High school graduate	59.5	51.0	51.0	230.8	137.8	52.4	
Some college	42.1	17.9	17.9	49.4	20.4	7.8	
Total	61.9	100.0	100.0	416.7	263.0	100.0	

*Based on responses of regular enlisted men in their first term of service to the question, "If there had been no draft and if you had no military obligation, do you think you would have volunteered for active military service?" Entries denote the percentage who responded, "Yes, definitely," or "Yes, probably."

†Figures may differ from force strength statistics due to elimination of nonrespondents and sampling variability.

‡Estimates of voluntary enlistments in FY 1970–75 if the draft is continued.

§Obtained by multiplying columns 1 and 4. Assumes that the draft is eliminated but pay and recruitment incentives are unchanged.

first-term military pay M to alternative civilian pay C. This supply equation implies that a 1 percent rise in relative pay leads to a β percent decline in the remainder (complement) of the population not in military service. The elasticity of supply ϵ is,

$$(2) \qquad \epsilon = \beta \left(\frac{1 - E}{E} \right)$$

An upper bound to the necessary pay increase is obtained by restricting the analysis to Army enlisted personnel. For a total strength of 2.65 million, the Army enlisted strength is 857 thousand. Under a continued draft, 159 thousand recruits are projected to volunteer while another 55.3 thousand will be drafted. In a steady state after the transition, a voluntary Army with its lower personnel turnover can be sustained by annual enlistments of only 144.6 thousand. If the draft is eliminated, Army enlistments are expected to fall by 43.2 percent to annual inputs of 90.3 thousand. The necessary increase in enlistments is thus given by the ratio of required accessions to voluntary supplies with no pay changes; that is, $144.6/90.3 = 1.601$. The pay increase (Y_1/Y_0) that will achieve this increase in enlistments is estimated from the complement supply equation.

$$(3) \qquad \left(\frac{1 - A}{1 - E} \right) = \left(\frac{Y_1}{Y_0} \right)^{-\beta}$$

The estimated Army supply equation revealed an estimate for β of .108 implying an initial elasticity of supply of 1.36. The necessary pay increase to meet manpower requirements on a voluntary basis was estimated to be 1.68.[15]

The 68 percent pay increase is presumed to apply to men on their first term. The mechanics of implementing this pay increase deserve brief mention. The annual income of a serviceman includes money payments for various reasons and some income in kind. In this paper, I shall use the concept of tax equivalent income, which includes (1) base pay, (2) money payments for subsistence, quarters, and uniforms, (3) the implicit value of subsistence and quarters if the serviceman receives no money allowances for these, and (4) the tax advantage.[16] The total military incomes of enlisted men classified by years of service appear in Table 19.6. It will be noticed that pay is extremely low in the first two years because pay increases prior to 1964 applied mainly to the career force. If first-term pay is raised by 68 percent, I assumed that the discontinuity in the pay structure would be eliminated so that the average

TABLE 19.5

Gross Flow Demands for a Force Strength of 2.65 Million Men

Component	Voluntary Force (no draft)	Mixed Force (with draft)	Ratio
Total required accessions			
to enlisted ranks	333.5	472.0	.707
Other services	188.9	257.7	.733
Army—total	144.6	214.3	.675
Volunteers*	144.6	159.0	.909
Inductions	0	55.3	–
Required accession of			
officers	28.4	35.7	.796
Total gross flow demands	361.9	507.7	.713

*Assumes a 5.5 percent unemployment rate.

TABLE 19.6

Annual Military Incomes of Enlisted Men
(For Pay Scales of FY 1963)

Years of Service	Total Income DOD	Army Total Income	Army Taxable Income	Army Base Pay	Base Pay as Percent of Total Income
1	1,830	1,900	1,058	1,055	55.5
2	2,143	2,304	1,359	1,382	60.0
3	2,991	3,247	2,199	2,002	61.7
4	3,344	3,711	2,392	2,433	65.6
5	4,130	4,248	2,691	2,575	60.6
6	4,462	4,465	2,792	2,725	61.0
7	4,649	4,596	2,937	2,858	62.2
8	4,741	4,797	3,037	3,003	62.6
9–12	5,235	5,377	3,409	3,280	61.0
13–16	5,926	6,043	3,918	3,885	64.3
17–20	6,387	6,414	4,245	n.a.	—

pay over the first three years of service would climb from $2,500 to $4,200. In order to prevent reversals in the pay structure, the career force would enjoy a 17 percent increase in annual tax equivalent incomes.

With these pay increases, the armed services should be able to meet strength objectives with voluntary supplies of personnel. Since the incidence of reluctant volunteers is higher for older, more educated men, the voluntary force can be expected to have a lower average educational attainment. Because of its lower personnel turnover, only 27.5 percent of qualified males is required to sustain a voluntary force of 2.65 million men.

The lower personnel turnover also raises the career ratio defined as the proportion of men on their second and later tours of duty. Hence, the move to a voluntary army raises the career ratio of regular Army enlisted men from .431 to .537. The age structure of the voluntary force was thus developed from the new retention profiles and appears in Table 19.7. Finally, the educational distribution of the voluntary force was inferred from the education mix of true volunteers. It was assumed that officer procurement programs for noncollege graduates would be expanded. The proportion of enlisted men with 0–8 years of education was small for two reasons. First, the minimum AFQT score is assumed to be held at 16, and second, the secular trend toward more education implies a slower growth for this population base. The hypo-

TABLE 19.7

ACTIVE DUTY FORCE STRENGTH BY YEARS OF SERVICE
(Hypothetical Voluntary Force, in Thousands)

Years of Service	Total	Officers	Enlisted
0	355.3	34.5	320.8
1	327.5	33.6	293.9
2	299.2	32.1	267.1
3	204.4	20.2	184.2
4	108.0	16.0	92.0
5–9	455.6	65.4	390.2
10–14	343.3	51.5	291.8
15–19	304.6	44.1	260.5
20–24	165.2	28.1	137.1
25 and over	86.9	14.5	72.4
Total	2,650.0	340.0	2,310.0

thetical educational distribution of Table 19.8 pertains to a voluntary force in a steady state after the transition period.

In analyzing the cost and characteristics of a voluntary force, I neglected several pertinent factors, of which at least three should be discussed: (1) the transitional period, (2) the savings which obtain from lower turnover, and (3) possible substitutions of civilians for uniformed men. In order to maintain force strengths in the transition, required accessions are likely to be at least 10 percent greater than in the steady state. The necessary first-term pay increase to sustain Army force strengths during the transition is estimated to be 94 percent as opposed to the previous 68 percent pay increase. The average annual military pay over the first term climbs from $4,200 to $4,850.

In the mixed force, at least 10 percent of the active duty force is involved in training. Since initial accessions to a voluntary force are some 30 percent smaller, the voluntary force strength could be reduced by at least 3 percent and still retain the same number of men in an "effective" status. In addition, if men who are engaged in training others are moved to other duty assignments, further savings could be realized. A cut in the size of a voluntary force which achieves the same effective strength implies a corresponding reduction in required accessions. Neglect of these savings from lower turnover thus imparts an upward bias to my estimate of the necessary pay increase.

TABLE 19.8

ACTIVE DUTY FORCE STRENGTH BY AGE AND EDUCATION
(Hypothetical All-Volunteer Force)

Age	Years of School Completed					Total
	0–8	9–11	12	13–15	16 and Over	
Total DOD						
17–19	25.7	145.1	212.1	18.0	—	400.9
20–21	30.3	170.8	248.6	26.5	4.8	481.0
22–24	28.8	133.9	194.0	31.8	41.1	424.6
25–29	22.6	127.3	188.7	41.0	84.6	464.2
30–34	17.1	100.5	147.5	29.7	52.5	347.3
35–44	20.7	124.1	182.7	39.6	74.5	386.9
45–54	3.1	19.1	28.8	8.6	30.2	89.7
55 and over	—	—	0	0	0.7	0.7
All ages	143.3	820.8	1,202.4	195.2	288.3	2,650.0

Many medical, clerical, food service, and maintenance positions which are now staffed by servicemen could be filled by civilians. Given current military pay scales, assignment of military personnel to these jobs may well produce the lowest budgetary cost. However, when military pay is sharply advanced, it becomes economical even from the viewpoint of budgetary cost to substitute civilians for uniformed men.[17] By implementing these substitutions, the size of the armed forces could be reduced without changing the tasks performed by the totality of civilians and military personnel. A careful study of these possibilities for substituting civilians should, in my opinion, be an integral part of moving toward a voluntary force.

II. The Financial Cost of the Armed Forces

According to the defense budget for FY 1965, the cost of active duty military personnel was $12,662 million; retirement benefits accounted for another $1,384 million.[18] A second estimate of the payroll cost is obtained by applying the annual military incomes of Table 19.6 to the age structure of the force. This estimate of $12,049 million differs from the DOD cost because my measure of miliary pay excludes many pay items.[19] This latter procedure is, however, the only way to estimate the budgetary cost of a voluntary force.

In order to achieve a voluntary force with the same strength as the mixed force, the entire pay profile is shifted upward with the largest pay increases applying to the first four years of service. In a voluntary force, larger fractions of men are in the career force with the result that the higher military incomes in later years receive more weight. If the higher pay profiles are applied to the probable age structure of a voluntary force, Table 19.7, I obtain an estimated payroll cost of $16,103 million.[20] These cost estimates thus imply that the defense budget must be increased by $4 billion per year to obtain a voluntary force of 2.65 million men. The budgetary cost of moving to an all-volunteer force would be even higher if one considered the transitional period and additional retirement benefits.

Turn next to the financial cost of the armed forces to the economy as a whole. In both mixed and voluntary forces, 2.65 million men are allocated to maintaining the defense of the nation and are thereby kept out of the civilian labor force. The alternative cost of the armed forces is the value of civilian goods and services that could otherwise have been produced by them. An ideal measure of this cost would require estimates of the marginal value products of men in military service. An approximation can, however, be obtained by assuming that civilian incomes are equal to marginal value products. Median civilian incomes in 1964 classified by age and educational attainment and adjusted for unemployment are shown in Table 19.9. If servicemen were relocated to the civilian sector, it is assumed that they could earn the same incomes as civilians of similar ages and educational attainment. Two pieces of evidence suggest that these incomes are too low. First, the median incomes of veterans were about 2.5 percent higher than incomes of all civilians.[21] Second, a DOD survey revealed that prior civilian earnings were somewhat higher for men in the upper mental groups. Since the mental distribution of servicemen is higher than that for the entire population (especially when education is held constant), their alternative civilian earnings should also be higher. The use of median civilian incomes thus imparts a downward bias to the alternative cost of labor resources allocated to the armed services.

If the mixed force described in Table 19.2 had earned the civilian incomes of Table 19.9, they would have received an aggregate annual income of $13,041 million. The corresponding financial cost for the voluntary force of Table 19.8 was $14,233 million or 9.1 percent greater

TABLE 19.9

MEDIAN INCOMES OF CIVILIAN MALE LABOR FORCE, 1964

| Age | Years of Education Completed | | | | |
	0–8	9–11	12	13–15	16+
17–19	2,010	2,926	3,196	3,147	—
20–21*	2,391	3,314	3,924	4,668	—
22–24†	3,160	4,026	4,789	5,168	5,280
25–29‡	3,673	4,500	5,366	5,502	6,213
30–34	4,296	5,339	6,167	6,910	8,353
35–44	4,710	5,860	6,528	7,389	9,853
45–54	4,717	5,636	6,549	7,855	10,846
55 and over	4,229	4,944	6,135	6,642	9,883

*Incomes for males 21 years of age and under estimated from DOD survey of civilian nonveterans, 16–21 years of age. Adjusted for unemployment.

†Incomes interpolated from data for ages 20–21 and 25–29.

‡Median total incomes taken from *Statistical Abstract of the United States, 1966*, Table 157, p. 115. Figures were adjusted for unemployment rates of 2.8 percent for males 25 and older and with more than 8 years of education, and 4.7 percent unemployment for males with less than 8 years of education.

than that of the mixed force. Although the voluntary force has more men with less than twelve years of schooling, it also contains more older men, and on balance, the age effect outweighs education.

These cost estimates do not take account of personnel turnover. In the mixed force, larger fractions of an age class enter active military service for shorter tours of duty. The critical question is, are civilian incomes in later life reduced by short (two to four years) tours of active duty? The relationship of income to age (given education) can be explained in two ways. One is that older men have acquired on-the-job training which is reflected in higher incomes. The second argues that age is a proxy for maturity and stability which commands higher income.[22] If the first explanation is correct and if military training is not a perfect substitute for civilian job experience, the financial cost of the mixed force must be increased to reflect the cost of postponing civilian job training for more members of an age class.

The financial costs of $13.0 and $14.2 billion for mixed and voluntary forces are only slightly larger than the payroll cost of $12.7 billion for the mixed force. Military pay is, however, considerably below alternative civilian incomes for men on their first tours, while men in the career force receive slightly higher incomes than their counterparts in civilian life. It should be emphasized that these financial costs disregard the occupational preferences of individuals, some of whom are involuntarily inducted into the mixed force. They simply provide a measure of technical efficiency in terms of the value of goods and services which the economy relinquishes to maintain a standing army.

III. The Full Economic Cost of the Draft

The full economic cost embraces the principle that equalizing income differentials are properly included in the opportunity cost of acquiring men for military service. A simple theory of occupational choice along the lines of Marshall[23] provides a useful analytic framework. The economy can be imagined to consist of two industries: military and civilian sectors. Since pay cannot be separated from conditions of employment, occupational preferences (utilities and disutilities of the job) necessarily affect supplies of labor. Suppose that an individual, A, could earn an income C in the civilian sector while current first-term military pay is M_o. If military and civilian pay were the same, $M_o = C$, an individual with an aversion for service life would elect to remain in civil life. Military pay could, however, be advanced by enough to compensate A for his disutility, thereby attracting him into the military sector. There is, in principle, some minimum supply price M with its accompanying equalizing differential δ such that A would be indifferent between employments in the two sectors when $M = (1 + \delta) C < Mo$, A would volunteer for military service.

Occupational preferences can thus be expressed in terms of equalizing differentials δ. If $\delta > 0$, the individual must be compensated before he would volunteer. It is possible that some men prefer military service, in which case δ would be negative. The supply of men to the armed forces is then determined by the joint frequency distribution of alternative civilian incomes C and equalizing differentials δ. At current military pay, the voluntary supply of recruits consists of those individuals for whom $M_o > (1 + \delta)C$. If pay is advanced, the armed forces could attract men with higher civilian incomes or with greater aversions (meaning larger values of δ) for service life. The complement supply curve given by equation (1) implies that over the relevant range, the frequency distribution of occupational preferences, δ, follows an exponentially declining function.

The draft imposes costs on men in the armed services in at least three ways. First, more men from an age class are demanded by the armed forces under a draft because of the high turnover of draftees and reluctant volunteers. Second, some men are involuntarily drafted while others are coerced to enlist by the threat of a draft without being compensated for their aversion to military employment. At sufficiently high levels of military pay, all of these reluctant service participants could, in principle, have been induced to volunteer. Finally, the true volunteers who would have enlisted irrespective of the draft law are denied the higher military pay that would prevail in a voluntary force. First-term military pay can be kept at low levels because the draft assures adequate supplies of initial accessions.

In the years ahead, FY 1970–75, it is projected that only 55.3 thousand men will be drafted each year. If the DOD survey responses of Table 19.4 are valid, another 153.7 thousand annual accessions to enlisted ranks can be classified as reluctant volunteers. These projected annual flows of reluctant participants are distributed by education and age at entry in Table 19.2. However, all 209 thousand reluctant entrants will not be demanded by a voluntary force which is likely to enjoy considerably lower personnel turnover. In fact, the projected annual flow of 263 thousand true volunteers would have to be increased by only 75 thousand to sustain a voluntary force of 2.65 million men: 55 thousand in the Army and 20 thousand in the other services.

To measure the economic cost of the draft, one must know the minimum supply price M at which each draftee and reluctant volunteer could be induced to become a true volunteer. Such data are simply unavailable, and some simplifying assumptions must be invoked to arrive at an estimate of this cost. It seems reasonable to suppose that the 153.7 thousand reluctant volunteers who entered as regular enlisted men in preference to being drafted have less aversion to military service when compared to draftees and men who never enter service.[24] Indeed, if the draft were abolished and military pay advanced, I suspect that most of these men would become regular volunteers. A lower bound to the economic cost is thus obtained by assuming that these reluctant volunteers have the lowest minimum supply prices. According to the complement supply curve for enlistments to all services, first-term pay must be raised by a factor of 1.88 to attract an additional 153.7 thousand recruits.[25]

The exposition is facilitated by referring to the supply curve of Figure 19.1. If the draft is eliminated with no pay changes, the annual

FIGURE 19.1

SUPPLY CURVE OF VOLUNTARY ENLISTMENTS TO TOTAL DOD

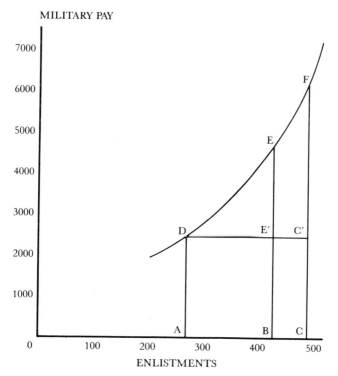

supply of voluntary enlistments is projected to be around 263 thousand men at a first-term pay M_o = \$2,500. If pay is increased by a factor of 1.88 to M_1 = \$4,700, the annual supply of recruits climbs to 416.7 thousand men; i.e., from OA to OB accessions. The reluctant volunteers (the line segment AB) enlist at the lower pay M_o in order to avoid being drafted. The difference between their minimum supply prices and the current first-term pay M_o represents an implicit tax which is borne by these men. The aggregate annual cost for the 153.7 thousand reluctant volunteers is thus given by the area of the triangle, $DB'E$, or \$141 million. This estimate tacitly assumes that each reluctant volunteer is compensated in a discriminatory fashion without compensating the true volunteers. If, however, pay were raised to \$4,700 for all recruits including true volunteers, the annual cost of the draft is increased by the additional amount M_oDEM_1 or \$917 million.[26] The lower annual cost of \$141 million which excludes rents represents an implicit tax levied against reluctant volunteers who were coerced to enlist by the draft liability. In a sense, each reluctant volunteer pays, on average, an implicit tax of \$915 in each of the 3.5 years of his first term of service. If the point estimate of β had been used in these calculations, the aggregate annual cost, $DB'E$, is estimated to be \$192 million.[27] Since each regular enlistee serves for 3.5 years, the total tax (excluding rents) borne by the reluctant volunteers in an age class is conservatively estimated to be \$493 million; the best estimate is \$672 million.

The economic cost of conscripting men into military service is harder to assess. The Selective Service System does not attempt to draft men with the least aversion for military life. The supposition that draftees were next in line above the point E in Figure 19.1 is less plausible than in the case of reluctant volunteers. However, a lower bound estimate is again obtained by assuming that draftees had the smallest equalizing income differentials and hence the lowest minimum supply prices. In Figure 19.1, first-term pay must be raised from M_1 = \$4,700 to M_2 = \$5,900 to attract the 55.3 thousand draftees (the line segment BC) on a voluntary basis. If each draftee is compensated in a discriminatory fashion, the implicit annual tax which is borne by involuntary draftees is given by the area $EB'C'F$ or \$175 million.[28] Since the average active duty tour for a draftee is about 1.9 years, the total implicit tax for draftees in an age class is \$333 million.

Each reluctant volunteer and draftee could, in principle, have been induced to enter active military service on a voluntary basis. The draft, however, compels some to serve while others are coerced to enlist at military pay scales which are below their minimum supply prices. The difference between minimum supply price and current first-term pay is simply an implicit tax—the economic cost of active military service for reluctant service participants. A lower bound estimate of this cost (for those who serve in enlisted ranks) is derived from the area $DC'F$ and is approximately equal to $826 million for reluctant participants in an age class. If the least squares estimate of the supply of voluntary enlistments were used in the supply curve of Figure 19.1, I obtain the middle estimates in the last column of the following summary table. The economic cost or implicit tax placed on men who were coerced to serve by the draft provides a lower bound estimate of the opportunity cost of acquiring enlisted men. The estimates shown in Table 19.10 are biased downward because the men who bear the cost are assumed to be those with the lowest supply prices in the absence of a draft. These estimates also neglect the rents that would have been paid to true volunteers in a competitive labor market. Under a draft, we not only tax the reluctant service participants but we also prevent true volunteers from collecting these rents. The full economic cost which includes these rents is estimated to be $5,364 million when I use the supply curve of Figure 19.1.

It is of some interest to separate the economic cost of the draft into (1) the loss of alternative civilian income during active duty service and (2) the net sum of equalizing income differentials to overcome aver-

TABLE 19.10

ESTIMATES OF THE IMPLICIT TAX
ON RELUCTANT SERVICE PARTICIPANTS

	Low Estimate ($\beta = .402$)	Middle Estimate ($\beta = .315$)
Annual first-term pay		
M_0	$2,500	$2,500
M_1	4,700	5,600
M_2	5,900	7,450
Annual cost excluding rents (millions)		
Reluctant volunteers ($DB'E$)	141	192
Draftees ($EB'C'F$)	175	243
Aggregate cost for an age class, excluding rents (millions)		
Reluctant volunteers	493	672
Draftees	333	462
Total	826	1,134

sions for service life. If the median 1964 civilian incomes of Table 19.9 are applied to the probable distribution of reluctant participants, Table 19.10, the average alternative civilian incomes are [as shown in Table 19.11]. The differential between alternative civilian and military incomes obviously varies, being larger for older, more educated men. The infrequent college graduate who is involuntarily inducted can expect a financial loss of over $3,000 a year. The aggregate financial cost to members of an age class (the difference between alternative civilian and current first-term pay) is estimated to be $691 million. This financial cost results from the abnormally low levels of first-term pay and is independent of the occupational preferences of reluctant service participants.

In this paper, the economic cost has only been estimated for men who serve in enlisted ranks because of the draft. A fuller analysis would include the costs borne by draft-motivated accessions to officer ranks and to reserve and National Guard units. The available evidence suggests that these men (especially those who enlist in Guard and reserve programs) have high aversions for military service.[29]

In addition to the direct costs borne by those who ultimately serve in the armed forces, the draft allegedly creates other indirect costs which derive from the mechanics of the selection process. Under the current Selective Service System, a youth can remain in a draft-liable status for seven and a half years. There is some evidence which suggests that employers discriminate against youths who are still eligible to be drafted.[30] The youth who elects to wait and see if he can avoid military service is likely to suffer more unemployment. He may be obliged to accept casual employment which does not provide useful job training for later life. Moreover, long periods of draft liability encourage youths to pursue activities which might bestow a deferment. When

TABLE 19.11

ESTIMATED ANNUAL CIVILIAN INCOMES
OF DRAFTEES AND RELUCTANT VOLUNTEERS

	Annual Flows (Thousands)	Civilian Income	Military Income	Ratio
Reluctant volunteers	153.7	$3,450	$2,500	.72
Draftees	55.3	3,810	2,100	.55
Total	209.0	3,545	2,400	.68

married nonfathers were placed in a lower order of call in September, 1963, it was followed by small increases in marriage rates of males in the draft-liable ages. It is also alleged that the draft prompts men to prolong their education or to enter occupations which grant deferments. These costs which derive from the uncertainty of the present draft are, in my opinion, small when compared to the direct economic costs incurred by those who are involuntarily inducted or who become reluctant volunteers.

If the current draft law is extended into the decade ahead, it is projected that only 38.5 percent of qualified males will be required to staff a mixed force of 2.65 million men. Since the draft assures adequate supplies of initial accessions, military pay can be kept at artificially low levels. Many servicemen on their first tour can correctly be called reluctant participants who pay substantial implicit taxes because they were coerced to serve. A conservative estimate of the economic cost (excluding rents) is $826 million—the amount of compensation which would have been demanded by these men to enter on a voluntary basis. If all recruits received the first-term pay needed to attract the last draftee, the opportunity cost of acquiring new accessions would exceed $5.3 billion.

An all-volunteer force offers a polar alternative to the draft. With its lower personnel turnover, a voluntary force of the same size could be sustained by recruiting only 27.5 percent of qualified males. The budgetary payroll cost would, however, have to be raised by $4 billion per year.

In closing, it should be emphasized that the figures appearing in this paper represent my estimates. The two crucial ingredients are the supply curve of voluntary enlistments in the absence of a draft and projected gross flow demands which are determined by personnel turnover. Complement supply curves were estimated from cross-sectional data on voluntary enlistment rates.[31] The retention profiles which were used to derive gross flow demands for an all-volunteer force generated an age structure of the force which closely approximates that of smaller professional armies in Canada and the United Kingdom. In the light of the data examined, I am reasonably confident of my cost estimates, at least for the assumed force strength of 2.65 million men.

If peacetime military requirements necessitate larger active duty forces, all costs necessarily climb. To sustain a force of 3.3 million men on a voluntary basis, the gross flow demand for new accessions rises by roughly 30 percent. Estimation of the pay increase to achieve this larger force involves an extrapolation of the supply curve beyond the range which I consider to be meaningful.[32] The high budgetary cost of a voluntary force is not the only relevant consideration. If men are procured under a draft, the high turnover of draftees implies that over 60 percent of qualified males would be demanded by the armed services to maintain a mixed force of 3.3 million men. The military payroll under a draft will be lower. However, the conscription of military personnel simply substitutes implicit taxes levied on reluctant service participants for explicit taxes on all citizens to finance the higher payroll of a voluntary force. The real economic cost of maintaining a large defense establishment is partially concealed since these implicit taxes never appear in the defense budget.

"The Economic Cost of the Draft," by Walter Y. Oi, from *American Economic Review*, Volume 57, Number 2 (May 1967), pages 39–62. Copyright © 1967 American Economic Association. Reprinted by permission of the publisher and the author.

Walter Y. Oi (1929–) is the Elmer B. Milliman Professor of Economics at the University of Rochester in New York. He was director of the economic analysis section of the Military Manpower Policy Study for the Department of Defense in 1964; consultant to the Office of the Assistant Secretary of Defense during 1964–1965; staff economist for the President's Commission on an All-Volunteer Force (Gates Commission) in 1969; and co-chairman of the Youth Task Force on the Draft and National Services for the White House Conference on Youths in 1970.

Notes

1. The current draft law (the Universal Military Training and Service Act of 1951 as amended and extended) expires on June 30, 1967. The proposed alternatives to an extension of the present law include (1) lottery at a younger age of induction, thereby shortening the period of draft liability, (2) universal military service, (3) equivalent national service wherein some youths could serve in the Peace Corps, VISTA, or other government sponsored programs, and (4) establishment of a voluntary professional army.

2. House of Representatives, 89th Cong., Second Sess., "Review of the Administration and Operation of the Selective Service System," Hearings before the Committee on Armed Services (June 22, 23, 24, 28, 29, and 30, 1966) (hereafter abbreviated as *House Hearings*), pp. 9923–59; see especially pp. 9936–40.

3. The effective strength is defined as the number of men who are not

in a "training status." Men who are being trained or who are engaged in training others are deducted from total force strength to arrive at the effective strength. A lower personnel turnover would therefore lead to a larger proportion in an "effective" status.

4. In the last decade, reservists were recalled to active duty in significant numbers only once. During the Berlin crisis of FY 1962, some 111 thousand Army and National Guard reservists were activated to raise Army force strengths from 858.6 to 1,066.4 thousand.

5. A few delinquents (mainly reservists who fail to attend drill meetings) are drafted into the other three services. The Navy drafted some men in FY 1956, and the Marines in FY 1966. Some voluntary enlistments serve in two-year active duty reserve programs offered by the Navy and Marine Corps. The Army offered a two-year reserve enlistment in 1956, but the program was dropped in 1958.

6. Confer *House Hearings,* p. 10011.

7. Approximately 16 percent of an age class is found to be physically unfit, while an additional 2.5 percent are rejected for moral reasons, mainly habitual criminals. These standards have remained quite stable over the last twenty years. Mental qualification standards have, however, been raised as supplies of enlistment applicants grew in relation to requirements. Currently, mental standards have been lowered to a percentile score of 16 on the Armed Forces Qualification Test. The overall rejection rate for all reasons was 40.8 percent for men with 0–11 years of education and 19.1 percent for college graduates.

8. These projections assume an unemployment rate of 5.5 percent, the average unemployment rate between 1957 and 1964. For details of the DOD projections, see *House Hearings,* p. 9954. If the unemployment rate is as low as 4.0 percent, voluntary enlistments can be expected to fall with an accompanying rise in inductions.

9. The total DOD force strength as of June 30, 1960, was 2,447 thousand males, but the Census enumerated only 1,715 thousand. The distribution shown in Table 19.2 thus invokes two assumptions. First, it is assumed that the same age-education distribution applies to men stationed in the U.S. and overseas. Second, if the draft is extended, future accessions and reenlistments will generate the distribution which was observed in 1960. I believe that these two assumptions impart a downward bias to the educational attainment of mixed forces in FY 1970–75.

10. These estimates contain a downward bias. It is likely that by FY 1970–75, the other services will enjoy excess supplies of enlistment applicants, some of whom will replace the reluctant volunteers. However, the shortfall in regular Army enlistments will persist.

11. Survey questionnaires try to determine the single most important reason for original entry. Two of several possible choices include "choice

of service" and "volunteered in preference to being drafted." Follow-up studies of respondents reveal that airmen selecting these responses had substantially lower reenlistment rates.

12. Over the period of 1957–64, the weighted average for first-term reenlistment rates of draftees was $R_d = 7.67$ percent as compared to $R = 22.06$ percent for regular Army enlistees. The observed rate for all enlistees, R, can be regarded as a weighted average of the rate for true volunteers R_v and of reluctant volunteers R_d which is assumed to be equal to that of draftees.

$$R = kR_v + 1 - k)R_d$$

where k is the proportion of true volunteers. In the case of the regular Army where $k = .568$ (the proportion of true volunteers), the first-term reenlistment rate is estimated to rise from $R = 22.1$ percent to $R_v = 33.0$ percent. Similar improvements in retention can also be expected of the other services as well as for officers.

13. True voluntary enlistment rates in relation to the civilian male labor force 17–20 years of age (adjusted for mental qualification) were estimated for the nine Census regions from the 1964 DOD survey. Two enlistment rates were developed corresponding to (1) total DOD enlistments in Mental Groups I to III and (2) Army enlistments in Mental Groups I to III. Voluntary enlistments of men in upper Mental Group IV (AFQT percentile scores of 20–30) were omitted since their enlistments were limited by recruitment quotas. The data which were used in the supply analysis can be found in *House Hearings*, p. 9957.

14. This functional relationship was suggested to me by Prof. A. C. Harberger. In estimating the parameters, an unemployment variable was included as an explanatory variable. I have deleted it here to simplify the exposition. Since unemployment is held constant in the projections, its influence is included in the constant term α. A fuller analysis of supplies of military personnel is contained in the paper by Altman and Fechter in this series.

15. My estimate of the necessary increase in first-term pay is lower than the DOD estimates. The DOD study presented three estimates corresponding to three values of β; namely, the point estimate of β and the point estimate plus or minus one standard error of the regression coefficient. For the case of a 5.5 percent unemployment rate, I have reproduced the estimated percentage increases in first-term pay; see *House Hearings*, p. 9958; DOD low estimate, 80; DOD best estimate, 111; DOD high estimate, 181; my estimate, 68. The difference between the DOD best and my estimates is due to different estimates of required accessions. My procedure deals with a steady state in which the Army enjoys the retention profile of a truly voluntary force.

16. Income in kind is clearly nontaxable. In addition, subsistence,

quarters, and uniform allowances are classified as nontaxable, thereby giving servicemen an indirect tax advantage which accounts for about 5.5 percent of tax equivalent income.

17. The stock demand for military personnel is not completely inelastic. At higher prices, fewer men would be demanded by the services. A consideration which operates in the opposing direction is the provision of rotational billets. Some jobs must be kept for men on rotation from overseas assignments. The demand for military men is likely to be determined by the anticipated peak load demand so that a considerable part of the force is always idle. This is as it should be and the reason for maintaining a standing army.

18. *Statistical Abstract of the U.S.*, 1966, Table 153, p. 112.

19. Flight pay, sea duty pay, and many other pay items were omitted in the annual tax equivalent incomes shown in Table 19.6. Another source of error is that the age structure of the force, Table 19.3, applies to years of active military service, while the pay profile of Table 19.6 is based on years of service for pay purposes; the latter is always equal to or greater than the former, thereby imparting a downward bias to my estimate of the payroll cost. Finally, I had only rough estimates of annual tax equivalent incomes for officers.

20. In arriving at this cost, I assumed that an enlisted man received $3,900 in his first year of service with annual increases of $300 over the next three years. Enlisted men's pay in later years was raised by 17 percent. The officers' pay profile was adjusted to eliminate the discontinuity in the pay profile. As a result, average annual pay for officers in their first three years of service rose by 20.1 percent. The additional payroll cost of a voluntary force contains an upward bias since I have neglected the savings from lower personnel turnover and possible substitutions of civilians for uniformed personnel. Finally, it may be cheaper to attract recruits with recruitment incentives other than higher annual military incomes. Initial enlistment bonuses, greater pay differentials for skilled personnel, or educational/training benefits could be incorporated into the pay structure.

21. A comparison of median incomes in 1959 revealed that veterans typically earned more than all males in the civilian labor force. Veterans 25–34 years of age with 12 years of education earned 2.3 percent more than all males. An opposing pattern is observed for veterans of World War II who were over 45 years of age in 1959; there, the veterans earned less than all males. These income estimates can be found in *U.S. Census of Population 1960*, "Earnings of Total Civilian Male War Veterans in Experienced Labor Force in 1959," Table 16 PC (2), 8C, "Earnings of Males 25–64 in Experienced Civilian Labor Force in 1959," Table 1, PC (2) 7B.

22. Becker argues that the age profile of income is mainly attributable

to investment in human capital via on-the-job training. See G. S. Becker, *Human Capital* (Columbia Univ. Press, 1964). The second thesis could be rationalized by my theory of fixed employment costs. Older men are more likely to be married and possess other attributes which are correlated with low labor turnover. If hiring and initial training costs are large, it behooves the firm to offer higher wages to men with longer expected periods of employment. See, W. Y. Oi, "Labor as a Quasi-fixed Factor," *J.P.E.*, Dec., 1962.

23. Alfred Marshall, *Principles of Economics* (8th ed., Macmillan, 1952), pp. 547–70.

24. It has long been alleged that many reluctant volunteers are prompted to enlist in preference to being drafted because of the uncertainties about whether they will be drafted, or if so, when. In his doctoral dissertation, David Bradford argues that men who become reluctant volunteers because of this uncertainty are those for whom the relative cost of later military service is the greatest. He further argues that the absolute cost of active military service is immaterial. I believe that his argument is specious because he considers only a dichotomous choice. The gist of his simple model can be put as follows. Let C_0 be the subjective cost to the individual of active military service now, while C_1 is the cost of entry at a later date and older age. If p is the subjective probability that he will be drafted later, this individual would prefer to enlist now if $C_0 < pC_1$ or $(C_0/C_1) < p$. Hence, only the ratio or relative cost of later entry, (C_0/C_1), matters. There is, however, a third option available to every draft liable youth; namely, securing a deferment. This may entail a cost C_d, especially if he must become a father or minister, or if he must pursue an occupation which bestows an occupational deferment. There are many reasons to suppose that the cost of acquiring a deferment, C_d, is independent of C_0 and C_1, the subjective cost of actually entering military service. Hence, if $C_d < C_0$, the individual would secure the deferment and never enter military service. Moreover, if C_d is the same for all individuals, Bradford's analysis applies only to men for whom the cost of active military service C_0 is greater than C_d. For the details of Bradford's analysis, the reader is referred to David F. Bradford, "The Effects of Uncertainty in Selective Service," Technical Report No. 144 (Inst. for Math. Studies in the Soc. Sci., Stanford Univ., 1966).

25. The complement supply curve, equation (1), for enlistments to total DOD revealed an estimate of β of .315 with a standard error of .087. In the absence of a draft, the enlistment rate (Mental Groups I to III) was estimated to be 27.8 percent of the qualified civilian labor force in an age class. In deriving the supply curve shown in Figure 19.1, I set β equal to .402, the point estimate plus one standard error. The elasticity of this supply curve at the initial enlistment rate was +1.04. Because of the upward bias in the supply elasticity, my procedure understates the magnitude of the economic cost.

26. In competitive labor markets, these rents are always included in the additional cost of acquiring larger supplies of labor. If college professors could be conscripted and compelled to work, or if the economic rents of teaching versus other occupations could be eliminated, the budgetary cost of higher education could be greatly reduced.

27. If the value of β is reduced from .402 to its least squares point estimate, .315, the elasticity of supply falls from 1.04 to 0.82. Using the point estimate, the necessary first-term pay M_1 to attract OB volunteers rises from \$4,700 to \$5,600.

28. Since the draftee serves for only two years, his annual military income of \$2,100 is less than the first-term pay of regular enlistees, $M_o = $ \$2,500. Hence, the annual cost is slightly greater than the area $EB'C'F$ in Figure 19.1. If β is set equal to .315, first-term pay must rise to $M_2 = $ \$7,450 to attract the draftees on a voluntary basis. In this event, the annual cost climbs to \$243 million, and the aggregate cost for the draftees in an age class rises from \$333 to \$462 million.

29. According to the 1964 DOD survey, draft-motivated enlistments accounted for 70.7 percent of total accessions to reserve and Guard components. Moreover, the percentage of reluctant volunteers was higher for individuals with higher alternative civilian earnings as revealed by the following excerpt from the *House Hearings* (p. 9956).

Annual Civilian Income	Percentage of Draft-Motivated Enlistments
Less than \$2,999	54.1
\$3,000–\$4,999	71.6
\$5,000–\$7,499	72.1
\$7,500 or more	82.2

30. A survey of college placement offices in 1964 indicated that 48 percent of employers placed restrictions on draft-liable males. According to the DOD survey of 22–25 year old civilians, 26 percent with draft classification I-A said that they had difficulty in securing employment. The credibility of this type of question is challenged by the finding that 17 percent of men with dependency deferments, III-A, also stated that they had difficulty securing employment because of their draft liability. The percentages having "difficulty" climbed with age and educational attainment. Further details of these surveys can be found in *House Hearings*, pp. 10008–10010.

31. Such data on a regional basis were only available for 1963. The recent enlistment experience is strongly influenced by the Vietnam build-up and the high draft calls. In any move toward a voluntary force, I would strongly recommend an on-going research effort on the determinants of the supply of volunteers as well as on manpower utilization practices of the armed forces.

32. The confidence interval for predictions from a regression equation

becomes extremely wide as one moves outside the range of the sample observations. Hence, the following estimates should be regarded as only indicative of orders of magnitude. In order to sustain a voluntary force of 3.3 million men, Army enlistments must be increased from 90.3 to 185 thousand per year; the latter gross flow demand of 185 thousand assumes a steady state. According to the complement supply curve, first-term pay would have to be raised from $2,500 to $6,350 to attract sufficient recruits. If part of the pay could be given as initial enlistment bonuses, the defense budget for active duty military personnel would be increased by $8 to $10 billion per year.

20

The Economics of
the Military Draft

by
Ryan C. Amacher, James C. Miller III,
Mark V. Pauly, Robert D. Tollison,
and Thomas D. Willett

Treating the military draft as a major tax-in-kind, the authors analyze the microeconomic (allocative and distributive) and macroeconomic effects of conscription relative to alternative methods of military manpower procurement. They conclude that conscription is inequitable, allocatively inefficient, and cost ineffective, and that it imposes dead-weight and utility losses on the economy as a whole.

The authors consider two alternatives to selective service: universal service and the lottery. They point out that universal service decreases intergenerational inequities, but is abusive of the rights of a greater number of persons than conscription. On the other hand, the lottery system constrains the discriminatory power of selective service boards, but amounts to a randomly levied tax, allowing inequity without clear assignment of social responsibility. Conscription is popular among those who need not serve because it is politically expedient: it taxes the few so that the many—the electing public—need not be inconvenienced by higher taxes or burdens of conscience.

Because individual free choice best approximates full compensation, and because gross national product losses to the economy at large are minimized, the authors conclude that the all-volunteer army is the most equitable and efficient means of military manpower procurement.

The military draft presents an ideal subject for basic economic analysis. The draft has allocative and distributive effects on the individual (microeconomics) and on the entire economy (macroeconomics). In analyzing the military draft we can develop some formal models and make use of statistical estimation. In short, an examination of the military draft will permit us to utilize a variety of economic tools.

The purpose of this model is to analyze the economic effects of draft policy per se. Generally, we will illustrate how the tools and methodology of economics can be used to examine questions relating to the military draft. In this manner we hope to demonstrate how economic analysis can be used to shed light on other questions of public policy, which at first glance may seem only peripherally related to economics as it is generally conceived.

We will begin our analysis with a discussion of the draft as a form of taxation, followed by an examination of the equity aspects of the military draft. The effects of conscription on allocative efficiency are examined in the third section, which is followed by a discussion of the alternative systems of conscription and their effects on the equity aspects of conscription. The remaining discussion is concerned with some not strictly economic issues surrounding draft reform and the use of economics to gain insights into these issues.

The Draft as a Tax

The draft is necessary because young men and young women do not volunteer at the current level of military pay in what the government regards as sufficient numbers. Consequently, men must be drafted into the armed forces.[1] Since a person would volunteer for something which in his own estimation made him better off, those who are drafted, and even some of those who volunteer because of the existence of the draft, must be made worse off in their own estimatior because of the fact that they are drafted. It is this reduction in the individual's level of well-being, as evaluated by himself, that is implicit in the view of the draft as a tax. That is, the draft is a tax because it compels individuals to do something which makes them in their own view worse off.

The proceeds of this tax are represented by the national defense which the draftees provide and for which they are not paid. Draftees receive some of this benefit because they are citizens, but certainly other members of the population who do not serve, who cannot serve, or who are not asked to serve obtain these benefits as well. This group includes individuals deferred from the draft, whether for good or bad reasons, women, and individuals who, during their draft-eligible years, were not called because they were not needed to attain the desired level of size of the military services. The purpose of this section is to show how the draft tax can be defined and measured.

Taxes in Kind

We usually think of taxes as money payments which individuals make to the government, but this is not the only way in which taxes can be paid. Rather than hand over to the government the money which he obtains from his labor, the individual could be required to provide the labor services directly. For example, in most cities people pay taxes which are used in part to clean litter off the streets. An alternative way of accomplishing the same goal would be for each individual to be required to devote a certain portion of the time, per day or per year, to picking up litter.[2] This would clearly provide the same kind of service as is now provided by money taxes, and all of those who benefit from cleaner streets would enjoy it. Moreover, a city which did require citizens to perform this function would have very low monetary (i.e., budgetary) costs for the cleaning of streets. Citizens in general would not count this as a very significant advantage, however, because in return for having to pay low money taxes they would have to give up a portion of their time to work for the government. If, however, we assume that only a subsection of the population—say, just the young or the black or people with red hair—were required to perform this service, most people would pay lower taxes and therefore might regard the situation as relatively desirable.

In fact we collect such taxes in kind very rarely. The major area in which we do use this method of obtaining services for the government is in the provision of military manpower.[3] Young men who are drafted clearly pay a draft tax. The tax that an individual pays is the reduction in his self-evaluated well-being caused by the existence of the draft. Viewed in this way, it is clear that the draft tax can be paid by more people than just those who are formally inducted. The draft tax also falls on families and friends of draftees, on those who were induced by the draft to volunteer, and on those who alter their lives in ways designed to avoid or change the effect the draft will have on them (and on those who are directly or indirectly affected by this behavior); it is even possible, some critics assert, to view much of the turmoil on campuses and the anomie of many of our nation's youth as a measure of the cost of the draft, even if an indirect one.

The following analysis will be mainly concerned with what might be called the direct tax cost of the draft—specifically, those direct costs which are borne by individuals who are eligible for the draft. What is required is a money measure of the change in the individual's well-being, as perceived by himself, which is caused by the existence of the draft. We shall first focus on those who actually do military service.

There is one critical assumption which underlies such a definition of the draft tax. It is that the individual's own evaluation of his well-being is the relevant measure of the change in his position which is produced by the draft. One might argue, and indeed some people have argued, that the draft is desirable (or at least not as undesirable as might otherwise be thought) because it produces improvements in individuals' situations which were not desired by, or not perceived by, those individuals prior to their military service. There is no easy philosophic answer to this objection. The fundamental consideration would seem to be whether, in a purportedly democratic and free society, individuals are to be permitted to have control over the conduct of their own lives. In a society which professes to value individual freedom and in which the individual is allowed to elect those who represent him and vote on the policies which they follow, the individual's own choice would seem to be the appropriate criterion for the desirability of alternative outcomes. The alternative view, which permits group choice to substitute for individual choice, seems to be inconsistent with basic assumptions of individualistic democracy. Insofar as reluctance to volunteer arises from ignorance about the potential benefits of extended military service, the appropriate remedy, consistent with individual freedom, would be to provide information about such benefits rather than to substitute collective choice for individuals' "uninformed judgments."[4]

Measurement of the Draft Tax

Initially, let us suppose that individuals who were qualified for military service were concerned in their choice of occupation only with the level of money income. Consider the case of an individual who is drafted and who would not have volunteered for service. The reason that he had to be drafted must be because his income as a soldier would be less than his civilian income. Since we are assuming income to be the only thing that matters to him, a measure of the extent to which being drafted makes him worse off would be provided by the difference between his civilian income and his income in the armed forces. Thus, if he could earn $10,000 as a civilian, and if his income (including the value of income in kind, such as the food, lodging, and medical services he is provided) in the armed forces was $5,000, the draft tax on him would be $5,000.[5]

In the example, this measure of the draft tax provides the answer to two conceptually different questions. First, if we were to ask what income it would take to induce the individual to volunteer for the armed forces, it is obvious that he would have to be paid an additional amount slightly above $5,000 in order to be induced to volunteer. If we ask what amount he would be willing to pay in order to avoid the draft obligation and if he were able to borrow against his future income, he should be willing to pay up to $5,000 in order to avoid being drafted. Insofar as markets for borrowing are less than perfect, in the sense that the individual could not borrow $5,000 even though he would be able to pay it back, some difference between these two measures might arise.

If we assume, as is more realistic, that aspects other than money income affect the individual's choice between military service and po-tential civilian occupations, it becomes somewhat more difficult to get a measure of the draft tax. The difficulty arises because it is necessary to put a dollar evaluation on the individual's perception of the difference between military life and civilian life. Suppose, for example, that at equal wages an individual would prefer his civilian job to that of being a soldier. If he were forced to serve as a soldier, even at equal wages, he would be made worse off in his own estimation. We would therefore want to include, as part of the measure of the draft tax, some measure of the extent to which he was made worse off. Consider the case of the individual who prefers being unemployed or working at a very low-paying civilian job to serving in the armed forces. Drafting him would cause him to pay a draft tax, even if he might be earning more dollars in the armed forces than as a civilian.

Let us suppose that we are considering individuals who, at equal wages, prefer civilian life. The problem then is to get a money measure of the value to the individual of what we might call his amenity for civilian life. There are two ways that a measure of the value of this amenity to an individual might be obtained. One is to ask him for what minimum price he would be willing to sell or give up his level of civilian amenity. The other is to ask what is the maximum price he would be willing to pay in order to retain that level of amenity. These two questions correspond to the two measures of the draft tax discussed above. In effect, by asking what is the minimum military income it would take to induce an individual to volunteer, one is asking what the minimum price is at which he would sell the combination of his civilian income and civilian amenity level. By asking the maximum amount an individual would be willing to pay in order to avoid the obligation to serve, one is asking the maximum amount he would be willing to pay for the combination of his civilian income and civilian amenity level. The critical difference is that in asking the individual for how much he would be willing to sell his amenity level, one implicitly assumes that initially he has the level of well-being which corresponds to that amenity level. On the other hand, in asking how much he would

FIGURE 20.1

TWO MEASURES OF IMPLICIT DRAFT TAX

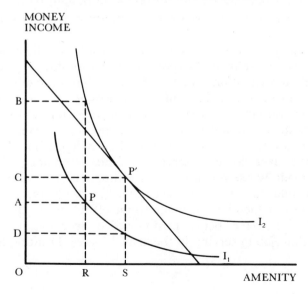

pay in order to avoid his draft obligation, one implicitly assumes that he has the amenity level corresponding to that in military service and is trying to buy back his civilian level.

Figure 20.1 illustrates this discussion through the use of indifference curve analysis. The two goods represented on the diagram are money compensation and civilian amenity measured in hypothetical homogeneous quality units. Indifference curves I_1 and I_2 trace the combinations of money income and civilian amenity between which the individual would be indifferent. Suppose that point P represents the combination of money income and amenity that the individual experiences in the military and P' represents the combination he would experience as a civilian. Figure 20.1 can thus be used to illustrate the fact that the two measures of the draft tax depend on which indifference curve is assumed as the starting point in the analysis. Given that amenity level OR is associated with the military, the minimum amount of money necessary to induce the individual to move from point P' to point P would be AB. BC dollars represents the value to the individual of the reduction in his amenity level from OS, the civilian level, to OR, the military level. AC represents the difference between the individual's civilian income (OC) and his income in the military (OA).

If instead we ask the amount the individual would be willing to pay to avoid military service, the measure is different. He would be willing to pay CD dollars, because at the combination of civilian amenity OS and disposable income OD, the individual would feel himself no better off than if he were in the armed forces at P. The value of the difference in amenity between civilian and military life here is measured by DA with, as before, AC dollars being the difference in civilian and military cash income. Note that these two measures are different; in particular, CB is greater than DA. CB represents the amount that would compensate a person for the reduction in amenity level (i.e., keep him as well off as if he were on the same indifference curve), given that he moved to point P from point P'. DA represents the amount he would be willing to pay for an increase in amenity level from the military to the civilian levels given that he moves to point P' from point P. The reason CB is greater than DA is that at the highest level of well-being represented by I_2, the individual is willing to pay more for civilian amenity than he is willing (and able) to pay at the lower level of well-being (real income) represented by I_1.

Which measure of the implicit draft tax is the proper one? The answer depends critically on what one assumes is the proper distribution of real income P that is, the proper distribution of the right to control one's own life. The measure of a draft tax as what a potential draftee would be willing to pay in order to avoid being drafted, or, what is the same thing, as what he would be willing to pay in order to hire a substitute, is an appropriate measure if one assumes that the government has a right to levy the burden of national defense on young men in this inequitable way. Given this assumption—which is implied by the mere existence of the draft—this measure is the one which is most appropriate from a theoretical viewpoint. The other measure, the minimum amount which the government would have to pay to a potential draftee to get him to volunteer, is an appropriate measure if one assumes that individuals do indeed have the right to remain civilians. This is really a specific illustration of the general principle that different distributions of property rights, because of income effects represented in Figure 20.1 by different budget lines, may lead to different measures of allocative results.[6]

From a theoretical viewpoint the measure of the tax as the amount a potential draftee would be willing to pay in order to avoid being drafted has much to recommend it, if one is willing to grant the assumption that individual property rights belong to the state. However, the second measure, the amount which would be required to induce an individual to volunteer, has considerable advantage from an empirical viewpoint. A rough measure of the draft tax is provided by simply determining the difference between the military and civilian wages of draftees or potential draftees. In addition this difference between military and civilian wages is an important part of both measures and is identical in each. To measure the value of civilian amenity with the current institutional arrangement, one is much more likely to use the minimum inducement to volunteer as an appropriate measure. The reason is that we do have some experience with inducing people to volunteer for various kinds of work, and we can thus estimate an elasticity of supply. In order to estimate empirically the alternative measure, the amount an individual would be willing to pay in order to avoid the draft, we would really have to observe a situation in which individuals were permitted either to buy their way out of the draft or to hire substitutes. Since such a situation has not existed since the Civil War, little empirical data exists which would provide us with a way of estimating the second measure of the tax.

The Distribution of the Draft Tax over Potential Draftees

In this section we will consider that portion of the draft tax borne by those who are potentially eligible—i.e., by men of draft-eligible age. These individuals may be classified into four categories:

1. those who are drafted
2. those who are true volunteers
3. those who volunteer only because of the existence of the draft
4. those who are not drafted

With the current lottery method of selecting individuals for the draft, the last group includes those who were deferred, for some reason or another, and also those who are eligible but were not taken. We shall consider each of these groups in turn.

Draftees. Those who were employed as civilians prior to being drafted clearly suffer, as part of the tax, a reduction in their money income from the civilian level to the level that they receive in the military. To this amount must be added some evaluation of the reduction in amenity which, most people would agree, is associated with the transition to military life. Empirically, it is difficult to make even this elementary separation of two components of the draft tax, because persons who are inducted into the army receive in addition to their cash income direct transfers of goods and services as income in kind. In order to estimate even the difference between civilian and military incomes, it is necessary to place some value on this income in kind. This income consists primarily of barracks housing, or other housing provided by the military, free medical care, food provided at military posts, clothing when provided by the military directly, and other items for personal life provided without monetary cost to the enlisted man. In empirical studies, these items are usually valued at their cost to the government. In theory, however, one really ought to value them at their value to the individual who receives them. It is conceivable, for example, that the value of living in a barracks might be even less to the individual who is compelled to live there than it costs the government to provide that housing. Or clothing for combat might be worth much less to the individual who received it than its cost to the government who provided it. If individuals in the army had a choice of free barracks housing or the equivalent cash income to be used for purchase of their own housing, we could value barracks housing at its cost to the government, since it is evident that provision of this housing is equivalent to providing the individual with the same amount of money income. But where individuals have no option but are required to take the housing, food, or medical care provided by the military, there is no easy way of placing a value on it.[7]

The purpose of this discussion is only to suggest that the most obvious measure of the draft tax is subject to some question. If we assume that individuals would prefer, other things being equal, to have the choice of the type of housing or food which they wish to buy, the measure of the draft tax as the difference between the civilian income and military income with income in kind evaluated at its cost will tend to understate the true tax being imposed on the individual. It would require an additional adjustment in the measure of the value of amenity level in order to offset it. Nevertheless, the measure of the difference in money income, or the economic cost imposed on the draftees, is useful as an approximate first measure of the draft tax.[8]

True volunteers. At first, it might appear that true volunteers bear no tax as a result of the draft. After all, they were willing to volunteer at the current rate of pay in the armed forces, and presumably did so because they would be better off. But there is a sense in which even true volunteers bear a tax as a result of the existence of the draft, although in their case the tax has no distortive allocative effects. The draft does, however, deprive them of income they would otherwise receive. If the draft were eliminated, and if wages had to be raised in order to induce more people to volunteer, those higher wages would be received not only by the new volunteers, but also by persons who volunteer at the current wage rate and who, therefore, would have been willing to volunteer for less. The difference between the income an individual gets and the minimum income for which he would be willing to stay on a particular job is economic rent. It is payment to a resource over and above the amount necessary to induce the resource to remain in a particular use; it is a payment in excess of the opportunity costs of the resource. It is obvious, however, that a tax on this surplus is still a tax, in the sense that it is a government-enforced policy that deprives a person of income he would otherwise earn.

To see this more clearly, consider the case of a college professor who receives $15,000 in income, but who is so in love with his subject that he would be willing to teach for a payment of only $6,000. Suppose the government took away from him $9,000 of his income. We would still call this a tax, and it would clearly fall on the individual concerned. It would have no effect on his behavior, of course, since he would still be willing to perform the same functions and take the same job at the lower income. Nevertheless, such a tax clearly does have distributive effects. It is in this sense that one can contend that a draft tax falls on even those who choose an army career. It is a tax in the sense that, in the absence of the draft, their incomes would be higher.

Induced volunteers. A significant portion of those who do volunteer do so only because of the existence of the draft. The Department of Defense estimates that at least 45 percent of volunteers in 1971 were draft-induced. It makes sense for an individual subject to the draft to volunteer because, by doing so, he can obtain many more of his first preferences with respect to his specialty in the armed forces and his location than if he is drafted. If he is risk-averse, he may also volunteer in order to avoid the risk of being drafted, in order to "get it over with." In particular, many of those in the National Guard are likely to be draft-induced volunteers.

Clearly, these induced volunteers are subject to the draft tax. If we assume that the other features of military life would not be changed, we would get a rough measure of the tax they bear by considering the difference between the wage at which they do volunteer when the draft is in existence and the wage at which they would be willing to volunteer if the draft were abolished.

Draft-eligibles who are not drafted.   Persons who are eligible for the draft but who are not drafted bear part of the draft tax if the existence of the draft induces them to alter their behavior from what it would have been in the absence of the draft. For example, if a young man decides to go to college because he can get a student deferment, and if he would not have done so had he not been threatened by the draft, some measure of the extent to which he is made worse off by choosing college over his most preferred alternative would be part of the draft tax. The less extensive and complicated the exemptions and deferments which are permitted, the smaller this tax will tend to be. Thus, abolition of occupational deferments means that it is no longer useful for a person to take a job he really does not prefer in order to avoid the draft.

Even if the draft does not directly affect a person's behavior it could cause utility loss from worrying over the draft. These psychological effects may affect work or academic performance. A student, for example, may be less than serious toward his studies if there is some probability he may be drafted. With the introduction of the lottery system in 1970 much of these parts of the draft tax were eliminated. To the extent that one can still, by altering his behavior, obtain exemption from the draft—for example, by seeking a conscientious-objector classification—the draft still imposes a tax. Even those who are subject to the lottery bear a kind of tax both before and after their number is drawn. It is probably safe to assume that most people are risk-averse in the sense that they would pay something (buy insurance) in order to avoid risk. Before a young man becomes 19, he knows that there is some positive probability that his birth date will have a low number assigned to it and that he will be drafted. This affects him in two ways. First, it means that he cannot really make plans for his future life until his number is drawn. He cannot get a job which requires a degree of permanency; he cannot plan his education. In addition, he clearly bears some psychological uncertainty which makes him worse off. Even after the drawing takes place, since the size of the draft call for any given year is never stated beforehand, some young men are still uncertain about whether their number will be one of the numbers reached in the process of calling draftees. Thus, they continue to bear the kind of risk described above and continue to be hindered in their ability to make plans for their future life. Obviously, the extent to which one bears this tax depends on how eager he is to make such plans at a particular point.

It is probably true, as was argued by the advocates of the lottery, that 19-year-olds are less desirous of making such plans than the 26-year-olds who were previously called first. Nevertheless, it is still true that this impediment to the ability of young men to take permanent jobs and make permanent plans at an early age imposes a cost on them. It is probably worth noting that this cost would tend to fall more heavily on lower-income persons who customarily cannot afford the luxury of four college years to decide what they want to do and who often need to get the best job they can as soon as they graduate from high school, or even before.[9]

All the components discussed above should be added in order to get a true measure of the draft tax. In the following section we discuss some equity aspects of the draft tax and provide a rough estimate of its magnitude.

Measurement and Equity Aspects of the Draft Tax

The previous sections showed how conscription is properly interpreted as a tax. This section is concerned with measurement and equity aspects of this tax. First, national defense as a collective good is discussed and suggested criteria for judging the equity of various means of financing military services are described. Second, there is a discussion of problems encountered in measuring the tax, and recent estimates of the tax and the tax rate are reviewed. The last sub-section examines the equity of the tax from several standpoints (vertical equity, horizontal equity, and intergenerational equity).

National Defense

National defense (of which military manpower is an important element) is a public good or collective good, meaning that provision by private persons has (positive) spillover or external effects [Buchanan 1972]. As a consequence, if private incentives operated alone, total expenditures would probably be suboptimal. Thus, external security has been collectivized, that is, provided by the government.

Like all governmental services, national defense must be financed by one or a combination of the following methods: taxing, inflation, or direct conscription of resources. Whatever the method, there are commonly accepted norms or criteria governing the equity of the financing scheme. These include (but are not necessarily limited to) the "benefit principle" and the "ability-to-pay principle."

According to the benefit principle, people should pay for a public service in proportion to the benefits they receive. The ability-to-pay principle would elicit greater payment from those whose income (or wealth) is higher—those who can "afford" to pay more. By either criterion, taxes for the provision of national defense should be higher for those with higher incomes. That is, people in the higher income brackets usually have greater wealth (i.e., more to protect), receive greater value from a given expenditure on national defense, and thus should pay more for the service. Obviously, those with higher incomes (or wealth) are better able to pay.

It is this frame of reference that governs our discussion of tax equity and should be kept in mind as the estimates of the implicit tax on military recruits are reviewed.

Estimates of the Tax

The previous section defined the implicit tax in two ways: (1) the amount a person would pay in order to avoid having to serve and (2) the difference between military income and that necessary to entice the recruit to enlist voluntarily. These two measures differ by what may be termed an income effect. Ideally, one could estimate the implicit tax corresponding to either definition. For example, it should be possible to perform individual experiments on induced recruits, obtaining their preferences for civilian life over military service in terms of the increased taxes they would be willing to pay in order to avoid service. However, data which would allow for even approximate measures of this version of the tax are not readily available.

As for the other definition—the difference between volunteer supply price and actual compensation—there are basically two estimating procedures. Conceptually the most appealing involves estimating the supply curve for those actually serving, determining their actual compensation, and computing the difference. But since supply curve estimating techniques (e.g., least-squares regression analysis) can determine only the relation for true volunteers, such estimates only approximate the supply relation for those actually serving. To the extent that some of the reluctant (induced) recruits have greater aversion to military service than those who would serve under an all-volunteer scheme, the difference between (volunteer) supply price and actual compensation underestimates the tax.

Figure 20.2 shows a supply curve for volunteer (first-term) enlistments. At military compensation level OX (i.e., monetary reward plus payment in kind), OA true volunteers will enlist yearly. If the Department of Defense requires OB recruits, then AB enlistments will be reluctant (i.e., draftees or induced volunteers). Since the supply curve shown is for a completely volunteer force, area CDE represents the implicit tax corresponding to those AB enlistees who would volunteer if the pay scale were raised to level OY. That is, for any rate of volunteer-

FIGURE 20.2

SUPPLY CURVE FOR VOLUNTEER ENLISTMENTS

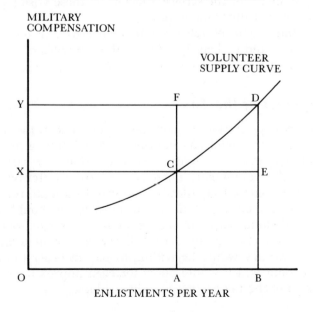

ing between *A* and *B,* the marginal recruit would volunteer at a pay level measured by the vertical distance from the horizontal axis to the point on the supply curve directly above. The tax is the difference between the supply price and actual compensation, *OX*. Area *CDE*, which simply aggregates the tax corresponding to those extra recruits who would serve voluntarily if pay were raised to *OY,* thus represents the minimum tax on actual induced recruits.

Using regression analysis, Walter Oi [1967] estimated the supply curve for volunteer enlistments, then derived a measure of average military compensation, and thus provided an estimate of area *CDE'*. Oi's estimate of the implicit tax is $316 million for 209,000 additional (volunteer) enlistees, meaning that at a minimum the 209,000 induced recruits projected to be in the armed services during the early 1970s paid on average $1,512 per year in implicit tax.

Of course, area *CDE* approximates only the implicit tax on those who serve reluctantly. Also at issue is the opportunity cost of true volunteers. That is, because there is a draft, true volunteers do not earn the economic rents they would earn if there were an all-volunteer army. If the military were on a completely volunteer basis and found it necessary to recruit *OB* enlistees, then the *OA* true volunteers would earn *OY* rather than *OX*, assuming that there would be no discrimination in hiring. The area *XYFC* thus represents the foregone rents of today's true-volunteer enlistees.[10] Oi estimated these rents to be $1,417 billion, or $3,400 per recruit.

Note also that area *CFD* represents an opportunity cost to those extra true volunteers who would serve when military compensation was raised to level *OY.* Whereas area *CDE* measures the implicit tax corresponding to these extra volunteers, area *CFD* represents the economic rents these recruits would earn if there were true volunteering at rate *OB*. Oi estimated this economic rent at approximately $395 million, or $1,888 per (additional) volunteer recruit.

Another way of estimating the implicit tax on induced recruits is to measure the difference between a recruit's foregone civilian earnings and his military compensation. This is a "financial cost" proxy measure because it presumes that a person is indifferent between civilian service and military service at comparable levels of pay. If induced recruits have an aversion for military services even if paid the civilian wage, then this financial-cost measure also underestimates the true implicit tax. Professors J. Ronnie Davis and Neil Palomba [1968] have attempted such a measure. By contrasting military incomes with median civilian earnings, they were able to estimate the implicit tax for individuals grouped by level of education (and income). Their results are listed in column [1] of Table 20.1 and show an implicit tax ranging from $2,684 (per year) for the induced recruit with grade school education to $8,717 for the induced recruit with a college degree.[11]

Actually, this approach may in some cases underestimate even the financial cost because it ignores the impact having to serve may have on lifetime civilian earnings after a person leaves service.[12] Thus, whenever an individual is forced into the military his financial loss is not only the earnings he foregoes while actually serving, but also how much the delay puts him "behind" in civilian employment. Data on civilian income streams indicate that typically a person's (civilian) income starts at one level, gradually rises as he becomes more proficient in his job, reaches a maximum, and then begins to fall as his productivity is slowly retarded by age.

Figure 20.3 (not drawn to scale) shows this phenomenon. The line *RUST* represents the civilian income stream. The broken line *XYZST* represents the income stream for one who serves for two years in the military then begins civilian employment. The implicit tax is represented by (the present value of) the area *XRSZY*.[13] The computations of Davis and Palomba measure area *XRUY* only, the loss for the two years of service. James C. Miller III and Robert D. Tollison [1971] used the lifetime earnings loss approach to estimate the implicit tax, and their results are listed in column [2] of Table 20.1. As shown, the implicit tax based on lifetime income loss ranges from approximately

TABLE 20.1

ESTIMATES OF IMPLICIT TAXES AND TAX RATES ON RELUCTANT
MILITARY RECRUITS, BY EDUCATION-INCOME GROUP

Years of School Completed	Implicit Tax		Tax Rate	
	Two Years of Service [1]	Lifetime Income Loss [2]	Two Years of Service [3]	Lifetime Income Loss [4]
0–8	$2,684	$ 0	.5855	.0000
9–11	4,304	1,046	.6937	.0074
12	5,250	2,978	.7347	.0175
13–15	6,219	4,748	.7660	.0251
16	8,717	9,256	.8210	.0361

SOURCE: Columns [1] and [3], Davis & Palomba; columns [2] and [4], Miller & Tollison.

zero for the induced recruit with some grade school education, up to $9,256 for the college graduate.[14]

Tax rates also may be computed, and these are shown in columns [3] and [4] of Table 20.2. Shown in column [3] are the tax rates derived by Davis and Palomba, computed as the ratio of the implicit tax to foregone civilian earnings. Thus, for example, the induced recruit with a high school education pays an implicit tax amounting to approximately 77 percent of his foregone civilian earnings. Miller and Tollison (like Bailey and Cargill) defined the tax rate differently, taking the ratio of the present value of civilian income. Their results are shown in column [4], and indicate, for example, that the induced recruit with a high school education loses nearly 2 percent of his lifetime income by having to serve in the military.

It is argued by those who advocate military service as a learning experience that, for some individuals, lifetime income may be higher because of military service. They would argue that line 1 in column [2] of Table 20.1 is positive rather than zero. Studies, however, show that the military work experience of lower-education-level people is not transferable to civilian occupations. The less qualified recruit or draftee is placed in a military occupation speciality (MOS) that has few, if any,

FIGURE 20.3

IMPACT ON CIVILIAN INCOME STREAMS OF THE DRAFT TAX

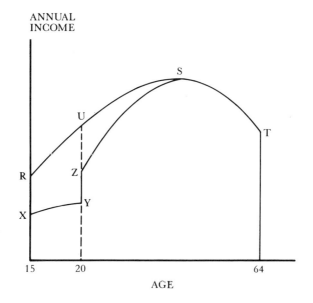

civilian equivalents (e.g., riflemen). Indeed most MOS classifications are not related very closely to civilian occupations [*Studies* 1970].

Equity of the Tax

Given the above estimates of the implicit tax on induced recruits, we may analyze the equity of this method of (partially) financing national defense, recalling our earlier discussion of criteria for equitable taxation.

Vertical equity. First, within the specially taxed group, there is general conformity with both the benefit principle and the ability-to-pay principle. That is, those in (succeeding) higher education-income groups pay higher implicit taxes, as shown in Table 20.1, columns [1] and [2]. Also, the tax rate is progressive, rising over the entire range for both sets of estimates, as shown in columns [3] and [4].

As compared with the general taxpaying population, however, the implicit tax is at odds with standards for fair taxation. For example, not until one reaches a taxable income (not counting deductions) of $13,699 does the federal government tax away more than $2,684, the lowest tax listed by Davis and Palomba (Table 20.1, column [1]). A taxable income of $32,136 is reached before the tax is $8,717, that for college educated induced recruits.[15]

Tax rate comparisons are even more striking. For example, taxable income must reach $263,818 before the (average) federal income tax is 59 percent, the lowest rate computed by Davis and Palomba (Table 20.1, column [3]). One's taxable income will never reach a rate where a civilian pays 82 percent (the rate paid by induced recruits fresh out of college), since the maximum marginal tax rate on income is only 70 percent.[16]

Horizontal equity. Another principle of equity most people would endorse is that individuals in like circumstances should be treated the same. If income level is taken to be the characteristic determining cohort relationships, then we may discuss the equity of the tax paid by induced recruits with the federal income tax paid by the *recruit's education-income cohort*.

Davis and Palomba determine from publications of the Census Bureau that median civilian incomes for the education-income groups listed in Table 20.1 are $4,584, $6,204, $7,150, $8,119, and $10,618, respectively. Federal income taxes on these amounts of taxable income are as follows: $731, $1,039, $1,218, $1,406, and $1,956. These should be contrasted with the implicit tax estimates shown in Table 20.1, column [1]. Cohort (average) federal income tax rates are .159, .167, .170, .173, and .184, to be contrasted with those shown in Table 20.1, column [2].

Intergenerational equity. The Marshall Commission recognized a basic issue of conscription when it raised the question, "Who Serves When Not All Serve?" [National Advisory Commission on Selective Service 1967]. Of course, the commission was referring to the problem of determining who among those of a specific age group would serve. Suppose, however, that within age groups equity were not a problem. Assume that means could be found where those in the draft-eligible generation were able to agree (among themselves) on an equitable recruiting scheme (a lottery, a system of taxes and payments, or whatever). Nevertheless, there would remain the problem of intergenerational equity, because military manpower requirements and draft calls are not constant over time.

Since the first peacetime draft was instituted in 1948, draft calls have fluctuated rather widely, as shown in Table 20.2. Quite noticeable, of course, are the buildups during the Korean and Vietnamese wars (especially 1951–1953; 1966–1968). Contrast these levels with draft calls for the late 1940s and late 1950s. Thus, succeeding generations of American males have paid different implicit military taxes, and

TABLE 20.2

U.S. DRAFT CALLS, 1948–1971

1948	25,000	1960	84,000
1949	10,000	1961	113,000
1950	210,397	1962	76,000
1951	524,680	1963	119,000
1952	413,608	1964	106,200
1953	430,000	1965	218,150
1954	251,000	1966	364,680
1955	151,000	1967	288,900
1956	149,000	1968	343,300
1957	136,958	1969	266,900
1958	136,000	1970	209,300
1959	94,000	1971	157,969

SOURCE: Office of the Director of Selective Service.

since there is no reason to expect military manpower requirements to even out in the future, continuation of conscription would perpetuate this intergenerational difference in tax burden.

Conscription and Economic Efficiency

In addition to the equity ramifications discussed in previous sections, military conscription affects the allocation of the nation's scarce resources.

Allocative Losses

We have previously shown that a true volunteer's supply price may be approximated by the civilian income he foregoes. It is important to realize, then, that excluding the interests of the individual himself the real cost to the rest of the economy of utilizing a recruit in the military may be approximated by the civilian income he would have earned. If, for a given job in the military, two people are equally qualified, yet the one with the higher civilian income is chosen, then the economy as a whole suffers more than if the person whose opportunity costs were lower had been selected. A volunteer army would generally select those people from the economy whose opportunity costs (in the sense of their ability to earn money in civilian employment) were least. In such manner, the real cost of providing recruits to the military would be minimized. To the extent that conscription chooses people who would not have volunteered (with higher pay and better living conditions), there is imposed on society a "deadweight loss" owing to this misallocation of resources.

Figure 20.4 illustrates this deadweight loss in the aggregate.[17] Assume that the demand curve for first-term recruits is given by D, and that the supply curve is measured by S. The volunteer army wage is given by W_v, and optimal output, in the sense that at the margin the value of an additional recruit is just offset by the wage he is paid, is given by X_v. Assume now that the military wage (payment in money and kind) is W_d. At this wage the military will "require" X_r recruits; X_e will enlist voluntarily, whereas $(X_r - X_e)$ will be conscripted. If X_t is the total pool of eligible recruits, and W_t is the minimum wage at which all would volunteer, then W_1 (which is the average of W_t and W_d) is the expected value under a "fair" lottery of the opportunity cost to a conscripted individual in the pool represented by $(X_t - X_e)$.

Thus, on average, conscriptees (or induced recruits) cost the civilian economy W_1.[18]

The effect of conscription is to impose a deadweight loss on the economy. Note that the value to the economy of the conscriptees is represented by the rectangle X_eBCX_r. If, instead of conscripting, X_r true volunteers had been attracted (by raising their wage to distance X_rE), the value loss to the civilian sector would be measured by the quadrangle X_eAEX_r. The difference between these two "costs" to the civilian sector is measured by the quadrangle $ABCE$. Thus, area $ABCE$ is the excess cost to the economy of conscripting individuals indiscriminately as opposed to enticing those with relatively low opportunity cost to volunteer.[19]

Excessive Military Costs

There are other ways in which conscription impacts on the real cost of providing national defense, some directly related to manpower utilization. For example, a perceived cost of manpower which is lower than the real cost leads the military to use excessive amounts of labor

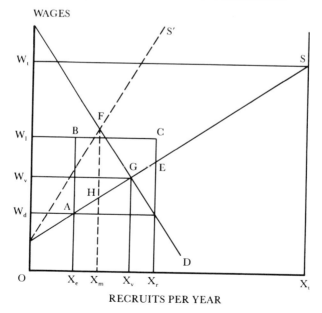

FIGURE 20.4

DEADWEIGHT LOSS CAUSED BY CONSCRIPTION

versus capital in its production of defense.[20] As illustrated in Figure 20.5, the military's perceived budget line has a different slope than the budget line which represents the real cost of labor. If the desired level of defense corresponds to the isoquant indicated in the figure, then the military will minimize its financial costs by choosing the input combination indicated by *B*. To minimize real cost, the input combination should be that indicated by *A*. Thus, keeping military wages artificially below the volunteer supply price encourages the military to use excessive amounts of labor in relation to capital. We thus witness grass being cut with old-fashioned hand equipment and don't find labor-saving food production (e.g., automatic peelers). Humanitarian considerations may prevent labor substitution in combat situations, but it has even been suggested as early as 1875 that human beings might be sacrificed to save capital (a cannon) when the humans can be conscripted at a zero explicit cost [von Thunen n.d.]. B. F. Kiker and J. Berkeli [1972] have attempted to calculate losses of human capital in Vietnam.

A number of criticisms may be made of this hypothesis. First, there may not be very much opportunity for the military to trade off capital and labor; second, with equal supply prices, the military would prefer drafting high-quality personnel which for many jobs may be used capi-

FIGURE 20.5

EFFECT OF CONSCRIPTION ON MILITARY FACTOR COMBINATIONS

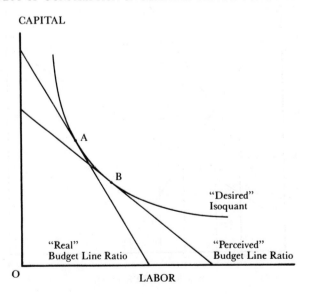

tal-intensively; and third, draft wages grossly underestimate the "cost" perceived by the military—that is, military decision makers feel political pressure whenever there is excessive utilization of the manpower pool. This takes the form of such statements as "nothing is too good for our fighting men."

A related cost of conscription results because inductees "cost" the military less than a market wage. Therefore, there is an incentive to use military personnel in capacities for which civilians are equally suited. For example, why should a clerk-typist on U.S. military bases (especially domestically) be in uniform? The same goes for mechanics, cooks, and people in other occupations. Ames Albro, in a study undertaken on behalf of the President's Commission on an All-Volunteer Armed Force [*Studies* 1970], concluded that "approximately 95,000 positions in a force of two million men could be staffed by civilians with no loss in effectiveness." It was estimated that such civilian substitution for military personnel could save the government (in real terms) between $90 million and $125 million per year.[21] The government has begun to make adjustments in this direction.

Even greater savings could be expected by virtue of lower training costs concomitant with a shift from conscription to volunteerism. Since draftees are required to serve a maximum of two years, a good deal of their time in service is spent in basic training. The savings that would be realized by utilizing four-year recruits (true volunteers) are apparent. Even the basic training a recruit receives is probably too little in terms of his job. Because he will "resign" in a very short period of time, the military has little incentive to train him for a skilled occupation. On the other hand, those who do enlist voluntarily for longer tenure receive (relatively) too much training. Also, because of the problem in training recruits, the military has an incentive to draft high-quality personnel, those which require less training to accomplish a specific task. With a lower rate of turnover, the proportion of the military personnel's budget going for training purposes would be much lower. This is because, for a given static force, fewer individuals at any one time would require training and those presently engaged in training others could be freed for a different type of work. Also, the higher average experience level would mean more productive personnel. The President's Commission estimates that an all-volunteer army would have a 17 percent annual turnover rate compared to a 26 percent turnover in a mixed (conscript/volunteer) army. This means that an equally effective volunteer force would need approximately 5 percent fewer personnel than a mixed force of conscripts and true volunteers. In real terms this could mean savings of up to $1 billion per year.[22]

External Costs

Additional costs of conscription can be identified, including the efforts of many young men to avoid the draft. For instance, in the past the Selective Service System has sought to "channel" young men into certain occupations by the use of selective deferments. Thus, oftentimes men have married earlier than they would have otherwise; they have had children which otherwise may not have been wanted; they have taken up occupations such as teaching for which they had no desire; and finally, our colleges and universities have been populated in good measure by those seeking to avoid conscription. In addition, certain individuals faced with imminent induction have actually chosen to leave the country rather than participate in an occupation they found grossly distasteful. Related to these efforts to escape the draft are the costs the government incurs in policing the draft. Both costs (i.e., escape and policing) are almost impossible to estimate.[23]

Even for those who make no overt attempt to escape conscription but on the other hand prefer to incur the risk rather than enlist, there are uncertainties. Such an individual finds it very difficult to plan his life. On the one hand, he may be discriminated against by employers who hesitate in making a commitment to someone who may leave very soon and be entitled to his job and seniority when he returns. On the other hand, as to his personal life, an individual may postpone a marriage, postpone having children, or postpone schooling in order to "wait it out," and "see what happens."[24] While no estimates of such costs have been attempted, by introspection one may conclude that they are considerable.[25]

Finally, conscription adversely affects the typical individual's allocation of consumption over time. Income is low at the beginning of an individual's career, rises until some maximum is reached shortly before retirement, and falls thereafter (see Figure 20.3). Typically, individuals find that they "need" higher incomes during the early parts of their lives, when the demands of family and schooling must be met, and given an imperfect capital market it is difficult to transfer future income into the present. The draft exacerbates this problem by giving still lower incomes during the early portion of a person's career, offset partially by a reduced tax liability in succeeding years. In so doing, conscription causes a transfer of income from times of very high marginal time preference to times of lower marginal time preference. This causes a utility loss to society as a whole [Thurow 1969, Willett 1968].

Analysis of Alternative Systems of Conscription

In previous sections we viewed the draft as a tax in kind and examined its equity aspects. This analysis and an examination of the allocative inefficiencies of conscription suggest that we examine more fully some alternative methods of conscription. We can divide these alternatives into three broad categories [Miller 1968]. Conscription can be carried out selectively (selective service), universally (universal military training or universal national service), or by a random process (lottery).[26]

A selective service system implies selectivity when manpower requirements dictate that universal service is unnecessary. Our present Universal Military Training Service Act, which has never been universal, requires that all men register at age 18, but contains much selectivity. Any one of several circumstances has, at one time or another, exempted or deferred eligible men.[27] Deferments are by far the most significant method of avoiding conscription. Of these deferments, paternity and student status have been the most important.[28] Economic theory can help us examine some implications of Selective Service policy.

The Granting of Deferments

Initially, we should recognize that the granting of a deferment or exemption to a certain group is, in fact, a relative subsidy to that group. Deferments reward (subsidize) students, fathers, farmers, and other occupational groups relative to their drafted counterparts. The net effect of this subsidy will be to lower the costs to individuals of becoming members of these groups. As a result, we will have at the margin more students, babies, and farm products than we would have had in the absence of any special treatment.[29] It may be the policy of the government to influence decision making through the draft. If, for example, the government wishes to encourage more people to become medical doctors, deferments or exemptions of medical students would be one way of doing so.

Given that we may wish to subsidize certain occupations or conditions in order to maintain "national health, safety, or interest," how should we proceed?[30] Historically, selective service has granted categorical "go/no go" deferments to "critical occupations." It can be shown that we should not be concerned about the value by group, but rather importance at the margin [Miller, Tollison & Willett 1968]. For instance, suppose we would agree that the engineering profession is somehow more important to national goals than is the law profession. Yet, if next year we had only ten lawyers compared to thousands of engineers, it is quite probable that the addition of the tenth lawyer would be considered more critical than the addition of the 10,000th engineer.

In Figure 20.6, the two groups of men are represented by the (perfectly inelastic) short run supply curves S_E (engineers) and S_L (lawyers). Assume that within each group persons have equal skills and will make equally good soldiers. We must conscript N soldiers from S_E and S_L. Average value (AV) and marginal value (MV) curves are drawn according to the law of decreasing value. That is, each additional member of any occupation has a net value to society less than the average value to society of persons already employed in that occupation. AV_E is greater at S_E than AV_L at S_L by design. Selective service policy makers would observe that engineers are of more value in their job than lawyers are in theirs. Applying their policy of categorical deferments, they would defer all engineers and conscript the men required from the law profession.

Using economic analysis we can find a more *efficient* policy. Given the goal of maximizing the total value to society of civilian employ-

FIGURE 20.6

MINIMIZING THE OPPORTUNITY COST OF CONSCRIPTION

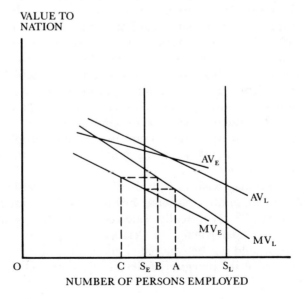

ment, subject to fulfilling manpower requirements, the efficient rule would be to equilibrate at the marginal values of the two classifications. In our graphical example the efficient rule calls for any $N - (S_L - A)$ to be taken from the law profession. But note, at A, that the marginal value of a lawyer is as great as the marginal value of an engineer at S_E. In cases where $N > (S_L - A)$, men should be conscripted from both classifications. An efficient solution where $(S_E - C) + (S_L - B) = N > (S_L - A)$ is illustrated. The marginal value of engineers at C is the same as the marginal value of lawyers at B. With this arrangement, the total value to the nation of civilian employment is maximized subject to meeting the manpower needs of the military. It is thus possible for selective service to minimize the opportunity cost associated with conscription for any *given* draft.

Universal Service

Under the proposed varieties of universal military training (UMT) or universal national service (UNS), all able-bodied men (and women) serve a short period in the military service or choose between the military and a social program. Proponents of this alternative are willing to increase intergenerational inequity in order to decrease intragenerational inequity. Advocates of universal service stress the benefits which would accrue to the individual and the nation when all are required to serve.

Former President Eisenhower, Senator Strom Thurmond, General Lewis B. Hershey, and the American Legion, among others, have emphasized the benefits of universal military service. Hershey, former director of the Selective Service System, testified in 1966, "I do not want to go along with a volunteer basis. I think a fellow should be compelled to become better and not let him use his discretion whether he wants to be smarter, more healthy, or honest." The American Legion maintains a position that "our nation should never be without an obligation for every youth to serve his country in a military capacity." Former President Eisenhower wrote that "above and beyond all [the] advantages of universal military training is the matter of attitude toward country." And according to Senator Strom Thurmond, "Military service would teach these young people patriotism and love of country and respect of the flag and discipline" [Miller 1968].

Margaret Mead and Robert McNamara recommended UNS to fight disease and poverty and to clean up the slums. They feel a country as rich as the United States can find a way to finance these humanitarian projects. One need not take issue with the "worthiness" of the projects they recommended to question the suggestion of conscripted labor as a means to that end. Conscripted labor does not lower the economic cost of these programs but only lowers their effective budgetary tax price vis-à-vis activities not utilizing conscripted labor, and at an additional cost in terms of violation of what many consider to be basic individual rights.[31] The labor which proponents of universal service call for is not unlike the "national service" the Chinese emperors "employed" centuries ago in order to build the Great Wall.[32]

The Lottery System

A lottery system in which few exemptions and deferments are allowed decreases the discriminatory power of the selective service boards. Proponents of the random lottery argue that it allows young men to plan their futures with more certainty, as it would limit their draft liability to a one-year period.[33] There are several shortcomings in the lottery system. A lottery with deferments, allowing the deferred individual to select his years of vulnerability, introduces elements of gaming. A shrewd individual can select his year of vulnerability reducing the probability of his being conscripted, thus achieving unequal treatment.[34] On equity grounds one can point to the inequity of a tax that is "collected" on a random basis. This type of tax is analagous to selecting a few people at random to bear the cost of the space program.[35] In effect, a lottery system only insures impartial inequity in the collection of the draft tax.

Equity and Conscription

The concept of equity, or what is fair, has run through this discussion of alternative methods of conscription. Almost everyone claims to want military procurement to be equitable, but disagreement over the lottery, universal service, and voluntarism is not uncommon. This disagreement often centers on which system is most equitable, or—better—least inequitable. We can gain some insights into this question by distinguishing between *ex post* and *ex ante* equity [Pauly & Willett 1972].

Returning to our space program example, suppose we have a population of ten people who vote to spend $1,000 in an attempt to reach the moon. How should the project be financed? The tax authority could charge each individual $100 or choose two $500 taxpayers at random. A decision on "fairness" depends upon the concept of equity employed. The random selection method is "fair" in an *ex ante* sense because each individual has an equal chance of "winning." The alternative, where all pay an equal amount, is equitable in an *ex post* sense. *Ex post* and *ex ante* equity are not mutually exclusive, but one does not imply the other.[36]

An ideal draft lottery presents equity in an *ex ante* sense, but not in an *ex post* sense. It is possible to approximate *ex post* equity with a lottery by compensating those who serve at a rate which makes them almost as well off as those who were not conscripted, but the costs of this compensation would generally be much greater than under a volunteer army, because military service would not follow the patterns of comparative advantage and preference which would be induced by voluntarism. Universal service guarantees intragenerational *ex post* equity. While it is possible to approximate *ex post* equity with conscription, voluntarism is the only system (ignoring the way it is financed) that guarantees both *ex post* and *ex ante* equity. We are insured of *ex ante* equity by a zero chance of being drafted. The soldier *choosing* military service has insured *ex post* equity by being fully compensated. Only voluntarism is compatible with both *ex post* and *ex ante* equity.

This examination has revealed that none of the alternative methods of conscription change its tax aspects. These forms of conscription are similar to an arbitrary and variable (by income opportunities) head tax. Some conscripted men, those who have many civilian alternatives, lose much; those with few opportunities lose little, and some may even gain by the training and medical care. All this generational inequity, the price of conscription, is carried out so that the general public need not be asked to pay more taxes. The recent move to a lottery has not made the draft more equitable; it has only helped create impartial inequity, thereby making the draft more politically palatable.

Draft Reform—Some Noneconomic Issues

In this essay we have concentrated on questions that concerned equity and efficiency and were very amenable to economic analysis. However, many issues raised in connection with draft reform concern questions of a political, sociological, or psychological nature and are, on the face of it, not directly susceptible to economic analysis. These questions ultimately involve noneconomic judgments by policy makers. In this section we will discuss several such issues in military manpower policy.

Flexibility

The demand for military manpower is not, of course, constant over time. It might be argued that whatever the static cost imposed by conscription, the essential role of conscription in times of rapid manpower buildup override all else.

One way to approach this issue is to postulate the conditions under which we might expect massive demands on our military personnel capability. The first is an all-out nuclear war. Under such circumstances, the prospect for training additional manpower would be totally irrelevant. Such a war would be fought by forces in being, and it would be difficult to conceive of the outcome's hinging on the nation's ability to mobilize additional manpower.

A second situation is that the country would once more become involved in a protracted conflict such as that in Vietnam, where over the course of many months (or perhaps years) our military forces would have to be augmented considerably. In such an event the first measure would be to observe the rate of volunteering. If, for example, such a war were popular, then one might expect the rate of volunteering to increase, even at the same pay. (For example, in the early days of World War II, the selective service mechanism was used mainly as a device for determining the order in which volunteers would be inducted.) If an insufficient number of volunteers failed to materialize, then two measures might be taken. First, call up the reserves (ostensibly, this is what they are for), and second, attempt to induce additional volunteering by raising the basic compensation. Special bonuses could be paid for those volunteering or committing themselves to be inducted in the future if the need arose. As a last resort, conscription could be temporarily reinstated, and if the mechanism were already in being, then the time lag would be trivial. This final solution requires the existence of stand-by draft mechanism for emergency situations.[37]

The flexibility lost if the draft were to be repealed is primarily the ability to adjust the quantity supplied to meet what are feared to be rapidly changing demand conditions. The loss of the very powerful lever conscription provides can be offset by flexibility in budgetary matters. With increased authority to vary methods and levels of pay, including enlistment bonuses, the quantity of manpower supplied can be adjusted to meet these changing demand conditions. It is even possible that by utilizing market forces these adjustments might be made more smoothly and quickly than they can be made by adjusting draft calls, which requires bureaucratic action.

A Black Army

The charge that a volunteer army would result in an all-black or predominantly black army can be shown to be considerably overstated. The appropriate question is whether a volunteer army would increase the proportion of black Americans serving in the armed forces (about 15 percent of current forces are black), and if so, by how much, and whether, if this happens, it should cause great concern to anyone. Elementary supply and demand analysis can be quite instructive here.

On the supply side it is important to recognize that although blacks are disproportionately represented in the lower-income categories of our society, for whom military service is often thought to be an attractive alternative, there are larger absolute numbers of whites in these categories. For example, whites outnumber blacks by a factor of 5.72 to 1.57 million in the less-than-$3,000-per-year category [U.S. Department of Commerce 1967]. Admittedly, these data are based on family units, but the presumption is that there is an absolutely higher supply of low-income poor whites that would be potentially competing for volunteer army jobs.

The effective manpower pools at these income levels would be affected by volunteer and mental and physical rejection rates. A predominantly black army could still emerge if, for example, volunteer rates were radically higher for blacks. First-term enlistment data are the best available evidence that we have on this problem and these data indicate that whites enlist at a higher effective rate than blacks (5.7 to 3.7 percent) [U.S. Department of Commerce 1967]. Since these are unadjusted rates, the effect of either blacks or whites enlisting under the threat of the draft is not discernible. But the discrepancy is probably large enough to hold in favor of higher white first-term enlistment rates after adjustment to the volunteer rates. Also, there is the fact that blacks fail more often in mental and physical examinations, which tends to reduce their effective volunteer rate.

Milton Friedman [1967] has argued that present levels of pay are comparatively more attractive to blacks than to whites and that, because of the existing opportunity differential, the increased wages of a volunteer army would attract proportionately more whites than blacks.[38]

On the demand side of this question, one could observe that present military production processes (using drafted manpower) are too labor-intensive due to the below-market wage paid for its labor input. Abolishing the draft in this context would affect military production processes by stimulating the increased use of capital inputs, using skilled labor. In other words, for any fixed size military "output level," total military employment of labor would be predicted to fall (due, for example, to economies in training operations). Moreover, the skill level of the higher-priced labor input under voluntarism might rise as the military moved to more capital-intensive operations. This result, if forthcoming, would further deter the prospects for considerably higher levels of black employment in a volunteer army [Miller 1968, Ford & Tollison 1969].

In short, the fears of an all-black army seem suspect when basic economic analysis is applied. More careful empirical work might add further evidence.

At the back of this discussion lurks the question of why anyone should worry about the possibility of an all-black army. To raise such a prospect seems racist. There are, however, arguments advanced by black leaders about the concern of the black community about losing its young, income-generating, family-producing males in war. This would seem to be a valid concern for blacks as a group, but it would have to be weighed in practice against the position that young black males, when volunteering for military service, know their own best interest.

An Army of Mercenaries

An often-heard argument against a volunteer army is that it would harbor more mercenary intentions than a drafted army. There are elements in this argument that make sense and elements that are faulty. The mercenary argument implies that there are some potential costs to not having a wide representation of the citizenry in the armed forces. The argument usually emphasizes the fear of a military takeover of civil authority. It is, of course, quite reasonable to worry about this kind of thing, but it should be recognized that the argument is largely independent of how enlisted men are procured. Historically, military takeovers have occurred with both volunteer and drafted armed forces, but there is no reliable historical evidence to suggest that either contributed to the coup.[39] The danger of a military takeover exists independently of the method of recruiting enlisted manpower.

The source and danger of a coup lie primarily in the professional officers corps, which is, by and large, volunteer manpower under any system. It might be argued that an enlisted force of professionals would be more obedient in a takeover attempt than draftees, but at best this sort of argument is inconclusive.[40] Military discipline and the point of a gun can invoke desired behavior in a large variety of circumstances from a draftee. But more emphatically, it should be obvious that support can be introduced for one side or the other in an argument such as this. For example, should better-paid, professional soldiers be more or less loyal? Should a more costly (budgetary) volunteer army be scrutinized more or less carefully by Congress and other civilian authorities? These are questions on which economic analysis cannot offer firm conclusions. Such arguments must be balanced against the other objectives of military manpower policy (efficiency, equity, etc.).

Citizen Opposition to the War

Another often-heard argument in favor of conscription is that a draft, where a wide range of the citizenry serve during war, stimulates widespread public opposition to military action, such as that in Vietnam [Reedy 1969].

Let us posit several cases of citizen attitude toward a given military action and compare potential differences in each case between a draft and a volunteer army. In the initial case, assume that there is a homogeneous attitude toward the military action in the polity—i.e., the people are unanimously opposed to or unanimously in favor of the action. If there were homogeneous opposition to the action, the volunteer system would increase citizen opposition where opposition is a function of the personal tax costs that the action imposes on a given citizen. In this case if, for example, the action were escalated through calling forth additional manpower resources, the costs of these resources under voluntarism would be high, due to general citizen opposition to the war (i.e., the supply of military manpower would be very inelastic with respect to the wage rate), and these costs would be spread generally over all taxpayers and not placed in a discriminatory manner on the young, as with the draft. Of course, a draft under these circumstances would also generate opposition, but a draft would lower the effective tax price of the action to those not drafted in the polity. Thus, one may be able to argue in this case that there is a differential amount of information about the cost of the war which flows to citizens under voluntarism relative to a draft system.

While this fact may not be terribly important where there is unanimous opposition to a military action, it is important in mixed cases where there is neither general opposition nor general support for the action. As a war is escalated, one would wish to calculate the marginal number of citizens each unit of escalation turns against the war. Under such conditions voluntarism *may* generate more marginal opposition to war than a draft system, by raising the marginal budget costs of escalation in terms of manpower resources more rapidly than a draft system.[41]

Let us pose a final alternative where there is a split in attitude on the war into two groups, one favoring and one opposing the action. Following the preceding logic in this case, one can see that a draft (e.g., a lottery with full compensation to those chosen) might generate more opposition to the war than a volunteer army. This could occur since under voluntarism those who intensely favored the war would enlist, presumably at relatively low wages. Unless the supply of hawks became exhausted the existence of groups having intense opposition would not influence the budgetary costs of a military buildup. For sake of comparison, if one drafted via a lottery and paid full compensation in this case, opposition (in the sense of the marginal costs of escalation in terms of additional manpower) would increase. Thus, in this instance one could argue that a draft might increase citizen opposition to war.

Another way in which the draft could cause greater opposition to a war would be if informed public opinion looked past budget costs to the total economic costs of the military. Then the higher economic costs of a draft system might increase political pressure for a smaller sized military.

Of course, we must emphasize again that the implicit model of narrow self-interest where opposition to war is a function of its tax cost to individual citizens is only applied in an illustrative way. Other arguments in taxpayers' utility functions such as the morality of the war or war in general may dominate the straight economic consequences of fighting or not fighting. Pacifists are a good example of this point. This discussion is not intended to answer the question about draft reform raised by citizen opposition but to better define the issue.

Economics and Social Questions

The intent of this section has been to gain insights into questions that involve sociopolitical decisions and as such are the concern of policy makers. To discuss these issues it was suggested that we widen the scope of our analysis of the draft to take account of political behavior and its relation to the military draft. This does not mean that we are abandoning economic explanations of individual behavior. The tools of economic analysis remain instructive in deciphering political behavior. Indeed, common sense suggests the extension of economic analysis in this regard since the consumer in the markets of traditional price theory also votes, protests, writes letters to his congressman, or abstains from participating in the political process on utility-maximizing grounds.[42]

Economic analysis cannot by itself offer answers concerning the desirability of incorporating social concerns into military manpower policy, but as has been illustrated it can be of substantial aid in clarifying numerous aspects of these questions and thus can be a major component in the making of "good" decisions concerning public policy.

Concluding Comments

In this essay we have sought to apply basic economic analysis to gain insights into the draft and the related social questions raised by military manpower policy. This exercise demonstrates a general approach that can be applied to other areas of public concern. Viewing the draft as a tax in kind and examining its equity aspects suggest that the incidence of other public programs be similarly viewed in order to determine who bears the real cost (and benefits) of these programs. The discussion of conscription and allocative efficiency might suggest studies of other areas where the prices of factor inputs are distorted and thereby affect resource allocation.

In concluding, it should be stressed that our purpose here was to analyze the draft objectively, and not to make a case for the volunteer army. The reader can weigh the relative merits of the alternatives and decide for himself which system he favors. If the reader senses our preference for voluntarism over conscription under most circumstances, it is perhaps a result of our training as economists. In view of the inequities and inefficiencies arising from conscription, we find little justification for its continuance.

Ryan C. Amacher, James C. Miller III, et al., *The Economics of the Military Draft* (Morristown, New Jersey: General Learning Corporation, 1973). Copyright © 1973 General Learning Corporation. Reprinted by permission of Silver Burdett Company.

RYAN C. AMACHER (1945–) is professor of economics at Clemson University. He is author of a number of publications, including the college texts *Principles of Microeconomics* and *Principles of Macroeconomics*.

JAMES C. MILLER III (1942–) received his graduate education at Georgia State and Texas A&M universities. He has served on the faculty of the University of Virginia, was assistant director of the Council on

Wage and Price Stability, and is co-director and resident scholar at the Center for the Study of Government Regulation of the American Enterprise Institute.

MARK V. PAULY (1941–) is professor of economics at Northwestern University and author of the forthcoming book *Doctors and Their Workshops*.

ROBERT D. TOLLISON (1942–) is executive director and professor of economics at the Center for the Study of Public Choice, Virginia Polytechnic Institute. Among his publications are two contributions to *Why the Draft? The Case for a Volunteer Army*, and "The Political Economics of the Military Draft," which appears in *Theory of Public Choice*, a volume he co-edited.

THOMAS D. WILLETT (1942–) was educated at William and Mary College and the University of Virginia. He is professor of economics at Claremont Graduate School and has served on the faculties of Cornell and Harvard universities. He is coeditor of *The Economic Approach to Public Policy* and contributes to a number of professional journals.

Notes

1. Women can volunteer for military service but are by law exempt from the draft. At present pay schedules the military service is a relatively attractive career for women. Queues of high quality women (as measured by the military) have developed and the services (particularly the Air Force and Navy) have recently taken steps to increase the use of these qualified women, thereby reducing the military demand for men.

2. During the recent presidential trip to China, newsmen reported the Chinese using this method to remove snow from the streets.

3. Another area which utilizes payment in kind is jury conscription. Many of the principles developed in examining the economic effects of the military draft can be applied to jury conscription [Martin 1972].

4. Our assumption that draft-age men should have control over the conduct of their lives is critical for many of our forthcoming arguments concerning the draft. At what age individuals "are no longer children" has recently resurfaced in the debate over lowering the voting age. It was argued that those who are called upon to fight are old enough to vote. Not wishing to waste needless space debating the merits of our assumption, we will merely state that we believe draft age individuals are sufficiently informed to make rational choices with regard to military service.

5. This assumes a zero net value of military training in later civilian employment.

6. If military life is preferred to civilian life, the individual would be

willing to give up money income to enter the military. The geometry of this case is left to the student.

7. In some cases the value of the in-kind transfer may exceed the cost to the government. This would be the case where government, because of economies of scale in purchasing, is able to supply items more cheaply than the soldier could buy them elsewhere. This is not too difficult a problem because, in almost all cases where the value of the in-kind transfer exceeds the cost to the government, the soldier is given the option of accepting the government issue or providing his own.

8. What of those whose actual civilian income is below that which they obtain in the armed forces? In particular, college students generally have very little income and might potentially be drafted into the armed forces. Do they pay a negative economic cost? The answer is no, because the draft tax is defined as the difference between what the individual could earn as a civilian and what he gets from the military. If a high school graduate could earn an income of, say, $10,000, but chooses to go to college instead, his choice of college over employment must indicate that going to college, even with positive tuition payments, is worth at least $10,000 of income to him. That is, he is willing to give up an opportunity to earn $10,000 of income in order to go to college. For college students, therefore, the economic cost of the draft is the difference not between what they do earn as civilians and their military earnings, but between what they could earn as civilians, plus the "excess" value of college life, and what they would get as draftees.

9. In some cases the military might expand the opportunities open to low-income groups through military training and postmilitary G.I. benefits. In instances where this applies we would expect proper information to induce such people to volunteer. Much of the discussion concerning the military being "good for the young man" is clouded by casual empiricism. Veterans argue that the military matured them and, as such, was a worthwhile experience. It is likely that this maturation process was coincidental to the military service, as witnessed by the fact that most young men mature in these same years even without the help of the military.

10. This increased salary would be paid out of general tax revenue and taxes would have to be raised to meet the increased payroll costs. The general tax increase that fell on servicemen would have to be deducted from the area $XYFC$. From an empirical view this deduction from $XYFC$ is probably not very large and is ignored here.

11. Professors Lee Hansen and Burton Weisbrod [1967] performed similar research on the implicit tax, estimating $1,799 for an induced recruit with 0–8 years of education, $1,340 for 9–11, $1,411 for 12, $1,627 for 13–15, and $2,675 for 16 (plus). These estimates are based on 1959 data and therefore considered out of date for purposes of comparison in Table 20.1. Professor R. E. Bierney [1969] has argued that a better

conceptual definition of the tax is derived by deflating the individual implicit tax estimate by the probability of being drafted. That is, once an induced recruit is serving, the tax is as Davis and Palomba and Hansen and Weisbrod have indicated.

12. Of course another consideration is the probability of not surviving military service.

13. Present value calculations, or discounting income streams, are calculations that are made to find the value of income (or costs) that are to be received (paid) at a future date. These calculations are necessary because the more distant in the future a good or service (income or goods), the lower the present price (value). A dollar of income today is significantly more valuable than a dollar earned next year and 50 to 75 times as valuable, depending on the opportunity cost of money (the interest rate), as a dollar earned 40 years from now. If, for example, you will receive a $10,000 inheritance in 10 years and the interest rate is 8 percent, the discounted value or present value of that $10,000 is $4,630.

That the implicit tax should be measured by the difference in the discounted future income stream was first pointed out by T. D. Willett [1968].

14. Using a similar technique but less aggregated data Duncan Bailey and Thomas Cargill [1969] estimated the present-value of the financial loss by comparing actual incomes of those who served in the military with incomes of their civilian cohorts. Their estimates are for high school and college graduates only.

15. Income tax comparisons in this and the following paragraph are taken from the 1969 *Federal Income Tax Rate Schedule II* ("Married Taxpayers Filing Joint Returns and Certain Widows and Widowers").

16. Unfortunately, no readily available means exist for making comparisons in terms of lifetime income loss. Since under this approach the implicit tax is considered to be spread out over the income cycle, equity comparisons would reveal somewhat less inconsistency with criteria for equitable taxation. However, it should be kept in mind that the lifetime income loss taxes listed in Table 20.1, column [3], are "taxes" incurred by induced recruits additional to those incurred by their civilian cohorts.

17. This discussion parallels the earlier work by Edward F. Renshaw [1960].

18. This is, of course, true only for a random lottery. It is quite probable that with selective deferments such as were available before the Vietnamese War, the average opportunity cost of induced volunteers and draftees (at the margin) was lower than the average opportunity cost of men in the entire pool. In such case, the welfare loss would be lower than that indicated above.

19. In a similar analysis, Thomas Borcherding [1971] has noted that a volunteer army may result in welfare losses or misallocations by virtue of

the military's being a monopsony purchaser of manpower. As shown on Figure 20.4, the military would face a marginal expense curve above the supply curve, noted by S'. On that basis, it would hire X_m manpower, where the value of the military is measured by $X_m F$, and the value in civilian employment is $X_m H$. In short, there is a welfare loss measured by triangle FGH. The implication is that unless the military is constrained to choosing manpower levels where demand and supply prices are equal, converting to a volunteer army may simply trade off one allocative inefficiency for another. Of course the relevant question is whether the loss measured by quadrangle $ABCE$ exceeds traingle HFG.

20. Roland McKean [1972] argues that he would not expect a volunteer army to lead to more efficiency in military manpower procurement policies because it will not give to officials the right to take home rewards for this efficiency.

21. These savings result from the fact that civilian substitution would lower the demand for military manpower and therefore reduce the increase in salary needed to achieve a volunteer force. The saving stems from the fact that military pay increases are generally across large categories of servicemen and therefore represent rents to many of them. Some of these rents are avoided by substituting civilians and women whenever possible.

22. This assumes that basic training has no positive spillover effects on civilian life. Arguments can be made pro and con; the available evidence on this point is inconclusive. See L. Sjaastad and R. Hansen in *Studies Prepared for the President's Commission on an All-Volunteer Armed Force* [1970].

23. The President's Commission made a very crude estimate of the escape costs and concluded that they were probably higher than those calculated as the implicit tax as usually computed [Sjaastad & Hansen in *Studies* 1970].

24. While a system of deferments may encourage premature marriages, children, and excessive schooling, the lottery may result, parodoxically, in excessive delays in family formation, schooling, and career development.

25. An analysis of the enlistment decision under draft uncertainty has been attempted by David F. Bradford [1968].

26. A lottery with disqualifications, deferments, and exemption might properly be classified as a subset of selective service, but is considered as a separate alternative to demonstrate its unique properties.

27. Congress has specifically exempted only a few classes of citizens from the draft: public health service officers, aliens not admitted for permanent residence, ministers and divinity students, certain public officials, and sole surviving sons. Deferments and exemptions were originally intended to be granted to advantage the public interest, health, and se-

curity, but in practice probably reflect the political pressure of certain groups. Organized professional groups try to secure deferments for their members and students in their field. College students are sons of the affluent, who participate more actively in politics than do other groups.

28. Paternity and student status deferments were held by 19.4 and 13.6 percent (respectively) of total registrants in ages of service liability during 1966 [U.S. House of Representatives 1966]. College student deferments fell to 8.5 percent of those registered in 1968. This was a result of the revocation of graduate student deferments [U.S. Department of the Army 1969].

29. These subsidies are often counterproductive, e.g., at a time when there was much concern over population growth, the government was subsidizing fatherhood. This type of subsidy affects marriage, family, and career plans. Studies conducted when deferments were given to married, childless males "suggest that a small, but significant percentage of young men in the most draft vulnerable groups accelerated their marriage plans presumably because of their draft status" [U.S. House of Representatives 1966]. General Hershey may have been Cupid's most productive ally.

30. An often-heard argument for deferment by occupational groups is that Congress and the Selective Service System should try to arrange deferments so as to minimize the GNP loss of conscription. A volunteer system of procurement would do this.

31. See for example Richard Flack [1966].

32. The argument that young men will be compelled to be better is best answered by our first assumption that draft-age men ought to have control over their own lives. The individuals who advocate military service for "character building" generally do so because it tends to produce attitudes they deem to be important. Dr. Spock and Senator Thurmond likely would disagree on the character-molding benefits of boot camp. Without supporting either contention it should be pointed out that voluntarism allows the individual to choose.

33. For an interesting discussion on the lack of randomness in the 1970 draft lottery see Stephen Feinberg [1971].

34. On efficiency grounds we might want to reward shrewdness.

35. Numbers could be drawn at random from Social Security files. One wonders if this would increase or decrease political support for such an expenditure. In any event the tax would probably be struck down by the country as inequitable. Renshaw [1960] notes an interesting trade-off between efficiency and equity implicit in our draft service obligation. On efficiency grounds, it would be better to have those so unlucky as to be drafted serve as long as 25 years. On equity grounds this seems excessive.

36. Preference for either tax scheme would depend on the risk characteristics of the individual in the society.

37. Such a stand-by draft was advocated by the President's Commission on an All-Volunteer Armed Force [*Studies* 1970].

38. Friedman is simply arguing that, because of the fact that there is at the current draft wage an opportunity cost differential between black opportunities in the civilian sector and those in the military sector, a higher percentage of blacks than whites who would be affected by the increased military wage are already in the military. In other words the elasticity of supply of whites exceeds the elasticity of supply of blacks in the relevant range (between the draft wage and volunteer wage).

39. See Desmond Wilson and Jessie Horack in *Studies Prepared for the President's Commission on an All-Volunteer Armed Force* [1970].

40. If average length of expected service affects loyalty to superiors an all-volunteer force might be more subservient to its commanders.

41. Counteracting this tendency is the fact that a draft increases the probability that an individual's son will be killed. This tends to increase opposition to war because of the draft.

42. In fact the manner in which military manpower is procured might affect demands for national defense [Wagner 1972, Tollison 1972].

Bibliography

Duncan Bailey and Thomas Cargill, "The Military Draft and Future Income." *Western Economic Journal*, December, 1969, 365–370.

R. E. Bierney, "The Incidence of the Draft—Is It Progressive?" *Western Economic Journal*, September, 1969, 244–247.

Thomas E. Borcherding, "A Neglected Social Cost of a Volunteer Army." *American Economic Review*, March, 1971, 195–196.

David F. Bradford, "A Model of the Enlistment Decision under Draft Uncertainty." *Quarterly Journal of Economics*, November, 1968, 621–638.

James M. Buchanan, *The Bases for Collective Action*. General Learning Press, 1971.

Ronnie J. Davis and Neil A. Palomba, "On the Shifting of the Military Draft as a Progressive Tax in Kind." *Western Economic Journal*, March, 1968, 150–153.

Stephen E. Feinberg, "Randomization and Social Affairs: The 1970 Draft Lottery." *Science*, January 22, 1971, 255–261.

Richard Flack, "The Draft in a Democratic Society." In Sol Tax, ed., *The Draft, A Handbook of Facts and Alternatives*, University of Chicago Press, 1966.

388 | RYAN C. AMACHER ET AL.

William F. Ford and Robert D. Tollison, "Notes on the Color of the Volunteer Army." *Social Science Quarterly*, December, 1969, 544–547.

Milton Friedman, "An All-Volunteer Army." *New York Times Magazine*, May 12, 1967.

Lee Hansen and Burton Weisbrod, "Economics of the Military Draft." *Quarterly Journal of Economics*, August, 1967, 345–421.

B. F. Kiker and J. Birkeli, "Human Capital Losses Resulting from U.S. Casualties of the War." *Journal of Political Economy*, September/October, 1972, 1023–1030.

Donald L. Martin, "The Economics of Jury Conscription." *Journal of Political Economy*, July/August, 1972, 680–702.

Roland N. McKean, "Property Rights within Government, and Devices to Increase Governmental Efficiency." *Southern Economic Journal*, October, 1972, 177–186.

James C. Miller III, ed., *Why the Draft? The Case for the Volunteer Army.* Penguin Books, 1968.

James C. Miller III and Robert D. Tollison, "The Implicit Tax on Reluctant Military Recruits." *Social Science Quarterly.* March, 1971, 924–931.

James C. Miller III, Robert D. Tollison, and Thomas D. Willett, "Marginal Criteria and Draft Deferment Policy." *Quarterly Review of Economics and Business*, Summer, 1968, 69–73.

National Advisory Commission on Selective Service, Report. U.S. Government Printing Office, 1967.

Walter Oi, "The Economic Cost of the Draft." *American Economic Review*, May, 1967, 39–62.

Mark V. Pauly and Thomas D. Willett, "Two Concepts of Equity and Their Implications for Public Policy." *Social Science Quarterly*, June, 1972, 8–19.

George E. Reedy, *Who Will Do Our Fighting for Us?* Meridian Books, 1969.

Edward F. Renshaw, "The Economics of Conscription." *Southern Economic Journal*, October, 1960, 111–117.

Paul A. Samuelson, "The Pure Theory of Public Expenditure." *Review of Economics and Statistics*, November, 1954, 387–389.

Studies Prepared for the President's Commission on an All-Volunteer Armed Force. U.S. Government Printing Office, 1970.

Lester C. Thurow, "The Optimum Lifetime Distribution of Consumption Expenditures." *American Economic Review*, June, 1969, 324–330.

Robert D. Tollison, "The Political Economy of the Military Draft." In

James M. Buchanan and Robert D. Tollison, ed., *Theory of Public Choice*. University of Michigan Press, 1972.

U.S. Department of the Army, *Supplement to the Health of the Army.* June, 1969.

U.S. Department of Commerce, Bureau of the Census, "Social and Economic Conditions of Negroes in the United States." *Current Population Reports, Series* P-23, No. 24. October, 1967.

U.S. House of Representatives, "Review of Administration and Operation of the Selective Service System." *Hearings before the Committee on Armed Services*, U.S. Government Printing Office, 1966.

Johann H. von Thunen, *Der isolierte Staat.* Vol. 2, Pt. 2. Translated by Bert F. Hoselitz. Comparative Education Center, University of Chicago, n.d.

Richard Wagner, "Conscription, Voluntary Service and Democratic Fiscal Choice." In James M. Buchanan and Robert D. Tollison, eds., *Theory of Public Choice*. University of Michigan Press, 1972.

Thomas D. Willett, "Another Cost of Conscription." *Western Economic Journal*, December, 1968, 425–462.

Part V

Universal National Service

21

The Spirit of National Service

by

Elihu Root

In September 1916, Elihu Root, who had held the positions of secretary of war, secretary of state, and U.S. senator, wrote Lieutenant-General S. B. M. Young, then president of the Association for National Service in Washington, D.C. In the letter, Root argues that universal national service for able-bodied male citizens is democratic and has precedent in the early history of the colonies; that developments in modern warfare have rendered the emergency volunteer system obsolete; and that the National Guard is inadequate for the task of national defense.

Clinton, N.Y., September 17, 1916.

My dear General:

I am obliged to you for sending me the papers relating to the Association for National Service. We certainly need the spirit of national service in our country. It is a mistake to suppose that a people can have good government, peace, order, and progress for any long period without any effort on their part. We in the United States need to have our patriotism awakened, to throw off our indifference, and to think more of our duties as well as of our rights.

Every one who is fit to be a citizen of a free country ought to be willing to serve the country when called upon, in accordance with his ability. The young men who are physically fit for military duty should hold themselves ready to fight for their country if need be, and if they are not ready when the need comes they will not long have any country, and they will not deserve to have any. The vast change in the way of carrying on war which has occurred within a very few years has created a situation in which it is perfectly plain that no country can be ready to defend her independence against foreign aggression except by universal military training and a resulting universal readiness for military service.

The old way of waiting until war came and then calling for volunteers has become obsolete, and is no longer effective. The National Guard system is not adequate and cannot be made adequate to meet the needs of national defense under any real assault upon our right. It is impossible to have an effective body of soldiers who serve two masters and are raised and organized to accomplish two different purposes. Universal training and readiness for service are not only demanded by plain common sense, but they are essentially democratic. They were required by law during the early years of our Republic, for every male citizen between the ages of eighteen and forty-five was required to be ready to fight for his country and was required to be trained and provided with arms in accordance with the simple needs of warfare in those days. It is only necessary now to apply the principles and requirements of the national law of May 8, 1792, adapted to present conditions.

You have my best wishes in your patriotic endeavors. With kind regards I am always faithfully yours,

ELIHU ROOT.

"The Spirit of National Service," by Elihu Root (letter, dated September 17, 1916, from Elihu Root to Lieutenant-General S.B.M. Young), from *The Military and Colonial Policy of the United States: Addresses and Reports*, edited by Robert Bacon and James Brown Scott (Cambridge, Massachusetts: Harvard University Press, 1916), pages 487–488. Reprinted by permission of the publisher.

ELIHU ROOT (1845–1937) was an active lawyer and statesman and winner of the Nobel Peace Prize in 1912 for his efforts on behalf of international peace. He was secretary of war under President McKinley and secretary of state under President Theodore Roosevelt and then served as U.S. senator from 1909 to 1915. He reorganized the Army, establishing the principle of rotation from staff to line, and created the Army War College in 1901.

22

A Moral Equivalent
for Universal Military Service

by

Randolph Bourne

Bourne's short article, which appeared just before World War I, is a classic appeal for some kind of universal national service. With utopian fervor, he calls for an "army of youth," which he pictures "swarming over the land, spreading the health knowledge, the knowledge of domestic science, of gardening, of tastefulness, that they have learned in school" and "organized in flying squadrons, so that [they] could travel widely and see and serve all kinds of men and communities." Bourne envisioned two years of compulsory state service for all young men and women between ages sixteen and twenty-one.

The current agitation for preparedness has set hosts of Americans to thinking out for the first time what a real national strength and readiness would mean. We suddenly realize that if we are to defeat that militaristic trend which we loathe we shall have to offer some kind of action more stirring and more creative. The call now upon every citizen is to be not nebulously patriotic, but clear and lucid as to America's aims, so that our national energy shall not be squandered and misused. There looms up as a crucial need that "moral equivalent for war" with which William James first roused our imaginations. It seems no longer so academic a proposal. Confronted with the crisis, we see that he analyzed the situation with consummate accuracy.

All around us we feel a very genuine craving for unity of sentiment, for service, for some new national lift and broadening which shall keep us out of the uneasy pettiness into which the American conscience has threatened to fall. In our hearts we know that to crystallize this desire into a meaningless sentiment, or into a piling-up of armaments or a proscribing of alien cultures, would not satisfy us. We want action, but we do not want military action. Even the wildest patriots know that America would have to go through the most pernicious and revolutionary changes to accept the universal military service which they advocate. We wish to advance from where we stand. We begin to suspect that military service, flag-reverence, patriotic swagger, are too much the weary old deep-dug channels into which national feeling always runs and is lost. The flooding river fills again its archaic and forsaken paths. Our present confusion expresses the dilemma we find ourselves in, when our instincts impel us into courses that our intelligence tells us we ought not to follow.

Our American danger is not so much that we become militarists as that we grope along, fretting and harrying each other into a unity which is delusive, and expressing our "Americanism" in activities that are not creative. The best will in America at the present time seems to crave some kind of national service but it veers off from military service. Until we satisfy that craving, we shall run at half-power, and suffer all the dissatisfaction and self-despising that comes from repressed energy. The question which all are asking, in the varied and disguised forms, is: How can we all together serve America by really enhancing her life?

To more and more of us the clue has come through James's conception of a productive army of youth, warring against nature and not against men, finding in drudgery and toil and danger the values that war and preparation for war had given. Ten years ago such an army seemed Utopian. We had neither the desire nor the technique. It seemed a project not to be realized without a reorganization of our life so radical as to make the army itself unnecessary. To-day, however, a host of new attitudes seem to give us the raw material out of which such a national service could be created. We hear much of universal military service as "education." The Plattsburgs* are sugar-coated as "civic training camps," "schools for citizenship." Universal service no longer stands on its old ground of mere preparation for war. It is frankly trying to get itself recognized as an indispensable mode of education. The next pertinent step is evidently to ask why, if universal service is valuable because it is educational, it should not be constructed on a strict educational foundation.

James's proposal sounded Utopian because it would require an entirely new and colossal national organization to put it into action. Universal military service in this country would certainly mean such a task. But if our national service is to be educational, we already have the organization in existence. The rapidly consolidating public school systems in the states provide the machinery for such an organization. As the public schools become better places for children to spend their time in, we are growing less tolerant of the forms of schooling outside of the public system. The tendency is towards the inclusion of all children in the public school. And the progressive states are requiring schooling up to the full age of sixteen years. We are rapidly creating a public school system, effectively administered by the states, which gives us the one universally national, compulsory service which we possess or are ever likely to consent to.

Education is the only form of "conscription" to which Americans have ever given consent. Compulsory military service would require decades of Napoleonic political evangelism to introduce. Compulsory education is universally accepted. For a national service which shall be educational you would have to convert nobody. The field is sown. No one denies the right of the state to conscript the child for education. But coupled with this assent is the insistence that the education shall be the freest, fullest and most stimulating that we know how to give. The current educational interest arises largely from the indignant demand that a state which takes all the children must meet the needs of every child. The very recent enthusiasm for "vocational education" means that we want a schooling that shall issue in capacity for fruitful occupation. A national educational service could give training for work at the same time that it gave opportunity for service.

It is only a national service of this kind that would really be universal. Military service is a sham universality. It omits the feminine half

---

*[Editor's note]: Training camps for civilians were called "Plattsburgs" because of the publicity they received at Plattsburg, New York, in 1915, when General Leonard Wood called for them to be used as part of the preparedness movement.

of the nation's youth. And of the masculine half it uses only the phys-ically best. France is the only country where the actual levy on men for military service has approximated the number liable. But worst of all, military service irons out all differences of talent and ability. It does not even tap the resources it enlists. It makes out of an infinitely varied group a mere machine of uniform, obeying units. The personal qualities, the individual powers of the youth it trains, are of no rele-vance whatever. Men are valuable exactly to the degree that they crush out these differences.

A national service for education would not be a sham. It would actually enlist the coöperation of every youth and girl. It would aim at stimulation, not obedience. It would call out capacity and not submerge it. It would organize varied tasks adapted to the capacities and strengths of its young citizenry. It would be universal, but it would be compulsory only in the sense that it called every one to the service. The tasks would not be enforced drudgery, but work that enlisted the will and toned up the aspirations.

Such a national service would be the logical outgrowth of our pub-lic school system. Suppose the state said: All children shall remain in school till the age of sixteen years. Between the ages of sixteen and twenty-one they shall spend two years in national service. This service shall be organized and administered by the state educational admin-istrations, but supervised and subsidized by the national government. The service would be performed as national service, but its work would be constructive and communal in its purposes and not military. Special military training could be given as a branch of this service to those who were best fitted for it. But defense would be but an incident in our constructive life, and not the sinew of our effort.

The tasks for such a national service would evidently be different from those contemplated by James. He thought of turning his army of youth into the drudgery of the world, where they might win in heroic toil and self-sacrifice the moral rewards which war had formerly given. But if our service is to be universal, it cannot be mere unskilled labor in mines and farms and forests. A large proportion of our youth would be disqualified. Furthermore, a service which made such frontal attack on industry would be bitterly resisted by those with whom its work com-peted. We are not prepared for a service which clashes too suddenly and harshly with the industrial system. What we need is a service which shall not so much do the old work of the world as create new demands and satisfy them. This national service could do the things which need to be done, but which are not now being done. It could have for its aim the improvement of the quality of our living. Our appalling slovenliness, the ignorance of great masses in city and country as to the elementary technique of daily life—this should be the enemy of the army of youth. I have a picture of a host of eager young missionaries swarming over the land, spreading the health knowledge, the knowledge of domestic science, of gardening, of tastefulness, that they have learned in school.

Such a service would provide apprentices for communal services in town and country, as many schools and colleges are already actually providing. Food inspection, factory inspection, organized relief, the care of dependents, playground service, nursing in hospitals—all this would be a field for such an educational service. On a larger scale, tree-planting, the care and repair of roads, work on conservation projects, the care of model farms, would be tasks for this army. As I was burning caterpillars' nests the other day in New Jersey and saw the trees sinister with grey webs, I thought of the destroying army of youth that should be invading the land clearing it of all insect pests. We might even come to the forcible rebuilding of the slovenly fences and outhouses which strew our landscape, and to an imposition of cleanness upon our American countryside. With an army of youth we could perform all those services of neatness and mercy and intelligence which our communities now know how to perform and mean to perform, but have not the weapons to wield.

The army could be organized in flying squadrons, so that its youth could travel widely and see and serve all kinds of men and communities. For its direction we would need that new type of teacher-engineer-community worker that our best school systems are already producing. Scientific schools, schools of philanthropy, are turning out men and women who could step into their places as non-commissioned officers for such an army. The service could be entirely flexible. Boys and girls could learn the rudiments of their trade or profession in actual service with the army. Book studies could be carried on, and college learning could come to its own as the intellectual fertilizer of a wholesome and stimulating life. Athletics and sports would be an integral part of the two years' service. There would be long periods of camping in the national parks or upon ocean beaches. The Boy Scouts and Camp-Fire Girls already give the clue to such an enterprise.

If objection is made that this national educational service would fail to bring out the sterner qualities of heroism and self-sacrifice, and would not be a genuine moral equivalent for war, the answer is that the best kind of a moral equivalent is a moral sublimation. We want to turn the energies of youth away from their squandering in mere defense or mere drudgery. Our need is to learn how to live rather than die; to be teachers and creators, not engines of destruction; to be inventors and pioneers, not mere defenders. Our cities and isolated farms alike are mute witnesses that Americans have never learned how to live. Suppose we had a national service which was making a determined assault for the enhancement of living. Would its standards and discipline be less rigorous? Rather would the ingenuity and imagination have to be of the finest.

Some such conception of national service is the only one which will give us that thrill of unity and vigor which we seek. An educational service built on the public school system puts the opportunity in our hands. The raw material in attitudes and desires is here. Every task that an army of youth might perform is already being done in some school or college or communal service. All we need to do is to coördinate and make universal what is now haphazard and isolated. An army of youth which focused school work would provide just that purpose that educators seek. The advocates of "preparedness" are willing to spend billions on a universal military service which is neither universal nor educational nor productive. Cannot we begin to organize a true national service which will let all serve creatively towards the toning up of American life?

"A Moral Equivalent for Universal Military Service," by Randolph S. Bourne, from *The New Republic,* Volume VII, Number 87 (July 1, 1916), pages 217–219.

RANDOLPH SILLIMAN BOURNE (1886–1918) was a forthright literary critic and essayist and a polemical spokesman for young radicals opposed to World War I. At his death he left a lengthy, unfinished manuscript, which presents a scathing indictment of the modern State and argues that, unfortunately, war is vital to the health of that institution.

23

The Logic of National Service

by

Morris Janowitz

Controversy over the Vietnam War led to a wide variety of suggestions for reforming the Selective Service System. Two major suggestions were the lottery and the all-volunteer force. Janowitz discusses the problems he perceives with these two methods of selection, and then presents his case for national service. After setting forth some of the demographic and organizational issues involved, he argues that national service is the most democratic alternative, as it avoids the undesirable consequences of both the lottery and the all-volunteer army.

In the spring of 1966, public discussion of the draft became widespread and intense for the first time since 1940 when the legislation was initially passed. One of the groups most critical of current policies is composed of college students who are opposed to war in Vietnam. By opposing the way in which the draft is managed they believe that they have found an acceptable and popular issue for agitating about Vietnam.

Public debate about the draft has now come to involve the widest segments of American society. Leading senators and congressmen, newspaper editors and columnists, educators and civic leaders have made it an important issue. The appointment of a Presidential Commission on the Draft means that it is no longer a question of whether the policies of the Selective Service System should be modified, but along what lines they will be altered.

Recommendations for change usually rest on an admixture of arguments based on moral justification, economic costs, and military efficiency, as well as on broad conceptions of national interest, both domestic and foreign. Three basic positions have emerged which contain some similar features but which express different conceptions of "who shall serve" in the armed forces of a political democracy.

First, there is the position that the armed forces should be a completely voluntary establishment based on a competitive pay scale, regardless of the costs. Immediate shortages in personnel should be made up by some form of lottery system. Selective service would be employed merely as a temporary device or to meet particular emergencies, and national policy should be to eliminate the Selective Service System as soon as possible.

Second, there is the position which seeks to reform the present Selective Service System. This approach assumes that the current system is inefficient as well as morally unjust because of the reliance placed on educational deferments. In this view, to rely exclusively on a "mercenary" army is politically risky and disruptive and it is probably not economically feasible. In the contemporary scene and in the foreseeable future, some form of selective service is required to produce manpower for the military establishment. To make use of educational deferments is to rely upon an unfair criterion which is biased against the lower classes, and immoral because it is a crude form of meritocracy which assumes that the intelligent should not serve their country. Moreover, it is disruptive of the operations of the university since it encourages many people to seek a refuge in higher education and introduces excessive amounts of uncertainty into making career decisions. This position seeks to reform current practice mainly by a lottery to augment the number of those who elect to serve on a volunteer basis.

Third is the viewpoint that leads to some form of national service. In this perspective, the question of selective service cannot be detached from broader problems of American education and American policy in international relations. Effective education as well as the pressures of social and political change underline the desirability of broad involvement of young people for a period of one or two years in various types of national service, both domestic and international. Selective service is required, but it must operate in a moral and political setting which makes it legitimate. National service is based on the widest degree of voluntary choice, but to insure military needs, selective service would rely on a lottery plus differential incentives. Those who do not serve in the military either as volunteers or as selectees would be expected (or, alternatively, required) to perform national service. The variety of forms of national service would be numerous and would involve many nongovernmental programs.

All three positions give a role to a lottery system, if only as a temporary or standby device. Civilians who urge this change must recognize that the idea of a lottery system strikes at a sensitive theme in the military self-image. The professional soldier often believes that he is perceived by civilians as one who has somehow failed in the occupational competition of the larger society. Many officers hold the view that a lottery for the selection of enlisted men would serve to strengthen and substantiate this stereotype of the military, that military service is a job for losers, as members of a luckless legion.

Moreover, the military services would still depend primarily on volunteers and professional soldiers, both as officers and as enlisted personnel. Frequently the military contend that it would be difficult to incorporate men selected by chance with those whose service is based on choice. They believe that the motivation of the soldier selected by a lottery might contaminate the attitudes of regular personnel and thus weaken efficiency.

There is a deeper moral issue for the professional officer. Military service always involves a chance of death in combat or even in training. However, the professional soldier views such a contingency as much more than an occupational risk. It is for him a supreme sacrifice for the welfare of the society. The professional officer feels that a lottery system might produce a moral definition which is highly undesirable. The man drafted on the basis of a lottery is a loser, a man who has lost in a game of chance. Having lost once, he runs the risk of losing again as a casualty in combat. It is wrong, in their opinion, to define potential casualties as losers in a chance situation. What will be the attitudes of society toward sacrifice resulting from being a two-time loser? Will it view the loss as simply another contingency and thus fail to support the men who fight?

The civilian may not fully understand this point of view, but there exists here a difference between military and civilian perspectives. The sense of professionalism among the military officers would lead them to accept such a lottery if it were made the law. But to the extent that they understand the limitations of the present system, and to the extent that modification would produce a more diversified source of skilled manpower, they would be more prepared to accept such a change.

The purpose of this paper is to set forth some of the demographic and organizational issues involved in a national service system, which I believe to be the most desirable format as a long-term objective, even though it clearly could not be launched overnight. In exploring the logic of a national service system, two elements are of crucial importance, although the arguments for and against any one of the basic three formats are complex and contain highly problematic elements. First, in my opinion, the national service system supplies a sound basis for coping with the deficiencies of any draft system, including one that must rely on a lottery. In other words, I do not object to arguing that some form of national service would make the lottery, if it had to be used, more acceptable to all involved. Second, and more crucial, the argument will be developed that a national service program supplies a powerful weapon for preventing the creation of a predominantly or even all-Negro enlisted force in the Army, an "internal foreign legion," which would be disastrous for American political democracy.

The Heritage of Selective Service

Demands for reorganizing the selective service are rooted, in part, in the strong public presumption that the system has worked with a definite social class bias. When selective service was reinstituted during the Korean conflict it was for a partial mobilization, in contrast to the more extensive mobilization of World War II. There was a military need for only part of the age cohorts from 19 through 26. There was also a belief in the necessity of continuing the flow of personnel into trained professional and scientific categories. In addition, selective service sought to remove itself from determining who should go on to higher education. As a result, occupational and educational criteria were used as the basis for deferment. In the public view, this had the result of placing the burden of military service on those who did not go to college, namely, on the lower socioeconomic groups, and has come to be viewed as unfair.

A set of demographic factors actually contributed to the validity of this perception. Steadily—since the Korean conflict until the period of the South Vietnam buildup—the size of the available manpower in age groups eligible for selective service has increased and the number to be drafted has decreased. The result was a greater and greater reliance on occupational and educational deferments. As a result, there is an important element of truth in the public's view of a selective service bias against the lower socioeconomic groups, but this view is so over-simplified as to be an inadequate and even dangerous basis for public discussion of selective service.

Unfortunately, social researchers have avoided serious and systematic analysis of selective service as a social and political institution. In fact, there is not a single major treatise on the subject. Nevertheless, as a result of the efforts of a handful of specialists, plus inferences that can be drawn from the operational statistics of government agencies and special government surveys, it is possible to piece together the social consequences of selective service. To this end, it is of prime importance to distinguish between the recruitment patterns of selective service and the allocation of manpower within the Armed Forces. For the period of the Korean hostilities, research has shown that the burdens of war, especially the incidence of casualties, fell disproportionately on lower socioeconomic groups. This was as much the result of the way manpower had to be utilized by the ground forces as it was of the social bias of selective service. At the officer level, casualties cannot be said to be distributed unequally as to social class. If anything, because of the emphasis on college graduation as a requirement for officers, there was a bias in the reverse direction. But among non-commissioned officers and enlisted men in the ground forces, where the bulk of casualties occurred, social scientists have documented the heavier incidence of casualties among lower socioeconomic groups. The division of labor in the military establishment meant that young men with better education (and higher socioeconomic position) were sent to advanced training and specialized units where the casualty rates were lower. Infantry units, those units which in the language of the military require "soft skills," were staffed with men of limited educational preparation. The result was that combat infantry units reflected a lower class and rural background.

After the Korean conflict, selective service, while it had definite biases, operated with a relative fairness, especially since there were no combat operations. The very few casualties occurred mainly in the Air Force among units engaged in routine aerial operations. These were officers of higher socioeconomic background and reflected the exposure to risks that a professional officer corps has to take.

The basic manpower requirements of the Armed Forces were met by two sources. Small quotas of young men were drafted and were assigned to the Army. The bulk of the requirements was met through volunteers who were responding in part to the pressure of the Selective Service System. This pressure generated not only contributions to the enlisted ranks but also men who joined the various short-term service officer programs. The Air Force and the Navy, because of their more attractive conditions of work and the specialized training they offered, could rely on volunteers exclusively. In fact, during the period after the end of the Korean conflict, standards of recruitment were being raised, thereby keeping out young men from low-income and Negro groups who would have served but who were ineligible because of educational requirements. The Marine Corps was also able to attract the personnel required because of its traditions and its image in American society. In addition, the Marine Corps had a two-year initial enlistment as opposed to the three-year term for the Army, which aided its recruitment. Since Vietnam, however, it has also drawn from Selective Service.

On the basis of available materials it is possible to describe the educational and social background of those who actually served in the Armed Forces during the period before the expansion of manpower for Vietnam. At this point we are interested in the incidence of all types of military service, whether a man volunteered or was drafted, whether he was an officer or an enlisted man, for all these types of military service are influenced by the operation of the Selective Service System. A good indicator is the military experience of men who were 27 to 34 in 1965; these men had already passed through the period of their eligibility for selective service. Of this group, those whose education ranged from having completed nine years of school to those who had completed college, roughly the same proportion (about 70 per cent) had had military service. At the lower end of the educational continuum the incidence of military service declines sharply; only one-third of those with less than grammar school education served in the military. At the upper end of the continuum, those who entered graduate and professional school, similarly only one-quarter entered active service.

The reasons are obviously different. Those with less than eight years of education were deferred on the basis of unfitness, a direct expression of their low educational achievement and related medical and psychiatric conditions. Graduate and professional study produced exemption on the basis of educational deferment, often supplemented by marital deferment. (This analysis does not include the limited number of agricultural deferments which tended to favor those with lower levels of education.)

Interestingly enough, we are dealing with the educational position of the son rather more than with that of the father. The relationship between father's education and son's military service is a much weaker relationship, although the same pattern holds true. In effect, the

United States has moved more and more toward an achievement society via education, and this has had the effect of decreasing a young man's chances of serving in the Armed Forces to the extent that he applies his energies to extending his education beyond four years of college.

But education in the United States is unequally distributed, and therefore in order to understand the social risks of the military service it is necessary to analyze these issues in terms of socioeconomic categories, particularly in terms of the interplay of social class and race. This interplay has meant that in the recent past the Negro has been underrepresented in the Armed Forces. This can be seen in two different ways. First, among men with less than 8th-grade education, Negroes have served to a lesser degree than whites. The same holds true among those with 9 to 11 grades of education—but among high school graduates, Negroes and whites have served in similar proportions. Second, among men of low socioeconomic background, the difference in military service between Negroes and whites has been marked, while the difference in military service between Negroes and whites with middle or medium socioeconomic background has declined.

Nevertheless, the integration of the Negro in the Armed Forces has been proceeding at a faster rate than in civilian society. This is the result of vigorous programs of desegregation and equal opportunity which have operated effectively despite the fact that until recently the criteria for selection based on education have served to depress the overall percentage of Negroes. Since 1962 the overall participation of Negroes has risen from 8.2 per cent to 9.0 per cent in 1965, and is most likely to continue to rise.

This rise needs to be related both to the procurement rate of new Negro personnel and more pointedly to the reenlistment rates of Negroes. During the period of 1962 to 1965, Negroes—both volunteers and inductees—were entering the Armed Forces at about their proportion in the civilian society or in slightly higher concentration for certain months. Given the attractiveness of a military career to low-income groups, this percentage still reflects the lack of educational preparation of Negroes. But the period 1962 to 1965 was one of an improvement in the quantity and quality of Negroes seeking admission to the Armed Forces. On the other hand, once there was an increase in Selective Service quotas because of Vietnam in the latter part of 1965, the procurement of Negroes by induction fell from 15.2 per cent during the month of July 1965 to 10.8 per cent in December 1965. A representative draft without college deferments would in the long run contribute to the elimination of any over-representation of Negro enlisted personnel.

However, more important in accounting for the representation of Negroes in the armed forces is the markedly higher reenlistment rate for Negro enlisted personnel. In 1965 the first-term reenlistments of white personnel was 17.1 per cent while for Negroes it was 45.1 per cent. Given their educational backgrounds and previous level of skills, Negroes have tended to concentrate in the combat arms of the Army where the opportunities are greatest for rapid advancement into non-commissioned officer positions. In some units such as the Airborne the percentage is near 40. Overall participation of Negroes in Vietnam was reported for the last part of 1965: the Army had the highest proportion of Negroes with 15.8 per cent, the Air Force 8.3 per cent, the Marines 8.9 per cent and the Navy 5.1 per cent.

The Armed Forces are aware of the dangers of creating units in which Negroes are concentrated. It is, of course, basic to their operations not to use racial quotas; on the contrary, they look with pride on the success of integrating the Negro into combat units, for success in combat units is the basis of military prestige. The armed services have a variety of personnel practices designed to distribute Negroes more equally throughout the services, but these are only slowly being implemented. Given the high rates of reenlistments among Negroes, it is not difficult to anticipate future trends.

Thus, in summary, it is clear that there have been distortions of the Selective Service System, mainly in the past, through the exclusion of low educational groups, especially Negroes, at one end of the scale, and through exclusion of persons following post-college education at the other. To some degree, exclusion at the lower levels will be modified as educational standards of the country rise and criteria for selection are altered. Efforts on the part of the Armed Forces to deal with this question by having special remedial battalions have not received congressional support, but special civilian or military programs are certain to emerge in the years ahead, not only because of the requirements of the military but because of broader social policy. Alternatively, distortions due to post-college education seem to be growing as the emphasis on such education increases. We must deal not only with the facts of distortion but with the growing public definition that education deferments per se are morally undesirable.

Assessment of the past performance of the Selective Service System must encompass more than the social characteristics of those who entered military service. The system operated in the past with a considerable degree of administrative effectiveness in meeting immediate and short-term requirements. In fact, its concern with month-to-month procurement in part prevented the development of a longer-range perspective and a capacity to meet changing requirements.

The organization represents an effective balance between highly centralized policy decision-making and decentralized implementation. Selective Service has worked with an amazing absence of personal corruption. The use of local community personnel has reduced hostility to rules and regulations. Moreover, there is a general feeling that local boards have been fair in applying national directives to the local situation. Decentralized operating procedure thus reduces local friction, but it produces considerable variation in practice from state to state. These differences have become a new source of criticism.

Selective Service and its local boards do not proceed on the basis of a national manpower pool which would take into consideration wide discrepancies in population characteristics among communities. Moreover, there have come to be wide variations in quotas on a month-to-month basis. Selective Service has emerged more and more as a procurement agency for the Department of Defense, without adequately representing the interests of the registrants or the larger society. While local boards are civilian, all other officials, from national headquarters to State Directors, tend to be military in rank and orientation.

However, the Selective Service System as it operated after the Korean War was adapted to the realities of the American political system and to American strategic commitments during a period of international tension without actual military operations. First and most basically, it was seen as temporary. The resistance to a permanent Selective Service System remained pervasive even after the end of World War II. Second, Selective Service operated with minimal disruption of civilian society even while it obtained manpower for the type of Armed Forces the executive branch wished to create. During the period of gradual expansion of the military establishment after 1960, Selective Service operated without great social strain or disruption. In good part this was due to the career opportunities the military establishment offered to the socially disadvantaged. Third, a temporary Selective Service System coupled with an extensive reserve component helped keep alive the citizen-soldier concept which has strong roots in the American scene. More tacitly than explicitly, the Selective Service System is seen—and in fact does operate—as a force for civilianizing the Armed Forces and overcoming the sharp segregation of the military from civilian society that characterized the Armed Forces before World War II.

The temporary nature of Selective Service operated to inhibit both long-range planning and public discussion of its operations since there was a pervasive feeling that at some future date it would no longer be needed. In fact, in 1964 President Johnson authorized a study to probe the possibility of its ultimate elimination. Instead, Vietnam has demonstrated the rigidities and inequalities of present procedure. During this period of actual military operations, the system operates ineffectively and produces considerable social and political strain. The standards of procurement have been judged too rigid and too arbitrary. Selection criteria have been lowered, but the Armed Forces have not developed the kinds of remedial programs which operated during World War II to utilize manpower which civilian society had not adequately prepared for adult responsibility and service in the military establishment. On the contrary, college deferments had to be altered to meet manpower requirements. Selective Service turned to the American Council on Education. In retrospect it is incredible that the Council did not engage in wider consultation with its constituency, but merely endorsed the repetition of a system that was used during the Korean hostilities. The changed political circumstances and heightened sensitivity to issues of social justice, as well as the arbitrary character of the system of deferments based on academic performance, have led to the current agitation. Secretary Robert McNamara's proposal for a system of national service has created the conditions for a careful scrutiny of immediate military requirements and, for the first time since the end of World War II, public discussion has been generated, oriented toward long-range requirements and national objectives.

The Organization of a National Service Program

To anticipate military manpower requirements for even a year or two in advance has been hazardous in the past. However, to describe the elements of a national service system, some assumptions must be made not only for the next two or three years but minimally for a ten- to twenty-year period. While the military manpower aspects of national service could be introduced very rapidly, other elements would have to be developed over a five-year period.

In Table 23.1, the actual number of new personnel procured by the Armed Forces in 1965 is shown to be over 570,000. This includes the small number in the special federal programs of the Coast Guard, U.S. Public Health Service, and the Merchant Marine Academy. For 1966—with the Vietnam buildup—this is certain to have gone well over 800,000. As a point of departure for planning a national service program, it is assumed that the required level of manpower will be equal to that before the current buildup. This implies a reduction of international tensions and in particular some degree of stabilization in Southeast Asia, without which even larger amounts of military manpower will be required. For the purposes of this analysis, 550,000 to 600,000 men, obtained through all the various procurement programs for officers and enlisted men, is projected as the need for the next ten years and then slowly decreasing during the tenth to the twentieth year.

Each year in the United States approximately 1,800,000 young men reach age 18, and this figure can be expected to increase slowly in the years ahead before it declines. To many manpower specialists this presents a real dilemma (see Table 23.2): We have too many young men to deal with only by a Selective Service System, yet military manpower requirements are too large to rely upon a voluntary system. Among other issues, a national service system is designed precisely to deal with this dilemma.

TABLE 23.1

NEW MILITARY MANPOWER ACTUALLY PROCURED IN 1965*

National military establishment		
Enlisted: First enlistments	318,209	
Inductions	102,555	
Reserves—active duty training	94,374	
Total		515,138
Officers: Commissioned	46,535	
Officer candidates		
Academy cadets (entering class)	2,449	
Aviation cadets and OCS	2,856	51,840
Total		566,978
Coast Guard		
Officers	385	
Enlisted: Regular terms	4,912	
Active duty training	3,038	
Total		8,335
U.S. Public Health Service		665
Merchant Marine Academy		200
Total new personnel		576,178

*Includes special federal programs (Coast Guard, U.S. Public Health Service, and Merchant Marine Academy).

National service is based upon a dual concept. Military manpower must be met by a fair and flexible selective service system, recognizing that there will be hardships and imperfections in any system. At the same time all young men should engage in some type of national service. The notion of national service applies to young women also, but for the purposes of this discussion it is given a second level of priority. For those young men who do not enter military service, either as volunteers or under a reformed system of selective service, national service would at the outset be voluntary. There must be a maximum amount of free choice in the type of national service and a heavy emphasis on the role of private and voluntary groups in developing opportunities to do national service. In short, our goal is to fuse together a reasonable selective service system with a broad concept of national service. The basic features and principles are strikingly simple.

First, each new group of 18-year-old men would be required to participate in a national registration at which each young man would make known his personal preference. He would have the opportunity to indicate his choice of three basic alternatives:

1. *Make known his intention to volunteer for military service* and indicate his interest in the various specialized procurement programs, including enlistment in a reserve program with active-duty training.

2. *Declare himself subject to selective service* and indicate what type of alternative volunteer national service he prefers in the event he is not selected by lottery for military service.

3. *Apply for exemption* on the basis of being a conscientious objector by virtue of religious conviction or other criteria set forth in the decisions of the U.S. Supreme Court. There would be no marital exemptions and while there would be some family and financial hardship exemptions, a federal allotment system would be used wherever required to eliminate gross inequalities. Deferment on the basis of critical skill (as defined by the Department of Labor) would be kept to a minimum, handled as under present arrangements, and administered by local Selective Service boards.

Second, entrance into the military service would take place during the next year when the young man is 19, or in an orderly fashion on a basis of completing a given school year. Those who wished to volunteer for the Armed Forces would be directly incorporated on the basis of their preference and qualifications. Volunteers, of course, must be matched against the available openings. Deficiencies in military manpower requirements beyond those generated by voluntary choice would be met by the Selective Service System operating on the basis of a lottery system. Normally, a young man would be subject to the selective service lottery only once during this period of initial registration, at age 18. Such an approach would eliminate the great uncertainty which exists in the present system. In the event of a major national emergency, cohorts between the ages of 19 and 26 would on a systematic basis be liable for subsequent exposure to the Selective Service procurement system. It would also be expected that young men who did not enter the Armed Forces would have completed their alternative volunteer national service by the time they reached 26 years of age.

Third, it is clearly recognized that there would be differential incentives and rewards. Those who served in the Armed Forces would receive a GI Bill of benefits while alternative national service would not have such features, or very limited ones in the case of the Peace Corps. Alternative service might very well be longer than military service. The Peace Corps, for example, requires 27 months as against 24 months of military service, reflecting an appropriate differential incentive and differential obligation. The type of alternative national service would depend on the skill and qualifications of the man involved as well as his preference. Where the person would perform his national service would be determined by his convenience and the time at which he is best prepared for doing so.

This system does not imply that the Armed Forces will become the manager of large numbers of young men. Rather, the administration of

TABLE 23.2

NUMBER OF MALES ATTAINING AGE 18
FOR SELECTED YEARS, JULY 1ST

1966	1,791,000
1967	1,787,000
1968	1,775,000
1969	1,823,000
1970	1,871,000
1971	1,938,000
1972	1,974,000
1973	2,028,000

SOURCE: *Current Population Reports*, Series P-25, No. 321, November 30, 1965, Table 4, p. 23.

selective service would rest in the present structure. Once military manpower needs are met, the Armed Forces have no involvement with the rest of the age group. For example, the Peace Corps would continue to operate as a volunteer organization; there would be no compulsion for any individual to enter, and young men could volunteer for it after they had been exposed to the lottery system. The same is true for all forms of alternative service described in detail below.

The national service concept emphasizes the maximum dependence on voluntary compliance along with the lottery which is designed to meet military manpower needs. But it is a system of voluntary service in the context of changing social and political definitions. It would be expected that when Congress modifies the Selective Service System it will express its intent and commitment to the idea that national service is a national goal. Expansion of the voluntary aspects would be based upon the creation of real and meaningful opportunities for fulfilling these goals which would require both public and private funds of noteworthy magnitude. This definition could become part of our educational system and its requirements. Thus, for example, Peace Corps volunteers are already given informal preference in selection for certain types of graduate school training programs. The basis of the national service concept could be that each young man be required by law to complete his service, but this seems to be unnecessary and would involve excessive compulsion. It may very well be that there are a limited number of types of national service activities which are either so burdensome, or so important to have done, that they could be specially designated as exempting an individual from the selective service lottery. This could be called substitute service and would include, as is presently the case, the U.S. Public Health Service, the Coast Guard, etc., as well as new programs such as a police cadet corps.

The Logistics of National Service

The sheer number of young men reaching 18 each year sets the scope of a national service program. The Selective Service System based upon a lottery could be instituted immediately, while it would seem to require at least three and perhaps five years to develop the full range of opportunities for alternative voluntary service. These programs would have to be phased in year by year.

The initial step in examining the logistics of national service is to recognize that the existing standards of eligibility for selective service—both medical and educational—are not relevant. In the past, of those young men who were subject to examination by Selective Service, 15 per cent were rejected on medical grounds. If one adds those rejected by reason of unacceptable educational standards and on administrative (moral and criminal) grounds, the percentage of rejection in specific years rose to over 45 per cent, the bulk of these falling in the educational category. Men who sought to volunteer for military service had, of course, a much lower rate of rejection. Thus, a more realistic rejection rate, on the basis of past military standards for the 18-year-old youth population, would be approximately 30 per cent ineligible. Thus under present arrangements the 1,800,000 young men of a given 18-year-old cohort would be allocated as follows: 600,000 enter military service; 600,000 rejected; and 600,000 surplus by various forms of exemptions and deferments.

But a basic objective of national service is to eliminate arbitrary educational standards, either through remedial efforts by the Armed Forces or by substitute service in a National Job Training Corps. Thereby, these young men would have a second chance to enter the mainstream of American life. Some greater flexibility in medical and psychiatric standards is clearly possible both for military service and for alternative forms of national service. However, it would be unrealistic to assume that all young men would be eligible by educational and medical and administrative standards to participate in some aspect of national service. There are those with severe medical problems, gross bodily deformities, incapacitating psychiatric maladjustments, mental retardation, or asocial personalities. There are, in addition, those young men who suffer from limited defects, especially medical ones, who would be better off not participating in any of the group experiences of national service. In all, we are dealing with approximately 15 per cent of the 18-year-old group, approximately 270,000 persons, leaving a total manpower pool of roughly 1,530,000. In Table 23.3, allocations of manpower to the various programs of a national service program are set forth on the basis of this figure. In addition to this reduction of eligibles for the volunteer programs, a goal of 80 per cent compliance within three years is set, although the figures presented are for the total group when it reaches age 19.

Armed Forces

If levels can be reduced to the size before the Vietnam buildup, the Armed Forces will require approximately 575,000 new men each year; 500,000 will be required for the normal intake of enlisted personnel, both volunteer and selected by a lottery system. Because of the impact of the operation of a lottery, the Air Force, Navy, and Marine Corps will be able as in the past to meet their military manpower requirements on the basis of volunteer three-year enlistments. The Army will have to rely on a mixture of volunteers and those procured by the lottery system.

In addition to meeting national security requirements, the manpower system of the armed services serves as a vast training system for basic technical skills as well as for a variety of more advanced occupa-

TABLE 23.3

MANPOWER ALLOCATIONS UNDER PROJECTED
NATIONAL SERVICE PROGRAM
(Distribution for 19-Year-Old Age Cohort)

Total age group (19 years old)		1,800,000
Not eligible for national service		
(15 per cent medical and administrative)		270,000
Eligible annual manpower		1,530,000
Projected annual allocations:		
National military establishment		
Enlisted personnel	500,000	
Officer personnel*	75,000	575,000
Military remedial programs		40,000
Special federal programs (substitute service)		
U.S. Public Health Service, Coast Guard,		
Merchant Marine		10,000
Police Cadet Corps (substitute service)		100,000
National Teacher Corps		150,000
National Health Corps		50,000
VISTA workers and similar public		
programs		70,000
Private domestic programs		30,000
Peace Corps		50,000
Private Peace Corps programs		20,000
National Job Training Corps		400,000
Conscientious objectors		10,000
Not allocated		25,000
		1,530,000

*Does not include the 90,000 enrolled in high school ROTC programs.

tions. In essence, the Armed Forces are the main source of vocational education in the United States and there is every reason to believe this will have to continue during the next decade.

The majority of those who serve a term as enlisted men, including volunteers, do not reenlist. In 1964, only 25 per cent of all Armed Forces regulars, for example, reenlisted. The Armed Forces, because of the realities of the marketplace, still tend to lag behind civilian pay, especially for trained technicians. Some improvement in reenlistment rates might be expected, more in the case of second and subsequent reenlistments than for first-term reenlistments, by improving work conditions, etc. But a high rate of personnel turnover at the enlisted level is to be expected. If the situation were otherwise, it might be dangerous, indicating that the Armed Forces did not have flexible policies and were being burdened with personnel who could not find comparable positions in civilian life. Moreover, it should be recognized that the men who do not reenlist bring into the civilian sector crucial skills required for economic growth and personal mobility. Their training proceeds with a high effectiveness because of the organizational environment. Perhaps an important area of change would be to reduce the first term of volunteer enlistment in the ground forces to two years so it would be comparable to the period of service for those drafted. Specialized training would come wherever possible after the first period of two years of service.

An additional 40,000 young men would be taken on a volunteer basis into the proposed specialized training and educational program designed to supply remedial education and health services. This would be only ten per cent of those eligible for such training and the remainder would be allocated to the National Job Training Corps.

To meet officer manpower needs, 75,000 men would have to enter the various procurement programs. This would include new entrants into the military academies and into the various college ROTC programs. This does not include the 90,000 cadets in the high school ROTC since the bulk of these would enter into service as volunteers and become non-commissioned officers or, in a minority of cases, participate in an officer training program.

Special Federal Programs

In the United States there are various national programs which provide substitutes for service in the Armed Forces. These include the Coast Guard, the Merchant Marine, and the Public Health Service.

Entrance into these programs has been and should continue to be considered a substitute for involvement in Selective Service. In all, approximately 10,000 men each year are involved.

Police Cadet Corps

One hundred thousand young men could do substitute service in some form of police work. Increasing the number and quality of police officers is a pressing issue in the United States and resembles the issues of procurement of military manpower. Police departments require a broader base from which to recruit personnel, and professionalization would be enhanced if there were an increase in the flow of personnel at the lower ranks. The opportunity for promotion of career police personnel would be increased with a category equivalent to short-term military service.

A number of arrangements could be worked out. Youngsters could be taken at the age of 16 or 17 to serve four or five years on cadet tours of duty. This kind of a program would emphasize recruitment into the police service at the end of the cadet's duty. An alternative approach would be to take men at age 21 to serve three years as police officers. In all cases, personnel would volunteer for police duty and have to meet the qualifications of the police departments involved. Such substitute service would exempt the person from Selective Service.

National Teachers Corps

One hundred fifty thousand teachers could be recruited annually for work in the inner city. Present policies and resources make it impossible for the inner city to have an adequate supply of teachers and teaching personnel. The whole trend in teaching is to make use of more personnel with general liberal arts background and special summer training. The teachers corps concept would also make use of semi-professionals with two years of college, and teacher aides with a high school background.

Service in the national teaching corps would be an alternative for national service and would not exempt an individual from being subject to the lottery system. In particular it is important to emphasize that the national teachers corps would be extremely valuable in supplying men for the inner city. Organized by the federal government along the lines of the Peace Corps, it would involve about 27 months of service. It is not far-fetched to look forward to the day when, formally or informally, entrance to the teaching profession would include some service in the national teaching corps.

National Health Corps

Similarly to the national teachers corps, 50,000 young men could be utilized in the health service field.

Peace Corps

The present Peace Corps could be expanded to include 50,000 young men each year. The organizational procedures are well worked out and involve 27 months of service. Because of the small number involved, Peace Corps service could be either substitute service that exempts individuals from the lottery, or merely alternative volunteer service which the individual would perform if he is not selected by the lottery system. In addition, opportunities could be created for 20,000 men annually in private equivalents of Peace Corps operations abroad.

Domestic VISTA Programs

Domestic equivalents of the Peace Corps under government sponsorship could employ 70,000. Private voluntary national service, under the auspices of church groups, voluntary associations, and the like, would involve another 30,000 young men in the United States.

Conscientious Objectors

Finally, there is the category of conscientious objectors. They, in effect, constitute a very small proportion of the population, even if present Supreme Court definitions are used which include both political and religious objectors. At a maximum, 10,000 men per year would be involved under the broadest definitions.

National Job Training Corps

Of special importance in a national service program is a National Job Training Corps along the lines of the Civilian Conservation Corps which would annually accommodate up to 400,000 young men. The United States is witnessing a crisis in the ability of its educational institutions to meet the needs of low-income groups. The entire thrust of federal aid to education has been thus far designed mainly for those entering college and those already prepared for various forms of specialized training.

We are faced by a problem of overwhelming magnitude. The public education system has been unresponsive to the needs of the most culturally depressed in the inner city. During the last three years we have witnessed an increase in social tension in the inner city to the point of outright explosion. It is unlikely that the schools can handle these problems. Initial halting steps have been taken by the Neighborhood Youth Corps and in some of the Job Training Centers. But the ideology of the professional educators and social welfare workers does not make possible the fundamental planning required to meet the needs of inner-city youths. We are particularly thinking of the years between dropping out or being forced out of school and of being available for employment. A National Job Training Corps under civilian jurisdiction with clear paramilitary elements would supply an opportunity for basic education and satisfactory achievement experience during this difficult period. In the past, the Armed Forces performed some of this job as a matter of routine. But this becomes more difficult as the Armed Forces become more automated and more technical. We are dealing with approximately 400,000 youths who have been failed by our society; at most 40,000 would have opportunities in the above-mentioned special remedial programs of the armed services. A total of 360,000 would be eligible for this type of service. Service in a National Job Training Corps would be a substitute for military service. After successful completion of National Job Training Corps experience, however, the young man would be in a position to volunteer for the armed services.

Long-Term Implications

For the next five- to ten-year period, the national service concept must be evaluated against a purely voluntary armed force based upon competitive economic compensation. From an economic point of view, an Armed Forces based on "competitive" salaries is not a real possibility because of the imperfections of the marketplace. The military would always be disadvantaged relative to the private sector which could raise its prices and salaries more rapidly. Each official inquiry into these topics produces higher and higher cost estimates.

The argument against a purely volunteer force is not merely economic: it is also political and professional. The Armed Forces reflect the social structure and the basis of their recruitment. Their effectiveness is linked to their social composition and ties to civilian society. In a communist society, professional standards and political control are maintained by a system of party control. It should not be overlooked that this system operates with a considerable degree of effectiveness, although it is incompatible with the standards of a democratic society. By contrast, the armed services in a political democracy cannot operate without a variety of social links to civilian society; executive and congressional control at the top level is not sufficient. The military must find its place in the larger society through a variety of contacts and points of interaction and control. A widely representative military personnel contributes to a willingness to accept the controls of the outer society. A long-term and highly professionalized force, especially at the enlisted man's level, is likely to be less representative and have weaker civilian ties. The inflow and outflow of civilian recruits is both a control device and a basis for positive morale and incentive in the military establishment.

But the case for national service is not to be based on a refutation of the volunteer force concept. The arguments for national service involve positive ideas of institution-building and facilitating social change, although they fundamentally must deal with the task of selecting men for the armed forces.

First, national service is an attempt of a democratic society to find an equitable approach to sharing the risks of military service without disrupting the management of our universities. The present system is unfair because of its reliance on educational deferments and inefficient because of the exclusion of those who do not meet contemporary standards. The present system is dangerous because of the disruptive impact on the administration of higher education. It has led students into postgraduate study as a way of avoiding military service. If the universities and colleges are to perform their educational functions, they can do this best if they are free from excessive involvement in the administration of selective service. On the other hand, the present system cannot be defended on the grounds that it maintains a supply of trained professionals. The supply of professionals depends on many basic factors such as graduate-study subsidies, available training opportunities, and the like. Moreover, to interrupt training either before college or between college and professional school would not radically alter the long-term supply of trained professionals.

Second, the present system cannot long endure regardless of the projected size of the military establishment. The United States is faced with the prospect of a segregated Negro enlisted men's ground force if the present trends are permitted to continue. In fact, the strongest argument against a volunteer force is that such a procedure would merely hasten this transformation.

A lottery system is an initial step toward the control of this form of disequilibrium. A national service system would be another important step, for it would both make the lottery system more meaningful and help bring the Negro into the mainstream of American life. To the extent that Negroes become integrated into the larger society and have the same medical and educational qualifications as their white counterparts, their concentration in particular sectors of the Armed Forces is likely to be reduced. Effective integration in the armed services requires in-service training and flexible personnel policies which would treat the armed services as a whole. Moreover, the armed services are abandoning an emphasis on merely retaining personnel in order to develop optimum policies of utilization which recognize the necessity and desirability of rotation and various forms of short-term service. These policies are likely to reduce the possibility of segregated units within the armed services. The case for a lottery and a system of national service can be made without reference to the position of the Negro in the Armed Forces, but this special problem only serves to emphasize the need for constructive reform.

Third, national service is an experiment in education. National service is more than an effort at rehabilitation and a second chance for those youngsters who come from the most deprived segments of our society. It is designed to deal with fundamental problems of personal maturation for all social levels. The present structure of American education is unable to supply those group experiences required for the socilization of successive generations. The search for personal development and individual identity in a social setting which has a narrow emphasis on individual classroom performance leads all too often to various forms of rebellion and withdrawal.

There is every reason to believe that the recent increased academic effectiveness of the American educational system, especially at the high school level, has been purchased at the price of complicating the process of personal development. In a democratic society it is particularly dangerous to make school and academic performance the exclusive route to social mobility. The results of this danger are already clearly manifested by the existing levels of hostility, negativism, and apathy toward "school." This is not to assert that the levels of hostility are higher than in the past; this is difficult to ascertain. Moreover, such a comparison is difficult to make since we are now keeping in school larger and larger segments of society whose education in the past was brief. Our problems derive from our higher aspirations and the necessity for more adequate levels of formal education.

National service should contribute positively toward innovation in education, broadly defined. Clearly, the military establishment has in the past performed educational functions, and continues to do so. It operates as the largest system of vocational education. It provides an avenue of social mobility for lower-class youth because it supplies social skills and a sense of self-respect to youngsters from the most deprived backgrounds. The Armed Forces, however, can have only a specific and delimited role in this process of social education. Professional requirements and organizational pressures in administering the military establishment preclude expansion. The United States is hardly an example of a nation which looks to its military to perform core tasks in education.

The Selective Service System and national service will nonetheless supply a system of national accounting of human resources. It will make clear how many young people are growing up without minimum health and education standards. In this sense national service will make a special contribution to the social welfare of the lowest income groups in our society.

But national service is designed to make contributions to the educational objectives of all social strata. It is designed to interrupt, at appropriate points, classroom experience so as to give the young man alternative educational experiences. These experiences are meant to develop intense and close group solidarity, based on collective rather than individualistic goals. They seem an essential aspect of personal maturing and are not supplied by classroom or academic education. In the complex and rapidly changing world, these experiences need to be intense and need to permit the expression of public service objectives.

It is particularly important to have these alternative life chances to overcome the boredom that comes from continuous exposure to classroom instruction. Young people particularly need exposure to a wide range of adults and teachers beyond subject-matter specialists. The broadening of the range of experience is crucial since at the university level there has been a rapid expansion of the faculty, a new large proportion of whom have achieved their teaching positions without any significant non-academic experience and who are therefore restricted in their capacity as effective teachers and role models.

Fourth, national service is an effort at "institutional building," to assist social change both at home and abroad. At home, it is an expression of the fact that traditional methods in education and social welfare need drastic adaptation. Abroad, it is part of the growing realization that United States foreign policy requires new approaches to produce economic, social, and political development.

National service is an innovation in the allocation of human resources, both of persons with motivation for labor-intensive jobs and of persons with highly trained skills. In dealing with the problem of the inner city and with selected aspects of overseas development, labor-intensive techniques have an important and crucial role to play. The terms volunteer, semi-professional, and para-professional are prestigious words to describe the fact that there are limits to the number and effectiveness of highly trained professionals. We are dealing not only with the results of the restrictive policies in the education and training of professionals, but with the inescapable fact that many operational tasks are better performed by persons who do not have trained-in capacities. One way of organizing these work situations is to have persons perform them for short periods of time but without having to confront the issues of a career in that particular vocation. Such experience is also vital preparation for more fully trained professional careers. The national service concept is designed particularly to meet this need, recognizing that there are limitations of the allocation of labor by economic incentives.

On the other hand, national service is a contribution to the reallocation of the most highly trained professional skills. In recent years the gap between the old nations and the new nations has not been closed rapidly. In fact, there has been a drastic drain-off of professionals from the new nations, especially doctors and scientists. The national service program is a device for making service abroad part of the education and responsibility of each generation of highly trained professionals. In the last analysis, national service is a form of enlightened self-interest on a worldwide scope.

"The Logic of National Service," by Morris Janowitz, from *The Draft: A Handbook of Facts and Alternatives*, edited by Sol Tax (Chicago: University of Chicago Press, 1967), pages 73–90. Copyright © 1967 The University of Chicago. Reprinted by permission of the publisher.

MORRIS JANOWITZ (1919–) received his doctorate in sociology from the University of Chicago, served as professor of sociology at the University of Michigan, and is now Distinguished Service Professor at the University of Chicago. He has been director of the Center for Social Organizational Studies, a member of the Social Sciences Advisory Board of the United States Arms Control and Disarmament Board, and chairman of the Interuniversity Seminar on Armed Forces and Society. He has written several books, including *The Professional Soldier* and *Social Conflict of the Welfare State.*

24

A National Service System
as a Solution to a
Variety of National Problems
by
Margaret Mead

*The debate on the draft during the late 1960s included some discussion
of the nonmilitary aspects of national service. In this article, Mead criti-
cizes the Selective Service System and the all-volunteer armed force,
arguing that a national service system would both provide needed military strength and solve a host of other national problems. She endorses
federally supported testing of youth that "would make it possible to assay the defects and potentialities of every young American on the
threshold of adulthood," maintaining that voluntarism is less congruent
with emergent national values than universal conscription.*

Problems of the Composition of the Armed Services

In considering the draft, it seems important to realize that the
armed services are not, as many critics believe, tied to types and levels
of warfare which should become progressively outdated. In the foreseeable future, every step toward the elimination of major warfare is
likely to be accompanied by an increase in violence on a smaller scale.

Types of conflict between small states, within states, and within local communities which were formerly suppressed as the direct or indirect consequence of the warmaking capacity of large nation-states proliferate under conditions within which massive nuclear weapons and major military confrontations are barred.

At the same time, such worldwide conditions as the population explosion, the spread of urbanization, the enormous increase in mobility and migration, and a climate of opinion which hails the humanity of members of all races and all classes inevitably result in a very large amount of social disorganization. Various forms of violence—border warfare, riots, massacres, massive destructions of life and property when urban concentrations and natural catastrophe are combined, communal conflict, civil wars overtly or covertly supported from outside the country, political coups, civil difficulties springing from unresolved ethnic loyalties, and renascent irredentism—will have to be controlled.

It seems clear that the United States will have to maintain large mobile forces, available for activities in different parts of the world—within international sanctions to the extent that international peace-keeping forces can be developed, nationally dispatched to troubled areas in the world where international peace-keeping forces cannot be used; and available for major domestic catastrophes and disorders. Such forces will have to be composed of young men who are physically and mentally fit, trained in combative activities, able to risk their lives and to kill if necessary.

A crucial question thus becomes whether such a force should be composed of volunteers for limited periods, of draftees, or of those who enter the armed services as a life career, or whether the three kinds of recruitment should be used in various proportions. A nationwide draft helps to underline a sense of national commitment and the urgency of total national involvement in the maintenance of an orderly world. A draft potentially touches every household in the nation, no matter how small the number who are actually drafted, and where it is conducted on any sort of lottery basis, it selects men of all types of temperament and character, and many kinds of social economic background and training. The substitution of volunteers for a limited period, even were it to provide a sufficient number of men, has the disadvantage of drawing on men with specific types of character and temperament. Armed services based on volunteers present a danger both to countries in which the population is as highly diversified as the United States, and to very homogeneous countries where the volunteer self-selection process is even more likely to select individuals to whom the particular ethos of the armed services, or of special branches of the services, is specially congenial. (Armed services in different countries have drawn historically on different kinds of character structure. In considering the Nazi period and the excesses of cruelty which occurred, the cruelty may be attributed to a selective process within which those who were willing to undertake careers of great responsibility were also those who were attracted to opportunities for excessive personal power, whereas in England, for example, responsibility was associated with requirements of impulse control and gentleness. The same kinds of differences can be found in the police forces of different countries; e.g., the contrast between those American police who were recruited from ethnic groups in which lawlessness had been a political virtue, and English police, who were selected for certain specific characteristics of strength and patience.)

However much they may differ from country to country, armed forces developed to defend against attack and control violence evolve a style that is antithetical to many of the values of ordinary democratic civilian society: discipline; uniform, unquestioning acceptance of orders; rank. Single items in the customary military repertoire may be removed or modified: excessive emphasis on polishing buttons may be diminished, over-insistence on rank at all times may be reduced, rank and routine requirements may be abrogated in front-line combat. But within our present cultural styles, the requirements for armed services are still differentiated from civilian life. And this holds for police forces also. The English policeman may carry nothing but a stick, but he wears a uniform and the force is hierarchically organized.

If the armed services—through some sort of nationwide draft—are continually faced with the task of absorbing recruits to whom the military way of life is basically uncongenial, or even repellent, there is a useful check on the development of a highly differentiated counter-civilian ethos. A professional army, with life-long career commitment, is even more cut off from civilian style, as those with inappropriate character can be cut off all through the recruitment and training and advancement process.

In summary, we will continue to need for the foreseeable future a sizable armed and disciplined force, however much it may become more acceptable to describe their activities as maintenance of order, peacekeeping, or post-disaster control, inside and outside the United States. Under these conditions, armed services which draw at least in part upon the entire male population of the United States, within specified age limits, and which rule out complete self-selection—such as that which obtains in a purely volunteer or professional army—are more congruent with our national values. Acceptance of this fact means acceptance of the greater cost in time and energy of training draft armed forces.

If a draft is to be continued, then the question of the relationship of those who are selected to their contemporaries becomes an urgent question. The draft may be phrased as a lottery in which those selected become losers. Alternatively, the draft may be embedded in a system of universal national services in which all of the other elements involved in the draft—except specific military requirements of greater risk and the moral requirement to use arms—are shared. These other elements, which now play such a conspicuous part in judgments made on the fairness of the Selective Service System, are many. Perhaps chief among them are: arbitrary interference with an individual career, and with educational and personal plans, minimal pay, curtailment of freedom of movement in favor of directed activity, and compulsory association with a cross-section of the national population involving the hazards of reevaluating one's place in the national society. If, through universal national service, every young male shared all of these perceived disadvantages of the draft, except the requirement of military service, would this substantially reduce the present perception of the unfairness of the system?

Let us ask first how universal national service would affect the draft, and those purposes which the draft is expected to fulfill, without discussing the merits of universal national service on any other grounds. This question can be explored independently of other questions about universal national service, such as the cost, whether it should involve everyone of a fixed age or within a fixed age period, the reasons for including women, and the relations of such a service to our changing educational needs and changing economy. A basic question then becomes the way in which the sense of fairness or inequity would be met, and whether, within such a universal service, some lottery system would still have to be used.

Many of the discussions of universal national service seem to ignore the functions of a draft army when it is a question of military service within universal national service. Then assumptions are made which would produce in effect a magnification of the present pressure for volunteering—which comes from the draft—to the end that all those who served in the various branches of the armed services would ultimately be self-selected. If this were done, one of the essential elements in the compulsory participation in a citizen army—the inclusion of those who dislike bearing arms but are not morally opposed to it—would be lost.

American Attitudes Toward Chance and Luck

The preservation of some element of chance, or lottery, among those from whom national service is required is the most immediately available method of assuring that the armed services would still be composed of draftees.

As a lottery would be a method of preserving the arbitrary character of the draft within universal national service, just as it is without universal national service, it is important to assay the way in which Americans view lotteries, prize winning, gambling and luck, and allegedly open competitions based on a mixture of luck and skill.[1] These are inextricably combined with notions of honesty and fairness, and with such ideas as having "pull," "the inside track," or "being born with a silver spoon in one's mouth." Americans handle the concept of luck itself in two ways: Those situations which give an individual an unfair advantage, such as ethnic origin, hereditary wealth, hereditary status or lack of status, are conceived of as either good luck or bad luck, but in either case essentially unfair, and inconsistent with the ideal of equal opportunity. On the other hand, when any individual outstrips his competitors to an extraordinary degree for which no unfair element in his past can be held accountable, or fails in spite of what looks like tremendous advantages, then the success or lack of success is again explained away by invoking luck. Luck can therefore be used both to excuse defeat and as a way of accepting one's own or another's success without challenging the ethic of equal opportunity. It is in these cases a way of affirming the reality of a system in which no one should win or lose unfairly in spite of apparently glaring exceptions.

Where a lottery is used, further considerations are involved. Because of our traditional ambivalence toward the ethics of gambling, many if not all forms of gambling have had to operate outside the law. Making an activity illegal almost inevitably produces corruption. The only form of gambling which could be completely regulated would be one in which no imponderables, such as the state of a race horse, the health of a jockey, or the fitness of a boxer, would be involved. The corruption involved in most gambling provides one of the principal attractions for gamblers who, far from being attracted by an impersonal fair system, combine their belief in its essential dishonesty with a hope that if they are lucky, they can beat the system.

So to the extent to which the American draft system is modeled on a gambling model, it will to that extent be invested with an expectation that it is intrinsically dishonest and that those who are involved will be working the system for their own benefit to evade the operation of the draft. (Veterans will be accused of working veterans' benefits in the same way.) The draft dodger who tries to beat the system and gets caught will be the scapegoat, and the man who is smart enough to beat the system will be envied and covertly admired. Those who are in line to be drafted, but are not drafted, will be subjected to certain kinds of hostility; their exemptions will not be credited to luck, even though the man who is drafted may try, along with his wife and parents, to assimilate this to his *bad* luck. The draft becomes personalized as a force which "catches up with you," or "gets you" if you aren't smart enough. When "Uncle Sam" is substituted for "the draft," the image of the federal government as a pursuing hostile figure out after young men becomes reinforced. When these attitudes are combined with the possibility of volunteering, instead of waiting to be caught because of a lack of skill, or with enough to escape, a man can volunteer and preserve the fiction of having made a free choice. Thus the draft does, in fact, increase the number of those who do volunteer by those who would never, without the pressure of the draft, have volunteered for military service. Such volunteers will have some of the characteristics which provide a useful challenge to the military ethos: an insistence on personal autonomy and an intolerance of submission to bureaucracy which is thought of as undue passivity or conformity. But the system of draft-induced volunteering also includes within it elements of resentment against those who are so sure they can escape military service altogether that they don't *have* to volunteer.

The less the lottery system contains elements which are seen as subject to manipulation, the less resentment there is. Ideally, therefore, what is needed is a draft system in which the lottery system works with impeccable impersonality. Obviously all exemptions for education, marriage, parenthood, hardship, or participation in an essential occupation are elements which reduce the impersonality and therefore the intrinsic impartiality of the system. Even exemption for gross physical defect, such as blindness, deafness or crippling, can be seen as an element which makes it possible to beat the system.

Congruently, the exemption of anyone who can be regarded as likely to win the sympathy of a draft board and the drafting of anyone who is underprivileged or likely to alienate the sympathies of a draft board is also suspect. Categories of types of individuals who may expect exemption or draft vary from year to year; current gossip may advise making certain kinds of political speeches or abstaining from them, or spraying on perfume, or shaving the armpits. But there continues to be the belief that a draft lottery is a form of gambling, and that because it has so many human and variable components, it can be "fixed."

The lottery model also fits in with the extent to which Selective Service activities appear to be capriciously extended or reduced from month to month. Last month a given man would have been exempted; this month he is called up. This, in turn, fits into an undesirable picture of the Armed Forces as irrational, likely to fit square pegs into round holes, denying the capabilities of recruits and setting everyone to the performance of inappropriate tasks. The lottery model as a model for the route into the service is very easily extended to the whole of the services.

There were certain elements in the Korean War call-up, such as the recall of reserves, which increased the sense of the armed services as wantonly capricious, and this sense was expressed in stories of busloads of passengers abandoned in the wilds (sic) when the long arm of the government had plucked the bus driver off the bus. This sense of the capriciousness and unpredictability of the whole selective service mechanism was then expressed by parents and teachers in advice to the young, who were told that it was now impossible to plan for a consistent career. They insisted that it was impossible for a young man to make a rational career design for study, marriage, and occupation because this would be interrupted. Although the armed services have made extensive attempts to show how military service can be related to life-career plans, such irrational attitudes as those aroused by the Korean War and perpetrated in the communication between adults and adolescents have prevented the recognition that Selective Service regulations actually made it easier to plan ahead than it had been in either World War I or World War II.

In summary it may be said that some form of lottery is necessary in order to have a draft component in the Armed Forces which directly, or at least indirectly by creating pressure for volunteering, will provide a citizen component essential for our kind of democratic society. The more impersonal the lottery, the fewer the exemptions and exceptions, in fact the fewer human decisions involved, the less there will be a feeling that decisions are fixed and arbitrary, and the greater the acceptance of the chance results will be.

The problem then becomes how large the draft component based on some form of lottery need be, and what form it should take, in order to provide the conditions for a citizen army, most but not all of whom will be volunteers, and a small number of whom will be professionals. And how is the question of a feeling that forms of drafting and exemption are unfair to be handled?

Universal national service would provide a setting within which the sense of unfairness could be enormously reduced. If every young adult were subjected to the same initial form of arbitrary involvement, the feeling that no particular young adults were luckier or more unlucky than the rest would decrease the feelings of envy or guilt which are presently being expressed both by those who feel a disproportionate burden and by those who feel—as many college students feel—that they are disproportionately privileged. Initially every individual, including the physically handicapped, the mentally defective, the emotionally disturbed, the totally illiterate, would be registered, and every one of these, according to their needs or potentialities, would be assigned to types of rehabilitation, education, and different kinds of services with different sorts of risks, benefits, and requirements. These categories, if seen in a national context, would be large. Within each category, including such categories as conscientious objectors, or those who desired to devote themselves to human welfare, or those who were determined to do something connected with aeronautics, there would again be choice, but at some point some element of chance could be preserved. A contrast can be drawn, for example, between the operation of chance in assignment to the Atlantic or Pacific theatres in World War II and the use of the point demobilization system at the end of World War II, where a rational evaluation of services performed and hardships experienced was used as a basis for priorities. If all those groupings *within* which chance finally played a role were *initially* composed of individuals from all parts of the country, all races, all ethnic groups, all class levels, then the operation of chance would seem less arbitrary. When it was finally necessary to choose those who were actually most fit for military service within such a group, choice could again operate. Failure to reach a standard of performance which admitted to officer training school, or qualified a registrant for training as a pilot, would be the end product of long periods of equably shared sacrifice and opportunity.

As it is vitally important to change the present attitude toward selective service as involving extreme inequities, the creation of a situation within which such a sense of inequity would be almost abolished seems important.

Universal National Service as a New Institution

We may now turn to the other arguments in favor of universal national service. Universal national service would make it possible to assay the defects and the potentialities of every young American on the threshold of adulthood. The tremendous disparity in schools and health conditions in different parts of the country and in different socio-economic groups which now results in the disqualification of such large numbers, both for military service and for participation in our society, could be corrected for the whole population. Currently, the bulk of the young people so handicapped are simply rejected and left to their own devices, or left to become the subject of inadequate and prohibitively expensive programs of reeducation or rehabilitation later.

Universal service would immediately do away with the present anomalous situation in which young people with a record are exempted. The juvenile delinquent is, in a majority of cases, a type of individual who most needs reeducation and rehabilitation. Where a professional army is compromised by a large number of members with court records, a universal national service could appropriately deploy young people into service specialties which would meet many of the unfulfilled desires which had led to their encounters with the law: a love of cars, speed, and risk.

Universal registration and evaluation would also serve to find the very extensive numbers of highly talented young people whose capacities are hidden by lack of education, medical care, or social experience, or by membership in deprived ethnic and racial groups. As our civilization becomes more and more technical, the demand for talent becomes ever more intense. Our present methods of talent search are terribly inadequate.

Universal national service would provide an opportunity for young adults to establish an identity and a sense of self-respect and responsibility as individuals before making career choices or establishing homes. At present a very large number go from dependency on their parents into careers that have been chosen for them, or use early marriage as a device to reach pseudo-adult status.

Universal national service would provide an opportunity for young adults to experience the satisfaction of services performed on behalf of the nation and of other fellow citizens—children, the sick, the aged, the deprived—which could serve as a paradigm for later social participation not immediately based on the standards of the marketplace. It should increase the capacity for dedication. Whatever methods are selected for distributing income in such a way as to separate productive ability from consumer need, universal national service could be set up as a suitable educational prelude. Universal national service, if set up in such a way that units were a cross section of the entire society, could compensate for the increasing fragmentation, ignorance, and lack of knowledge of their fellow citizens and the rest of the world which are characteristic of those reared in our economically segregated residential pattern, in which both the poor and the rich, the highly technologically gifted and those with obsolescent skills, the white collar and the blue collar, are each reared in almost total ignorance of the others.

Universal national service could be a preparation for later periods of reeducation and reevaluation which may become a necessary feature of a society faced with increasing longevity and rapid technological change.

Universal national service could be made into a tremendous system of incentives for pupils in elementary and secondary school. If it were widely known that every child would someday have to serve in a service unit, and that his skills and abilities would give him a chance at particular kinds of service, then the incentives, which now operate for the privileged group who know they must study in order to enter college, would be extended to the whole population. The present frequency of dropouts is due not only to poor backgrounds and poor teaching, but also to lack of incentive for those young people who have, at present, no vision of higher education. Higher education as an incentive to hard work on the part of privileged American students is not wholly an academic or economic incentive; it is primarily a promise that they will be able to participate for two years, or four, or six, in the kind of life that they want to live, associate with others with the same aspirations, and find the kinds of wives they want to marry. Universal national service could extend this kind of aspiration to young people who are not capable of or interested in higher education, but who are quite capable of dreaming of living in the city instead of the country, at the seaside instead of on the plains of Kansas, who want to work near airplanes instead of at mine pitheads, or in zoos, or forestry preserves, or in something connected with science or medicine. Just as the armed services have been able to make training for a chosen but often otherwise unobtainable vocation an incentive to the recruitment of young adults, the opportunities which would be opened for choice in universal national service could be widely disseminated to the young. The hopeless, unemployed young corner boys might never reach the corner if they knew that, no matter who they were, they would have a chance, at 18, at a wider world.

Universal national service would provide for an interval within our very prolonged educational system in which actual, responsible work experience would precede further educational and vocational choices. Our present changing society demands—instead of individuals who will learn one job and, driven by the fear of hunger, will stick to it all their lives—people who are flexible, able to learn new skills and perform new tasks, who will be motivated by a desire to participate in work situations rather than by a simple fear of starvation. Universal national service should prepare them for this kind of participation where parents and immediate elders, who have been reared in a world of scarcity and limitation of opportunity, are not able to give them the necessary training.

Universal national service would provide opportunities for service abroad in a variety of capacities, service in different parts of the country, service in different climes and conditions. It should broaden all young people in the way in which those who have taken full advantage of service overseas and of the Peace Corps have been broadened and prepared for responsible citizenship and wider understanding of national and world problems.

The Inclusion of Women

The inclusion of women on the same basis as men is absolutely essential for the accomplishment of the goals listed above. Universal national service for men only would be so handicapped that it might be wiser to retain the present system of selective service and the present numerically few minor activities like the Peace Corps and the Job Corps. It is necessary to include women because:

Women form half of the age group involved, and a failure to include them will promote a split in the experience of men and women at a time when it is essential that they should move in step with each other, economically and politically.

The position of women today has become so identified with ideas of non-discrimination, non-segregation, and equality of privilege that failure to include women will automatically touch off latent fears of other kinds of class, race, and ethnic discrimination. The association of women with disadvantaged minorities in recent legislation, and in the thinking of many developing nations, continually reinforces this attitude. Women are not, of course, actually a minority in the same sense as racially or ethnically disadvantaged groups, and there are cogent reasons for some discrimination between the sexes (which will be discussed below), but the national and world climate of opinion treats them as such.

One of the most important goals of universal national service is the identification and correction of physical and educational handicaps. These are as significant for women, as mothers of the next generation and as a large part of the labor force, as they are for men. If the women are left behind in isolated rural regions, in the slums or in ghettos, the broadening educational effects for men will be at least partially nullified because their wives will not be able to maintain the standards their husbands have learned to respect.

Universal national service will serve as a gigantic and effective talent search. Half of our intelligent and gifted citizenry are women. Because of the persistence of traditional ideas about women's aptitude, we are at present losing more highly gifted women than highly gifted men. Girls with mathematical ability are discouraged from going into the sciences or into any kind of technology; they are either shunted off into typewriting or, if they persist with academic interests, into the humanities. Furthermore, it has been found that women who reenter the work force later are more likely to follow up leads which they started in college than to enter entirely new fields. The chance to assay their ability during universal national service would provide a background for appropriate career choices when they wish to reenter the labor market and are seeking additional education.

Women form a very substantial element in opinion formation and in political decision-making, especially at the local level. During the last two decades, much of the contra-suggestibility to scientific careers for men has come from women who have been alienated from the type of preparatory literature—science fiction and technical magazines—on which future scientists have been nourished. Failure to include women in universal national service would result in an imbalance in the capacity for advancement and higher standard of living which universal national service should give its participants, in a widening of the educational gap between men and women, and in a sharpening of irrational opposition both to the military and to the application of technology and automation. The two-party type of democracy rests upon giving women enough education so that children experience two parents, who often disagree, but who are both well informed and trustworthy.

Ways in Which Universal National Service
Would Differ for Women

Throughout human history, with very few and brief exceptions, women have never been given weapons or asked to take part in overt aggressive activity. Although women were given tools when tools were invented—the stone or bone knife, the needle, the scraper, the digging stick—we have no record of women in very technologically primitive societies wielding weapons of war. Either some very deep biocultural objection to giving weapons to women operated in all early societies, or those societies which did permit women to use weapons did not survive. History cannot, of course, provide a complete guide to the future and the fact that women have only very occasionally been given offensive weapons is not a conclusive proof that this would be an undesirable course for a society to take. But whenever such a cultural choice is very widespread, it is worthwhile considering its significance. Recent work on aggression in the animal world has emphasized the amount of ritual combat between males of the same species, in which competitive and rivalrous behavior was kept within biologically structured bounds. The females of the same species, when they fight, fight in defense of their young and fight to the death. The controls which operate on male aggression seem to be lacking in females. Among human beings, where cultural controls replace biological controls, the ability to use violence in a disciplined way seems to be dependent upon early experiences and learning how to subject aggressive physical behavior to rules of fair play and appropriateness. (It is notable that the massive killings within the same society which have occurred since World War II have occurred in societies in which open aggression is deprecated: India and Indonesia, especially Bali, where children of both sexes are restrained from any show of aggression whatsoever.)

The historical and comparative material at least suggests that it may be highly undesirable to permit women, trained to inhibit aggressive behavior, to take part in offensive warfare. Defensive warfare, on the other hand, does not have the same disadvantages, as it invokes the biological basis of defense of the nest and the young.

On the other hand, there seems to be no objection to permitting women to assume risks, and it is possible that defense of the young may be a very appropriate biological underpinning for risk. Nor does there seem to be any objection to women playing significant roles within the military establishment, as technicians, physicians, teachers, etc., except probably in the training of those special units where the whole emphasis is upon the development of techniques of face-to-face combat.

The other problem involved in including women in universal national service is the need to protect women as future mothers from inappropriate types of physical strain, and to protect them during a service period from pregnancy. Protection from pregnancy involves either adequate chaperonage or adequate contraception. In the present climate of opinion it should be possible for a choice to be made by each girl: for a sheltered and protected environment within which she could carry out her national service, caring for children or the sick or the aged under appropriate chaperonage; or for contraception. In either case, pregnancy could be treated as a severe breach of contract, comparable to going AWOL in males. Part of the institution of universal national service would be the postponement of marriage until the service was completed, if universal national service takes the form of a nationwide call-up at 18, or the possibility of the entry into national service as a working couple if proposals for extending the service period into the late 20's were to be adopted. Universal national service would replace for girls, even more than for boys, marriage as the route away from the parental home, and provide a period of responsible and directed reappraisal before marriage and parenthood were assumed. The postponement of marriage until the age of 20 would cut down on the number of divorces due to immaturity, reduce the number of fatherless families, and contribute to the control of the population explosion. Choice between chaperonage and contraception should meet the demands of religious groups who are still able to protect their young girls from premarital sex experimentation.

The coeducational aspects of the universal national services could be varied to suit the different circumstances, allowing for groups of both boys and girls who wished for time to mature before being forced into the continuous company of the opposite sex.

Others have dealt with the question of what types of service could be performed by the number of young people who would be called up each year, so this paper will not go into this except to suggest that any attempt to make part of the civilian services local and voluntary, without the mediation of a national agency, would defeat many of the purposes discussed here. Furthermore, a major part of the educational impact of universal national service is experience away from own home, own town, own class, own ethnic group, and an opportunity to gain a sense of independent identity and citizenship amid the diversities of the modern world. Any program of self-selection or local control which permitted immediate choice of locale or type of service would segregate young people into the kinds of groups that resident and non-resident colleges, low-level and high-level high schools, privileged rich communities and ghettos, slums and deprived rural areas, segregate them today. This is true of such organizations as the Peace Corps and the Job Corps. In any consideration of types of service, a primary emphasis should be on types of group residence and initial training which would serve to eliminate all deficiencies of experience due to various types of segregation.

Universal national service, in addition to solving the problem of fairness for those who are asked to serve in the military, in contrast to those who are not, is above all a new institution for creating responsible citizens alert to the problems and responsibilities of nationhood in a rapidly changing world.

"A National Service System as a Solution to a Variety of National Problems," by Margaret Mead, from *The Draft: A Handbook of Facts and Alternatives*, edited by Sol Tax (Chicago: University of Chicago Press, 1967), pages 99–109. Copyright © 1967 The University of Chicago. Reprinted by permission of the publisher.

MARGARET MEAD (1901–1979) received her graduate education in anthropology from Columbia University and is well known for her many works on the cultural conditioning of sexual behavior, and on national character and cultural change in nonliterate Oceanic and contemporary complex societies. She became controversial for her popular lectures on contemporary social issues. Among her numerous writings are *Coming of Age in Samoa*, *Culture and Commitment*, and *Blackberry Winter*, an autobiography of her early years.

Note

1. M. Janowitz, in "The Logic of a National Service System" for this Conference [University of Chicago Conference on the Draft, 1966], has discussed the attitudes of the military and those concerned with problems of morale on the undesirability of treating the drafted group as double losers. This is a special instance of the wider problem of how those who participate in a lottery, as either winners or losers, are viewed in American culture. [*Editor's note:* For Janowitz's discussion, see Chapter 23.]

25

The Courage to Compel

by
*Terrence Cullinan**

Cullinan argues in favor of national service, which offers equivalent military and nonmilitary alternatives, on the grounds that it benefits both the individual and society. He claims that it would act as a social panacea, provide a sense of national spirit, widen the horizons of participants, and expand their capabilities. He concludes: "Is national service the future solution? If so, should the hesitancy in approaching it be reexamined? Should we not finally muster the courage to compel?"

The United States has reached a crisis point in its national life. True individuality cannot exist without order. It cannot develop without opportunity. It is of little value without an accompanying sense of personal satisfaction. A means of providing these conditions without limiting the individual potential would clearly be consistent with both democracy and particularity.

---

*[Editor's note]: In a personal communication (September 22, 1979) to this editor, Mr. Cullinan commented that though many of the specifics in this article have changed over time, the basic thrust of its argument remains relevant.

National Service

The concept of *National Service* is one which would provide this consistency and could simultaneously move toward dramatic correction of the shortcomings in contemporary American society. National service provides for equivalent military and non-military options for required service obligations. Were such a program currently operational in the United States, for example, qualifying non-military service could include such public organizations as VISTA, the Job Corps, and the Peace Corps; and such private programs as the Red Cross, International Voluntary Service, and those local civic action, community progress, and educational programs approved by Congress or some special organization established by Congress. Satisfactory completion of non-military service tours would be legally equivalent to the present two-year military obligation.

Basically, national service calls upon members of a national community to render service to that community for some period of time as a responsibility of membership in and a contribution to general community progress. It provides manpower to wrestle with major community problems, gives its participants a sense of purpose, brings members of the community together for common experiences and the benefits thereof, and creates a pride of accomplishment. Service is particularly effective if performed at a young age, when educative values are significant, physical capabilities at a peak, social (family) encumbrances at a minimum, and level of idealistic enthusiasms possibly greatest. National service specifically is not limited to traditional military service, although such service may be one of several forms it may take.

President Franklin Roosevelt was the first political figure to draw the parallel of non-military and military power. In his first inaugural in 1933, in time of great social crisis, he called on Congress for "broad Executive power to wage war against the emergency, as great as the powers that would be given me if we were in fact invaded by a foreign foe." At that time, military service was not subject to a compulsory draft. Nearly thirty years later, in 1960, it was. In that year, Hubert Humphrey, then a Senator, made the first national service proposal in which compulsion played a role. He was the first to suggest a "Peace Corps" of 30,000 to 50,000 national servicemen to serve three years in civilian development work as an alternative to two years' military service under the draft.

The past two years have witnessed new efforts in broadening the service concept. Secretary of Labor Willard Wirtz called for a program of service for all youth. Speaking in Montreal, Canada, on May 18, 1966, Secretary of Defense Robert McNamara outlined the commitment and dedication of the idealistic major segment of American youth, and then said:

> As matters stand, our present Selective Service System draws on only a minority of [these] young men. This is an inequity.
>
> It seems to me that we could move toward remedying that inequity by asking every young person in the United States to give two years of service to his country—whether in one of the military services, in the Peace Corps, or in some other volunteer developmental work at home or abroad.

President Johnson asked a special Advisory Commission on Selective Service to answer the specific question: "Can we—without harming national security—establish a practical system of non-military alternatives to the draft?" (The Commission's answer: hopefully, yes, once further study has been made of program implementation.) Johnson has not given up this goal. "I wish," he told a group of Peace Corps workers in August of last year, "there were as many of you as there are of soldiers, sailors, and marines. The more we have of you, the less we will need of them."

That these suggestions have support in the world beyond our shores is at least suggested by the past developments and present trends in other countries. Twenty-six countries now have compulsory national service programs of some type. Secretary General U Thant of the United Nations apparently approves the pattern. He looks forward to the time when " . . . [people everywhere] will consider that one or two years of work for the cause of development either in a far-away country or in a depressed area of his own community is a normal part of one's education."[1]

Potential Values to the United States

An American national service program would respond immediately to four national needs: absolute, psychological, sociological, and democratic.

Absolute needs may be easily quantified; the National Commission on Technology, Automation, and Economic Progress estimates that a total of 5.3 million new sub-professional jobs need to be filled in the public service area shown in Table 25.1. A 1965 analysis prepared for

the Office of Economic Opportunity and covering only selected manpower requirements cited more than 4 million unfilled jobs at the sub-
professional level [see Table 25.2]. The impact which manpower in
these positions would have on the educational system, ghetto problems,
minority group handicaps, and the other major social issues of the day
needs no elaboration.

Psychological needs are not completely quantifiable. Study after
study, however, has shown that youth in the United States need to feel
that they as individuals are making a positive contribution to the betterment of the world in which they live. In other countries, this contribution was an economic or a physical assist to the family unit. Today,
however, such contributions are not required of the affluent majority,
and the underprivileged minority lack the skills and education to participate economically. National service could be the means for effecting
psychological satisfactions for today's disenchanted youth, and thereby
removing a major sore from the national spirit.

Sociological shortcomings in the United States have been similarly
demonstrated through studies and ongoing Federal programs. All segments of American society need exposure to one another. This value of
broadening contacts was noted by President Kingman Brewster of
Yale, a member of the President's Advisory Commission on Selective
Service, when he spoke of the value of "an intimate awareness of the
extent to which values, expectations, standards of living and ways of

TABLE 25.1

ESTIMATES OF POTENTIAL MANPOWER NEEDS
THROUGH PUBLIC SERVICE EMPLOYMENT*

(Estimated from Various Unpublished Sources) Source of Employment	Job Potential in Millions
Medical institutions and health services	1.2
Educational institutions	1.1
National beautification	1.3
Welfare and home care	0.7
Public protection	0.35
Urban renewal and sanitation	0.65
Total	5.3%

*"Technology and American Economy," *Report of the National Commission on
Technology, Automation, and Economic Progress*, February, 1966, vol. 1, p. 36.

life can be totally different from what . . . [has been] . . . inherited and experienced."

Immediate practical benefits of such contacts are felt strongly by the underprivileged, who find through such exposure "new worlds" of which previously they were virtually unaware. The more privileged, for their part, receive an awakening to existing shortcomings. National service could provide the needed sociological "melting pot" by stressing work and problem-solving projects including representatives from diverse strata of society. The understanding and friendships gained in the course of such common effort would significantly lessen the level of inter-group tensions.

Democratic contributions of national service would be multiple. First, by broadening the definition of "service" beyond strictly military service, responsibility for national welfare would be distributed among a greater number of persons. At present, only about 33 per cent of those reaching age 26 serve (all in the military); this is a patent inequity. Second, by broadening the definition of "service" to include "making oneself capable of performing in mid-20th century society," educative and developmental opportunities could be extended to the underprivileged. Third, by exposing American youth to national needs

TABLE 25.2

SUMMARY OF MANPOWER NEEDS BY FIELD OF SERVICE*

Field of Service	Manpower Requirement
Health, including hospitals and mental health	1,355,000
Education	2,016,900
Day care	14,000
Recreation and beautification	136,000
Libraries	62,700
Public welfare	65,000
Probation and parole	16,000
Institutions, dependent and delinquent children	38,500
Public works	150,000
Police and fire	50,000
Prisons	24,000
Defense	350,000
Total	4,280,100

*Greenleigh Associates, Inc. *A Public Employment Program for the Unemployed Poor*, November, 1965, pp. 28–9.

and service capabilities, a widespread "social conscience" would inevitably carry over into servicemen's adult lives and have significant effects on national domestic attitude patterns.

Potential Values to the Individual

The concept of national service is totally harmonious with changing views of the educative process. Two such views are of particular interest, one concerning those experiencing long years of schooling, one concerning terminal "dropouts" from the scholastic system.

The "Interlude" Benefit

National service could provide an "interlude" period in the formal education cycle for individuals planning extended periods of schooling beyond that required by compulsory education laws. There is now strong evidence that such non-academic interludes are of considerable value to most people. Existing studies are well documented,[2] from the outstanding performance of World War II's GI Bill veterans through the postgraduate records of returned Peace Corps Volunteers.

Recent studies indicate that the interlude is becoming a purposefully selected part of the development of college-level students. Prior to the 1950's, 65–70 per cent of all college-level "dropouts" were for "required" reasons; of these, about 85 per cent were academic or disciplinary. Today, however, causal statistics for dropping out are now almost the reverse: 67 per cent of all dropouts are for nonrequired reasons. A 1956 study at Princeton[3] found that

> . . . the problems of poor motivation and immaturity are consistently noted as contributing to withdrawal. In most cases poor motivation was attributed to a general lack of interest ("just didn't want to study"), boredom, apathy, dislike for the curriculum, getting nothing out of college, a lack of goals, and a lack of certainty as to what to major in.

Similarly, the National Merit Scholarship Foundation found that uncertainty about what to study is the reason their talented students most frequently give for dropping out of college.

There is a steady increase in reports of positive effects of the interlude period on education when resumed. Trends in students' attitudes are thus consistent with the steady increase in the number of college deans and counselors who regard dropping out as a beneficial part of the overall educative pattern for many students.[4]

Reasons for and reactions to non-academic college interludes were most recently surveyed by TERRYBUKK, INCORPORATED. In the Fall of 1966, interviews were held with 300 Stanford University undergraduates who had dropped out of and returned to college. Those surveyed were randomly selected from males who had (1) started college immediately after high school, (2) dropped out of college at some time for at least 12 consecutive months, and (3) been back in college for at least 12 consecutive months at time of survey.

Each student was asked to describe his reason for dropping out and indicate his reaction to the non-academic period. Survey results are summarized below:

Reason for dropping out
To do something different	33.0%
To get military service out of the way	28.5
Consciously "to find self"	16.5
Enforced by college—academic or administrative	13.0
Enforced by noncollege necessity	9.0

Desire to drop out
Wanted to drop out	83.5
Did not care either way	5.0
Did not want to	11.5

Original plans for interlude period
Military service	35.5
Work	27.0
Travel for educational purposes or non-academic study	19.5
"Bum around"	11.5
Concern with family problems	6.5

Length of interlude duration
24 months or more	41.5
18–24 months	10.5
12–18 months	48.0

School attended prior to drop out
Stanford	77.0
Other schools	23.0

Respondents were last asked what impact the non-academic interlude had on their subsequent academic interest and purpose. Responses were:

Negative influence	1.0%
Neither negative nor positive influence	4.5
Improvement	30.5
Significant improvement	64.0

Most respondents (94.5 per cent) felt that the interlude had been beneficial to their education, even though 11.5 per cent had not wanted to drop out at all and another 5 per cent had been noncommittal. Only three respondents felt that the interlude had had a negative influence; these and six of those who felt that there had been no influence one way or the other had all dropped out to help in some family problem. The data suggest that an interlude period can be a profitable experience for students dropping out both voluntarily and involuntarily. Questions remain as to whether particular dropouts get maximum benefits, during the interim between leaving and returning to college, from the random types of experiences in which they now engage.

The "New Horizons" Benefit

More than 1 million high school and college students will leave the American educational system in 1968 before graduating. From these will come the major percentage of our "hard core" dropouts, the societal problem children. From these, too, will come most of our lost "soft core" dropouts, unmotivated and purposeless, who adopt new ways of life not from intellectual curiosity, but from boredom and nonfulfillment. The creative outlets national service could offer the latter are self-evident. The Job Corps and the Army's former "Pioneer" and ongoing "Project 100,000" programs, all of which had the purpose of rehabilitating undereducated high school dropouts, give evidence that national service could benefit this group educationally to a considerable extent, as well.

Twenty per cent of those leaving the Job Corps are presently accepted into the military; whereas 60 per cent of those same qualifiers had previously been rejected by the military on grounds of mental or physical inability. A report on 29 of the Army Pioneer test cases (accepted in spite of their being mentally unqualified by military standards) summarized:

> Nearly all had come from either broken homes or those in which argument and violence were common. Several of the young men had been affected by over-control, nagging, and excessive physical punishment. More had been affected by insufficient control. Almost all of them had found it necessary to go to work at an early age.

Four had prison records. Only three of the 29 had ever learned to play baseball or other common games. A defeatist attitude in competition characterized the entire group. As a group they were easily swayed.

After six months of training, 59 per cent of the group met minimum Army standards. For the remainder, six months had not sufficed to make up for the deficiencies of 18 years. Yet all 12 asked to be allowed to remain in the Army and receive further training; hope had been awakened if not fulfilled. National service could provide the same educative benefits for the under-educated and follow such training with service assignments to instill pride of participation and accomplishment in the serviceman.

A final group which would benefit from expansion of outlook are those terminating formal education upon graduation from high school. Dr. Dorothy Knoell of the American Association of Junior Colleges in Washington, D.C., has found that nearly all such graduates want an escape—most often temporary—from the environment in which they grow up. A physical change of scene is the primary goal, usually accompanied by the wish for a change of "atmosphere." Little hostility to the historical environment exists; the desire is simply for diversity of experience and an opportunity for independence. Dr. Knoell concludes:

> . . . in each group of seniors [there] are some who have the potential to achieve goals they dare not dream of, if they can be given a second and sometimes still another chance. The way needs to be kept open for them to move up the educational ladder after high school as they demonstrate new potential . . . so that each may become all he is capable of being. There is a gap of monstrous proportions in the . . . services offered most youth during the years when they make critical decisions about education and life work.

The Courage to Compel

Compulsion is a pejorative word. The United States was founded on a doctrine of freedom for the individual. Yet this very doctrine is a compulsive one: it demands that *each* individual *have* that freedom to develop which is the Constitutional basis for this nation. There can be no dispute that the promise of such freedom is today unfulfilled for a substantial American minority. The requirement now is to rectify that shortcoming.

Under a non-compulsory and therefore non-universal national service system, the goals of true democracy simply will not be attainable. Social frustrations will continue to mount and social integration of the deprived and disadvantaged will remain unaccomplished. The tremendous energies of youth will continue unsatisfied. The American dream will remain unrealized.

Compulsory education and the compulsory taxation which finances it are not universally desired. Yet the overwhelming majority of Americans believes literacy to be imperative for the good of both the nation and the individual. Compulsory national service, similarly, is an imperative if both the manpower needs for freedom in society and the developmental bases for freedom of the individual are to be provided.

American history has demonstrated that compulsion is the reverse side of the coin of societal freedoms. Absolute economic individualism—the completely free-enterprise system—proved inadequate early in that history. In spite of cries of absolute economic individualism, compulsory economic constraints of increasing sophistication have been steadily introduced in the majority interest. Today the cry is for absolute social individualism. Yet without compulsion, would *any* progress toward racial integration have taken place? We are *still* waiting for adequate non-compulsory manning of woefully understaffed schools, health facilities, poverty programs. Without compulsion, our major national social ills will keep on compounding. Without compulsion, our national promise will go unfulfilled.

From the viewpoint of individual freedoms, failure to make national service compulsory would deny its values to those needing them most. The most disadvantaged, smothered in ghettos or in rural isolation, would simply not respond to a voluntary system, even in the unlikely event that they learned of it: there is conclusive evidence that the social inertia of these deprived individuals can only be overcome by positive compulsory action. Conversely, the affluent and unconcerned—those for whom a final explosion of social tensions would be most dangerous—are unlikely to grasp the full significance of those tensions unless forced into confrontation with them. The entire problem of communication is involved here: only compulsory intercourse seems even marginally capable of creating the framework for dialogue which is today so desperately needed.

The best proof of the value of compulsion to the advantaged is the established Ethiopian compulsory programs. Since 1964, Ethiopian university students have been required to spend one year in rural service as a requirement for university graduation. Reaction by the initial participants is illuminating.[5] As participants started their year of service, reaction was decidedly negative: 60 per cent of the participants felt the service was an unfair imposition; 78 per cent strongly opposed its coercive aspects. Strongest resentment was felt at being made to participate in programs not directly related to specific vocational interests.

On conclusion of their service these same participants were surveyed again. At the end of these 12 months: 90 per cent felt the service was *not* an unfair imposition; 87 per cent said the program should be continued (only 1 per cent disagreed); 81 per cent stated that the service experience should be required of all Ethiopian students; 63 per cent believed the service would not be successful if made voluntary (only 25 per cent thought it would); and 72 per cent felt they had been of real service to their country through the program.

Of further interest, the initial resentment felt by the first service group has not been shared by subsequent groups, and an increasingly large percentage of the new groups are found to actually look forward to the opportunity to serve.

Of Courage and Compulsion

It is never easy to call for sacrifice and commitment on the part of a complacent society. With a majority both well-fed and unconcerned, it is simpler to ignore even deep rifts in that satisfaction. Even when the rifts explode temporarily, emergency palliatives seem capable of smoothing the surface.

Yet beneath the surface lie extreme dangers. We have witnessed major outbursts in 1966, 1967, and (already) 1968. Indications are that compulsory remedial programs do work both for the society sponsoring them and the participants therein. The courage to *compel* such enduring benefits has regrettably failed to materialize thus far in the United States.

The Philosophical Questions

Suggestions of compulsory national service in the United States immediately raise philosophical objections from some individuals. Several of the common objections are dealt with below.

Compulsory National Service Will Spawn a Hitler Youth. This is simply absurd. The United States of 1968 is not the bitter, defeated Germany of the 1930's. American national temperament is one of diversity, not conformity. Any compulsory program would contain so many options under so many sponsors that firm central control would be impossible. The United States Congress, one of the world's most independent bodies, would have full ultimate supervisory responsibility. No such question has ever been of issue in countries—such as France—which have had compulsory national service programs for years.

A Goverment-Sponsored Program Would Mean Regimentation and Lack of Individuality. As indicated previously, any compulsory national service program would include a vast array of alternative opportunities. Any individual could find some option consistent with his own particular interests and talents. Again, since sponsorship would be diverse, regimentation would not be a danger. Government participation in privately sponsored options would be limited to establishment of general guidelines and perhaps financial support.

Compulsory National Service Destroys Individual Capability for Life-Planning. National service tours would probably be approximately two years in length. Before and after such service, an individual would be free to do whatever he wished, wherever he wished. During his service tour, as previously cited, he would have the widest possible latitude to choose his own field of activity interest. A two-year pause hardly threatens an individual's lifetime plans.

Volunteers Are Far Superior to Compulsory Servicemen. The number of "volunteers" in United States national service-type programs today (Peace Corps, VISTA, etc.) has always been far too small to make any significant impact on the problems these organizations face. These volunteers are, in addition, an "elitist" group, requiring high educational and technical backgrounds. The majority of the nation's youth cannot qualify for these limited programs.

The superiority of "volunteer" service itself is questionable. Many previous Peace Corps Volunteers, for one example, unquestionably would not have "volunteered" had they not viewed the Corps as the unofficial but *de facto* alternative to military service it largely has been. There is no proof that because these volunteers joined under pressure, they did not perform well. There are good and bad volunteers of all kinds; there would also be good and bad compulsory servicemen.

Alternative Service Cannot Match Military Service for Danger. Only a very small percentage of the United States military faces hostile fire, even during time of war. In peacetime, of course, there is virtually no danger. At present, the national death rate for men of military age is 1.6 per thousand. Since the 1966 escalation, battle deaths per year per thousand men in uniform have ranged between 1.3 and 2.0 in Viet Nam. The comparison between injuries from civilian accidents and numbers wounded in military action is actually favorable to the military: 52 out of 1000 for civilian activity; 25 in World War I; 8 in World War II, and 6 in Korea and Viet Nam among military actions.

National Service in the United States Today

In the Public Sector

The past two years has witnessed constant public complaint over inequities in the Selective Service System and equally constant public confusion over just what to do about them. Attention, unfortunately, has been focused on Viet Nam and the traditional military draft.

The concept of National Service is broader than the average citizen can consciously consider in an atmosphere of military crisis. Yet in a largely ignored poll in June, 1966, Gallup specifically asked participants if they "favor requiring all young men to give two years of service—either in military forces or in *non*-military work here or abroad, such as the Peace Corps." A remarkable 72 per cent of those polled said yes, with only 21 per cent opposed.[6] And it is true that no matter how many soldiers Viet Nam required, the military will be able to absorb only a relatively small percentage of the available draft manpower. The social programs of the Great Society, meanwhile, languish due to lack of manpower or rapid depletion of funds by expensive private labor.

In the Private Sector

A privately sponsored pilot program for national service will be sponsored during 1968–1970 by the National Service Foundation of Palo Alto, California,[7] as a direct response to the Presidential Advisory Commission's request for such a program. The National Service Secretariat of Washington, D.C., an established clearing house for national service materials and information, is providing consultive services to the Foundation.

In Congress

Congressional support for national service has been mixed. Congressmen Fraser (Minn.), Ryan (N.Y.), and Kastenmeier (Wisc.) introduced Congressional resolutions[8] in 1966 calling for a Joint Senate-House Committee on National Service and the Draft. This Committee was to "make a complete study of the Selective Service System and of alternative forms of national service." All together some 35 Congressmen and 9 Senators made national proposals in that year (1966). On the other hand, several Congressmen rose to denounce the whole idea. Congressman Abernethy, giving special attention to the Peace Corps, said: "Two years in the all-expense paid adventurous Peace Corps, which is more like an economy vacation abroad than anything else I can think of, is hardly comparable to two years of roughing and toughing in Uncle Sam's Army."[9]

Bills similar to the Fraser-Ryan-Kastenmeier bill have been introduced each year, in 1968 by Senators Edward and Robert Kennedy.

In the Military

The military understandably opposes Universal *Military* Training (UMT) and other suggestions it considers either uneconomic or an outright impairment of its combat preparedness. However, it has always been surprisingly (to some) open to rather radical proposals for basic changes in service orientation. "The Army," according to an interim report on UMT as far back as 1947, "wants to send [a boy] back to his home trained to be a soldier *if necessary*, but *primarily* equipped to lead a better life and earn a better living in a *peacetime* democratic society" (italics supplied).

The Army has indicated that five months' military training makes a soldier basically duty proficient.[10] This would leave considerable latitude for adjusting both his post-proficiency service time and scope of service activities, if the military participated in alternative-service programs.

In the Future

With an end to Viet Nam perhaps in sight, it is time to turn seriously to the problems which face the nation and have repeatedly been cited above. National service—compulsory national service—deserves high priority consideration in the search for solutions. At minimum, alternative services should be certified immediately from among those obviously pertinent. This single step would permit some flexibility in manpower allocation and allow some independence of choice by those wishing to define national service as including, but more than, the military.

To quote again from Edward Hall:

> In 1940 National Service meant active military service. The military threat to national survival was our emergent and exclusive concern. In 1968 our concern is equally with national survival, but the vital interest of the commonwealth is no longer seen as principally military. Not yet fully grown up, the nation is a little more accustomed to our unsought role of world leadership, and a little more aware of what individual freedom means at home. We realize that at home an educated and enlightened few cannot thrive unless all of us develop to our fullest potentials. We realize that in the world we cannot achieve freedom and peace unless all nations progress toward those goals.
>
> This broadened outlook creates a correspondingly broader concept of National Service.

Is national service the future solution? If so, should the hesitancy in approaching it be reexamined? Should we not finally muster the courage to compel?

"The Courage to Compel," by Terrence Cullinan, from *The Forensic Quarterly*, Volume 42, Numbers 1–3 (May 1968), pages 211–224. [Originally published in *Compulsory Service Systems: A Critical Discussion and Debate Source Book* (Columbia, Missouri: Artcraft Press, Publishers, 1968), the contents of which were also published, under the title *Compulsory Service Systems*, as the May 1968 issue of *The Forensic Quarterly*.] Copyright © 1968 The Forensic Quarterly. Reprinted (with omission of one footnote) by permission of the author and *The Forensic Quarterly*.

TERRENCE CULLINAN (1940–) received his M.B.A. degree from Stanford University in 1964 and served in executive positions in a number of firms involved in resource allocation and recreational development. He directs research on manpower, land use, recreation, and tourism at SRI International in California, is the author of a number of draft-related articles, and has testified before the House Armed Services Committee.

Notes

1. In *A Profile of National Service*, edited by Donald J. Eberly, p. 54.

2. See, for example, Terrence Cullinan, "National Service and the American Educational System," in *The Draft*, University of Chicago, 1967.

3. See Lawrence A. Pervin, "A New Look at College Dropouts," *Princeton Quarterly*, Winter 1964–65.

4. Developed programs which include service experience in the educational process exist at Anderson College (Indiana), California State College at Los Angeles, Dartmouth College, Franconia College (New Hampshire), Harvard College, Idaho State University, Iowa Wesleyan College, Lewis and Clark College, Lincoln University, Marymount College (New York), Mercer County Community College (New Jersey), Northeastern Junior College (Colorado), Radcliffe College, University of Washington, Wilmington College (Ohio), and the State College at Old Westbury (New York). On another level, San Mateo (California) High School has begun an experimental part-time service curriculum for some of its students.

5. David C. and Frances F. Korten, "Ethiopia's Use of National University Students in a Year of Rural Service," *Comparative Education Review*, October 1966.

6. As Edward Hall of the Litchfield, Connecticut, *Enquirer* points out: "Contrary to widespread belief, service in the regular armed forces might be the first, rather than the last, to be overfilled. Despite the emphatic expression and wide reporting of anti-military sentiment, the glamour of the military tradition retains a powerful hold on a great many American males. In reply to a question (in the same poll) whether they would rather have a son in military or non-military National Service, 62.6 per cent of those expressing choice preferred the military option. Recognition and esteem is a powerful motive for all human beings, and the uniform represents a cachet that identifies the wearer with the heroic aspects of male egotism. Parachute boots are cumbersome and heavy, but anyone able to wear them legitimately or by intrigue rarely appears dressed otherwise. There may be a sophisticated unfashionableness to such elemental emotion in the current scene, but the elemental will always prove more durable than the fashionable."

7. Particulars from the National Service Foundation, 457 California Street, Palo Alto, California 94027.

8. H. Con. Res. 662, 663, and 664.

9. *Congressional Record*, May 19, 1966, p. 10563. Some people familiar with both the Peace Corps and peacetime Army overseas post life think the Congressman had his order reversed.

10. Letter to the author from Roy K. Davenport, Deputy Assistant Secretary of Defense, dated April 22, 1966.

Part VI

Foreign Conscription

26

Compulsory Military Service
in England

by

H. B. Simpson

This essay argues that the Common Law of England recognized that every able-bodied male was liable to render military service to the State when required to do so for its defense. Simpson refutes the widespread belief that conscription was not part of the English tradition, as he traces "ten centuries of unbroken custom, recognised and sanctioned in innumerable statutes." He clearly demonstrates that the notion that able-bodied men do not have an obligation to defend their nation with their lives is a relatively recent one in the history of mankind.

The dictum that the Common Law of England recognises on the part of every able-bodied adult male a liability to render military service, when required to do so in the defence of the realm, has caused much surprise among those to whom obligatory military service means nothing less than militarism of the purest Continental type. But if ten centuries of unbroken custom, recognised and sanctioned in innumerable statutes, are sufficient to constitute a law, the law in question can be proved. Its history may be divided into three periods: the first, when the liability existed, but we have little or no information how it operated or by what means it was enforced; the second, when it was enforced by statute and the machinery of government; the third, when it was not enforced at all.

Nothing in early English law is more familiar to the general reader than the *trinoda necessitas,* the threefold obligation on all freemen in Saxon times, which included the obligation to take arms in defence of the realm against invasion or for the maintenance of internal order. It was, we are told, by a general levy of the whole population that the early wars against the Danes were fought: in each county the *ealdorman* summoned the *fyrd,* and when the realm was so fortunate as to have a military genius for its king the war might have a successful issue. With an Alfred for king and savages like the early Danish raiders to contend against, there is no difficulty in understanding how the system worked. But in later days, when the English after their period of storm and stress settled into an unadventurous peace, from the death of Edmund Ironside and the accession of Canute onwards, it is not easy to understand how the *fyrd* was in fact collected. In Stubbs's *Select Charters* extracts are given from Domesday Book as illustrating the customs with regard to military service found in different parts of the country. "When the king went on an expedition" Oxford sent him twenty of her burgesses or paid 20*l.* in lieu. "Qui monitus ire in expeditionem non vadit, c. solidos regi dabit." In Berkshire, "si rex mittebat alicubi exercitum, de quinque hidis tantum unus miles ibat," and each hide paid 4*s.* for his pay and victualling for two months. "These monies were given not to the king but to the soldiers." It is impossible, however, to avoid the suspicion that such entries describe not so much the ancient militia law of the country, but either the particular customs of a particular town or district—the first beginnings perhaps of the regular military tenures—or what the Conqueror's Commissioners of Inquiry in 1086 wished to be considered the law. It is of some significance that in the earlier Anglo-Saxon laws that are still extant no similar references appear to occur. The references in Domesday are, on the one hand, too rare, and, on the other hand, too precise to form a satisfactory foundation for the national system which unquestionably existed before the Conquest, and leave us in complete doubt as to the means whereby that system was enforced.

We are told that Canute's *hus-carls,* his personal retainers, formed the nucleus of a standing army, which was imitated by his successor. But the host that followed Harold to victory at Stamford Bridge and to disaster at Senlac, what was the motive that gathered them together?

At a time when the ancient divisions of shire and hundred had lost much of their original meaning and the conception of England as a single realm was still a comparative novelty, when the tradition of fighting to obtain land to settle on and make a home in was dim and faded and, on the other hand, there had not been for generations the need to fight for very life against ruthless invasions from the North, it is difficult to understand how that primary obligation to render military service for the common good was enforced and what machinery of the law could be invented to keep it effectively alive. We know that in some way or other it did survive. Whether knight-service—that is to say, the tenure of land by military service—was a natural growth in England or, according to another theory, was introduced, as it were, at a blow by the Conqueror, it is certain that feudalism, once established, tended to obliterate the more ancient law of the *fyrd*. The Norman king would look for help in his wars to the great nobles whose landed possessions depended on a strict compliance with the conditions on which they had been granted, rather than to a shadowy law which existed before the Normans came to England, and which had failed to organise a successful resistance to their invasion. Throughout medieval times it is probable that the feudal system supplied an army more consistently and more effectively than the ancient law of the land, but apart from it the law still subsisted, coming into greater prominence as feudalism decayed and triumphantly surviving when feudal tenures were finally abolished.

Some random notes on the evolution of the law of compulsory military service and the establishment of the Militia of our own days may be of interest at this time when the question of national defence must inevitably be in the thoughts of everyone. That the County Militia was pre-eminently the oldest and most constitutional of the military forces of the Crown is so much of a commonplace that we are apt to think it untrue or at all events more of a rhetorical statement than a fact of history. But the continuity of English law from the earliest ages can scarcely be more strikingly illustrated than by reference to the history of the Militia, and it may even be of practical utility to realise that an obligation to render military service when required, as exemplified by the Militia ballot, is no mere creation of statute, no importation from abroad, however nearly it may approximate to the "conscription" of foreign countries, but one of the most deeply rooted of all English institutions.

In Florence of Worcester's Chronicle under the year 1094 we have a glimpse of what seems to be the survival of the ancient system under the Norman kings. He tells us how Rufus in the course of his wars in Normandy finds himself in need of reinforcements, how he summons 20,000 foot-soldiers from England, how they assemble at Hastings, each one having with him 10s. for his victualling. Then Ranulph Flambard, by the king's direction, takes their money, sends them home again, and transmits the funds so obtained to the king in Normandy. One may look on this as an example of the iniquity of an ill-advised king making money out of the patriotism of his subjects, or one may look at it as a sensible measure by which money was obtained to pay for a well-trained army of professional soldiers in place of such an ill-equipped and undisciplined host as thirty years before lost the day at Hastings; but, whichever view is fairer, the incident itself is a clear illustration of the traditional law of the land, and the assembly at Hastings was an exact prototype, even down to the detail of the "conduct-money" each man carried with him, of the levies which we shall find mustered five hundred years later for Elizabeth's foreign expeditions.

It is, however, in the Assize of Arms of 1181 that we have set down for the first time in statutory form a comprehensive scheme of universal military service. The first clause requires every holder of a knight's fee to be possessed of certain armour, and later clauses impose analogous obligations on men who cannot be supposed to be bound by any tenure of land: every freeman whose goods or income amount to 16 marks is to have a hauberk, helmet, shield, and lance; if he is worth 10 marks his arms are to be of a cheaper kind; all "burgenses et tota communa liberorum hominum" are to have helmet and lance and *wambais*—apparently some kind of mail coat that differed from both the *lorica* and the *aubergel*. These they were to keep by them for service when required, neither selling, pledging nor lending them, and to leave to their heirs or their heirs' guardians, and no more than these were they allowed to keep. They might not sell arms to anyone to take out of England, nor might they themselves take them out of England except by the king's command. Finally, elaborate provision is made for an inquiry by the king's Justices, through sworn jurors in every hundred and town, to ascertain how many men there were falling under each category.

It is significant that the Assize does not attempt to specify what is the amount of military service required from the lieges. This is taken for granted as part of the Common Law: all that the king is concerned with is to see that the lieges are properly equipped for discharging the obligations incumbent on them. We know that forty days' service in the year was generally reckoned as the amount required from each holder of a knight's fee, but we know also that constant disputes arose as to the occasions on which it might be required, and even the limit of forty days "seems to have existed rather in theory than in practice, and its theoretic existence can hardly be proved for England out of any authoritative document."[1] It is scarcely likely that the more general obligation to military service was ever more clearly defined. We should be disposed to assume that it did not extend to service beyond the seas if it were not that impressment for the Navy, which was based in a precisely similar manner on the immemorial Common Law, and to which we shall refer again later, involved necessarily obligatory service outside the realm. As it would seem that this obligatory service was always paid for, it is a fair conjecture that at every period of our history the law, though compulsion was always in the background, was so administered as to secure an amount of voluntary service sufficient to obviate any necessity actually arising for defining with precision the length to which compulsion might be carried.

The press-gang forms a prominent feature in literary pictures of the past: the hardship of being torn from home was no doubt keenly felt; numerous Acts of Parliament—which perhaps were not very strictly complied with—alleviated the hardship by granting exemption to special classes of the community, and the Courts of Law were constantly called on to decide whether the press had not been illegally applied; but it does not appear that occasion ever arose for determining how long a seaman impressed against his will might be compelled to serve. The same vagueness to this day attends jury-service. A juryman *may* in certain circumstances obtain a certificate which will exempt him from further service on juries for a time, but this is not of very general application, and it would almost seem that the law which requires or required us to render service to the State as soldiers, or sailors, or jurymen whenever the State has need of such service fixes no limit within which such services must be restricted. The subject was much discussed in the early part of the sixteenth century, when the powers of the Crown were undoubtedly strained beyond the limits of the law; but it cannot be said that the limits of the law were even then very precisely ascertained.

At least we may be sure that in the early part of the thirteenth century military service was not felt generally as a hardship. The sixty-three chapters of Magna Charta enumerate in great detail all kinds of evil practices by the Crown for which a remedy is demanded, from such great matters as the freedom of the Church, the right to a *judicium parium,* or the encroachments of the Forest Law, down to the repair of bridges (Cap. 23), the commandeering of horses and carts for transport purposes (Cap. 30), and the removal of unauthorised fish-weirs (Cap. 33), but never a word can we find with regard to compulsory military service! The Charter is one long catalogue of the matters in which the king had used his powers illegally or oppressively, but military service is not one of them.

In later times traces begin to appear in the statute-book of the obligation to serve in the king's army having been enforced with harshness, but in such a connexion as to show clearly that the obligation itself was beyond question. Thus 18 Edward III. stat. 2 cap. 7 provides that the pay of soldiers "chosen to go in the king's service out of England" shall fall on the king from the day they leave the county in which they were chosen to serve till the day of their return. 1 Edward III. stat. 2 cap. 5 declared that no man should be charged to arm himself or to go out of his shire otherwise *than had been customary in times past* for the defence of the realm. 25 Edward III. stat. 5 cap. 8 again appears to point to a certain confusion between military service arising out of the feudal tenures and the much older Common Law liability. Under it no man was to be constrained to find men-at-arms, hoblers, or archers, except by tenure or common assent and grant of Parliament. These and other similar references have much significance as showing that, vague and undefined as the common law liability to bear arms in defence of the realm may have been, the fact of its existence was beyond dispute.

Curiously enough, it was in Philip and Mary's reign that the law was most clearly defined. An Act of 1557 (4 & 5 P. & M. cap. 2) lays down with great minuteness the arms with which each citizen was required to furnish himself, and sect. 7 positively enacts that this obligation should not in any way lessen obligations arising from the tenure of lands. It is, in fact, a re-casting for the purpose of more modern requirements of the Assize of Arms of 1181, with a very important amendment. It was the Sheriff of each county on whom, as the local representative of the Crown, the responsibility of enforcing the law had hitherto devolved, but by the sixteenth century the dignity and authority of the Sheriff's office had greatly declined, and now the Act transferred this duty to specially selected Justices of the Peace empowered by Commissions under the Great Seal to ensure compliance with the Act in each county.

This is the statutory origin of the County Lieutenancy as it exists in our own time. It has been commonly said that Lords Lieutenant were first instituted by Henry the Eighth, and it has been inferred that the institution of the office was due to the centralising policy of the Tudor kings. But, like most other English institutions, it seems rather to have been a natural outgrowth of an earlier system. The Sheriff, whose undoubted duty it was to muster the levies in each county, was sinking in importance, and more particularly in military importance, throughout the Middle Ages. His jurisdiction was limited to his own shire. When the county levies were required for the suppression of internal disorder the Sheriff naturally took command; and as for this purpose alone military force might often be required, it is in vain that we attempt to draw a sharp line between the *posse comitatus* summoned to maintain good order and headed by the Sheriff in person and the county levies mustered by him for service in the king's army. When the king himself was in command, the Sheriff's duties would be ended when he delivered over the quota required from his county, but when the king himself ceased to take command, it became necessary to appoint some deputy or Lieutenant of the king. For a time, no doubt, the feudal levies marching under the banners of great barons, and held together by the bond of land tenure, supplied the place of the county Militia; but the Wars of the Roses broke the power of the barons, and during the Tudor period it was usual for the Crown to appoint by special commissions nobles of high standing to command the levies which the Sheriffs under the older law had summoned for military service. The Acts of the Privy Council during the Tudor reigns illustrate the process by which these Lieutenants of the king, at first appointed in special emergencies, became in time part of the permanent machinery of government. Thus, in 1542 letters were sent by the Council to the Sheriffs to have the county levies mustered and arrayed in anticipation of an incursion by the Scots, and the Duke of Norfolk was appointed the King's Lieutenant to command the army of the North. In 1547 Commissions of Array were issued to certain great nobles, both to collect and to arm troops. In 1551 commissions were issued for a similar purpose to persons of high standing in twenty-eight different counties. In some counties more than one Lieutenant were appointed, and on the other hand the same Lieutenant was sometimes appointed for more counties than one. A similar practice prevailed, in spite of the statute of 1557, up to the end of the century. The Principality of Wales was commonly treated as a separate unit, and again the Lord President of the Council of the North was regarded as the King's Lieutenant for all counties within his jurisdiction. Further commissions were issued for the summer of 1552, and again in 1553. It is noteworthy that the Lieutenants were at the first resorted to for other than merely military purposes. In 1552 a circular was issued to them with instructions to make search for counterfeiters of money, and in 1558 they were directed to appoint collectors of certain taxes. On the other hand, instructions were issued from time to time to Sheriffs and Justices with regard to the county levies, and in 1586 the Council expressed Her Majesty's pleasure that the Earl of Bath, who had been appointed Lieutenant, should, by reason of his youth, consult his Deputy-Lieutenants in the discharge of his duties.

We can perhaps best see how this machinery worked by reference to 1588, the year in which the peril of invasion was more insistent, or at least was thought to be more insistent, than it has ever been since then. Lords Lieutenant were well established by that time, and instructions were sent them on the 1st of April to call out the county levies, but the system was not complete; it was apparently only in the southern half of England that the Lords Lieutenant were held responsible. In the minutes of the Privy Council we hear little of the northern counties, except that the Earl of Huntingdon, who was Lieutenant of Leicestershire, was also "Lord President of the Northe Partes," and in that capacity was instructed on the 17th of June to see to the fortifications of Tynemouth and Newcastle, in case the Spaniards should attempt a landing there. He, rather than the local authorities, appears to have organised the measures for the defence of the realm.

Again, Norfolk appears to have been without its Lord Lieutenant, all instructions being sent to the Deputy-Lieutenants. Both in this country and Suffolk the inhabitants, finding the encampment on the sea coast "greatlye chargeable and burthensome unto them," the Council "thought meete the same should continue onelye for one month," one company relieving another at the end of that time. In those parts Sir Thomas Leighton was given a special commission to review the local levies and report to the Council thereon. The Sheriffs of Norfolk, Suffolk, and Essex were bidden to render him assistance. Sir John Norris was sent on a similar mission to Kent, Sussex, Hants, and Dorset.

Again, the Lord Chancellor being Lord Lieutenant of Middlesex, it appears that the County Justices took the levies in hand. They were first required to find 1500 soldiers, but pleaded that large numbers claimed exemption on the ground that they either were servants or officers of the Queen, or were citizens of London, or belonged to the Tower Hamlets, or had houses elsewhere, and consequently were charged elsewhere for military service. The number was accordingly reduced from 1500 to 1000.

Lastly, the Council appears to have communicated with the Earl of Pembroke, Lord President of Wales, rather than with the Lieutenants of the Welsh counties. Here, too, a special Commissioner (Sir Thomas Morgan) was sent down from London to organise the troops.

It soon became apparent that persons liable to military service were not furnished with the necessary arms and armour, and instructions were sent to the various County Lieutenants to take for the purpose all arms sequestered from recusants two years before, and to seize any more that might now be found in the possession of recusants. These were to be sold to the persons requiring them, and the price paid over to the owners.

A main army, called the Queen's Guard, was formed under the Lieutenancy of the Earl of Leicester, the Lord Steward. The retainers of any peer summoned to attend Her Majesty were to join this Guard instead of serving in the county levies, and from many of the counties the greater part of the musters raised were summoned to London and thence to Tilbury in August—the whole of the Hertfordshire levies (1500); 1500 out of the 1871 raised in Surrey; 1500 out of 1900 for Berks; 1150 out of 1164 for Oxfordshire; 2500 out of 4000 for Gloucestershire; 3000 out of 4239 for Suffolk; and so on. Arms were issued from the Tower of London to this army, and instructions were sent to the Lord Mayor that he should tell the City brewers to "carrye some quantitie of beere thither where they should finde readie moneye."

The Deputy-Lieutenants, however, stayed in their own counties, sending off the trained bands under the captains they had appointed, with the "coat and conduct money," for which each county was liable. There appears to have been some chicanery about the raising of this money. In Devon the Council are given to understand that far greater sums had been collected by precepts from the Justices than were ever used. In some parishes money was exacted, but "never a souldier trayned." Men had been pressed and discharged again on payment of monies, their places being taken by untrained recruits, some of the Justices being themselves under suspicion of complicity in such malpractices. It is clear that the picture drawn by Shakespeare in 2 *Henry IV.* iii. 2, of Falstaff's recruiting expedition into Gloucestershire may well have reproduced his own experience in the year of the Armada, and have exaggerated the facts to no great extent. Indeed, one cannot but suspect some knavery having been the occasion of a reference to the levies for this very county in the Privy Council's minute-book under the date of 18th of August. Thomas and Joseph Baynham, having been given by the Lord Lieutenant of Gloucestershire the charge of "trayning and conducting" 200 soldiers apiece, "wherein they had taken great care and diligence," complained that the charge had been afterwards assigned to others. The Lord Lieutenant was ordered to look into the matter. The "forwardness" of the Deputy Lieutenants of Somerset in collecting for the quota required from their county men "well-chosen and of willing minds" called forth a week before a special letter of thanks. In Hertfordshire, on the other hand, strict measures had to be taken with "divers gentlemen and others" who fraudulently changed the good and serviceable horses they had furnished at the musters for very bad ones.

On the whole, if we may judge the temper of the times from the proceedings of the Privy Council, the patriotism shown in our present day of stress need not fear comparison with the "spacious days" of Queen Elizabeth.

One more extract from the Acts for the Armada year may be quoted as illustrating how the novel Tudor militia system superseded the older county institutions. The Council were on the 27th of October informed that, though a Commission under the Great Seal had been issued to the Sheriff of Cambridgeshire to take unto him the *posse comitatus* for the enforcement of a decree in Chancery whereby one William Redman, Archdeacon of Canterbury, was to be put in possession of the manor of Great Shelford, yet the Sheriff, meeting with resistance "to the hurte of some of his companie," had after several attempts failed to carry out the law. Lord North, then Lieutenant of the county, was accordingly commanded to go to the Sheriff's assistance and arrest the offenders, sending them up to London or taking sureties in 200*l.* each for their appearance before the Council.

The proceedings of the Privy Council during 1589 illustrate our subject from a somewhat different standpoint. The military operations for this year were chiefly concerned with the retaliatory expedition to Portugal fitted out by Drake, Sir John Norris, and other "adventurers," of whom the Queen was one. Though this could not in any sense be called an operation for the defence of the realm, instructions were sent early in January to the County Lieutenants in the south of England to levy troops for the purpose, and measures were taken for the impressment of trumpeters, drummers, fifers, surgeons, and armourers to join the expedition. There seems to have been no general opposition to these measures, and it may be further noted that instructions were sent to the Lord Chief Justice, the Lord Treasurer, and the Lord Mayor and Sheriffs of London to prevent the arrest of any persons enlisted for the expedition, and to set free any who had been arrested (otherwise than in execution) since enlistment. The men from Hampshire, however, were ill-supplied with arms, and a letter had to be written to the Lords Lieutenant (of whom there were then two for the county), pointing out that 5*s.* for a coat and 3*s.* 4*d.* for a sword was "verie lyttle," and asking that further allowance should be made. In May letters were again sent out to the Lieutenants for mustering, arming, and arraying the county levies. It is not clear what was the occasion of this. It may have been done on account of bad news from Portugal, where Drake and Norris's forces were not prospering as well as the Council may have anticipated; but from a letter sent to one of the Lords Lieutenant of Hampshire on the 13th of May it would appear that the Council was by no means satisfied with either the quality or the quantity of the troops levied in this and the preceding year. His lordship was enjoined to take counsel with such of the County Justices as he should think meet how these defects might be remedied.

Soldiers were also required to garrison the "cautionary towns" of the Low Countries, such as Flushing, Ostend, and Bergen-op-Zoom, where the English were helping the Dutch in their struggle against Spain. Most of these appear to have been obtained by impressment, and the Lord Mayor of London was told on the 6th of May to collect some forty or fifty from the City, where were "divers masterless men to be found that lived idly, and might well be spared." It was probably one of these who was brought before the Council on the 4th of June by a pursuivant for having used "contemptuous woordes when he was to be presed as a drommer to goo towards Ostende." It does not appear what was eventually done with him. No other contumacy of the kind is recorded during the year. In all, some 500 were levied or "imprested" from London for Ostend alone, 404 of whom had to be supplied with arms from Government stores: 150 of them being said to be "verie bare apparelled" and "in naked sort," the Lord Mayor was enjoined to take order that they should be furnished with "necessarie rayment" at the cost of one mark apiece. On the 8th of June the Lord Mayor was told that in future all levies should be raised in the City through him, instead of by officers sent expressly by the Council. From various instructions issued, it is plain that the Council had reason to fear peculation in the matter of the soldiers' pay after their arrival at Ostend.

Lastly, we may mention that inquiry into the frauds of 1588 in connexion with the Devonshire musters was continued in 1589, with the result that the monies fraudulently obtained were apparently, after much trouble, refunded. Similar frauds were discovered in Wiltshire. Forty shillings seems to have been an ordinary price for a man to pay to a Justice or his servant for discharge after having been impressed.

It is probable that a thorough examination of the daily minutes of the Privy Council for three successive years, at a time when military service was being freely enforced in accordance with the Common Law, will give a fairer idea of the operation of the law than would be given by a selection of the more striking entries during an extended period. No excuse, therefore, is needed for quoting further references to the subject in the year 1590. In this year an expedition was fitted out for France under the command of Sir John Norris to help Henry the Fourth against the League. It was at first intended that the greater part of the troops should come from the garrisons of the "Cautionary Towns," but deference was paid to objections raised by the Dutch States, and instructions were sent in January to the County Lieutenants to have their quotas ready for service. Out of every hundred men, forty were to be armed with pikes and corslets, five to be halberdiers, twenty musketeers, and the rest "shot with callivers" (an arquebus lighter and shorter than a musket, which was fired without a rest). But to save the county expense in each case, the levies might be short by ten per cent., "though the Queen's Majestie is to make her paie to the full number without saving any penie therebie." It is not clear in what proportion the monies raised in the counties for "coat and conduct" were ordinarily supplemented by allowances from the Exchequer, but it would appear that some controversy had arisen with regard to the heavy cost of the levies constantly raised during Elizabeth's reign for military purposes. Later in the month further instructions were issued, with a special recommendation to summon such persons to the muster "as have served as soldiers aforetyme," but much was left to the discretion of the Lieutenants as they should find "most convenient both for the service and the ease of the contrie." Later in the year, when the levies were ordered to march to various ports to embark for foreign service, 4s. a head was allowed by Her Majesty "for everie coate," and for "conduct" either a halfpenny for each mile or 8d. for each day from the time they left their respective counties. The soldiers were also to be given their ordinary wages till they embarked, further allowances on board ship, and when they landed in France to "enter into the monethlie paie." Great care was to be taken to have an inventory of their arms and "apparrellinge," so that all might be restored on the army's return from foreign service.

It is clear from these and other similar entries that while service abroad in the Queen's armies was recognised as obligatory, the machinery for raising the necessary forces was not so well established but that disputes might arise with regard to it, and fresh instructions had constantly to be sent to the officers charged with the duty of enforcing the obligation. The difference in the operation of this law and that for impressment for the Navy, which appears to have had a precisely similar traditional origin, is very remarkable. The press-gang lingers in our memory mostly for the hardships it entailed and the efforts made to evade it: impressment for the County Militia carries with it no such associations. Whether it be that military service is more congenial to the Englishman than service on board ship, or that it was less onerous to him through being enforced by his neighbours and known officials instead of by strangers; or (which is perhaps the most probable reason) it was easier from the earliest times to escape it by providing a substitute, it has certainly left no such memories as the naval press-gang has. Further, while statutes for the purpose of enforcing military service are very numerous, naval impressment appears in our statute-book merely as a burden which Parliament has from time to time found it necessary to alleviate by granting exemption to certain classes of persons or by restricting the powers of the Crown with respect to it.

But however this may be, the reign of Elizabeth saw the last of obligatory military service in the strictest sense—that is to say, the sense in which service in the Navy was enforced up to the last century. The Act of 1557 was repealed in James the First's reign (1 Jac. I. cap. 25): an Act of Charles the First (16 Car. I. cap. 28) declared impressment by the Crown for the Army was illegal, though it authorised Justices of the Peace by order of Parliament to impress all men between 18 and 60 for the war. In the disputes between King and Parliament it would appear that Parliament repudiated not so much the ancient obligation to military service as the methods by which the Crown had enforced it. In the Petition of Right it is martial law as imposed by Royal Commissions that is mainly impugned. Nevertheless, it would not have been surprising if, in the welter of civil strife that followed these disputes, the ancient law of the realm had been finally and irrevocably submerged; and it is perhaps the strongest evidence of its tenacity that it reappeared in a comprehensive and carefully elaborated form in one of the earliest Acts of the Restoration Parliament. The law of 1557 was reestablished in a modified form. In each county there was to be a Lord Lieutenant, who should appoint Deputy Lieutenants to undertake the duty of mustering the county levies when occasion required, the soldiers to be provided by owners of property in proportion to their income. Some relics of the older system remained in that certain great Crown officers, the Lord Warden of the Cinque Ports, the Warden of the Stannaries, the Governor of the Isle of Wight, discharged this function within their several jurisdictions in the place of County Lieutenants, and to this day the City of London has a Commission of Lieutenancy but no Lord Lieutenant.

Then when the Seven Years' War put a severe strain on our military resources more stringent measures were necessary for reaping the full benefit of the County Militia, and the Militia ballot was introduced by an Act of 1757. Under this the liability of every able-bodied adult to military service might have been made a reality, but it would appear that in fact the ballot was not put in force till 1775, and from the first every man balloted was allowed to find a substitute. During the Napoleonic period various experiments were made for the purpose of obtaining a Reserve Army from the material supplied by the oldest of our constitutional forces, and Militia Acts have been very numerous. Mr. Fortescue, in his *County Lieutenancies and the Great War*, gives a full account of the system during 1802–14. He points out that in all the discussions on the subject it was taken for granted that no one balloted for the Militia would serve in person, and notes that in one year in the Middlesex Militia out of more than 45,000 men there was only one principal—i.e. only one who was not a substitute for an original ballot-tee! Whatever may be said of the suspension of the existing Militia Ballot Act, which has for long been an annual ceremony, it cannot be contended that under the existing Acts any approach to universal personal service could be made. The Militia Acts are a remarkable illustration of the law by which civic freedom involves a liability to military service whenever national interests demand it; but Mr. Fortescue has pointed out in a very convincing manner that their actual operation has been in the past by no means favourable to the national interests whenever those interests have made a large increase in the Regular Army necessary.

Any novel application of the law which we have traced from the eleventh century onwards would form a subject of discussion quite beyond the limits of the present article. Such application would obviously require the creation of administrative machinery not so far in existence.

The Acts relating to the Militia form an almost impenetrable tangle into which no one is likely to enter unnecessarily, but so far as the ballot is concerned the law at present, according to the officially authorised *Manual of Military Law*, appears to stand as follows: Those provisions of a Consolidation Act of 1802 (42 Geo. III. c. 90) which relate to the ballot are still in force, though they have been amended by some later Acts. No ballot for the Militia appears to have been held since 1810, except in the years 1830 and 1831. First in 1816 under a temporary Act, and then in 1817 under a permanent Act, the provisions for annual training were suspended year by year by Orders in Council. Next, from 1829 to 1865, annual Acts were passed suspending all proceedings for raising Militia by ballot, except when specially authorised by Order in Council, as happened in 1830 and 1831. The Act of 1865 (28 & 29 Vict. c. 46), though for one year only, has been continued in force since 1865 by Annual Expiring Laws Continuance Acts.

Lastly, in 1808 and 1812, independently of the legislation referred to above, special Acts were passed for raising by ballot in each county a force of men between 18 and 30, which was styled "Local Militia," and is said in the *Manual of Military Law* to represent the old general levy. Each man balloted must serve in person for four years and receives no bounty. No force has been raised under these Acts since 1815. From 1815 to 1832 Orders in Council were annually passed suspending the operation of the Acts, but the Act authorising the issue of these Orders was itself repealed as obsolete in 1873. The "Local Militia," as distinguished from the regular Militia with which we are more familiar, does not seem to have ever been of actual importance; but the provisions relating to it are of interest as showing at what a comparatively recent date the ancient law of military service was embodied by Parliament in a statutory form.

"Compulsory Military Service in England: A Retrospect," by H. B. Simpson, from *The Nineteenth Century and After*, Volume LXXVII, Number 458 (April 1915), pages 816–829.

HARRY BUTLER SIMPSON (1861–1940) was educated at Oxford University. He practiced law and was assistant secretary to the House Office from 1884 to 1925. He is the author of *Cross Lights* and of a number of magazine articles on British institutions.

Note

1. Pollock and Maitland's *History of English Law*, i. 233.

27

The Social and Political Aspects of Conscription: Europe's Experience

by

Herman Beukema

Colonel Beukema analyzes the historical roots of conscription in English tradition and European experience. Regarding it as a function of social and political institutions, he examines its three major types— democratic or universal conscription, despotic conscription corrupted by exemptions, and autocratic conscription—giving examples of each as they relate to modern practice. He concludes that, whereas autocratic conscription is unquestionably the most efficient for developing a powerful strike force, the high morale associated with democratic conscription compensates for its lesser efficiency on the front and also helps solve postwar problems at home.

As defined by Colonel F. N. Maude, English scholar and soldier, conscription is "the selection by lot or otherwise of a proportion of men of military age for compulsory service in the naval and military forces of their country." The definition appears to be both simple and all-inclusive. At first glance, one would anticipate no difficulty in the attempt to survey either the social conditions which have underlain the resort to conscription at various times in history or the social consequences to the nations which have adopted it. We discover our error when we note that compulsory service has been not only the tool of the despot but the freely accepted weapon of embattled democracy. On one occasion we find conscription universally applied to all men of fighting age, as in the *levée en masse;* on others we find the principle modified by exemptions—either selective, for the best interests of the state and the individual, or corrupted by purchase and influence to the detriment of both. With rare exceptions compulsory military service has been regarded as the role of the males, but those exceptions are now in the ascendant.

Here then are enough variants, all conforming in principle to Colonel Maude's definition, to make it clear that any investigation of the social aspects of conscription must be a study in contrasts. Moreover the casual investigator may easily repeat the double error into which some past surveys have fallen: first, in attributing to conscription rather than to war the social effects, good or evil, which have ensued; secondly, in failing to compare the effects which stem directly from conscription and those resulting from the partial or complete reliance on voluntary enlistment or some other method of induction. Incorporation of any such errors in analysis may well invalidate the conclusions reached.

The present study of conscription is necessarily confined to an examination of the more important variations cited above, beginning with its employment as a democratic weapon. Consideration is then given to the degeneration of democratic conscription into the better-known despotic type. Lastly, brief comment is made on instances of the draft where, throughout its course, it was a function of autocratic rule.

Ancient history furnishes two striking examples of democratic conscription: one in Athens and one under the early Roman Republic. The Athenian hoplites and sailors of Marathon and Salamis were true citizen levies of a democratic people. They received no pay; they furnished their own arms and equipment. Citizenship meant for them not merely privileges but duties and obligations as well. Whatever they lacked in military efficiency was compensated for by their sense of a common determination to accept death in combat rather than life under an Oriental despotism. Delbrück states that in the Periclean Age more than 80 percent of Athens's male citizenry were enrolled in the citizen-militia. From that figure it is evident that only the physically disabled, the very aged, and the children were exempted from military duty. The victories achieved by common sacrifice were duly credited by contemporaneous writers for their share in the social unification and spiritual vitalization which made inevitable the coming of the Golden Age of Athens. Modern criticism not infrequently sees in that development evidence of the particularism which kept Hellas in discord until she collapsed before the foreign invader. Whatever the truth of that contention, the manner of Athens's victory over Persia remains as a triumph for democratically exercised conscription. Moreover its contrast with the Spartan equivalent should be noted. The Spartan youth, literally conscripted in his infancy, trained by the state under a system so rigorous that the weaklings were "liquidated," lived only as a soldier, a cog in the state machine. The Athenian saw his own world through the eyes of a citizen; his soldier status was secondary, called into being only through the dictates of necessity. Both systems have been classed as democratic. One, however, energized the individual to the achievement of his highest potentialities, the other tended to reduce him to a cipher. The Athenian system gave to civilization the Golden Age; the Spartan, a blank page.

From Rome we have borrowed the word "conscription," derived from the Latin *conscribere milites,* the enrollment or registration of men chosen for the legion from the whole body of freeborn Roman citizens capable of bearing arms. Men from seventeen to sixty were liable to service. The Roman conscript received no pay. Like his Athenian prototype, he provided his own arms and equipment, a requirement which automatically placed the wealthy in the cavalry, the less well-to-do into various categories of heavy and light infantry, and left the *proletarii,* a numerous class, at home as "getters of children." Men of no property, they were deemed devoid of patriotism. The system was admirably suited to the needs of the Republic in its early years, when the rather numerous wars were of relatively short duration, permitting the citizen-soldier to fill his double role. In spite of the emphasis on class distinction resulting from the assignment to arm of service according to wealth, the mutual sharing of hazards was a powerful social factor in knitting together the early Romans not only for war but for the constructive duties of peace as well.

The Middle Ages furnish few instances of conscription unless we fall into the frequent error of considering the soldier-serf a conscript. To quote General Crowder, the serfs "did not come to arms in the service of a common cause, but in payment of a debt of fealty to which they were not a party." One notable example of conscription which, with few lapses, has transmitted its influence through 650 years to express itself finally in the democratic institutions of the Switzerland of today, was born in 1291 when the three forest cantons—Uri, Schwyz, and Unterwalden—discovered in universal liability to service the means of defending their independence against overwhelmingly stronger enemies. All males of sixteen and upwards were liable to service. The physically unfit paid a tax in lieu of service; the physically fit draft evader suffered heavy punishment and became an outcast. The Swiss system marked a distinct social advance over the Athenian and Roman policies, because of its broader underlying basis of citizenship. Whereas Athens disbarred from military service not less than 80 percent of her populace as non-citizens, and Rome rejected her *proletarii,* the Swiss cantons imposed the obligation on all males. In sharing the common dangers and sacrifices entailed by war, the Swiss achieved a sense of social and spiritual unity which ever since has evoked the admiration of the historian.

The thirteenth century furnishes a short-lived example of conscription in the north Italian communes, which for a brief period approached democracy in their social and political organization. Internecine strife led to the substitution of the mercenary, the professional soldier, for the less efficient citizen levy. With the collapse of democracy went its democratic counterpart, universal conscription. In the Low Countries the free cities of Ghent, Bruges, and Ypres launched an abortive effort in the same direction. Effective for a while in curbing the rapacity of the nobles, it was too weak to withstand the rising tide of nationalism. One of the most interesting experiments in this direction was made by Sweden after the Protestant party gained control in the early seventeenth century. To maintain the armies of Charles IX and Gustavus Adolphus, the Riksdag decreed the organization of an army to be recruited by fixed quotas from the various districts. In return the conscripts, officers and men, were provided with sufficient land to support themselves and their dependents. Military service was thus tied to the soil by the "indelta" system. This curious combination of the medieval and modern social concepts immediately won the support of every element in the nation—a support which vanished when the ambitions of Charles XII converted conscription into a tool of despotism which so far drained the nation's resources that Sweden's subsequent status as a third-class power was ensured.

Except for the English fyrd, to be discussed later, the principle of conscription vanished for some centuries, to be reborn in the stress of revolutionary France's wars with the Royalists. Its advent then was an abrupt and complete reversal of the initial stand of the revolutionaries, who at first looked on conscription as an instrument of oppression, a wasteful consumer of national income, and the earmark of militarism. By December, 1789, Dubois Crance was declaring to the Assembly: "I lay it down as an axiom that every citizen must be a soldier, and every soldier a citizen; or we shall never have a real constitution. . . . We must have a truly national conscription. Every man must be ready to march as soon as the country is in danger." The Assembly, however, turned down the proposal and placed its dependence on the volunteer system. Unable to stem the advance of the Austrians and Prussians, the Republican government in February, 1793, hastily "requisitioned" 300,000 men of the National Guard and followed that act with a general levy of all able-bodied men between the ages of eighteen and twenty-five. There were no exemptions except for the physically disabled, and the guillotine promptly put a period to such popular resistance as developed. However, all soldiers were known as "volunteers," a fact which has created no little confusion among the historians. Jourdain's law of 1798 incorporated conscription into the constitution, prescribing universal liability to a five-year term of military service for the age group mentioned above. That step placed the seal of approval on the results obtained by the emergency levy of 1793, of which Colonel Maude speaks as follows: "Raw enthusiasm was replaced by a systematic and unsparing conscription, and the masses of men thus enrolled, inspired by ardent patriotism and directed by the ferocious energy of the Committee on Public Safety, met the disciplined formalist with an opposition before which the attack completely collapsed." The nation's call to arms in fact produced in a few months more than a million men. That call incidentally presaged the almost universal dependence of European states on conscription as a basis of recruitment from that day down to the present.

Contrary to popular opinion, English history affords one of the longest and most interesting pictures of conscription recorded. Although its origin is not absolutely certain, it appears to have been brought to England's shores with the waves of Angles and Saxons who overran the country in the fifth century of our era. If this supposition is true, John Lothrop Motley's *Rise of the Dutch Republic* presents a clear picture of the completely democratic organization of the early German tribes, both for peace and for war, which became the parent of the English fyrd. Certainly it was well established before King Alfred's day. The privilege (not to be evaded) of taking the oath of arms was conferred on all able-bodied men between the ages of sixteen and sixty. Like the Roman legionary of republican days, the English militiaman equipped himself. His equipment, assignment to branch of service, and rank depended almost wholly on his property status. Training, placed by custom at two months annually in King Alfred's time, was rarely either regular or thorough. Nevertheless the fyrd remained through centuries the principal dependence of the English monarchs for home defense. It acquitted itself magnificently on many battlefields and was a powerful factor in developing the sturdy qualities of the yeomanry who wiped out the French armies at Crécy, Poitiers, and Agincourt. The English soldier of those battles was a volunteer, it is true, but he was accepted for service only after he had demonstrated his capacities in the militia. In its long history down to 1908, when it was finally absorbed into the "special reserve" of the regular army, the fyrd survived many vicissitudes, usually from the hands of rulers like the Stuarts who mistrusted the democratic attitude of the citizen-soldiers. Its disappearance was due to several factors, chief among them England's increasing dependence on sea power after the sixteenth century and the need of a long-service professional soldiery for her foreign garrisons after she was launched on her program of imperial expansion.

Prussia's military revival after Jena is the one other important example of democratic conscription prior to the World War. How complete its reversal from Prussian tradition is evident from Frederick William II's rejection in 1794 of a proposal to summon the *levée en masse* in answer to France's resort to the "nation in arms." The Prussian king declared that it was "infinitely dangerous [politically] to assemble such a mass of men." After Prussia's humiliation at Napoleon's hands he had no choice except to take his councillors' advice. Scharnhorst's scheme circumvented the stipulations of the Treaty of Tilsit, with the limit of 42,000 as the strength of the Prussian Army, by passing the entire young manhood of the nation through the ranks of that army. The recruit received no more than a few months' training in fundamentals before his transfer to the reserve. What he lacked in military efficiency at the end of his period of training was more than compensated for by the high average level of intelligence of the group—a true cross-section of the nation's manhood—and the patriotic ardor roused by the wiping out of class distinctions in the imposition of a universal obligation. In that respect, Prussia's experience followed revolutionary France's earlier precedent. And, like that precedent, the social leveling and welding vanished with the restoration of autocratic rule.[1]

The conscript system of recruitment, as already stated, had become the accepted practice throughout Europe before the outbreak of the first World War. A varying cadre of professional troops provided the nucleus of instructors for the annual contingents called to the colors. Historians of the period are wont to speak of the democratic basis on which the great standing armies of 1914 were created. The description fits only if the term democratic can be whittled down to refer merely to the theoretical obligation of all able-bodied men to render military service. But this, too, overlooks the devices of exemption and substitution by which very considerable numbers evaded service; it assumes at the same time that the military agencies of an autocracy like Russia can be democratic in theory or in fact. Candid analysis dismisses the notion of Europe's democratic conscription until it turns to Switzerland, where national defense, like all other functions of the state, was on a fully democratic basis. Great Britain, it should be added, is outside the discussion inasmuch as she maintained a small, long-service professional army of volunteers.

The heavy losses suffered by all the belligerents compelled them early to revise their methods of recruitment. Before the end of 1915 the various loopholes of exemption, substitution, and other means of evading service had been generally eliminated. Great Britain's experience in building an army was particularly significant, inasmuch as her costly errors taught the United States what to avoid when the time came to draft our Selective Service Act of May 18, 1917. Contrasting America's success from the outset with the long agony of England's failure, General Crowder remarks:

> Not so fortunate was England. Imbued with our own heresy, she did not escape the deadly cost, which we happily avoided. How she blindly struggled to maintain the volunteer doctrine; how, step by step, she receded from it, first through the importuning of her wiser leaders, then through an overwhelming national necessity; how she yielded first in principle, then in partial practice, until the realization of the awful toll was thrust upon her and she took the whole drastic step, this is . . . a story of vital national interest.

British "muddling through" in this instance ensured the early transfer to the "Roll of Honour" of the best and bravest of her young manhood; ensured also the repeated and prolonged disruption of production as tens of thousands of her key men in industry "joined up." It was not merely the fact that Britain's best blood, in the broadest sense of the word "best," stood almost alone under German drumfire for two years of war but the fact that guns and shells for their support were inadequate that remains as an unanswerable indictment of Britain's policy. It was not until July 15, 1915, that Parliament provided for registration of the men of fighting age, a job so badly bungled that two years later the minister in charge confessed to Parliament that the National Register could not be depended on for its accuracy before the middle of 1918. No thoroughgoing provision for conscription was made until passage of the second Military Service Act, May 25, 1916. And in

August, 1917, three months after the United States had placed conscription on a selective basis to maintain the proper military-industrial balance, England followed suit. Throughout those years of bungling every form of pressure, including social ostracism, was resorted to in order to push the proper individuals into uniform. Too many of the wrong men got there instead. The resulting social cleavages and the general bitterness which ensued played no little part in the refusal of the British citizen and his representatives in Parliament to face the truth of European developments after 1933. So it happens that Britain pays not once, but twice for her stubborn and stupid reluctance in the first World War to espouse thoroughgoing democratic selective military service.

The decade after 1919 witnessed Europe's general return to the peacetime conscription prevalent before 1914. Exceptions were Great Britain, relying once more on volunteers and repeatedly finding herself unable to fill the ranks even though recruiting standards were seriously reduced; the defeated Central Powers, which by treaty were compelled to content themselves with small long-service professional armies; and Soviet Russia, which frankly resorted to the nation-in-arms principle, the first important instance of its peacetime employment. Russia in fact was the one power of importance which maintained in full the obligation of all able-bodied men to military service. Her policy was the first step toward the inauguration of what we may call the 1939 concept of the "nation-in-arms," to be discussed later.

Before glancing at totalitarian war, and its underlying peacetime mobilization of all resources, human and material, we must note a few outstanding examples of conscription which bear no relation to democratic concepts of social and political organization. They are in fact quite the reverse, based as they are on the despotic use of human raw material for the attainment of some militarist's ambitions. Unhappily humanity has had far more experience with compulsory service as a function of militarism than as a democratic means of defense. It is even more regrettable that truly democratic conscription has all too often degenerated into pure militarism when the infatuation of the mob with its leader has blinded men to the nation's true interests. Just so, imperial Athens, launched on a program of conquest, placed her destiny in the hands of soldier-adventurers and their armies of mercenaries. It was all too late when Demosthenes exhorted the decadent Greeks: "Recruit your armies, man your fleets, not with the offscourings of Hellas and Asia, but with the best of your freeborn citizens, and you may yet conquer." The native Athenian had ceased to be a soldier.

Rome's record in this respect differs in no essential from that of

Greece, unless one takes the position that the Punic Wars were defensive in character. Long before 146 B.C., the amateur Roman generals had been replaced by professionals like Scipio Africanus, and the warrior-farmers in the ranks had likewise given way to the professional legionaries. Soldiering had become a lifetime career. The veteran who survived the campaigns to win at last his retirement and the farm granted him by the state was usually a social encumbrance, too old to marry, too proud or too inept to till his land. Meanwhile the great mass of the citizens, concerned only with their peacetime activities, lost all sense of obligation toward the defense of the state. Imperial Rome, in fact, leaned more and more on the recruitment of barbarians as mercenaries. In the hour of Rome's final crisis, she had no reserve of citizen-soldiers to fall back upon. The fat years of "bread and circuses" had so far sapped the native-born Roman's will and capacity to fight for his beliefs or his country that it was but a question of time when she must collapse before the onset of a more virile people. And, interestingly, that people was one which had held to its prehistoric traditions requiring every citizen to be a soldier, every soldier a citizen; democracy at its crudest and with its fangs displayed, but democracy nevertheless.

The full story of the degeneration of Rome's system of universal compulsory service stretches through the better part of two centuries. Seventeen centuries later revolutionary France traversed a similar road in the span of two years when she fell under the spell of Napoleon Bonaparte's leadership. For a brief period the fiction of emancipating the oppressed of Europe deluded the impressionable who marched behind the Corsican's banners and gave them the *élan* to press home the bayonet attack at the critical moment. When that delusion ended, there remained a solid nucleus of superbly trained veterans, professional soldiers all, fanatically attached to the "Little Corporal." They became the central cadre around which Napoleon organized army after army by conscripting everything male and human that was fit to carry a musket. His system drained not only the lifeblood of France but of the subject territories as well. Whatever vestige of democracy existed in his method was destroyed when exemption by purchase—a very handsome purchase—permitted the well-to-do to escape service. Napoleon reaped the fruits of his militarism when in 1810 more then 80 percent of the annual French quota failed to appear for registration. To hunt down the bands of *Réfractaires,* sixteen flying columns of his best troops, more than 40,000 men all told, were diverted from their normal duties. The Napoleon of ten years earlier, not yet quite a megalomaniac, would have read the lesson aright, with its augury of the wholesale defections that helped to make a hell of his retreat from Moscow—prelude to the final disasters of Leipzig and Waterloo.

It was a trick of fate that gave to Prussia, briefly espousing democratic principles in the rejuvenation of her national vitality, a major role in administering the deathblow to Napoleonic tyranny. But hardly had the reports from Leipzig been digested in Berlin when a long-term service law, finally enacted in 1814, put an end to the momentary appearance of the Prussian citizen-soldier. The rank and file of the armies which fought at Sadowa, Gravelotte, and Verdun were primarily soldiers, rather than citizens. The only vestige of the democratic principle remaining from Scharnhorst's day was the universality of obligation. Even that was vitiated by the manner in which exemptions were regulated. All the distinctions of caste adhering to the individual in his civilian status accompanied him into the ranks. Like the prototype of Frederick the Great's day, the Prussian (later, German) army after 1814 was the bludgeon of the autocrat.

There remains a final general classification of conscription which at no time approached the democratic principle, either in purpose, in application, or in the political and social organization of the people upon whom it is employed. Despotism has filled more pages of history than all other forms of social and political organization lumped together. A categorical account of the despots' employment of conscription would do likewise and in the end would leave the reader with a sense of monotonous repetition. The autocrats of Imperial Egypt and Assyria were brothers under the skin to Genghis Khan and Tamerlane of the East, to Louis XIV and Frederick the Great of the West, in their attitude to their subjects, whether peasant, artisan, or soldier. Necessarily the soldier suffered more than his civilian brother, at least in terms of physical sacrifice. On the whole, neither the men-at-arms nor the civilian subjects of these autocrats received more consideration than that which a careless ranchman of today gives to his herd. To the ruler, these men were no more than intelligent livestock, *homo sapiens* in uniform.

The principal variants in the general picture relate to the efficiency and intelligence with which the despot used his human cattle. Genghis Khan and Frederick the Great demonstrated that an ethnologically homogeneous group could be welded by hard training and clever leadership into a striking force of great potency; moreover that victory and loot were ample compensation to the rank and file for the sacrifices endured. Let that leadership ossify, however, as it did in Germany after the death of Frederick the Great, the outcome may spell Jena and Tilsit. And when the despot brings into the ranks a motley of unassimilated peoples, his military host is as apt to be a mob as an army, a fact well demonstrated at Arbela and Actium.

The totalitarian war of today presents the world with a concept of conscription far more sweeping than anything witnessed since the practice of wholesale extermination of defeated peoples was ruled out as an uneconomic procedure. Soviet Russia gave the cue with her Compulsory Service Law of August 15, 1930, establishing liability for all citizens regardless of sex. Women are accepted for military duty in peacetime and may be drafted in time of war. Italy goes a step further with a premilitary training program beginning for both sexes at the age of six. As a result, when the Italian youth is drafted for military service at the age of 21, he is already a trained soldier. Nazi Germany, with its particularly efficient system of military and premilitary training, has decreed that all citizens, women as well as men, shall be obligated to render service over and above strictly military duty. France, all too late, was moving toward totalitarian mobilization when her defenses collapsed. Only then did Great Britain move to the passage of an Emergency Powers Defense Bill, enacted May 22, 1940. It provides for the draft of all British resources, human and material, during the period of the emergency. Its application thus far falls well short of the rigors inherent in the provisions of the Act. Dictatorship is there—to be applied as needed, whether in a bombed area, a munitions plant, or a channel of distribution. To round out the picture of a world under arms, the Oriental appendage of the Axis, with its National Mobilization Law of 1938 and the decrees of the Konoye Ministry, is living under a system of conscription at least as inclusive as that which obtains in the unconquered regions of Europe.

For the five hundred million people under the totalitarian rule conscription has become the wartime extension of a peacetime social concept which reduces the individual to the status of a fraction of the state. He lives only in the contribution which he makes to the collective output of the whole, whether in goods or carnage. Shouting "Heil Hitler" or "Workers of the World Unite," he goes forward with his fellows in mass formation to almost certain death in the hope that a few of his comrades may be pushed through the enemy line to disrupt communications. Fanatically he adheres to the "party line," or if reason intrudes to chill his enthusiasm until he deviates so far as to express an independent thought, he pays for his rashness with the loss of liberty or life. And, except for the bit of ribbon or the trinket which may be pinned on his breast, he finds his reward in the glory of his nation's conquests. Whatever social terraces may remain as a heritage of the past tend to level to a common plain through the erosions of common sacrifice, confiscatory taxation, and the swifter scoop-shovel action of the state's periodic decrees. The net result is a social, mental, and spiritual horizon no higher than that enjoyed in ancient days by the warriors of Assyria or Sparta. The despot's conscription does, however, leave one terrace, one upper level from which the conscript may look down upon the peoples enslaved through his collective, regimented efforts. He enjoys that satisfaction so long, and only so long, as his social order produces a fighting machine superior to the forces sent into action by the collective will and common sacrifice of democratic conscription.

The examples cited afford us no more than a glance at three types of conscription; two, in fact, if one chooses to class all instances of the despotically administered draft under a single head. They are, however, typical. Further analysis, covering the full range of military history, would not vitiate the major conclusions which may properly be drawn as to the social and political conditions which have produced these types of conscription and the effects of their employment on the nations involved. First, it is evident that conscription for the autocrat, whether ancient, medieval, or modern, whether the scion of an established line of autocrats like Frederick the Great, or the adventurer who subverts democracy into despotic rule as did Napoleon, is the most efficient device for converting the human raw material under his control into a striking force of terrific power.

The autocrat finds justification for his action in his military successes. The historian, concerned chiefly with the social consequences of such successes to the people rather than with the aggrandizement of the monarch, encounters not only the harsh treatment of the vanquished but the absence of any betterment in the lot of the victors. The spurious prosperity resulting from the inflow of captured treasure and subsequent tribute which has usually followed on the heels of military victory have not served to change the fundamental status of the subjects of the despot. There has been no relaxation in the harshness of his controls. The change, if any, has been in the contrary direction, aimed at securing still greater military efficiency for the furtherance of the ruler's ambitions. In the lot of the French citizen in 1813, in that of the Japanese, Italian, and German citizens today, in the bread lines standing in the snow of Russia's richest agricultural area all winter while the Soviet armies were pounding the Finnish lines, we find the perfect picture of the consequences of despotic conscription.

By contrast democratic conscription has in every instance occurred as the voluntary dedication of a nation's resources to the cause of defense. The armies so raised have not always been notable for their efficiency; often, the contrary. Frequently deficient in training and led by commanders whose experience in troop leading was necessarily limited, they have had to depend on morale to make up for their technical shortcomings. And that morale, that spirit of a common cause, has not only been the product of the social conditions which democracy alone makes possible, but it has served as a priceless asset for the problems of peace remaining after the war. A proviso must be added—the benefits of democratic conscription have persisted to the day of peace only for the nations which in the heat of war have not lost sight of their own true interests. Napoleon's early successes blinded the French people to the fact that their liberties were being wiped out. A gullible people, dazzled by military success, are all too apt to overlook the necessity of qualifying a grant of power to the nation's leaders with the proviso "for the period of the emergency" only, and of leaving in being the popularly elected instrumentalities which shall determine when the emergency has in fact ended. Therein, as history has clearly shown, lie the greatest social and political dangers of democratic conscription.

"The Social and Political Aspects of Conscription: Europe's Experience," by Herman Beukema, from *War as a Social Institution: The Historian's Perspective* (New York: Columbia University Press, 1941), pages 113–129. Copyright © 1941 Columbia University Press. Reprinted by permission of the publisher.

HERMAN BEUKEMA (1891–1960) graduated from the U.S. Military Academy at West Point in 1915 and returned to join the faculty in 1928. In his twenty-six-year career at West Point, he reached the rank of brigadier general, served as professor and chairman of the Department of Economics, Government and History, and led a decade-long campaign to make military instruction a regular part of nonmilitary college education. Among his books on U.S. military policy and education are *Defense Policy of the United States, 1775–1944* and *The Economics of National Security.*

Note

1. G. C. Coulton records in his *Compulsory Military Service* that during the American Revolutionary War, the Landgrave of Hesse-Cassel supplied the British Army with 23,000 conscripts at a net profit of nearly $23,000,000. Modern history provides no cruder example of cold-blooded barter in human flesh.

28

Selection for Military Service in the Soviet Union

by
Raymond Garthoff

Garthoff analyzes universal military obligation in the Soviet Union in an attempt to provide perspective on the draft in the United States. He examines the relevant clause of the USSR Constitution, discussing its practical implications, and concludes that Soviet citizens appear to regard their system as reasonably equitable despite the fact that no opportunity is given for public discussion of the subject. Garthoff notes that a percentage of Soviet conscripts are assigned nonmilitary or "paracivilian" duties, rendering their system transitional between universal military and universal national service.

Following the Bolshevik seizure of power in Russia, the first law on compulsory military service was enacted on May 29, 1918. On June 12, 1918, a decree ordered the conscription of certain age groups "of workers and peasants who do not exploit the labor of others." By the end of the Russian Civil War in 1921, over five million men were under arms. This large army was rapidly cut back to a little over half a million regular troops, and it was not until the latter half of the 1930's that the Soviet armed forces again increased substantially in numbers. During the 1920's and the 1930's a series of conscription laws succeeded one another. The 1936 Constitution of the USSR, which is still in effect, abolished class distinctions as a qualification for military service, and stated (in Article 132) that "Universal military obligation shall be law." On September 1, 1939, the Supreme Soviet passed a law "On Universal Military Obligation," which (with minor amendments) remains in effect today.

The law "On Universal Military Obligation" explicitly bases itself on Article 132 of the Constitution, and states (in Article 3): "All male citizens of the USSR without distinction as to race, nationality, religion, educational qualification, or social origin and position, shall be obliged to render military service in the ranks of the Armed Forces of the USSR." The law further spells out (Article 5) that: "Military service shall consist of active service and of service in the reserves of the army and the navy." In addition, the military establishment is accorded the right "to register and accept for service" women who have medical and special technical training, and in time of war to induct such women into the armed forces.

Voluntary Service

There is no provision for "volunteers" for military service (except for reenlistees, and except for those choosing to enter military cadet and officer candidate schools). A voluntary youth organization, DOSAAF (The Voluntary Society for Support of the Army, Air Force, and Navy), conducts a large-scale preinduction training program in military-related activities such as parachute jumping, preflight training, marksmanship, and the like. Subsequent military service assignments are in part based on skills and premilitary training in DOSAAF. This organization is an adjunct of the Ministry of Defense, with the dual functions of preinduction training and civil defense training. In addition, a preservice military familiarization course is given in secondary schools (i.e., the 8th through 10th grades). This school course involves two hours of instruction per week, and includes brief summer field camp training between the 9th and 10th grades.

Since World War II, there have been a number of military and naval preparatory cadet schools. For a number of years some of these schools, established in 1943 and named "Suvorov" and "Nakhimov" (in honor of distinguished Imperial Russian military commanders), were open to boys at the age of ten with a seven-year course. These schools, which are military boarding schools, were opened primarily for the orphans and children of career military officers. However, at present all cadet schools are limited to the three-year secondary school level. Upon graduation, cadets are given preferential admission to officer candidate schools, which have an additional three-year curriculum.

During World War II, there was, in addition to the draft, a "Universal Military Training" program under which all men between 16 and 50 years of age were subject to a 110-hour course of military training supplementing their regular schooling or employment.

Induction

Registration and induction for military service is administered through a network of rural and urban precinct "military commissariats." These commissariats, usually headed by a field-grade military officer, are associated with the local government authorities but are subordinate to the appropriate Military District of the Ministry of Defense.

All males register in January or February following the year in which they reach the age of 17 (lowered from age 18 in July, 1962). At the time of registration, each young man is presumably asked his preference for arm of military service, but—according to many former Soviet servicemen—in practice this preference is usually ignored. Those selected for induction are called up some time between June and December of the following year. Since August 1, 1960, the timing of induction varies according to the location and the arm of service in which the draftee would serve. Prior to that time (and for most conscriptees at present) the call-up is in September.

Active Duty

The duration of active service for those conscripted depends upon the branch of service to which the man is assigned. In 1939, soldiers in the ground forces served for two years, in the air force for four years, and in the navy for five years. In much of the postwar period the term of active service was three years for the army, four years for the air force, and five years for the navy. At present, it is three years for all services except the navy, where the term of service is four years. Conscriptees serve not only in the regular army, navy, and air force, but also in the paramilitary internal security troops, border guards, and coast guard of the KGB (Committee for State Security).

The system of an annual age-class call-up, although slightly modified by the spread of induction over a several month period, is related to an annual training cycle in the armed forces. Since new trainees fill the places vacated by those leaving at the end of their three-year term, roughly one-third of the privates are new each year. By the same token, two-thirds are "veterans" of the repetitive annual training cycle, and in this manner the combat effectiveness of all units is presumably preserved.

Selection for Service

It is evident that the number of young men conscripted each year will be a function of two factors: the size of the age class for call-up, and the personnel level desired for the armed forces. During the early 1960's, there was a manpower shortage of young men of military age caused by the "birth gap" of 1941–45. That gap has now been passed. As a very rough generalization, on the order of half of each age class is at present called up for active service. However, only a small minority are rejected on grounds of physical or mental disability.

Theoretically, the Soviet system of conscription is not a selective service system. But in fact, it is—a system based, however, on the principle of "selection out," rather than "selection in." Liberal deferments are granted for reasons of health, family hardship, and continued education. Marriage is, however, *not* a basis for deferment or non-selection. On the other hand, being the only support of a family (mother or brothers and sisters) is basis for non-selection. (Those who have been previously convicted of a crime by a legal court are also not drafted.)

Educational deferment is granted for secondary school pupils to age 20. Deferment is also granted to all full-time students enrolled in college-level schooling. Most college students serve after graduation in the ranks for one year, and are then commissioned in the reserve, but some (e.g., in engineering or medicine) are simply placed at once in the reserve. There also is a voluntary ROTC program in Soviet higher educational institutions.

Inadequate education is not generally a basis for non-selection. Those conscripted who do not have an eighth-grade level of education are given special after-duty schooling to bring them up to that level.

Those not called up for service are placed on the reserve rolls.

Non-Commissioned Officer Service and Reenlistment

Some NCO's are career reenlistees, but conscripts during their initial obligatory three-year term of service comprise most of those of non-commissioned rank. The term of service of non-commissioned officers is the same as that for private soldiers. Reenlistment, particularly but not only by non-commissioned officers, is encouraged. A few privates, and a larger number of non-commissioned officers, do reenlist, and some continue to reenlist as career NCO's. Ordinarily, reenlistment brings a one-step promotion.

Conditions and Privileges of Enlisted Service

Enlisted men receive, of course, all the necessities of life, plus very modest pay. Pay is based primarily on rank and position held, and to a lesser extent on length of service, with increments beginning with the third year of service and with each promotion. In addition, there is supplementary pay for specialist service of various categories. Pay of servicemen is tax free. Allotments are given to dependents only in cases where such dependents are unable by virtue of age, health, or other factors to be gainfully employed. Among the few statutory "fringe" benefits are accident insurance, reduced transportation charges, and free mail to and from servicemen.

Reserve Service

Under the basic military service law, obligations include enlisted reserve service up to age 50. Upon completion of the regular term of active duty, the conscript is automatically discharged into the reserve. Up to 35 years of age, the reservist is in the "first class" of the reserve, and is liable—apart, of course, from the possibility of call-up to active duty in time of emergency—to call-up six times for two-month refresher training tours (or, if he has been deferred and never served on active duty, nine such tours). From age 35 to 45 the reservist is in the "second class" and is subject to five additional calls for one-month refresher duty. Finally, from 45 to 50, the "third class" of the reserves may be called up for a single one-month refresher course. (Candidates for promotion within the reserve are liable for slightly longer periods of short-term active duty.) In practice, it appears that actual calls of reservists for short-term refresher duty are much less frequent.

The active and reserve service of officers differs according to rank, and reserve officers are kept in the respective grades of the reserve for longer periods than enlisted men. For example, a university student who has been commissioned into the reserve after completion of his deferred one-year service in the ranks would, if he had reached the rank of army captain in the reserve, be kept in the first class until age 50, the second class until age 55, and the third class until age 60. Upon reaching the age limit for being in the reserve, officers are retired, while enlisted personnel are simply discharged.

Until 1939, there existed "territorial troops" roughly along the lines of our National Guard. However, since that date there has been no equivalent of our National Guard.

Concluding Observations

Soviet citizens appear to regard the system of conscription in the USSR as a reasonably equitable one. There has, of course, been no opportunity for public discussion of the subject. While there is no provision for alternative civilian duty for eligible young men who may not be needed for military service, as has been proposed in the United States, it should perhaps be noted that some components of the Soviet armed forces such as the construction troops and the railroad troops engage in what might be termed "paracivilian" activities. In addition, units of the regular army are on occasion shifted to meet non-military requirements such as "crash" harvesting. To date, probably largely by coincidence, the available pool of those eligible for induction into military service seems to have coincided reasonably well with the personnel requirements of the armed forces. When there has been a discrepancy, the slack (or squeeze) of the need for conscription has been met by tightening or loosening deferments and by evening out differences in annual age classes by postponing induction of some eligible men for a year or two. In the future, especially if the size of the Soviet armed forces should decline, it may be more difficult to avoid an evident selective service system. However, even in that case, the Soviet leadership would probably use indirect adjustments to regulate the flow of induction rather than alter the formal obligation—and image—of universal military service.

"Selection for Military Service in the Soviet Union," by Raymond L. Garthoff, from *The Draft: A Handbook of Facts and Alternatives*, edited by Sol Tax (Chicago: University of Chicago Press, 1967), pages 167–170. Copyright © 1967 The University of Chicago. Reprinted by permission of the publisher.

RAYMOND LEONARD GARTHOFF (1929–) is a researcher and foreign service specialist in U.S.-Soviet relations. He has served on the faculties of George Washington University, the School for Advanced International Studies at Johns Hopkins University, and the NATO Defense College. He was foreign affairs adviser to the Department of the Army and deputy director for political-military affairs in the Department of State, served as adviser on political and military affairs for NATO and as ambassador to Bulgaria, and participated in the U.S.-USSR SALT negotiations, 1969 to 1972.

Part VII

Conscription: Pro

29

Recommendations
for a Federal Draft

by

James Monroe

*In 1814, Secretary of War James Monroe, at the request of William B.
Giles, chairman of the Senate Committee on Military Affairs, submitted
four plans for improving the nation's military establishment. Giles's request stemmed from problems encountered in securing sufficient numbers of volunteer regular soldiers of adequate strength and skill to fight
the War of 1812. Secretary Monroe (who was to become president in
1817) proposed a federal draft of male citizens between the ages of
eighteen and forty-five, on the grounds that a federal draft is not inconsistent with the Constitution because the power the Constitution grants
Congress to raise armies necessarily implies giving it the means to put
that power into effect. Monroe further argued that conservation of the
State is a duty paramount to all others, and that to this end a commonwealth has a right to the service of all its citizens.*

*Monroe's "first plan" was largely the basis of the Conscription Bill
of 1814, which was not passed; Congress enacted his "fourth plan" instead. Except for a provision that draftees could furnish substitutes,
Monroe's recommendations contain most of the principles of the Selective Service System that the United States set up a century later.*

Explanatory Observations

In providing a force necessary to bring this war to a happy termination, the nature of the crisis in which we are involved, and the extent of its dangers, claim particular attention. If the means are not fully adequate to the end, discomfiture must inevitably ensue.

It may fairly be presumed that it is the object of the British Government, by striking at the principal sources of our prosperity, to diminish the importance, if not to destroy the political existence, of the United States. If any doubt remained on this subject, it has been completely removed by the despatches from our ministers at Ghent, which were lately laid before Congress.

A nation contending for its existence against an enemy powerful by land and sea, favored, in a peculiar manner, by extraordinary events, must make great exertions, and suffer great sacrifices. Forced to contend again for our liberties and independence, we are called on for a display of all the patriotism which distinguished our fellow-citizens in the first great struggle. It may be fairly concluded that if the United States sacrifice any right, or make any dishonorable concession to the demands of the British Government, the spirit of the nation will be broken, and the foundations of their union and independence shaken. The United States must relinquish no right, or perish in the struggle. There is no intermediate ground to rest on. A concession on one point leads directly to the surrender of every other. The result of the contest cannot be doubtful. The highest confidence is entertained that the stronger the pressure, and the greater the danger, the more firm and vigorous will be the resistance, and the more successful and glorious the result.

It is the avowed purpose of the enemy to lay waste and destroy our cities and villages, and to desolate our coast, of which examples have already been afforded. It is evidently his intention to press the war along the whole extent of our seaboard, in the hope of exhausting equally the spirits of the people and the national resources. There is also reason to presume that it is the intention to press the war from Canada on the adjoining States, while attempts are made on the city of New York, and other important points, with a view to the vain project of dismemberment or subjugation. It may be inferred likewise, to be a part of the scheme, to continue to invade this part of the Union, while a separate force attacks the State of Louisiana, in the hope of taking possession of the city of New Orleans, and of the mouth of the Mississippi, that great inlet and key to the commerce of all that portion of the United States lying westward of the Alleghany [sic] mountains. The peace in Europe having given to the enemy a large disposable force, has essentially favored these objects.

The advantage which a great naval superiority gives to the enemy, by enabling him to move troops from one quarter to another, from Maine to the Mississippi, a coast of two thousand miles extent, is very considerable. Even a small force, moved in this manner, for the purposes avowed by the British commanders, cannot fail to be sensibly felt; more especially by those who are most exposed to it. It is obvious that, if the militia are to be relied on, principally, for the defence of our cities and coast against these predatory and desolating incursions, wherever they may be made, that, by interfering with their ordinary pursuits of industry, it must be attended with serious interruption and loss to them, and injury to the public, while it greatly increases the expense. It is an object, therefore, of the highest importance, to provide a regular force with the means of transporting it from one quarter to another, along our coast, thereby following the movements of the enemy, with the greatest possible rapidity, and repelling the attack wherever it may be made. These remarks are equally true as to the militia service generally, under the present organization of the militia, and the short terms of service prescribed by law. It may be stated with confidence, that at least three times the force, in militia, has been employed at our principal cities, along the coast and on the frontier, in marching to, and returning thence, than would have been necessary in regular troops; and that the expense attending it has been more than proportionably augmented, from the difficulty, if not the impossibility of preserving the same degree of system in the militia as in the regular service.

But it will not be sufficient to repel these predatory and desolating incursions. To bring the war to an honorable termination, we must not be contented with defending ourselves. Different feelings must be touched, and apprehensions excited, in the British Government. By pushing the war into Canada, we secure the friendship of the Indian tribes, and command their services, otherwise to be turned by the enemy against us; we relieve the coast from the desolation which is intended for it, and we keep in our hands a safe pledge for an honorable peace.

It follows, from this view of the subject, that it will be necessary to bring into the field, next campaign, not less than one hundred thousand regular troops. Such a force, aided, in extraordinary emergencies, by volunteers and the militia, will place us above all inquietude as to the final result of this contest. It will fix on a solid and imperishable foundation, our union and independence, on which the liberties and happiness of our fellow-citizens so essentially depend. It will secure to the United States an early and advantageous peace. It will arrest, in the further prosecution of the war, the desolation of our cities and our coast, by enabling us to retort on the enemy, those calamities which our citizens have been already doomed to suffer—a resort which self defence alone, and a sacred regard for the rights and honor of the nation, could induce the United States to adopt.

The return of the regular force now in service, laid before you, will show how many men will be necessary to fill the present corps; and the return of the numerical force of the present military establishment will show how many are required to complete it to the number proposed. The next and most important inquiry is, how shall these men be raised? Under existing circumstances, it is evident that the most prompt and efficient mode that can be devised, consistent with the equal rights of every citizen, ought to be adopted. The following plans are respectfully submitted to the consideration of the committee. Being distinct in their nature, I will present each separately, with the considerations applicable to it.

First Plan

Let the free male population of the United States, between eighteen and forty-five years, be formed into classes of one hundred men each, and let each class furnish four men for the war, within thirty days after the classification, and replace them in the event of casualty.

The classification to be formed with a view to the equal distribution of property among the several classes.

If any class fails to provide the men required of it, within the time specified, they shall be raised by draught on the whole class, any person, thus draughted, being allowed to furnish a substitute.

The present bounty in land to be allowed to each recruit, and the present bounty in money, which is paid to each recruit by the United States, to be paid to each draught by all the inhabitants within the precinct of the class within which the draught may be made, equally, according to the value of the property which they may respectively possess; and if such bounty be not paid within ———— days, the same to be levied on all the taxable property of the said inhabitants; and, in like manner, the bounty, whatever it may be, which may be employed in raising a recruit, to avoid a draught, to be assessed on the taxable property of the whole precinct.

The recruits to be delivered over to the recruiting officer in each district, to be marched to such places of general rendezvous as may be designated by the Department of War.

That this plan will be efficient cannot be doubted. It is evident that the men contemplated may soon be raised by it. Three modes occur by which it may be carried into effect: 1st. By placing the execution of it in the hands of the county courts throughout the United States: 2d. By relying on the militia officers in each county: 3d. By appointing particular persons for that purpose in every county. It is believed that either of these modes would be found adequate.

Nor does there appear to be any well founded objection to the right in Congress to adopt this plan, or to its equality in its application to our fellow-citizens individually. Congress have a right, by the constitution, to raise regular armies, and no restraint is imposed on the exercise of it, except in the provisions which are intended to guard generally against the abuse of power, with none of which does this plan interfere. It is proposed that it shall operate on all alike; that none shall be exempted from it except the Chief Magistrate of the United States, and the Governors of the several States.

It would be absurd to suppose that Congress could not carry this power into effect, otherwise than by accepting the voluntary service of individuals. It might happen that an army could not be raised in that mode, whence the power would have been granted in vain. The safety of the State might depend on such an army. Long continued invasions, conducted by regular, well disciplined troops, can best be repelled by troops kept constantly in the field, and equally well disciplined. Courage in an army is, in a great measure, mechanical. A small body, well trained, accustomed to action, gallantly led on, often breaks three or four times the number of more respectable and more brave, but raw and undisciplined troops. The sense of danger is diminished by frequent exposure to it, without harm; and confidence, even in the timid, is inspired by a knowledge that reliance may be placed on others, which can grow up only by service together. The grant to Congress to raise armies, was made with a knowledge of all these circumstances, and with an intention that it should take effect. The framers of the constitution, and the States who ratified it, knew the advantage which an enemy might have over us, by regular forces, and intended to place their country on an equal footing.

The idea that the United States cannot raise a regular army in any other mode than by accepting the voluntary service of individuals, is believed to be repugnant to the uniform construction of all grants of power, and equally so to the first principles and leading objects of the federal compact. An unqualified grant of power gives the means necessary to carry it into effect. This is an universal maxim, which admits of no exception. Equally true is it, that the conservation of the State is a duty paramount to all others. The commonwealth has a right to the service of all its citizens; or, rather, the citizens composing the commonwealth have a right, collectively and individually, to the service of each other, to repel any danger which may be menaced. The manner in which the service is to be apportioned among the citizens, and rendered by them, are objects of legislation. All that is to be dreaded in such case, is, the abuse of power; and, happily, our constitution has provided ample security against that evil.

In support of this right in Congress, the militia service affords a conclusive proof and striking example. The organization of the militia is an act of public authority, not a voluntary association. The service required must be performed by all, under penalties, which delinquents pay. The generous and patriotic perform them cheerfully. In the alacrity with which the call of the Government has been obeyed, and the cheerfulness with which the service has been performed throughout the United States, by the great body of the militia, there is abundant cause to rejoice in the strength of our republican institutions, and in the virtue of the people.

The plan proposed is not more compulsive than the militia service, while it is free from most of the objections to it. The militia service calls from home, for long terms, whole districts of country. None can elude the call. Few can avoid the service; and those who do are compelled to pay great sums for substitutes. This plan fixes on no one personally, and opens to all who choose it a chance of declining the service. It is a principal object of this plan to engage in the defence of the State the unmarried and youthful, who can best defend it, and best be spared, and to secure to those who render this important service an adequate compensation from the voluntary contributions of the more wealthy, in every class. Great confidence is entertained that such contribution will be made in time to avoid a draught. Indeed, it is believed to be the necessary and inevitable tendency of this plan to produce that effect.

The limited powers which the United States have in organizing the militia may be urged as an argument against their right to raise regular troops in the mode proposed. If any argument could be drawn from the circumstance, I should suppose that it would be in favor of an opposite conclusion. The power of the United States over the militia has been limited, and that for raising regular armies granted without limitation. There was doubtless some object in this arrangement. The fair inference seems to be, that it was made on great consideration; that the limitation, in the first instance, was intentional, the consequence of the unqualified grant in the second. But it is said, that, by drawing the men from the militia service into the regular army, and putting them under regular officers, you violate a principle of the constitution, which provides that the militia shall be commanded by their own officers. If this was the fact, the conclusion would follow. But it is not the fact. The men are not drawn from the militia, but from the population of the country. When they enlist voluntarily, it is not as militia men that they act, but as citizens. If they are draughted, it must be in the same sense. In both instances, they are enrolled in the militia corps; but that, as is presumed, cannot prevent the voluntary act in the one instance or the compulsive in the other. The whole population of the United States, within certain ages, belong to these corps. If the United States could not form regular armies from them, they could raise none.

In proposing a draught as one of the modes of raising men, in case of actual necessity, in the present great emergency of the country, I have thought it my duty to examine such objections to it as occurred, particularly those of a constitutional nature. It is from my sacred regard for the principles of our constitution, that I have ventured to trouble the committee with any remarks on this part of the subject.

Should it appear that this mode of raising recruits was justly objectionable, on account of the tax on property, from difficulties which may be apprehended in the execution, or from other causes, it may be advisable to decline the tax, and for the Government to pay the whole bounty. In this case, it is proposed that, in lieu of the present bounty, the sum of fifty dollars be allowed to each recruit or draught, at the time of his engagement, and one hundred acres of land in addition to the present bounty in land, for every year that the war may continue.

It is impossible to state, with mathematical accuracy, the number which will be raised by the ratio of 4 to 100, or 1 to 25, nor is it necessary. It is probable that it will be rather more than sufficient to fill the present corps. The extra number, in that case, may form a part of the local force in contemplation, a power to that effect being given to the President.

No radical change in the present military establishment is proposed. Should any modification be found necessary, on further consideration, it will form the subject of a separate communication. It is thought advisable, in general, to preserve the corps in their present form, and to fill them with new recruits, in the manner stated. All these corps have already seen service, and many of them acquired in active scenes much experience and useful knowledge. By preserving them in their present form, and under their present officers, and filling them with new recruits, the improvement of the latter will be rapid. In two or three months, it will be difficult to distinguish between the new and old levies.

The additional force to be provided amounts to forty thousand men. Of this it is proposed that local corps be raised, to consist partly of infantry, partly of mounted men, and partly of artillery. There is reason to believe that such corps may be raised in the principal cities, and even on the frontiers, to serve for the war, under an engagement as to the limit beyond which they should not be carried. Every able bodied citizen is willing and ready to fight for his home, his family, and his country, when invaded. Of this we have seen in the present year the most honorable and gratifying proofs. It does not suit all, however, to go great distances from home. This generous and patriotic spirit may be taken advantage of, under proper arrangements, with the happiest effects to the country, and without essential inconvenience to the parties.

The officers who may be appointed to command these corps should be charged with recruiting them. Local defence being their sole object, it may be presumed that the corps will soon be raised. Patriotism alone will furnish a very powerful motive. It seems reasonable, however, that some recompense should be made to those who relieve others from the burthen; one hundred acres of land and fifty dollars to each recruit will, it is presumed, be deemed sufficient.

It is proposed that this additional force shall form a part of any plan that may be adopted.*

Second Plan

This plan consists of a classification of the militia, and the extension of their terms of service.

Let the whole militia of the United States be divided into the following classes, viz.

All free male persons, capable of service, between the ages of 18 and 25, into one class; all those between the ages of 25 and 32, into another class; and those between 32 and 45, into a third class.

It is proposed, also, that the President shall have power to call into

---

* [Editor's note]: For an eloquent argument against this plan, see Chapter 41.

service any portion of either of these classes which, in his judgment, the exigencies of the country may require, to remain in service two years from the time each corps shall be assembled at the appointed place of rendezvous.

It is believed that a shorter term than two years would not give to these corps the efficiency in military operations that is desired, and deemed indispensable; nor avoid the evils that are so sensibly felt, and generally complained of, under the present arrangement. It requires two campaigns to make a complete soldier, especially where the corps, officers, and men, are alike raw and inexperienced. In the interim, the numbers must be multiplied, to supply the defect of discipline; and it requires the extension of the term of service, to avoid the additional proportional augmentation of having so many in the field at the same time, in marching to the frontier, and returning from it. The inconvenience to the parties, and loss to the community, in other respects, need not be repeated. It is proper to add, only, that, if substitutes are allowed in this service, it must put an end to the recruiting of men for the regular army, especially the old corps. Of the justice of this remark what has occurred in the present year has furnished full proof. It follows that, if this plan is adopted, the militia must be relied on principally, if not altogether, in the farther prosecution of the war.

The additional force for local service, amounting to forty thousand men, will likewise form a part, as already observed, of this plan.

Third Plan

It is proposed by this plan to exempt every five men from militia service, who shall find one to serve for the war. It is probable that some recruits might be raised in this mode, in most or all of the States. But it is apprehended that it would prevent recruiting in every other mode, by the high bounty which some of the wealthy might give. The consequence would probably be very injurious, as it is not believed that any great number could be raised in this mode.

Fourth Plan

Should all the preceding plans be found objectionable, it remains that the present system of recruiting be adhered to, with an augmentation of the bounty in land. Should this be preferred, it is advised that, in addition to the 160 acres of land now given, 100 be allowed annually for every year while the war lasts.

These plans are thought more deserving the attention of the committee than any that have occurred. The first, for the reasons stated, is preferred. It is believed that it will be found more efficient against the enemy, less expensive to the public, and less burthensome on our fellow-citizens.

It has likewise the venerable sanction of our Revolution. In that great struggle, resort was had to this expedient for filling the ranks of our regular army, and with decisive effect.

It is not intended by these remarks, should the first plan be adopted, to dispense altogether with the service of the militia. Although the principal burthen of the war may thereby be taken from the militia, reliance must still be placed on them for important aids, especially in cases of sudden invasion. For this purpose it will still be advisable that the men be classed according to age, and that their term of service be prolonged. Even should this plan be attended with all the advantages expected of it, such an arrangement could not fail to produce the happiest effect. The proof which it would afford of the impregnable strength of the country, of the patient virtue and invincible spirit of the people, would admonish the enemy how vain and fruitless his invasions must be, and might dispose him to a speedy, just, and honorable peace.

Of the very important services already rendered by the militia, even under the present organization, too much cannot be said. If the United States make the exertion which is proposed, it is probable that the contest will soon be at an end. It cannot be doubted that it is in their power to expel the British forces from this continent, should the British Government, by persevering in its unjust demands, make that an object with the American people. Against our united and vigorous efforts, the resistance of the enemy will soon become light and feeble. Success in every fair and honorable claim is within our easy grasp. And surely the United States have every possible inducement to make the effort necessary to secure it. I should insult the understanding, and wound the feelings of the committee, if I touched on the calamities incident to defeat. Dangers which are remote, and can never be realized, excite no alarm with a gallant and generous people. But the advantages of success have a fair claim to their deliberate consideration. The effort which we have already made has attracted the attention and extorted the praise of other nations. Already have most of the absurd theories and idle speculations on our system of government been refuted and put down. We are now felt and respected as a Power, and it is the dread which the enemy entertains of our vast resources and growing importance, that has induced him to push the war against us, after its professed objects had ceased. Success by the discomfiture of his schemes, and the attainment of an honorable peace, will place the United States on higher ground, in the opinion of the world, than they have held at any former period. In future wars, their commerce will be permitted to take its lawful range unmolested. Their remonstrances to foreign Governments will not again be put aside unheeded. Few will be presented, because there will seldom be occasion for them. Our union, founded on interest and affection, will have acquired new strength by the proof it will have afforded of the important advantages attending it. Respected abroad, and happy at home, the United States will have accomplished the great objects for which they have so long contended. As a nation, they will have little to dread; as a people, little to desire.

From James Monroe, Communication to William B. Giles, October 17, 1814, in *American State Papers*, Class V, *Military Affairs* (Washington: Gales and Seaton, 1832), Volume 1, pages 14–17.

JAMES MONROE (1758–1831) survived fighting in the War of Independence to become fifth president of the United States. Author of the Monroe Doctrine, a warning to European nations not to intervene in the Western hemisphere, he also served as governor of Virginia, secretary of state, secretary of war, minister to Great Britain, and minister and envoy extraordinary to France during the purchase of Louisiana.

30

Comments on
Compulsory Military Service:
Annual Report of
the War Department, 1916
by
Hugh Scott

This is a partial text of the 1916 Annual Report of the War Department in which Hugh Scott, then chief of staff, advocates compulsory military service. As a basis for his position, he outlines the nation's military needs (in the year before the United States entered World War I) and notes that those needs are not being met through a voluntary system of procurement. Justifying conscription, he argues that the granting of equal privileges in a free society implies equal sharing of responsibilities, both in civil affairs and in national defense.

Military Policy

In compliance with instructions of the Secretary of War, the War College Division of the General Staff Corps prepared a Statement of a Proper Military Policy for the United States, which was submitted to the Secretary of War, September, 1915 . . . .

. . . This report was based upon the actual needs of the country, as they existed at that time, leaving to Congress the ways and means to provide the men. The first 500,000 mentioned was to be composed of the Regular Army and its reserve, the reserve to be produced by a term of enlistment of eight years, two with the colors and six with the reserve. The second 500,000 mentioned above was to be composed of citizen soldiers, to be given nine months' military training in time of peace and three months' additional training on or before the outbreak of war before they would be prepared for war service.

The General Staff prepared a plan of organization for the first 500,000 which called for 7 infantry divisions of 9 regiments each, and 2 cavalry divisions of 9 regiments each, with necessary field artillery, engineer and signal troops to complete the divisions. In addition, there was to be provided a total of 263 companies of coast artillery. . . .

Congress accepted the recommendation of the General Staff in regard to the number of organizations, but at practically two-thirds of the strength recommended. . . .

. . . The recommendation of the General Staff that a citizen volunteer army of 500,000 men, with a minimum of nine months' training in time of peace, be created was not accepted by Congress. This recommendation was attacked on various grounds as being radical, unnecessary, and impracticable, and as being particularly aimed at the Organized Militia, which the General Staff recommended be maintained as it existed at the date of the report. . . .

. . . In the consideration of this question, the constitutional limitations regarding the militia occupied most of the attention of Congress to the exclusion of the standard of training necessary to prepare troops for service in the first line. Congress believed, as shown by the national defense act, that the constitutional questions that were raised were not serious enough to interfere to any extent with the transformation of the Organized Militia into a citizen force substantially in number as recommended by the General Staff, and the bill, as passed, provides that at the end of five years the National Guard will consist of about 17,000 officers and 440,000 men, the period of enlistment in the National Guard being six years, three with the colors and three with the reserve of the National Guard. A liberal provision is made in the bill for the payment. . . .

. . . The debate in Congress and the discussion in the press of the country indicated that there is a very widespread, serious and vital misconception in this country in regard to the time it takes to train the individual soldier and the organization of which he is an element.

In the belief that soldiers can be very quickly trained and armies improvised, we not only run counter to the military opinion and practice of practically all the other great nations of the world, but we run counter as well to our own experience as a nation in war. The time required for the training of armies depends largely on the presence or absence of trained officers and noncommissioned officers. If there be a corps of trained officers and noncommissioned officers and a tested organization of higher units with trained leaders and staff officers, the problem of training is largely limited to the training of the private soldier. This has been satisfactorily accomplished in Europe as is being demonstrated in the present war by giving the soldiers in time of peace two years of intensive training with the colors and additional training in the reserve.

It should be obvious to any unprejudiced mind that if we are to *defeat* highly trained and splendidly disciplined armies of our possible enemies, our own forces when called upon for battle should have training and discipline at least equal to that of our opponent. While we have splendid material for soldiers, for us seriously to claim that the average American youth can be trained and disciplined in less time than the average English, French, German, or Japanese youth argues a decided lack of understanding on the part of our people of the progress and character of the English, French, German, or Japanese people. . . .

. . . If we can not increase the period of training for the National Guard to the minimum laid down as essential by the General Staff, and it is very doubtful if we will be able to do so and keep the force recruited to the maximum authorized by Congress, we are confronted by a serious situation. The difficulty that is being now experienced in obtaining recruits for the Regular Army and for the National Guard in service on the [Mexican] border and at their mobilization camps raises sharply the question of whether we will be able to recruit the troops authorized by Congress in the national-defense act, both Regular Army and National Guard.

It is, in my judgment, a cause for very sober consideration on the part of every citizen of the country when the fact is fully understood that the units of the National Guard and the Regular Army have not been recruited to war strength in the crisis which we have just passed through. The number of units in both organizations are relatively small and the total number of men needed to recruit them to war strength certainly not great—almost negligible, in fact, when considered in relation to the total male population in the United States of military age; that is, men between 18 and 45 years. Many of the elements which favor recruiting under a volunteer system in this country existed at the time of the call for mobilization for the militia. Among others may be enumerated:

1. The agitation for preparedness that has swept over the country, due largely to the lessons of the European war.

2. The public press of the country generally, regardless of party, had given liberal space in the news and editorial columns in favor of military preparation for months previous to the call.

3. Preparedness parades in which thousands had participated had recently been held in many of the principal cities of the country.

4. Congress had but recently, in response to public sentiment, passed a new national-defense act, which will ultimately almost double the size of our small Regular Army and almost quadruple the size of the Organized Militia.

5. In response to the same national sentiment, Congress has passed, since the National Guard was called to active service, a naval bill giving the largest naval increase in the history of the country.

These facts are mentioned to show that public interest in the Army and Navy, and the national defense generally, had been aroused to a comparatively high degree; yet, in what is considered by the Government a grave emergency the National Guard is mobilized for service on the southern frontier to protect the lives of American men, women, and children, recruiting is found so difficult that many of its organizations have not yet, over three months after the call, been raised to even minimum peace strength, and likewise the units of the Regular Army have not been recruited to the minimum peace strength authorized in the new national-defense act. . . .

. . . In my judgment, the country will never be prepared for defense until we do as other great nations do that have large interests to guard, like Germany, Japan, and France, where everybody is ready and does perform military service in time of peace as he would pay every other tax and is willing to make sacrifices for the protection he gets and the country gets in return. The volunteer system in this country, in view of the highly organized, trained, and disciplined armies that our possible opponents possess, should be relegated to the past. There is no reason why one woman's son should go out and defend or be trained to defend another woman and her son who refuses to take training or give service. The only democratic method is for every man in his youth to become trained in order that he may render efficient service if called upon in war.

Universal Military Training

... Universal military training has been the corner stone upon which has been built every republic in the history of the world, and its abandonment the signal for decline and obliteration. This fact was fully recognized by the makers of our Constitution and evidenced in our early laws. A regular army was regarded as inconsistent with the principles of free government, dangerous to free institutions, and apart from the necessities of the times. All were imbued with a patriotism which would make them stand shoulder to shoulder in upholding the laws, and in the defense of the common country, sharing equally the blessings of peace and the hardship of war. The law required every able-bodied male between 18 and 45 years to keep himself provided with rifle and ammunition and to attend muster, and was in effect compulsory military service. They were called together for training at muster time only, for the outdoor life of the early settlers was considered sufficient training for any military duty they were then liable to be called upon to perform. Unfortunately the doctrine of States' rights crept in to prevent the enforcement of Federal law, and each State was left to build up its militia. The Regular Army existed as a small force to protect the western march of civilization from Indian foray, and notwithstanding its brilliant record, the attitude of a great mass of our people continued hostile to the soldier, so much so that several States and Congress have in recent times had to pass laws to insure respect to the uniform and its wearers in public places. Some of our States, while extending the right to vote to aliens of a few months' residence who have declared their intention to become citizens, deny it absolutely to persons in the military and naval service of the United States, putting them in a class with the criminal and insane.

It is vital that our ideas with reference to military service be regenerated. For our small army we go into the labor market for recruits. When the demand for labor is lax, the stipend of the soldier attracts; when the daily wage goes up, recruiting is at its lowest ebb. There is no appeal to patriotism, no appeal for the individual to obtain military training as the highest duty of his citizenship. Enlistment is held out as a job in which the individual gets small pay but is well cared for, with an outdoor, wholesome life and retirement on three-quarters pay and allowances after thirty years of service, and it is accepted as a job. . . .

... A few years ago we reached across the seas and assumed responsibilities of insular possessions and alien races. In the interest of advancing civilization we have built the Panama Canal. We have given a fiat to the world that on this hemisphere at least must survive the principle that rulers derive their just powers from the consent of the ruled. We claim an enlightened civilization of over a hundred million people and stand the richest country in the world. As a nation we are devoted to the peaceful avocations of industrial and commercial life. We treat others as we desire to be treated. Few have knowledge of war and fewer still any training for its rigors. We are entering fully into the affairs of the world and as the greatest of nations we must be ready to uphold and protect our institutions.

It is fundamental with a free people that equal opportunities and protection under the law brings equal responsibility in upholding and maintaining the law. Each owes to the body politic his duty not only in civil affairs but also in the defense of the nation. But with us thousands have been inculcated with the belief that wars were to be ended and that the United States should, as the exponent of the highest civilization, set an example in a minimum of military preparedness, and some even advocated the Army and Navy be disbanded. The country became apathetic in the training of its people for national defense. But the awful cauldron of war into which Europe was suddenly plunged has served to awaken us in a measure to a realization that we must believe in ourselves, and as the exponents of a democracy that should regenerate the political systems of the world, we must be ready to hold our place in the councils of the world, and to do this we must be physically fit, or we shall be brushed aside by the vigorous manhood of other races who sacrifice self that the nation may live.

During the months of May and June hundreds of thousands marched in so-called preparedness parades to the plaudits of onlookers. But when the militia was called out in June to protect our border, it was with the utmost difficulty that its units were recruited to the small number required, and some were never filled. The spirit was rife to let somebody else do it. Not only is there evidence of the volunteer spirit being moribund, but the States have for years been unable to make an efficient showing with the militia, even with the generous assistance of the General Government in qualified instructors and supplies. It would seem that the self-reliance of the individual, like that of the States, had given way to dependence upon others. The fine volunteer spirit of the States' militia was injured in the demand for Federal pay in time of peace. It sounded the knell of patriotic military training for individuals and commercialized the highest duty that a State can demand from its people. We have fallen away from the teaching of the Fathers, for there is no longer instilled into our people the fundamental doctrine that every man owes a military as well as a civil obligation to his Government. . . .

"Comments on Compulsory Military Service," by Hugh Scott, from *War Department Annual Reports, 1916* (Washington, D.C.: Government Printing Office, 1917), Volume I, pages 155–162.

HUGH LENOX SCOTT (1853–1934) graduated from the U.S. Military Academy at West Point in 1876, after which he served in Indian campaigns. A student of Indian sign languages, he became a negotiator with various Indian tribes. He was chief of staff of the U.S. Army from 1914 to 1917 and, though retired for age in 1917, remained on active duty until 1919.

31

The Basic Purpose
and Objective of the
U.S. Selective Service System
by
Lewis B. Hershey

This highly controversial letter sent by General Hershey, then director of the Selective Service System, to all local selective service boards on October 26, 1967, calls their attention to actions that may be taken against Vietnam War protestors. It demonstrates clearly the ease with which conscription can be used for political ends, and with rare succinctness and candor presents a widely held view of military obligation.

Letter to all Members of the Selective Service System

The basic purpose and the objective of the Selective Service System is the survival of the United States. The principal means used to that end is the military obligation placed by law upon all males of specified age groups. The complexities of the means of assuring survival are recognized by the broad authority for deferment from military service in the National health, safety, or interest.

Important facts too often forgotten or ignored are that the military obligation for liable age groups is universal and that deferments are given only when they serve the National interest. It is obvious that any action that violates the Military Selective Service Act or the Regulations, or the related processes, cannot be in the National interest. It follows that those who violate them should be denied deferment in the National interest. It also follows that illegal activity which interferes with recruiting or causes refusal of duty in the military or naval forces could not by any stretch of the imagination be construed as being in support of the National interest.

The Selective Service System has always recognized that it was created to provide registrants for the Armed Forces, rather than to secure their punishment for disobedience of the Act and Regulations. There occasionally will be registrants, however, who will refuse to comply with their legal responsibilities, or who will fail to report as ordered, or refuse to be inducted. For these registrants, prosecution in the courts of the United States must follow with promptness and effectiveness. All members of the Selective Service System must give every possible assistance to every law enforcement agency and especially to United States Attorneys.

It is to be hoped that misguided registrants will recognize the long-range significance of accepting their obligations now, rather than hereafter regretting their actions performed under unfortunate influences of misdirected emotions, or possibly honest but wholly illegal advice, or even completely vicious efforts to cripple, if not to destroy, the unity vital to the existence of a nation and the preservation of the liberties of each of our citizens.

Demonstrations, when they become illegal, have produced and will continue to produce much evidence that relates to the basis for classification and in some instances, even to violation of the Act and Regulations. Any material of this nature received in National Headquarters or any other segment of the System should be sent to State Directors for forwarding to appropriate Local Boards for their consideration.

A Local Board, upon receipt of this information, may reopen the classification of the registrant, classify him anew, and if evidence of violation of the Act and Regulations is established, also declare the registrant to be a delinquent and process him accordingly. This should include all registrants with remaining liability up to 35 years of age.

If the United States Attorney should desire to prosecute before the Local Board has ordered the registrant for induction, full cooperation will be given him and developments in the case should be reported to the State Director and by him to National Headquarters.

Evidence received from any source indicating efforts by non-registrants to prevent induction or in any way interfere illegally with the operation of the Military Selective Service Act or with recruiting or its related processes, will be reported in as great detail as facts are available to State Headquarters and National Headquarters so that they may be made available to United States Attorneys.

Registrants presently in Classes IV-F or I-Y who have already been reported for delinquency, if they are found still to be delinquent, should again be ordered to report for physical examination to ascertain whether they may be acceptable in the light of current circumstances.

All elements of the Selective Service System are urged to expedite responsive classification and the processing of delinquents to the greatest possible extent consistent with sound procedure.

Extract from "The Basic Purpose and Objective of the U.S. Selective Service System," by Lewis B. Hershey, from *The Forensic Quarterly*, Volume 42, Numbers 1–3 (May 1968), pages 71–72. [Originally published in *Compulsory Service Systems: A Critical Discussion and Debate Source Book* (Columbia, Missouri: Artcraft Press, Publishers, 1968), the contents of which were also published, under the title *Compulsory Service Systems*, as the May 1968 issue of *The Forensic Quarterly*.] Copyright © 1968 The Forensic Quarterly. Reprinted by permission of *The Forensic Quarterly*.

LEWIS B. HERSHEY (1893–1977) was a general who began his military career in 1911 as a private in the Indiana National Guard. He subsequently served as assistant professor of military science and tactics at Ohio State University, as a member of the Joint Army and Navy Selective Service Commission, and as deputy director and, from 1941 to 1970, director of the Selective Service System. He administered the Selective Service and Training Act of 1940, mobilizing U.S. manpower in World War II, and eventually became a symbol of the draft.

32

Inequities in the Draft

by
Edward M. Kennedy

In this brief article Senator Kennedy states that an all-volunteer army is inherently inequitable because, under it, the bulk of enlistees are the economically disadvantaged. Kennedy, in opposing an all-volunteer military, further argues that voluntary systems exclude those who make the decisions to go to war from having to fight those wars. He advocates eliminating deferments and limiting the number of conscripts the president can call without the consent of Congress.

Although I share with many of my colleagues a deep and abiding respect for the concept of voluntarism in a democratic society, I cannot believe it should be raised above the demands of social justice. For that reason, I remain unalterably opposed to a volunteer army in wartime.

While Americans continue to die in Vietnam, Cambodia and Laos, the inequities inherent in a volunteer army far outweigh any of the benefits described by its promoters.

Adoption of the volunteer army proposal would mean that the economically disadvantaged would form the bulk of the entries into the armed forces under the inducement of higher pay. Even more repugnant is the special $3,000 bonus for combat service which would program most of these less affluent youths into the divisions where there is the highest risk of death.

Some dispute the argument that given the limited opportunities available in the private sector, we would be channeling the poor into the front lines to fight the battles based on decisions made by others in our society. Yet I would challenge any of the proponents of a volunteer army to travel to college campuses, as I have, to ask for volunteers. Nearly all raised their hands when I asked how many favored a volunteer army but there were almost none who kept their hands up when I asked: "Would you volunteer?"

If this nation repeals the draft today while men die in Indochina, it will be saying that the best option for the less affluent is front-line duty. I cannot believe this nation wants to rely upon such an inequitable policy when some citizens are being called upon to give their lives.

So it is that if we are to force some of our young men to fight the continuing war in Indochina, then the responsibility must be spread evenly throughout all sectors of the society. Failing that, we face the risk of muting the most articulate and the most resourceful voices in this land, voices that have proved vital in dissent and effective in causing some change in the direction of the war's escalation.

The wisdom of insulating middle and upper middle class men from the horrors of war by shifting the burden of the draft from their sons to those of the less affluent is open to serious question in a democracy.

On the other hand, in a nation at peace, the concept of a volunteer army can be considered without addressing the moral question of whether only certain segments of society are being called upon to risk their lives.

There is one element, however, in the all-volunteer plan that is vital to the future course of this nation's foreign policy deliberations. The Goldwater-Hatfield legislation would require the President to come to the Congress to request a reinstatement of the draft. By so doing, it reasserts the constitutional responsibility of Congress to raise the armies.

However, that goal can be just as effectively written into the draft law, as I have sought to do this year, by legislating a ceiling on the number of men the President can draft. I would place that limit at 150,000, which is less than any year since 1964. Any request for more men to be drafted would have to be ratified by Congressional action. In so doing, the President might request, but the Congress would decide.

But placing a ceiling on the draft would not remedy the defects of

the draft mechanism. Reform is needed. The bill which I have introduced seeks to end existing inequities.

First, it requires by statute that the random selection system be
operated on a national basis.

Second, the bill also would end current student deferments. The
present undergraduate college deferment permits too many to escape
the draft. It means that the university student may postpone induction until there is no Vietnam; but the mechanic must face the draft
immediately.

Third, there must be guarantees of due process, including the right
to personal appearances and legal counsel.

Fourth, the regulations and practices of the Selective Service system
must more accurately reflect the recent Supreme Court decisions on the
definition of conscientious objectors. Contrary to the assertion of Senator Goldwater that there has been an enormous increase since that decision, the proportion of C.O. deferments in the 1-A pool has risen by
less than a single percentage point.

Finally, by reorganizing the system and taking the classification
decision out of the hands of the 4,000 volunteer local boards, greater
uniformity can be assured.

These are the reforms that are needed to establish a draft system
that is fair and certain and just.

"Inequities in the Draft," by Edward M. Kennedy, from *The New York Times*, February 24, 1971, page 41. Copyright © 1971 by The New York Times Company. Reprinted by permission.

EDWARD MOORE KENNEDY (1932–) has served as U.S. senator from
Massachusetts since 1962 and is the author of *Decisions for a Decade*.

33

Doubts About
an All–Volunteer Army

by
Joseph A. Califano, Jr.
Reply by *Roger T. Kelley*
Rejoinder by *Joseph A. Califano, Jr.*

In this interchange between Joseph Califano and then Assistant Secretary of Defense Roger T. Kelley, Califano—one-time special assistant to Secretary of Defense McNamara—argues that abolition of the draft would greatly increase the cost of defense while disproportionately subjecting those at the bottom of the economic and social ladder to military service. In rebuttal, Kelley maintains that a living wage is an honorable attraction to all classes, not just to the economically disadvantaged; and that, in any case, it is superior to the coercion of the draft. Califano, in his cross-rebuttal, asserts that the billions of dollars that must be invested in "volunteer mercenaries" are too high a price to pay. And he fears that when we remove the middle class "from even the threat of conscription, we remove perhaps the greatest inhibition on a President's decision to wage war."

The President has proposed a budget outlay of $268.7 billion for fiscal 1974 with receipts of $256 billion for a deficit of $12.7 billion, and he has warned that if the Congress appropriates more money than he asks for he will try to impound it. If that fails he will spend it and blame any tax increase on the Democrats. The Democrats are thus being neatly boxed in to support a spending ceiling to exculpate themselves from the blame for any tax boost. The political virtuosity of the President's performance can best be appreciated in light of the economic reality that such an increase seems inevitable during his second term.

Lost in constitutional rhetoric and political bickering between the Hill and the White House may be the hope of any serious debate about some of the real choices that have quietly been made in the fiscal 1974 budget. Foremost among these is the decision to achieve an all-volunteer force through pay rates high enough to attract sufficient manpower.

An all-volunteer military is a very expensive proposition, since raising pay at the bottom requires increases in higher ranks and in retired pay as well. As in the case of so many weapons systems the Pentagon has already confronted a cost overrun: the 1974 budget outlays projected for an all-volunteer force are about four times the original estimate for a military manpower force of comparable size.

Three years ago the President's Commission on an All-Volunteer Force, chaired by former Defense Secretary Thomas Gates, estimated that:

★ To attract an all-volunteer force of two million men the nation would have to pay $1.5 billion per year more than it was then paying.

★ To attract 2.5 million men would cost $2.1 billion more.

★ To attract three million men would cost $4.6 billion more.

★ The projected 20 percent increase in manpower from 2.5 to three million men required more than a 100 percent increase in cost to the nation: from $2.1 billion to $4.6 billion a year. But the cost of achieving an all-volunteer force in fiscal 1974 far exceeds estimates in the Gates report.

The fiscal 1974 budget Nixon sent to the Congress carefully avoids telling us precisely what the taxpayer will have to put out for the all-volunteer force; it nevertheless contains some interesting figures. The defense budget shows an increase of $5.4 billion over fiscal 1973—from $76.4 billion to $81.8 billion. This increase, the budget message tells us, is "primarily as the result of an additional $4.1 billion required to maintain military and civilian pay levels comparable to those in the private sector, to raise pay and benefit levels sufficient to achieve an all-volunteer force, to meet normal price increases, and to pay for higher military retirement annuities." The detailed manpower cost explanations are more revealing:

★ The proportion of the defense budget devoted to manpower costs in all-volunteer force fiscal 1974 will be 56 percent; in fiscal 1968, the proportion for the combined draft and volunteer force was 42 percent.

★ In 1968 manpower costs were $32.6 billion; in 1974 they will be $43.9 billion.

★ In 1968 the end strength of the armed forces was 3,547,000 men and women; in 1974 it will be 2,233,000.

Thus we will pay an additional $12.3 billion for a military manpower force reduced by 1,314,000 men and women. Put another way an all-volunteer force 37 percent smaller than a combined volunteer and draft force will cost over 30 percent more. True, some of the $12.3 billion will go to higher retirement pay, but that increase is required to bring current retirement pay in line with new pay levels needed to attract the volunteers.

Thus even with a generous allotment for inflation, the nation will be spending some six billion dollars more in fiscal 1974 for only two-thirds of the number of soldiers, sailors, marines and airmen that it had on active duty in 1968. This is some 300 percent more than the amount estimated in 1971 as the cost of an all-volunteer force of this size by the President's Commission on an All-Volunteer Force. That new six billion dollar investment is more than twice the amount committed to the Office of Economic Opportunity in the peak anti-poverty war years of Lyndon Johnson.

By design and incentive an all-volunteer army is structured to bring into the armed forces the poor and near poor and to free of even the danger of military service the middle- and upper-middle-class young. The draft never achieved perfect egalitarianism in distributing the burdens of military service, but at least it made the attempt. The all-volunteer concept—and the investment of billions to make it a reality—is consistent with the overall thrust of the administration's budget for fiscal 1974: a budget designed to appeal to the more affluent majority. It legislates into government policy the Civil War practice of having the better-off hire the worse-off to serve their time in the military. In effect with the all-volunteer army we write into law the concept of one man's money for another man's blood. This six billion dollar investment strikes a harmonious chord in a budget that also eliminates 100 programs for the disadvantaged and protects the present tax structure and distribution of wealth. The concept strikes a perfect note on a scale of human values that protects the haves.

It is appalling that so many antiwar congressmen have climbed and stayed on the volunteer army bandwagon. Many have done so because of their revulsion at the Vietnam war and because they can rationalize the concept as providing that only those who "volunteer" will have to go to war.

This is a gross misreading of one of the central historical lessons of the war in Southeast Asia. What turned this nation around on Vietnam was not demonstrations in the street or the demagogic rhetoric of Dellinger, Hayden and Spock. It was, in quite readable political terms to the Presidents who agonized over Vietnam, the realization that the vast middle class of America would not permit *their* sons to die in a war which they considered meaningless. It was middle- and upper-class Americans who know how to contact congressmen, influence their local communities—and most all of whom vote and know finance campaigns—who posed the sharp dilemma to Washington: get out of Vietnam or get out of office. An all-volunteer force that subjects only the ones at the bottom to military service will effectively reduce the need for future leaders to be concerned about the more affluent majority of America and its judgments about foreign adventures, at least until those adventures are so far along that they will be virtually impossible to stop. It is no accident that the ardor of the campus antiwar movement cooled in lock step with the reduction of the draft and ended with the advent of the all-volunteer force.

It is ironic that those who express such concern about the debilitating impact of welfare on the will to work can so enthusiastically accelerate the erosion of the American will to sacrifice and pander to the protective cocoons in which the affluent already live. But it is truly Kafkaesque thinking for public officials who call themselves liberals to support this six billion dollar investment of scarce public sector resources so the lower class can fight our wars.

If we think history will read this concept of paid military service as a step forward in national development then we had better review the ABCs of the Roman and Greek empires, of German mercenaries and of the French Foreign Legion. The long-term maintenance of an all-volunteer force of two million or more paid mercenaries fighting our wars is no more likely to provide the sense of common commitment necessary for national cohesion than it is likely to build the personal character of the affluent teenagers in suburban America whose daddies' dollars and influence have bought their way out of military service. Perhaps most unfortunate is that the investment in this new human weapons system is being made as quietly as so many other investments in material weapons systems have been made over the past few years.

Reply by Roger T. Kelley

Sirs:

Your March 3 edition included an article by Mr. Joseph Califano ("Doubts about an All-Volunteer Army") replete with errors and false charges about the all-volunteer force. As the Defense official closest to that program for the past four years, I want to set the record straight.

Chief among Mr. Califano's charges are 1) the all-volunteer force is "a very expensive proposition" and among the "choices that have been quietly made in the fiscal 1974 budget," and 2) "an all-volunteer army is structured to bring into the armed forces the poor and near-poor . . ."

I am confident that the informed public's own experience discredits the claim that the all-volunteer force was a choice "quietly made in the fiscal 1974 budget." Mr. Nixon, while campaigning for President in 1968, announced his firm intention to end the draft and move to a peacetime all-volunteer force. The goal and the related volunteer activities have been reported almost continuously since the Gates Commission was convened by the President in 1969. These are facts well known to Congress, the news media and the general public.

The simple cost and related pay facts are these: For 13 years, 1952 to 1964, military first termers received *no* pay increases—a period in which virtually every wage and salary earner in our society received at least annual pay adjustments. Until their pay hike of November 1971, the total compensation of military first termers—basic pay plus allowances—was $600 a year less than the federal minimum wage!

The big amount invested in military pay in the past two years was in fact fair and equitable catch-up, due the military members. Would Mr. Califano have avoided these expenditures in pay, thus making the poor poorer?

Our nation was still drafting men into military service when the big pay increase occurred, and it seemed unconscionable to the Nixon administration to continue drafting men into depressed levels of pay. To do so would have been, as pointed out by the Gates Commission in its report, an insidious and burdensome tax on the military member.

Mr. Califano's claim that the all-volunteer system is designed to attract "the poor and the near-poor" is baseless. Since when has a living wage become a lure to attract only the poor? Entry into the armed forces is on the basis of meeting physical, mental and moral standards.

It doesn't matter how rich or poor a candidate is. If a young person who is poor qualifies for the armed forces, and is thus relieved of his poverty, so much the better for the nation and for him.

The all-volunteer force is attracting a typical cross-cut of Main Street, USA—rich, poor and middle class. Seventy-five percent of the entries have high school or better educations. Eighteen percent are racial minorities, which is virtually their proportion of the national population. The number of new volunteer entries during the past year—over 400,000—and their varied backgrounds belie the charge that they are, by plan, dominated by the "poor and near poor."

Finally if Mr. Califano would reject the all-volunteer force, what would he substitute in its place—the draft? For this nation to draft its young citizens is an important policy action, justified only if our national defense requires it. The alternative—voluntary enlistment—is working well. It has been demonstrated that we don't need the draft to meet our peacetime military requirements.

The draft has ended and we have achieved the all-volunteer force. It is a better military organization than its draft-heavy predecessor of four years ago. Mr. Califano may prefer the draft, but he shouldn't attempt to discredit this historic achievement by spinning "rich man–poor man" yarns that are unsupported by the facts.

ROGER T. KELLEY
ASSISTANT SECRETARY OF DEFENSE

Rejoinder by Joseph A. Califano, Jr.

By the administration's own figures, the fiscal 1968 manpower costs for roughly a 3.5 million-man armed force totaled $32.6 billion; fiscal 1974 costs for a force of roughly 2.2 million men are estimated at $43.9 billion. This represents a difference of $11.3 billion (inadvertently misstated as $12.3 billion in my March 3 article)—a 30 percent dollar increase for an all-volunteer force in fiscal 1974, some 37 percent smaller than a combined volunteer and draft force in fiscal 1968. In my judgment, half the difference, or $5.65 billion, is roughly the incremental cost of the all-volunteer force.

While Mr. Kelley gives no cost figures in his letter, in his press conference on March 23, he estimated the fiscal 1974 incremental cost for the all-volunteer force at $3.1 billion (a figure, incidentally, some $1 billion less than the $4 billion incremental cost used in the Office of Systems Analysis in the Pentagon). I believe the $3.1 billion figure to be decidedly on the low side in terms of fiscal 1974. Moreover maintaining an all-volunteer force of the same size will clearly be more expensive in later years, not simply because of inflation, but also because the fiscal 1974 costs are computed in an environment of sharp reduction in the number of men in the armed forces, an increase in 31,000 civilians to take over military jobs and an increase in the number of women from 31,500 in fiscal 1972 to 53,600 in fiscal 1974 to take over military jobs. But whether the cost is closer to $3.1 billion or $5.65 billion, it is still too much to invest in volunteer mercenaries at this stage of our history.

The "quiet decision" point in my March 23 article was not intended to imply that the all-volunteer army concept was announced with a muted trumpet. What was orchestrated in such muted tones was the *cost* of achieving an all-volunteer force; what has been missing from our national life been a serious and, if you will, noisy public debate over whether those extra billions—$3.10 or $5.65—are better spent creating a force of military mercenaries or on our domestic needs.

In his press conference of March 23, as reported in *The Washington Star-News*, Mr. Kelley rejected as "irrelevant" and as a matter that "doesn't concern me" whether the all-volunteer force concept will "attract people from the lower economic range" to wage war for the rest of us. In his letter Mr. Kelley appears to back off from this position, asserting that the all-volunteer force is attracting "a typical crosscut of main street USA—rich, poor and middle class," and that "75 percent of the entries have high school or better educations." The assertions are somewhat contradictory to the March 1973 special report of Secretary of Defense Elliot Richardson on the all-volunteer force. In that report Secretary Richardson expresses concern at "a sharp decline in the percentage of high school graduates among Army enlistees" and notes that "the overall percentage of high school graduates among enlistees for all of the Armed Services dropped from 71 percent in [fiscal] 1972 to 63 percent in the first half of [fiscal] 1973." In the army, where the tough, dangerous, dirty work of fighting ground wars is done, the percentage of high school graduates among enlistees dropped from 70 percent in fiscal 1972 to 52 percent in the first half of fiscal 1973. High school graduates are particularly important for the armed services not simply because they have, in the words of Secretary Richardson's special report, "consistently performed better in their military jobs," but because such graduates "have had fewer disciplinary problems than those who have not graduated." The comments of the secretary of defense are consistent with the analysis of the all-volunteer force by Morris Janowitz in the March 1973 *Annals of the American Academy of Political and Social Science*. There Janowitz concludes that "progress toward numerical quotas in part is the result of compromises in quality."

Finally Mr. Kelley ignores the central points of the case against an all-volunteer force. There is no question but that recruitment for an all-volunteer force levels its appeal at the mercenary instinct of the potential enlistee; the special report of the secretary of defense is full of financial goodies to attract them, up to a request in the $225 million Special Pay Act for "authority to pay up to $15,000 to an individual during critical retention years." Aside from the offense that a mercenary force of this kind commits against the concept of social justice in a democracy, among its potent political impacts will be to remove the need for the President to have any concern about drafting middle- and upper-class Americans before he decides to embark upon bellicose adventures around the world. It is my profound belief that every reasonable inhibition should be placed upon those who have the power to make the decisions of war and peace in the 1970s and that a critical defect in the proposal for the volunteer army is that it could make it too cheap and easy for national leaders to make the initial decision to wage a war. As we all know, it is from that initial decision of one or a few men that it is so difficult for subsequent leaders and an entire nation to retreat. By removing the middle class from even the threat of conscription, we remove perhaps the greatest inhibition on a President's decision to wage war, at a time when the *de facto* constitutional power and logistic capabilities of Presidents to station US forces in any part of the world and intervene in any war is markedly greater than at any time in our history.

At the policy-making level, civilian control of the military is no easier than civilian control of the civilian bureaucracy or mayoral control of a local police force. As powerful and well connected as the military establishment is in corporate and congressional America, there is at least the continuing check of turnover in both the officer and enlisted corps of scores of thousands of men who enter and leave the military each year and make their career in civilian professions. What, for an extreme but true example, would the chance have been of exposing the Mylai massacre if the only Americans present had been soldiers who were totally dependent upon the army for their active career and their retirement pay? The congressional seniority system, the steel industry and some labor unions bear eloquent witness to the dangers of excessively sustained professional parochialism.

Moreover from the point of view of a military increasingly (and too often unfairly) suspect by the civilian establishment and the most educated classes in our nation, it would seem important to continue to have a constant flow of young draftees and temporary reserve officers from military life to civilian life. In that way, the military has in the civilian society a number of citizens who have experienced military life, understand it and more frequently than not support the military establishment.

Mr. Kelley asks what I would substitute for the volunteer army—"the draft?" My response is a resounding yes—I would rather draft a broad cross-section of society to defend our national security than be totally dependent on "paid mercenaries" for that task. I might in turn ask Mr. Kelley: What are we to say of a society that can no longer inspire its young men to serve in its armed forces or fight for its national security policies? Not simply (I hope) that it is fortunate that we have enough money to buy mercenary volunteers.

What is of such profound concern to me is that so many of our national leaders on both sides of the aisle so wholeheartedly support this move to ease the burden of the affluent and thus make it easier politically to engage in military adventures abroad at a time when our nation desperately needs a real measure of inspired sacrifice at home and the strictest inhibitions of further military adventures in far-off lands. Whether the cost is $3.1 billion, as Mr. Kelley contends, the $5.65 billion that I contend, or some billions in between, I am one citizen who would rather distribute the burden of military service equally across the social, educational and economic classes of our nation and use the special bonuses Mr. Kelley offers to potential military mercenaries to assist the disadvantaged of our society.

JOSEPH A. CALIFANO, JR.

"Doubts About an All-Volunteer Army," by Joseph A. Califano, Jr., from *The New Republic*, Volume 168, Number 9 (March 3, 1973), pages 9–11; with reply by Roger T. Kelley and rejoinder by Joseph A. Califano, Jr., from *The New Republic*, Volume 168, Number 16 (April 21, 1973), pages 30–32. Reprinted by permission of *The New Republic*, Copyright © 1973, The New Republic, Inc.

JOSEPH A. CALIFANO, JR. (1931–) received his law degree from Harvard University and has served in a number of capacities in government, including general counsel for the Department of the Army, special assistant to Secretary of Defense McNamara, special assistant to President

Johnson for domestic affairs, and secretary of the Department of Health, Education, and Welfare.

ROGER T. KELLEY (1919–) received his graduate education in business administration from Harvard University and served as assistant secretary of defense for manpower and reserve affairs from 1969 to 1973. He is currently vice-president of the Caterpillar Tractor Company, where he has held executive positions since 1946.

34

We Must Suspend
Many Rights and Privileges
by
James W. Wadsworth

One of the earliest congressional proponents of national service, former Congressman Wadsworth delivered this plea during World War II to impress men into industrial as well as military service. He claims there is no fundamental distinction between conscripting some men to serve in the front lines and conscripting others to manufacture the goods they need to fight.

We have proceeded a certain distance along toward mobilization [thus far in World War II]. To a very large degree we have mobilized industry. The Congress of the United States has placed it within the power of the Federal Government by statutes duly enacted to take over any industrial plant in America and operate it in the war effort. The government, in accordance with laws passed by the Congress, may step up to any employer or owner of a plant and say, "You must proceed to make a certain type of supply." That owner must do it lest the government take over the management and operation of the plant.

By laws enacted by the Congress, every contract made by an employer who is furnishing supplies to the government may be and is renegotiated, with the government the complete master of the final decision.

In accordance with an act of the Congress, the wages and salaries of every person employed in a plant from top to bottom may be and are fixed by executive order based upon law. Our tax laws, also enacted by the Congress, are devised, and I think correctly, to reduce profits to a minimum. The excess profits taxes on corporate incomes run as high as 90 per cent and correspondingly high on individual incomes. In other words, by the laws of the land, industry has been mobilized. We have not yet, however, by the process of any law whatsoever mobilized manpower. . . .

In some of the steps taken in the last two or three months in the direction of mobilizing manpower . . . the element of compulsion is present. I refer, for example, to the Work or Fight Order, directed to men between 18 and 38 years of age, registered in the draft, with the clear intimation that if those men did not immediately or by April 1— and they are given leeway until May 1—find jobs in essential industry, they may be reclassified under the draft and put into the army or the navy. That is the threat. There is your element of compulsion. I think I can say to you that when the Congress passed the Selective Service Law it never expected or intended that that law should be used as a club to drive a citizen from one place to another.

And the recent order, well intended—I am not criticizing the intention of these steps—to the effect that no man may leave his job in an essential industry to take another job at a higher pay lest he be subjected to fine or imprisonment or both, cannot be found in any statute of the United States. It rests presumably upon the Stabilization Act of October 1942, but in that act the Congress authorized the government to freeze prices of commodities, salaries, and wages—not men, they are not mentioned.

So I think it well to dispel the idea that we are proceeding solely in the voluntary spirit. I can mention some other orders because the element of compulsion, the implied threat, the indirect pressure, is back of nearly all of them.

We are the only great nation engaged in this war that is not completely mobilized . . . as to industry and manpower. Great Britain is completely mobilized, so is Australia, so is New Zealand, and, heaven knows, they are liberty-loving countries just as we are. Russia is completely mobilized. Every man and woman in Canada above the age of 16 is registered, and of course it goes without saying that our enemies are also completely mobilized. We alone stand halfway along this road. . . .

You have heard, of course, of the great pool of workers engaged in nonessential industries, men and women, upon which we must draw if we are to meet the demands of 1943–1944. The trouble is . . . that thousands and thousands of men and women anxious to work, anxious to help their country, don't know where to go or how to get there, and if they do find their way to the place, they don't know where they are going to live. There is no law on the subject whatsoever. The War Manpower Commission cannot today, for example, pay the traveling expenses of a person who moves from one community to another to take a war job. The War Manpower Commission has no power under the law today to see to it that proper housing awaits that person. The War Manpower Commission has no power, direct or implied, in the existing statutes, to assure that person that when the emergency is over he may return to his former employment and recover it. Not a word in any law we have! And unless my investigations are completely wrong, I find that the great deterrent standing in the way today of the recruiting of war workers from the nonessential industries is that atmosphere of complete uncertainty. They don't know.

More than that, many of them will tell you, as they have told me, "Yes, I am willing to go, leaving my nonessential job, into an essential job, if everybody else like me is treated the same way." There is no equality of obligation suggested by law to the people of the United States, none whatsoever.

It is a little disturbing to look ahead and measure this thing, if we can do so. It was not a pleasant thing to have Admiral [Emory S.] Land [U.S. Maritime Commission Chairman] come before the Military Affairs Committee of the House the other day and state that in the first quarter of the year 1943 he was short 70,000 men in the shipyards and couldn't get them. He will need another 150,000 before the year 1943 is over. "Yes," he admitted, "we broke all shipbuilding records in 1942, have never known anything like it, 8.2 million tons of ships, but the program for 1943 is almost 19 million tons of ships," and his great danger is that he can't find the men to do it, and there is no adequate machinery to produce them in orderly fashion.

The thing I have pleaded for from the beginning of this discussion is the orderly distribution of workers, systematic, and we can use to a very large degree the volunteer spirit.

Let me say a word about [the proposed Austin-Wadsworth] . . . bill. In its first section it sets forth a fundamental principle, to the effect that every civilian adult in the United States otherwise competent and with certain liberal exemptions owes it as a duty to serve in a civilian capacity where he or she is most needed in support of the armed forces and the winning of the war.

That declaration of principle runs exactly parallel to the declaration of principle contained in the draft law, which says, in effect, that every man of military age otherwise competent and not needed in a more important undertaking owes it as a duty to serve in the armed forces of the United States. There is no difference, whatsoever, my friends, between those two declarations of principle, and both are democratic, absolutely in accord with the democratic spirit. . . .

Many steps have been taken in an endeavor to cure the situation. I call to mind the condition in the copper mines. Copper is a very critical material, as you all know. We are falling down in the production of copper. There isn't any doubt about it. It is conceded we need more of it. Is it because we haven't enough copper in the ground? No, it is because we haven't got enough men mining the copper, and in a desperate endeavor to get miners for copper mines, the government, through the exercise of some mysterious power—where it comes from I do not know—ordered the closing down of all gold mines in the belief that gold miners would go to the copper mines. It just didn't happen, and we are still short of copper.

There is another side of this problem with which I come into very intimate contact, and that is the shortage of labor on the farms. The figures show that 60 per cent of all the men drained away from the land have gone to industry and 40 per cent to the armed forces. It is a curious thing that a country like the United States should be threatened as we hear with a food shortage; that is rather dismaying, disconcerting, to say the least. By comparison, you look across the ocean to England where complete mobilization of manpower has been achieved for three years, and we find that the British have so succeeded in the orderly distribution of workers in industry, in the services, and on the land, that England has increased her food production in the last three years by 50 per cent, and ours is threatening to go down by comparison. . . .

We are fighting to save ourselves from involuntary servitude. If we lose, we shall have it. We ought to employ everything we can muster to save our freedom, yes, suspend many of our rights, many of our privileges, even suspend some of our traditions, if you please, while this great war is on, but in suspending them, be conscious of the fact that when we have won it we recover them all and can live in safety and our children and our grandchildren can live in safety. It isn't involuntary servitude that we propose, nothing like it.

Is there any difference between tapping a young man on the shoulder and telling him, "Put on a uniform and go to New Guinea or North Africa and perhaps die" and tapping another civilian on the shoulder and saying, "You are needed in that factory; you will be well paid while you are there, but you are needed there to help that man in North Africa"? Surely we cannot distinguish between those two things.

"We Must Suspend Many Rights and Privileges," address delivered by James W. Wadsworth before the Chamber of Commerce of the United States, April 27, 1943. From *Vital Speeches of the Day*, Volume 9 (June 1, 1943), pages 508–510. Reprinted by permission of the publisher.

JAMES WOLCOTT WADSWORTH (1877–1952) was educated at Yale University and fought in the Spanish-American War as a volunteer. As U.S. senator (1915–1927) he sponsored the National Defense Act of 1920, and as U.S. representative (from 1933) he sponsored the Selective Service and Training Act of 1940.

35

Department of Defense
Report on Study of the Draft, 1966
by
Thomas D. Morris

Thomas D. Morris, as assistant secretary of defense for manpower procurement, presented this statement before the House Committee on Armed Services on June 30, 1966. Summarizing a Department of Defense study on the draft, he concludes that conscription is indispensable for maintaining adequate troop numbers and quality at a reasonable cost.

In April 1964 a comprehensive study of the present draft system was undertaken by the Department of Defense. A major objective of the study was to assess the possibility of meeting our military manpower requirements on an entirely voluntary basis in the coming decade. The basic conclusions of this study were contained in Secretary McNamara's posture statement to the Congress early this year. We have now brought the analyses upon which the study was based up to date, and find that experience in recent months confirms in all respects our earlier findings and conclusions.

At the outset, I would like to stress that it has been, and is, our firm policy to meet a maximum of our requirements through voluntary enlistments, and that we depend upon the draft only for the residual number of people required from month to month. There are many reasons for this. Reliance upon volunteers to the greatest extent possible in peacetime is in accord with the American tradition. The volunteer, moreover, serves initially one or two years longer than the draftee, and is more likely to seek a military career.

To encourage and facilitate voluntary enlistments, the Military Services maintain a substantial recruiting organization; currently there are more than 3,000 recruiting stations throughout the United States, manned by 7,000 recruiters. The Navy, Marine Corps, and Air Force have—with limited exceptions—depended entirely upon volunteers. The Army, in most recent years, has obtained over half of its personnel through enlistments and its enlistment totals have exceeded those of any other Service.

Nonetheless, our studies fully confirm the essentiality of the draft, both to supply the residual number of men needed to man our forces, and to encourage a larger number of volunteers.

In this statement I will review five questions which have been considered:

1. What has been our experience with the Selective Service System since passage of the Act in 1948?

2. What are the problems in the Selective Service process?

3. Can foreseeable manpower requirements be met without the draft under present military manpower policies?

4. If not, would improvements in pay and other manpower practices enable us to sustain an all-volunteer force?

5. Finally, if the draft must be continued, are there ways of improving the process of choosing those men who must serve in uniform?

Scope of Study

Before outlining our answers to these five questions, I would like to indicate the comprehensive basis for our studies. Altogether, these studies have assessed the experience and attitudes of several hundred thousand men. They were conducted by the Military Departments, by the Bureau of Census, by the Departments of Labor and Health, Education, and Welfare, and by the Selective Service System.

— Selective Service reviewed the records of 288,000 registrants as of July 1964 to obtain information, for each age class, on those who had served and those who had not.
— The Military Departments obtained information on the attitudes of 102,000 men on active duty and 46,000 Ready Reservists, in order to determine their reasons for entering the Service, including the influence of the draft.
— The Bureau of Census made a nationwide survey of both non-veterans and veterans, ages 16–34 in 35,000 households, to determine their military service plans, experience, and attitudes, with particular reference to the draft.
— Finally, the Labor Department and the Public Health Service assisted us in special studies. The Labor Department surveyed over 2,700 employment and training officials in industry, colleges, and public employment offices, to determine the effect of the draft on employment and training opportunities of draft-liable young men. The Public Health Service assisted us in evaluating the special problems of medical manpower supply and requirements.

[Examination of Five Basic Questions]

I. What Has Been Our Experience With Selective Service?

Between September 1950 and June 1966, 188 draft calls were placed with the Selective Service System—one in every month except May and June 1961. During this period, 11.3 million men have entered or been called to active service as enlisted men, of whom 3.5 million—nearly one in three—were draftees. This has meant an average monthly rate of inductions of about 18,600.

The draft has proven to be a very flexible tool during the past 16 years [see Table 35.1]. It has adjusted rapidly to widely varying annual requirements. In 1953, it was called upon to supply 564,000 men (59% of new entrants), while in 1961 draft requirements dropped to 60,000 (14% of new entrants). In the past 12 months (FY 1966) it has been necessary to issue draft calls for 334,500 men in spite of a record volume of new enlistments. These requirements have been met promptly.

Clearly, there is no question about the success of the draft in meeting military manpower requirements, nor can there be any reasonable doubt as to the need for the draft in the present period.

A principal problem affecting the operation of the draft system in the past has been the growing supply of draft-age men in relation to military requirements. A decade ago, only 1,150,000 men were reaching age 18. In 1965, the number of 18-year-olds had increased by 50% to more than 1,700,000. This trend will continue into the coming decade; by 1974, the number of men reaching draft age will total more than 2,100,000—over 80% above the 1955 level. [See Table 35.2].

As a consequence of this trend, a steadily decreasing percentage of the Nation's manpower in the draft ages 19 through 25 has been called on to serve, and this trend may continue downward in the future. . . . In 1958 70% of men reaching age 26 had seen military service; in 1962

TABLE 35.1

ENLISTED PERSONNEL ENTRIES BY MAJOR SOURCE, FY 1948–1966[1]
(Numbers in Thousands)

	Total	Enlistees[2]	Draftees	Reserve Recalls	Percent Draftees
1948	281	281	—	—	—
1949	398	368	30	—	7.5%
1950	182	182	—	—	—
1951	1,826	630	587	609	32.1
1952	991	532	379	80	38.2
1953	961	397	564	—	58.7
1954	647	382	265	—	41.0
1955	695	480	215	—	30.9
1956	583	446	137	—	23.5
1957	576	396	180	—	31.3
1958	453	327	126	—	27.8
1959	451	340	111	—	24.6
1960	439	349	90	—	20.5
1961	446	386	60	—	13.5
1962	715	409	158	148	22.1
1963	447	373	74	—	16.6
1964	527	376	151	—	28.7
1965	454	351	103	—	22.7
1966[3]	933	598	335	—	35.9

[1] Excluding reenlistments.

[2] Includes male regular enlistments, other than prior service, and enlisted reservists voluntarily entering active duty tours of two years or more.

[3] Estimated.

58% of those reaching age 26 had served; today the figure is about 46%. By 1974, at pre-Vietnam force levels, only 34% of those reaching age 26 will be required to serve. If the current 3 million strength level were sustained in the future, the percentage serving would decline to 42%.

One consequence of the growing imbalance in supply versus requirements in the past decade was a trend towards more liberal deferment policies. These actions were based on the objective of providing the armed services with fully qualified men, while minimizing disruption to the careers of as many men as possible when justified in the national health, safety, and interest. Recent high draft calls have made it necessary to reverse this trend, as discussed later in this statement.

To keep the Selective Service process responsive to local conditions and to minimize processing time, a high degree of decentralization is practiced. Classification of men, granting of deferments, and the issuance of induction orders are the responsibilities of over 4,000 local Draft Boards. The benefits of this decentralization have been well stated by the Director of Selective Service.

> No system of compulsory service could long endure without the support of the people. . . . The Selective Service System is, therefore, founded upon the grass roots principle, in which boards made up of citizens in each community determine when registrants should be made available for military service.

The examination of men under Department of Defense fitness standards is conducted by the 74 Armed Forces Examining and Entrance Stations, which are jointly staffed by all Military Services and administered by the Army. In order to assist the Selective Service System in meeting current high draft calls, the Department of Defense has made a strenuous effort to assure that its examination results are re-

TABLE 35.2

MEN REACHING AGE 18

(000's)

Year	Number	% Increase
1955	1,150	—
1960	1,330	16
1965	1,720	50
1970	1,930	68
1974	2,210	84

ported on a timely basis to the draft boards. As a result, the backlog of incomplete cases in the Armed Forces Examining and Entrance Station has dropped 32% in the past few months; and 85% of all completed cases are now handled in six days or less.

II. What Are the Problems in the Selective Service Process?

Criticisms of the Selective Service process in recent years have emphasized four principal points:

First, the present selection procedure calls the oldest men first—those who are most settled in their careers.

Second, past deferment rules have favored college men—those who may be the more fortunate economically.

Third, past deferment rules have favored married men without children—thus putting a premium on early marriages.

Fourth, Department of Defense standards in recent years have disqualified men with lesser mental ability and educational attainment—those who may have been culturally deprived.

We have examined each of these criticisms with the following findings.

A. The Present Selection Procedure Calls the Oldest Men First.

Present draft rules operate to lift the median age of involuntary inductees during times of a surplus in supply versus requirements; and this trend is sharply decreased during periods of high draft calls. During the past five years, the median age of draftees has ranged from a high of 23.7 in 1963 to today's low of 20.3.

The outlook for the next decade is again an upward trend in the median age, due to the growing supply of draft-liable men, particularly if military strengths return to the pre-Vietnam level.

This is the most undesirable feature of the present selection procedure, both from the military viewpoint and from the standpoint of the individual. Combat commanders prefer the younger age group, and about eight out of ten volunteers are in the age group under 20.

We have also ascertained that older draft-liable men face personal hardships. In our surveys, we found that:

— 39% of enlisted men who had originally entered service at ages 22–25 had been told by at least one prospective employer that they could not be hired because they might be drafted. College men had the greatest difficulty with restrictive hiring practices.

— 54% of this group reported some difficulty in their personal planning, prior to entering service, because of the uncertainty of their draft status.

B. Past Deferment Rules Have Favored College Men.

Our analysis of Selective Service records of men reaching age 26 as of June 1964 revealed that only 40% of the college graduates had served, compared to 60% of the college drop-outs, 57% of the high school graduates, and 50% of the non–high school graduates. Since nearly all physicians and some other officers enter service after age 26, the percentage of college graduates in this age class who will have served will be somewhat larger than 40%.

There are many reasons why past draft rules tended to favor the college graduate under the high draft ages in effect in the early 1960's. He has had more opportunity to reach age 26 without serving—by receiving an occupational deferment, by continuing graduate study, or by acquiring dependents. In fact, 11% of the 26-year-old college graduates had an occupational deferment as of June 30, 1964, compared to less than 1% of all other men who were age 26 on this date.

There are arguments, however, in favor of college student deferment. Present student deferment rules were originally developed in 1951, based on the views of leading educators and Federal policy makers, in order to provide an assured flow of college trained manpower, both for the civilian economy and for the Armed Services. The Military Departments, in fact, look to civilian colleges for 90% of their new officers. Under the much lower current draft age and the tighter deferment rules now in effect, the percentage of college graduates serving will be much higher than in the recent past.

C. Past Deferment Rules Have Favored Married Men Without Children.

In September 1963, when the median age of inductees reached a peak, it was decided that married men without children should be placed in an order of induction after single men, a procedure then tantamount to deferment. After two years of experience, it was found that men in the 20–21-year age group had accelerated their marriage plans, presumably because of this deferment incentive. Last summer, it became clear that continuation of the lower order of call for these men was not desirable, either from a manpower supply standpoint or in terms of social and equity considerations. An Executive Order was thus issued on August 26, 1965, providing that registrants married after that date would no longer be placed in a lower order of call.

Our experience with this deferment policy suggests that it should not be reinstituted in the future.

D. DOD Standards in Recent Years Have Disqualified Men with Lesser Mental Ability and Educational Attainment.

Department of Defense qualification standards are of three types: mental, physical, and moral. The latter two categories have been evolved over long years of experience and have not changed materially. We are engaged in a thoroughgoing review of these particular standards and their application.

The principal area of opportunity, however, lies in reassessing our mental standards, which have been increased substantially since 1958. The legal minimum requires that the new recruit pass the Armed Forces Qualification Test (AFQT) with a score in the 10th percentile or above (that is, in the upper 90% of the population tested). The law, however, permits the Secretary of Defense to raise these standards in peacetime.

The legal minimum standard was used from Korea until 1958, at which time permission to raise peacetime standards was granted by Congress. Between 1958 and 1963, standards were raised by adding the requirement for a passing score in three out of seven areas of an aptitude test battery given to those with low AFQT scores.

Last summer, a reexamination was begun to determine whether these standards were unnecessarily disqualifying men who, during the normal training cycle, could be made fully suitable by adequate "remedial" programs and acceptable "screening-out" procedures. Our examination led to revisions in standards which are now qualifying an additional 40,000 men annually. The first revision, made on November 1, 1965, provides that any high school graduate scoring in the 16th AFQT percentile or above will be accepted, regardless of his aptitude test scores. This revision was based on extensive research which showed that high school graduates, at any mental level, had a better performance record than non-high school graduates. The second revision, made on April 1, 1966, accepts an individual in the 16th percentile or above, who scores well in any two aptitude areas.

The results of these changes are being carefully scrutinized, and further revisions will be instituted if found feasible.

In order to accept men with lesser aptitudes in a sound manner, the Services have instituted remedial training programs and screening procedures to assure that only fully suitable men are retained. These safeguards are important not only under today's revised standards, but also for the future should the need arise to accept all men who meet the legal minimum. They will enable us to avoid many of the problems of discipline and marginal performance which were experienced during and after Korea.

In the future, we feel that a more comprehensive program of remedial education and physical rehabilitation should be conducted to qualify an even larger group of men. This program would accept men who have physical defects that can be remedied (with minor surgery, if required), or who need educational upgrading requiring up to three to six months beyond the basic training cycle. We believe that this is an investment we must make, both in the interest of broadening the pool from which manpower can be drawn, and to assure a more even distribution of the military obligation among our youth.

* * *

In the light of the problems described above, and the objective of the Department of Defense to draw to a maximum on volunteers, the next question examined by our study [concerned manpower requirements].

III. Can Foreseeable Manpower Requirements Be Met Without the Draft Under Present Manpower Policies?

While the draft has been called on to produce less than one-third of new enlisted entrants since 1950, it has long been apparent that the pressure of the draft has a decided influence on the decision of many of the remaining two-thirds who volunteer. To document this influence, a questionnaire survey was made of a representative sample of active duty and ready reserve personnel on their first tour, to determine the extent to which the draft influenced their decision to enter military service. The results [shown in Table 35.3] provide a significant measure of draft motivation.

Using these findings, we have estimated the probable numbers of men who could be expected to enlist voluntarily without the pressure of the draft, if no changes were made in pay or other incentives. These estimates allow for the expected growth in military-age population. Separate estimates were produced (1) under an unemployment level of 5.5%, the average for the ten years ending in 1965; and (2) under the current unemployment level of 4%. The findings clearly demonstrate that an all-volunteer force, under present policies, would fall far short of any force level which has been required since 1950.

A. New Enlisted Accessions Would Drop Sharply by 1970 Without the Draft.

After making full allowance for the increasing supply of men in the younger age classes, it is estimated that the annual volume of enlisted accessions would drop by 1970, [as shown in the tabulation below].

Unemployment Rate	Estimated Number of Volunteers
4.0%	235,000
5.5%	274,000

In comparison, the annual enlisted requirements for the active force between 1960 and 1965 (which were relatively low intake years) averaged 480,000. Hence, the annual all-volunteer enlisted flow would be only 50% to 60% of pre-Vietnam requirements. Officer accessions would also decline. Further, there would be an even larger drop in men volunteering for the reserve forces, where our questionnaire survey showed that only 29% would have volunteered in the absence of the draft.

B. As a Consequence, Force Levels Much Above the 2 Million Level Could Not Be Sustained in the 1970's.

It is projected that by 1973 the maximum all-volunteer force which could be sustained at a 4% unemployment rate would be about 2.0 million. At a 5.5% unemployment rate, the force level sustainable

TABLE 35.3

PERCENTAGE WHO WOULD NOT HAVE
VOLUNTEERED WITHOUT THE DRAFT

Group Queried	All Services	Army	Navy	Air Force	Marine Corps
Regular Enlistees	38%	43%	33%	43%	30%
Officers	41%	48%	40%	39%	27%
Reserve Enlistees (including National Guard)	71%	72%	75%	80%	50%

would be approximately 2.2 million. Contrasting these levels with the pre-Vietnam average of almost 2.7 million [shows that] a deficit of between 475,000 and 650,000 men might be experienced.

Even greater deficits would emerge in the reserve forces. For example, enlistments in the Army National Guard would shrink from an average level of 88,000 in 1964–65 to about 40,000 a year in the 1970's.

C. The Qualitative Deficits of Military Personnel Would Be Much More Severe Than Suggested by These Estimates.

In the absence of the draft, our surveys indicate that the sharpest reduction in voluntary enlistments would occur among individuals with above-average educational attainment and with higher-than-average scores on aptitude tests. These individuals are the major source of trainees for the many highly technical military occupational specialities.

These include such diverse skills as electronics maintenance technicians, missile repairmen, intelligence analysts, meteorological aides, and computer programmers—among many others. Increasing reliance upon sophisticated weapons systems and equipment has greatly increased the relative importance of these skills, and this trend will continue in the future.

Similar problems of specialist shortages would be encountered in officer procurement programs. The medical and dental corps would experience particularly severe shortages in view of the heavy reliance upon the draft in staffing these professional positions.

IV. Would Improvements in Pay and Other Manpower Practices Enable Us to Sustain an All-Volunteer Force?

Having found that elimination of the draft, with no new incentives, would make it impossible to sustain force levels of the size required during the past 16 years, we next examined the potentials for attracting a larger number of volunteers by (1) increasing pay, (2) offering more liberal educational and fringe benefits, and (3) replacing military with civilian employees.

To examine these opportunities, we requested the Bureau of Census to survey non-veterans, ages 16 to 34, to determine their attitude toward military service versus civilian employment and the factors they considered most important in choosing a job or career.

A. *The Cost of Sustaining an Adequate All-Volunteer Force Would Be Prohibitive.*

Surprisingly, responses of the 16–19-year-old group revealed that pay alone is a less potent factor than might be expected.

This group was asked: "If there were no draft, what condition would be most likely to get you to volunteer?" The responses revealed:

— That "equal pay" with civilian life was considered the most important inducement by less than 4%.

— That "considerably higher" pay than in civilian life was considered most important by only 17%.

These findings generally confirmed other analyses of enlistment rates versus wage levels in various sections of the United States. By relating the rate of voluntary enlistments, unemployment, and the differential between military and civilian pay by region, we were able to establish estimates of the additional payroll costs required to attract an all-volunteer force.

It was found that pay increases for officers during their first two years would have to be in the range of 20%–50% to attract an all-volunteer officer force. For enlisted personnel, much steeper increases would be needed:

Unemployment Rate	Range of Pay Increases Required
4.0%	110–280%
5.5%	80–180%

Translating these findings into dollars required to support a 2.7 million (pre-Vietnam) all-volunteer active force gave the following results:

Unemployment Rate	Range of Increased Payroll Costs
4.0%	$6–17 Billion
5.5%	$4–10 Billion

The above estimates make allowance for the offsetting savings which would later result from lower turnover and the higher career content of an all-volunteer force.

But these are not the total new costs which would be required. Still greater increases in the pay of reserve personnel would be needed, due to the very low volunteer response without the draft. While less precise analyses were made, it is estimated that at least an additional $1 billion would be required in order to attract an all-volunteer reserve force of present size.

In the medical field, it would be impracticable to induce 3,000 or more physicians annually—nearly 50% of those graduating each year—to voluntarily enter service through increased pay.

Finally, the above estimates are representative of the costs required to sustain the pre-Vietnam force level. To obtain increases above this level would necessitate greater-than-proportionate increases for each increment added to the force.

B. Improvement in Fringe Benefits Would Have Limited Effect as an Enlistment Inducement.

The Bureau of Census study of non-veterans requested the respondents to designate the factor "most important" in choosing a job or career. Fringe benefits placed eighth out of nine factors, with less than 3% ranking it most important. This bears out experience from other studies of the career motivation of young men, and confirms the view that leave, retirement, and medical and other such benefits are of primary importance to men already in service, particularly at career decision points.

Thus, while we must continue to press forward with improvements in such areas to improve morale and career retention rates, it is unlikely that these improvements will contribute significantly to attracting a larger number of volunteers.

The one possible exception to the above finding is in the field of educational benefits [as shown in Table 35.4].

The last named incentive is provided under the recently enacted "GI Bill of Rights." In respect to the first two, the Services are offering such training and educational incentives on an extensive scale, and those surveyed recognized that military service is superior to civilian careers in these respects. Thus, while further improvements should be made whenever possible, the opportunities to increase volunteers through such incentives cannot be counted on to overcome more than a small fraction of the deficit we would face without the draft.

C. Replacement of Military with Civilian Personnel Can Reduce Requirements, But Not Enough to Solve the Volunteer Deficit.

Early in our study, analyses were made of the opportunities for greater substitution of civilians in support-type jobs now performed by military personnel. As a result, plans were implemented in the fall of 1965 to release 74,300 military personnel for combat-type assignments by substituting 60,500 civilians. The elimination of 13,800 additional military jobs is accounted for primarily by a reduction in the number of trainees and related support jobs.

We are watching carefully the experience in this substitution program, and continuing to search for additional support-type jobs which might qualify for substitution. However, there are practical limitations on the extent to which civilian substitution is feasible due to the need:

— To provide billets for the training and development of military personnel in many specialties, such as logistics, required in combat theaters; and

— To provide rotational billets for military personnel returning from tours at sea and in overseas areas.

* * *

In summary, we find that it is theoretically possible to "buy" an all-volunteer force, at a cost ranging up to $17 billion (depending upon unemployment conditions in the nation). This is the cost to sustain pre-Vietnam force levels. Other policy changes and techniques to attract more volunteers do not appear collectively to offer the potential of meeting the deficit anticipated under an all-volunteer force. However, these techniques must be aggressively pursued to help us hold our competitive position in the labor market, under conditions of full employment, and to continue attracting more volunteers.

TABLE 35.4

PERCENTAGE WHO FELT THEY WOULD BE INDUCED TO VOLUNTEER, WITHOUT A DRAFT (16–19 YEARS OLD)

	Non-Students	Students
If guaranteed training in a job or skill useful in civilian life	29%	20%
If sent to school or college at Government expense, before or during military service	18%	31%
If sent to school or college at Government expense, after military service	8%	12%

V. Are There Ways of Improving the Process of Choosing Those Who Must Serve?

The final question considered in our studies was whether—given the continuing need for some form of conscription—there are better ways of choosing those who must serve.

One fact stands out as the key criterion for future improvements— that is, the need for concentrating military service among the younger age classes.

A nationwide poll, reported in late 1964, asked: "If you had a son who had to spend two years in a military service, at what age would you like him to begin his service?" The following responses were received:

Age	Percent
16–17	6%
18	48
19–20	20
21	18
22 or over	8

The desirability of service at a young age is fully confirmed by:
— The experience of military commanders, as discussed earlier.
— Less disruption of school plans, since it would permit men to fulfill their obligation after high school and before college (if they prefer). It would, likewise, offer the opportunity to more men to earn GI benefits before entering college.
— Less disruption to marriage plans. Fifty percent of men marry by age 22, and 70% by age 26.

By way of illustration, the following approach might be considered as a way of concentrating the major requirement for military service among a young age class, such as 19 or 20:
— All men would be classified, as at present by local boards. Present deferment rules would be continued in respect to student status, occupational status, dependency status, and ROTC and Reserve status.
— Inductions of men from the Class I-A available pool in any one year would be made from a priority category consisting in large part of the current 19- or 20-year olds.
— For those men preferring to complete their college education before serving, deferments could be granted until the student completed or

terminated his education. At that time, he would have equal exposure along with the 19- or 20-year olds of that year.

— The priority category—called after draft delinquents and volunteers for induction—would thus consist of: (1) available 19- or 20-year-olds, and (2) older men up to age 35, who become available for service in the current year after expiration of their student or other temporary deferments.

— Men not reached for induction by the end of the year would be placed at the bottom of next year's draft list, after men in the new class of 19- or 20-year-olds and the newly available ex-students.

The principal feature of a system such as that illustrated above is that it reverses the present policy of calling the oldest men first to one of calling young men either at age 19 or 20, or upon completion of school (if later).

It is, thus, our conclusion that the "young age class" system deserves thoroughgoing evaluation, in preparation for its application when military strengths stabilize at a level which would result in a renewed trend towards higher induction ages. Immediate introduction is not required in view of the low median age (20.3) which now exists.

Conclusions

The foregoing studies have led to five conclusions:

First, we cannot look forward to discontinuing the draft in the next decade unless changing world conditions reduce force levels substantially below those needed since Korea.

Second, increases in military compensation sufficient to attract an all-volunteer force cannot be justified. Nor would other incentives do more than help us hold our competitive position in the labor market under conditions of full employment.

Third, we should continue to maximize service by volunteers; to eliminate unnecessary requirements for military men where civilians can perform the task; and to perfect techniques of remedial training and physical rehabilitation so as to make military service available to every man who wishes it and is able to serve.

Fourth, with recent changes, the principle of deferments (on such grounds as dependency, student status, occupation, and unfitness) is basically sound. However, experience must be continuously monitored to assure broad participation among the various population groups.

Fifth, looking to the future, the draft selection system should be redesigned to concentrate military service among the younger age class—and older students when they leave school—when force levels are reduced and stabilized.

"Department of Defense Report on Study of the Draft, June 1966," by Thomas D. Morris, from *Dialogue on the Draft*, edited by June A. Willenz (Washington, D.C.: American Veterans Committee, 1967), pages 115–126.

THOMAS DALLUM MORRIS (1913–) has held a number of positions in the Department of Defense, including deputy assistant secretary for supply and logistics, assistant to the deputy secretary of defense (1956–1957), and assistant secretary for manpower (1967–1969). He was also assistant director for management and organization in the Bureau of the Budget (1959–1961). Since 1977 he has served as inspector general of the Department of Health and Human Services (until 1979 called the Department of Health, Education, and Welfare).

Part VIII

Conscription: Con

36

Conscription and Conscience
by
A. J. Muste

Arguing from the point of view of Christian morality, Muste makes a case for individual conscience as the final arbiter in decisions whether to comply with the draft, on the grounds that ultimate values are embodied in individuals, not in institutions or systems. He also counters a number of social welfare arguments then (at the height of World War II) being presented in favor of conscription.

The Case for Conscience

According to the Christian faith, ultimate values are incarnated in the individual human being, not in any institution or system. This does not mean that the individual exists apart from his fellows and from society. But it does mean that in the final analysis "the Sabbath was made for man and not man for the Sabbath." Economic and political institutions are human beings living together in certain relationships, and the relationships are mere words and abstractions apart from human personalities.

This does not mean that each human being is a law unto himself. It means rather that he is subject to a higher law, i.e., to the command of God. He cannot function as a responsible human being, he cannot therefore discharge his obligations to his fellow-men, unless he remains substantially free to order his own life, to make crucial decisions, to obey the voice of God as it comes to him. Each human being is a child of God, and therefore in himself of infinite worth, with his own distinctive contribution to make. He has direct access to the Inner Light and is responsible, therefore, for seeking the will of God. *He must obey his own conscience.* In order that it may be worthy of obedience, it must remain free, sensitive to the new light which is yet to break forth from God.

To Kill or Not to Kill?

Conscription is a basic evil because it robs the human being of this freedom to make his own decisions, to obey the voice of God as it leads him on. Specifically it does this with regard to the ultimate question as to whether or not he shall kill or be killed, be trained or not trained for organized killing. It was this that constituted the chief foundation of the famous "No Conscription Fellowship" in Great Britain during World War I. Clifford Allen, its president, said at its opening conference:

> Whatever else a State may or may not do, whatever infringement of individual liberty a State may or may not effect, there is one interference with individual judgment that no State in the world has any sanction to enforce—that is, to tamper with *the unfettered free right of every man to decide for himself the issue of life and death.* The individual conscience alone must decide whether or not a man will sacrifice his own life or inflict death upon other people in time of war. . . . The right of private judgment in this particular must be left to the individual, since human personality is a thing which must be held sacred.

In his address at the closing convention of the N.C.F., Clifford Allen returned to the same theme. War "involves actions that are so fundamental, and results that are so irreparable, that only the most passionate belief in the righteousness of a cause can justify a man in giving up his life or inflicting death. It is a fatal debasement of human dignity to force men to do these things against their will or without conviction as to the justice of their actions."

Having made for the individual by external compulsion the decision that he must submit to training for organized killing, conscription introduces the individual into, and holds him for a portion of his life, in a regime based on the principle of unquestioning obedience or conformity. The decision whether he is to engage in this form of killing or that; whether as the line-up among national powers shifts he is to regard a whole people as his enemies or his friends; whether he is to kill other soldiers or also civilians; whether after he has shared in the destruction of so many hundreds of thousands of human beings he shall call a halt or keep on; whether after a great city has been frightfully bombed nine times he shall or shall not join in a tenth expedition against it; whether he shall spare or not spare an enemy at a given moment; whether he shall lie or tell the truth, where the military fortunes of his own side are involved—all these decisions involving obviously the gravest moral issues and his own survival as a responsible moral being, a soul made in the image of God, are made for him by others, by the impersonal mechanism which has swallowed him up.

Does Conscription Reduce Hysteria?

The opinion is sometimes expressed that once war is decided upon, conscription is not only the most democratic way to provide for military and other national service, but the least open to objection even from the pacifist point of view because less flag-waving is necessary, individuals are not so likely to be "high-pressured" into enlistment by being called "yellow," and the public is generally less hysterical. There is no question that during the time when efforts are made to secure "volunteer" enlistments, there is tension in the community and "unpleasant incidents" occur. But this is simply the proof that war agencies are having a difficult time in inducing people to enlist "voluntarily" and that individuals are having a difficult time in making the fateful decision for or against participation in war. Painful as these things are, this is as it should be. The process of ethical decision and moral growth is in the nature of the case costly and painful. The fact that dictatorship works more "smoothly" than democracy is not necessarily and in every instance a reflection upon democracy. It simply means that democracy partakes of the nature of life and dictatorship of the nature of death. When a government by means of conscription and the other devices of indoctrination and regimentation which are available to it puts an end to discussion, dissent, and tension, and multitudes who are not inwardly deeply convinced are thus induced to acquiesce in war, that is not cause for rejoicing. Experience demonstrates, furthermore, that *the personal and social tension is not removed when conscription is enforced, but only suppressed, and that it will break forth in more destructive and painful forms for having been suppressed.* The psychiatric casualties of war, on the one hand, and the social upheavals marking the end of war and the collapse of totalitarian regimes, on the other hand, illustrate this point.

Does Conscription Develop Self-discipline?

It may be well to make one other observation of an elementary character in passing. People often justify conscription on the ground that none of us can have our own way; throughout life we are subject to restrictions of all kinds, we have to take account of other men and their desires and interests, and "anyway, discipline, having to do things you don't like to do, is good for you." It is true that both in the world of nature of which we are a part and in the world of human society to which we also belong, we are confronted with conditions with which we have to reckon, which provide us, as it were, with the raw materials out of which we must fashion our lives. But it is the very essence of rational and ethical living that the human mind and spirit should not be inert clay in the hands of the environment but that the elements in the environment should be the clay out of which men fashion life. When men are deprived of the freedom to react intelligently and of their own volition to the concrete situations that arise in a dynamic universe, they are robbed of that which makes them men and sons of God. So far as adults at any rate are concerned, the only discipline that produces results is that which is voluntarily accepted because the reason for it is understood. Forcing men to do things for which there is no reason they can understand and accept, is not discipline but tyranny and torture.

Does Conscription Benefit Youth?

Conscription of youth at an early age is especially reprehensible because it forces upon them an awful decision which they are not mature enough to face. In many cases their whole future life-attitude will be determined by the course which the State forces upon them. *At a critical period in their adolescence, at a most impressionable age, they are subjected to training based on an acceptance of militarism and on a philosophy of mechanical, unquestioning obedience which is bound to unfit them for responsible citizenship in a democracy.* One of our most severe and most generally accepted criticisms of the various totalitarian regimes has been precisely that they took children at an early age and indoctrinated them with ideas of war and the glories of the regimented life in which the individual does not count and the power of ethical decision is taken from him. Now many propose permanently to fasten this institution on the youth of the United States.

Does Conscription Level Social Barriers?

There are not a few educators and liberal-minded citizens like Mrs. Eleanor Roosevelt who have been advocating a year of "service to society," by which they mean the government or the State, by all young people. Many of them would prefer to have this service civilian in character but involving physical toughening, such as forestry, road building, perhaps nursing for women, and so on. One argument advanced which seems to have a strong attraction for a good many people is that young people have too much the idea that democracy is a matter of rights and not enough sense of obligation to society. Still another is that for a year at least this would throw people of all social rank together, would put the rich man's son on a level with the poor man's since both would be drafted and so would develop a spirit of fraternity among them.

All such proposals seem to me dangerous, even sinister in their implications. In the first place, it is most unlikely that in this era any such program will be adopted unless it is largely military in content and emphasis. If the war-minded should find it absolutely impossible to put over military training, they might settle temporarily for universal, compulsory civilian training as a first step toward their goal. In any event, the civilian aspect of such a program would be the sugar-coating by which the unwary were induced to accept what they dreaded and opposed. I doubt whether any thoughtful and reasonably informed person can believe that a military training program once adopted would, short of a revolution, be transformed into a genuinely civilian one. On the other hand, an ostensibly civilian one could easily be made increasingly military and militaristic.

In the second place, the argument that compulsory military training will level barriers between economic groups will not bear a moment's scrutiny. Has that been, save in isolated individual cases, the effect of conscription and militarization in the countries like Germany and France where these have been tried out most fully? Even in the armed forces, social and economic distinctions are maintained and even emphasized and intensified. *After conscript training men go back ordinarily into the circles out of which they came. Army and navy commands and officer groups become castes of their own, drawing most rigid caste distinctions.* When have men ever looked, except in brief moments of revolution, to armies for anything but preservation of the status quo or reaction?

So far as Negroes are concerned, since Jim Crow is the accepted pattern in the armed forces, the adoption of compulsory training is likely to mean that this pattern is further set and hardened.

Does Conscription Solve Unemployment?

Back of this talk about compulsory training, plain or sugar-coated, though some of its advocates may not be aware of this, is the idea that nations can no longer put their unemployed to work at normal, peace-time occupations. Something has to be done, therefore, to take young people off the streets, occupy their minds, give them something to do. Compulsory training, if not frankly military, will mean setting up a permanent W.P.A., P.W.A., or C.C.C. Do the American people really want this? *If we cannot put our unemployed to work, it would be better to admit it and set about honestly solving the problem rather than rationalizing ourselves into the adoption of conscription by evading the real issue.* Furthermore, if we have come to the time when a large percentage of our young people constitute an unneeded and unwanted drug on the market, do we believe that we shall make them feel they are wanted, that they deeply and truly "belong" to and in a free society, by the process of conscription and a permanent C.C.C.? And if conscription is a means to get a sizable amount of public work done, we need also to face the fact that this will constitute another step toward a regimented, State-controlled economy and have to ask ourselves whether this is the direction in which we wish to move in our economic life. Certainly the fairly numerous advocates of conscription who also clamor for the restoration of "free enterprise" in our economic system are sawing off the limb on which they are sitting.

Does Conscription Mould Responsible Citizens?

Even more important, it seems to me, than such considerations as we have named is this. The extent and seriousness of irresponsibility among American youth are frequently exaggerated. We heard a good deal about it a couple of years ago from college professors whose students were reluctant about accepting a war program because they still believed what the professors had been telling them about war during the 'thirties. Whether one agrees with the position the students took, one must grant that they were acting responsibly and not otherwise in not tossing overboard without serious reflection what they had come to believe on high authority and as a result of their own best thinking. But it is a fact that a good deal of social irresponsibility and lack of devotion to democracy may be found. How would true believers in democracy go about remedying such a condition when it is found in young people who, be it recalled, have gone through our American school system? Surely the procedure would be to try to discover the causes and to remove them, confident that then the symptom would also disappear. This might lead us to investigate and revamp the school system itself. We might surmise that a generation of youth for whom society seems to have no jobs, no responsible task in other words, can hardly be expected to have a deep devotion for that society and that the thing to do is to place responsibility upon them, i.e., put them to work. We might see that Negroes can hardly feel "responsible" in a society which says they are inferior and cannot be given full responsibility. It is, I am convinced, only by giving our youth real and growing responsibility that we can develop a deep devotion for democracy, not by resorting to a favorite device of dictators all over the world, namely the forced labor camp. *Devotion to democracy in the very nature of the case must come from within, must be freely given, cannot be imposed from without or generated by any system of conscription.*

Can Fellowship Be Forced?

We have been speaking of the individual, the person, as of infinite value, a creation of spirit, in whom the Light of God dwells, who is therefore clothed with moral responsibility and must in the final analysis obey the leading of God and his own conscience. This is not, however, as some appear to think, synonymous with individualism. It is indeed as a theory and a way of life at the opposite pole from individualism. The key word is fellowship rather than freedom if freedom is thought of as an attribute and right of the isolated individual rather than as a condition and a fruit of fellowship.

The individual was made by and for community. As modern life has become more mechanical and the individual has been cut adrift—the landless, jobless, rootless multitudes—he has been stricken with fear and other spiritual ills. Totalitarianism, conscription, and war have transformed nearly the whole world into a barracks. This takes place because the individual cannot bear his isolation. In desperation he submits to an impersonal, mechanical collectivity which, though it destroy him as a person, nevertheless takes him in and gives him a place.

It does little good to exhort him to assert his independence, and not to surrender his autonomy. It is precisely his "independence" and "freedom" in their present-day form that he wants to rid himself of. Escape into primitive life, though there are those who seek to find it, is not possible. The result for those who seek it is that they descend to the animal, or more accurately sub-animal level, or simply go to pieces. The economic conditions, for example, for the restoration of primitive society do not exist. Even if they did, it is psychologically impossible for modern man, who has become self-conscious and introspective, who has inherited a civilized culture, who has been faced with the possibility and the necessity of using scientific methods in his thought and life, to go back to primitive living.

If men are to be saved and society on the human level is to be maintained, men must be integrated into another type of community. *It must be a fellowship which they deliberately choose to join and to help create and extend. The fellowship in which they find true satisfaction cannot be one into which they are simply born or forced.* It must be what they choose, and they must, in helping to bring it into being, find use for their highest powers.

Yet this community cannot be a temporary and superficial association which enlists in its activity a part of man's self and leaves the rest, the core of his being, still without a home. The new community must give men the satisfactions, supply the profound integration of the part and the whole, the individual and society, which the simpler communities provided. The new community must also grow from within, not be manufactured and imposed from without.

Removing the Occasion of All Conscription

Religion, and religion alone, supplies the key for the solution of this problem. Man "belongs" in a spiritual universe. He is the creation, that is, the child of God. As Christianity teaches, this is true of all men. Thus men know each other as brothers, as bound together in a profound and ultimately indissoluble unity in the family of God, the divine-human society. Each loves his neighbor as himself, not in obedience to a moral exhortation, as a matter of duty, but because the neighbor is the other self in whom, and in God, we live and move and have our being. I can no more think of wanting to put my neighbor in the wrong, wanting to injure or kill him, than I can think of wanting to do these things to myself. Obviously this outlook upon life, this way of life, "taketh away the occasion of all wars."

This does not mean that there may not be a place in life for various types of human association, including economic enterprises, cultural associations, educational institutions, labor unions, political organizations and institutions, and government. But the religious view of life and society to which we are committed *does* mean that allegiance to God and his Kingdom has precedence over loyalty to any of these institutions, that it is as they contribute to the growth of the Kingdom and the divine-human community that they have validity and worth and that none of them may claim final and complete authority over human life. The moment one of them does so it can no longer serve the purposes of life and growth but it is trying to take the place of God, it becomes anti-Christ. The State is the institution which has frequently, and most flagrantly in modern times, sought to assert absolute authority.

When we spoke of the unity of human beings in God and in the true divine-human society we pointed out that the spirit which is the creator and the very soul of such a society is the spirit which "taketh away the occasion of all wars." Is it not clear that it is just as surely and utterly the spirit which taketh away the occasion of all conscription?

"Conscription and Conscience," by A. J. Muste, from *Sourcebook on Conscience and Conscription and Disarmament,* compiled by American Friends Service Committee (Wallingford, Pennsylvania: Pendle Hill, 1943), pages 3–8. Copyright © 1943 American Friends Service Committee. Reprinted with permission of the American Friends Service Committee, Philadelphia, Pennsylvania.

ABRAHAM JOHANNES MUSTE (1885–1967) was a Quaker theologian and sociologist who wrote extensively on conscientious objection, pacifism, and organized labor. From 1926 to 1929 he was chairman, and from 1940 to 1953 executive director, of the Fellowship for Reconciliation.

37

Why the Draft Should Go
by
John M. Swomley, Jr.

One-time director of the National Council Against Conscription, Swomley opposes conscription on individualist grounds. He discusses the impact of the draft on social relationships and institutions, refuting a number of popular arguments in its favor. Swomley concludes that conscription can never be equitable, and that, in the final analysis, the issue is not equality under compulsion but freedom to follow individual human values.

The United States has had military conscription for almost thirty years, and few Americans now remember how little influence the armed forces had in the nation's life when the draft was first adopted in 1940. Conscription and the increase of military influence have gone hand in hand, so that for many Americans military values and compulsory military duty have come to be a part of the culture.

The reluctance to abandon conscription is today evident chiefly in liberal circles where largely new arguments are being used. These imply that conscription is needed to foster anti-war values, to encourage a limited war strategy instead of nuclear war, to keep the Army from becoming all black and thus forcing Negroes to bear the brunt. An examination of these and similar arguments is essential if they are not to become part of the popular wisdom.

One major argument for the draft is stated simply: A professional-volunteer-career army is more of a threat to peace or to involvement in empire than a citizen army. However, "citizen army" is a term not to be equated with conscription. It refers basically to militia such as the National Guard, which could be raised either by voluntary or compulsory means. The essence of a professional army is an officer and noncommissioned officer group that makes a career out of the military. Such an army may enlist short-term volunteers or use a draft. The United States today has a professional force which uses the draft as a method to raise additional manpower—during the war in Vietnam, the Air Force, the Navy, the bulk of the Marine Corps and the Army have been made up of volunteers.

Conscript armies are no less destructive than volunteer armies. The armies of Napoleon, the Kaiser, Hitler and Stalin were raised by conscription and supported either imperialist or totalitarian purposes. The United States used volunteer armies in the Mexican and Spanish-American Wars to add foreign territory to its empire. It has employed volunteers to invade Latin American countries and conscripts to invade Vietnam or occupy other Asian countries. Drafted men do not prevent the use of armies for imperialism or war. The crucial decisions are made at a different level, by generals, presidents or emperors.

A second widely held belief about the draft is that campus and GI protests against the war in Vietnam would have been much less vigorous if the government had been able to get along with volunteers only. Campus protests are only partly draft motivated. There have been significant protests against military recruiters, Dow Chemical personnel recruiters, ROTC and university involvements with military research. Although the draft is part of this whole complex it cannot be said to have motivated students in the early protests when all students including graduate students were automatically deferred. This argument implies also that the resistance within the Army has come chiefly from conscripts, whereas much of the evidence points the other way.

Most men subject to the draft who resist the military do so before induction by filing as conscientious objectors, accepting voluntary exile in Canada or going to prison. According to Arlo Tatum of the Central Committee on Conscientious Objectors, "the majority of deserters in Sweden are volunteers." His colleague, Mike Wittels said: "The volunteer is a man who wants to control his own life, and is more likely to resist." My own contacts with numerous friends and relatives of those who visit military prisoners in the Army Disciplinary Barracks in nearby Leavenworth confirm this impression. There are, however, no reliable statistics. What is certain is that both volunteers and draftees have resisted war duty.

Sometimes it is asserted in support of the draft that its repeal would result in smaller armed forces and would mean, therefore, greater reliance on nuclear weapons. There is, however, no necessary relation between the draft and the size of the armed forces. It is possible to have a pre-Vietnam size army without the draft if, as a Pentagon report indicates, adequate pay were used as an inducement for enlistment. Or the military could have a combat army of the present size if civilians were hired for noncombat work in the United States. Only about 20 per cent of the army is ever involved in combat. Or it could lower recruiting standards, since not all army jobs demand the high test scores now required of recruits.

Neither is there a necessary relation between the absence of a draft and reliance on nuclear weapons. Nuclear weapons were developed and used during World War II when the largest draft army in United States history was in the field. Both bomber and missile installations have been equipped with nuclear weapons during the peacetime draft. If nuclear weapons were used for other than deterrent, pre-emptive or retaliatory purposes (none of which has any relation to a draft) they would be used to escalate a conventional war when defeat seems otherwise likely. In that case it would be possible to argue, as President Truman did, that nuclear weapons were employed to save the lives of drafted men, or to win the war more quickly or decisively or because an adversary permitted no alternative.

Another argument is that an end to the draft would mean an increased reliance on troops of the developing world to fight our wars, as British and French imperialists relied on Asian and African troops. One response to this is the historical record that the United States has relied on South Korean troops both in Korea and in Vietnam while there was a draft. During the draft, United States troops were not used in Iran, the Congo, Guatemala or elsewhere where the CIA with ample funds managed *coups d'état* or assisted pro-American native forces to consolidate power.

The Army has steadily pursued during the peacetime draft a policy of training for counterinsurgency the armies of Thailand, Latin America and other nations. The United States did not rely fully on the troops of the South Vietnamese Government only because they were unreliable, showing a high desertion rate and an unwillingness to kill other Vietnamese.

It is frequently asked: "But wouldn't a volunteer army mean a mercenary army?" The word "mercenary" refers to the hiring of foreign troops to fight a nation's battles as the English employed Hessians during the American Revolution. In the United States Army, all officers and enlisted men, whether volunteers or draftees, are paid at the same rate for their rank. The presence or absence of a draft has nothing to do with whether men are paid. The only point at issue here is that the Pentagon, to raise an all-volunteer army, might have to offer an adequate wage to men of the lower ranks.

Some political leaders have claimed that foreign policy changes must come first, including big-power agreements for disarmament; only then, they say, will nations be secure enough to end the draft. Such a position assumes that nations want disarmament, or that foreign policy is changed independently of the military capabilities of nations. Military power is one of the most decisive factors influencing foreign policy. It is the ability of the United States to garrison other nations and invade, with or without invitation, nations such as Vietnam and the Dominican Republic that makes possible the dominance known as the Pax Americana. Such actions can be undertaken with or without the draft. But the draft, even in stand-by form, gives the Joint Chiefs of Staff and the President a blank check on the nation's manpower to escalate any overseas action into a major war without Congressional approval. It thus helps determine foreign policy.

If we assume, first, that nations will ever negotiate disarmament and, second, that the draft is essential to real military strength, then a vigorous campaign to repeal the draft would be an important way of telling those in power to begin serious negotiation toward an international abolition of conscription. Any way one looks at it, foreign policy and military policy are intertwined; both must be changed. Support of the foreign policy goals of the military-industrial complex necessarily implies whatever means are essential for such support, such as access to unlimited manpower via the draft. Likewise, support of the means, including a blank check on manpower, nuclear weapons, etc., is support of the goals of those who can use these means.

Leaders who are disinclined to talk disarmament say the United States needs the draft until such time as we work out binding treaty arrangements with China and the Soviet Union, since these nations are the chief source of potential military threat. Even if the United States were to draft its every man, woman and child we would be outnumbered by the Chinese millions; no military man suggests the draft as a way to subdue either China or Russia. Nuclear weapons, missiles, submarines, control of air, seas, etc., are much more in the minds of military strategists than land warfare against more densely populated nations with larger land areas. The proposal that we need the draft until we work out agreements with China and Russia is an excuse, not a reason. We have made little or no effort to explore the overtures of these nations toward nonaggression pacts or other treaties decreasing tensions.

Sometimes racists and sometimes liberals, for differing reasons, claim that a volunteer army would probably in time be all black, since black youth is denied access to other jobs with decent pay and turns in increasing numbers to the Army. This argument is based on the fact that the black re-enlistment rate is currently higher than the white. But white initial enlistment is higher than black even at existing pay rates. If higher pay for recruits were authorized, the Army would attract ample numbers of young white men as well as those from other racial groups.

Among the factors discouraging black enlistments are the following: (1) Black militants encourage youth to avoid the army because it serves the white power structure. (2) The black discovery of power, begun under Dr. Martin Luther King, Jr., has made it necessary for hitherto white schools, businesses and industry to employ Afro-Americans if they are to receive black support. This competition for skilled or educated personnel is likely to continue. (3) Because of inadequate economic, educational and other opportunities there are not enough qualified black youth among the approximately 250,000 who turn 18 each year to fill up the armed forces even if every qualified black youth did enlist.

Still another argument against ending the draft is the idea that a volunteer army is better trained, shows higher morale and a greater eagerness to fight, and is, therefore, a greater threat to world peace. The level of training is determined by length of enlistment. If a man is drafted for two years and re-enlists, is he more of a threat to world peace than he was when a draftee? If so, this is an argument not for the draft but against re-enlistment, and for requiring the armed forces to discharge everyone before they can develop a vested interest in war. No advocate of the draft seriously suggests ending all voluntary re-enlistment or enlistment. In fact, the Air Force and Navy are built with volunteers and the Army relies chiefly on re-enlistments.

Finally, it is claimed that the injustice and inequity of the draft can be corrected by modifying rather than repealing the law. Against this is the argument that a lottery or any other chance approach is not more equitable than human decision. The lottery, whatever its impersonal values, has two serious defects. First, it assumes that inequality of treatment is the primary defect of the draft and that the national or world interest is served best by disregarding a man's abilities, education and potential when forcing him to enter the Army. The second weakness in present lottery proposals is the camouflage it provides for a traditional Army demand. The Army has always wanted boys in their teen-age years, when they are most malleable and least able to resist complete regimentation. Liberals in Congress are now offering teenagers to the Army under the guise of an "equitable" lottery instead of via the more naked military formula of the younger the better.

Actually, the draft can never be equitable because some will be drafted and others not; of those who are drafted some are sent to battle and others remain in safer areas. Some are killed in battle; others not. The fundamental injustice is that a man who is compelled to enter the Army feels a loss of freedom. The American system of freedom, insofar as it operates in employment, is one of persuading or inducing persons to engage in work rather than in compelling them to do so. It is a cardinal point in our religious faith as well as our democratic philosophy that ultimate values reside in the individual human being. The idea that the individual must be subjected to the state, or that compulsory "service" is preferable to a voluntary society, contributes to the alienation of young people. The power to reach into every family, to take a boy from his home and subject him to complete military discipline for months or years is the most serious limitation America places on freedom.

In the final analysis, the issue is freedom, rather than equality under compulsion.

"Why the Draft Should Go," by John M. Swomley, Jr., from *The Nation Magazine,* Volume CCIX, Number 4 (August 11, 1969), pages 108–110. Copyright © 1969 The Nation Associates. Reprinted by permission.

JOHN M. SWOMLEY, JR. (1915–) is a Methodist minister who has been professor of social ethics at the St. Paul School of Theology in Kansas City since 1960. He was executive director of the National Council

Against Conscription from 1944 to 1952, during which time he was also editor of *Conscription News*. Formerly a national president of the United Methodist Peace Fellowship, he is the author of numerous articles and books, among the latter being *The Military Establishment* and *Religion, the State and the Schools*.

38

The Draft:
Unjust and Unnecessary
by
Thomas B. Curtis

Curtis discusses the practical and ethical ramifications of adopting a volunteer military in lieu of the draft. He examines the philosophical dilemmas confronted by an otherwise free society when it incorporates a compulsory system, concluding that such action threatens the very ideals American society exists to preserve.

The Spectrum of Values to Be Considered

The defense of a nation's values by military force presents difficult choices for any society. For the American people, born under the aegis of individual liberty and maximum freedom from arbitrary governmental interference in the lives of independent men, such choices are especially hazardous. For an inappropriate system of national defense may threaten those very ideals our society exists to preserve. Thus, a discussion of manpower procurement policies for the military carries us into a consideration of the very basic values which our form of government was established to protect. It is important that this be foremost in the minds of those who discuss the question of the draft and its alternatives.

In addition to the question of justice and individual freedom, military manpower procurement policy raises questions of economics and strategic preparedness. Our modern technological society has produced a new concept of warfare for which old ideas of manpower procurement, and former views of the skills necessary for military preparedness and civilian economic strength, are no longer adequate. No longer do the principles of mass warfare conducted by massive armies across wide expanses of ground with primitive weapons hold true. The modern soldier is a specialist, a technician of war, a "knight on horse-back" who rides to battle in tanks, helicopters, and armored personnel carriers, and is equipped with a bewildering array of sophisticated weapons and implements of war. War, which was once the sport of royalty, is now a conflict between civilizations, and the entire economy and productive capacity of nations are part of the field of conflict.

Therefore, this discussion of a voluntary system of military manpower procurement is intended to be in the context of these basic ethical, economic, and strategic considerations.

The Ethics of a Volunteer Army

The Arithmetic of Ethics. There are approximately two million men now reaching draft age each year. At present our armed forces require the services of slightly more than one-third of them. This percentage is most likely to decrease as the population reaching draft age each year increases, and with the hoped-for cessation of military hostilities in Asia. With these basic figures the ethical question is immediately thrown into relief. The military does not need approximately two-thirds of draft age men. What is the fairest way of selecting that minority it does need?

The present system, based as it is upon compulsion, is inherently inequitable and inconsistent with the ideals of a free society. The method currently employed under the selective service law of cutting out the unneeded two-thirds is through a leaky system of deferments and exemptions which generally favors the physically limited, fathers, farmers, clergymen, reservists, and scholars—provided their subject of study is continually within a shifting area of priorities dictated by the government. Those young men who do not fit into one of these and a few other categories make up that directly compelled one-third. It is also fair to say that many of the remaining two-thirds feel the indirect compulsion of government when they choose their future careers and activities with a wary eye on selective service draft deferment categories.

Today's Obstacles to Choice. To compound the inequity very little effort is made by the Selective Service System to afford the would-be draftee an "eyes-open" choice. Bruce Chapman, in his recent book *Wrong Man in Uniform*, describes the draft registrant's selection opportunities in the following terms:

> ... young men born since World War II ... meet the draft in a Kafkaesque experience of bewilderment and frustration that most older adults do not understand. There are nowadays some sixty optional programs through which one can fulfill his military obligation, with a strange maze of attendant procedures and processes; and there are countless ways of not serving at all. Despite such complexities, no counseling is made available to young men as a matter of course and even if one seeks out his draft board, the information supplied by the busy and businesslike clerk is likely to be skeletal. It is surprising that nearly all young men even know that they must go to their draft board to register at age 18, yet the law deals firmly indeed with him who does not. "Those registrants whose infractions of the law are not deliberate," reads a report by the Director of Selective Service, "usually are not brought to trial, but they are subject to accelerated induction into the Armed Forces and they occupy the highest position in the sequence of selection for induction."
>
> When a man does register he is given a tiny flyer whose chief function is to list the eighteen different categories of Selective Service classification—without explaining what they are and how one gets assigned to them. One is told that any appeal of classification must be entered to the local board in writing no more than ten days after notification, but one is not told under what circumstances an appeal should be made or what to put in the appeal. The terse flyer's parting shot is the hardly reassuring advice that "Classifications are subject to change by the local board at any time," and that "Failure to comply with an order from your local board may make you subject to fine or imprisonment."
>
> Even a bright and determined young man—usually the one with bright and determined parents—might have a hard time compiling all the information relevant to his rights, obligations and choices. Yet at no single time does the Government or the educational system automatically provide the full facts of the draft and military service to youngsters who face it.

Contrast this briefly with what would be the required procurement procedure for a voluntary career army. The basic premise upon which procurement rests is that a modern technological army is seeking skills and not bodies. Therefore manpower procurement procedure need not be essentially different from civilian jobs offered by the government or the private sector. Skills in demand must be paid the going rate, and additional benefits, such as greatly improved living conditions, better schools for servicemen's families, and an upgrading of the concept of military service in the eyes of the community, would be part of the inducement package. There must be a multitude of reforms in military life.

Professionals or Mercenaries? Increase in pay, even along with other necessary reforms, to induce voluntarily the necessary number of enlistments has brought about the charge that a volunteer career army would be an army of "mercenaries" and this is philosophically or morally undesirable to many Americans. Although I feel that the charge of "mercenaries" is a distortion of both the term "mercenary" and the concept of a volunteer army, it is important to discuss the various ethical questions at the base of this objection.

To students familiar with American history, the term "mercenary" brings to mind the German Hessians hired by the British to fight the rebellious American colonists. After all, the Americans won the Revolutionary War, and could it be that part of this may be due to the underlying unreliability of the mercenary Hessians, who had no interest in the cause for which they were fighting? Certainly, and this concept of the word "mercenary" accurately carries with it a justified fear of unreliability in battle.

However, there are two different concepts contained in the word "mercenary." The first is that of a soldier hiring for service in an army not of his own country, like the Hessians in the American Revolution. The second is acting merely for pay or monetary reward. The first definition is used to denigrate the value of a volunteer army by its opponents, although only the second definition even comes close to describing accurately the concept, and this isn't very close. A voluntary career army is one in which citizens of the same country are hired into that country's armed services. The derogatory import of the term "mercenary" is then manifestly unfair.

Any charge of unreliability of one who serves in his own country's army for a salary commensurate to what he could be earning in a civilian occupation is difficult to sustain. Indeed, some of those who have yelled the loudest that "they would not want to be defended by an army of mercenaries" are themselves mercenaries in the sense that they serve for pay or make their living at their work. The career director of the Selective Service System, General Lewis B. Hershey, is then a mercenary even though he winces at the thought of being defended by them. It is also true in this sense that he and all of us receive medical treatment and legal advice and accept political regulation from "mercenaries."

To the extent then that there is any danger of unreliability from a professional army, we already face it. Most every officer above the rank of major is properly considered a professional career man. It is only the lowly enlistee and the draftee who would be replaced if a voluntary career system of manpower procurement were instituted. It can hardly be said that draftees infuse the system with a healthy civilian influence which counterbalances judgments made by their career officers. Anyone who thinks so has not had first-hand observation of the system in operation and a draftee's influence on military policy.

The notion of paying a soldier what he might be worth in his civilian occupation, far from being ignoble, is eminently just and our failure to do so is a national shame. The beginning pay of an enlisted man in the United States Army, whether he has volunteered or is a draftee, is $90.60 per month. To this base rate must be added the approximate value of housing and food he receives, and the Department of Defense has estimated that this is $73.31 per month for a newly enlisted man. Both these figures rise slightly during his early promotions in grade. Thus the newly enlisted soldier receives in his first year of service approximately $2122.47 in pay and benefits. This figure must be adjusted slightly because of the 5.6 per cent basic pay increase across the board for all services enacted in 1967. Even with this the yearly benefits are approximately $2191.77 in the first year of service.

This figure is scandalously low—below the statutory minimum wage, below the proclaimed minimum "poverty level," and, according to *The New York Times*, only slightly more than the pay of a peasant on a collective farm in Rumania. Small wonder enlistments do not meet requirements! But within these figures there is an additional moral question which must be faced by our society. The difference between the $2191.77 which the soldier makes in the service and the amount he could have made in his civilian occupation is an additional cost to him. It should be legitimately considered part of the cost of our national defense. However, note who must bear this cost. Not the well-to-do American taxpayer who is receiving all the benefits of the defense, but the draftee who, in addition to having to bear this extra economic loss, is possibly risking life and limb as well.

Professor Milton Friedman, of the University of Chicago, accurately characterizes this discrepancy as an additional tax which must be borne by the service man, and adds that "adequate pay alone may not attract, but inadequate pay can certainly deter" the young man in choosing the military as a career. We are being a bit nonsensical and unreasonable if we expect this difference to be made up by patriotism as some do. As Bruce Chapman points out "men should not be paid for their patriotism, but neither should they be punished for it."

The Composition of a Volunteer Army. A further ethical or philosophical consideration which has been raised with regard to a volunteer army is the representativeness of its members. It is particularly feared by some, including Senator Edward Kennedy, that an all volunteer army would contain a disproportionate number of Negroes and other minority and lower income groups. The statistics in fact bear this out. The Department of Defense has reported that in the first eleven months of fiscal year 1966, 12.9 per cent of the draftees were nonwhite, compared to 11.1 per cent of the entire United States population which is non-white. Additionally, the National Advisory Commission on Selective Service found that while Negro soldiers comprised only 11 percent of United States personnel in Viet Nam, they accounted for 14.5 per cent of all army combat units, and that they represented 22.4 per cent of all army troops killed in action.

More significant in consideration of the composition of an all volunteer army is the fact that Negro re-enlistment rates were double those of white troops as reported by the National Advisory Commission. These figures indicate that it can reasonably be expected that a greater proportion of Negroes and other lower income groups would make up our armed services if procurement were solely by voluntary enlistment. However, I feel that those who condemn the concept of an all volunteer army on moral grounds because of this must answer two additional ethical questions. First, isn't the fact that more Negroes re-enlist a condemnation of the civilian conditions from which many of them come, and should we then object to a military procurement system because it affords them greater opportunities than our civilian society? And, second, since a greater percentage of Negroes under the present system are drafted anyway from their total population than are whites, is it better to see these Negroes drafted against their will, or volunteer because they want to?

The Ethics of the Alternatives. Although the preferable moral and ethical values of the voluntary procurement system can be best seen by affirmatively setting forth the case for that system, some brief mention of the philosophical detractions of the competing systems may be in order.

There are those who feel that some form of a lottery system would be the best method of military manpower procurement. I have said that I would prefer a lottery to the present draft system with all its inequities and deferments, but I think we can do much better than either. Those who turn to a lottery to obtain military manpower are figuratively throwing up their hands in the face of complexity. A rational system of military manpower procurement—a voluntary system—can be achieved through study of the various skills needed by the military which have counterparts in the civilian society, development of the necessary variety of rewards to induce the proper enlistments, and raising the role of military service in the eyes of the nation.

Furthermore, any lottery must itself inevitably have some exemptions and deferments. The physically handicapped for example cannot serve in combat positions, and there may be others who are selected by the lottery whom we may not want to have serve, such as our nuclear physicists. Certain exemptions must then be made, and once this process is begun it may be difficult to find a rational place to stop. The result would probably be a completely new set of inequitable exemptions, and should this be the case any young man selected will hardly feel better because he was singled out through mechanical irrationality rather than human irrationality.

Another commonly discussed alternative to the draft is a system of national service. The philosopher William James once discussed this as the "moral equivalent of war" and in so doing captured the imaginations of social planners and governmental activists ever since. Basically the idea of national service would require all young people to give a few years in service to their country, and, in lieu of the military, this service could consist of social work for society's improvement. Those activities commonly considered as acceptable alternatives today are the Peace Corps, VISTA, poverty work, and the like.

Philosophical and moral objections to this concept run very deep and are not immediately apparent to those who strongly favor the objectives of groups like the Peace Corps and VISTA. The idea that a citizen owes his government a certain number of years of service is foreign to this nation's principles of limited government; and a system of national service, by starting out to expand liberties, would end by severely curtailing them. Consider for example who or what agency is to make the decision as to what is valuable social work and what is not, and therefore whether that work can be an alternative to military service. Political judgments would necessarily have to be made on a scale so broad as to affect virtually every member of society in a certain age group. Could activities of a private charitable nature be selected instead of a governmental activity? If not, isn't this saying that government programs are somehow more worthy than private individual action? If so, who is to determine which private activities will qualify—churches, religious institutions, political parties, black power groups, white citizens councils, etc?

The administrative difficulties of national service are no less staggering than the philosophical. Recall that one of the underlying reasons that the draft has been declared inequitable is because only one-third of the available manpower was needed for military service. National service, instead of devising a rational system to cut down the interference of government on the lives of those two-thirds that are not needed, expands government to touch them all. If there are approximately 2 million men in each year of the draft age population, and approximately 2 million women, we are dealing with between 30 to 35 million young people. The administrative costs of dealing with such a large segment of our population would be great. And to this must be added costs of training; for example, the training costs for one Peace Corps worker alone is on the average $7800. The costs of national service may be enormously large, much larger than that of a volunteer army discussed subsequently. In addition, most of these charitable and social organizations operate to a great extent on the impetus of volunteerism and individual initiative. We could reasonably expect that many of them would be overwhelmed and severely damaged by an influx of an extremely large number of indirectly coerced young people.

The Economic and Strategic Considerations

The accurate costs of a volunteer service must reflect the savings obtained through the abolition of the draft system.

The High Cost to the Draftee. The cost of our present system of procuring military manpower is enormous. At first glance it may seem otherwise to some because the draft is a means of acquiring very cheap labor. [But,] as Professor John Kenneth Galbraith has stated, "the draft survives principally as a device by which we use compulsion to get young men to serve at less than the market rate of pay. We shift the cost of military service from the well-to-do taxpayer, who benefits by lower taxes, to the impecunious young draftee. This is a highly regressive arrangement which we would not tolerate in any other area." However, in addition to the social costs implicitly underlying Professor Galbraith's criticism, there are also grave economic costs. The draft has served as a crutch for the military services and allowed them to avoid the development of sound personnel policies. Our modern army requires specialists and technicians much more than automatons with rifles. The present procurement policies require the army to waste millions in training these draftees in skills which the military will lose in a few years and which the trainee will generally never have a use for in later life. The present personnel policies encourage further waste by deterring re-enlistments.

Military pay in the lower grades is lower in the United States than in any of the other NATO powers, including those like France and West Germany which have compulsory service. A private E-1 in the United States makes approximately $90 a month, hardly enough to support himself, much less a wife and family. With an increasingly lower average age for marriage in this country, it is not surprising that many married draftees in the military services are forced to depend on relief payments to support themselves. For example, in 1964, the Air Force alone identified more than 5000 men who were receiving relief support. Such economic facts hardly encourage volunteering and certainly discourage re-enlistments.

The High Cost of Low Re-enlistment Rates.   Department of Defense figures reveal that only about 8 per cent of draftees stay in the service and only 25 per cent of first-term volunteers re-enlist. In 1964, the re-enlistment rate for inductees was down to 2.8 per cent and the percentage has never been greater than 20 per cent. Thus approximately 90–95 per cent of all the manpower which is obtained by the draft is "temporary" and the skills of these men, which took about $6000 per draftee to train, are wasted in the process. The cost, in wasted training and lost skills alone, is approximately 2.4 billion dollars a year for an army that depends on compulsion to secure its manpower. This cost must be borne by Professor Galbraith's "well-to-do taxpayers" and is the penalty we pay for our inefficient manpower procurement system.

The High Costs of Ignoring Technological Changes.   In addition, the draft ignores the basic changes which have occurred in the technology of war during the past two decades. Back in 1957, a report prepared by a blue-ribbon commission headed by Ralph Cordiner observed:

> It is foolish for the Armed Services to obtain highly advanced weapons systems and not have men of sufficient competence to understand, operate, and maintain such equipment. . . . The solution here, of course, is not to draft more men to stand and look helplessly at the machinery. The solution is to give the men already in the armed forces the incentives required to make them want to stay in the service long enough and try hard enough to take these higher responsibilities, gain the skill and experience levels we need and then remain to give the services the full benefit of their skills.

Our modern army requires more highly skilled technicians and less manual laborers in order to operate and maintain its sophisticated weapons systems. But it is precisely these skilled personnel who leave the military services for higher paying, more satisfying jobs in civilian life. The draft, to be sure, provides ample quantity, but what is needed increasingly today is men of special skills or quality. The latter are uninterested in remaining in the services and, because they are also the most expensive to train, the army is faced with a discouraging inverse relationship between degree of costs of skills obtained and re-enlistment.

The army, with its alleged traditional talent for putting "square pegs into round holes," has aggravated the situation with the misuse of the skills and talents it has at its disposal. A General Accounting Office study, noted by Senator Gaylord Nelson in 1964, revealed that at least 35,000 soldiers were employed in the wrong jobs wasting some $48 million. The GAO described the Army's handling of men as a personnel system that generates mismanagement. Examples cited were helicopter pilots serving as dog handlers and airplane mechanics as military policemen.

Unfortunately the military has also been shown to be unable to make effective use of available scientific talent. On August 30, 1962, Senator Proxmire read into the *Congressional Record* a study prepared by a former Army engineer which showed that "the effective utilized time of the enlisted scientist or engineer spent on work commensurate with his qualifications is 10 per cent." This astounding figure was confirmed by the Army's Adjutant General's Office.

For comparison, it is interesting to examine the personnel policies of the Navy Seabees during World War II. The Seabees' practice of placing already trained bull-dozer operators, engineers, and other skilled personnel immediately in jobs commensurate with their ability and skills resulted in large savings in time and costs. In addition it encouraged enlistments as the enlistee was assured of an opportunity to make use of his skills and talents. Regrettably even the Seabees have dropped this policy today.

The High Cost of the Draft on the Civilian Economy.

Equally important with the distorting effects on the military are the effects of the draft's inefficiency on the civilian sector of our society. The current military buildup in Viet Nam has intensified pressures on business firms faced with severe shortages of skilled labor due to the draft. In June, 1966, a trade journal published by Prentice-Hall, entitled "Personnel Management—Policies and Pressures," contained a survey of 192 American business firms showing that 35 per cent faced severe shortages of skilled labor. Furthermore, these firms cannot find their way out of their dilemma by instituting job training programs as there is great difficulty in finding young workers to train. The very fact of the draft liability of those presently available makes a company balk at providing expensive training. The Department of Defense reported during the hearings on the draft last June that 39 per cent of the draftees between the ages of 22–25 were refused jobs because of their liability.

A *de jure* attempt was once made to provide some measure of insulation from the draft to key employees of essential industries in the name of the "national interest." The little known "Department of Commerce List of Currently Essential Activities" and the "Department of Labor's List of Critical Occupations" set down recommendations for jobs which should enjoy draft exemption. Unfortunately this list has not been revised since 1963, despite the new demands for manpower and the current shortage. The lists also use job descriptions which are now out of date according to the 1965 revised edition of the *Dictionary of Occupational Titles* published by the Department of Labor. Furthermore, the committee responsible for compiling these lists, and thus coordinating military and civilian manpower needs, has concentrated solely on "defense" jobs. Critical occupations in the civilian sector have gone unconsidered. For example, a manufacturer of electrical fuses with a large share of the civilian market but only a small number of defense contracts could not qualify for the Commerce list and thus has experienced great difficulties in keeping its trained employees. This failure of the selective service to coordinate its selection process with the needs of the civilian society is damaging to our defense efforts because the health of the civilian economy is an important aspect of our military strength.

During the debate on the floor of the House in June of 1967, when the amendments to the Selective Service Act were being considered, the job of compiling lists of critical skills and essential activities was transferred to the National Security Council with no discussion whatever of the efforts of that agency's predecessor in the task. Subsequently, in February, 1968, the National Security Council announced that it had totally suspended the list of "Currently Essential Activities" even though it never really had one, and with it suspended all except a few occupational deferments, even though it had no knowledge of how many occupational deferments had been granted and were outstanding and in what industries the holders of these deferments might have been employed.

A further ramification of the total lack of coordination between the civilian sector of our economy and the military is the sorry state of the Reserve and National Guard. Originally established in 1955 to serve as an available source of trained manpower in the event of a buildup, the Reserves have become a repository for over-aged former servicemen and young men seeking a way to avoid the draft. For the most part, Reserve units are untrained. A study prepared by the Governors' Advisory Committee on the National Guard indicated that 90,000, or 30 per cent of the total strength of the Guard, had never received training. General Hershey stated at the Armed Services Committee hearings in June of 1967 that 50,000 Reservists were in control units and had never received training. This lack of preparedness was illustrated when the Army recently completed a program whereby selected reserve units were given up-to-date training in order to bring them to combat readiness. Unfortunately to achieve this a redistribution of the personnel and material resources of the remaining 70 per cent of the Reserve was necessary. Thus, to get a few Reserve units ready for callup the Army was forced to let the remainder deteriorate.

The lack of coordination of skills between the Reserves and the civilian sector makes any large-scale callup dangerous if not impossible. In 1961 the Reserves were called to meet the Berlin crisis resulting in chaos in many communities. The same effect would result if the Reserves were called up today. As an illustration, Lambert Airport in St. Louis, where many key employees are also reservists, might have to be shut down.

The Alternative of Volunteerism

My proposal focuses on the major elements necessary to achieve a modern career military force. I argue that such a force—sustained by volunteers through increased pay and other benefits and both regular and ready reserves—would have a higher morale, be better trained, and more able to meet the immediate military threats to our country. The essential elements of a career force would include [the five considerations examined below].

I. Higher Pay, Better Housing, and Other Benefits Which Would Make Military Life More Comparable to Civilian Life in Similar Jobs Utilizing Similar Skills

This is basic to attracting and keeping a career army and ready reserves. Unfortunately the possibilities have never been given the detailed study necessary. The Defense Department sweepingly argues that it would cost too much to rely on volunteers. In the last days of the hearings held by the House Armed Services Committee in June, 1966, the Defense Department finally came forward with the year-late report. This report, or more correctly, a "report of their report," contained cost estimates ranging from $4 to $17 billion. These figures unfortunately were based on the Department's estimates on what it would cost to "hire" 500,000 new men annually without any other changes in personnel policies. I requested supplemental data from the author of the report, Assistant Secretary of Defense Thomas D. Morris, and was advised in a letter that "no estimates were made for the draft study of the combined effects of improvements in fringe benefits upon the rate of volunteering . . . since these benefits—with the exception of training and educational opportunities—were not found to be effective inducements for *initial* enlistment." (Emphasis added.) Thus the military establishment responded with figures so vague as to be almost meaningless and based them upon inadequate considerations. They have in effect created an artificial monetary barrier to an all-volunteer army at the outset. Fortunately I have been advised in a succeeding letter from Assistant Secretary Morris that further study will be done on the effect of higher pay and benefits on re-enlistments and the concomitant savings which would be realized by the military.

The National Advisory Commission on the Selective Service, otherwise known as the Marshall Commission, fared no better in this area than the previous Defense Department "studies." After exclusive hearings behind closed doors, and refusals to release its working papers for public examination, the Marshall Commission announced its unsubstantiated verdict on the volunteer army in its report released in March of 1967. The Marshall Commission said only that a volunteer army "would be expensive although the Department of Defense gives no solid estimate of what it would cost."

Others have offered some estimates in this area. Dr. Walter Oi, an economist at the University of Washington and former employee of the Department of Defense, estimates that the total extra payroll costs would be around $3–$4 billion a year for armed forces equivalent to 2.7 million men under present methods of recruitment and not more than $8 billion a year for armed forces equivalent to the present higher number of men, around 3.1 to 3.2 million. Dr. Oi's exhaustive analysis is found in his paper "The Costs and Implications of an All Volunteer Force," which was presented to the University of Chicago's Conference on the Draft on December 4, 1966. Dr. Milton Friedman, of the University of Chicago, in a paper submitted to the same conference, concurred in these figures. Bruce Chapman, using 1965 figures leaked from the Pentagon study, has estimated that a pay increase totaling $3 billion would reduce—through higher re-enlistments—from 500,000 to 150,000 the number of new army personnel needed each year. One can safely assume that higher fringe benefits and other improvements in military life could bring down the number even further. In this regard I would like to add that greater consideration must be given to making the military life more commensurate to civilian in many respects. To attract career men certain improvements must be made which need not entail a corresponding decrease in discipline. Such things as better family housing and schools for children of servicemen are imperatives.

II. Much Greater Coordination of the Utilization of Skills Between the Civilian and Military Sectors of Our Society

Almost 90 per cent of the technical skills which are used by the military are also employed by the civilian economy. Civilian personnel can then be substituted for the military in many cases. Under a program begun in 1965 by Secretary of Defense McNamara, 74,300 military jobs were replaced by 60,500 civilian positions. This program of "civilianization" resulted in a net decrease of 13,800 jobs, since trainers and manpower support requirements could be eliminated entirely for the civilian positions. Assistant Secretary Morris also promised me that further study would be done in this area. He did, however, point out that the military is limited in replacement programs of this type by the requirement that many positions be retained in the military in order to rotate combat troops into stateside jobs. Nevertheless significant reductions can still be carried out.

Furthermore, savings may be realized by utilizing existing civilian training establishments, including college campuses, vocational schools, high schools, and on-the-job vocational training programs, to train personnel for the skills the military needs. At the present time the military establishment persists in maintaining costly duplicate and I would say highly inefficient training facilities. This is true even though 80–90 per cent of the military jobs are congruent with jobs in the civilian economy, according to the Department of Labor Statistics. Thus military programs could conceivably be reduced to train only the 10–20 per cent of combat or direct combat support positions which need military as opposed to vocational training. The resulting savings would be extensive, could have the possible additional effect of encouraging business investment in our manpower resources, and could produce a greater amount of skilled labor for the civilian economy.

III. Lowering Physical Standards Where Possible to Use Less Than I-A Specimens in Non-combat Jobs.

Many non-combat positions could easily be filled by men now exempted from the draft under present selective service regulations. Utilization of all our manpower resources is essential to an efficient procurement system. The Department of Defense's physical and mental standards for induction are unduly high as the old saw that "every man must be able to carry a rifle" has rarely been borne out in wartime experience and is certainly wasteful.

IV. Improving the Capabilities of Reserve Units So That They May Serve as a Means of Retaining and Maintaining Needed Skills for Potential Military Usage, and Coordinate Reserve Organizations with the Civilian Society

American military theory has always centered around a relatively small standing army with a strong Reserve. Therefore improving the present Reserve system should be one of our first priorities. A vital Reserve could and should be a repository for maintaining crucial skills for possible military use and be coordinated with the civilian economy so that any callup would not endanger the strength of the economy. An effective program would call for a voluntary army of the peacetime size of 2.7 million men, plus a well trained reserve of 1 million men.

V. Revising the Uniform Code of Military Justice to Include Only Those Personnel Engaged in Combat or Training for Combat Under the Aegis of Direct Military Authority, and Limiting Severely Its Application to Non-combat Stateside Occupations

In making military life more comparable to civilian life consideration should be given to the necessity of maintaining a strict uniform code of military justice across the board to non-combat troops. Military law maintaining discipline and control over combatants' and support troops' activities outside battle areas is essential. However, we should revise the present Code to cover only those activities which need to be under direct military control.

Conclusion

The peacetime draft has only been justifiable as a measure of necessity; if it is not necessary, it is not justifiable. Alternatives should be studied in their broadest aspects. The problem of manpower utilization is more than a military one. The arguments I have advanced for a volunteer army affect the civilian sector, our American value system, and the whole universe of military and civilian life.

"The Draft: Unjust and Unnecessary," by Thomas B. Curtis, from *The Forensic Quarterly*, Volume 42, Numbers 1–3 (May 1968), pages 165–179. [Originally published in *Compulsory Service Systems: A Critical Discussion and Debate Source Book* (Columbia, Missouri: Artcraft Press, Publishers, 1968), the contents of which were also published, under the title *Compulsory Service Systems*, as the May 1968 issue of *The Forensic Quarterly*.] Copyright © 1968 The Forensic Quarterly. Reprinted by permission of the author and *The Forensic Quarterly*.

THOMAS BRADFORD CURTIS (1911–), a lawyer who has taught at several universities, served as U.S. representative from Missouri from 1951 to 1960. He was a member of the Commission on an All-Volunteer

Armed Force under President Nixon, was vice-president and general counsel of Encyclopaedia Britannica, Inc., from 1969 to 1973, and was chairman of the Federal Election Commission during 1975–1976. He is the author of *87 Million Jobs: A Dynamic Solution for Unemployment* and *The Kennedy Round: The Future of U.S. Trade.*

39

The All-Volunteer Armed Force
by
Richard M. Nixon

During the 1968 presidential campaign, Richard Nixon pledged to end the draft "once our involvement in the Vietnam War is behind us." In his campaign speech, Nixon outlines his proposal for an all-volunteer armed force. In arguing for the proposal, he cites a significant change in conditions since the initiation of the draft just before World War II, inequities in the existing draft system, and the fundamental opposition of the draft to the principles of individual liberty upon which the United States was founded.

I speak tonight about a matter important to us all, but especially to young Americans and their parents.

I refer to compulsory military service—or, as most of us know it, "the draft."

We have lived with the draft now for almost thirty years. It was started during the dark uncertainty before the Second World War, as a temporary, emergency measure. But since then we have kept it—through our ordeals in Korea and Vietnam, and even in the years of uneasy peace between.

We have lived with the draft so long, in fact, that too many of us now accept it as normal and necessary.

I say it's time we took a new look at the draft—at the question of permanent conscription in a free society.

If we find we *can* reasonably meet our peacetime manpower needs by other means—then we should prepare for the day when the draft can be phased out of American life.

I have looked into this question very carefully. And this is my belief: once our involvement in the Vietnam war is behind us, we move toward an all-volunteer armed force.

This means that just as soon as our reduced manpower requirements in Vietnam will permit us to do so, we should stop the draft and put our Selective Service structure on stand-by.

For the many years since World War II, I believed that, even in peacetime, only through the draft could we get enough servicemen to defend our nation and meet our heavy commitments abroad. Over these years it seemed we faced a Hobson's choice: either constrict the freedom of some or endanger the freedom of all.

But conditions have changed, and our needs have changed. So, too, I believe, our defense manpower policies should change.

Tonight, I would like to share with you some of the reasons why I think this is so.

First, let me talk about what we cannot do.

First of all, we must recognize that conditions in the world today require us to keep a powerful military force. Being prepared for war is our surest guarantor of peace. While our adversaries continue to build up their strength, we cannot reduce ours; while they continue to brandish the sword, we cannot lay aside our shield.

So any major change in the way we obtain military manpower must not keep us from maintaining a clearly superior military strength.

In the short run we need also to recognize the limits imposed by the war in Vietnam. However we might wish to, we can't stop the draft while we are in a major war.

What we can do—and what we should do now—is to commit ourselves as a nation to the goal of building an all-volunteer armed force.

The arguments about the draft center first on whether it's right, and second, on whether it's necessary.

Three decades ago, Senator Robert Taft declared that the draft "is absolutely opposed to the principles of individual liberty which have always been considered a part of American democracy."

I feel this way: a system of compulsory service that arbitrarily selects some and not others simply cannot be squared with our whole concept of liberty, justice and equality under the law. Its only justification is compelling necessity.

The longer it goes on, the more troublesome are the questions it raises. Why should your son be forced to sacrifice two of the most important years of his life, so that a neighbor's son can go right along pursuing his interests in freedom and safety? Why should one young American be forced to take up military service while another is left free to make his own choice?

We all have seen, time and time again, how hit-or-miss the workings of the draft are. You know young people, as I do, whose lives have been disrupted first by uncertainty, next by conscription. We all have seen the unfairness of the present system.

Some say we should tinker with the present system, patching up an inequity here and there. I favor this too, but only for the short term.

But in the long run, the only way to stop the inequities is to stop using the system.

It does not work fairly—and, given the facts of American life, it just can't.

The inequity stems from one simple fact—that some of our young people are forced to spend two years of their lives in our nation's defense, while others are not. It's not so much the way they're selected that's wrong, as it is the *fact* of selection.

Even now, only about 40 percent of our eligible young people ever serve. As our population grows, and the manpower pool expands, that percentage will shrink even further. Ten years ago about a million men became of draft age each year. Now there are almost two million.

There has also been a change in the armed forces we need. The kinds of war we have to be prepared for now include not only conventional war and nuclear war, but also guerrilla war of the kind we are now experiencing in Vietnam.

In nuclear war huge ground armies operating in massive formations would be terribly vulnerable. That way of fighting, where nuclear weapons are in use, is a thing of the past.

An all-out *non*-nuclear war, on the other hand—that is, what we knew before as large-scale conventional war—is hard to see happening again. Of course, a sudden Soviet ground attack from Eastern Europe could mix Soviet forces with the populations in the West and thereby prevent swift resort to nuclear weapons. But even in this situation a massing of huge ground units would be impossible because of their nuclear vulnerability. So again, even this kind of struggle would break up into smaller unit actions.

In a guerrilla war of the Vietnam type, we face something else entirely. Here we need a highly professional, highly motivated force of men trained in the techniques of counterinsurgency. Vietnam has shown us that success in such wars may depend on whether our soldiers are linguists and civil affairs specialists, as well as warriors. Also, the complex weapons of modern war demand a higher level of technical and professional skill.

Of course, we will still need conventional forces large by standards of only a few decades ago to guard our vital interests around the world. But I don't believe we will need them in such quantity that we cannot meet our manpower needs through voluntary enlistments.

Conscription was an efficient mechanism for raising the massive land armies of past wars. Also, it is easier—and cheaper—simply to order men into uniform rather than recruiting them. But I believe our likely military needs in the future will place a special premium on the services of career soldiers.

How, then, do we recruit these servicemen? What incentives do we offer to attract an adequate number of volunteers?

One kind of inducement is better housing, and better living conditions generally. Both to recruit and to retain the highly skilled specialists the services need, military life has to be more competitive with the attractions of the civilian world.

The principal incentives are the most obvious: higher pay and increased benefits.

The military services are the only employers today who don't have to compete in the job market. Supplied by the draft with the manpower they want when they want it, they've been able to ignore the laws of supply and demand. But I say there's no reason why our military should be exempt from peacetime competition for manpower, any more than our local police and fire departments are exempt.

A private in the American army is paid less than a $100 a month. This is a third of the minimum wage in the civilian economy. Now to this we should add food, uniforms and housing which are furnished free. Taken all together, a single young man can probably get by on this. But it's hardly competitive with what most people can earn in civilian life. Even with allowances, many married servicemen in enlisted ranks have actually been forced to depend on relief payments to support their families.

These pay scales point up another inequity of the draft system. Our servicemen are singled out for a huge hidden tax—the difference between their military pay and what they could otherwise earn. The draftee has been forced by his country not only to defend his neighbors but to subsidize them as well.

The total cost of the pay increases needed to recruit an all-volunteer army cannot be figured out to the dollar, but authoritative studies have suggested that it could be done for 5 to 7 billions of dollars more a year. While this cost would indeed be heavy, it would be increasingly offset by reductions in the many costs which the heavy rate of turnover now causes. Ninety-three percent of the Army's draftees now leave the service as soon as their time is up—taking with them skills that it costs some $6,000 per man to develop. The *net* additional annual cost of shifting to an all-volunteer armed force would be bound to be much less.

It would cost a great deal to move to a voluntary system, but unless that cost is proved to be prohibitive, it will be more than worth it.

The alternative is never-ending compulsion in a society consecrated to freedom. I think we can pay a great deal to avoid that.

In any case, in terms of morale, efficiency and effectiveness, a volunteer armed force would assuredly be a better armed force.

Today, seven out of every ten men in the Army have less than two years' military experience. As an Army Chief of Personnel put it: "As soon as we are able to operate as a unit, the trained men leave and we have to start all over again." A volunteer force would have a smaller turnover; it would be leavened by a higher percentage of skilled, motivated men; fewer would be constantly in training; and fewer trained men would be tied down training others.

The result would be, on the average, more professional fighting men, and less invitation to unnecessary casualties in case of war.

The same higher pay scales needed to get more volunteers would also strengthen incentives for career service. I am sure the spirit and self-confidence of the men who wear the nation's uniform would be enhanced.

In proposing that we start toward ending the draft when the war is over, I would enter two cautions: first, its structure needs to be kept on stand-by in case some all-out emergency requires its reactivation. But this can be done without leaving 20 million young Americans who will come of draft age during the next decade in constant uncertainty and apprehension.

The second caution I would enter is this: the *draft* can't be ended all at once. It will have to be phased out, so that at every step we can be certain of maintaining our defense strength.

But the important thing is to decide to begin and at the very first opportunity *to* begin.

Now, some are against a volunteer armed force because of its cost, or because they're used to the draft and hesitant to change. But three other arguments are often raised. While they sound plausible, I say they don't stand up under examination.

The first is that a volunteer army would be a black army, so it is a scheme to use Negroes to defend a white America. The second is that a volunteer army would actually be an army of hired mercenaries. The third is, a volunteer army would dangerously increase military influence in our society.

Now, let's take these arguments in order:

First, the "black army" one. I regard this as sheer fantasy. It supposes that raising military pay would in some way slow up or stop the flow of white volunteers, even as it stepped up the flow of black volunteers. Most of our volunteers now are white. Better pay and better conditions would obviously make military service more attractive to black and white alike.

Second, the "mercenary" argument. A mercenary is a soldier of fortune—one who fights for or against anyone for pay. What we're talking about now is American soldiers, serving under the American flag. We are talking about men who proudly wear our country's uniform in defense of its freedom. We're talking about the same kind of citizen armed force America has had ever since it began, excepting only the period when we have relied on the draft.

The third argument is the threat of universal military influence. This, if ever it did come, would come from the top officers ranks, not from the enlisted ranks that draftees now fill—and we already have a career officer corps. It is hard to see how replacing draftees with volunteers would make officers more influential.

Today all across our country we face a crisis of confidence. Nowhere is it more acute than among our young people. They recognize the draft as an infringement on their liberty—which it is. To them, it represents a government insensitive to their rights—a government callous to their status as free men. They ask for justice—and they deserve it.

So I say, it's time we looked to our consciences. Let's show our commitment to freedom by preparing to assure our young people theirs.

"The All-Volunteer Armed Force," an address by Richard M. Nixon on the CBS Radio Network, October 17, 1968 (New York: Nixon/Agnew Campaign Committee, 1968), pages 1–10 (full text).

RICHARD MILHOUS NIXON (1913–) was the thirty-seventh president of the United States. Following up on his campaign pledge to end the draft, he instituted the all-volunteer force in 1973. He thus, for the first time in the nation's history, made it official national policy for the armed forces to rely totally on volunteers for its personnel.

40

The Debate on an
All-Volunteer Armed Force

by
*The President's Commission
on an All-Volunteer Armed Force*

In March 1969, President Nixon created the President's Commission on an All-Volunteer Armed Force, chaired by former Secretary of Defense Thomas Gates, to study in depth what, if any, changes should be made in military manpower procurement in the United States when the Selective Service Act expired on June 30, 1971. In 1970 the commission released its unanimous recommendation to establish an all-volunteer armed force. This chapter from the Gates Commission Report summarizes major arguments about the feasibility of the all-volunteer armed force, and gives the commission's answers to each argument.

"We have lived with the draft so long," President Nixon has pointed out, "that too many of us accept it as normal and necessary." Over the past generation, social, political, and economic arrangements have grown up around conscription that touch our lives in a great many ways. The elimination of the draft will inevitably disrupt these arrangements and may be disturbing to some. But beyond these narrow, often overlooked interests lie broader considerations which have prompted defenders of conscription to argue that an all-volunteer armed force will have a variety of undesirable political, social, and military effects.

In our meetings we have discussed the opposing arguments extensively. As our recommendations disclose, we have unanimously concluded that the arguments for an all-volunteer force are much the stronger. Yet, there can be no question of the sincerity and earnest conviction of those who hold the views we have rejected. In fairness to them, and to acquaint the Nation with both sides of the issues, this chapter summarizes the main arguments raised against the volunteer force and offers answers to them. . . .

A general point should be made here. The elimination of conscription admittedly is a major social change, but it will not produce a major change in the personnel of our armed forces. The majority of men serving today are volunteers. And many who are now conscripted would volunteer once improvements were made in pay and other conditions of service. Therefore, the difference between an all-volunteer force and a mixed force of conscripts and volunteers is limited to that minority who would not serve unless conscripted and who would not volunteer in the absence of conscription. An all-volunteer force will attract men who are not now conscripted and who do not now volunteer but who will do so when military service imposes less of a financial penalty than it currently does.

Contrary to much dramatic argument, the reality is that an all-volunteer force will be manned largely by the same kind of individuals as today's armed forces. The men who serve will be quite similar in patriotism, political attitudes, effectiveness, and susceptibility to civilian control. The draft does not guarantee the quality of our armed forces, and neither will voluntarism. There are no simple solutions or shortcuts in dealing with the complex problems that must always concern us as a free people.

Arguments against an all-volunteer force fall into fairly distinct, though sometimes overlapping categories, one of which is feasibility. Summarized below are some of the main objections under this heading.

Objection 1: An all-volunteer force will be very costly—so costly the Nation cannot afford it.

Answer: The question of how much the armed forces cost is confused with the question of who bears those costs. It is true that the budget for a voluntary force will generally be higher than for an equally effective force of conscripts and volunteers; but the cost of the voluntary force will be less than the cost of the mixed force. This apparent paradox arises because some of the costs of a mixed force are hidden and never appear in the budget.

Under the present system, first-term servicemen must bear a disproportionately large share of the defense burden. Draftees and draft-induced volunteers are paid less than they would require to volunteer. The loss they suffer is a tax-in-kind which for budget purposes is never recorded as a receipt or an expenditure. We estimate that for draftees and draft-induced volunteers the total tax amounts to $2 billion per year; an average of $3,600 per man. If Government accounts reflected as income this financial penalty imposed on first-term servicemen, it would become clear that a voluntary force costs less than a mixed force. One example of real cost savings that will accrue is the reduction in training costs as a result of the lower personnel turnover of a voluntary force.

Conscription also imposes social and human costs by distorting the personal life and career plans of the young and by forcing society to deal with such difficult problems as conscientious objection.

Objection 2: The all-volunteer force will lack the flexibility to expand rapidly in times of sudden crises.

Answer: Military preparedness depends on forces in being, not on the ability to draft untrained men. Reserve forces provide immediate support to active forces, while the draft provides only inexperienced civilians who must be organized, trained, and equipped before they can become effective soldiers and sailors—a process which takes many months. The Commission has recommended a standby draft which can be put into effect promptly if circumstances require mobilization of large numbers of men. History shows that Congress has quickly granted the authority to draft when needed.

Others contend that an all-volunteer force will have undesirable political and social effects. Some of these objections are given below.

Objection 3: An all-volunteer force will undermine patriotism by weakening the traditional belief that each citizen has a moral responsibility to serve his country.

Answer: Compelling service through a draft undermines respect for government by forcing an individual to serve when and in the manner the government decides, regardless of his own values and talents. Clearly, not all persons are equally suited for military service—some are simply not qualified. When not all our citizens can serve, and only a small minority are needed, a voluntary decision to serve is the best answer, morally and practically, to the question of who should serve.

Objection 4: The presence of draftees in a mixed force guards against the growth of a separate military ethos, which could pose a threat to civilian authority, our freedom, and our democratic institutions.

Answer: Historically, voluntary service and freedom have gone hand in hand. In the United States and England, where voluntarism has been used most consistently, there is also the strongest tradition of civilian control of the military. There are responsibilities to be met in maintaining civilian control, but they must be exercised from above rather than at the lowest level of the enlisted ranks. They reside in the Halls of Congress, and in the White House as well as in the military hierarchy.

In either a mixed or volunteer force, the attitudes of the officer corps are the preponderant factor in the psychology of the military; and with or without the draft, professional officers are recruited voluntarily from a variety of regional and socioeconomic backgrounds. It is hard to believe that substituting a true volunteer for a draftee or a draft-induced volunteer in one of every six positions will so alter the military as to threaten the tradition of civilian control, which is embodied in the Constitution and deeply felt by the public. It is even less credible when one considers that this substitution will occur at the lowest level of the military ladder, among first-term enlisted men and officers, and that turnover of these first-term personnel in an all-volunteer force will be approximately three-fourths of that in a comparable mixed force.

The truth is, we already have a large professional armed force amounting to over 2 million men. The existing loyalties and political influence of that force cannot be materially changed by eliminating conscription in the lowest ranks.

Objection 5: The higher pay required for a voluntary force will be especially appealing to blacks who have relatively poorer civilian opportunities. This, combined with higher reenlistment rates for blacks, will mean that a disproportionate number of blacks will be in military service. White enlistments and re-enlistments might decline, thus leading to an all-black enlisted force. Racial tensions would grow because of white apprehension at this development and black resentment at bearing an undue share of the burden of defense. At the same time, some of the most qualified young blacks would be in the military—not in the community where their talents are needed.

Answer: The frequently heard claim that a volunteer force will be all black, or all this or all that, simply has no basis in fact. Our research indicates that the composition of the armed forces will not be fundamentally changed by ending conscription. Negroes presently make up 10.6 percent of the armed forces, slightly less than the proportion of blacks in the Nation. Our best projections for the future are that blacks will be about 14 percent of the enlisted men in a conscripted force totalling 2.5 million officers and men, and 15 percent in an all-volunteer force of equal capability. For the Army, we estimate that the proportion of blacks will be 17 percent for the mixed force and 18 percent for the voluntary force as compared to 12.8 percent in the Army today. To be sure, these are estimates, but even extreme assumptions would not change the figures drastically.

If higher pay does make opportunities in an all-volunteer force more attractive to some particular group than those in civilian life, then the appropriate course is to correct the discriminations in civilian life—*not* introduce additional discriminations against such a group.

The argument that blacks would bear an unfair share of the burden of an all-volunteer force confounds service by free choice with compulsory service. With conscription, some blacks are compelled to serve at earnings below what they would earn in the civilian economy. Blacks who join a voluntary force presumably have decided for themselves that military service is preferable to the other alternatives available to them. They regard military service as a more rewarding opportunity, not as a burden. Denial of this opportunity would reflect either bias or a paternalistic belief that blacks are not capable of making the "right" decisions concerning their lives.

Objection 6: Those joining an all-volunteer force will be men from the lowest economic classes, motivated primarily by monetary rewards rather than patriotism. An all-volunteer force will be manned, in effect, by mercenaries.

Answer: Again, our research indicates that an all-volunteer force will not differ significantly from the current force of conscripts and volunteers. Maintenance of current mental, physical, and moral standards for enlistment will ensure that a better-paid, volunteer force will not recruit an undue proportion of youths from disadvantaged socioeconomic backgrounds. A disproportionate fraction of the 30 percent presently unable to meet these standards come from such backgrounds, and these men would also be ineligible for service in an all-volunteer force. Increasing military pay in the first term of service will increase the attractiveness of military service more to those who have higher civilian earnings potential than to those who have lower civilian potential. Military pay is already relatively attractive to those who have very poor civilian alternatives. If eligible, such individuals are now free to enlist and, moreover, are free to remain beyond their first term of service when military pay is even more attractive.

Finally, how will "mercenaries" suddenly emerge in the armed forces as a result of better pay and other conditions of service? The term "mercenary" applies to men who enlist for pay alone, usually in the service of a foreign power, and precludes all other motives for serving. Those who volunteer to serve in the armed forces do so for a variety of reasons, including a sense of duty. Eliminating the financial penalty first-term servicemen presently suffer, and improving other conditions of service, will not suddenly change the motives and basic attitudes of new recruits. Also, can we regard as mercenaries the career commissioned and noncommissioned officers now serving beyond their first term?

Objection 7: An all-volunteer force would stimulate foreign military adventures, foster an irresponsible foreign policy, and lessen civilian concern about the use of military forces.

Answer: Decisions by a government to use force or to threaten the use of force during crises are extremely difficult. The high cost of military resources, the moral burden of risking human lives, political costs at home and overseas, and the overshadowing risk of nuclear confrontation—these and other factors enter into such decisions. It is absurd to argue that issues of such importance would be ignored and the decision for war made on the basis of whether our forces were entirely voluntary or mixed.

To the extent that there is pressure to seek military solutions to foreign policy problems, such pressure already exists and will not be affected by ending conscription. The volunteer force will have the same professional leadership as the present mixed force. Changes in the lower ranks will not alter the character of this leadership or the degree of civilian control.

A decision to use the all-volunteer force will be made according to the same criteria as the decision to use a mixed force of conscripts and volunteers because the size and readiness of the two forces will be quite similar. These military factors are key determinants in any decision to commit forces. Beyond initial commitment, the policy choice between expanding our forces by conscription or by voluntary enlistment is the same for both the all-volunteer force and a mixed force of conscripts and volunteers. The important difference between the two forces lies in the necessity for political debate before returning to conscription. With the all-volunteer force, the President can seek authorization to activate the standby draft, but Congress must give its consent. With the mixed system, draft calls can be increased by the President. The difference between the two alternatives is crucial. The former will generate public discussion of the use of the draft to fight a war; the latter can be done without such public discussion. If the need for conscription is not clear, such discussion will clarify the issue, and the draft will be used only if public support is widespread.

Other critics of an all-volunteer force argue that it will gradually erode the military's effectiveness. Some of their main concerns are taken up below.

Objection 8: A voluntary force will be less effective because not enough highly qualified youths will be likely to enlist and pursue military careers. As the quality of servicemen declines, the prestige and dignity of the services will also decline and further intensify recruiting problems.

Answer: The Commission has been impressed by the number and quality of the individuals who, despite conscription, now choose a career in the military. The fact that we must resort in part to coercion to man the armed services must be a serious deterrent to potential volunteers. A force made up of men freely choosing to serve should enhance the dignity and prestige of the military. Every man in uniform will be serving as a matter of choice rather than coercion.

The Commission recognizes the importance of recruiting and retaining qualified individuals. It has recommended improved basic compensation and conditions of service, proficiency pay, and accelerated promotions for the highly skilled to make military career opportunities more attractive. These improvements, combined with an intensive recruiting effort, should enable the military not only to maintain a high quality force but also to have one that is more experienced, better motivated, and has higher morale.

Objection 9: The defense budget will not be increased to provide for an all-volunteer force, and the Department of Defense will have to cut back expenditures in other areas. Even if additional funds are provided initially, competing demands will, over the long term, force the Department of Defense to absorb the added budgetary expense of an all-volunteer force. The result could be a potentially serious deterioration of the nation's overall military posture.

Answer: Ultimately, the size of the military budget and the strength of our armed forces depend upon public attitudes toward national defense. Since World War II, our peacetime armed forces have been consistently supported at high levels. The public has supported large forces because it has felt them essential to national security. The change from a mixed force of volunteers and conscripts to an all-volunteer force cannot significantly change that feeling.

The contention that an all-volunteer force is undesirable because it

THE PRESIDENT'S COMMISSION

would result in smaller defense forces raises a serious issue regarding the conduct of government in a democracy. Conscription obscures a part of the cost of providing manpower for defense. When that cost is made explicit, taxpayers may decide they prefer a smaller defense force. If so, the issue has been resolved openly, in accord with the Constitution, and in the best tradition of the democratic process. Those who then argue that too little is being devoted to national defense are saying that they are unwilling to trust the open democratic process; that, if necessary, a hidden tax should be imposed to support the forces they believe are necessary.

"The Debate," from The President's Commission on an All-Volunteer Force, *The Report of the President's Commission on an All-Volunteer Armed Force* (Washington, D.C.: Government Printing Office, 1970), pages 11–20.

The following biographical information on members of the President's Commission on an All-Volunteer Force—as of 1970—is reproduced from their Report. For further data on Thomas Curtis and Milton Friedman, see pages 600 and 632.

THOMAS GATES, CHAIRMAN. Chairman of the Executive Committee of Morgan Guaranty Trust Co. Former Secretary of Defense. New York City

THOMAS CURTIS. Vice-President and General Counsel, Encyclopaedia Britannica. Former Congressman from Missouri and ranking Republican on Joint Economic Committee, United States Congress. St. Louis, Missouri

FREDERICK DENT. President, Mayfair Mills. Spartanburg, South Carolina

MILTON FRIEDMAN. Paul Snowdon Russell Distinguished Service Professor of Economics, University of Chicago. Chicago, Illinois

CRAWFORD GREENEWALT. Chairman, Finance Committee, E. I. duPont de Nemours and Co. Wilmington, Delaware

ALAN GREENSPAN Chairman of the Board, Townsend-Greenspan & Co. Economic consultants. New York City

ALFRED GRUENTHER. Former Supreme Allied Commander, Europe. Washington, D.C.

STEPHEN HERBITS. Student, Georgetown University Law Center. Washington, D.C.

THEODORE HESBURGH. President, University of Notre Dame. Chairman, U.S. Commission on Civil Rights. South Bend, Indiana

JEROME HOLLAND. President, Hampton Institute. Hampton, Virginia

JOHN KEMPER. Headmaster, Phillips Academy. Andover, Massachusetts

JEANNE NOBLE. Professor, New York University. Vice-President, National Council of Negro Women. Former member, National Advisory Commission on Selective Service. New York City

LAURIS NORSTAD. Chairman of the Board, Owens-Corning Fiberglas Corp. Former Supreme Allied Commander, Europe. New York City

W. ALLEN WALLIS. President, University of Rochester. Rochester, New York

ROY WILKINS. Executive Director, NAACP. New York City

41

Why Not a Volunteer Army?

by

Milton Friedman

In the late 1960s, arguments favoring an all-volunteer armed force on practical, economic, and ethical grounds gave new impetus to the anti-draft movement in the United States. During this period one of the most articulate and influential arguments was made by economist Milton Friedman, who argued that the volunteer army would not only be more consistent with human freedom but also economically more efficient than the draft. Friedman maintains that an all-volunteer armed force would eliminate the hidden costs the draft imposes on draftees; increase reenlistment rates, thereby reducing training costs; and increase overall military effectiveness.

Manning our military forces currently requires the services of only a minority of young men. At most, something like one-third will have seen military service by the time they reach age 26. This percentage is scheduled to decline still further as the youngsters born in the postwar baby boom come of age. Hence, some method of "selective service"— deciding which young man should serve and which two or three should not—is inevitable. However, the present method is inequitable, wasteful, and inconsistent with a free society.

On this point there is wide agreement. Even most supporters of a draft like the present one regard it as at best a necessary evil. And representatives of all parts of the political spectrum have urged that conscription be abolished—including John K. Galbraith and Barry Goldwater; the New Left and the Republican Ripon Society.

The disadvantages of our present system of compulsion and the advantages of a voluntary army are so widely recognized that we can deal with them very briefly. The more puzzling question is why we have continued to use compulsion. The answer is partly inertia—a carryover from a total war situation when the case for a voluntary army is far weaker. But even more, the answer is the tyranny of the status quo. The natural tendency of an administrator of a large, complex, and ongoing activity is to regard the present method of administering it as the only feasible way to do so and to object strenuously that any proposed alternative is visionary and unfeasible—even though the same man, once the change is made and it becomes the existing method, will argue just as strenuously that *it* is the only feasible method.

This bureaucratic standpattism has been reinforced by a confusion between the apparent and the real cost of manning the armed forces by compulsion. The confusion has made it appear that a voluntary army would be much more expensive to the country and hence might not be feasible for fiscal reasons. In fact, the cost of a voluntary army, properly calculated, would almost surely be less than that of a conscripted army. It is entirely feasible to maintain present levels of military power on a strictly voluntary basis.

The other disadvantages that have been attributed to a voluntary army are that it might be racially unbalanced, would not provide sufficient flexibility in size of forces, and would enhance the political danger of undue military influence. While the problems referred to are real, the first and third are in no way connected with the use of voluntary or compulsory means to recruit enlisted men and do not constitute valid arguments against abolishing the draft. The second has more merit, but devices exist to provide moderate flexibility under a voluntary as under a compulsory system.

There is no reason why we cannot move to volunteer forces gradually—by making conditions of service more and more attractive until the whip of compulsion fades away. This, in my opinion, is the direction in which we should move, and the sooner the better.

The Disadvantages of Compulsion and Advantages of a Voluntary Army

Military Effectiveness

A voluntary army would be manned by people who had chosen a military career rather than at least partly by reluctant conscripts anxious only to serve out their term. Aside from the effect on fighting spirit, this would produce a lower turnover in the armed services, saving precious man-hours that are now wasted in training or being trained. It would permit also intensive training and a higher average level of skill of the men in the service. And it would encourage the use of more and better equipment. A smaller, but more highly skilled, technically competent, and better armed force could provide the same or greater military strength.

Individual Freedom

A voluntary army would preserve the freedom of individuals to serve or not to serve. Or, put the other way, it would avoid the arbitrary power that now resides in draft boards to decide how a young man shall spend several of the most important years of his life—let alone whether his life shall be risked in warfare. An incidental advantage would be to raise the level and tone of political discussion.

A voluntary army would enhance also the freedom of those who now do not serve. Being conscripted has been used as a weapon—or thought by young men to be so used—to discourage freedom of speech, assembly, and protest. The freedom of young men to emigrate or to travel abroad has been limited by the need to get the permission of a draft board if the young man is not to put himself in the position of inadvertently being a law-breaker.

A conspicuous example of the effect on freedom of a voluntary army is that it would completely eliminate the tormenting and insoluble problem now posed by the conscientious objector—real or pretended.

Arbitrary Discrimination

A by-product of freedom to serve would be avoidance of the present arbitrary discrimination among different groups. A large fraction of the poor are rejected on physical and mental grounds. The relatively well-to-do are in an especially good position to take advantage of the possibilities of deferment offered by continuing their schooling. Hence the draft bears disproportionately on the upper lower classes and the lower middle classes. The fraction of high school graduates who serve is vastly higher than of either those who have gone to college or those who dropped out before finishing high school.

Removal of Uncertainty for Individuals Subject to Draft

A volunteer army would permit young men, both those who serve and those who do not, to plan their schooling, their careers, their marriages, and their families in accordance with their own long-run interests. As it is, the uncertainty about the draft affects every decision they make and often leads them to behave differently from the way they otherwise would in the correct or mistaken belief that they will thereby reduce the chance of being drafted. This disadvantage could be avoided under a compulsory system by, for example, a universal lottery that at age 16, say, assigned youngsters categories such as: certain to be called, likely to be called, possibly will be called, unlikely to be called, certain not to be called. The size of each category would be determined by estimates of future military needs.

Effect on Rest of Community

Substitution of a voluntary army (or of a lottery) for the present draft would permit colleges and universities to pursue their proper educational function, freed alike from the incubus of young men—probably numbering in the hundreds of thousands—who would prefer to be at work rather than in a school but who now continue their schooling in the hope of avoiding the draft and from controversy about issues strictly irrelevant to their educational function. We certainly need controversy in the universities—but about intellectual and educational issues, not whether to rank or not to rank.

Similarly, the community at large would benefit from the reduction of unwise earlier marriages contracted at least partly under the whip of the draft and from the probable associated reduction in the birth rate. Industry and government would benefit from being able to hire young men on their merits, not their deferments.

Defects Unavoidable Under Compulsion

So long as compulsion is retained, inequity, waste, and interference with freedom are inevitable. A lottery would make the arbitrary element in the present system overt. Universal national service would only compound the evil—regimenting all young men, and perhaps women, to camouflage the regimentation of some.

The Situation in Time of Major War

If a very large fraction of the young men of the relevant age groups are required—or will be used whether required or not—in the military services, the advantages of a voluntary army become very small. It would still be technically possible to have a voluntary army, and there would still be some advantages, since it is doubtful that literally 100 per cent of the potential candidates will in fact be drawn into the services. But if nearly everyone who is physically capable will serve anyway, there is little room for free choice, the avoidance of uncertainty, and so on. And to rely on volunteers under such conditions would then require very high pay in the armed services, and very high burdens on those who do not serve, in order to attract a sufficient number into the armed forces. This would involve serious political and administrative problems. To put it differently, and in terms that will become fully clear to non-economists only later, it might turn out that the implicit tax of forced service is less bad than the alternative taxes that would have to be used to finance a voluntary army.

Hence for a major war, a strong case can be made for compulsory service. And indeed, compulsory service has been introduced in the United States only under such conditions—in the Civil War, World War I, and World War II. It is hardly conceivable that it could have been introduced afresh in, say, 1950, if a system of compulsory service had not so recently been in full swing. As it was, the easiest thing to do when military needs for manpower rose was to reactivate the recent wartime technique.

Possible Disadvantages of a Voluntary Army

Is a Voluntary Army Feasible?

Under present conditions, the number of persons who volunteer for armed service is inadequate to man the armed forces, and—even so—

many who volunteer do so only because they anticipate being drafted. The number of "true" volunteers is clearly much too small to man armed forces of our present size. This undoubted fact is repeatedly cited as evidence that a voluntary army is unfeasible.

It is evidence of no such thing. It is evidence rather that we are now grossly underpaying our armed forces. The starting pay for young men who enter the armed forces is now about $45 a week—including not only cash pay and allotments but also the value of clothing, food, housing, and other items furnished in kind. When the bulk of young men can command at least twice this sum in civilian jobs, it is little wonder that volunteers are so few. Indeed, it is somewhat surprising that there are as many as there are—testimony to the drives other than pecuniary reward that lead some young men to choose military service either as a career or for a few years.

To man our armed forces with volunteers would require making conditions of service more attractive—not only higher pay but also better housing facilities and improved amenities in other respects. It will be replied that money is not the only factor young men consider in choosing their careers. That is certainly true—and equally certainly irrelevant. Adequate pay alone may not attract, but inadequate pay can certainly deter. Military service has many non-monetary attractions to young men—the chance to serve one's country, adventure, travel, opportunities for training, and so on. Not the least of the advantages of a voluntary army is that the military would have to improve their personnel policies and pay more attention to meeting the needs of the enlisted men. They now need pay little attention to them, since they can fill their ranks with conscripts serving under compulsion. Indeed, it is a tribute to their humanitarianism—and the effectiveness of indirect pressures via the political process—that service in the armed forces is not made even less attractive than it now is.

The personnel policies of the armed forces have been repeatedly criticized—and, with no spur, repeatedly left unreformed. Imaginative policies designed to make the armed forces attractive to the kind of men the armed services would like to have—plus the elimination of compulsion which now makes military service synonymous with enforced incarceration—could change drastically the whole image that the armed services present to young men. The Air Force, because it has relied so heavily on "real" volunteers, perhaps comes closest to demonstrating what could be done.

The question of how much more we would have to pay to attract sufficient volunteers has been studied intensively in the Department of Defense study of military recruitment. Based on a variety of evidence collected in that study, Walter Oi [has estimated] that a starting pay (again including pay in kind as well as in cash) of something like $4,000 to $5,500 a year—about $80 to $100 a week—would suffice. This is surely not an unreasonable sum. Oi estimates that the total extra payroll costs (after allowing for the savings in turnover and men employed in training) would be around $3 billion to $4 billion a year for Armed Forces equivalent to 2.7 million men under present methods of recruitment and not more than $8 billion a year for Armed Forces equivalent to the present higher number of men (around 3.1 or 3.2 million men). Based on the same evidence, the Defense Department has come up with estimates as high as $17.5 billion. Even the highest of these estimates is not in any way unfeasible in the context of total federal government expenditures of more than $175 billion a year.

Whatever may be the exact figure, it is a highly misleading indication of the cost incurred in shifting from compulsion to a voluntary army. There are net advantages, not disadvantages, in offering volunteers conditions sufficiently attractive to recruit the number of young men required.

This is clearly true on the level of individual equity: the soldier no less than the rest of us is worth his hire. How can we justify paying him less than the amount for which he is willing to serve? How can we justify, that is, involuntary servitude except in times of the greatest national emergency? One of the great gains in the progress of civilization was the elimination of the power of the nobleman or the sovereign to exact compulsory servitude.

On a more mundane budgetary level, the argument that a voluntary Army would cost more simply involves a confusion of apparent with real cost. By this argument, the construction of the Great Pyramid with slave labor was a cheap project. The real cost of conscripting a soldier who would not voluntarily serve on present terms is not his pay and the cost of his keep. It is the amount for which he would be willing to serve. He is paying the difference. This is the extra cost to him that must be added to the cost borne by the rest of us. Compare, for example, the cost to a star professional football player and to an unemployed worker. Both might have the same attitudes toward the army and like—or dislike—a military career equally. But because the one has so much better alternatives than the other, it would take a much higher sum to attract him. When he is forced to serve, we are in effect imposing on him a tax in kind equal in value to the difference between what it would take to attract him and the military pay he actually receives. This implicit tax in kind should be added to the explicit taxes imposed on the rest of us to get the real cost of our Armed Forces.

If this is done, it will be seen at once that abandoning the draft would almost surely reduce the real cost—because the armed forces would then be manned by men for whom soldiering was the best available career, and hence who would require the lowest sums of money to induce them to serve. Abandoning the draft might raise the apparent money cost to the government but only because it would substitute taxes in money for taxes in kind.

Moreover, there are some important offsets even to the increase in apparent money cost. In addition to the lower turnover, already taken into account in the estimates cited, the higher average level of skill would permit further reductions in the size of the army, saving monetary cost to the government. Because manpower is cheap to the military, they now tend to waste it, using enlisted men for tasks that could be performed by civilians or machines, or eliminated entirely. Moreover, better pay at the time to volunteers might lessen the political appeal of veteran's benefits that we now grant after the event. These now cost us over $6 billion a year or one-third as much as current annual payroll costs for the active armed forces—and they will doubtless continue to rise under present conditions.

There are still other offsets. Colleges and universities would be saved the cost of housing, seating, and entertaining hundreds of thousands of young men. Total output of the community would be higher both because these men would be at work and because the young men who now go to work could be used more effectively. They could be offered and could accept jobs requiring considerable training instead of having to take stopgap jobs while awaiting a possible call to service. Perhaps there are some effects in the opposite direction, but I have not been able to find any.

Whatever happens to the apparent monetary cost, the real cost of a voluntary army would almost surely be less than that of the present system and it is not even clear that the apparent monetary cost would be higher—if it is correctly measured for the community as a whole. In any event, there can be little doubt that wholly voluntary armed forces of roughly the present size are entirely feasible on economic and fiscal grounds.

Would a Voluntary Army Be Racially Unbalanced?

It has been argued that a military career would be so much more attractive to the poor than to the well-to-do that volunteer armed services would be staffed disproportionately by the poor. Since Negroes constitute a high proportion of the poor, it is further argued that volunteer armed forces would be largely Negro.

There is first a question of fact. This tendency is present today in exaggerated form—the present levels of pay are *comparatively* more attractive to Negroes than the higher levels of pay in voluntary armed forces would be. Yet the fraction of persons in the armed forces who are Negro is roughly the same as in the population at large. It has been estimated that even if every qualified Negro who does not now serve were to serve, whites would still constitute a substantial majority of the armed forces. And that every qualified Negro who does not now serve *would* serve is a wholly unrealistic possibility. The military services require a wide variety of skills and offer varied opportunities. They have always appealed to people of varied classes and backgrounds and they will continue to do so. Particularly if pay and amenities were made more attractive, there is every reason to expect that they would draw from all segments of the community.

In part, this argument involves invalid extrapolation from the present conscripted army to a voluntary army. Because we conscript, we pay salaries that are attractive only to the disadvantaged among us.

Beyond this question of fact, there is the more basic question of principle. Clearly, it is a good thing not a bad thing to offer better alternatives to the currently disadvantaged. The argument to the contrary rests on a political judgment: that a high ratio of Negroes in the armed services would exacerbate racial tensions at home and provide in the form of ex-soldiers a military trained group to foment violence. Perhaps there is something to this. My own inclination is to regard it as the reddest of red herrings. Our government should discriminate neither in the civil nor in the military services. We must handle our domestic problems as best we can and not use them as an excuse for denying Negroes opportunities in the military service.

Would a Voluntary Army Have Sufficient Flexibility?

One of the advantages cited for conscription is that it permits great flexibility in the size of the armed services. Let military needs suddenly increase, and draft calls can be rapidly stepped up, and conversely.

This is a real advantage—but can easily be overvalued. Emergencies must be met with forces in being, however they are recruited. Many months now elapse between an increase in draft calls and the availability of additional trained men.

The key question is how much flexibility is required. Recruitment by voluntary means could provide considerable flexibility—at a cost. The way to do so would be to make pay and conditions of service more attractive than is required to recruit the number of men that it is anticipated will be needed. There would then be an excess of volunteers—queues. If the number of men required increased, the queues could be shortened and conversely.

The change in scale involved in a shift from conditions like the present to a total war is a very different matter. If the military judgment is that, in such a contingency, there would be time and reason to expand the armed forces manyfold, either universal military training, to provide a trained reserve force, or standby provisions for conscription could be justified. Both are very different from the use of conscription to man the standing army in time of peace or brushfire wars or wars like that in Vietnam which require recruiting only a minority of young men.

The flexibility provided by conscription has another side. It means that, at least for a time, the administration and the military services can proceed fairly arbitrarily in committing U.S. forces. The voluntary method provides a continuing referendum of the public at large. The popularity or unpopularity of the activities for which the Armed Forces are used will clearly affect the ease of recruiting men. This is a consideration that will be regarded by some as an advantage of conscription, by others, including myself, as a disadvantage.

Is a "Professional Army" a Political Danger?

There is little question that large Armed Forces plus the industrial complex required to support them constitute an ever-present threat to political freedom. Our free institutions would certainly be safer if the conditions of the world permitted us to maintain far smaller armed forces.

The valid fear has been converted into an invalid argument against voluntary armed forces. They would constitute a professional army, it is said, that would lack contact with the populace and become an independent political force, whereas a conscripted army remains basically a citizen army. The fallacy in this argument is that the danger comes primarily from the officers, who are now and always have been a professional corps of volunteers. A few examples from history will show that the danger to political stability is largely unrelated to the method of recruiting enlisted men.

Napoleon and Franco both rose to power at the head of conscripts. The recent military takeover in Argentina was by armed forces recruiting enlisted men by conscription. Britain and the U.S. have maintained freedom while relying primarily on volunteers; Switzerland and Sweden, while using conscription. It is hard to find any relation historically between the method of recruiting enlisted men and the political threat from the armed forces.

However we recruit enlisted men, it is essential that we adopt practices that will guard against the political danger of creating a military corps with loyalties of its own and out of contact with the broader body politic. Fortunately, we have so far largely avoided this danger. The broad basis of recruitment to the military academics, by geography as well as social and economic factors, the ROTC programs in the colleges, the recruitment of officers from enlisted men, and similar measures, have all contributed to this result.

For the future, we need to follow policies that will foster lateral recruitment into the officer corps from civilian activities—rather than primarily promotion from within. The military services no less than the civil service need and will benefit from in-and-outers. For the political gain, we should be willing to bear the higher financial costs involved in fairly high turnover and rather short average terms of service for officers. We should follow personnel policies that will continue to make at least a period of military service as an officer attractive to young men from many walks of life.

There is no way of avoiding the political danger altogether. But it can be minimized as readily with a volunteer as with a conscripted army.

The Transition to a Volunteer Army

Given the will, there is no reason why the transition to volunteer armed forces cannot begin at once and proceed gradually by a process of trial and error. We do not need precise and accurate knowledge of the levels of pay and amenities that will be required. We need take no irreversible step.

Out of simple justice, we should in any event raise the pay and improve the living conditions of enlisted men. It if were proposed explicitly that a special income tax of 50 per cent be imposed on enlisted men in the armed services, there would be cries of outrage. Yet that is what our present pay scales plus conscription amount to. If we started rectifying this injustice, the number of "real" volunteers would increase, even while conscription continued. Experience would show how responsive the number of volunteers is to the terms offered and how much these terms would have to be improved to attract enough men. As the number of volunteers increased, the lash of compulsion could fade away.

This picture is overdrawn in one important respect. Unless it is clear that conscription is definitely to be abolished in a reasonably short time, the armed services will not have sufficient incentive to improve their recruitment and personnel policies. They will be tempted to procrastinate, relying on the crutch of conscription. The real survival strength of conscription is that it eases the life of the top military command. Hence, it would be highly desirable to have a definite termination date set for conscription.

Conclusion

The case for abolishing conscription and recruiting our armed forces by voluntary methods seems to me overwhelming. One of the greatest advances in human freedom was the commutation of taxes in kind to taxes in money. We have reverted to a barbarous custom. It is past time that we regain our heritage.

"Why Not a Volunteer Army?" by Milton Friedman, from *New Individualist Review*, Volume 4, Number 4 (Spring 1967), pages 3–9. Copyright © 1967 Liberty Fund, Inc. Reprinted by permission of the author and the Liberty Fund.

MILTON FRIEDMAN (1912–), a Nobel laureate in economics, is well known for his many writings supporting individualism and free enterprise. He served on the President's Commission on an All-Volunteer Force and has written a number of books, the latest (with his wife, Rose, as coauthor) being *Free to Choose.*

42

An Unpublished Speech

by

Daniel Webster

The speech that Daniel Webster delivered on the floor of the House of Representatives on December 9, 1814, is well known among the foes of conscription, but though many may be familiar with one or two heavily edited excerpts, few have ever read the entire speech.

The speech was not published at the time Webster gave it, and early editions of Webster's works made no mention of it. One of his biographers, George Ticknor Curtis, wrote in 1872 that "it was never published, and the manuscript is not now to be found." Happily, around the turn of the century, the complete manuscript was discovered deep in the archives of the New Hampshire Historical Society and published by C. H. Van Tyne, a senior fellow at the University of Pennsylvania, in his edition of the Letters of Daniel Webster, *in 1902.*

Webster's speech is an eloquent, powerful attack on the idea of conscription and was instrumental in defeating the 1814 bill that proposed to draft all males in the United States between the ages of eighteen and forty-five.

Mr. Chairman,

After the best reflection which I have been able to bestow on the subject of the bill before you, I am of opinion that its principles are not warranted by any provision of the constitution. It appears to me to partake of the nature of those other propositions for military measures, which this session, so fertile in inventions, has produced. It is of the same class with the plan of the Secretary of War; with the bill reported to this House by its own committee for filling the ranks of the regular army by classifying the free male population of the United States; & with the resolution recently introduced by an honorable gentleman from Pennsylvania (Mr. Ingersoll), & which now lies on your table, carrying the principle of compulsory service in the regular army to its utmost extent.

This bill indeed is less undisguised in its object, & less direct in its means, than some of the measures proposed. It is an attempt to exercise the power of forcing the free men of this country into the ranks of an army, for the general purposes of war, under color of a military service. To this end it commences with a *classification,* which is no way connected with the general organization of the Militia, nor, to my apprehension, included within any of the powers which Congress possesses over them. All the authority which this Government has over the Militia, until actually called into its service, is to enact laws for their organization & discipline. This power it has exercised. It now possesses the further power of calling into its service any portion of the Militia of the States, in the particular exigencies for which the Constitution provides, & of governing them during the continuance of such service. Here its authority ceases. The classification of the whole body of the Militia, according to the provisions of this bill, is not a measure which respects either their general organization or their discipline. It is a distinct system, introduced for new purposes, & not connected with any power, which the Constitution has conferred on Congress.

But, Sir, there is another consideration. The services of the men to be raised under this act are not limited to those cases in which alone this Government is entitled to the aid of the militia of the States. These cases are particularly stated in the Constitution— "to repel invasion, suppress insurrection, or execute the laws." But this bill has no limitation in this respect. The usual mode of legislating on the subject is abandoned. The only section which would have confined the service of the Militia, proposed to be raised, within the United States has been stricken out; & if the President should not march them into the Provinces of England at the North, or of Spain at the South, it will not be because he is prohibited by any provision in this act.

This, then, Sir, is a bill for calling out the Militia, not according to its existing organization, but by draft from new created classes;—not merely for the purpose of "repelling invasion, suppressing insurrection, or executing the laws," but for the general objects of war—for defending ourselves, or invading others, as may be thought expedient;—not for a sudden emergency, or for a short time, but for long stated periods; for two years, if the proposition of the Senate should finally prevail; for one year, if the amendment of the House should be adopted. What is this, Sir, but raising a standing army out of the Militia by draft, & to be recruited by draft, in like manner, as often as occasion may require?

This bill, then is not different in principle from the other bills, plans & resolutions, which I have mentioned. The present discussion is properly & necessarily common to them all. It is a discussion, Sir, of the last importance. That measures of this nature should be debated at all, in the councils of a free Government, is cause of dismay. The question is nothing less, than whether the most essential rights of personal liberty shall be surrendered, & despotism embraced in its worst form.

I have risen, on this occasion, with anxious & painful emotions, to add my admonition to what has been said by others. Admonition & remonstrance, I am aware, are not acceptable strains. They are duties of unpleasant performance. But they are, in my judgment, the duties which the condition of a falling state imposes. They are duties which sink deep in his conscience, who believes it probable that they may be the last services, which he may be able to render to the Government of his Country. On the issue of this discussion, I believe the fate of this Government may rest. Its duration is incompatible, in my opinion, with the existence of the measures in contemplation. A crisis has at last arrived, to which the course of things has long tended, & which may be decisive upon the happiness of present & of future generations. If there be anything important in the concerns of men, the considerations which fill the present hour are important. I am anxious, above all things, to stand acquitted before GOD, & my own conscience, & in the public judgments, of all participations in the Counsels, which have brought us to our present condition, & which now threaten the dissolution of the Government. When the present generation of men shall be a matter of history only, I desire that it may then be known, that you have not proceeded in your course unadmonished & unforewarned. Let it then be known, that there were those, who would have stopped you, in the career of your measures, & held you back, as by the skirts of your garments, from the precipice, over which you are plunging, & drawing after you the Government of your Country.

I had hoped, Sir, at an early period of the session, to find gentlemen in another temper. I trusted that the existing state of things would have impressed on the minds of those, who decide national measures, the necessity of some reform in the administration of affairs. If it was not to have been expected that gentlemen would be convinced by argument, it was still not unreasonable to hope that they would listen to the solemn preaching of events. If no previous reasoning could satisfy them, that the favorite plans of Government would fail, they might yet be expected to regard the fact, when it happened, & to yield to the lesson which it taught. Although they had, last year, given no credit to those who predicted the failure of the campaign against Canada, yet they had seen that failure. Although they then treated as idle all doubts of the success of the loan, they had seen the failure of that loan. Although they then held in derision all fears for the public credit, & the national faith, they had yet seen the public credit destroyed, & the national faith violated & disgraced. They had seen much more than was predicted; for no man had foretold, that our means of defence would be so far exhausted in foreign invasion, as to leave the place of our own deliberations insecure, & that we should, this day, be legislating in view of the crumbling monuments of our national disgrace. No one had anticipated, that this City would have fallen before a handful of troops, & that British Generals & British Admirals would have taken their airings along the Pennsylvania Avenue, while the Government was in full flight, just awaked perhaps from one of its profound meditations on the plan of a Conscription for the conquest of Canada. These events, Sir, with the present state of things, & the threatening aspect of what is future, should have brought us to a pause. They might have reasonably been expected to induce Congress to review its own measures, & to exercise its great duty of inquiry relative to the conduct of others. If this was too high a pitch of virtue for the multitude of party men, it was at least to have been expected from Gentlemen of influence & character, who ought to be supposed to value something higher than mere party attachments, & to act from motives somewhat nobler than a mere regard to party consistency. All that we have yet suffered will be found light & trifling, in comparison with what is before us, if the Government shall learn nothing from experience but to despise it, & shall grow more & more desperate in its measures, as it grows more & more desperate in its affairs.

It is time for Congress to examine & decide for itself. It has taken things on trust long enough. It has followed Executive recommendation, till there remains no hope of finding safety in that path. What is there, Sir, that makes it the duty of this people now to grant new confidence to the administration, & to surrender their most important rights to its discretion? On what merits of its own does it rest this extraordinary claim? When it calls thus loudly for the treasure & the lives of the people, what pledge does it offer, that it will not waste all in the same preposterous pursuits, which have hitherto engaged it? In the failure of all past promises, do we see any assurance of future performance? Are we to measure out our confidence in proportion to our disgraces, & now at last to grant away every thing, because all that we have heretofore granted has been wasted or misapplied? What is there in our condition, that bespeaks a wise or an able Governement? What is the evidence, that the protection of the country is the object principally regarded? In every quarter, that protection has been more or less abandoned to the States. That every town on the coast is not now in possession of the enemy, or in ashes, is owing to the vigilence [*sic*] & exertions of the States themselves, & to no protection granted to them by those on whom the whole duty of their protection rested.

Or shall we look to the acquisition of the professed objects of the war, & there find grounds for approbation & confidence. The professed objects of the war are abandoned in all due form. The contest for sailors' rights is turned into a negotiation about boundaries & military roads, & the highest hope entertained by any man of the issue, is that we may be able to get out of the war without a cession of territory.

Look, Sir, to the finances of the country. What a picture do they exhibit of the wisdom & prudence & foresight of Government. "The revenue of a State," says a profound writer, "is the state." If we are to judge of the condition of the country by the condition of its revenue, what is the result? A wise Government sinks deep the fountain of its revenue—not only till it can touch the first springs, & slake the present thirst of the Treasury, but till lasting sources are opened, too abundant to be exhausted by demand, too deep to be affected by heats & droughts. What, Sir, is our present supply, & what our provision for future resource? I forbear to speak of the present condition of the Treasury; & as to public credit, the last reliance of Government, I use the language of Government itself only, when I say it does not exist. This is a state of things calling for the soberest counsels, & yet it seems to meet only the wildest speculations. Nothing is talked of but Banks, & a circulating paper medium, & Exchequer Notes, & the thousand other contrivances, which ingenuity, vexed & goaded by the direst necessity, can devise, with the vain hope of giving value to mere paper.

All these things are not revenue, nor do they produce it. They are the effect of a productive commerce, & a well ordered system of finance, & in their operation may be favorable to both, but are not the cause of either. In other times these facilities existed. Bank paper & Government paper circulated, because both rested on substantial capital or solid credit. Without these they will not circulate, nor is there a device more shallow or more mischievous, than to pour forth new floods of paper without credit as a remedy for the evils which paper without credit has already created. As was intimated the other day by my honorable friend from North Carolina (Mr. Gaston) this is an attempt to act over again the farce of the Assignats of France. Indeed, Sir, our politicians appear to have but one school. They learn every thing of modern France; with this variety only, that for examples of revenue they go to the Revolution, when her revenue was in the worst state possible, while their model for military force is sought after in her imperial era, when her military was organized on principles the most arbitrary & abominable.

Let us examine the nature & extent of the power, which is assumed by the various military measures before us. In the present want of men & money, the Secretary of War has proposed to Congress a Military Conscription.* For the conquest of Canada, the people will not enlist; & if they would, the Treasury is exhausted, & they could not be paid. Conscription is chosen as the most promising instrument, both of overcoming reluctance to the Service, & of subduing the difficulties which arise from the deficiencies of the Exchequer. The administration asserts the right to fill the ranks of the regular army by compulsion. It contends that it may now take one out of every twenty-five men, & any part or the whole of the rest, whenever its occasions require. Persons thus taken by force, & put into an army, may be compelled to serve there, during the war, or for life. They may be put on any service, at home or abroad, for defence or for invasion, according to the will & pleasure of Government. This power does not grow out of any invasion of the country, or even out of a state of war. It belongs to Government at all times, in peace as well as in war, & is to be exercised under all circumstances, according to its mere discretion. This, Sir, is the amount of the principle contended for by the Secretary of War.

Is this, Sir, consistent with the character of a free Government? Is this civil liberty? Is this the real character of our Constitution? No, Sir, indeed it is not. The Constitution is libelled, foully libelled. The people

*[Editor's note]: For Secretary of War James Monroe's proposal, see chapter 28.

of this country have not established for themselves such a fabric of despotism. They have not purchased at a vast expense of their own treasure & their own blood a Magna Charta to be slaves. Where is it written in the Constitution, in what article or section is it contained, that you may take children from their parents, & parents from their children, & compel them to fight the battles of any war, in which the folly or the wickedness of Government may engage it? Under what concealment has this power lain hidden, which now for the first time comes forth, with a tremendous & baleful aspect, to trample down & destroy the dearest rights of personal liberty? Who will show me any constitutional injunction, which makes it the duty of the American people to surrender every thing valuable in life, & even life itself, not when the safety of their country & its liberties may demand the sacrifice, but whenever the purposes of an ambitious & mischievous Government may require it? Sir, I almost disdain to go to quotations & references to prove that such an abominable doctrine has no foundation in the Constitution of the country. It is enough to know that that instrument was intended as the basis of a free Government, & that the power contended for is incompatible with any notion of personal liberty. An attempt to maintain this doctrine upon the provisions of the Constitution is an exercise of perverse ingenuity to extract slavery from the substance of a free Government. It is an attempt to show, by proof & argument, that we ourselves are subjects of despotism, & that we have a right to chains & bondage, firmly secured to us & our children, by the provisions of our Government. It has been the labor of other men, at other times, to mitigate & reform the powers of Government by construction; to support the rights of personal security by every species of favorable & benign interpretation, & thus to infuse a free spirit into Governments, not friendly in their general structure & formation to public liberty.

The supporters of the measures before us act on the opposite principle. It is their task to raise arbitrary powers, by construction, out of a plain written charter of National Liberty. It is their pleasing duty to free us of the delusion, which we have fondly cherished, that we are the subjects of a mild, free & limited Government, & to demonstrate by a regular chain of premises & conclusions, that Government possesses over us a power more tyrannical, more arbitrary, more dangerous, more allied to blood & murder, more full of every form of mischief, more productive of every sort & degree of misery, than has been exercised by any civilized Government, with a single exception, in modern times.

The Secretary of War has favored us with an argument on the

constitutionality of this power. Those who lament that such doctrines should be supported by the opinion of a high officer of Government, may a little abate their regret, when they remember that the same officer, in his last letter of instructions to our ministers abroad, maintained the contrary. In that letter, he declares, that even the impressment of seamen, for which many more plausible reasons may be given than for the impressment of soldiers, is repugnant to our constitution.

It might therefore be a sufficient answer to his argument, in the present case, to quote against it the sentiments of its own author, & to place the two opinions before the House, in a state of irreconcilable conflict. Further comment on either might then be properly foreborne, until he should be pleased to inform us which he retracted, & to which he adhered. But the importance of the subject may justify a further consideration of the argument.

Congress having, by the Constitution a power to raise armies, the Secretary contends that no restraint is to be imposed on the exercise of this power, except such as is expressly stated in the written letter of the instrument. In other words, that Congress may execute its powers, by any means it chooses, unless such means are particularly prohibited. But the general nature & object of the Constitution impose as rigid a restriction on the means of exercising power, as could be done by the most explicit injunctions. It is the first principle applicable to such a case, that no construction shall be admitted which impairs the general nature & character of the instrument. A free constitution of Government is to be construed upon free principles, & every branch of its provisions is to receive such an interpretation as is full of its general spirit. No means are to be taken by implication, which would strike us absurdly, if expressed. And what would have been more absurd, than for this constitution to have said, that to secure the great blessings of liberty it gave to Government an uncontrolled power of military conscription? Yet such is the absurdity which it is made to exhibit, under the commentary of the Secretary of War.

But it is said, that it might happen that an army would not be raised by voluntary enlistment, in which case the power to raise armies would be granted in vain, unless they might be raised by compulsion. If this reasoning could prove any thing, it would equally show, that whenever the legitimate powers of the Constitution should be so badly administered as to cease to answer the great ends intended by them, such new powers may be assumed or usurped, as any existing administration may deem expedient. This is a result of his own reasoning, to which the Secretary does not profess to go. But it is a true result. For if it is to be assumed, that all powers were granted, which might by possibility become necessary, & that Government itself is the judge of this possible necessity, then the powers of Government are precisely what it chooses they should be. Apply the same reasoning to any other power granted to Congress, & test its accuracy by the result. Congress has power to borrow money. How is it to exercise this power? Is it confined to voluntary loans? There is no express limitation to that effect, &, in the language of the Secretary, it might happen, indeed, it has happened, that persons could not be found willing to lend. Money might be borrowed then in any other mode. In other words, Congress might resort to a *forced* loan. It might take the money of any man, by force, & give him in exchange Exchequer notes or Certificate of Stock. Would this be quite constitutional, Sir? It is entirely within the reasoning of the Secretary, & it is a result of his argument, outraging the rights of individuals in a far less degree, than the practical consequences which he himself draws from it. A compulsory loan is not to be compared, in point of enormity, with a compulsory military service.

If the Secretary of War has proved the right of Congress to enact a law enforcing a draft of men out of the Militia into the regular army, he will at any time be able to prove, quite as clearly, that Congress has power to create a Dictator. The arguments which have helped him in one case, will equally aid him in the other. The same reason of a supposed or possible state necessity, which is urged now, may be repeated then, with equal pertinency & effect.

Sir, in granting Congress the power to raise armies, the People have granted all the means which are ordinary & usual, & which are consistent with the liberties & security of the People themselves; & they have granted no others. To talk about the unlimited power of the Government over the means to execute its authority, is to hold a language which is true only in regard to despotism. The tyranny of Arbitrary Government consists as much in its means as in its ends; & it would be a ridiculous & absurd constitution which should be less cautious to guard against abuses in the one case than in the other. All the means & instruments which a free Government exercises, as well as the ends & objects which it pursues, are to partake of its own essential character, & to be conformed to its genuine spirit. A free Government with arbitrary means to administer it is a contradiction; a free Government without adequate provision for personal security is an absurdity; a free Government, with an uncontrolled power of military conscription, is a solecism, at once the most ridiculous & abominable that ever entered into the head of man.

Sir, I invite the supporters of the measures before you to look to their actual operation. Let the men who have so often pledged their own fortunes & their own lives to the support of this war, look to the wanton sacrifice which they are about to make of their lives & fortunes. They may talk as they will about substitutes, & compensations, & exemptions. It must come to the draft at last. If the Government cannot hire men voluntarily to fight its battles, neither can individuals. If the war should continue, there will be no escape, & every man's fate, & every man's life will come to depend on the issue of the military draught. Who shall describe to you the horror which your orders of Conscription shall create in the once happy villages of this country? Who shall describe the distress & anguish which they will spread over those hills & valleys, where men have heretofore been accustomed to labor, & to rest in security & happiness. Anticipate the scene, Sir, when the class shall assemble to stand its draft, & to throw the dice for blood. What a group of wives & mothers, & sisters, of helpless age & helpless infancy, shall gather round the theatre of this horrible lottery, as if the stroke of death were to fall from heaven before their eyes, on a father, a brother, a son or an husband. And in a majority of cases, Sir, it will be the stroke of death. Under present prospects of the continuance of the war, not one half of them on whom your conscription shall fall, will ever return to tell the tale of their sufferings. They will perish of disease & pestilence, or they will leave their bones to whiten in fields beyond the frontier. Does the lot fall on the father of a family? His children, already orphans, shall see his face no more. When they behold him for the last time, they shall see him lashed & fettered, & dragged away from his own threshold, like a felon & an outlaw. Does it fall on a son, the hope & staff of aged parents. That hope shall fail them. On that staff they shall lean no longer. They shall not enjoy the happiness of dying before their children. They shall totter to their grave, bereft of their offspring, & unwept by any who inherit their blood. Does it fall on a husband? The eyes which watch his parting steps may swim in tears forever. She is a wife no longer. There is no relation so tender or so sacred, that, by these accursed measures, you do not propose to violate it. There is no happiness so perfect, that you do not propose to destroy it. Into the paradise of domestic life you enter, not indeed by temptations & sorceries, but by open force & violence.

But this father, or this son, or this husband goes to the camp. With whom do you associate him? With those only who are sober & virtuous & respectable like himself? No, Sir. But you propose to find him companions in the worst men of the worst sort. Another Bill lies on your table offering a bounty to deserters from your enemy. Whatever is most infamous in his ranks you propose to make your own. You address yourselves to those who will hear you advise them to perjury and treason. All who are ready to set Heaven & earth at defiance at the same time, to violate their oaths, & run the hazard of capital punishment, & none others, will yield to your solicitations. And these are they whom you are allowing to join your ranks, by holding out to them inducements & bounties with one hand, while with the other you are driving thither the honest & worthy members of your own community, under the lash & scourge of conscription. In the line of your army, with the true levelling of despotism, you propose a promiscuous mixture of the worthy & the worthless, the virtuous & the profligate; the husbandman, the merchant, the mechanic of your own country, with the beings whom war selects from the excess of European population, who possess neither interests, feelings or character in common with your own people, & who have no other recommendation to your notice than their propensity to crimes.

Nor is it, Sir, for the defense of his own house & home, that he who is the subject of military draft is to perform the task allotted to him. You will put him upon a service equally foreign to his interests & abhorrent to his feelings. With his aid you are to push your purposes of conquest. The battles which he is to fight are the battles of invasion; battles which he detests perhaps & abhors, less from the danger & death that gather over them, & the blood with which they drench the plain, than from the principles in which they have their origin. Fresh from the peaceful pursuits of life, & yet a soldier but in name, he is to be opposed to veteran troops, hardened under every scene, inured to every privation & disciplined in every service. If, Sir, in this strife he fall—if, while ready to obey every rightful command of Government, he is forced from home against right, not to contend for the defence of his country, but to prosecute a miserable & detestable project of invasion, & in that strife he fall, 'tis murder. It may stalk above the cognizance of human law, but in the sight of Heaven it is murder; & though millions of years may roll away, while his ashes & yours lie mingled together in the earth, the day will yet come, when his spirit & the spirits of his children must be met at the bar of omnipotent justice. May God, in his compassion, shield me from any participation in the enormity of this guilt.

I would ask, Sir, whether the supporters of these measures have well weighed the difficulties of their undertaking. Have they considered whether it will be found easy to execute laws, which bear such marks of despotism on their front, & which will be so productive of every sort & degree of misery in their execution? For one, Sir, I hesitate not to say, that they can not be executed. No law professedly passed for the purpose of compelling a service in the regular army, nor any law, which under color of military draft, shall compel men to serve in the army, not for the emergencies mentioned in the Constitution, but for long periods, & for the general objects of war, can be carried into effect. In my opinion, it ought not to be carried into effect. The operation of measures thus unconstitutional & illegal ought to be prevented, by a resort to other measures which are both constitutional & legal. It will be the solemn duty of the State Governments to protect their own authority over their own Militia, & to interpose between their citizens & arbitrary power. These are among the objects for which the State Governments exist; & their highest obligations bind them to the preservation of their own rights & the liberties of their people. I express these sentiments here, Sir, because I shall express them to my constituents. Both they & myself live under a Constitution which teaches us, that "the doctrine of non-resistance against arbitrary power & oppression, is absurd, slavish, & destructive of the good & happiness of mankind."[1] With the same earnestness with which I now exhort you to forbear from these measures, I shall exhort them to exercise their unquestionable right of providing for the security of their own liberties.

In my opinion, Sir, the sentiments of the free population of this country are greatly mistaken here. The nation is not yet in a temper to submit to conscription. The people have too fresh & strong a feeling of the blessings of civil liberty to be willing thus to surrender it. You may talk to them as much as you please, of the victory & glory to be obtained in the Enemy's Provinces; they will hold those objects in light estimation, if the means be a forced military service. You may sing to them the song of Canada Conquests in all its variety, but they will not be charmed out of the remembrance of their substantial interests, & true happiness. Similar pretences, they know, are the graves in which the liberties of other nations have been buried, & they will take warning.

Laws, Sir, of this nature can create nothing but opposition. If you scatter them abroad, like the fabled serpents' teeth, they will spring up into armed men. A military force cannot be raised, in this manner, but by the means of a military force. If administration has found that it can not form an army without conscription, it will find, if it venture on these experiments, that it can not enforce conscription without an army. The Government was not constituted for such purposes. Framed in the spirit of liberty, & in the love of peace, it has no powers which render it able to enforce such laws. The attempt, if we rashly make it, will fail; & having already thrown away our peace, we may thereby throw away our Government.

Allusions have been made, Sir, to the state of things in New England, &, as usual, she has been charged with an intention to dissolve the Union. The charge is unfounded. She is much too wise to entertain such purposes. She has had too much experience, & has too strong a recollection of the blessings which the Union is capable of producing under a just administration of Government. It is her greatest fear, that the course at present pursued will destroy it, by destroying every principle, every interest, every sentiment, & every feeling, which have hitherto contributed to uphold it. Those who cry out that the Union is in danger are themselves the authors of that danger. They put its existence to hazard by measures of violence, which it is not capable of enduring. They talk of dangerous designs against Government, when they are overthrowing the fabric from its foundations. They alone, Sir, are friends to the union of the States, who endeavor to maintain the principles of civil liberty in the country, & to preserve the spirit in which the Union was framed.[2]

From *The Letters of Daniel Webster*, edited by C. H. Van Tyne (New York: McClure, Phillips & Company, 1902), pages 56–68.

DANIEL WEBSTER (1782–1852) is best remembered as an orator, lawyer, and statesman who practiced prominently before the U.S. Supreme Court. He served as congressman (1813–1817 and 1823–1827), as senator (1827–1841 and 1845–1850), and as secretary of state under Presidents Harrison, Tyler, and Fillmore, and thrice unsuccessfully sought the presidency. He was an articulate and enthusiastic advocate of business interests, and his forceful nationalist arguments significantly influenced the constitutional views of Chief Justice John Marshall.

Notes

1. New Hampshire Bill of Rights.

2. See "Private Correspondence of Daniel Webster," vol. i., p. 248. In this letter to Ezekiel [Webster], Webster says "after the best reflection which I have been able to bestow" he has decided not to publish this speech on the conscription bill. It is merely mentioned in the Register of Congressional Debates.

Index

Education (*continued*)
universal national service, 339, 402, 417, 424–25, 438–39, 440, 447–48, 460; motivational problems in, 450–52; benefits to, by abolishing conscription, 624
Educational deferments and exemptions, 339, 370, 371, 385–86, 402, 409, 434, 529, 553, 586; criticism of, 404, 553; in Soviet Union, 496
Edward III (England), 468
Efficiency, economic, and conscription, 366–70
Egypt, 143, 310, 488
Eisenhower, Dwight D., 113, 373
Eliot, Andrew, 244
Eliot, Charles W., 27
Elizabeth I (England), 470–75 *passim*
Ellsworth, Oliver, 253
El Paso, Texas, 70
Emergency Powers Defense Bill of 1940 (Great Britain), 489
England, *see* Great Britain
English Service Act of 1916, 222, 237
Enlistments, 548; proposed amendments to restrict term, 265, 377; rate of, 346, 581; supply curve for, 360–61. *See also* Accessions
Enthusiasm: compulsion, conscription, and, 36, 37
Equal Rights Amendment, 95–96
Equity issue: draft tax and, 358, 364–66; and conscription systems, 374–75; *ex post* and *ex ante* equity, 374–75; national service and, 423; and Soviet conscription, 498; AVF and conscripted force compared, 527–29, 582
Espionage Act, 281
Essex, England, 470
Ethiopia, 454–55
Europe: conscription in, 479–91
Euxine Sea, 310
Exemptions, 10, 105–6, 203, 385–86, 586–87, 595; in French conscription, 8; in colonial period, 51; for conscientious objectors, 147–48, 151, 197–99, 357; from Civil War conscription, 208, 216–17, 276; from World War I draft, 220–21, 228;

Exemptions (*continued*)
economics of, 371–73; to national service, 414; in lottery system, 434–35; in British military service, 470, 485; in Monroe's 1814 proposal, 507
External costs of conscription, 370

Fabianism, 77
Falstaff, 471
Fascism, 42. *See also* Totalitarian conscription
Federalist Papers, The, 235, 255–59, 272, 288
Federalists, 250. *See also* Hamilton, Alexander; Madison, James
Feudalism: conscription and military organization under, 3–6, 60, 302, 464–68, 481–82; and concept of citizenship, 88; militia, 312
Finland, 108, 490
Firearms: impact on military organization of, 62, 306–7, 314
First Amendment, 228
Fitzsimons, Thomas, 292
Flambard, Ranulph, 466
Florence of Worcester, 465
Flushing, Netherlands, 473
Food Administration, 32
Force levels of U.S. military, 318–31
Foreign policy: conscription as determinant of, 580
Forsythe, George I., 124
Fort Benning, Ga., 117, 124–26, 129
Fort Carson, Colo., 124
Fortescue (English author), 476
Fort Ord, Calif., 124
Fort Polk, La., 128
Fourteenth Amendment, 219, 228
France: conscription in, 7–8, 36, 482–83, 487–88, 489, 490, 518, 638; war between U.S. colonies and, 14, 16; and 1745 uprising of Prince Charles, 23; decline of army in World War I, 37; origins of modern conscription and mass army, 62–63, 74, 237; U.S. in undeclared war with, 73, 271; German invasion of, 282; professional army in, 308; compulsory national service in, 456, 571; wars with England, 474, 484; use of

About the Author

MARTIN ANDERSON is Assistant to the President for Policy Development and a member of the Military Manpower Task Force established by President Reagan in 1981. He is also a Senior Fellow (on leave) at the Hoover Institution at Stanford University, and served as a member of the Defense Manpower Commission (1975–76) established by President Ford to study the short- and long-term manpower requirements of the Department of Defense.

While serving as Special Assistant and Special Consultant to President Nixon (1969–1971), Dr. Anderson was deeply involved in the formulation of military manpower policy. He served as the chairman of an interagency task force that evaluated the report of the President's Commission on an All-Volunteer Armed Force and developed the legislation that abolished the draft in 1971.

A summa cum laude graduate of Dartmouth, Anderson received a Ph.D. in Industrial Management from the Massachusetts Institute of Technology and taught economics and corporate finance at Columbia University's Graduate School of Business for six years before becoming involved in national politics. He is the author of *Conscription: A Select and Annotated Bibliography* (1976), *Welfare: The Political Economy of Welfare Reform in the United States* (1978), and *The Federal Bulldozer: A Critical Analysis of Urban Renewal, 1949–62* (1964).

DATE DUE

Wars and Conscription

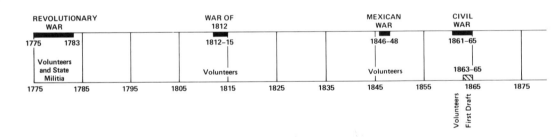

REVOLUTIONARY WAR			WAR OF 1812			MEXICAN WAR	CIVIL WAR
1775 1783			1812–15			1846–48	1861–65
Volunteers and State Militia			Volunteers			Volunteers	1863–65
1775 1785	1795	1805	1815	1825	1835	1845 1855	1865 1875

Volunteers
First Draft

UB340 .M55 1982   c.1
                                   100107 000
The military draft :

3   00044502 1
GOSHEN COLLEGE-GOOD LIBRARY